Demosthenes

Select private orations of Demosthenes

Demosthenes

Select private orations of Demosthenes

ISBN/EAN: 9783337276867

Printed in Europe, USA, Canada, Australia, Japan

Cover: Foto ©ninafisch / pixelio.de

More available books at **www.hansebooks.com**

SELECT PRIVATE ORATIONS

OF

DEMOSTHENES

PART I

CONTAINING

CONTRA PHORMIONEM, LACRITUM, PANTAENETUM, BOEOTUM DE NOMINE, BOEOTUM DE DOTE, DIONYSODORUM.

WITH

INTRODUCTIONS AND ENGLISH COMMENTARY

BY

F. A. PALEY, M.A., LL.D.

EDITOR OF HESIOD, THE GREEK TRAGIC POETS, ETC.; LATE EXAMINER IN CLASSICS TO THE UNIVERSITY OF LONDON,

WITH SUPPLEMENTARY NOTES BY

J. E. SANDYS, LITT. D.

FELLOW AND TUTOR OF ST JOHN'S COLLEGE, AND PUBLIC ORATOR IN THE UNIVERSITY OF CAMBRIDGE.

EDITED FOR THE SYNDICS OF THE UNIVERSITY PRESS.

SECOND EDITION, REVISED.

CAMBRIDGE:
AT THE UNIVERSITY PRESS.
1886

PREFACE.

WE have endeavoured in this edition to promote and facilitate the study of a most important and most interesting part of the writings of Demosthenes, the *Private Orations*. To this end we have selected twelve, which either from the nature of the subjects or from the manner of treatment or for both reasons appeared to afford the best and the most copious illustrations of the laws and general polity of Athens. It is remarkable that (with the exception of a small volume, long ago out of print, published by the late Mr Penrose) no such work as the present exists, even in Germany[1].

The importance, however, of these shorter but more technical orations, in illustrating the details of finance, mercantile transactions, loans, securities, interest on money, banking and mining operations, the laws of citizenship, &c., may be judged of in two ways. The pages of Boeckh's well-known work on the Public

[1] The Speeches against *Aphobus* and *Onetor* alone are included in Bremi's *Orationes Selectae* (1829),—and only those against *Conon* and *Eubulides* in A. Westermann's *Ausgewaehlte Reden des Demosthenes* (ed. 2, 1865). Mr Penrose's selection included the Speeches against *Aphobus*, *Onetor*, *Zenothemis*, *Apaturius*, *Phormio*, and *Lacritus* (1843; ed. 2, 1853).

Economy of Athens are filled with references to the *Private Orations*, which are indeed the principal sources of his information. Secondly, a mere glance at the index of the present volume will show the considerable amount of legal and political usages alluded to or discussed and (as far as space would permit) explained in these pages. In a literary point of view, and regarded as specimens of acute legal argument, of rhetorical skill, or consummate grace of style and diction, the interest of these orations can hardly be overrated. Hitherto, they have been accessible to general students only through the English Translation (a very excellent one) and Dissertations by the late Charles Rann Kennedy, or through the *variorum* notes of G. H. Schaefer. We have endeavoured to bring together all the references of importance in Boeckh's great work, the Public Economy[1], and have so compiled in a brief form all the necessary explanations of the text from various sources,

[1] Translated by G. C. Lewis, 1828; ed. 2, 1842. Mr Sandys has occasionally added references to the Second *German* Edition of 1851 (translated by Anthony Lamb, 1857). He has also availed himself of K. F. Hermann's *Lehrbuch der Griechischen Privat-alterthümer* (ed. Stark, 1870, ed. Blümner, 1882), *Rechtsalterthümer* (ed. Thalheim, 1884); of Büchsenschütz, *Besitz und Erwerb im Griechischen Alterthume* (1869); and of Arnold Schaefer's *Demosthenes und seine Zeit* (1858), the second part of the third volume of which (pp. 130—322) contains admirable introductions to the Private Orations; also of the volume on Demosthenes in the excellent work of Blass, entitled *die Attische Beredsamkeit*, Vol. iii, 1877. Lastly, he has occasionally referred with advantage to the notes appended to M. Rodolphe Dareste's translation of the Private Orations, *Les Plaidoyers Civils de Démosthène*, 1875.

PREFACE.

that we have reason to hope this volume will be found useful alike for school and for college use.

Most of the earlier orations of Demosthenes, besides others of the principal and longest of the speeches, e.g. *De Corona, De Falsa Legatione, Contra Aristocratem*, are almost entirely historical, and therefore come under quite a different branch of study from the legal points which are so numerously and so curiously brought out in the *Private Orations*. Others, as the *Midias*, the *Leptines*, the *Androtion*, and the *Timocrates*[1], equally well known and perhaps as much read in the schools, are rich in illustrations of Attic law, and as examples of Attic oratory and composition they can hardly be surpassed. But there are countless details of domestic life dispersed throughout the *Private Orations*, such as could hardly enter into the great public questions of the policy of Philip and his opponents and partisans. What Aristophanes is to the private life of the Athenians half a century earlier, the same for his own times is Demosthenes, whose earliest speeches are separated by an interval of some thirty years from the latest plays of the comic poet. We feel very confident, from several points of view, that the study of the *Private Orations* will be found as useful as it is interesting. It is not from dictionaries of antiquities, or from other books of reference,

---

[1] The two last named have been edited with very useful notes by Mr Wayte, since the publication of our former edition.

however excellent, that such questions and practices of the Attic law can be fully understood. They must be studied in their bearing on actual life, and in their connexion with real causes that have come before the Attic courts.

It may be added, that there can be no better introduction to the study of English law than the speeches of the Attic orators. These, indeed, cannot be fully appreciated without some general acquaintance with the principles of our own legal practice. And perhaps some at least of those students who have laid a good foundation on a knowledge of the Greek Orators gained at School and College, will not rest satisfied without acquiring some further knowledge of Roman and English jurisprudence, even if legal practice is not their object in life. "Of what use," asks Mr Kennedy[1], "can it be to an English gentleman to cram his head with the terms of Attic process, when he is utterly ignorant of that of his own country? It is only by some acquaintance with the latter that he is competent to understand the former."

With regard to the text, we have thought it best, on the whole, for the convenience of schoolmasters and students alike, to follow the third and latest edition of W. Dindorf in the Teubner series. At the same time, as Dindorf's edition hardly claims the authority of a *Textus Receptus*, Mr Sandys has given a careful colla-

[1] Appendix x, p. 395.

tion throughout with the text printed by Baiter and Sauppe in the Zürich edition of the *Oratores Attici*, noting all the varieties under the text in each page. We advise every student to use the Teubner text with our edition, because, for brevity's sake, we have referred to the different speeches, for the most part, merely by the *number of the oration and the marginal paragraph* (e.g. Or. 40 § 20). Besides, as some schoolmasters object to the use of notes under each page—while we could not reconcile ourselves to the less convenient arrangement of notes collected at the end—we recommend the general use of the cheap and accurate *Teubner* text along with our own commentary[1].

The entire work is strictly that of both editors conjointly, though Mr Paley is directly responsible for the major part or general body of the notes in this volume, and Mr Sandys for those in Part II, which contains the *Pro Phormione*, the two speeches against *Stephanus*, and those against *Nicostratus*, *Conon*, and *Callicles*. The passages inserted in each volume under the respective initials (S. or P.) will be understood as the interpolations of either editor, for the sake of fuller or clearer explanation in the notes of the other. Mr Sandys had the advantage of attending Professor Kennedy's lectures on the last three Orations in this

---

[1] The *Teubner* text of Demosthenes may be obtained in *Parts* as well as *Volumes*. Vol. II Part II consists of Orations 24—40, and includes all the speeches in this volume except the last.

PREFACE.

volume during the Lent Term of 1874; and with the Professor's kind permission a few of his renderings have been inserted, with an acknowledgment in each case of the source to which they were due. It is hoped that no serious want of uniformity or useless repetition will be found to arise from this joint editorship. Of course, there is some liability to slight divergences of opinion, and some varieties in style and method of treatment will perhaps be detected in a commentary written by two hands. But all the notes in manuscript, and all the proofs of both volumes, have passed through the hands and undergone the separate revision of each of the editors.

In carefully revising the notes for a second edition, advantage has been taken of the Rev. Joseph Bickersteth Mayor's friendly criticisms in Vol. VI of the *Journal of Philology* (pp. 240—252), and his suggestions and corrections have been in all cases duly weighed and generally adopted. Many new references have been also inserted, especially in connexion with points of Attic law; and a plate of illustrative coins, with descriptive letterpress, has been added by Mr Sandys.

F. A. P.
J. E. S.

October, 1886.

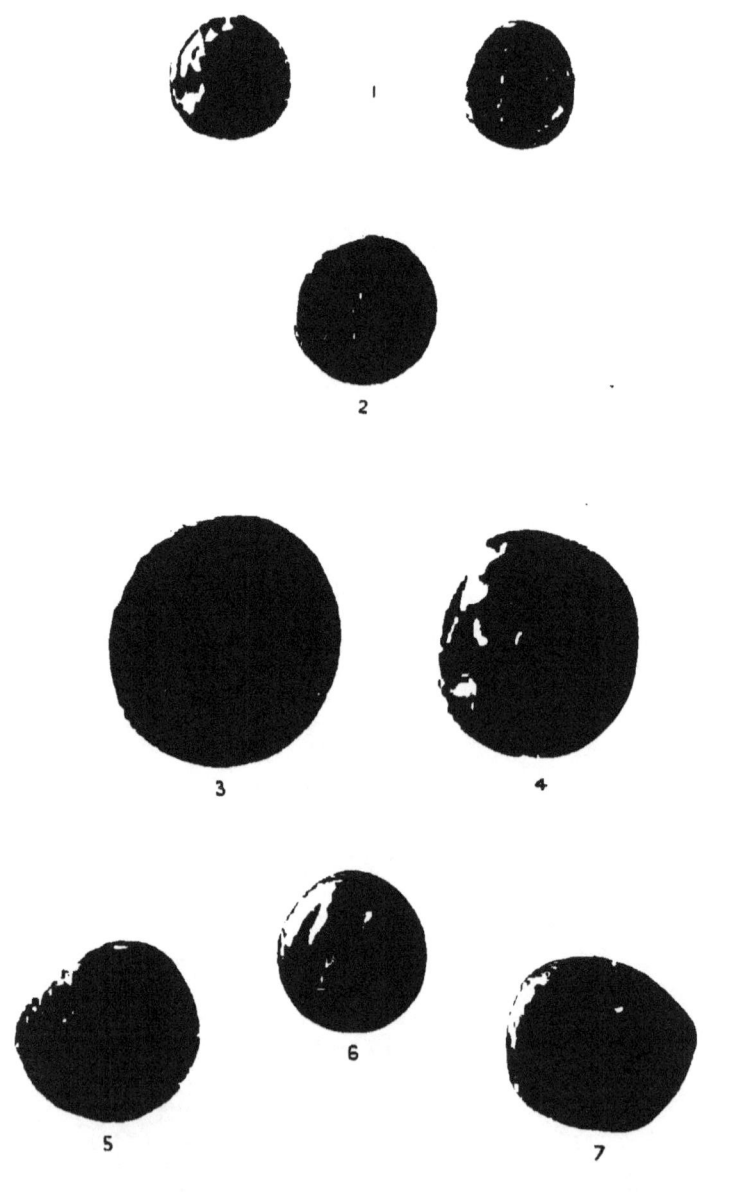

DESCRIPTION OF ILLUSTRATIVE COINS.

1. SILVER HALF-DRACHMA OF ATHENS (ἡμίδραχμον Pollux VI 160), the daily fee of the Athenian δικαστής, the τριώβολον of Aristophanes, Eq. 51, 255, 800, Av. 1541, Vesp. 609, 684, 690 and 1121. Cf. Boeckh's *Public Economy of Athens*, book II, chap. xiv. Dem. Or. 39 § 17, εἰ μισθὸς ἐπορίσθη τοῖς δικαστηρίοις, εἰσῆγον ἂν δῆλον ὅτι.

On the *obverse* is a head of Athene, of archaic style, looking to the right. On the *reverse* is the legend $\begin{smallmatrix}A\\ \exists\ \odot\end{smallmatrix}$ for 'Αθηναίων, a form of spelling retained on the coins of Athens long after H had come into use. In the centre, under an arch formed of two sprigs of olive, is an owl, facing to the front and with wings closed (Ar. Aves 1106, γλαῦκες ὑμᾶς οὔποτ' ἐπιλείψουσι Λαυρειωτικαί). Photographed from a cast of the specimen (III 29) in the selection from Leake's Greek Coins exhibited in the Fitzwilliam Museum, Cambridge. Weight 33 grains (Leake's *Numismata Hellenica*, European Greece, p. 25). Cf. Mr B. V. Head's *British Museum Guide to the Coins of the Ancients* II B 23.

2. COPPER COIN OF PEPARETHUS, one of the northern Sporades, N. of Euboea. On the *reverse* is a diota, with tendril and grapes hanging from the mouth of the vase on either side. In the field to the right and left in two lines is the legend ΓΕΠΑ. [On the *obverse*, not given here, a head of Dionysus, crowned with ivy, to right.] From the Leake Collection, *Numismata Hellenica*, Insular Greece, p. 30. The types on both sides of the coin allude to the wine of the island, or (more strictly speaking) to Dionysus, its patron-god, and thus illustrate Or. 35 § 35, εἰς τὸν πόντον ὁ οἶνος εἰσάγεται ἐκ Πεπαρήθου καὶ Κῶ καὶ Θάσιος καὶ Μενδαῖος. Its vines are referred to in Soph. Philoct. 548 τὴν εὔβοτρυν Πεπάρηθον, and in Heraclides Ponticus, Allegoriae Politicae, 13 αὕτη ἡ νῆσος εὔοινός ἐστι (cf. Plin. N. H. 14 § 76). It has been identified with the island now named Σκόπελος (Bursian, *Geogr.* II 387), the chief produce of which is a light and pleasant red wine, which the inhabitants export to the Black Sea, as in the days of Demosthenes (Murray's *Greece* 1884, II 597).

3. SILVER TETRADRACHM OF MENDE, on the peninsula of Pallene. *Reverse:* ΜΕΝΔΑΙΟΝ surrounding a linear square, in which is a vine with four bunches of grapes, all in a shallow incuse square. [*Obverse*, not given here, Dionysus reclining on the back of an ass.] From an electrotype in the Leake Collection, *Num. Hell.*, European Greece, p. 73. For a specimen on which the vine is on a larger scale, see *British Museum Guide* II B 9. The celebrity of its wine is attested by the writers cited by Athenaeus, I 29 D, E; IV 129 D οἴνων...Θασίων καὶ Μενδαίων καὶ Λεσβίων, VIII 364 D (Menander) Μενδαῖον, Θάσιον, and XI 784 C. Alciphron III 2 describes an Athenian supper including στάμνια τοῦ Μενδησίου, νέκταρος εἴποι τις ἄν, πεπληρωμένα, and Eubulus (ap. Athen. I 23 A) makes a toper swear μὰ Δία Μενδαῖον (Leake *l.c.*). Or. 35 § 35 οἶνος...Μενδαῖος.

4. SILVER TETRADRACHM OF THASOS. *Obverse;* head of bearded Dionysus, wearing a wreath of ivy. The wreath is remarkably graceful and Mr Ruskin observes that it rather resembles a growth than a composition (Babington's *Catalogue of Selections from the Leake Coins* V 59). [*Reverse*, ΘΑΣΙΟΝ. Hercules, kneeling on right knee and drawing a bow.] From an electrotype from the *Bibliothèque Nationale*, in the Leake Collection, Insular Greece, p. 44. There is a fine specimen in the *British Museum Guide* II B 7, on which Dr Percy Gardner remarks that the head of Dionysus is a work of great beauty and in dignity resembles Zeus rather than the god of revels (*Types of Greek Coins* p. 133). The wine of Thasos is mentioned in Athenaeus I 28 E, F; 29 A, 32 A; IV 129 D; VIII 364 D. Or. 35 § 35 οἶνος...Θάσιος.

5. ELECTRUM OR PALE GOLD STATER OF PHOCAEA, on the Ionian coast. *Obverse*, a seal (φώκη), a *type parlant* alluding to the name Φώκαια. (An early silver coin of Phocaea with the same type may be seen in *British Museum Guide* I A 23.) The letter below, though apparently a *theta*, has a small projection at the upper right-hand extremity, and was probably intended for the first letter of Φωκαέων. This extremely rare specimen is of a remote antiquity when the same letter varied in its form in different places (Leake's *Num. Hell.*, supplement p. 81). [*Reverse*, two incuse squares.] From Leake's Selected Coins II 70, an electrotype from the Munich Collection. Cf. Gardner's *Types of Greek Coins* Plate IV 7. See further in note on Or. 40 § 36 στατῆρας Φωκαεῖς.

6. ELECTRUM STATER OF CYZICUS, in the Propontis off the coast of Mysia. *Obverse;* in the centre is the ὀμφαλὸς of Apollo at Delphi, decorated with strands of wool (Aesch. Eum. 40; Passow's *Vermischte Schriften* p. 254, and K. O. Müller's *Dissertation* § 27). Above are the two golden eagles

ILLUSTRATIVE COINS. xiii

mentioned by Pindar (Pyth. IV 4 χρυσέων Διὸς αἰητῶν οὐκ ἀποδάμου 'Απόλλωνος τυχόντος ἱρέα χρῆσεν). Below is the tunny-fish which was the mint-mark of Cyzicus. [*Reverse*, four *quadrata incusa* in a square.] From a specimen in the British Museum, see *Guide* II A 12. The types are extremely numerous, including the lion and the bull (sometimes their heads only), the ram, Hercules, Victory, Cecrops, and Harmodius and Aristogeiton. Cf. Gardner's *Types*, plate x 4 and p. 143, where it is noticed that Cyzicus alone among Greek mints borrows its types from the beliefs and traditions of the most varied regions. Owing partly to this great variety of type, and to the absence of inscriptions upon these coins, it was long before they were identified as staters of Cyzicus. Thus Eckhel, *Num. Vet.*, Prolegomena IX p. xli—iii, observes 'pari fama fuerunt stateres Cyziceni aurei sed verisimiliter imaginarii tantum.' As many as 21 specimens are exhibited in the *Bibliothèque Nationale*. See note on Or. 34 § 23 εἴκοσι στατῆρας Κυζικηνοὺς and cf. Or. 35 § 36 ἑκατὸν στατῆρες Κυζικηνοί. In the descriptive letterpress to *British Museum Guide* II A 6—19, it is observed that these staters 'circulated in immense numbers from about B.C. 478 to 387, and *perhaps later*'. As the date of Or. 35 is either 351 or 341 B.C., and that of Or. 34 is after B.C. 329, the doubt here implied may be readily removed. I find, however, from the writer, Mr B. V. Head, that he intended the above dates to indicate the period during which these staters were originally *coined*, and not that in which they continued to circulate. He informs me that 'out of the 150 types of Cyzicene staters, there are none which appear to be of the more recent style of art which we should expect to see after the early part of the fourth century'.

7. ELECTRUM STATER OF CYZICUS. *Obverse*, a lion stepping toward the left, with a tunny-fish below it. [*Reverse*, four *quadrata incusa* in a square.] Weight 246·5 grains. The original in Leake's Selected Coins II 21 (*Num. Hell.* supplement p. 44) is an actual coin, wrongly described in the note on 34 § 23 as an electrotype from the British Museum. This description really applies to another specimen, with a bull for its type, to which greater prominence is accidentally given by its appearing not in the supplement, but in the body of the work, in *Num. Hell.*, Asiatic Greece, p. 50.

J. E. S.

*** For a Table of Attic Money see Part II p. xviii.

EXPLANATION OF THE SYMBOLS USED IN THIS EDITION IN RECORDING VARIOUS READINGS.

As a general rule, wherever our text (that of W. Dindorf's third Edition) agrees with that of the Zürich editors, we have not thought it necessary to notice any variations in the MSS. Where Dindorf differs from the Zürich editors, the difference is in most cases due to the greater weight given by the latter to the readings of the Paris MS Σ.

Z stands for the *Zürich* text of Demosthenes as printed by J. G. Baiter and H. Sauppe in their excellent edition of the *Oratores Attici*, in one volume (1850).

Bekk. Bekker's Berlin edition of 1824. Bekker's stereotyped edition (*Bekker* st.) was published at Leipzig in 1854, including a list of all the variations between the two editions; and this list is incorporated in the critical notes to the present volume. When Dindorf differs from the Zürich editors, he generally agrees with Bekker. When a note begins with Bekk., it is meant that Dindorf's text is supported by Bekker's Berlin and Leipzig editions: then, after a slight space, follows the reading of the Zürich editors (Z) with the MSS supporting it, introduced by the word *cum*.

The MSS thus quoted by the Zürich editors are as follows:

Σ. [Cited by some editors as S] in the *Bibliothèque Nationale*, Paris (No. 2934), on parchment; of century X. This is admitted on all hands to be the best MS, and its readings are very often accepted by Bekker and still more frequently by the Zürich editors. (For a protest against *excessive* deference to its authority, see the Preface of Mr Shilleto's fourth edition of the *De falsa legatione*, pp. vii, viii, xiv.)

F. *Codex Marcianus*, in the Library of St Mark's, Venice (No. 416), on parchment; of century XI. This MS generally agrees with the *Codex Bavaricus* (B).

Φ. In the same Library (No. 418), on parchment; of century XI.

r. In the *Bibliothèque Nationale*, Paris (No. 2936), on parchment *forma maxima;* of century XIII.

A¹. *Augustanus primus*, formerly at Augsburg (*Augusta Vindelicorum*), now at Munich (No. 485), on parchment, *paene quadratus;* of century XI (according to Dindorf), or XII (according to the Zürich editors).

B. *Bavaricus*, now at Munich (No. 85), on cotton-paper ('bombycinus'), *forma maxima;* of century XIII.

γρ. A contraction for γράφεται, used in the MSS themselves to introduce the marginal citation of a various reading.

J. E. S.

CORRIGENDUM.

On p. 67, note on διοπεύων, for '*An* overlooker' read '*As* overlooker.'

CONTENTS.

ORATION		PAGE
XXXIV.	ΠΡΟΣ ΦΟΡΜΙΩΝΑ ΠΕΡΙ ΔΑΝΕΙΟΥ . .	1
XXXV.	ΠΡΟΣ ΤΗΝ ΛΑΚΡΙΤΟΥ ΠΑΡΑΓΡΑΦΗΝ . .	49
XXXVII.	ΠΑΡΑΓΡΑΦΗ ΠΡΟΣ ΠΑΝΤΑΙΝΕΤΟΝ . .	89
XXXIX.	ΠΡΟΣ ΒΟΙΩΤΟΝ ΠΕΡΙ ΤΟΥ ΟΝΟΜΑΤΟΣ .	136
XL.	ΠΡΟΣ ΒΟΙΩΤΟΝ ΠΕΡΙ ΠΡΟΙΚΟΣ ΜΗΤΡΩΙΑΣ	176
LVI.	ΚΑΤΑ ΔΙΟΝΥΣΟΔΩΡΟΥ ΒΛΑΒΗΣ . . .	223

Lampis, to sail back to Athens without him, promising that he would soon follow. It so happened that Lampis' ship was wrecked; and though Phormio, having no goods on board, was not in any way a loser by the accident, he evaded his liability by falling back on a clause in the contract, which exempted him from payment if his goods on the return-voyage should be lost at sea. It is on this point that the action turns. Chrysippus gives evidence that Phormio never thought of disputing his liability at first, on his return to Athens, but trumped up the excuse at a subsequent time in collusion with Lampis.

Chrysippus then brings an action, of the class called ἐμπορικαὶ δίκαι, to compel Phormio to pay his claims. Phormio objects that the suit cannot be maintained, because he has done nothing to violate the terms of the contract. This objection is now answered by Chrysippus, and, at a later part of the oration (probably beginning at § 21 or 22), by his partner. This speech therefore is directed against the παραγραφὴ or demurrer which had been pleaded by Phormio, and shows grounds why the action can be and ought to be tried.

The liability to pay had been at first admitted by Phormio; but he afterwards denied it, and when the case was submitted to arbitration by mutual consent (§ 18) he had suborned Lampis (who on a former occasion had, virtually at least, admitted that he had not been paid anything by Phormio) to swear that he had received the money from him in the Bosporus, and had lost it in the ship which had been wrecked. Chrysippus handles the accounts in a very dexterous way, and convicts Phormio of falsehood by showing that the money he pretended to have paid Lampis was a great deal too much. He dwells also on the improbability of so large

ΠΕΡΙ ΔΑΝΕΙΟΥ.

a sum having been paid without any witness to the transaction, and urges that the clause in the contract, making the safety of the ship a condition of the liability, must be taken in close connexion with another clause, which compels the borrower to put goods on board for the home voyage; which Phormio had been unable to do.

The παραγραφή, or special plea, might have been put in, says Chrysippus, if the transaction had not been made in, or in connexion with, the Attic mart. But the law is explicit in stating (§ 42) that all disputes about contracts so made shall be brought before the Attic courts. And the defence set up, viz. that the money was paid, is not a ground for a special plea at all; it is simply a defence in an ordinary action (εὐθυδικία).

The Phormio in this suit πρὸς Φορμίωνα is quite a distinct person from the Phormio in *Or*. 36, ὑπὲρ Φορμίωνος, who was a liberated slave, and concerned in a banking transaction.

The date of this oration is approximately fixed by the mention of Paerisades in § 8, as king of the Bosporus, which office he held from B.C. 348 to 310, but much more closely by the allusion in § 38 to the capture of Thebes by Alexander, B.C. 335. [The famine-prices of § 34 probably belong to the years 330—326. If so, the speech belongs, at earliest, to the year 329. A. Schaefer, *Demosthenes und seine Zeit* III 268 ff., III 2. 300 n. On the speech in general, cf. Blass, *die Attische Beredsamkeit* III 515—520. S.]

ΠΡΟΣ ΦΟΡΜΙΩΝΑ ΠΕΡΙ ΔΑΝΕΙΟΥ.

ΥΠΟΘΕΣΙΣ.

Φορμίων ἔμπορος δανείζεται παρὰ Χρυσίππου μνᾶς εἴκοσι πλέων εἰς Βόσπορον. ἀφικόμενος δὲ ἐκεῖσε κατέλαβεν ἀπρασίαν τῶν φορτίων ὧν ἐκόμιζε. διόπερ τοῦ ναυκλήρου Λάμπιδος ἀποπλεῖν βουλομένου Ἀθή-

905 Reiske.

πρὸς Φορμίωνα περὶ δανείου] The speech is quoted under the same title in Pollux ix 45, ἐν τῷ πρὸς Φορμίωνα περὶ δανείου. Harpocration, however, in explaining the use of ἐπεθήκαμεν in § 28, s.v. ἐπιθέτους ἑορτὰς, gives the fuller and more accurate title ὑπὲρ Χρυσίππου πρὸς τὴν Φορμίωνος παραγραφήν, which is also found at the end of the speech in the Paris MS, and at the beginning in the *Augustanus primus*. Harpocr. s.v. ἔφεκτος τόκος, quoted on § 23, has the shorter title ἐν τῷ ὑπὲρ Χρυσίππου. S.]

3. *Argument.* κατέλαβεν, κ.τ.λ.] 'He found there was no market for the wares he was bringing.' What these were, does not appear. Probably it was a mixed cargo on speculation. He called it ῥῶπος, 'trash,' in a fit of ill-temper at his failure, inf. p. 910 init., § 9.

ibid. ὧν ἐκόμιζε] This is an instance of attraction to an antecedent which is expressed, whereas the usage is much more common when the antecedent is omitted, and the case of the word to be supplied is shifted as it were on to the relative, by which the ellipse is sufficiently indicated. This attraction takes place *only* where the proper case of the relative is the accusative. We may say κατάλογος βιβλίων ὧν ἔχομεν or ἃ ἔχομεν, but not ὧν χρώμεθα, because ὧν may represent ἅ, but not οἷς.

4. ναυκλήρου] 'The skipper.' The word seems properly to mean one who has a share or interest in a ship; a part-owner, or one who has hired it for a time (Phot. in v.). Hesych. explains it by ὁ δεσπότης τοῦ πλοίου. Lampis, however, was only a slave (§ 5), and perhaps was representing his master. [Cf. Lacrit. § 33 (μαρτυρίαι) 'Τβλήσιος ἐναυκλήρει...κοινωνεῖν δὲ καὶ αὐτὸν τῆς νεὼς 'Τβλησίῳ, καὶ συμπλεῖν ἑαυτοῦ οἰκέτας ἐν τῇ νηί. Arnold Schaefer, *Demosthenes und seine Zeit* (III 2. 305), quotes Bekker's *Anecdota*, p. 282, ναύκληρος σημαίνει μὲν καὶ τὸν τῆς νεὼς κύριον, σημαίνει δὲ καὶ τὸν ἐπιπλέοντα αὐτῇ ἐφ' ᾧ τὰ ναῦλα λαμβάνειν. S.]

6 XXXIV. ΠΡΟΣ ΦΟΡΜΙΩΝΑ [Argument

5 ναζε, καὶ κελεύοντος αὐτὸν ἐνθέσθαι τῇ νηὶ τὰ ἀγοράσματα τῶν χρημάτων τῶν παρὰ Χρυσίππου (τοῦτο γὰρ ἔφραζεν ἡ συγγραφὴ) οὔτε φόρτον τινὰ ἐνέθετο οὔτε ἀργύριον, ἀλλ' ἔφη πρὸς τὸν Λάμπιν ἀδυνάτως ἔχειν ἐν τῷ παρόντι ποιῆσαι ταῦτα, μικρὸν δ' ὕστερον
10 ἐφ' ἑτέρας ἐκπλεύσεσθαι[a] νεὼς ἅμα τοῖς χρήμασιν. ἡ μὲν οὖν τοῦ Λάμπιδος ναῦς ἀναχθεῖσα διαφθείρεται, καὶ μετ' ὀλίγων ὁ Λάμπις ἐν τῷ λέμβῳ σώζεται, καὶ ἀφικόμενος Ἀθήναζε μηνύει Χρυσίππῳ τὸ εὐτύχημα τοῦ Φορμίωνος, ὡς ἀπελείφθη τε ἐν τῷ Βοσπόρῳ καὶ
15 εἰς τὴν ναῦν οὐδὲν ἐνέθετο. ὁ δὲ Φορμίων, καταπλεύσας ὕστερον καὶ τὸ ἀργύριον ἀπαιτούμενος, τὸ μὲν πρῶτον, ὡς ἔφη Χρύσιππος, καὶ ὀφείλειν ὡμολόγει καὶ ἀποδώσειν ὑπισχνεῖτο, ἔπειτα ὡς ἀποδεδωκὼς Λάμπιδι μηδὲν ὀφείλειν ἔλεγε· τὴν γὰρ συγγραφὴν
20 κελεύειν παθούσης τι κατὰ θάλατταν τῆς νεὼς ἀπηλλάχθαι τοῦ ὀφλήματος τὸν Φορμίωνα· ἔλαχεν οὖν δίκην αὐτῷ ὁ Χρύσιππος. ὁ δὲ παρεγράψατο. καὶ

[a] ἐκπλευσεῖσθαι Z.

5. τὰ ἀγοράσματα] The goods purchased with, or in place of (i.e. as security for), the money he had borrowed from Chrysippus.—ἀργύριον, the money he ought to have made by the transaction, and given to Lampis to hand over to Chrysippus on his return.

12. ἐν τῷ λέμβῳ] Lampis, with a few of the crew (some thirty being lost, inf. p. 910, § 10), gets safe to land in the ship's boat.

16. ἀπαιτούμενος] 'On being asked for payment.' [For ἀπαιτεῖν, rem debitam reposcere, cf. § 12 and note on Or. 53 § 10. For the passive of the person, cf. Xen. Apol. 17, ἀπαιτεῖσθαι εὐεργεσίαν, and] Theocr. xiv 63, αἰτεύμενος οὐκ ἀνανεύων.

19. τὴν γὰρ συγγραφὴν] 'The compact expressly says that if anything happens to the ship at sea, Phormio is discharged from his debt to Chrysippus.' Loans on bottomry partook of the nature of insurance also, i.e. the profit on the loan was so large (§ 23), that it covered some total losses resulting from wrecks, or loss of goods from pirates, storms, or other unavoidable mishaps.

22. παρεγράψατο] Phormio put in a demurrer or bar to the suit, trying to show there was no ground for action at all, as he had abided by the terms of the contract.

P. 906] ΠΕΡΙ ΔΑΝΕΙΟΥ. 7

Λάμπις ἐμαρτύρησε παρὰ τῷ διαιτητῇ ὡς ἀπειληφὼς
εἴη παρὰ Φορμίωνος ἐν Βοσπόρῳ τὰ χρήματα καὶ
25 ἀπολωλεκὼς μετὰ τῶν ἄλλων ἐν τῇ ναυαγίᾳ. πρότερον δὲ τἀναντία τούτων εἰρήκει πρὸς Χρύσιππον, ὡς 906
οὐδὲν ὁ Φορμίων εἰς τὴν ναῦν ἐντέθεικεν. ἐλεγχόμενος
δὲ ἐπὶ τούτοις ὁ Λάμπις ἐξεστηκέναι τότε ἔφησεν, ὅτε
ἐκεῖνα πρὸς τὸν Χρύσιππον ἔλεγε. τούτων ἀκούσας ὁ
30 διαιτητὴς καὶ μηδὲν ἀποφηνάμενος εἰς τὸ δικαστήριον
τὸ πρᾶγμα πέπομφε. καὶ ὁ ἀγὼν ὀνόματι μέν ἐστι
παραγραφικός, τῷ δὲ ἀληθεῖ τὴν εὐθεῖαν[b] γίγνεται· εὖ
γὰρ καὶ ὁ ῥήτωρ κατ' ἀρχὰς ἐπισημαίνεται ὡς οὐκ

[b] παρὰ τὴν εὐθεῖαν Z.

23. παρὰ τῷ διαιτητῇ] Lampis had given false testimony when the case was brought before the arbitrator, Theodotus, § 18, for he had been bribed by Phormio to say anything to get him off. It appears from § 18 that a witness was not likely to be prosecuted for ψευδομαρτυρία given before an arbitrator.

27. ἐντέθεικεν] This perfect is one of the middle-Attic forms. It occurs first in Eur. El. 7, ὑψηλῶν δ' ἐπὶ νηῶν τέθεικε σκῦλα πλεῖστα βαρβάρων, with which compare παρεῖκεν, the perfect of παρίημι, in Hel. 1059. ἀφεικότα occurs Or. 37 § 1. For the (generally) medial use of τέθειμαι see inf. § 16.

28. ἐξεστηκέναι] That he was out of his sober senses—not himself, as we say. [οὐκ ἐντὸς ὢν αὑτοῦ, §§ 20, 35, 49. Eur. Bacch. 359, μέμηνας ἤδη καὶ πρὶν ἐξέστης φρενῶν. S.]

29. ἐκεῖνα] 'that other account.'

30. μηδὲν ἀποφηνάμενος] 'Without delivering judgment.' In classical Greek, of course, οὐδὲν would be required. Cf. ὅτι μὴ inf. 44.—πέπομφε, a rather rare perfect (Thuc. VII 12). Perhaps πεπόμφει, or ἐπεπόμφει, 'had sent.' Otherwise we should expect the aorist. In this late Greek the Latin usage, which has one tense only for aorist and perfect, misit, is perhaps incorrectly followed. Cf. Or. 39, Arg. 18. See Winer's Grammar, p. 136 ed. Moulton.

32. τὴν εὐθεῖαν γίγνεται] It takes the course of an ordinary or regular action, εὐθυδικία. The accusative here is strangely and irregularly used, and perhaps παρὰ should be preferred, 'according to the ordinary practice.' In showing that a demurrer cannot be pleaded in this case, Chrysippus, or his advocate, goes into all the facts, just as they would appear in a common trial.

33. ἐπισημαίνεται] 'Remarks;' another late usage.—κατ' ἀρχὰς, see § 4.—τὸ λέγειν, the saying a man has done all the contract required him to do is no ground at all for pleading that the action

ἔστιν ὅλως ͨ παραγραφὴ τὸ λέγειν πεποιηκέναι πάντα
35 κατὰ τὰ συγκείμενα, ἀποδιδόναι τὰ χρήματα Λάμπιδι,
κελευούσης τοῦτο τῆς συγγραφῆς καὶ ἀφιείσης ἐπὶ
τοιούτῳ πάθει τὸ ὄφλημα· ταῦτα γάρ ἐστι τὴν εὐθυδικίαν ἀγωνιζομένου καὶ τοῖς ἐπιφερομένοις ἐγκλή-
μασιν ἀπαντῶντος, ἀλλ' οὐχὶ ἀναιροῦντος τὸν περὶ
40 αὐτῶν ἀγῶνα καὶ τὴν εἰσαγωγὴν τῆς δίκης· παραγραφὴν δέ, φησὶν, ὁ νόμος δίδωσι περὶ τῶν μὴ γενομένων ὅλως Ἀθήνησι μηδὲ εἰς Ἀθήνας συμβολαίων.
 Τετήρηται δὲ ἐν τῷ λόγῳ ταὐτὸν ὅπερ καὶ περὶ τὸν
κατὰ Νεαίρας, ὅτι μὴ ὑφ' ἑνὸς εἴρηται προσώπου.
45 ᵈἀλλ' ἐκεῖ μὲν ἑκατέρουᵈ διαστολὴ φανερά, ἐνταῦθα δὲ
συγκέχυται. δοκεῖ δὲ ἔμοιγε ἐντεῦθεν ὁ δεύτερος λέγειν
"ἀκούσας τοίνυν ἡμῶν, ὦ ἄνδρες Ἀθηναῖοι, Θεόδοτος
πολλάκις, καὶ νομίσας τὸν Λάμπιν ψευδῆ μαρτυρεῖν."
δῆλον δὲ ὅτι κοινωνοί τινές εἰσιν οἱ πρὸς τὸν Φορμίωνα
50 ἀγωνιζόμενοι.

Δίκαια ὑμῶν δεησόμεθ', ὦ ἄνδρες δικασταὶ, ἀκοῦ- 907

ͨ Bekk. st.   ὅλον Z.   ᵈ⁻ᵈ ἀλλ' ἡ θατέρου Z.

cannot be brought. *That,* he says, is the plea of one who is defendant in an ordinary trial, and rebuts a charge brought against him; not the plea of one who wants to show that there is no case against him at all. A *παραγραφή*, in fact, turned solely on the *inadmissibility* of a suit, e.g. on the ground that it belonged to another court or different jurisdiction. He quotes as a case of this in the next sentence, that contracts not made at or for a voyage to Athens could not be brought before an Athenian court.

43. *τετήρηται*] 'The same peculiarity is observed here as in the speech against Neaera, viz. that it is not spoken by one party only; but whereas there the division is plain, here it is confused and obscure: it appears to me however' (i.e. to the grammarian Libanius) 'that the second speech begins at ἀκούσας, &c. (§ 21). Anyhow, it is clear that they are *partners* who bring this action against Phormio.'

p. 907. §§ 1, 2. *The proeme, or introduction. Chrysippus begins by showing that he and his partner are reasonable men,*

σαι ἡμῶν μετ᾽ εὐνοίας ἐν τῷ μέρει λεγόντων, γνόντας ὅτι ἰδιῶται παντελῶς ἐσμεν, καὶ πολὺν χρόνον εἰς τὸ ὑμέτερον ἐμπόριον εἰσαφικνούμενοι καὶ συμβόλαια πολλοῖς συμβάλλοντες οὐδεμίαν πώποτε δίκην πρὸς ὑμᾶς εἰσήλθομεν[e], οὔτ᾽ ἐγκαλοῦντες οὔτ᾽ ἐγκαλούμενοι ὑφ᾽ ἑτέρων. οὐδ᾽ ἂν νῦν, ἀκριβῶς ἴστε, ὦ ἄνδρες 2

[e] ἤλθομεν Z cum Σ.

who can bear a loss if it is a just and unavoidable one, and not συκοφάνται or lovers of law.

ἐν τῷ μέρει] 'In our turn,' and at a disadvantage, because they had been abused and misrepresented in every way. Phormio, the party accused, in pleading a demurrer, had the first speech; consequently the actual plaintiffs, Chrysippus and partner, speak after him. This is the meaning of κατηγορεῖν τοῦ διώκοντος in § 4. See Or. 45 § 6. Kennedy renders it, 'as we take our turns of addressing you,'—apparently referring it to the two partners speaking in succession. But this appears a less likely meaning; [and the rendering in question was disapproved by Shilleto].

ἰδιῶται] Unprofessional as far as the art of speaking is concerned. [Cf. Isocr. Paneg. § 11, τῶν λόγων τοῖς ὑπὲρ τοὺς ἰδιώτας ἔχουσι καὶ λίαν ἀπηκριβωμένοις, and ib. § 44 n. S.]

πολὺν χρόνον, κ.τ.λ.] 'Long as we have been in the habit of coming into your market, and many as are the merchants with whom we have had transactions about loans, we have never yet commenced any suit either as plaintiffs or defendants; and even now, be well assured, if we had really thought the money that we lent to Phormio had been lost on the ship that was wrecked, we should not have brought this action against him: no! we are not so shameless nor so inexperienced in losses.'

συμβόλαια] A general term for any kind of contract or mutual compact, besides those of money-loans or commerce. Plat. Soph. p. 225 c, τοῦ ἀντιλογικοῦ ὅσον περὶ τὰ ξυμβόλαια ἀμφισβητεῖται. Eur. Ion 411, ἅ τε νῷν συμβόλαια πρόσθεν ἦν ἐς παῖδα τὸν σόν, μεταπέσοι βελτίονα. See Or. 37 § 49, and 33 § 3, ὅσα ἐμοὶ καὶ τούτῳ ἐγένετο συμβόλαια.

2. οὐδ᾽ ἂν—οὐκ, κ.τ.λ.] In this sentence the οὐκ is superfluously repeated after the οὐδέ, by a not very common idiom. We might have expected καὶ νῦν—οὐκ ἄν ποτε ἐλάχομεν κ.τ.λ., but the negative sentence is continued, οὐδεμίαν πώποτε δίκην εἰσήλθομεν, οὐδ᾽ ἂν νῦν—ἐλάχομεν, and the second οὐκ is added before the verb in order to carry the favourite combination οὐκ ἄν, the simple verb ἐλάχομεν being too far removed from the preceding οὐδ᾽ ἂν νῦν. Compare Mid. p. 557, § 129, οὐδ᾽ εἰ τὸ παρ᾽ ἀμφοτέρων ἡμῶν ὕδωρ ὑπάρξειε,—οὐκ ἂν ἐξαρκέσειεν. Aesch. Agam. 1612 (1634 Dind.), ὃς οὐδ᾽ (Mss οὐκ) ἐπειδὴ τῷδ᾽ ἐβούλευσας μόρον, δρᾶσαι τόδ᾽ ἔργον οὐκ ἔτλης αὐτοκτόνως. Other examples occur in Soph. Ant. 6, Trach. 158 and 1014, Phil. 416, and

10   XXXIV. ΠΡΟΣ ΦΟΡΜΙΩΝΑ   [§§ 3—5

Ἀθηναῖοι, εἰ ὑπελαμβάνομεν ἀπολωλέναι τὰ χρήματα ἐπὶ τῆς νεὼς τῆς διαφθαρείσης, ἃ ἐδανείσαμεν Φορμίωνι, οὐκ ἄν ποτ᾽ ἐλάχομεν τὴν δίκην αὐτῷ· οὐχ οὕτως ἡμεῖς ἀναίσχυντοί ἐσμεν οὐδ᾽ ἄπειροι τοῦ ζημιοῦσθαι. πολλῶν δ᾽ ἡμᾶς κακιζόντων, καὶ μάλιστα τῶν ἐν Βοσπόρῳ ͉ ἐπιδημησάντων ἅμα Φορμίωνι, οἵπερ τοῦτον ᾔδεσαν οὐ συναπολέσαντα τὰ χρήματα ἐν τῇ νηὶ, δεινὸν ἡγούμεθ᾽ εἶναι τὸ μὴ βοηθῆσαι ἡμῖν αὐτοῖς ἀδικουμένοις ὑπὸ τούτου.

3   Περὶ μὲν οὖν τῆς παραγραφῆς βραχύς ἐστιν ὁ λόγος· καὶ γὰρ οὗτοι οὐ τὸ παράπαν συμβόλαιον ἐξαρ-

͉ + ἐμπόρων τῶν Z.

perhaps the difficult lines Oed. Tyr. 328—9 may be explained (reading τἄμ᾽ ὡς ἂν εἴπῃς, 'however you may speak of *my* conduct') by the repetition of μὴ immediately before the verb. Not unlike this is Or. 37 § 59, οὐδέ γε ἂν ὁ παθὼν αὐτὸς ἀφῇ—οὐδενὶ τῶν λοιπῶν συγγενῶν ἔξεστιν ἐπεξιέναι. There is another instance in Androt. p. 603, Or. 22 § 32, ἐν ταῖς ὀλιγαρχίαις, οὐδ᾽ ἂν ὦσιν ἔτ᾽ Ἀνδροτίωνός τινες αἴσχιον βεβιωκότες, οὐκ ἔστι λέγειν κακῶς τοὺς ἄρχοντας. In other cases (Or. 37 § 16) the οὐδὲ placed at the beginning negatives the whole sentence. See also Mid. § 57.

κακιζόντων] 'Taunting us with cowardice,' i.e. with the fear of being called συκοφάνται. So Or. 54 § 5, λοιδορηθέντος αὐτοῖς ἐκείνου καὶ κακίσαντος αὐτούς. Mid. § 73, οἳ τὸν μὲν κακιεῖν οἷς ἔπραξε—ἔμελλον. Eur. Ion 984, οἴμοι, κακίζει.

Βοσπόρῳ] [Also called Panticapaeum (*Kertsch*), Lacrit. § 31, the capital of the Bosporus Cimmerius. Cf. Dem. Lept. Or. 20

§§ 29—36. S.] See the note on Or. 35 § 10.

τὸ μὴ βοηθῆσαι] Not to seek redress; not to do all we could to assist our own cause, by appearing in person. This is a favourite word with Demosthenes in appealing to the law or the judges.

§§ 3, 4. *Phormio's plea for a* παραγραφή, *i.e. his ground for denying that the action can be tried, is this:* 'I don't deny that the loan was made in your market (your Exchange, we should say), but I deny that, after the shipwreck, I am any longer bound by the contract to pay.' *But that plea is no real ground: the law says,* 'an action cannot be tried if the compact was not made at Athens, nor for the Athenian market;' *which does not hold in this case. His defence, in fact, is only applicable to an ordinary trial,* εὐθυδικία, *in which the action relies solely on the merits of the case.*

καὶ γὰρ οὗτοι] 'For *even* the defendants,' i.e. Phormio and Lampis.

νοῦνται μὴ γενέσθαι ἐν τῷ ἐμπορίῳ τῷ ὑμετέρῳ, ἀλλ' οὐκέτι εἶναί φασι πρὸς ἑαυτοὺς οὐδὲν συμβόλαιον· πεποιηκέναι γὰρ οὐδὲν ἔξω τῶν ἐν τῇ συγγραφῇ γεγραμμένων. οἱ μὲν οὖν νόμοι, καθ' οὓς ὑμεῖς δικασταὶ κάθησθε, οὐχ οὕτω λέγουσιν, ἀλλ' ὑπὲρ μὲν τῶν μὴ γενομένων ὅλως συμβολαίων Ἀθήνησι μηδ' εἰς τὸ Ἀθηναίων ἐμπόριον παραγράφεσθαι δεδώκασιν, ἐὰν δέ τις γενέσθαι μὲν ὁμολογῇ, ἀμφισβητῇ δὲ ὡς πάντα πεποίηκε τὰ συγκείμενα, ἀπολογεῖσθαι κελεύουσιν εὐθυδικίαν εἰσιόντα, οὐ κατηγορεῖν τοῦ διώκοντος. οὐ μὴν ἀλλ' ἔγωγε ἐλπίζω καὶ ἐξ αὐτοῦ τοῦ πράγματος δείξειν εἰσαγώγιμον τὴν δίκην οὖσαν. σκέψασθε δ', ὦ ἄνδρες Ἀθηναῖοι, τί ὁμολογεῖται παρ' αὐτῶν τούτων καὶ τί ἀντιλέγεται· οὕτω γὰρ ἂν ἄριστα ἐξετάσαιτε. οὐκοῦν δανείσασθαι μὲν τὰ χρήματα ὁμολογοῦσι καὶ συνθήκας ποιήσασθαι τοῦ δανείσματος, φασὶ δ' ἀποδεδωκέναι τὸ χρυσίον Λάμπιδι τῷ Δίωνος οἰκέτῃ ἐν Βοσπόρῳ. ἡμεῖς τοίνυν οὐ μόνον τοῦτο δείξομεν, ὡς οὐκ

οὐδὲν συμβόλαιον] 'No obligation by virtue of the contract.' Hesych. συνάλλαγμα.
4. οἱ μὲν οὖν νόμοι, κ.τ.λ.] Cf. Or. 32 (Zenoth.) § 1 οἱ νόμοι κελεύουσιν...τὰς δίκας εἶναι τοῖς ναυκλήροις καὶ τοῖς ἐμπόροις τῶν Ἀθήναζε καὶ τῶν Ἀθήνηθεν συμβολαίων, καὶ περὶ ὧν ἂν ὦσι συγγραφαί· ἂν δέ τις παρὰ ταῦτα δικάζηται, μὴ εἰσαγώγιμον εἶναι τὴν δίκην. S.]
ἀμφισβητῇ] 'should plead on the other side.' Lit. 'should question the justice of the action by saying that he has done all that the contract required.'
οὐ κατηγορεῖν] See on § 1, ἐν τῷ μέρει.
οὐ μὴν ἀλλὰ, κ.τ.λ.] 'Not but that I hope'—lit. 'I do not however (dwell on this point, viz. what is the true ground of a παραγραφή), but I hope,' &c. Translate: 'Still I hope to show from the facts of the case itself that this suit of mine is one that can be tried. And now observe well what is admitted by the defendants themselves, and what is denied; for by these means you will best investigate the truth of my charges.' The sense is, that as the law does not here apply which allows a special plea on contracts not made at or for Athens, the facts of the case are such that Phormio's conduct is clearly actionable.
5. συνθήκας ποιήσασθαι] 'They had contracts duly made to secure the loan.'

ἀποδέδωκεν⁵, ἀλλ' ὡς οὐδ' ἐξῆν αὐτῷ ἀποδοῦναι. ἀναγκαῖον δ' ἐστὶ βραχέα τῶν ἐξ ἀρχῆς διηγήσασθαι ὑμῖν.

6 Ἐγὼ γὰρ, ὦ ἄνδρες Ἀθηναῖοι, ἐδάνεισα Φορμίωνι τούτῳ εἴκοσι μνᾶς ἀμφοτερόπλουν εἰς τὸν Πόντον ἐπὶ ἑτέρᾳ ὑποθήκῃ, καὶ συγγραφὴν ἐθέμην παρὰ Κίττῳ

⁵ ἀπέδωκεν Z cum Σ.

οὐδ' ἐξῆν αὐτῷ] 'That he could not have paid,' since he could not realize the value of his wares, § 8. Kennedy misses the sense in translating 'it was not even lawful for him to pay.' §§ 6, 7. *Statement of the circumstances and nature of the loan, and of the way in which Phormio violated it at the very first by illegal acts.*
ἐγὼ γὰρ, κ.τ.λ.] 'I on my part lent the defendant twenty minae' (about £85) 'for the double voyage to Pontus and back, on the security of twice that amount of goods.' The meaning of ἐπὶ ἑτέρᾳ ὑποθήκῃ has been doubted; but the context leaves it pretty clear that it is a brief legal term for ἐφ' ἑτέρῳ τοσούτῳ. Cf. Or. 35 § 18, ἐδανείζοντο παρ' ἡμῶν τὰς τριάκοντα μνᾶς, ὡς ὑπαρχούσης αὐτοῖς ὑποθήκης ἑτέρων τριάκοντα μνῶν. Phormio borrowed 20 minae = 2000 drachmae, and should have put on board goods worth 4000 drachmae, this transaction leaving an ample margin for a bad market, or for actual losses. Mr Joseph Bickersteth Mayor (in *The Journal of Philology*, VI p. 242) thinks the phrase means 'on a separate, distinct, independent security,' and to this he refers οὔτε γὰρ τὴν ὑποθήκην παρέσχετο in § 7, and ὑποθήκην οὐκ ἔχων in § 22. Would not this be ἐπ' ἄλλῃ ὑποθήκῃ? (Compare however ἐφ' ἑτέρας νεὼς in § 9.) If the goods (of whatever amount) were the security, and (what is nowhere expressly stated, though it seems probable) the ship itself also was pledged, the not bringing the ship back to the Peiraeus would be alluded to in § 7. Kennedy follows Seager in rendering it 'on the security of the single cargo,' i.e. the return cargo; but it does not appear how the Greek can mean this. [M. Dareste renders it: 'avec affectation sur un chargement d'une valeur double;' thereby coinciding with Mr Paley's view, which, however, says Shilleto, 'cannot be right'. The disputed phrase should perhaps be altered into ἐπ' ἐλευθέρᾳ ὑποθήκῃ, 'on an unencumbered security.' Cf. Or. 35 § 21 ὑποτιθέασι ταῦτ' ἐλεύθερα and § 22 ἐπ' ἐλευθέροις τοῖς χρήμασι δανειζόμενοι. S.]
ἀμφοτερόπλουν] sc. δάνειον, 'For the double voyage,' as ἑτερόπλους (§ 22) is for the single or outer voyage. See Or. 56, Διονυσ. §§ 6 and 29. It was usual in the latter case to pay the loan and interest either to a partner on the spot, under letter of advice, or to an agent who was on board during the voyage.
ἐθέμην] 'I deposited the bond with Kittus the banker.' [Possibly son of the Kittus mentioned in the τραπεζιτικὸς of Isocr. as a servant of the noted banker Pasion. S.] It was the custom

τῷ τραπεζίτῃ. κελευούσης δὲ τῆς συγγραφῆς ἐνθέσθαι εἰς τὴν ναῦν τετρακισχιλίων φορτία ἄξια, πρᾶγμα ποιεῖ πάντων δεινότατον· εὐθὺς γὰρ ἐν τῷ Πειραιεῖ ἐπιδανείζεται λάθρᾳ ἡμῶν παρὰ μὲν Θεοδώρου τοῦ Φοίνικος τετρακισχιλίας πεντακοσίας δραχμὰς, παρὰ δὲ τοῦ ναυκλήρου Λάμπιδος χιλίας[h]. δέον δ' αὐτὸν καταγοράσαι 7 909 φορτία Ἀθήνηθεν μνῶν ἑκατὸν καὶ δέκα καὶ πέντε[i], εἰ

[h] + δραχμάς Z cum Σ.   [i] δεκάπεντε Z. Reiske, approved by A. Schaefer, conjectures πεντήκοντα. '*ortus est error lectionis ex errore librarii qui ΔΠ i.e.* δεκάπεντε *dedit pro* ΔΙ, πεντάκις δέκα *i.e.* πεντήκοντα.'

then, as with us, to place valuable deeds in the custody of bankers. See Or. 33 § 15; 35 § 14.

εὐθύς] 'At the very outset,' before he left the harbour.—ἐπιδανείζεται, 'he raises another loan on the same security.' This was illegal, as a second mortgage would be on property already mortgaged to its full value. Or. 35 § 21, μετὰ δὲ ταῦτ' ἔστιν ἐν τῇ συγγραφῇ ὅτι ὑποτιθέασι ταῦτ' ἐλεύθερα καὶ οὐδενὶ οὐδὲν ὀφείλοντες.

Θεοδώρου] 'La traduction grecque du nom phénicien Ionathan ou Nathaniel, ou du nom carthaginois Baalitan ou Mathanélim.' Dareste. S.]

τοῦ Φοίνικος] 'The Phoenician.' [The Phoenicians of Tyre and Sidon carried on a considerable trade with Greece (Odyss. xv 415—480) and many of that mercantile people were settled in Athens. There is a decree extant granting the Sidonians resident in Athens exemption from the μετοίκιον and other taxes. Cf. Büchsenschütz, *Besitz und Erwerb im Griechischen Alterthume*, pp. 443, 275, 362, and Isocr. Trapez. § 4, συστή-

σαντός μοι Πυθοδώρου τοῦ Φοίνικος Πασίωνα, ἐχρώμην τῇ τούτου τραπέζῃ. S.]

7. καταγοράσαι] The word technically means 'to purchase goods against, or as a set-off to, a sum of money.'

μνῶν ἑκατὸν, κ.τ.λ.] As 100 drachms = 1 mina, and therefore twice the amount of the whole ἐπιδανεισμὸς (of 4500+1000) is 11000 drachmae or 110 minae, and as καταγοράσαι implies the doubling, without including, the loan of 2000 drachms, it is not very clear why the sum is put at 115 minae, unless 5 minae in addition should have been spent in provisioning the ship, ἐπισιτισμός.

[If the terms of the agreements with Theodorus and Lampis were identical with those of the original agreement with Chrysippus, Phormio was bound to put on board not 115 minae, but 150, i.e. *double* the value of the three loans, amounting in all to 7500 dr. = 75 minae. The copyist may have failed to understand what more than one critic has conjectured as the right reading, viz. 150 minae. He was probably led to alter

ἔμελλε^j τοῖς δανεισταῖς πᾶσι ποιήσειν τὰ ἐν ταῖς συγγραφαῖς γεγραμμένα, οὐ κατηγόρασεν ἀλλ' ἢ πεντακισχιλίων καὶ πεντακοσίων δραχμῶν, σὺν τῷ ἐπισιτισμῷ· ὀφείλει δ' ἑβδομήκοντα μνᾶς καὶ πέντε. ἀρχὴ μὲν οὖν αὕτη ἐγένετο τοῦ ἀδικήματος, ὦ ἄνδρες Ἀθηναῖοι· οὔτε γὰρ τὴν ὑποθήκην παρέσχετο οὔτε τὰ χρή-

^j ἤμελλε Z.

this into 115, on finding that the latter happened to be the total of the sums mentioned in the text. He thus makes the blunder of including the original loan of 20 minae in the estimated total value of the goods which should have been put on board. Thus:
ἐδάνεισα εἴκοσι μνᾶς = 2000 dr.
κελεύει ἡ συγγραφὴ
ἐνθέσθαι τετρακισχι- } = 4000 dr.
λίων φορτία ἄξια ...
ἐπιδανείζεται
παρὰ Θεοδώρου...... = 4500 dr.
παρὰ Λάμπιδος...... = 1000 dr.
———
11,500 dr.
= μναῖ ἑκατὸν δεκάπεντε. Shilleto, however, remarks that 115 minae 'seems right.' S.]
Mr H. W. Lucas writes from Stonyhurst College:—"Reiske's conjecture (150 minae for 115 minae) seems to me probable; since then the amount of the goods shipped will be just double the value, as you remark, of the δανεισμὸς plus the two ἐπιδανεισμοί, which latter it is not unreasonable to suppose were negociated on the same terms as the original δανεισμός (viz. security of a cargo of double value)."
There is some uncertainty as to how τοῖς δανεισταῖς includes all the three creditors, πᾶσι, viz. Chrysippus, Theodorus, and Lampis. The whole sum borrowed was 7500 drachms, the double of which is too much, viz. 150 minae. What Phormio did do, perhaps, was to put on board goods only equal in value to the ἐπιδανεισμοί (5500) singly; thus leaving the original loan of 2000 (20 minae) from Chrysippus unsecured. See § 40. This is the πρᾶγμα δεινότατον, or the chief point of it, in § 6.

οὐ κατηγόρασεν, κ.τ.λ.] He did not buy goods of the value of more than 5500 dr.

ἀλλ' ἢ] [This formula is used only after an actual or an implied negative. Cf. Isocr. Paneg. § 7 n. S.] Originally, it seems to have represented ἄλλο or ἄλλα ἤ. Cf. Ar. Pac. 475, οὐδ' οἶδε γ' εἷλκον οὐδὲν ἀργεῖοι πάλαι, ἀλλ' ἢ κατεγέλων τῶν ταλαιπωρουμένων.

σὺν] i.e. including the provisions for the crew, which should have been paid for in addition.

ὀφείλει] He owes 7500 drachms to the three lenders, viz. 2000 + 4500 + 1000 = 7500 = 75 minae.

τὴν ὑποθήκην] It seems from p. 922, § 50, that the penalty of death attached to the not producing or handing over the security. In this case, either the ship might have been made over to Chrysippus, or double the value of his loan put on board. Phormio did neither, as

μάτ' ἐνέθετ' εἰς τὴν ναῦν, κελευούσης τῆς συγγραφῆς ἐπάναγκες ἐντίθεσθαι. καί μοι λαβὲ τὴν συγγραφήν.

ΣΥΓΓΡΑΦΗ.

Λαβὲ δὴ καὶ τὴν τῶν πεντηκοστολόγων ἀπογραφὴν καὶ τὰς μαρτυρίας.

ΑΠΟΓΡΑΦΗ. ΜΑΡΤΥΡΙΑΙ.

Ἐλθὼν τοίνυν εἰς τὸν Βόσπορον, ἔχων ἐπιστολὰς 8 παρ' ἐμοῦ, ἃς ἔδωκ' αὐτῷ ἀπενεγκεῖν τῷ παιδὶ τῷ ἐμῷ παραχειμάζοντι ἐκεῖ καὶ κοινωνῷ τινι, γράψας ἐν τῇ ἐπιστολῇ τό τε ἀργύριον ὃ ἐδεδανείκειν καὶ τὴν ὑποθήκην, καὶ προστάξας, ἐπειδὰν τάχιστ' ἐξαιρεθῇ τὰ

all the goods on board only covered the value of the ἐπιδανεισμοί.

ἀπογραφὴν] The entry made by the collectors of the two per cent. duties on all exports and imports. In the time of the Peloponnesian war these tolls seem to have been less; for we read of τὰς πολλὰς ἑκατοστὰς in Ar. Vesp. 658. [Cf., however, Boeckh, *P. E.* III v p. 321 Lewis (=p. 429 Lamb):—'We are not justified in assuming that this hundredth was an import duty, which was levied at a particular period in place of the fiftieth; for we find the fiftieth mentioned both *in the earlier time of Andocides* (whose lease of the custom duties... falls in the first years after the anarchy), and also in the time of Demosthenes; and an alteration in this tax cannot be assumed without any proof.' Boeckh conjectures that the ἑκατοστὴ was a *harbour duty*, separate from the *custom duty* or πεντηκοστή. S.]

§§ 8, 9. *Arrived at the Bosporus (Panticapaeum) he again* acted *fraudulently in not delivering the advices I had written to my agent there, which were, that he should keep his eye on Phormio. And at last, being unable to sell his goods, and finding it difficult to pay the ἐπιδανεισμοί (which he had borrowed only for the outer voyage), instead of shipping goods from the Pontus to Athens, as he was bound to do by his contract with me, he told Lampis to set out for Athens, and promised that he would follow on another ship.*

ἃς ἔδωκα] 'Which I had given him to deliver to a servant of mine who was wintering there, and a certain partner.' It might seem doubtful whether παιδὶ means 'son' or 'slave,' but we have οὔτε τὸν παῖδα τὸν ἡμέτερον οὔτε τὸν κοινωνὸν § 28, Λάμπιδι τῷ Δίωνος οἰκέτῃ § 5, and μετὰ τῶν ἄλλων παίδων τῶν Δίωνος inf. § 10:

τὴν ὑποθήκην] viz. that the security was the cargo, and therefore that a counter-cargo must be sent from the Pontus back to Athens.

ἐπειδὰν, κ.τ.λ.] 'As soon as

16   XXXIV. ΠΡΟΣ ΦΟΡΜΙΩΝΑ [§§ 9, 10

χρήματα, ἐξετάζειν καὶ παρακολουθεῖν, τὰς μὲν ἐπιστολὰς οὐκ ἀποδίδωσιν οὗτος, ἃς ἔλαβε παρ' ἐμοῦ, ἵνα μηδὲν εἰδείησαν ὧν ἔπραττεν οὗτος, καταλαβὼν δ' ἐν τῷ Βοσπόρῳ μοχθηρὰ τὰ πράγματα διὰ τὸν συμβάντα πόλεμον τῷ Παιρισάδῃ[k] πρὸς τὸν Σκύθην, καὶ τῶν φορτίων ὧν ἦγε πολλὴν ἀπρασίαν, ἐν πάσῃ ἀπορίᾳ ἦν· καὶ γὰρ οἱ δανεισταὶ εἴχοντο αὐτοῦ οἱ τὰ ἑτε-

[k] Παρεισάδῃ Z.

ever the goods were (shall have been) unloaded, that he should take stock (inventory) of them and keep close to him,' viz. lest he should give him the slip. This use of ἐξετάζειν is idiomatic. See Ar. Eccl. 728, ἐγὼ δ', ἵν' εἰς ἀγοράν γε τὰ σκεύη φέρω, προχειροῦμαι κἀξετάσω τὴν οὐσίαν. Kennedy's rendering 'to inspect' does not fully give the sense.

καταλαβών] 'Finding business in the Bosporus bad, through the war that had broken out between Paerisades and the Scythian (king), and great difficulty in selling the goods he had brought.' Paerisades is mentioned inf. § 36 as an ally and friend of Athens. He is identical with a king of that name who is said by Diodorus Siculus (xvi ch. 52 fin.) to have reigned in Pontus Ol. 107. 4 (B.C. 349); ἅμα δὲ τούτοις πράττομένοις ἐν τῷ Πόντῳ Σπάρτακος ὁ τοῦ Πόντου βασιλεὺς ἐτελεύτησεν ἄρξας ἔτη πέντε, τὴν δ' ἡγεμονίαν διαδεξάμενος ὁ ἀδελφὸς Παρισάδης ἐβασίλευσεν ἔτη τριάκοντα ὀκτώ. Again, in lib. xx ch. 22 and 24 we have mention of Παρυσάδης as βασιλεὺς τοῦ Κιμμερικοῦ Βοσπόρου, B.C. 310, and of a grandson of the same name, ὁ παῖς ὁ Σατύρου Παρυσάδης. Strabo (VII 4 § 4) speaks of Leuco, Satyrus, and Paerisades as μόναρχοι of Panticapaeum, and says the last had divine honours paid to him. He mentions a Παιρισάδης ὁ ὕστατος who gave up his kingdom to Mithridates. The Paerisades of the text is different from the Paerisades, or Βηρισάδης (Or. 23, contr. Aristoc. p. 623, §§ 8—10), who succeeded Cotys, king of Thrace, B.C. 358. Like many eastern appellatives, the word perhaps was not so much a proper name as a title of dignity. [Paerisades, king of Bosporus (B.C. 348—310), is the Birisides of Dinarchus in Dem. § 43 (compare infr. § 36 n.), but is different from Berisades, king of Thrace, who, as may be seen from Dem. Aristocr. § 10, was already dead in B.C. 352. Penrose has apparently confounded them. For the king of Thrace, cf. Strabo VII fragm. 48, 'Οδρύσας δὲ καλοῦσιν ἔνιοι πάντας τοὺς ἀπὸ Ἕβρου καὶ Κυψέλων μέχρι Ὀδησσοῦ τῆς παραλίας (sc. Odessa) ὑπεροικοῦντας, ὧν ἐβασίλευσεν Ἀμάδοκος καὶ Κερσοβλέπτης καὶ Βηρισάδης καὶ Σεύθης καὶ Κότυς.——For a dissertation on the Kings of Bosporus, see Clinton, Fasti Hellenici II, Appendix, chap. 13, and cf. Grote, chap. 98. S.]

οἱ δανεισταί] viz. Theodorus

ρόπλοα δανείσαντες. ὥστε τοῦ ναυκλήρου κελεύοντος 9
αὐτὸν κατὰ τὴν συγγραφὴν ἐντίθεσθαι τὰ ἀγοράσματα
τῶν ἐμῶν χρημάτων, εἶπεν οὗτος ὁ νῦν φάσκων ἀποδεδωκέναι τὸ χρυσίον ὅτι οὐκ ἂν δύναιτο ἐνθέσθαι εἰς
τὴν ναῦν τὰ χρήματα. ἄπρατον γὰρ εἶναι τὸν ῥῶπον.
κἀκεῖνον[1] μὲν ἐκέλευεν ἀνάγεσθαι· αὐτὸς δ', ἐπειδὰν
διαθῆται τὰ φορτία, ἐφ' ἑτέρας νεὼς ἔφη ἐκπλεύσεσθαι.
καί μοι λέγε ταύτην τὴν μαρτυρίαν.

ΜΑΡΤΥΡΙΑ.

Μετὰ ταῦτα τοίνυν, ὦ ἄνδρες Ἀθηναῖοι, οὗτος 10

[1] καὶ ἐκεῖνον Z.

and Lampis.——καὶ γὰρ, i.e. they *also*, besides the other demands on him to ship a cargo for Athens.

9. τὰ ἀγοράσματα] The goods bought with, or as a set-off to, my money. Hesych. ἀγοράσματα· ὤνια. Cf. § 33.

ὅτι οὐκ ἂν δύναιτο, κ.τ.λ.] His actual words would be, οὐκ ἂν δυναίμην, μὴ διατιθέμενος τὰ φορτία.

τὸν ῥῶπον] 'the trash,' 'the common wares.' *Vilia scruta*, Hor. Epist. I 7, 65. Aeschylus fragm. Φρύγες (242 Dind.) ναυβάτην φορτηγὸν ὅστις ῥῶπον ἐξάγει χθονός. [Strabo VIII p. 376 says of Aegina: Ἐμπόριον γὰρ γενέσθαι διὰ τὴν λυπρότητα τῆς χώρας τῶν ἀνθρώπων θαλαττουργούντων ἐμπορικῶς, ἀφ' οὗ τὸν ῥῶπον Αἰγιναῖαν ἐμπολὴν λέγεσθαι. Eustath. on Iliad, XIII 199, ῥῶπος μέντοι λεπτὸς καὶ ἀτελὴς (qu. εὐτελὴς) φόρτος, ὡς δὲ Αἴλιος Διονύσιος λέγει, καὶ ποικίλος. Bekker's *Anecd.* 299, ῥῶπος ὁ παντοδαπὸς φόρτος. Hesych. ῥωποπῶλαι· μυροπῶλαι. S.] Hesych. ῥῶπος· ῥωπικόν· ἀντὶ τοῦ οὐδενὸς ἄξιον. ὁ γὰρ λεπτὸς ῥῶπος, ἤγουν ὁ φόρτος, μίγματα, χρώματα, ὅσα ζωγράφοις, βαφεῦσι, μυρεψοῖς χρησιμεύει. With this word (μυρεψοῖς) τὸν ῥῶπον well agrees, and § 13 καταλαμβάνομεν πρὸς τοῖς μυροπωλείοις τουτονί. He may have done a small business in perfumery.

κἀκεῖνον] 'And Lampis he ordered to get under weigh at once, and said that he himself, so soon as he should (shall) have disposed of his wares, would sail out in another ship.' We have the subjunctive as expressing a result pending at the time described. The idiom is not English unless in *oratio recta*: we suppose him to have said, 'I will follow you on another ship,' &c.—διατίθεσθαι, precisely our word 'to dispose of,' comes naturally from the idea of settling and arranging goods to be kept back or taken away.

§ 10. *Lampis sails while Phormio is left behind. But the ship, being over-freighted, is lost, with some of the crew, and Lampis is picked up in the boat. Evidence is given that Phormio was congratulated for not having any goods on board.*

18   XXXIV. ΠΡΟΣ ΦΟΡΜΙΩΝΑ [§§ 10—12

μὲν ἐν τῷ Βοσπόρῳ κατελέλειπτο^m, ὁ δὲ Λάμπις ἀναχθεὶς ἐνανάγησεν οὐ μακρὰν ἀπὸ τοῦ ἐμπορίου· γεγεμισμένης γὰρ ἤδη τῆς νεὼς, ὡς ἀκούομεν, μᾶλλον τοῦ δέοντος, προσανέλαβεν ἐπὶ τὸ κατάστρωμα χιλίας βύρσας, ὅθεν καὶ ἡ διαφθορὰ τῇ νηὶ συνέβη. καὶ αὐτὸς μὲν ἀπεσώθη ἐν τῷ λέμβῳ μετὰ τῶν ἄλλων παίδων τῶν^n Δίωνος, ἀπώλεσε δὲ πλέον ἢ τριάκοντα σώματα χωρὶς τῶν ἄλλων. πολλοῦ δὲ πένθους ἐν τῷ Βοσπόρῳ ὄντος, ὡς ἐπύθοντο τὴν διαφθορὰν τῆς νεὼς, ηὐδαιμόνιζον τὸν Φορμίωνα πάντες τουτονὶ ὅτι οὔτε συνανήχθη

^m 'Optime Dindorfius restituit' Cobet, Nov. Lect. 582. κατελείπετο Z cum Σ.   ^n τοῦ Z cum Σ.

ἀναχθείς] Cf. note on Or. 53 (Nicostr.) § 3, ἀνήγμαι.
γεγεμισμένης, κ.τ.λ.] 'The ship had already been overloaded when Lampis took on deck besides 1000 hides, which was the real cause of the wreck.' Hides are very heavy; and the deckload would so alter the centre of gravity as to make the ship very unmanageable in a heavy sea. [For the βύρσαι of Bosporus, cf. Lacrit. § 34 (μαρτυρ.) δέρματα αἴγεια and Strabo XI 3, p. 493, Τάναϊς κτίσμα τῶν τὸν Βόσπορον ἐχόντων Ἑλλήνων...ἐμπόριον κοινὸν τῶν τε Ἀσιανῶν καὶ τῶν Εὐρωπαίων νομάδων καὶ τῶν ἐκ τοῦ Βοσπόρου τὴν λίμνην (Sea of Azov) πλεόντων τῶν μὲν ἀνδράποδα ἀγόντων καὶ δέρματα ...τῶν δὲ ἐσθῆτα καὶ οἶνον...ἀντιφορτιζομένων. S.]
λέμβῳ] Hesychius has λήμβωνι· ἐν σκαφίδι, ἢ ἐν πλοιαρίῳ.
παίδων] 'slaves.' See on § 8. Lampis himself was Δίωνος οἰκέτης, § 5. τριάκοντα of the Paris ed. of 1570 is much more plausible than the manuscript reading τριακόσια (found in Σ and other MSS), which could only be explained on the supposition that it was a slave-ship, bringing Θρᾷκες or Σκύθαι to Athens (cf. Strabo, supr.). Whether σώματα means 'slaves' or merely 'hands,' i.e. crew, is uncertain; but the former is more probable, as half-a-dozen men would easily work such a ship. [One MS the August. primus has the interpolation πλείω ἢ διακόσια σώματα ἐλεύθερα, which is accepted by Reiske, but rightly rejected by Bekker and the Zürich editors. In later Greek, the use of σώματα for 'slaves' became common, e.g. Revelation xviii 13; Atticists like Pollux (iii 78) protested against this usage, σώματα ἁπλῶς οὐκ ἂν εἴποις ἀλλὰ δοῦλα σώματα. Cf. Dem. Lept. p. 480 § 77, αἰχμάλωτα σώματα. In Plat. Leg. p. 908 A, σώματα is used of any kind of men, slaves or free, indiscriminately. S.]—
χωρὶς τῶν ἄλλων, 'besides his cargo.'
πένθους] 'mourning,' the regular meaning of this word.

ΠΕΡΙ ΔΑΝΕΙΟΥ.

οὔτ' ἐνέθετο εἰς τὴν ναῦν οὐδέν. συνέβαινε δὲ παρά τε τῶν ἄλλων καὶ παρὰ τούτου ὁ αὐτὸς λόγος. καί μοι ἀνάγνωθι ταύτας τὰς μαρτυρίας.

ΜΑΡΤΥΡΙΑΙ.

Αὐτὸς μὲν τοίνυν ὁ Λάμπις, ᾧ φησιν ἀποδεδωκέ- 11 ναι τὸ χρυσίον (τούτῳ γὰρ προσέχετε τὸν νοῦν), προσελθόντος αὐτῷ ἐμοῦ, ἐπειδὴ τάχιστα κατέπλευσεν ἐκ τῆς ναυαγίας Ἀθήναζε, καὶ ἐρωτῶντος ὑπὲρ τούτων, ἔλεγεν ὅτι οὔτε τὰ χρήματα ἔνθοιτο εἰς τὴν ναῦν οὗτος κατὰ τὴν συγγραφήν, οὔτε τὸ χρυσίον εἰληφὼς εἴη παρ' αὐτοῦ° ἐν Βοσπόρῳ τότε. καί μοι ἀνάγνωθι τὴν μαρτυρίαν τῶν παραγενομένων.

ΜΑΡΤΥΡΙΑ.

Ἐπειδὴ τοίνυν, ὦ ἄνδρες Ἀθηναῖοι, ἐπεδήμησε 12 Φορμίων οὑτοσὶ σεσωσμένος ἐφ' ἑτέρας νεώς, προσῄειν

° παρὰ τούτου Z.

καὶ παρὰ τούτου] i. e. Phormio was heard to congratulate himself. With συνέβαινε we might supply γενέσθαι, but perhaps the sense is rather 'coincided.'

§ 11. *When I went to Lampis immediately after his arrival in Athens, he declared that Phormio had neither put goods on board the lost vessel nor given him any remittance for Athens. Evidence is adduced of his statement to that effect.*

ἐκ τῆς ν.] Either 'from' or 'after' the wreck.

ἔνθοιτο] Compounds of τίθεσθαι, but not the simple verb, often assume this form of the uncontracted optative, though mss commonly present the other form ἐνθεῖτο, ἐπιθεῖτο &c. Many examples of both are given by Veitch, *Irreg. Gk. Verbs*, p. 636–7. mss generally

vary in the forms πρόοιντο, προοῖντο, προεῖντο and similar compounds of ἵεσθαι.

οὔτε τὸ χρυσίον] The change of subject might have been more clearly expressed by οὔτ' αὐτὸς τὸ χρυσίον κ.τ.λ.

τῶν παραγενομένων] Of those present at the interview between me and Lampis at Athens.

§§ 12, 13. *And when Phormio himself arrived somewhat later, he told substantially the same story, that is, he admitted his liability. Afterwards, however, there was a collusion between them, and he then said he had paid Lampis the money at the Bosporus.*

προσῄειν] Like ᾔδειν and ᾖν, this word takes the ν even in the first person in the middle and later Attic. The older forms were πρόσῃα, ᾔδη, ἦ, as forms

2—2

20   XXXIV. ΠΡΟΣ ΦΟΡΜΙΩΝΑ   [§§ 12—16

αὐτῷ ἀπαιτῶν τὸ δάνειον. καὶ οὗτος κατὰ μὲν ἀρχὰς οὐδεπώποτ', ὦ ἄνδρες Ἀθηναῖοι, εἶπε τὸν λόγον τοῦτον ὃν νυνὶ λέγει, ἀλλ' ἀεὶ ὡμολόγει ἀποδώσειν· ἐπεὶ δ' ἀνεκοινώσατο τοῖς νῦν παροῦσιν αὐτῷ καὶ συνδικοῦσιν, 13 ἕτερος ἤδη ἦν καὶ οὐχ ὁ αὐτός. ὡς δ' ᾐσθόμην αὐτὸν διακρουόμενόν με, προσέρχομαι τῷ Λάμπιδι, λέγων ὅτι οὐδὲν ποιεῖ τῶν δικαίων Φορμίων οὐδ' ἀποδίδωσι τὸ δάνειον, καὶ ἅμα ἠρόμην αὐτὸν εἰ εἰδείη ὅπου ἐστὶν, ἵνα προσκαλεσαίμην αὐτόν. ὁ δ' ἀκολουθεῖν μ' ἐκέλευεν ἑαυτῷ, καὶ καταλαμβάνομεν πρὸς τοῖς μυροπωλίοις τουτονί[p]. κἀγὼ κλητῆρας ἔχων προσεκαλεσά-14 μην αὐτόν[q]. καὶ ὁ Λάμπις, ὦ ἄνδρες Ἀθηναῖοι, παρὼν

[p] μυροπωλείοις αὐτόν· Z.   [q] τουτονί. Z et Bekk. st.

like τετύφη seem to be older than ἐτετύφειν, &c. Thus κεχήνη is the first person of the pluperfect in Ar. Ach. 10. [Plato Apol. 31 E, πάλαι ἂν ἀπολώλη καὶ οὔτ' ἂν ὑμᾶς ὠφελήκη κ.τ.λ. *Elucidations of Curtius' Gk. Gr.* § 283. S.]

ὃν νυνὶ λέγει] viz. that he paid Lampis.——ἀνεκοινώσατο, 'when he had entered into a secret understanding.'

συνδικοῦσιν] συνδίκοις οὖσιν, advocates for the defence. Perhaps we should read συναδικοῦσιν, meaning Lampis in particular. Cf. §§ 28 and 46, Λάμπιδος τοῦ συναδικοῦντος.——παρεῖναι, *adesse* is often used of friends and advocates, e.g. Mid. § 182.

13. προσέρχομαι] Cf. προσελθόντος in § 11, which was the first, this being the second interview.——τῷ Λάμπιδι, 'this Lampis,' said with some contempt.

ὁ δὲ] 'Accordingly he, Lampis, bade me go with him, and we find the defendant at the shops for perfumery.' See Hesych. quoted on § 9, τὸν ῥῶπον. [The shops of the perfumers, like those of the barbers and the cobblers, were favourite places of lounge at Athens, cf. Lysias Or. 24 § 20, ἕκαστος γὰρ ὑμῶν εἴθισται προσφοιτᾶν ὁ μὲν πρὸς μυροπωλεῖον, ὁ δὲ πρὸς κουρεῖον, ὁ δὲ πρὸς σκυτοτομεῖον. S.]

§§ 14, 15. *Though Lampis was present when I served Phormio with a summons, he never said, as he would have done had the story been true, that Phormio had already paid the money to him.* A negative argument ἐκ τῶν εἰκότων, as the rhetoricians called it. It was not *likely* that Lampis would be silent. "Between τεκμήρια and εἰκότα there is strictly this difference: the former are the evidentiary facts, the latter the results which are obtained by combining such facts together and reasoning upon them." Kennedy, Append. VI to Vol. IV of Demosth. p. 369. So Or. 30 § 10, δῆλον δὲ καὶ ἐκ τῶν εἰκότων ὅτι τούτων ἕνεχ' ὧν εἴρηκα ὀφείλειν εἵλοντο.

ΠΕΡΙ ΔΑΝΕΙΟΥ.

προσκαλουμένῳ μοι οὐδαμοῦ ἐτόλμησεν εἰπεῖν ὡς ἀπείληφε παρὰ τούτου τὸ χρυσίον, οὐδ' ὃ εἰκὸς ἦν εἶπε, "Χρύσιππε, μαίνει· τί τοῦτον προσκαλεῖ; ἐμοὶ γὰρ ἀποδέδωκε τὸ χρυσίον." ἀλλὰ μὴ ὅτι ὁ Λάμπις ἐφθέγξατο[r], ἀλλ' οὐδ' αὐτὸς οὗτος ἠξίωσεν εἰπεῖν, παρεστηκότος τοῦ Λάμπιδος, ᾧ νῦν φησιν ἀποδεδωκέναι τὸ χρυσίον. καίτοι εἰκός γ' ἦν αὐτὸν εἰπεῖν, ὦ ἄνδρες 15 Ἀθηναῖοι, "τί με προσκαλεῖ, ἄνθρωπε; ἀποδέδωκα γὰρ τούτῳ τῷ παρεστηκότι τὸ χρυσίον," καὶ ἅμα ὁμολογοῦντα παρέχειν τὸν Λάμπιν· νῦν δ' οὐδέτερος αὐτῶν οὐδ' ὁτιοῦν εἶπεν ἐν τοιούτῳ καιρῷ. καὶ ὅτι ἀληθῆ λέγω, λαβέ μοι τὴν μαρτυρίαν τῶν κλητήρων[s].

ΜΑΡΤΥΡΙΑΙ.

Λαβὲ δή μοι καὶ τὸ ἔγκλημα ὃ ἔλαχον αὐτῷ πέρυ- 16 σιν· ὅ ἐστιν οὐδενὸς ἔλαττον τεκμήριον ὅτι οὐδέπω τότ'[t] ἔφησε Φορμίων ἀποδεδωκέναι τὸ χρυσίον Λάμπιδι.

ΕΓΚΛΗΜΑ.

Τοῦτο τὸ ἔγκλημα ἔλαχον ἐγώ, ὦ ἄνδρες Ἀθηναῖοι,

[r] μὴ ὅτι Λάμπις οὐκ ἐφθέγξατο Z.   [s] κλητόρων Z.
[t] οὐδεπώποτ' Z.

μὴ ὅτι] Both this and οὐχ ὅτι are used in the sense of non modo or non modo non. In the former case there is an ellipse of λέγειν, in the latter, of λέγω. Translate, ' Not only did Lampis not utter a word, but not even Phormio himself thought fit to say he had paid it, though Lampis was actually standing by, to whom he now says he paid the money.' Cf. Or. 56 § 30.

εἰκὸς ἦν] Lit. 'it was reasonable for him to have said.' Hence in such expressions as δίκαιον ἦν, ἐχρῆν, &c., the Greeks never use ἄν, as some might expect, deceived by the difference of our idiom, 'it would have been natural for him to say,' &c. [See Goodwin's Gk. Moods and Tenses, § 49, 2, p. 97—100, ed. 3. S.]

15. παρέχειν] To have brought him forward at the time, viz. as a ground for withdrawing the summons.

§§ 16, 17. Another proof of Phormio's falsehood is, that in moving for a demurrer to a suit I brought against him last year, he never pleaded payment. And yet the sole ground of my action was the report of Lampis that he had not paid, or put any goods on board.

οὐδαμόθεν ἄλλοθεν σκοπῶν ἀλλ' ἢ ἐκ τῆς ἀπαγγελίας
τῆς Λάμπιδος, ὃς οὐκ ἔφασκεν οὔτε τὰ χρήματα ἐντε-
θεῖσθαι τοῦτον οὔτε τὸ χρυσίον ἀπειληφέναι· μὴ γὰρ
οἴεσθέ με οὕτως ἀπόπληκτον εἶναι καὶ παντελῶς μαινό-
μενον ὥστε τοιοῦτο^u γράφειν ἔγκλημα ὁμολογοῦντος
τοῦ Λάμπιδος ἀπειληφέναι τὸ χρυσίον, ὑφ' οὗ ἔμελ-
λον^v ἐξελεγχθήσεσθαι.

17 Ἔτι δ', ὦ ἄνδρες Ἀθηναῖοι, κἀκεῖνο σκέψασθε·
αὐτοὶ γὰρ οὗτοι παραγραφὴν διδόντες πέρυσιν, οὐκ
ἐτόλμησαν ἐν τῇ παραγραφῇ γράψαι ὡς ἀποδεδώκασι
Λάμπιδι τὸ χρυσίον. καί μοι λαβὲ ταύτην τὴν παραγραφήν.

ΠΑΡΑΓΡΑΦΗ.

Ἀκούετε, ὦ ἄνδρες Ἀθηναῖοι, ὅτι οὐδαμοῦ γέγραπται ἐν τῇ παραγραφῇ ὡς ἀποδέδωκε τὸ χρυσίον
Φορμίων Λάμπιδι, καὶ ταῦτ' ἐμοῦ διαρρήδην γράψαν-

^u τοιοῦτον Z.   ^v ἤμελλον Z.

ἐντεθεῖσθαι] In the middle sense, as is usual with the passive perfect of τίθεσθαι and its compounds. [Infr. § 34, ὡς ἐντεθειμένος. The perfect passive of τίθημι and its compounds is almost invariably borrowed from κεῖμαι, e.g. Plat. Leg. 793 B, (νόμων) τῶν ἐν γράμμασι τεθέντων τε καὶ κειμένων (not τεθειμένων) καὶ τῶν ἔτι τεθησομένων. Isocr. ad Dem. § 36 n. S.]

μὴ γὰρ, κ.τ.λ.] 'For don't suppose I am so crazy, or, rather, so downright mad, as to put into writing such a charge as that, if Lampis had admitted that he had received the money; since I was sure to be refuted in my claim by him.'

[ἀπόπληκτον, κ.τ.λ., noted by Blass III 519 as a peculiar expression, finds its parallel in the Meidias § 143, οὐχ οὕτως εἰμὶ ἄφρων οὐδ' ἀπόπληκτος ἐγώ. S.]

17. παραγραφὴν διδόναι] A notable synonym of παραγράφεσθαι.

οὐκ ἐτόλμησαν] This would have been the ordinary defence in a εὐθυδικία, and was not a true ground for a παραγραφή (§ 4), but it would have been an argument, if they could have pleaded it, in favour of the court granting a bar to the suit.

καὶ ταῦτα] 'And that too when I had expressly written in the charge against him, which you have just heard read, that he had neither put the goods on board nor paid the money.' If he could have given so direct

ΠΕΡΙ ΔΑΝΕΙΟΥ.

τος εἰς τὸ ἔγκλημα ὃ ἠκούσατ' ἀρτίως, ὅτι οὔτε τὰ χρήματ' ἔνθοιτο εἰς τὴν ναῦν οὔτ' ἀπέδωκε τὸ χρυσίον. τίνα οὖν ἄλλον χρὴ περιμένειν ὑμᾶς μάρτυρα, ὅταν τηλικαύτην μαρτυρίαν παρ' αὐτῶν τούτων ἔχητε[w]; Μελλούσης δὲ τῆς δίκης εἰσιέναι εἰς τὸ δικαστή- 18 ριον ἐδέοντο ἡμῶν ἐπιτρέψαι τινί· καὶ ἡμεῖς ἐπετρέψαμεν Θεοδότῳ ἰσοτελεῖ κατὰ συνθήκας. καὶ ὁ Λάμπις μετὰ ταῦτα νομίσας αὐτῷ ἀσφαλὲς ἤδη εἶναι πρὸς διαιτητῇ μαρτυρεῖν ὅ τι βούλοιτο, μερισάμενος τὸ ἐμὸν χρυσίον μετὰ Φορμίωνος τουτουὶ ἐμαρτύρει[x] τἀναντία οἷς πρότερον εἰρήκει. οὐ γὰρ ὅμοιόν ἐστιν, ὦ ἄνδρες 19

[w] At this point the Zürich editors (and A. Schaefer) mark a break in the speech. 'Alterum actorem hinc nobis videri incipere lineola significavimus (cf. § 20).'   [x] om. Z cum Σ.

an answer to so direct a charge,. he would have done so; not indeed as in itself sufficient as a bar to the suit (see *supra* on the argument), but as an additional reason why it need not be tried.
τηλικαύτην] tam gravem.
§§ 18—20. *When the suit last year was coming on, the defendants asked for an arbitration, to which I consented. Lampis, having no fear of being prosecuted for perjury before an arbitrator, and being bribed by Phormio, then said that Phormio had paid the money to him, though before he had denied it. When I confronted him with witnesses who heard him say he had not been paid by Phormio, he admitted he had said so, but pretended he didn't then know what he was saying.*
ἐπιτρέψαι] See note on Or. 54 § 26.
ἰσοτελεῖ] A privileged sojourner (denizen), i.e. a μέτοικος who paid equal taxes with

an ἀστός, and no more. They were specially exempted from the tax called μετοίκιον. See F. A. Wolf, Pref. to Leptines (p. 27, Beatson), who remarks that this passage shows they were not wholly excluded from holding offices, as had been generally supposed. He appears to think they could even sit as dicasts. There is some depreciation of the position in § 44.
ἀσφαλές] That there was no great danger of a prosecution. This is explained by οὐ γὰρ, &c. *infra*.——ἤδη, viz. as he was not now in court.
μερισάμενος] Compare ἐπεὶ ἀνεκοινώσατο, § 12.
19. ὅμοιον—καί] 'The same as it is to do so before an arbitrator.' It does not seem certain from this passage whether a man *could* not be prosecuted for perjury before an arbitrator. It may mean, that in practice it was seldom done, and so the risk was not great.

Ἀθηναῖοι, εἰς τὰ ὑμέτερα πρόσωπα ἐμβλέποντα τὰ ψευδῆ μαρτυρεῖν καὶ πρὸς διαιτητῇ· παρ' ὑμῖν μὲν γὰρ καὶ ὀργὴ μεγάλη καὶ τιμωρία ὑπόκειται τοῖς τὰ ψευδῆ μαρτυροῦσι, πρὸς δὲ τῷ διαιτητῇ ἀκινδύνως καὶ ἀναισχύντως μαρτυροῦσιν ὅ τι ἂν βούλωνται.
20 ἀγανακτοῦντος δέ μου[y] καὶ σχετλιάζοντος, ὦ ἄνδρες Ἀθηναῖοι, ἐπὶ τῇ τόλμῃ τοῦ Λάμπιδος, καὶ παρεχομένου πρὸς τὸν διαιτητὴν τὴν αὐτὴν μαρτυρίαν ἥνπερ καὶ νῦν πρὸς ὑμᾶς παρέχομαι, τῶν ἐξ ἀρχῆς προσελθόντων αὐτῷ μεθ' ἡμῶν, ὅτε οὔτε τὸ χρυσίον ἔφη ἀπειληφέναι παρὰ τούτου οὔτε τὰ χρήματ' αὐτὸν ἐνθέσθαι εἰς τὴν ναῦν, οὕτως ὁ Λάμπις κατὰ κράτος[z] ἐξελεγχόμενος τὰ[a] ψευδῆ μαρτυρῶν καὶ πονηρὸς ὢν ὡμολόγει μὲν εἰρηκέναι ταῦτα πρὸς τοῦτον, οὐ μέντοι

[y] δ' ἐμοῦ Z. [z] κατακράτος Z.
[a] om. Z et Bekk. st. cum Σ.

ὑπόκειται] 'Is in store.'
20. τῶν ἐξ ἀρχῆς] Of those who had been present at the first interview (§ 11) between me and Lampis.——παρέχομαι, as distinct from παρέχω, always contemplates the person *from* whom a thing comes, not *to* whom it is given. It is subjective, while the active is objective. Thus, ἐγὼ παρέχομαι ἀρετήν, 'I show or exhibit virtue,' but παρέχω σοι χρήματα, &c. 'Producing witnesses' implies that it was for the object and interest of the party producing them.
κατὰ κράτος] *luculenter et invicte* (Reiske). Being convicted, in a way that he could not evade, of telling falsehoods.——[κατὰ κράτος is probably not found elsewhere with ἐξελέγχεσθαι, which is usually coupled with adverbs such as περιβοήτως or (more commonly) φανερῶς. S.]
——πονηρός, 'a fellow without principle,' i. e. preferring κέρδος to τὸ δίκαιον.
πρὸς τοῦτον] There is some difficulty in this, first, as to taking it with ὡμολόγει or with εἰρηκέναι, secondly, as to the person meant. It can hardly mean, as G. H. Schaefer, Voemel and Kennedy take it, the arbitrator Theodotus; it may mean Phormio, the defendant, if construed with εἰρηκέναι, but then we must assume that Phormio was also present at the interview, which is not stated in § 11. Or, possibly, if the δευτερολογία, or second partner's speech, commences at § 21, πρὸς τοῦτον may mean the other partner. The sense would then be, 'Lampis admitted he had told my partner here (anonymous) that Phormio had not paid him.' But

γε ἐντὸς ὢν εἰπεῖν αὐτοῦ. καί μοι ἀνάγνωθι ταύτην τὴν μαρτυρίαν.

ΜΑΡΤΥΡΙΑ.

Ἀκούσας τοίνυν ἡμῶν, ὦ ἄνδρες Ἀθηναῖοι, ὁ 21 Θεόδοτος πολλάκις, καὶ νομίσας τὸν Λάμπιν ψευδῆ μαρτυρεῖν, οὐκ ἀπέγνω τῆς δίκης, ἀλλ' ἐφῆκεν ἡμᾶς εἰς τὸ δικαστήριον· καταγνῶναι μὲν γὰρ οὐκ ἐβουλήθη[b] διὰ τὸ οἰκείως ἔχειν Φορμίωνι τούτῳ, ὡς ἡμεῖς ὕστερον ἐπυθόμεθα, ἀπογνῶναι δὲ τῆς δίκης ὤκνει, ἵν' αὐτὸς μὴ ἐπιορκήσειεν. ἐξ αὐτοῦ δὴ τοῦ πράγματος 22 λογίσασθε, ὦ ἄνδρες δικασταί, παρ' ὑμῖν αὐτοῖς ὁπόθεν ἔμελλεν[c] οὗτος ἀποδώσειν τὸ χρυσίον. ἐνθένδε

[b] ἠβουλήθη Z.   [c] ἤμελλεν Z.

this supposition is not without difficulty. [M. Dareste takes it of Chrysippus, whose brother, he considers, is now speaking. S.]
§ 21. That the second speech begins here seems probable from οὗτος in § 23, which appears to mean Chrysippus. If we could fix the division at any paragraph before, then the τοῦτον just discussed might equally mean Chrysippus. [G. H. Schaefer and Voemel think the second speech begins at § 22, ἐξ αὐτοῦ δὴ τοῦ πράγματος. This seems not unlikely, as the second speaker would naturally commence with a brief summary of the facts that had been brought forward. The Zürich editors and Arnold Schaefer (*Dem. u. s. Zeit* III 2. 305) consider the second speech to begin at § 18, μελλούσης δὲ τῆς δίκης. The latter view is followed by M. Dareste. Nitsche, *dissert. de traiciendis partibus in Dem. or.* Berlin, 1863 (quoted by Blass III 519), assigns §§ 1—17, 30—31, 34—52, to Chrysippus; and §§ 18—29, 32-33, to his brother. S.]
ἀκούσας, κ.τ.λ.] 'Theodotus, after several hearings, believing that Lampis was giving false evidence, did not acquit Phormio, but sent us to the court; for he did not like to decide against the defendant, being a friend or relation of his, as we afterwards heard; and he did not like to acquit him, that he might not break his own oath,' viz. to decide according to the merits of the case.—ἐφῆκεν, by the process called ἔφεσις, an appeal to a higher court. See a good note of Mr Wayte's, Timocr. § 54.
§ 22. *Now ask yourselves how he could have paid the money to Lampis. He left Athens without sufficient goods as a security, and additionally in debt to other lenders. At the Bosporus the market was so dull, that he could hardly pay those who had lent him for the outer voyage only.*

μὲν γὰρ ἐξέπλει οὐκ ἐνθέμενος εἰς τὴν ναῦν τὰ χρή- 914
ματα καὶ ὑποθήκην οὐκ ἔχων, ἀλλ' ἐπὶ τοῖς ἐμοῖς
χρήμασιν ἐπιδανεισάμενος· ἐν Βοσπόρῳ δ' ἀπρασίαν
τῶν φορτίων κατέλαβε, καὶ τοὺς τὰ ἑτερόπλοα δανεί-
23 σαντας μόλις ἀπήλλαξεν. καὶ οὗτος μὲν ἐδάνεισεν
αὐτῷ δισχιλίας δραχμὰς ἀμφοτερόπλουν, ὥστ' ἀπολαβεῖν Ἀθήνησι δισχιλίας ἑξακοσίας δραχμάς· Φορμίων δέ φησιν ἀποδοῦναι Λάμπιδι ἐν Βοσπόρῳ ἑκατὸν
καὶ[d] εἴκοσι στατῆρας Κυζικηνοὺς (τούτῳ γὰρ προσέ-

[d] om. Z.

οὐκ ἐνθέμενος] It is clear that the goods worth 5500 drachms in § 7 were purchased with the ἐπιδανεισμοί, and did not cover the loan of Chrysippus. See sup. on § 6.

ἀπήλλαξεν] See note on Or. 36 § 25.

§ 23. '*Phormio pretends to have paid a sum to Lampis which I can show to be more than he owed me at Athens; and therefore it is very improbable that he paid it.*' Again an argument ἐκ τῶν εἰκότων.

οὗτος] My partner Chrysippus.——δισχιλίας, cf. § 6, where the sum is called 20 minae.
——ὥστε, 'on condition of receiving at Athens 2600 drachms.' The interest therefore was very large, but so also was the risk considerable.

στατῆρας] A Cyzicene stater was a gold coin (with a female head on one side and a lion's head on the other) worth about one guinea, an Attic drachma being taken at a trifle less than ten-pence. A high rate of exchange is here adopted to make as large a total as possible. According to the ordinary rate, a stater was equivalent to 20 drachms only. Hesych. Κυζι-

κηνικοὶ στατῆρες· διεβεβόηντο ὡς εὖ κεχαραγμένοι. πρόσωπον δὲ ἦν γυναικὸς ὁ τύπος.

["Demosthenes (Or. 34 § 23) speaking of this money informs us that its current value was 28 Attic drachmae. The weight of the Cyzicene stater is uniformly about 248 grains. As the Attic and Macedonian staters which weighed 133 grains were equivalent to 20 Attic drachmae, while the Cyzicene, weighing 248 grains, passed for no more than 28, it is evident that the silver alloy of the electrum of which these pieces are made was deducted and considered of no value, not being in fact worth the cost of extraction. Mr Burgon estimates the alloy of ancient electrum at about ¼. Then as 133 is to 20, so is ¾ of 248 or 186 to 28, exactly the equivalent in drachmae of the Cyzicene stater as given by Demosthenes." Leake's Numismata Hellenica (Asiatic Greece), p. 50. An electrotype from the specimen in the British Museum may be seen in Leake's Collection at the Fitzwilliam Museum, Cambridge, Div. II 21, and there are two genuine ones in Trin. Coll. Library. Their types vary, some-

ΠΕΡΙ ΔΑΝΕΙΟΥ.

χετε τὸν νοῦν) δανεισάμενος ἐγγείων τόκων. ἦσαν δὲ ἔφεκτοι οἱ ἔγγειοι τόκοι, ὁ δὲ Κυζικηνὸς ἐδύνατο ἐκεῖ εἴκοσι καὶ ὀκτὼ δραχμὰς Ἀττικάς. δεῖ δὴ μαθεῖν 24 ὑμᾶς ὅσα φησὶ χρήματ᾽ ἀποδεδωκέναι. τῶν μὲν γὰρ ἑκατὸν καὶ[e] εἴκοσι στατήρων γίγνονται τρισχίλιαι τριακόσιαι ἑξήκοντα, ὁ δὲ τόκος ὁ ἔγγειος ὁ ἔφεκτος[f] τῶν τριάκοντα μνῶν καὶ τριῶν καὶ ἑξήκοντα, πεντακόσιαι δραχμαὶ καὶ ἑξήκοντα· τὸ δὲ σύμπαν κεφάλαιον γίγνεται τόσον καὶ τόσον[g]. ἔστιν οὖν, ὦ ἄνδρες 25 δικασταί, οὗτος ὁ ἄνθρωπος ἢ γενήσεταί ποτε, ὃς ἀντὶ δισχιλίων καὶ ἑξακοσίων δραχμῶν τριάκοντα

[e] om. Z.
[f] ὁ ἔγγειος ἔφεκτος Z. ὁ ἔγγειος Σ. ἔγγειος ὁ F. Φ. ὁ ἔγγειος ὁ ἔφεκτος Bekker.
[g] τὸ δὲ—καὶ τόσον glossema videntur esse. Sauppe.

times the head of a bull or lion, generally with a tunny-fish below; sometimes the head of Proserpine. See *Plate of Coins*. Cf. Hesych. quoted above, and Boeckh's *Publ. Econ.* bk. I, chap. v, pp. 36—38 (ed. Lamb). S.]

δανεισάμενος] 'By borrowing it (at the Bosporus) on the interest paid for loans on land,' i.e. on real security. This being ἔφεκτος, i.e. a sixth part added to the sum lent (e.g. £70 for £60, or somewhat more than 16 per cent.), makes up the following sums; 120 staters = 3360 dr. = 33 min. 60 dr., which + interest at ⅙ or 560 amounts to 3920 dr. = 39 min. 20 dr.

ἔφεκτοι] Harpocr. s. v. ἔφεκτος τόκος: ὁ ἐπὶ τῷ ἕκτῳ τοῦ κεφαλαίου· Δημοσθένης ἐν τῷ ὑπὲρ Χρυσίππου.

ἐδύνατο ἐκεῖ] This shows that the value of money differed, as with us, in different places. [Cf.

Xenoph. de Vectig. III 2, καὶ οἱ ἀργύριον ἐξάγοντες (ἐκ τῶν Ἀθηνῶν) καλὴν ἐμπορίαν ἐξάξουσιν. ὅπου γὰρ ἂν πωλῶσιν αὐτὸ πανταχοῦ τοῦ ἀρχαίου λαμβάνουσι. K. F. Hermann, *Griech. Privatalterthümer*, § 47, 17 = p. 451 ed. Blümner. S.]

24. τόσον καὶ τόσον] '*Comes to so much*, namely thirty-nine minas twenty drachms, which he does not here specify, because it is mentioned immediately after.' Penrose. Kennedy translates, 'and the whole sum is the amount of the two;' which is the literal sense. [Cf. Or. 57 § 29, ἔτη τόσα καὶ τόσα· Hesych. ἢ τοσαῦτα. S.]

25. ἀντὶ δισχιλίων, κ.τ.λ.] Instead of the sum he really owed.

———τριάκοντα κ.τ.λ., the sum he pretended to have paid in staters, not including the interest. (He here expresses it not as 33 minae, but as 30 minae 300 drachmae, &c.)

μνᾶς καὶ τριακοσίας καὶ ἑξήκοντα ἀποτίνειν προεί-
λετ' ἄν, καὶ τόκον πεντακοσίας δραχμὰς καὶ ἑξήκοντα δανεισάμενος, ἥς φησιν[h] ἀποδεδωκέναι Φορμίων
Λάμπιδι, τρισχιλίας ἐννακοσίας εἴκοσιν; ἐξὸν δ'
αὐτῷ ἀμφοτερόπλουν Ἀθήνησιν ἀποδοῦναι τὸ ἀργύριον, ἐν Βοσπόρῳ ἀπέδωκε[i], τρισὶ καὶ δέκα μναῖς
26 πλέον; καὶ τοῖς μὲν τὰ ἑτερόπλοα δανείσασι μόλις
τἀρχαῖα ἀποδέδωκας, οἳ συνέπλευσάν σοι καὶ προσ-
ήδρευον· τούτῳ δὲ τῷ μὴ παρόντι οὐ μόνον τἀρχαῖα

[h] ἑξήκοντα, δανεισάμενος ἅ φησιν Z.   [i] ἀποδέδωκε Z.

δανεισάμενος] 'As having borrowed it at the interest on land,' i.e. the τόκος was added *because* he had to borrow it.

τρισχιλίας ἐννακοσίας εἴκοσι] It will be observed that the interest (560 dr.) on the sum borrowed in the Bosporus, though really due to the lender, is here unfairly reckoned with the amount paid to Lampis as agent of Chrysippus. See A. Schaefer, *Dem. u. s. Zeit*, III 2. 306. S.]

ἐξὸν δ' αὐτῷ, κ.τ.λ.] 'And when he might have paid the money back at Athens after the double voyage, are we to believe that he paid it in the Bosporus (i.e. as ἑτερόπλους), and too much by 13 minae?' For he said he had paid 3920 instead of 2600, which is too much by 1320; or 13 minae 20 dr. In the reckoning by a round sum, he omits the 20 dr. See on Or. 37 § 50. For πλέον τρισί, 'more by three,' compare Thuc. I 36 fin., ἕξετε πρὸς αὐτοὺς πλείοσι ναυσὶ ταῖς ἡμετέραις ἀγωνίζεσθαι, i.e. 'with a fleet the larger by the accession of our (the Corcyrean) ships.' (Arnold here wrongly reads ὑμετέραις, and Shilleto renders it 'with a larger navy even ours).'

[If Phormio's loan of 1000 dr. from Lampis (§ 6 fin.) was at the same interest as the 2000 dr. from Chrysippus (§ 23 init.) he would owe Lampis exactly 1300 dr. or 13 minae. It is therefore open to Phormio to reply that the alleged overpayment included the sum due to the skipper himself. S.]

§ 26. Another improbability. *You found it difficult to pay the loan on the outer voyage only; and yet you pretend to have paid before the full time, and when there was no pressure on you for payment, the principal and the interest, and the penalty besides, when you were not bound to pay that at all.*

προσήδρευον] Who kept close to you, and watched your proceedings. Cf. Lacrit. § 29, τούτοις προσῇμεν καὶ ἅμ' ἐσκοποῦμεν κ.τ.λ.

τῷ μὴ παρόντι] Logically, τῷ οὐ παρόντι is more correct; but there is a tendency to say ὁ μὴ παρών, because the formula generally refers to some indefinite person. Conversely, in Eur. Suppl. 227, θεὸς τοῖς τοῦ νοσοῦντος πήμασιν διώλεσε τὸν οὐ νοσοῦντα, we might have looked

p. 915]   ΠΕΡΙ ΔΑΝΕΙΟΥ.   29

915 καὶ τοὺς τόκους ἀπεδίδους, ἀλλὰ καὶ τὰ ἐπιτίμια τὰ
ἐκ τῆς συγγραφῆς ἀπέτινες, οὐδεμιᾶς σοι ἀνάγκης
οὔσης; κἀκείνους μὲν οὐκ ἐδεδίεις, οἷς αἱ συγγραφαὶ 27
ἐν Βοσπόρῳ τὴν πρᾶξιν ἐδίδοσαν τοῦ δανείου· τούτου
δὲ φῂς φροντίζειν, ὃν ἐξ ἀρχῆς[j] εὐθὺς ἠδίκεις οὐκ
ἐνθέμενος τὰ χρήματ' εἰς τὴν ναῦν κατὰ τὴν συγγραφὴν Ἀθήνηθεν; καὶ νῦν μὲν εἰς τὸ ἐμπόριον ἥκων,
οὗ τὸ συμβόλαιον ἐγένετο, οὐκ ὀκνεῖς ἀποστερεῖν τὸν
δανείσαντα· ἐν Βοσπόρῳ δὲ πλείω τῶν δικαίων φῂς
ποιεῖν, οὗ δίκην οὐκ ἔμελλες δώσειν; καὶ οἱ μὲν ἄλλοι 28

[j] + ὥς φησιν Z.

for τὸν μὴ, yet here there is a kind of attraction to what next follows, κοὐδὲν ἠδικηκότα. See on Or. 37 § 28, ἐμοὶ τῷ μὴ παρόντι, and ibid. § 25, and 57.
p. 915. καὶ τὰ ἐπιτίμια] He appears to call the 1320 drachms overpaid 'the penalty,' not in serious earnest, since it was not likely the sums would agree exactly. Phormio had incurred the penalty by not putting the goods on board as security; but no necessity was laid on him at the time for paying it. The amount mentioned in § 33 as a penalty for not shipping the goods according to the contract, is 5000 drachms, the risk being greater if there was no cargo.
27. κἀκείνους] The lenders of the money on the ἑτερόπλους agreement.
οὐκ ἐδεδίεις] Phormio had paid these (at least the ἀρχαῖον, though not perhaps the interest, § 26), but μόλις, perhaps after being 'dunned' and threatened. Cf. Or. 37 § 38, καὶ ταῦτ' ἀπειληφότι γλίσχρως καὶ μόλις παρὰ τούτου. The sense is, 'it was more likely that you would have been afraid of them, than that you would have had such special care for Chrysippus, whom you had wronged before you left the harbour.'—πρᾶξιν, the right to enforce payment, by seizing your goods.
καὶ νῦν κ.τ.λ.] Further arguments ἐκ τῶν εἰκότων. 'At Athens, where the compact was made (and therefore where you can be sued at law), you don't scruple to defraud the lender, while in the Bosporus, where you were not likely to be sued, you pretend to have paid more than was due.' There is an assumption here of fraudulent intention in οὐκ ὀκνεῖς ἀποστερεῖν, which is hardly fair.
28. καὶ οἱ μὲν ἄλλοι] 'Most people, who borrow for the outward voyage, on leaving their places of business, take care to have plenty of witnesses present, and call on them to attest that the lender is risking his money on the voyage just going to commence (ἤδη). And yet you rely (lit. lean) on a single witness, and that too one who has taken part in the wrong (Lampis); you did not make my slave nor my partner witnesses

30   XXXIV.   ΠΡΟΣ ΦΟΡΜΙΩΝΑ   [§§ 28—31

πάντες οἱ τὰ ἑτερόπλοα[k] δανειζόμενοι, ὅταν ἀποστέλλωνται ἐκ τῶν ἐμπορίων, πολλοὺς παρίστανται, ἐπιμαρτυρόμενοι ὅτι τὰ χρήματα ἤδη κινδυνεύεται τῷ δανείσαντι· σὺ δ' ἑνὶ[l] σκήπτει[m] μάρτυρι αὐτῷ τῷ συναδικοῦντι, καὶ οὔτε τὸν παῖδα τὸν ἡμέτερον παρέλαβες ἐν Βοσπόρῳ ὄντα οὔτε τὸν κοινωνὸν, οὐδὲ τὰς ἐπιστολὰς ἀπέδωκας αὐτοῖς, ἃς ἡμεῖς ἐπεθήκαμεν, ἐν αἷς ἐγέγραπτο παρακολουθεῖν σοι, οἷς ἂν πράττῃς; 29 καίτοι, ὦ ἄνδρες δικασταὶ, τί οὐκ ἂν πράξειεν ὁ τοιοῦτος, ὅστις γράμματα λαβὼν μὴ ἀποδέδωκεν ὀρθῶς καὶ δικαίως; ἢ πῶς οὐ φανερόν ἐστιν ὑμῖν τὸ τούτου κακούργημα ἐξ αὐτῶν ὧν ἔπραττεν;·καίτοι, ὦ γῆ καὶ θεοὶ, προσῆκέ γε τοσοῦτο χρυσίον ἀποδιδόντα, καὶ πλέον[n] τοῦ δανείσματος, περιβόητον ποιεῖν ἐν τῷ ἐμπορίῳ, καὶ παρακαλεῖν πάντας ἀνθρώπους, πρῶτον δὲ τὸν παῖδα 30 τὸν τούτου καὶ τὸν κοινωνόν· ἴστε γὰρ δήπου πάντες ὅτι δανείζονται μὲν μετ' ὀλίγων μαρτύρων, ὅταν δ'

[k] ἀμφοτερόπλοα Bekk. 1824.   [l] δὲ Bekk. 1824.
[m] σκήπτῃ Z.   [n] πλεῖον Z.

of the payment in the Bosporus, nor deliver the letters to them with which we charged you, and in which a written order had been given that they were to follow you closely in whatever matter you might happen to be engaged.'——τὸν παῖδα τὸν ἡμέτερον, called τὸν τούτου in § 29, see sup. § 4.

ἐπιστολὰς...ἐπεθήκαμεν] Harpocr. s.v. ἐπιθέτους ἑορτάς·...λέγειν γὰρ ἦν εἰθισμένου ἐπέθηκεν ἐπιστολὴν ἀντὶ τοῦ παρέδωκεν, ὡς Δημοσθένης ἐν τῷ ὑπὲρ Χρυσίππου πρὸς τὴν Φορμίωνος παραγραφήν. Id. s. v. ἀντεπιτίθησιν: ἀντὶ τοῦ ἀντεπιστέλλει Ἰσαῖος ἐν τῷ πρὸς Καλλιπίδην. S.]

29. ὅστις—μὴ ἀποδέδωκεν] qui non dederit.

προσῆκέ γε] Irony: 'Surely, when he was paying back so large a sum of money, and even more than he had borrowed, he ought to have had it talked about on the Mart, and to have invited all men to witness the act, but above all the servant and partner of Chrysippus' (sup. § 8).

§ 30. Continued irony: 'men don't get more witnesses than is necessary to see that they borrow, but as many as they can to see that they pay, and that their honesty and respectability in their dealings may be talked about. How then was it that you acted so differently in the matter of your pretended payment?'

p. 916] ΠΕΡΙ ΔΑΝΕΙΟΥ. 31

ἀποδιδῶσι, πολλοὺς παρίστανται μάρτυρας, ἵν' ἐπιεικεῖς δοκῶσιν εἶναι περὶ τὰ συμβόλαια. σοὶ δ' ἀποδιδόντι τό τε δάνειον καὶ τοὺς τόκους ἀμφοτέρους, ἑτε-
ροπλόῳ τῷ ἀργυρίῳ κεχρημένῳ, καὶ προστιθέντι ἑτέρας
τρεῖς καὶ δέκα μνᾶς, πῶς οὐχὶ πολλοὺς ἦν παραληπτέον μάρτυρας; καὶ εἰ τοῦτ' ἔπραξας, οὐδ' ἂν εἰς
σοῦ μᾶλλον τῶν πλεόντων ἐθαυμάζετο. σὺ δ' ἀντὶ
τοῦ πολλοὺς μάρτυρας τούτων ποιεῖσθαι πάντας
ἀνθρώπους λανθάνειν ἐπειρῶ, ὥσπερ ἀδικῶν τι. καὶ
εἰ μὲν ἐμοὶ τῷ δανείσαντι ἀπεδίδους, οὐδὲν ἔδει μαρ-
τύρων· τὴν γὰρ συγγραφὴν ἀνελόμενος ἀπήλλαξο ἂν

τοὺς τόκους ἀμφοτέρους] 'The interest on both voyages, though you had used the money only for the outer voyage,' and so might have employed it in some other investment till your return to Athens.
καὶ εἰ τοῦτ' κ.τ.λ.] 'And, if you had acted so,' viz. had secured many witnesses, 'no one of the trading merchants would have been more looked up to (for honesty) than you.' The indefinite πλεῖν and οἱ πλέοντες for 'trading' and 'traders' is to be noticed. So Ar. Pax 341, ἤδη γὰρ ἐξέσται τόθ' ὑμῖν πλεῖν, μένειν, οἴκοι καθεύδειν. Plat. Gorg. p. 467 D, οἱ πλέοντές τε καὶ τὸν ἄλλον χρηματισμὸν χρηματιζόμενοι. Dem. Or. 37 § 54, ὅστις δὲ εἴργασται μὲν ὥσπερ ἐγὼ πλέων καὶ κινδυνεύων.
31. σὺ δέ, κ.τ.λ.] 'Whereas you, instead of making many persons witnesses of these acts, did all you could to escape observation! One would almost think you were doing something dishonest.' The satire is very keen, and must have been effective as an answer to Phormio's pretences.

ἐμοί] 'To me in person,' not to an agent, and for me. In that case, he says, you would have got the bond cancelled, and so have been rid of the liability at once. 'But, paying as you say you did, to an agent, at a distance, when the contract was with me and not with Lampis, and when the risk of a voyage was at hand, it seems that you never asked any one to be your witness; either slave or free.' It does not appear from all this that a witness of the payment to an agent was legally necessary. A receipt of some kind would have been enough, probably. But Phormio appears to have thought that his bare assertion would be accepted by the court.
ἀνελόμενος] Lit. 'taking up (or 'getting back,' Mr Mayor p. 242) the bond deposited against you.' Kennedy translates, 'you would have taken up the agreement and got rid of the obligation. The active in the sense of 'destroying,' 'cancelling,' occurs in § 33, καὶ τοῦτ' ἀνῃρηκὼς αὐτός. In Or. 48 § 46, we read ἐχρῆν

XXXIV. ΠΡΟΣ ΦΟΡΜΙΩΝΑ [§§ 31—33

τοῦ συμβολαίου· νῦν δ' οὐκ ἐμοὶ, ἀλλ' ἑτέρῳ ὑπὲρ ἐμοῦ ἀποδιδοὺς, καὶ οὐκ Ἀθήνησιν, ἀλλ' ἐν Βοσπόρῳ, καὶ τῆς συγγραφῆς σοι κειμένης Ἀθήνησι καὶ πρὸς ἐμὲ, καὶ ᾧ τὸ χρυσίον ἀπεδίδους ὄντος θνητοῦ καὶ πέλαγος τοσοῦτον μέλλοντος πλεῖν, μάρτυρα οὐδέν' 32 ἐποιήσω, οὔτε δοῦλον οὔτ' ἐλεύθερον. ἡ γὰρ συγγραφή με, φησὶ, τῷ ναυκλήρῳ ἐκέλευεν ἀποδοῦναι τὸ χρυσίον. μάρτυρας δέ τοι° οὐκ ἐκώλυε παρακαλεῖν, οὐδὲ τὰς ἐπιστολὰς ἀποδοῦναι. καὶ οἴδε μὲν πρὸς σὲ δύο συγγραφὰς ἐποιήσαντο ὑπὲρ τοῦ συμβολαίου, ὡς ἂν οἱ μάλιστ' ἀπιστοῦντες· σὺ δὲ μόνος μόνῳ φῂς δοῦναι

° γ' Bekk. 1824.

γὰρ αὐτὸν—παραλαβόντα πολλοὺς μάρτυρας ἀξιοῦν ἀναιρεῖσθαι τὰς συνθήκας παρὰ τοῦ Ἀνδροκλείδου. And Or. 33 § 12, ἐναντίον πολλῶν μαρτύρων τὰς συγγραφὰς ἀνειλόμεθα.

32. τῷ ναυκλήρῳ] There seems to have been ·a clause in the bond to the effect that, if Phormio should be detained in the Bosporus, he should pay the money to the skipper; or, as Kennedy suggests, that he should have the option of so paying it if he did not choose to ship the goods.

οἴδε] The partners here present. This is certainly obscure. The speech commences in the plural, δίκαια δεησόμεθα, &c., but in § 6 Chrysippus speaks for himself, ἐγὼ γὰρ, κ.τ.λ., and in § 21 the other partner, who is supposed to be still addressing the court. It would seem therefore that several were concerned in the loan to Phormio; for no account is here taken of the ἐπιδανεισμοί. Again, the δύο συγγραφὰς is obscure. Penrose thinks it only means that two copies were made. It is evidently spoken of as an additional security; and perhaps it means that each of the principal partners had his own bond against Phormio.

ὡς ἂν, κ.τ.λ.] Supply δράσαιεν. So Mid. p. 519 § 14, καὶ θόρυβον καὶ κρότον τοιοῦτον ὡς ἂν ἐπαινοῦντές τε καὶ συνησθέντες ἐποιήσατε. Thuc. I 33, ὡς ἂν μάλιστα μετ' ἀειμνήστου μαρτυρίου τὴν χάριν καταθήσεσθε (καταθεῖσθε and καταθῆσθε are mistakes resulting from ignorance of the idiom).

μόνος μόνῳ] A forcible and idiomatic collocation (like πολλὰ πολλοῖς, πᾶσι πάντως, &c.); oftener found in such contexts than the simple μόνος. [As an instance of the former we have De Cor. p. 273, 1 τῷ ὑπὸ τῶν πολεμίων πεμφθέντι μόνος μόνῳ συνῄει, of the latter Fals. Leg. p. 430, 22, οὐδαμοῦ μόνους ἐντυγχάνειν Φιλίππῳ which Cobet (Variae Lectiones, p. 112) would alter into μόνους μόνῳ. Mr Shilleto however quotes passages from the poets which do not admit of such alteration, e.g. Ar. Pax 660, ἡ δ' ἀλλὰ πρὸς σὲ

τῷ ναυκλήρῳ τὸ χρυσίον, εἰδὼς κατὰ σοῦ κειμένην Ἀθήνησι συγγραφὴν πρὸς τοῦτον[p].

Λέγει δ' ὡς ἡ συγγραφὴ σωθείσης τῆς νεὼς αὐ- 33
τὸν ἀποδοῦναι κελεύει τὰ χρήματα. καὶ γὰρ ἐνθέσθαι τἀγοράσματα εἰς τὴν ναῦν κελεύει σε, εἰ δὲ μή, πεντακισχιλίας δραχμὰς ἀποτίνειν. σὺ δὲ τοῦτο μὲν τῆς συγγραφῆς οὐ λαμβάνεις, παραβεβηκὼς δ' εὐθὺς ἐξ ἀρχῆς καὶ τὰ χρήματα οὐκ ἐνθέμενος ἀμφισβητεῖς πρὸς ἓν ῥῆμα τῶν ἐν τῇ συγγραφῇ, καὶ τοῦτ' ἀνῃρηκὼς αὐτός. ὁπότε γὰρ ἐν τῷ Βοσπόρῳ φῇς μὴ τὰ

[p] The Zürich editors (and A. Schaefer) here mark another break. '*Post hanc paragraphum Chrysippum* (cf. § 35, 4 ἐμέ) *denuo loqui videri notavimus.*'

σμικρὸν εἰπάτω μόνον (v. *Journ. of Class. and Sacred Philol.* vol. 4, p. 310). S.]—κατὰ σοῦ, i.e. ἀλλ' οὐ κατὰ Λάμπιδος.—πρὸς τοῦτον, with Chrysippus.
§§ 33—5. *Phormio pleads, as a bar to the suit, that the payment was conditional, and not binding on him if the ship should be wrecked. The reply is, that this non-payment is again conditional on the goods being put on board, which was not done. Therefore the actual wreck is no release from liability.*
σωθείσης τῆς νεώς] Emphatic, as the condition of ἀποδοῦναι. Or. 32 Zenothem. § 5, οὐσῶν τῶν συγγραφῶν ὥσπερ εἰώθασιν ἅπασαι, σωθείσης τῆς νεὼς ἀποδοῦναι τὰ χρήματα. Or. 56 Dionysid. § 31.——καὶ γάρ, κ.τ.λ. 'very true; for it bids you,' &c.——πεντακισχιλίας, a very heavy ἐπιτίμιον (§ 26), and nearly double the amount due with interest (2600 dr., § 23). Kennedy thinks this was the penalty to which Phormio was bound, in case he neither shipped the goods at Bosporus nor paid the stipulated sum to Lampis. This he accounts for by the increased risk incurred by the lenders through the doubtful respectability of Lampis, who though he resided at Athens was a foreigner by extraction.—Hesychius: ἀγοράσματα· ὤνια.
σὺ δέ, κ.τ.λ.] You take exception to, or do not admit, this clause, viz. ordering you to ship the goods, and yet found an objection to my claims on the phrase σωθείσης τῆς νεώς, though you have yourself made the phrase null and void by *not* shipping the goods from the Bosporus. Of course, the exemption from payment in the event of a wreck depended solely, in equity, on the heavy loss of the borrower's goods.
ὁπότε γάρ, κ.τ.λ.] *Dum dicis*, &c. A conditional and idiomatic use of ὁπότε, when *time* is not considered, but simply the allegation of a fact. (Some examples are given in the note on Aesch. Suppl. 1030.) So

χρήματ' ἐνθέσθαι εἰς τὴν ναῦν, ἀλλὰ τὸ χρυσίον τῷ ναυκλήρῳ ἀποδοῦναι, τί ἔτι περὶ τῆς νεὼς διαλέγει[q]; οὐ γὰρ μετέσχηκας τοῦ κινδύνου διὰ τὸ μηδὲν ἐν-
34 θέσθαι. καὶ τὸ μὲν πρῶτον, ὦ ἄνδρες Ἀθηναῖοι, ὥρμησεν ἐπὶ ταύτην τὴν σκῆψιν, ὡς ἐντεθειμένος τὰ χρήματα εἰς τὴν ναῦν· ἐπειδὴ δὲ τοῦτο ἐκ πολλῶν ἔμελλεν ἐλεγχθήσεσθαι[r] ψευδόμενος, ἔκ τε τῆς ἀπογραφῆς τῆς ἐν Βοσπόρῳ παρὰ τοῖς ἐλλιμενισταῖς καὶ ὑπὸ τῶν ἐν τῷ ἐμπορίῳ ἐπιδημούντων κατὰ τὸν αὐτὸν χρόνον, τηνικαῦτα μεταβαλλόμενος συνίσταται μετὰ τοῦ Λάμπιδος καὶ φησὶν ἐκείνῳ τὸ χρυσίον ἀποδεδω-
35 κέναι, ἐφόδιον μὲν λαβὼν τὸ τὴν συγγραφὴν κελεύειν, οὐκ ἂν ἡγούμενος δ' ἡμᾶς εὐπόρως ἐξελέγξαι ὅσα μόνοι

[q] -ῃ Z.   [r] ἐξ- Z.

ὅπου is used inf. § 45. Or. 41 § 25 (πρὸς Σπουδ.), ὁπότε γὰρ καὶ νόμους ἔχω παρέχεσθαι,—τί δεῖ μακρῶν ἔτι λόγων; Compare also Or. 56 § 13, and ὁπηνίκα in Mid. p. 527, § 42. Xen. Conviv. II § 12 οὗτοι τούς γε θεωμένους τάδε ἀντιλέξειν ἔτι οἴομαι ὡς οὐχὶ καὶ ἡ ἀνδρεία διδακτόν, ὁπότε αὕτη καίπερ γυνὴ οὖσα οὕτω τολμηρῶς εἰς τὰ ξίφη ἵεται.
84. τὸ μὲν πρῶτον] 'The contract ordered him to put the goods on board, which he did once pretend to have done, only, knowing that he was sure to be detected, he changed his story and pretended that he paid the amount to Lampis in gold.' Penrose.——ὥρμησεν ἐπί, 'he thought to rely on,' 'he had recourse to.'
ἐλλιμενισταῖς] 'The harbourmasters,' who had to see that no vessel cleared out without paying duty. Cf. § 7.
μεταβαλλόμενος, κ.τ.λ.] 'Then he changes his tack, conspires with Lampis to defraud me, and says he paid *him* in *money*.' Both words are emphatic; 'he no longer says he put the goods on board, but that he placed the amount in his hands to give to Chrysippus.'
ἐφόδιον] A support to his plea; σκῆψιν, πρόφασιν. [For this rare metaphorical use of ἐφόδιον, cf. Hyperides Eux. col. xxxi 15, ἐφόδιον ἑαυτῷ εἰς τὸν ἀγῶνα τὸ ἐκείνης ὄνομα παραφέρων. S.]
35. οὐκ ἂν ἡγούμενος] i.e. ὅτι οὐκ ἄν, &c., 'thinking that *we* (here at Athens) would not find it easy to get to the truth respecting transactions that had passed between themselves alone.' Like οὐ φημί, οὐ δοκῶ &c., οὐχ ἡγοῦμαι means 'I think not,' and the ἄν follows the οὔκ by the usual attraction, though its force is exerted on ἐξελέγξαι.—ὅσα πράξειαν, quae ipsi inter se fecissent.

ΠΕΡΙ ΔΑΝΕΙΟΥ.

πρὸς αὐτοὺς αὐτοὶ πράξειαν. καὶ ὁ Λάμπις, ὅσα μὲν εἶπε πρὸς ἐμὲ πρὶν ὑπὸ τούτου διαφθαρῆναι, οὐκ ἐντὸς ὢν αὐτοῦ φησιν εἰπεῖν· ἐπειδὴ δὲ τὸ χρυσίον τοὐμὸν ἐμερίσατο, τότ᾽⁸ ἐντὸς εἶναί φησιν αὐτοῦ καὶ πάντ᾽ ἀκριβῶς μνημονεύειν.

Εἰ μὲν οὖν, ὦ ἄνδρες δικασταὶ, ἐμοῦ μόνου κατε- 36 φρόνει Λάμπις, οὐδὲν ἂν ἦν θαυμαστόν· νῦν δὲ πολλῷ δεινότερα τούτου πέπρακται αὐτῷ πρὸς πάντας ὑμᾶς. κήρυγμα γὰρ ποιησαμένου Παιρισάδουᵗ ἐν Βοσπόρῳ, ἐάν τις βούληται Ἀθήναζε εἰς τὸ Ἀττικὸν ἐμπόριον σιτηγεῖν, ἀτελῆ τὸν σῖτον ἐξάγειν, ἐπιδημῶν ἐν τῷ

⁸ τότε Z.   ᵗ Παρεισάδου Z.

οὐκ ἐντὸς ὢν] See § 20 and ὑποθ. l. 28 n.

ἐμερίσατο] See § 18.——μνημονεύειν, like the convenient memory of Strepsiades in Ar. Nub. 485, ἐὰν δ᾽ ὀφείλω, σχέτλιος, ἐπιλήσμων πάνυ.

§ 36. *The conduct of Phormio has been such that the public have been wronged as well as myself. He has fraudulently availed himself of the remission of the corn-duty to convey corn from the Pontus to Macedonia.*

πέπρακται αὐτῷ πρὸς πάντας] The usual construction with this passive perfect (or aorist). It is a very common use with Demosthenes.

κήρυγμα γὰρ——ἐξάγειν] In the speech against the law of Leptines for abolishing ἀτέλεια, or exemption from taxes and burdensome duties in reward for important services to the state, Demosthenes dwells at length on the benefits conferred on Athens by Leucon king of Bosporus, who had himself received this ἀτέλεια with the citizenship, and had signally assisted the Athenian importation of the corn of the Euxine by exempting from tolls all vessels bound for Athens, and by giving public notice that they should be freighted before all others. (Lept. p. 466 § 31, τὸν Λεύκωνα τοῖς ἄγουσιν Ἀθήναζε ἀτέλειαν δεδωκέναι καὶ κηρύττειν πρώτους γεμίζεσθαι τοὺς ὡς ἡμᾶς πλέοντας.) Leucon after reigning from 393 to 353 B.C. was succeeded by his son Spartacus, who after a short reign was succeeded in 348 B.C. by his son Paerisades who in the present passage is described as granting a privilege to the Athenian corn-trade (ἀτελῆ τὸν σῖτον ἐξάγειν) similar to that which had been granted by his grandfather Leucon. It appears that, by a proposal of Demosthenes, a bronze statue was set up in his honour in the market-place of Athens (Deinarchus I 43 p. 95). His reign ended in 310 B.C. S.]

Παιρισάδου] See § 8 n.

ἐπιδημῶν, κ.τ.λ.] 'Lampis happening then to be in the Bosporus, took to exporting corn, and got the remission of duty in the name of the state.

3—2

Βοσπόρῳ ὁ Λάμπις ἔλαβε τὴν ἐξαγωγὴν τοῦ σίτου καὶ τὴν ἀτέλειαν ἐπὶ τῷ τῆς πόλεως ὀνόματι, γεμίσας δὲ ναῦν μεγάλην σίτου ἐκόμισεν εἰς "Ακανθον κἀκεῖ 918 διέθετο προσκοινωνήσας τούτῳ ἀπὸ τῶν ἡμετέρων 37 χρημάτων. καὶ ταῦτ' ἔπραξεν, ὦ ἄνδρες δικασταί, οἰκῶν μὲν 'Αθήνησιν, οὔσης δ' αὐτῷ γυναικὸς ἐνθάδε καὶ παίδων, τῶν δὲ νόμων τὰ ἔσχατα ἐπιτίμια προτεθεικότων, εἴ τις οἰκῶν 'Αθήνησιν ἄλλοσέ ποι[u] σιτηγήσειεν ἢ εἰς τὸ 'Αττικὸν ἐμπόριον, ἔτι δ' ἐν τοιούτῳ καιρῷ ἐν ᾧ ὑμῶν οἱ μὲν ἐν τῷ ἄστει οἰκοῦντες διεμε-

[u] ἄλλοθί που Bekk. 1824.

And so he loaded a large ship with corn, but took it to Acanthus (in Chalcidice) and there disposed of it, having entered into a partnership with Phormio, and that though the money they traded with was mine.' He regards it as an aggravation of the offence, that the money of an Athenian citizen was used for a contraband transaction.— See Boeckh, *P. Econ.* p. 85 (ed. 2 of trans. by G. C. Lewis [= p. 118 of Lamb's trans. of ed. 2].

ἔλαβε] This verb is adapted to τὴν ἀτέλειαν rather than to τὴν ἐξαγωγήν. In Lept. p. 466 § 31 the orator remarks that Athens depended more than any other state on its importation of corn, πλείστῳ τῶν πάντων ἀνθρώπων ἡμεῖς ἐπεισάκτῳ σίτῳ χρώμεθα.

§ 37. *Further aggravations of the offence. He, Lampis, was an Athenian citizen, and the time was one of special scarcity, so that every cargo that could be had, was wanted at Athens.*

οὔσης, κ.τ.λ.] The definition of an ἀστὸς seems to be the having an οἶκος (i.e. not merely an οἰκία, but a family) resident in Attica. Perhaps, however, the mere *residence* was pressed by the law, οἰκῶν 'Αθήνησιν, since of course a citizen did not cease to be so by residing elsewhere for a time.

τῶν νόμων—ἐμπόριον] Cf. Or. 35 § 50, Lycurgus adv. Leocratem 27, οἱ ὑμέτεροι νόμοι τὰς ἐσχάτας τιμωρίας ὁρίζουσιν, ἐάν τις 'Αθηναίων ἄλλοσέ ποι σιτηγήσῃ ἢ ὡς ὑμᾶς, cf. Or. 58 § 12 πλεύσαντα δικαίως οἱ προσῆκεν, and 56 § 6. S.]

διεμετροῦντο] 'Were having measured out to them their barley-meal in the Odeum, while those in the Peiraeus (a δῆμος, contrasted with τὸ ἄστυ) were getting their loaves by pennyworths at a time in the arsenal and at the long warehouse, and having their barley-meal doled out to them at a gallon a-piece, and nearly trampled to death in the crush.' A curious picture of corn at famine price. [Arnold Schaefer places this time of high prices in the period between 330 and 326 B.C. when Demosthenes was σιτώνης. *Dem. u. s. Zeit* III p. 268—271, III 2, p. 300, 339. Cf. Blass, *Att. Ber.*, III 516. S.]

τροῦντο τὰ ἄλφιτα ἐν τῷ ᾠδείῳ, οἱ δ' ἐν τῷ Πειραιεῖ ἐν τῷ νεωρίῳ ἐλάμβανον· κατ' ὀβολὸν τοὺς ἄρτους καὶ ἐπὶ τῆς μακρᾶς στοᾶς, τὰ ἄλφιτα καθ' ἡμίεκτον μετρούμενοι καὶ καταπατούμενοι. καὶ ὅτι ἀληθῆ λέγω, λαβέ μοι τήν τε μαρτυρίαν καὶ τὸν νόμον.

ΜΑΡΤΥΡΙΑ. ΝΟΜΟΣ.

Φορμίων τοίνυν τούτῳ χρώμενος κοινωνῷ καὶ 38 μάρτυρι οἴεται δεῖν ἀποστερῆσαι τὰ χρήμαθ' ἡμᾶς, οἵ γε σιτηγοῦντες διατετελέκαμεν εἰς τὸ ὑμέτερον ἐμπόριον, καὶ τριῶν ἤδη καιρῶν κατειληφότων τὴν πόλιν ἐν οἷς ὑμεῖς τοὺς χρησίμους τῷ δήμῳ ἐξητάζετε,

ᵛ διελάμβανον Z cum Σ. ἐλάμβανον Bekker. ʷ στοᾶς τὰ ἄλφιτα, Z.

ἐν τῷ ᾠδείῳ] The Odeum [of Pericles] was a music school or minor theatre, lying just to the east of the great theatre under the Acropolis, and sometimes (Ar. Vesp. 1109) used as a law court, and the present passage shows that it was made generally useful. [Or. 59 § 52 λαχόντος δίκην σίτου εἰς ᾠδεῖον and Pollux VIII 33. Cf. Bekker's *Anecd.* 317 ᾠδεῖον· θέατρον Ἀθήνησιν, ὃ πεποίηκε Περικλῆς εἰς τὸ ἐπιδείκνυσθαι τοὺς μουσικούς· ἐν ᾧ καὶ δικαστήριον ἦν σίτου καὶ ἄλφιτα διεμετρεῖτο ἐκεῖ. S.] The μακρὰ στοά seems to have been a cornstore. It is mentioned in Ar. Ach. 548, as in a state of activity during preparation for war, στοᾶς στεναχούσης, σιτίων μετρουμένων. [Schol. τῆς λεγομένης ἀλφιτοπώλιδος ἦν ᾠκοδόμησε Περικλῆς ὅπου καὶ σῖτος ἐπέκειτο τῆς πόλεως. ἦν δὲ περὶ τὸν Πειραιᾶ. Leake (*Athens*, I p. 382) appears to distinguish between the μακρὰ στοά of the Peiraeus and the στ. ἀλφιτοπῶλις or meal-bazaar. See Thuc. VIII 90 § 6, and cf.

Pausan. I 1 § 3 (of the Peiraeus) ἔστι δὲ τῆς στοᾶς τῆς μακρᾶς ἔνθα καθέστηκεν ἀγορὰ τοῖς ἐπὶ θαλάσσης. It is clear that it was not, as Mr Penrose thought, in the city, apparently confounding it with the μακρὰ στοά in the quarter called Melite (Scholiast on Ar. Aves 998). There were many στοαί, like the *porticos* at Rome. See Boeckh, *P. E.* p. 88, = pp. 83, 121 trans. Lamb. S.]

καθ' ἡμίεκτον] a medimnus held 48 choenices, so that 8 choenices were a sixth, and 4 choenices a half-sixth. Hence the joke in Ar. Nub. 645, περὶ ὅου νῦν ἐμοί, εἰ μὴ τετράμετρόν ἐστιν ἡμιεκτέον.

§§ 38, 9. *Phormio, in collusion with this fellow, thinks to rob us, who on the contrary have not ceased to import corn into your mart during all these hard times.*

οἵ γε] The same nearly as οἵτινες, 'yes, *us*, who have,' &c.

ἐξητάζετε] 'Put to the test,' as in the common phrase ἐξετάζεσθαι φίλος.

ούδενὸς τούτων ἀπολελείμμεθα, ἀλλ' ὅτε μὲν εἰς Θήβας 'Αλέξανδρος παρῄει, ἐπεδώκαμεν ὑμῖν τάλαν-
39 τον ἀργυρίου, ὅτε δ' ὁ σῖτος ἐπετιμήθη πρότερον καὶ ἐγένετο ἑκκαίδεκα δραχμῶν, εἰσαγαγόντες πλείους ἢ μυρίους μεδίμνους πυρῶν διεμετρήσαμεν ὑμῖν τῆς

ἀπολελείμμεθα] 'We have been defaulters in none of these.'

'Αλέξανδρος παρῄει] On the murder of his father Philip, Alexander ascended the throne at the early age of 20, and one of his first expeditions was against Thebes, which had taken an active part against him, but submitted on his approach. The meaning of the phrase probably is 'entered Thebes.' It is hard to see how it means 'advanced against,' which is the ordinary rendering. Mr Mayor (p. 243) gives the literal sense 'was marching along to Thebes,' and Shilleto renders οὐκ ἔνεστι παρελθεῖν in De Fals. Leg. p. 367 fin., 'it is not in his power to accomplish the pass,' and just before παρῆλθεν, 'marched through,' 'marched up near the place.' It simply means, 'entered Phocis.' Xen. Conviv. I § 7, οἱ δὲ καὶ λουσάμενοι παρῆλθον, i.e. came in, or came forward to join the rest in the house. Compare the use of παρελθεῖν, Or. 39 § 16, Thuc. I 63, and so we have ἔσω πάρειμι in Eur. Hel. 451.—The date of this event, B.C. 335, is three years before this speech, which is one of the later ones. [The allusion to the period of scarcity (B.C. 330—326) in § 37 makes it probable that the speech was not delivered until B.C. 329 or even later. I. Hermann, *Einleit. Bemerk. zu Dem. paragr. Reden.* S.]

ἐπεδώκαμεν] The ἐπίδοσις was a free gift or 'benevolence' made by a rich citizen through φιλοτιμία, or public spirit, at any time of urgent need. We can hardly say how far these presents were really voluntary. Considering the burden of the λειτουργίαι, we may wonder at so disinterested a patriotism if there were no ulterior motives. [Boeckh, *P. E.* IV xvii p. 758 Lamb. Theophr. Char. 6 (23) ἐν τῇ σιτοδείᾳ...ὡς πλείω ἢ πέντε τάλαντα γένοιτο αὐτῷ τὰ ἀναλώματα διδόντι τοῖς ἀπόροις τῶν πολιτῶν, where the very same period of famine is probably alluded to. A. Schaefer, *Dem. u. s. Zeit* III 269 n. S.]

39. ἐπετιμήθη] 'When the price of corn was raised, and got up to 16 drachms (about 13 shillings) the medimnus.' As this was about one bushel and a half, the price does not seem so extravagantly high, unless indeed we take into account the very different value of money. Cf. Or. 50 § 6 (πρὸς Πολυκλ.), ὁρῶντες ἐν τῷ Πειραιεῖ τὸν σῖτον ἐπιτιμώμενον.

διεμετρήσαμεν] 'We measured it out to you at the average, or usual market-price.' This, Mr Penrose remarks, is at the rate of about a guinea a quarter, (less than half our average current prices. Notice the active as distinct from the middle διαμετρεῖσθαι.)

ΠΕΡΙ ΔΑΝΕΙΟΥ.

καθεστηκυίας τιμῆς, πέντε δραχμῶν τὸν μέδιμνον· καὶ ταῦτα πάντες ἴστε ἐν τῷ πομπείῳ διαμετρούμενοι· πέρυσι δ' εἰς τὴν σιτωνίαν τὴν ὑπὲρ τοῦ δήμου τάλαντον ὑμῖν ἐπεδώκαμεν ἐγώ τε καὶ ὁ ἀδελφός. καί μοι ἀνάγνωθι τούτων τὰς μαρτυρίας.

MAPTYPIAI.

Ἀλλὰ μὴν εἴ γε δεῖ καὶ τούτοις τεκμαίρεσθαι, οὐκ 40 εἰκὸς ἦν ἐπιδιδόναι μὲν ἡμᾶς τοσαῦτα χρήματα, ἵνα παρ' ὑμῖν εὐδοξῶμεν, συκοφαντεῖν δὲ Φορμίωνα, ἵνα καὶ τὴν ὑπάρχουσαν ἐπιείκειαν ἀποβάλωμεν.

Δικαίως ἂν οὖν βοηθήσαιτε ἡμῖν, ὦ ἄνδρες δικασταί· ἐπέδειξα γὰρ ὑμῖν οὔτ' ἐξ ἀρχῆς τὰ φορτία ἐνθέμενον τοῦτον εἰς τὴν ναῦν ἁπάντων ὧν ἐδα-

πομπείῳ] The hall [near the Dipylum] in which the sacred vessels, dresses, &c. were kept for the use of the Panathenaic procession. [Leake, *Athens*, I p. 108 n., Boeckh, *Public Economy*, I 121 trans. Lamb, Wordsworth's *Athens and Attica* XXII p. 145 ed. 1855. S.] In Androt. p. 615 § 61, the vessels and furniture themselves are called τὰ πομπεῖα.——ἴστε, 'you remember.'

πέρυσι] probably 327 B.C. The evidence of inscriptions connected with the Athenian navy proves that these contributions for the purchase of corn were made shortly before 326 (*Seeurkunden* xiii° 1 ff. referred to by Blass, *Att. Ber.* III 516). S.]

σιτωνίαν] The purchase of corn undertaken by the state in behalf of the people.

ἀδελφός] Probably to be identified with the partner of Chrysippus. Blass, *Att. Ber.* III 517. S.]

40. 'If o ur characters may be tested by such proofs, we were not likely to spend so much money for the sake of gaining credit, and then to bring an unjust action against Phormio for the mere purpose of losing that credit.' Again we have the favourite rhetorical argument from the εἰκότα of the case. See Plat. Phaedr. p. 266 fin., and 273 B.

ἐπιείκειαν] Our character for respectability. The καὶ here means, '(not only not gain, but) lose *even* what we had.'

ἁπάντων ὧν ἐδανείσατο] He put on board only the goods sufficient to cover the actual value of the ἐπιδανεισμοί, § 7. The simple genitive is used in nearly all cases where equivalence of value is expressed. Thus τῶν ἐν Βοσπόρῳ πραθέντων apparently means that Phormio settled part of the claims with, or by the money obtained for, the goods sold. It might however be the genitive absolute, and

νείσατο Ἀθήνηθεν, τῶν τ' ἐν Βοσπόρῳ πραθέντων τοὺς τὰ ἑτερόπλοα δανείσαντας μόλις διαλύσαντα, 41 ἔτι δ' οὔτ' εὐποροῦντα οὔθ' οὕτως ὄντ' ἀβέλτερον ὥστ' ἀντὶ δισχιλίων καὶ ἑξακοσίων δραχμῶν τριάκοντα μνᾶς καὶ ἐννέα ἀποδοῦναι, πρός τε τούτοις, ὅτε ἀποδοῦναί φησι τὸ χρυσίον τῷ Λάμπιδι, οὔτε τὸν παῖδα παραλαβόντα τὸν ἐμὸν οὔτε τὸν κοινωνὸν ἐπιδημοῦντα ἐν Βοσπόρῳ. ἐμοὶ δὲ Λάμπις αὐτὸς μαρτυρῶν φαίνεται ὡς οὐκ ἀπείληφε τὸ χρυ- 42 σίον, πρὶν ὑπὸ τούτου διαφθαρῆναι. καίτοι εἰ καθ' ἓν ἕκαστον οὕτως ἐδείκνυε Φορμίων, οὐκ οἶδ' ὅπως ἂν ἄλλως ἄμεινον ἀπελογήσατο. ὑπὲρ δὲ τοῦ τὴν δίκην εἰσαγώγιμον εἶναι ὁ νόμος αὐτὸς διαμαρτύρεται,

shortly put for τῶν τ' ἐς Βόσπορον κομισθέντων ἐν Β. πραθέντων.

διαλύσαντα] Or. 37 § 12; 36 § 50; 30 § 8.

§ 41. 'Moreover, Phormio was not well off at the time, and not so foolish as to pay 3900 drachms (39 minae) instead of 2600; and if he had, he certainly would have taken my slave and partner as a witness.' For the sums here mentioned see § 25. The 20 drachms in addition are here omitted.

τὸν παῖδα τὸν ἐμὸν] In § 8, it is Chrysippus who speaks of τῷ παιδὶ τῷ ἐμῷ καὶ κοινωνῷ τινι. If the other partner is now speaking, they must be supposed to proceed on the maxim κοινὰ τὰ τῶν φίλων. In § 28 we have τὸν παῖδα τὸν ἡμέτερον.

πρὶν ὑπὸ τούτου, κ.τ.λ.] This is to be construed with μαρτυρῶν φαίνεται. See § 18.

42. καίτοι, κ.τ.λ.] 'I have proved (ἐπέδειξα, § 40) every point thus clearly; (therefore Phormio is guilty;) and yet, if he had tried to make his case out equally plainly, it would have been the best possible defence to the charge,' i.e. if the case had come on in the usual way, and he had not moved for a rule to set it aside. In fact, the defence would have been sufficient to secure an acquittal, and he need not have pleaded a bar to the suit at all. Cf. § 4, οἱ νόμοι—ἀπολογεῖσθαι κελεύουσιν εὐθυδικίαν εἰσιόντα, οὐ κατηγορεῖν τοῦ διώκοντος, i.e. οὐ παραγράφεσθαι. The prosecutor's object, as the next sentence shows, is to object to the παραγραφὴ, and to show that the suit can be and ought to be brought on. He seems to say that Phormio need not have moved for the rule, nor objected to the trial, if his case for the defence had been equally good.

ὁ νόμος αὐτὸς] The law itself is explicit, and no judge need give an opinion. [διαμαρτύρεται, lit. 'protests solemnly' (cf. obtestari),—here, by a rare metaphor, applied to 'the law.' S.]

p. 920] ΠΕΡΙ ΔΑΝΕΙΟΤ. 41

κελεύων τὰς δίκας εἶναι τὰς ἐμπορικὰς τῶν συμβολαίων τῶν Ἀθήνησι καὶ εἰς τὸ Ἀθηναίων ἐμπόριον, καὶ οὐ μόνον τῶν Ἀθήνησιν, ἀλλὰ καὶ ὅσ' ἂν γένηται ἕνεκα τοῦ πλοῦ τοῦ Ἀθήναζε. λαβὲ δή μοι τοὺς νόμους.

NOMOI.

Ὡς μὲν τοίνυν γέγονέ μοι τὸ συμβόλαιον πρὸς 43 Φορμίων' Ἀθήνησιν, οὐδ' αὐτοὶ ἔξαρνοί εἰσι, παραγράφονται δὲ ὡς οὐκ εἰσαγώγιμον τὴν δίκην οὖσαν. 920 ἀλλ' εἰς ποῖον δικαστήριον εἰσέλθωμεν, ὦ ἄνδρες δικασταί, εἰ μὴ πρὸς ὑμᾶς, οὗπερ τὸ συμβόλαιον ἐποιησάμεθα; δεινὸν γὰρ ἂν εἴη, εἰ μὲν ἕνεκα τοῦ

κελεύων τὰς δίκας εἶναι, κ.τ.λ.] Possibly we should read κελεύων Ἀθήνησι τὰς δίκας εἶναι κ.τ.λ. The Ionic dative in -ησι is a remnant, perhaps, of an old Solonian law. If the text is right, it seems that we must supply εἰσαγωγίμους. 'The law says that mercantile actions about contracts made at Athens, or indeed anywhere else, if for the Athenian trade, shall be admissible.' Therefore, this suit is admissible, and it is no case for a παραγραφή. Or thus, perhaps: 'that the mercantile actions are those for contracts made,' &c. This would give a precise definition of ἐμπορικαὶ δίκαι, in harmony with § 43.

§§ 43—5. *The point and gist of Phormio's παραγραφὴ is not that he has acted rightly, but that the action cannot be tried here. Why, where can it be tried, if not here? Besides, by accepting the arbitration before Theodotus, they virtually admitted it could be tried. And if they say it can't, when the arbitrator expressly sent it to this court, what would they have said if he had dis-* missed the case altogether?

παραγράφονται τὴν δίκην] The original meaning seems to have been, 'they have a note made on the side (or back) of the suit, not admissible.' Otherwise, ὡς οὐκ οὖσαν must be taken for an accusative absolute.

δεινὸν γὰρ, κ.τ.λ.] 'For it would be hard indeed, supposing I had been wronged in some matter relating to the voyage to Athens, that I should be able to get satisfaction from Phormio in your court; while, now the agreement between us has actually been made *in* your mart, these men should say that they will not be tried before you.' He thus refers to the two preceding clauses of the law τῶν Ἀθήνησι καὶ (τῶν) ἐς τὸ Ἀθηναίων ἐμπόριον. The context seems to show, that either of these two conditions justifies a δίκη ἐμπορικὴ being brought. He puts the case thus: a bargain made *in* Athens is more under the direct cognisance and protection of the jury than one for Athens, i.e. for trading to it.

42 XXXIV. ΠΡΟΣ ΦΟΡΜΙΩΝΑ [§§ 43—46

πλοῦ τοῦ Ἀθήναζε ἠδικούμην, εἶναί μοι παρ' ὑμῖν τὸ
δίκαιον λαβεῖν παρὰ Φορμίωνος, ἐπειδὴ δὲ τὸ συμβόλαιον ἐν τῷ ὑμετέρῳ ἐμπορίῳ γέγονε, μὴ φάσκειν
44 παρ' ὑμῖν τούτους ὑφέξειν τὴν δίκην. καὶ ὅτε μὲν
Θεοδότῳ τὴν δίαιταν ἐπετρέψαμεν, ὡμολόγησαν εἶναι
καθ' αὑτῶν ἐμοὶ τὴν δίκην εἰσαγώγιμον· νυνὶ δὲ
τοὐναντίον λέγουσιν ὧν πρότερον αὐτοὶ συγκεχωρή-
κασιν, ὡς δέον παρὰ μὲν τῷ Θεοδότῳ τῷ ἰσοτελεῖ
ὑποσχεῖν αὐτοὺς δίκην ἄνευ παραγραφῆς, ἐπειδὴ δὲ
εἰς τὸ Ἀθηναίων δικαστήριον εἰσερχόμεθα, μηκέτ'
45 εἰσαγώγιμον τὴν δίκην εἶναι. ἐνθυμοῦμαι δ' ἔγωγε τί
ἄν ποτε εἰς τὴν παραγραφὴν ἔγραψεν, εἰ ὁ Θεόδοτος
ἀπέγνω τῆς δίκης, ὅπου νῦν γνόντος τοῦ Θεοδότου
ἀπιέναι ἡμᾶς εἰς τὸ δικαστήριον οὔ φησι τὴν δίκην
εἶναι εἰσαγώγιμον παρ' ὑμῖν, πρὸς οὓς ἐκεῖνος ἔγνω
ἀπιέναι. πάθοιμι μεντἂν τὰˣ δεινότατα, εἰ οἱ μὲν
νόμοι τῶν Ἀθήνησι συμβολαίων κελεύουσι τὰς δίκας
εἶναι πρὸς τοὺς θεσμοθέτας, ὑμεῖς δ' ἀπογνοίητε τῆς
δίκης ὀμωμοκότες κατὰ τοὺς νόμους ψηφιεῖσθαι.

ˣ om. Z.

44. ὡς δέον] 'As if, forsooth, it was quite right that they should be tried before an obscure half-alien umpire, without pleading a bar to the suit, and then, when we rely on the justice and dignity of an Athenian jury, they should refuse to appear.' It is evident that there is some irony in ὁ Θεόδοτος ὁ ἰσοτελής, conveyed by the double article.

45. ἐνθυμοῦμαι, κ.τ.λ.] 'For my part, I am trying to conceive what in the world he would have written in the demurrer, if Theodotus had acquitted him, and decided against me, when now, after that Theodotus has expressly sent us (decided that we should go) into your court, he says the trial cannot be held before you, to whom that official told us to go.' The sense is, as Mr Penrose gives it, 'if his pretexts are so insolent and imperious now, what would they have been then?' For ἀπέγνω see § 21.

ἀπογνοίητε] i.e. were to acquit him by allowing the validity of the παραγραφή.

§ 46. *There is the fullest proof of the borrowing, while of the payment there is only the evidence of an interested witness. Lampis has contradicted himself; but of his two statements the former, and the true one,*

Τοῦ μὲν οὖν δανεῖσαι ἡμᾶς τὰ χρήματα αἵ τε συν- 46
θῆκαι καὶ αὐτὸς οὗτός ἐστι μάρτυς· τοῦ δ' ἀποδεδωκέναι οὐδείς ἐστι μάρτυς ἔξω τοῦ Λάμπιδος τοῦ
συναδικοῦντος. καὶ οὗτος μὲν εἰς ἐκεῖνον μόνον ἀνα-
φέρει τὴν ἀπόδοσιν, ἐγὼ δ' εἴς τε τὸν Λάμπιν αὐτὸν
καὶ τοὺς ἀκούσαντας αὐτοῦ ὅτι οὐκ ἔφη ἀπειληφέναι
τὸ χρυσίον. τούτῳ μὲν οὖν τοὺς ἐμοὺς μάρτυρας
ἔξεστι κρίνειν, εἰ μή φησι τἀληθῆ μαρτυρεῖν αὐτούς.
ἐγὼ δ' οὐκ ἔχω τί χρήσωμαι τοῖς τούτου μάρτυσιν, οἵ
φασιν εἰδέναι τὸν Λάμπιν μαρτυροῦντα ἀπειληφέναι
τὸ χρυσίον. εἰ μὲν γὰρ ἡ μαρτυρία ἡ τοῦ Λάμπιδος
κατεβάλλετο ἐνταῦθ', ἴσως ἂν ἔφασαν οὗτοι δίκαιον

viz. that he was not paid, is confirmed by witnesses who heard it. And whereas the witnesses for me may be prosecuted for perjury if they say what is false, one cannot so deal with a mere witness of a witness, especially when his written evidence is not put in. Therefore, the witnesses on my side are more trustworthy.

συναδικοῦντος] See § 28.

οὗτος μὲν] i.e. Phormio rests the proof of the repayment on the sole unsupported testimony of Lampis.

ὅτι] i.e. λέγοντος ὅτι κ.τ.λ.

κρίνειν] This is the criterion or test of the honesty of my witnesses, viz. that Lampis is an interested witness, while mine are not.

τί χρήσωμαι] 'How to deal with.' This kind of evidence, he says, is an intangible thing; there is nothing we can produce as a ground of prosecution, οὐδὲν βέβαιον ἐνέχυρον. My witnesses say that Lampis declared he had not, his witnesses say 'they know that Lampis acknowledged that he had received the money from Phormio.'

κατεβάλλετο] viz. εἰς τὸν ἐχῖνον. 'If Lampis' own evidence had been put into court in writing, they might have asked, Why don't you prosecute him, if you believe what he now says is true?'

ἐπισκήπτεσθαι] 'bring to trial for false witness.' The technical term for this particular prosecution is given just below. It is so used in Plat. Theaet. p. 145 c, but in the active, πάντως γὰρ οὐδεὶς ἐπισκήψει αὐτῷ, where Stallbaum compares ἐπισκῆψαι so used by Aeschines, adv. Timarch. p. 142. The middle occurs in Or. 48 § 45, ἐπεὶ εἰ μή ἐστι ταῦτ' ἀληθῆ ἃ λέγω, διὰ τί οὐκ ἐπεσκηψάμην ἐγὼ τότε τοῖς μάρτυσι τοῖς ταῦτα μαρτυροῦσιν; [Lysias, Or. 23 § 14, ἐπισκηψάμενος δὲ τῷ μάρτυρι οὐκ ἐπεξῆλθεν. Aristot. Pol. II 12 § 11, Χαρώνδου δ' ἴδιον μὲν οὐδέν ἐστι πλὴν αἱ δίκαι τῶν ψευδομαρτυρίων, πρῶτος γὰρ ἐποίησε τὴν ἐπίσκηψιν. Bentley's Phalaris, I p. 408, 9, ed. Dyce. S.]

44 XXXIV. ΠΡΟΣ ΦΟΡΜΙΩΝΑ [§§ 46—48

εἶναι ἐπισκήπτεσθαί μ᾿ʸ ἐκείνῳ· νῦν δ᾽ οὔτε τὴν μαρτυρίαν ταύτην ἔχω, οὑτοσί τε οἴεται δεῖν ἀθῷος εἶναι οὐδὲν βέβαιον ἐνέχυρον καταλιπὼν ὧν πείθει 47 ὑμᾶς ψηφίζεσθαι. πῶς δ᾽ οὐκ ἂν εἴη ἄτοπον, εἰ αὐτοῦ Φορμίωνος ὁμολογοῦντος δανείσασθαι, φάσκοντος δ᾽ ἀποδεδωκέναι, τὸ μὲν ὁμολογούμενον ὑπ᾽ αὐτοῦ τούτου ἄκυρον ποιήσετε, τὸ δ᾽ ἀμφισβητούμενον κύριον ψηφιεῖσθε· καὶ ὁ μὲν Λάμπις, ᾧ οὗτος σκήπτεται μάρτυριᶻ, ἔξαρνος γενόμενος τὸ ἐξ ἀρχῆς ὡς οὐκ ἀπείληφε τὸ χρυσίον, νῦν τὰ ἐναντία μαρτυρεῖ, ὑμεῖς δὲ γνόντες ὡς οὐκ ἀπείληφ᾽ ἐκεῖνος, οὐκ ἐστὲ

ʸ με Z.
ᶻ σκήπτεται μαρτυρεῖ (omissis infra νῦν—μαρτυρεῖ) Z et Bekker st. cum F et Φ. σκ. μάρτυρι Bekker 1824.

οὑτοσί] Phormio thinks to get off free because Lampis cannot be reached; whereas, if Lampis could be prosecuted for false witness, Phormio might also have been prosecuted for collusion (κακοτεχνιῶν), and because the false evidence was given in his favour. Kennedy translates, 'the defendant thinks fit to secure his own impunity, by leaving no pledge for the verdict which he urges you to pronounce.'

§ 47. *Phormio admits that he borrowed but (falsely) says that he paid. It would be strange if, by a verdict in his favour (viz. that he is not bound to pay, and that he cannot be sued for payment), you were to stultify his assertion that he borrowed, and accept as true the very point which we dispute, viz. his having paid Lampis.* 'Would it not be absurd—that you should make a nullity of what he himself confesses, and give effect to what he disputes?' Kennedy. There is a rhetorical antithesis, of course, between ἄκυρον and κύριον: 'you say that he did borrow, but is not bound to pay!' There is a very similar sentence inf. § 49.

ἔξαρνος γενόμενος τὸ ἐξ ἀρχῆς] 'After denying at first that he received the money from Phormio.'—ὡς οὐκ, i.e. λέγων ὡς οὐκ, κ.τ.λ.

οὐκ ἐστὲ μάρτυρες] 'while you, knowing well that Lampis did not receive the money, refuse the evidence of your verdict in the matter.' This is an example of a bi-membered sentence, the initial question πῶς δ᾽ οὐκ ἂν εἴη being continued even beyond μάρτυρες τοῦ πράγματος, and the long sentence really ending with ὑπολάβατε εἶναι; Mr Joseph Mayor observes (p. 243) "there are three pairs of antitheses opposed by μέν and δέ. 'How monstrous it would be that you should attach weight to a disputed statement, while you refuse to believe what is agreed by all parties; that

p. 921]   ΠΕΡΙ ΔΑΝΕΙΟΤ.   45

μάρτυρες τοῦ πράγματος· καὶ ὅσα μὲν εἶπε μετὰ τῆς 48
ἀληθείας, μὴ χρῆσθε τεκμηρίῳ, ἃ δ' ἐψεύσατο τὸ
ὕστερον, ἐπειδὴ διεφθάρη, πιστότερα ταῦθ' ὑπολάβοιτε εἶναι; καὶ μὴν, ὦ ἄνδρες Ἀθηναῖοι, πολὺ δικαιότερόν ἐστι τοῖς ἐξ ἀρχῆς ῥηθεῖσι τεκμαίρεσθαι μᾶλλον
ἢ τοῖς ὕστερον τεκταινομένοις. τὰ μὲν γὰρ οὐκ ἐκ

Lampis should come forward to give evidence of that which he formerly denied, and you should refuse to give the evidence of your verdict though fully convinced of the fact; that you should not listen to Lampis when he speaks the truth, but place implicit confidence in the story which he was bribed to tell.'" Kennedy: 'and when Lampis, on whose testimony the defendant relies, after originally denying that he had received the money, now gives evidence to the contrary; that you, who know that he has never received payment, should not be witnesses to the fact?' The meaning seems to be, 'as we have not got Lampis' evidence that he *was* paid by Phormio (§ 46), your verdict in our favour will be equivalent to evidence that he was not.' The Zürich edition gives μαρτυρεῖ for μάρτυρι, and this is a good reading, if we take ἔξαρνος—ἀρχῆς as a separate clause, 'after denying at first,' and either insert δὲ after the following νῦν, or omit νῦν —μαρτυρεῖ.

48. καὶ ὅσα] The sentence is still continued from πῶς οὐκ ἄτοπον ἂν εἴη εἰ, κ.τ.λ. Hence the optative ὑπολάβοιτε. Mr Penrose is wrong in saying 'it can hardly be tolerated.' The present μὴ χρῆσθε refers to the fact, and is usual in bi-membered sentences of this kind.

Generally however (as in οὐκ ἐστὲ μάρτυρες just above), οὐ and not μὴ is used with the primary clause, as Shilleto has shown at length in a good note on Thuc. I 121 § 7. Compare Or. 38 § 18 (p. 989), ἢ δεινόν γ' ἂν εἴη, εἰ τῶν μὲν ἐξ ἀρχῆς ἀδικημάτων οὐ δίδωσιν ἔξω πέντε ἐτῶν τὰς δίκας τοῖς ὀρφανοῖς ὁ νόμος—πρὸς δὲ τοὺς ἐξ ἐκείνων ἡμᾶς—εἰκοστῷ νῦν ἔτει δίκην τελέσαισθ' ὑμεῖς. Lysias, Or. 30, κατὰ Νικομ. § 32, δεινὸν δέ μοι δοκεῖ εἶναι, εἰ τούτου μὲν ἑνὸς ὄντος—οὐκ ἐπεχείρησαν δεῖσθαι, —ὑμᾶς δὲ—ζητήσουσιν πείθειν ὡς, κ.τ.λ. Id. Or. 31, κατὰ Φίλωνος, § 31, σχέτλιον δ' ἂν εἴη, εἰ οὗτος μὲν ἅπαντας τοὺς πολίτας περὶ οὐδένος ἡγήσατο, ὑμεῖς δὲ τοῦτον ἕνα ὄντα μὴ ἀποδοκιμάσαιτε. Or. 54, κατὰ Κον. § 29, εἰ δ' ἄρ' ἠγνόησε ταῦτα καὶ—οὐ παρεσκευάσατο ὑπὲρ τηλικούτου κινδύνου, κ.τ.λ. The question of οὐ or μὴ turns, of course, on the clause being regarded as stating a fact or a mere supposition or possibility. Thus here ἄτοπον εἰ ὑμεῖς οὐκ ἐστὲ means, 'it is strange that you refuse to be witnesses to the non-payment.'

τεκταινομένοις] Patched up, fabricated, put together. Ar. Equit. 462, ταυτὶ μὰ τὴν Δήμητρά μ' οὐκ ἐλάνθανεν τεκταινόμενα τὰ πράγματ'.

ἐκ παρασκευῆς] As the result of a plot.

παρασκευῆς, ἀλλ' ἐκ τῆς ἀληθείας ἔλεγε, τὰ δ' ὕστερον
49 ψευδόμενος καὶ πρὸς τὸ συμφέρον αὐτῷ. ἀναμνήσθητε
δ', ὦ ἄνδρες Ἀθηναῖοι, ὅτι οὐδ' αὐτὸς ὁ Λάμπις ἔξαρνος
ἐγένετο ὡς οὐκ εἴη εἰρηκὼς ὅτι οὐκ ἀπείληφε τὸ χρυσίον, ἀλλ' εἰπεῖν μὲν ὡμολόγει, οὐ μέντοι γ' ἐντὸς ὢν
αὑτοῦ εἰπεῖν. οὐκ οὖν ἄτοπον, εἰ τῆς ἐκείνου μαρτυρίας τὸ μὲν πρὸς τοῦ ἀποστεροῦντος πιστῶς ἀκούσεσθε,
τὸ δ' ὑπὲρ τῶν ἀποστερουμένων ἄπιστον ἔσται παρ' 922
50 ὑμῖν; μηδαμῶς, ὦ ἄνδρες δικασταί. ὑμεῖς γάρ ἐστε
οἱ αὐτοὶ οἱ τὸν ἐπιδεδανεισμένον ἐκ τοῦ ἐμπορίου
πολλὰ χρήματα καὶ τοῖς δανεισταῖς οὐ παρασχόντα
τὰς ὑποθήκας θανάτῳ ζημιώσαντες εἰσαγγελθέντα ἐν
τῷ δήμῳ, καὶ ταῦτα πολίτην ὑμέτερον ὄντα καὶ πατρὸς

πρὸς τὸ συμφέρον αὐτῷ] Supply βλέπων ἔλεγε.

49. εἴη εἰρηκὼς] Shilleto on De Fals. Leg., Append. A, observes that the orators 'generally if not always express the perfect subjunctive and optative by the auxiliary verb and the participle.' Examples however of -ήκῃ and -ήκοι are not wanting in the best Attic writers.

τὸ μὲν πρὸς τοῦ, κ.τ.λ.] If you accept the part of Lampis' evidence that makes for the defrauding party, viz. the assertion that he was paid. See sup. § 47.—τὸ ὑπὲρ τῶν, κ.τ.λ., 'that part of the evidence of Lampis which tells in favour of the injured party,' viz. his first statement that he had not been paid. (J. B. Mayor.)

μηδαμῶς] sc. πιστῶς ἀκούσητε τὰ τοιαῦτα.

§ 50. *You dicasts once sentenced to death a person impeached by εἰσαγγελία*. The commonly accepted meaning of this term is, 'an impeachment before the senate or the people for all extraordinary crimes committed against the state, and for which there was no special law provided.' In an excellent and exhaustive article on εἰσαγγελία in the *Journal of Philology*, Vol. IV p. 74—112, by Dr Herman Hager (referred to also by Mr Wayte, in a good note on Timocr. § 63), an opinion is expressed (p. 94), which might have been fully proved by citing this passage, that 'an eisangelia was also applicable to offences committed against the commercial laws.' The condemnation here mentioned is one of the many proofs how little human life was valued by the Athenians when balanced against the letter of the law. There are many startling instances of this in the oration against Midias. See, for instance, § 182.

τὸν ἐπιδεδανεισμένον] In the medial sense. See sup. § 6.—
οὐ παρασχόντα, § 7.

πατρὸς ἐστρατηγηκότος] The Athenians had an extraordinary

p. 922] ΠΕΡΙ ΔΑΝΕΙΟΥ. 47

ἐστρατηγηκότος. ἡγεῖσθε γὰρ τοὺς τοιούτους οὐ μό- 51
νον τοὺς ἐντυγχάνοντας ἀδικεῖν, ἀλλὰ καὶ κοινῇ βλάπ-
τειν τὸ ἐμπόριον ὑμῶν, εἰκότως[a]. αἱ γὰρ εὐπορίαι τοῖς
ἐργαζομένοις οὐκ ἀπὸ τῶν δανειζομένων, ἀλλ' ἀπὸ τῶν
δανειζόντων εἰσί, καὶ οὔτε ναῦν οὔτε ναύκληρον οὔτ'
ἐπιβάτην ἔστ' ἀναχθῆναι, τὸ τῶν δανειζόντων μέρος
ἂν ἀφαιρῆτε. ἐν μὲν οὖν τοῖς νόμοις πολλαὶ καὶ καλαὶ 52
βοήθειαί εἰσιν αὐτοῖς· ὑμᾶς δὲ δεῖ συνεπανορθοῦντας
φαίνεσθαι καὶ μὴ συγχωροῦντας τοῖς πονηροῖς, ἵν' ὑμῖν
ὡς πλείστη ὠφέλεια παρὰ τὸ ἐμπόριον ᾖ. ἔσται δ',
ἐὰν διαφυλάττητε τοὺς τὰ ἑαυτῶν προϊεμένους, καὶ μὴ
ἐπιτρέπητε ἀδικεῖσθαι ὑπὸ τῶν τοιούτων θηρίων.

[a] ὑμῶν. εἰκότως· Z.

regard for a στρατηγὸς, and his character was regarded almost as 'sacrosanct.' Hence the crime of Clytemnestra is exaggerated in Aesch. Ag. 1605, ἀνδρὶ στρατηγῷ τόνδ' ἐβούλευσας μόρον, compared with Eum. 434, 595, Soph. El. 1, ὦ τοῦ στρατηγήσαντος ἐν Τροίᾳ ποτὲ Ἀγαμέμνονος παῖ. ibid. 694, τοῦ τὸ κλεινὸν Ἑλλάδος Ἀγαμέμνονος στράτευμ' ἀγείραντός ποτε. Timocr. p. 742 § 135, Ἀρχίνου υἱὸς τοῦ —πολλὰ καὶ καλὰ πεπολιτευμένου καὶ ἐστρατηγηκότος πολλάκις.

51. τοὺς ἐντυγχάνοντας] 'Those who have dealings with them.' Hence the later use, e.g. in Theophrastus, of ἔντευξις for 'behaviour.'

αἱ εὐπορίαι] The resources, the supplies of ready money, αἱ ἀφορμαί. εὐπορεῖν and συνευπορεῖν (Or. 37 § 49) are specially used in this sense. 'The accommodation required by traders comes not from those who borrow, but from those who lend; and no ship, no ship-owner, no passenger-merchant can go to sea if you judges (by your vote on this occasion) make null and void the part taken by those who make the advances. Well, gentlemen, in the laws there are many excellent principles laid down in their support, and it is for you to show that you aid the laws in correcting abuses, and not that you make concessions to the dishonest, in order that you may get as much benefit as possible from (lit. through, or along of) your market.'—ὑμᾶς, sc. οἱ δικάζοντες δίκας ἐμπορικάς. It is reasonable to suppose that such juries would be selected from men acquainted with business. See Or. 56 § 16.

52. προϊεμένους] 'Who lend on risk.'—θηρίων, a strong word, used in Or. 35 § 8, οὐδὲν ᾔδει οἵοις θηρίοις ἐπλησίαζε. Or. 24, κατὰ Τιμοκρ. p. 745 § 143, οὐκ ἂν φθάνοι τὸ πλῆθος τοιούτοις θηρίοις δουλεῦον, on which Mr Wayte observes, 'the word θηρίον is freely applied by the orators in invectives.'

Ἐγὼ μὲν οὖν ὅσαπερ οἷός τ' ἦν εἴρηκα· καλῶ δὲ καὶ ἄλλον τινὰ τῶν φίλων, ἐὰν κελεύητε.

καὶ ἄλλον τινὰ] Demosthenes himself, perhaps. See Or. 56 fin., ἀξιῶ δὲ καὶ τῶν φίλων μοί τινα συνειπεῖν. δεῦρο, Δημόσθενες. It is clear that in such a case Demosthenes had written the speech to be delivered by another, and that he was not known at the time to have been the author of it.

OR. XXXV.

ΠΡΟΣ ΤΗΝ ΛΑΚΡΙΤΟΥ ΠΑΡΑΓΡΑΦΗΝ.

THE speech against Lacritus affords another example of παραγραφή or special plea in bar of a suit. Here too, as in the preceding speech, and indeed in that next following, the pleader for the demurrer speaks first, and Androcles, the real claimant, follows, his object being to show that this is no case for a παραγραφή.

The plaintiff had lent money on bottomry to Artemo, a merchant of Phaselis in Pamphylia. Lacritus, the defendant, also of Phaselis (§ 15), was Artemo's brother, and being present at the transaction, had verbally (it seems) engaged to be responsible for the repayment. Artemo having died without discharging his debt to Androcles, Lacritus is sued, both as the inheritor of his brother's property, and as having pledged himself to see that the loan should be repaid.

Lacritus was a *Sophist*, one of the pupils of Isocrates. The plaintiff taunts him (much in the tone and style in which Aristophanes taunts the professors of wisdom in the "Clouds,") with perverting his knowledge of right and wrong to evade the just claim now made upon him. Indeed, the prosecutor seems to rely somewhat on the

general unpopularity of Sophists for getting a verdict in his own favour (§ 41). The answer of Lacritus is, that Androcles cannot show any written proof or affidavit by which he has become legally liable for his brother's debt; and further, as he has given up the property, he is entitled to be discharged also from any debts upon it.

Two parties are concerned as principals on each side, viz.: Androcles of Athens and Nausicrates of Carystus (in Euboea) as lenders, and the brothers Artemo and Apollodorus [1], of Phaselis, as borrowers [2]. The conditions were, that they (the brothers) should sail with goods to Pallene (in Macedonia), take in a specified number of jars of Thracian wine, thence sail to the Bosporus (Crimea), and after selling the wine, return to Athens with a counter-cargo and so discharge the debt on the double voyage (ἀμφοτερόπλους). The usual conditions were inserted in the contract, that the money should be paid liable only to certain drawbacks in the event of storms, wreck or leakage, capture by pirates, &c. And the security offered was a cargo of wine to be taken in at Pallene, the lenders having the right to take possession, on the return to Athens, of the return-cargo, until the loan should be paid.

"It is stated by Androcles, the speaker, that this agreement was violated in several ways by the borrowers;

---

[1] [That Apollodorus (as well as Artemo) was a brother of Lacritus has been inferred from § 15, οἱ ἀδελφοὶ οἱ τούτου, cf. 42. But cf. 7, Ἀρτέμωνι τῷ τούτου ἀδελφῷ καὶ Ἀπολλοδώρῳ and §§ 3, 15, 36, where Artemo alone is described as brother of Lacritus. Artemo is dead (3); and L. is his sole heir. This would be impossible if Apollodorus also, who is apparently still alive, had been a brother of L. Blass, Att. Ber. III 502. S.]

[2] Kennedy inclines to think that the action lay solely between Androcles and Lacritus, as the custom at Athens was to make contracts between parties both joint and several. See on § 34.

ΠΑΡΑΓΡΑΦΗΝ. 51

that they failed to ship the stipulated quantity of wine; that they took up a further loan upon the security given to himself and his partner; that they did not purchase a sufficient return-cargo; that, instead of entering into the regular port of Athens, they put into a creek used only by thieves or smugglers; and, when the creditors demanded their money, they and their brother Lacritus falsely represented that the vessel had been wrecked[1]."

It does not seem clear that Lacritus was legally liable. All that he appears to have done was to have gone with his brothers, as a "referee" or guarantee for their respectability and solvency, to the money-lenders, and to have assured them that it was "all right." Demosthenes is somewhat abusive in speaking of Lacritus, and it has been thought he had a personal dislike of or feeling of jealousy against Isocrates, the teacher of Lacritus (see § 40). It is clear that the death of Artemo may have suggested to Androcles the attempt to make Lacritus personally liable, though at first he had trusted to Lacritus' character and credit, and influence with his brothers. His general abuse of the merchants of Phaselis (§ 1) implies vexation at a loss rather than conscious justice.

The special plea put in by Lacritus turned, as usual, on a denial that the action was maintainable. He simply denied all complicity, and pleaded that, having resigned his brother's property, he could not be saddled with his debts. And there seems no reason to doubt that this was a fair and just defence.

Mr Penrose says "This speech is of uncertain date;" and there appears to be no safe criterion for forming any conclusion in any part of the oration. [But it may be noted (1) that Isocrates, the teacher of Lacritus, is re-

[1] C. R. Kennedy.

XXXV. ΠΡΟΣ ΤΗΝ ΛΑΚΡΙΤΟΤ Π.

ferred to in terms implying that he is still actively engaged as a teacher of Rhetoric (§ 40), while Lacritus himself is already gathering pupils around him (§ 41). Hence the speech may belong to the later years of Isocrates, at any rate before his death in B.C. 338.—(2) We have an express allusion to the prompt settlement of commercial cases during the winter months, a reform probably due to the administration of Eubulus and fully established when the speech on Halonnesus (Or. 7) was delivered, B.C. 343—2. (See § 46 n.).—(3) The commercial relations of Athens, in particular the trade with the Euxine, with the islands of the Northern Aegean and the towns of Chalcidice, remain unbroken (§ 35, &c.). These considerations with others, stated in detail by Arnold Schaefer (*Dem. und seine Zeit* III 2, 290), point to the period preceding the outbreak of the last war with Philip, and make it probable that the speech may be approximately placed in the year B.C. 341. Blass, *Att. Ber.* III 503, prefers placing it in 351, the year after the peace between Athens and Chalcidice. S.]

XXXV.
ΠΡΟΣ ΤΗΝ ΛΑΚΡΙΤΟΥ ΠΑΡΑΓΡΑΦΗΝ.

ΥΠΟΘΕΣΙΣ.

Ἀνδροκλῆς δανείσας χρήματα Ἀρτέμωνι Φασηλίτῃ τὸ γένος, ἐμπόρῳ, τελευτήσαντος ἐκείνου πρὶν ἀποδοῦναι τὸ ἀργύριον, εἰσπράττει τὸν ἀδελφὸν αὐτοῦ Λάκριτον τὸν σοφιστήν, δύο προβαλλόμενος δίκαια, ὅτι τε πα-
5 ρόντος Λακρίτου καὶ ἀναδεξαμένου τὸ ἀργύριον ἐδάνεισε τῷ Ἀρτέμωνι, καὶ ὅτι κληρονόμος ἐστὶ τῶν Ἀρτέμωνος Λάκριτος. ὁ δὲ τῆς μὲν κληρονομίας ἀφίστασθαί φησι, παραγράφεται δὲ τὴν δίκην, λέγων μηδὲν ἑαυτῷ πρὸς Ἀνδροκλέα συμβόλαιον εἶναι μηδὲ συγγραφὴν μηδε-
10 μίαν. πάντως δὲ καὶ τὸ ἀναδεδέχθαι ἔξαρνος γίνεται· οὐδὲ γὰρ ἂν τοῦτο ὁμολογῶν ἠγνωμόνει πρὸς τὴν ἔκτισιν.

Οὐκ ὀρθῶς δέ τινες ἐνόμισαν τὸν λόγον μὴ γνήσιον

3. *Argument.* εἰσπράττει, κ.τ.λ.] 'Endeavours to make his brother Lacritus pay, putting forward two pleas. (1) That he made the loan to Artemo in the presence of Lacritus and on his promise to be a guarantee. (2) That Lacritus has succeeded to his brother's property.'

8. παραγράφεται] See on 34 § 43.

ibid. μηδὲν συμβόλαιον] 'No transaction (or obligation) between himself and Androcles, nor any *written* bond.' See Or. 34 § 3, and Or. 41 § 5, ἕως μὲν ὁ Λεωκράτης ἦν κληρονόμος τῶν Πολυεύκτου, πρὸς ἐκεῖνον ἦν μοι τὸ συμβόλαιον.

10. τὸ ἀναδεδέχθαι] He denies altogether the having given security for his brother; for, he adds, if he allowed *that*, he would not have been churlish in regard to the payment in full.

13. οὐκ ὀρθῶς, κ.τ.λ.] 'Some critics have wrongly thought this speech is not genuine, deceived by some obscure indications.

XXXV. ΠΡΟΣ ΤΗΝ [Argument

εἶναι, ἀμυδροῖς ἀπατηθέντες τεκμηρίοις. τὸ μὲν γὰρ
15 τῆς φράσεως ἀνειμένον οὐκ ἀπρεπὲς ἰδιωτικοῖς ἀγῶσι,
τὸν δὲ Δία τὸν ἄνακτα κατὰ τὴν τοῦ προσώπου τοῦ
ὑποκειμένου συνήθειαν δῆλός ἐστιν ὠνομακὼς, πρὸς
δὲ τὴν παραγραφὴν ἀσθενέστερον ἀπήντηκε διὰ τὸ
πρᾶγμα τὸ πονηρόν.

For the laxity of the diction is not unsuited to private orations; and the oath by Zeus as the 'King of the gods' (see note on § 40) was evidently taken in accordance with the familiar use of the character in the speech.' (Lit. 'it is clear that he has named,' i.e. the author of the speech.)

['Libanius sets no high value on the above objections; but we cannot so lightly dismiss a suspicion that the style and expression do not bear the stamp of Demosthenes (e.g. οἷα ἐτοιχωρύχησαν οὗτοι περὶ τὸ δάνειον in § 9 and εὐθὺς ἀπ' ἀρχῆς ἀρξάμενοι in § 27; also the loose and straggling structure of §§ 3, 4 and 7). Again, the piquant wit we here find, strikes us as unlike Demosthenes. Whether he would have spoken so disparagingly of Isocrates in § 40 is difficult to decide; Benseler at any rate doubts it. The strongest objections, however, are the feebleness of the argument even in crucial points of the whole case, and the wasting of words over irrelevant details, as when (in §§ 47—49) the jurisdiction of the Eleven, the first three Archons and the Generals is described at length, simply to prove that it is no part of their business to settle mercantile matters.' For these reasons, A. Schaefer agrees with Fynes Clinton (*Fasti Hellenici* II 357) in thinking that the evidence preponderates against our ascribing the speech to the authorship of Demosthenes. (From *Dem. u. seine Zeit* III 2 p. 291.) The same view is also taken by Blass (*Attische Beredsamkeit*, III 502, 504), who is led by considerations of style to ascribe the speech to the same writer as those against Macartatus (Or. 43) and Olympiodorus (Or. 48). It is also rejected by M. Dareste, I 316. S.]

Boeckh (*Publ. Econ.* Bk. I chap. xxii), in commenting at some length on this oration, expresses no doubt of its genuineness.

18. διὰ τὸ πρᾶγμα τὸ π.] i.e. διὰ τὴν πονηρίαν τοῦ πράγματος. The double article however (§ 19) seems here somewhat strangely used. If the subject is Lacritus, the grammarian seems to say that his plea of a demurrer is the weaker because he has behaved badly in the transaction. If Androcles is here said ἀπαντᾶν, 'to confront or meet the παραγραφὴ of Lacritus,' the sense will be that his claim against Lacritus is utterly unsound. And so Mr Penrose explains it. Perhaps we should read, διὰ τὸ πρᾶγμα ὂν πονηρόν, or διὰ τὸ τοῦ πράγματος πονηρόν. [The subject of ἀπήντηκε is the same as that of δῆλός ἐστιν ὠνομακὼς, viz.

Οὐδὲν καινὸν διαπράττονται οἱ Φασηλῖται, ὦ ἄνδρες δικασταί, ἀλλ' ἅπερ εἰώθασιν. οὗτοι γὰρ δεινότατοι μέν εἰσι δανείσασθαι χρήματ' ἐν τῷ ἐμπορίῳ, ἐπειδὰν δὲ λάβωσι καὶ συγγραφὴν συγγράψωνται ναυτικήν, εὐθὺς ἐπελάθοντο καὶ τῶν συγγραφῶν καὶ τῶν νόμων καὶ ὅτι δεῖ ἀποδοῦναι αὐτοὺς ἃ ἔλαβον, καὶ 2 οἴονται, ἐὰν ἀποδῶσιν, ὥσπερ τῶν ἰδίων τι τῶν ἑαυτῶν ἀπολωλεκέναι, ἀλλ' ἀντὶ τοῦ ἀποδοῦναι σοφίσματα εὑρίσκουσι καὶ παραγραφὰς καὶ προφάσεις, καὶ εἰσὶ πονηρότατοι ἀνθρώπων καὶ ἀδικώτατοι. τεκμήριον δὲ τούτου· πολλῶν γὰρ ἀφικνουμένων εἰς τὸ ὑμέτερον ἐμπόριον καὶ Ἑλλήνων καὶ βαρβάρων, πλείους δίκαι εἰσὶν ἑκάστοτε αὐτῶν τῶν Φασηλιτῶν ἢ τῶν ἄλλων ἁπάντων. οὗτοι μὲν οὖν τοιοῦτοί εἰσιν. ἐγὼ δ', ὦ 3

the composer of the speech, who (Libanius holds) is Demosthenes. The sense is: ' The writer, I admit, uses rather feeble arguments in meeting and combating the special plea raised on the other side; but the weakness of his reasoning is accounted for by the badness of his case.' S.]

§§ 1, 2. *The merchants of Phaselis have earned a very bad name for borrowing and forgetting their obligation to pay. There are more actions brought against them at Athens on this score than against all the other merchants put together.*

2. The words τῶν ἑαυτῶν read like a gloss on τῶν ἰδίων τι. Lit. 'they think they have lost something of the private property that belonged to themselves,'—a needless tautology. Compare inf. § 12, καὶ ἐκ τῶν τούτων ἁπάντων.

ἀλλά, κ.τ.λ.] '(And so they do not pay at all) but instead of it devise sophisms and special pleas and other excuses, and thus show themselves the most unprincipled of men as well as the most dishonest.'

ἀφικνουμένων] See Or. 34 § 1.

ἑκάστοτε] On each occasion when the courts sit to try ἐμπορικαὶ δίκαι. Kennedy translates 'year after year.' See on § 47.

αὐτῶν] ' The Phaselites alone.' Mr Penrose thinks "we must make considerable allowance for exaggeration here."

§§ 3, 4. *Statement of the case. I lent Artemo, in accordance with the laws of the Athenian mart, a sum of money for trading to Pontus and back. As he died before repaying me, I have brought the claim against his brother Lacritus as the same laws allow me to do, on the ground that he is his brother's heir and is liable for his debts.*

οὗτοι μὲν οὖν τοιοῦτοί εἰσιν] Or. 43 (Macart.) § 68, Or. 48 (Olymp.) § 56. These parallels

ἄνδρες δικασταί, χρήματα δανείσας Ἀρτέμωνι τῷ τούτου ἀδελφῷ κατὰ τοὺς ἐμπορικοὺς νόμους, εἰς τὸν Πόντον καὶ πάλιν Ἀθήναζε, τελευτήσαντος ἐκείνου πρὶν ἀποδοῦναί μοι τὰ χρήματα, Λακρίτῳ τούτῳ εἴληχα τὴν δίκην ταύτην κατὰ τοὺς αὐτοὺς νόμους τούτους
4 καθ' οὕσπερ τὸ συμβόλαιον ἐποιησάμην, ἀδελφῷ ὄντι τούτῳ ἐκείνου καὶ ἔχοντι ἅπαντα τὰ Ἀρτέμωνος, καὶ ὅσ' ἐνθάδε κατέλιπε[a] καὶ ὅσα ἦν αὐτῷ ἐν τῇ Φασήλιδι, καὶ κληρονόμῳ ὄντι τῶν ἐκείνου ἁπάντων, καὶ οὐκ ἂν ἔχοντος τούτου δεῖξαι νόμον ὅστις αὐτῷ δίδωσιν ἐξουσίαν ἔχειν μὲν τὰ τοῦ ἀδελφοῦ καὶ διῳκηκέναι ὅπως ἐδόκει αὐτῷ, μὴ ἀποδοῦναι δὲ τἀλλότρια χρήματα, ἀλλὰ λέγειν νῦν ὅτι οὐκ ἔστι κληρονόμος, ἀλλ' ἀφίσ-
5 ταται τῶν ἐκείνου. ἡ μὲν τουτουὶ Λακρίτου πονηρία τοιαύτη ἐστίν· ἐγὼ δ' ὑμῶν δέομαι, ὦ ἄνδρες δικασταί, εὐνοϊκῶς ἀκοῦσαί μου περὶ τοῦ πράγματος τουτουί· κἂν ἐξελέγξω αὐτὸν ἀδικοῦντα ἡμᾶς τε τοὺς δανείσαντας καὶ ὑμᾶς οὐδὲν ἧττον, βοηθεῖτε ἡμῖν τὰ δίκαια.

[a] κατέλειπε Z. κατέλειπεν Σ. κατέλιπε Bekker.

are from speeches attributed by Blass to the same author as the present speech, *Att. Ber.* III 505. Similar instances of inartistic transition are found below in §§ 24, 35, 52. S.]

4. ἀδελφῷ ὄντι τούτῳ] More simply, οὗτος γὰρ ἀδελφός τε ἦν καὶ ἅπαντα τἀκείνου εἶχε.

ἐν τῇ Φασήλιδι] Whether Artemo had a house at Athens, or in Pamphylia, or both, or what was the nature of his property at either place, is not stated, nor the total amount of it.

ἔχειν μέν] 'To be in actual possession of his brother's property, and to have administered it as he pleased—but to say now (i.e. to pretend) that he declines to take what belonged to him.' The actual words, ἀφίσταμαι τῶν ἐκείνου, 'I have nothing to do with *that man's* property,' seem quoted against him, as unbrotherly as well as plainly false. But see on 40 § 28.

5. τὰ δίκαια] 'In our rights,' a somewhat anomalous accusative which seems to depend on some suppressed participle like ἀποδόντες or παρασχόντες. Mr Mayor (p. 244) regards it as a cognate accusative. The same phrase occurs in Or. 54 § 2; 27 § 3; 38 § 2.

§§ 6—8. *Further details of the case. I myself knew nothing of these men, but they were*

p. 925]   ΛΑΚΡΙΤΟΥ ΠΑΡΑΓΡΑΦΗΝ.   57

Ἐγὼ γὰρ, ὦ ἄνδρες δικασταὶ, αὐτὸς μὲν οὐδ' ὅπωσ- 6
τιοῦν ἐγνώριζον τοὺς ἀνθρώπους τούτους· Θρασυμήδης
925 δ' ὁ Διοφάντου υἱὸς, ἐκείνου τοῦ Σφηττίου, καὶ Μελά-
νωπος ὁ ἀδελφὸς αὐτοῦ ἐπιτήδειοί μοί εἰσι. καὶ χρώ-
μεθ' ἀλλήλοις ὡς οἷόν τε μάλιστα. οὗτοι προσῆλθόν
μοι μετὰ Λακρίτου τουτουὶ, ὁπόθεν δήποτε ἐγνωρισ-
μένοι τούτῳ (οὐ γὰρ οἶδα), καὶ ἐδέοντό μου δανεῖσαι 7
χρήματ' εἰς τὸν Πόντον Ἀρτέμωνι τῷ τούτου ἀδελφῷ
καὶ Ἀπολλοδώρῳ, ὅπως ἂν[b] ἐνεργοὶ ὦσιν, οὐδὲν εἰδὼς,
ὦ ἄνδρες δικασταὶ, οὐδ' ὁ Θρασυμήδης τὴν τούτων
πονηρίαν, ἀλλ' οἰόμενος εἶναι ἐπιεικεῖς ἀνθρώπους καὶ

[b] ὅπως Bekker. ἂν addidit Dind. ex Σ et Ar.

introduced to me by some friends of mine. They wanted a loan for trading to the Pontus, in the joint names of Artemo and Apollodorus. My friends entertained no doubt of their respectability, and Lacritus was surety for the payment; and accordingly I lent them 30 minae.

ἐκείνου τοῦ Σ.] The words imply that Diophantus was well known, and all this is said to show that every reasonable precaution was taken by Androcles. [The latest certain mention we find of this Diophantus (apparently now no longer alive) is as a witness in the speech de Falsa Legatione, B.C. 343 (p. 403 § 128), and in p. 436 § 297 he is named as a man of mark, one of those who ἐπὶ καιρῶν γεγόνασιν ἰσχυροί. Melanopus, son of Diophantus, appears to have been called after his maternal uncle, the Melanopus who is attacked by Dem. in Or. 24, Timocr. §§ 125—130, and is described by Harpocration as κηδεστὴς Διοφάντου τοῦ ῥήτορος. A. Schaefer, Dem. u. s. Zeit, III 2. 290. S.]

χρώμεθα] In trade-transactions, perhaps. So in Or. 33 § 7, χρώμενος δ' Ἡρακλείδῃ τῷ τραπεζίτῃ ἔπεισα αὐτὸν δανεῖσαι τὰ χρήματα λαβόντα ἐμὲ ἐγγυητήν. And ibid. § 5, τούτοις τοῖς ἐκ Βυζαντίου καὶ πάνυ οἰκείως χρῶμαι διὰ τὸ ἐνδιατρίψαι αὐτόθι.

οὗτοι] Thrasymedes and Melanopus, not οἱ ἄνθρωποι οὗτοι, the two brothers accompanied by Lacritus. For he goes on to say that Lacritus had somehow or other made acquaintance with them; and it is clearly implied that the whole affair was a swindle.

7. ὅπως ἄν, κ.τ.λ.] 'That they might be engaged in a trading enterprise.' The more usual phrase is ὅπως ἔσονται. According to Hermann, the addition of the ἄν implies result rather than mere purpose. Kennedy accordingly renders it 'so that they might be profitably employed.'

οὐδ' ὁ Θ.] Thrasymedes did not know what rogues the defendants were, any more than the speaker, Androcles, did.

ἐπιεικεῖς] 'Respectable.'

οἱοίπερ προσεποιοῦντο καὶ ἔφασαν εἶναι, καὶ ἡγούμενος ποιήσειν αὐτοὺς πάντα ὅσαπερ ὑπισχνεῖτο καὶ ἀνεδέ-
8 χετο Λάκριτος οὑτοσί. πλεῖστον δ' ἄρ' ἦν ἐψευσμένος, καὶ οὐδὲν ᾔδει οἵοις θηρίοις ἐπλησίαζε τοῖς ἀνθρώποις τούτοις. κἀγὼ πεισθεὶς ὑπὸ τοῦ Θρασυμήδους καὶ τοῦ ἀδελφοῦ αὐτοῦ, καὶ Λακρίτου τουτουὶ ἀναδεχομένου μοι πάντ' ἔσεσθαι τὰ δίκαια παρὰ τῶν ἀδελφῶν τῶν αὐτοῦ, ἐδάνεισα μετὰ ξένου τινὸς ἡμετέρου Καρυστίου
9 τριάκοντα μνᾶς ἀργυρίου. βούλομαι οὖν, ὦ ἄνδρες δικασταί, τῆς συγγραφῆς ἀκοῦσαι ὑμᾶς πρῶτον, καθ' ἣν ἐδανείσαμεν τὰ χρήματα, καὶ τῶν μαρτύρων τῶν παραγενομένων τῷ δανείσματι· ἔπειτα περὶ τῶν ἄλλων ἐπιδείξομεν, οἷα ἐτοιχωρύχησαν οὗτοι περὶ τὸ δάνειον. λέγε τὴν συγγραφήν, εἶτα[c] τὰς μαρτυρίας.

ΣΥΓΓΡΑΦΗ[d].

10 ['Εδάνεισαν Ἀνδροκλῆς Σφήττιος καὶ Ναυσικράτης Καρύστιος Ἀρτέμωνι καὶ Ἀπολλοδώρῳ Φασηλίταις

[c] Σ. ἔπειτα Z.
[d] 'Syngraphen et testimonia omnia om. Σ.' Bekker. 'Nos omnia cancellis sepsimus.' Z.

ὑπισχνεῖτο, κ.τ.λ.] 'All that Lacritus promised and engaged they should do.' Hesych. ἀνεδέξατο· ὑπέσχετο, ὡμολόγησεν.

8. ἄρ' ἦν] 'It seems, however, that Thrasymedes was very greatly deceived, and had no idea what monsters he was coming in the way of by his acquaintance with these fellows.' For θηρίοις see Or. 34 § 52. Mr Penrose is wrong in taking ἐπλησίαζε transitively, in the sense of ἐπέλαζε. (An instance is cited in Liddell and Scott from Xen. de Re Equest. II 5, but πλησιάζειν is there also intransitive.)

πεισθείς, κ.τ.λ.] He gives three reasons for consenting, or rather perhaps four, since Nausicles of Carystus also thought the offer a reasonable one, and shared in making the advance.

ἀργυρίου] 'In cash.'

9. ἐτοιχωρύχησαν] 'How they acted like burglars in the matter of this loan.' A strong and invidious expression, like θηρίοις above. Cf. Or. 54 (Conon) § 37 and Or. 45 § 30, κακουργῆσαι καὶ διορύξαι πράγματα.

§§ 10—13. *The contract.* Like all the laws, depositions, and (as in the Pantaenetus, Or. 37) ἐγκλήματα, or grounds of accusation, actually quoted in Demosthenes, this document is

p. 926]   ΛΑΚΡΙΤΟΥ ΠΑΡΑΓΡΑΦΗΝ.   59

δραχμὰς ἀργυρίου τρισχιλίας Ἀθήνηθεν εἰς Μένδην ἢ
Σκιώνην καὶ ἐντεῦθεν εἰς Βόσπορον, ἐὰν δὲ βούλωνται,
τῆς ἐπ' ἀριστερὰ μέχρι Βορυσθένους καὶ πάλιν Ἀθήναζε, ἐπὶ διακοσίαις εἴκοσι πέντε τὰς χιλίας, ἐὰν δὲ
μετ' Ἀρκτοῦρον ἐκπλεύσωσιν ἐκ τοῦ Πόντου ἐφ' Ἱερὸν,

liable to the charge of spuriousness. All such citations are inclosed in brackets in W. Dindorf's edition; and the language of many of them is so evidently post-Attic that they cannot stand the test of a rigid criticism. How they were foisted into the text we do not know; but of the supposed quotations from the law it may plausibly be said, that, as the code of written Attic law was doubtless in existence at a late period, it was competent for any grammarian to extract and interpolate such portions as he considered to bear on the text. [On this subject see a monograph by Anton Westermann: *Untersuchungen über die in Attischen Redner eingelegten Urkunden*, p. 136, Leipzig, 1850 (*Abhandl. d. Lpz. Gesellschaft der Wissenschaften* I). Pages 81—90 are devoted to an examination of the depositions in the present speech alone. Cf. A. Schaefer III B 286, 3. See also Sauppe,*Philologenversammlung in Halle* 1869. Blass, *Att. Ber.* III 502, holds that the forgery of the documents in the present speech would be a task far beyond the skill of a later writer. They are repeatedly quoted by Harpocration s. v. Μένδη (§ 10), σύλας (13), διοπεύων (20). S.]

The genuineness of the contract here cited does not seem to have been suspected by Boeckh, who calls it however 'a carelessly written instrument.' He has given a full analysis of it in *Publ. Econ.* Book I chap. xxiii p. 137 seqq. ed. Lewis[2] = p. 190 ed. Lamb.

ἢ Σκιώνην] The alternative was given, probably in consideration of the state of the wind and the equal safety of the moorings. Scione (Thuc. IV 120, V 2, &c., Ar. Vesp. 210) was on the south coast of the promontory of Pallene, and Mende a little to the west of it, behind an elbow or headland sheltering it from the east.

εἰς Βόσπορον] To Panticapaeum, perhaps. See on Or. 34 § 2. As however this town is mentioned by name in § 32, a doubt is thrown on the identity of the two terms in this place. Strabo, C. 309, calls Panticapaeum ἡ μητρόπολις τῶν Βοσποριανῶν, but he speaks just before of οἱ τοῦ Βοσπόρου δυνασταί as if the word was not exactly a synonym. Boeckh (*Publ. Econ.* p. 90 ed. Lewis[2]) observes that "by Bosporus and Pontus the same kingdom is signified."

τῆς ἐπ' ἀριστερὰ] 'On the left coast,' Kennedy. Rather, 'for the voyage to the left (i. e. the northern, to a ship sailing eastward) parts of the Pontus as far as the river Borysthenes' (Dnieper).

ἐπὶ διακοσίαις] On terms of paying 225 per 1000, i.e. 22½ per cent. (lit. 'the thousand for two hundred and twenty-five').

μετ' Ἀρκτοῦρον] After the rising of Arcturus [about Sept.

ἐπὶ τριακοσίαις τὰς χιλίας, ἐπὶ οἴνου κεραμίοις Μενδαίοις τρισχιλίοις, ὃς πλεύσεται ͤ ἐκ Μένδης ἢ Σκιώνης
11 ἐν τῇ εἰκοσόρῳ, ἣν Ὑβλήσιος ναυκληρεῖ. ὑποτιθέασι δὲ ταῦτα, οὐκ ὀφείλοντες ἐπὶ τούτοις ἄλλῳ οὐδενὶ οὐδὲν ἀργύριον, οὐδ' ἐπιδανείσονται. καὶ ἀπάξουσι τὰ χρήματα τὰ ἐκ τοῦ Πόντου ἀντιφορτισθέντα

ͤ *cum* A et r.   πλευσεῖται Z.

20] stormy weather was expected to set in, and the sailing season, ὥρα, was then practically at an end. So the danger of a voyage is magnified ἀμφὶ Πλειάδων δύσιν, in November, Aesch. Ag. 826. See Hes. Opp. 616—28. Virg. Georg. 1 204. Plautus, Rudens, Prolog. 69, where Arcturus says, 'increpui hibernum et fluctus movi maritumos. Nam Arcturus signum sum omnium acerrimum; vehemens sum exoriens, quum occido, vehementior.' [Or. 50, πρὸς Πολυκλέα, § 23, συνέβη τῆς νυκτὸς ὥρᾳ ἔτους ὕδωρ καὶ βροντὰς καὶ ἄνεμον μέγαν γενέσθαι, ὑπ' αὐτὰς γὰρ Πλειάδων δύσεις οἱ χρόνοι οὗτοι ἦσαν. S.]——ἐφ' Ἱερόν, to the town so called from the temple of Ζεὺς Οὔριος, on a promontory near the entrance to the Euxine, on the Asiatic side of the Thracian Bosporus.

ἐπὶ τριακοσίαις (δράχμαις)] i.e. 30 per cent., the risk being greater and the voyage also longer.

ἐπὶ οἴνου, κ.τ.λ.] 'On security of 3000 jars (or crocks) of Mendean wine.' Cf. § 35, n. Hesych. κεράμιον. οἴνου ἢ ὕδατος σταμνίον. Mr Penrose says it was two-thirds of an ἀμφορεὺς, and held very nearly six gallons; but he does not give his authority. The whole value of the wine would be double the amount of the loan, according to the usual custom, i.e. each jar of wine was worth two drachmae (Penrose, from Boeckh).

ὃς πλεύσεται] 'Which shall be conveyed,' κομισθήσεται.

Μένδης] Harpocr. s.v. Μένδη: Δημοσθένης κατὰ Λακρίτου. μία πόλις ἐστὶ τῶν ἐν Παλλήνῃ Μένδη, ὑπὸ Ἐρετριέων ᾠκισμένη. S.]

ἐν τῇ εἰκοσόρῳ] 'in the twenty-oared boat of which Hyblesius is skipper' (Or. 34 arg. 1. 4). From § 52 it appears that this man also was a native of Phaselis. The word εἰκόσορος contains the root of ἐρέσσειν, and it is a curiously clipped compound. It occurs in Od. ιx 322, ὅσσον θ' ἱστὸν νηὸς ἐεικοσόροιο μελαίνης. The vessel, Mr Penrose observes, must have been of considerable size.

11. ὑποτιθέασι] 'They hypothecate these goods, not owing upon them any money to any other person, nor will they borrow anything further upon them.' Kennedy. For ἐπιδανείσονται see Or. 34 § 6 n.

τὰ ἐκ, κ.τ.λ.] 'The goods put on board *in* Pontus as a return cargo.' The idiom is the same as in the well-known οἱ ἐκ πόλεως ἔφευγον, &c.—ἐν τῷ αὐτῷ πλοίῳ. This clause is designed to forbid the use of any less sea-worthy vessel.

Ἀθήναζε πάλιν' ἐν τῷ αὐτῷ πλοίῳ ἅπαντα. σωθέντων δὲ τῶν χρημάτων Ἀθήναζε ἀποδώσουσιν οἱ δανεισάμενοι τοῖς δανείσασι τὸ γιγνόμενον ἀργύριον κατὰ τὴν συγγραφὴν ἡμερῶν εἴκοσιν, ἀφ' ἧς ἂν ἔλθωσιν Ἀθήναζε, ἐντελὲς πλὴν ἐκβολῆς, ἣν ἂν οἱ σύμπλοι ψηφισάμενοι κοινῇ ἐκβάλωνται, καὶ ἄν τι πολεμίοις ἀποτίσωσιν· τῶν δ' ἄλλων ἁπάντων ἐντελές. καὶ παρέξουσι τοῖς δανείσασι τὴν ὑποθήκην ἀνέπαφον κρατεῖν, ἕως ἂν ἀποδῶσι τὸ γιγνόμενον ἀργύριον κατὰ τὴν συγγραφήν. ἐὰν δὲ μὴ ἀποδῶσιν ἐν τῷ συγκει- 12 μένῳ χρόνῳ, τὰ ὑποκείμενα τοῖς δανείσασιν ἐξέστω ὑποθεῖναι καὶ ἀποδόσθαι τῆς ὑπαρχούσης τιμῆς· καὶ ἐάν τι ἐλλείπῃ τοῦ ἀργυρίου, ὃ δεῖ γενέσθαι τοῖς δανεί-

ᶠ A et r.   πάλιν Ἀθήνας Z.

τὸ γιγνόμενον] See on Or. 37 § 5.
ἡμερῶν, κ.τ.λ.] 'within twenty days after' (lit. 'counting from that on which') ' they shall have returned to Athens.' It is convenient to call this a ' genitive of limitation of time' (past or future), as if ἐντὸς were in the writer's mind.

ἐκβολῆς] *Jactura*, 'jettison,' goods lost by being thrown overboard to lighten a ship in a storm. To prevent fraud, it is specified that none can be allowed as a drawback, except such as the passengers have agreed to be necessary for their common safety. This partial jettison Aeschylus calls βαλεῖν σφενδόνης ἀπ' εὐμέτρου, Agam. 1010. Cf. Acts xxvii 18, 38. M. Dareste refers to the Digest xiv 2, *de lege Rhodia de iactu*.

ἀνέπαφον] A word properly applied to a cargo unmolested by pirates, came to mean *integram*, entire and without deduction. See on Aesch. Suppl.

309 (P.). Hesych. ἀνέπαφος· ἀψηλάφητος.
12. ὑποθεῖναι, κ.τ.λ.] 'To pledge or even to sell at the market value' ('for such price as can be obtained,' Kennedy). It seems here a synonym of καθεστώσης.

καὶ ἐάν τι, κ.τ.λ.] 'And if there is any deficiency in the money which is due to the lenders under the agreement, it shall be lawful for the lenders, both or either of them, to levy the amount by execution against Artemo and Apollodorus and against all their property, whether on land or sea, wheresoever they may be, in the same manner as if a judgment had been recovered against them, and they had committed default in payment.' Kennedy. This clause, of course, gives absolute right of seizure of any property to one or both, so that in the event of only one debtor being dishonest, the other is liable for the whole.

62   XXXV. ΠΡΟΣ ΤΗΝ   [§§ 12—14

σασι κατὰ τὴν συγγραφὴν, κατὰ Ἀρτέμωνος καὶ
Ἀπολλοδώρου ἔστω ἡ πρᾶξις τοῖς δανείσασι καὶ ἐκ
τῶν τούτων ἁπάντων, καὶ ἐγγείων καὶ ναυτικῶν, πανταχοῦ ὅπου ἂν ὦσι, καθάπερ δίκην ὠφληκότων καὶ 927
ὑπερημέρων ὄντων, καὶ ἑνὶ ἑκατέρῳ τῶν δανεισάντων
13 καὶ ἀμφοτέροις. ἐὰν δὲ μὴ εἰσβάλωσι, μείναντες ἐπὶ
κυνὶ ἡμέρας δέκα ἐν Ἑλλησπόντῳ, ἐξελόμενοι ὅπου
ἂν μὴ σῦλαι ὦσιν Ἀθηναίοις, καὶ ἐντεῦθεν καταπλεύ-
σαντες Ἀθήναζε τοὺς τόκους ἀποδόντων τοὺς πέρυσι
γραφέντας εἰς τὴν συγγραφήν. ἐὰν δέ τι ἡ ναῦς πάθῃ
ἀνήκεστον ἐν ᾗ ἂν πλέῃ τὰ χρήματα, σωτηρία ἔστω

13. εἰσβάλωσι] 'Make the entrance of Pontus.' A nautical term, probably, familiar to navigators in that sea and to those coasts.——ἐπὶ κυνί, 'after the rising of the dog-star.' 'Bad weather seems to have been generally expected in the dog-days [July 25 to August 5].' Penrose.

ὅπου ἂν μὴ σῦλαι ὦσιν] 'Wherever the Athenians have no rights of reprisal' (letters of marque justifying the seizure of goods). It is evident, that if a ship from the Pontus put into any port where property was allowed to be seized by the Athenians, the cargo and crew would be endangered, even though they might afterwards be liberated if it should appear that they were bona fide Athenian traders. Inf. § 26, ὥσπερ δεδομένων συλῶν Φασηλίταις κατ' Ἀθηναίων.
[Harpocration s. v. σύλας: Δημοσθένης ἐν τῷ περὶ στεφάνου τῆς τριηραρχίας (page 1232, 4) κἂν τῷ πρὸς τὴν Λακρίτου παραγραφὴν "ἐξελόμενος ὁπόταν (sic) μὴ σῦλαι ὦσιν Ἀθηναίοις..." S.]

τοὺς πέρυσι γραφέντας] 'The amount of interest (i.e. not more) inserted in the bond for last year.' If the legal year should have expired, the interest is to remain the same. ['L'année commençait au mois de juin, au solstice d'été. La saison de la navigation allait d'avril à octobre, et, par suite, les intérêts convenus au mois d'avril ne pouvaient être payés que l'année suivante, au retour du navire.' Dareste. S.]

πάθῃ ἀνήκεστον] Like ἀφανίζεσθαι, 'to be missing,' this is a euphemistic formula for being lost, or wrecked.

σωτηρία] 'Let there be salvage of the hypothecated goods for the benefit of the lenders.' The simplest sense seems to be, that if the ship be wrecked, but any of the goods be recovered, they shall belong to the lenders, i.e. the wreck shall not exonerate the borrowers from all further obligation. Or we might read σωτήρια in the plural, 'let costs be allowed for salvage.'—τὰ περιγενόμενα, 'any goods that may be saved be the property of both lenders alike.' By κοινά (in which Kennedy "can see no force") is meant

τῶν ὑποκειμένων[g]· τὰ δὲ περιγενόμενα κοινὰ ἔστω τοῖς δανείσασιν. κυριώτερον δὲ περὶ τούτων ἄλλο μηδὲν εἶναι τῆς συγγραφῆς.

Μάρτυρες Φορμίων Πειραιεύς, Κηφισόδωρος Βοιώτιος, Ἡλιόδωρος Πιτθεύς.]

Λέγε δὴ καὶ τὰς μαρτυρίας. 14

ΜΑΡΤΥΡΙΑΙ.

[Ἀρχενομίδης Ἀρχεδάμαντος Ἀναγυράσιος μαρτυρεῖ συνθήκας παρ' ἑαυτῷ καταθέσθαι Ἀνδροκλέα Σφήττιον, Ναυσικράτην Καρύστιον, Ἀρτέμωνα, Ἀπολλόδωρον, Φασηλίτας, καὶ εἶναι παρ' ἑαυτῷ ἔτι κειμένην τὴν συγγραφήν.]

Λέγε δὴ καὶ τὴν τῶν παραγενομένων μαρτυρίαν.

ΜΑΡΤΥΡΙΑ.

[Θεόδοτος ἰσοτελής, Χαρῖνος Ἐπιχάρους Λευκονοεύς, Φορμίων Κηφισοφῶντος Πειραιεύς, Κηφισόδωρος Βοιώτιος, Ἡλιόδωρος Πιτθεὺς μαρτυροῦσι παρεῖναι, ὅτ' ἐδάνεισεν Ἀνδροκλῆς Ἀπολλοδώρῳ καὶ Ἀρτέμωνι ἀργυρίου τρισχιλίας δραχμὰς, καὶ εἰδέναι τὴν συγγραφὴν καταθεμένους παρὰ Ἀρχενομίδῃ Ἀναγυρασίῳ.]

[g] (σωτηρία δ' ἔσται τῶν ὑποκειμένων), τὰ περιγενόμενα Z cum Ar; but Bekker agrees with Dindorf.

that neither lender shall claim it in discharge of *his* part of the loan, but both shall share the benefit of it.

The Zürich editors, by making σωτηρία δ' ἔσται part of the protasis, and commencing the apodosis with τὰ περιγενόμενα, adopt a solecistic syntax, ἐὰν—ἔσται, which could only be justified on the theory that this is a spurious and late document.

κυριώτερον] i.e. the terms of this bond shall be absolute, and not superseded by any law, conditions, or stipulations whatever to the contrary.

§ 14. *Evidence is put in (1) to identify the document; (2) to attest that the parties to the transaction are the present litigants.*

Anagyrus, Sphettus, Leuconoë or Leuconium (Photius), Piraeus and Pitthis, were all Attic *demi*. A Θεόδοτος ἰσοτελής is mentioned in Or. 34 § 18.

15 Κατὰ τὴν συγγραφὴν ταύτην, ὦ ἄνδρες δικασταί, ἐδάνεισα τὰ χρήματα Ἀρτέμωνι τῷ τούτου ἀδελφῷ, κελεύοντος τούτου καὶ ἀναδεχομένου ἅπαντ' ἔσεσθαί 928 μοι τὰ δίκαια κατὰ τὴν συγγραφὴν, καθ' ἣν ἐδάνεισα τούτου αὐτοῦ γράφοντος καὶ συσσημηναμένου, ἐπειδὴ ἐγράφη. οἱ μὲν γὰρ ἀδελφοὶ οἱ τούτου ἔτι νεώτεροι ἦσαν καὶ μειράκια παντάπασιν, οὑτοσὶ δὲ Λάκριτος
16 Φασηλίτης, μέγα πρᾶγμα, Ἰσοκράτους μαθητής· οὗτος ἦν ὁ πάντα διοικῶν, καὶ ἑαυτῷ με τὸν νοῦν προσ-

§§ 15—17. *Continuation of the narrative. At the personal request and engagement of Lacritus that justice should be done, I lent Artemo the money, and Lacritus actually put his seal to the bond. I thought him a man of consideration, and was charmed by his plausible words. No sooner, however, had they got the money than they violated all the terms of the compact, and this at the instance of Lacritus himself.*

συσσημηναμένου] 'Joining in the signature.' Or. 41 § 22 (πρὸς Σπουδίαν):—τί δὲ συνεσημαίνετο πάλιν τὰ μηδὲν ὑγιὲς ὄντα μηδ' ἀληθῆ γράμματα; We cannot say how far this made Lacritus legally liable. Perhaps it was only a plausible show of acceptance; but it was not necessarily done fraudulently, as Androcles implies.

μέγα πρᾶγμα] 'A great man,' δοκῶν εἶναί τις. Penrose compares Herod. III 132, ἦν μέγιστον πρῆγμα Δημοκήδης τῷ βασιλέϊ.

Ἰσοκράτους μαθητής] Cicero, *Brutus*, § 32, 'Isocrates, cuius domus cunctae Graeciae quasi ludus quidam patuit atque officina dicendi.' Quintilian II 8, 11, 'Clarissimus ille praeceptor Isocrates, quem non magis libri bene dixisse, quam discipuli bene docuisse testantur.' Amongst his best-known pupils were the orators Isaeus, Hyperides, Lycurgus; the historians Theopompus and Ephorus; also Timotheus the celebrated general, and Androtion the orator and demagogue attacked by Demosthenes; who describes him as τεχνίτης τοῦ λέγειν καὶ πάντα τὸν βίον ἐσχολακὼς ἐνὶ τούτῳ (Dem. Androt. § 4), and who is said to have spent special pains on his speech because he had to confront an orator who had learned his art in the school of Isocrates. (See further Isocr. Paneg. § 189 n.)

More than 40 of his pupils are discussed by P. Sanneg (*de Schola Isocratea*, p. 60), who describes Lacritus as 'demagogus magis et callidus versutusque vir quam literis deditus, tamen in arte rhetorica—si fides habenda Pseudo-Demostheni Or. in Lacr. 41—tradenda versatus. Ea enim oratio adeo disciplinae Isocrateae maledicit, ut e more Demosthenis fieri nequibat.' Cf. note on ὑπόθεσις l. 13. S.]

16. ἑαυτῷ προσέχειν] 'To attend to *him*,' i.e. to trust him rather than Artemo for the fulfilment of the engagement. Here also the words seem vague,

ἔχειν ἐκέλευεν· αὐτὸς γὰρ ἔφη ποιήσειν μοι τὰ δίκαια ἅπαντα καὶ ἐπιδημήσειν Ἀθήνησι, τὸν δ' ἀδελφὸν ἑαυτοῦ[h] Ἀρτέμωνα πλεύσεσθαι[i] ἐπὶ τοῖς χρήμασι. καὶ τότε μὲν, ὦ ἄνδρες δικασταί, ὅτ' ἐβούλετο τὰ χρήματα λαβεῖν παρ' ἡμῶν, καὶ ἀδελφὸς ἔφη εἶναι καὶ κοινωνὸς τοῦ Ἀρτέμωνος, καὶ λόγους θαυμασίως ὡς πιθανοὺς ἔλεγεν· ἐπειδὴ δὲ τάχιστα ἐγκρατεῖς ἐγένοντο τοῦ ἀρ- 17 γυρίου, τοῦτο μὲν διενείμαντο καὶ ἐχρῶντο ὅ τι ἐδόκει τούτοις, κατὰ δὲ τὴν συγγραφὴν τὴν ναυτικήν, καθ' ἣν ἔλαβον τὰ χρήματα, οὔτε μέγα οὔτε μικρὸν ἔπραττον, ὡς αὐτὸ τὸ ἔργον ἐδήλωσεν. οὑτοσὶ δὲ Λάκριτος ἁπάντων ἦν τούτων ὁ ἐξηγητής. καθ' ἕκαστον δὲ τῶν γεγραμμένων ἐν τῇ συγγραφῇ ἐπιδείξω τούτους οὐδ' ὁτιοῦν πεποιηκότας ὑγιές.

Πρῶτον μὲν γὰρ γέγραπται ὅτι ἐπ' οἴνου κεραμί- 18 οις τρισχιλίοις ἐδανείζοντο παρ' ἡμῶν τὰς τριάκοντα μνᾶς, ὡς ὑπαρχούσης αὐτοῖς ὑποθήκης ἑτέρων τριά-

[h] αὐτοῦ Z cum Σ.   τὸν αὐτοῦ Bekk. cf. § 36.
[i] πλευσεῖσθαι Z.

and to fall short of any legal liability. As Artemo was to sail with (ἐπὶ) the goods, and Lacritus said he should be in town, it was natural to trust to him rather than to Artemo. There is some satire in the language, especially in the λόγοι θαυμασίως ὡς πιθανοί. The passage is important as showing the same feeling against the Sophists which had prevailed so long before. See especially the opinion of Aristotle, Eth. Nic. x 9, 20.

17. ὅ τι ἐδόκει (χρῆσθαι)] 'for whatever purpose they chose.' The almost unvarying idiom is τί χρήσομαι τῷδε; rarely ἐπί or πρὸς τί.

οὑτοσὶ δὲ κ.τ.λ.] Perhaps we should transpose the article, which should not be used in the predicate and read οὑτοσὶ δὲ ὁ Λ. ἁπάντων ἦν τούτων ἐξηγητής, 'This fellow Lacritus was the author of the whole plot.' Mr Mayor (p. 244) objects that 'the article is of course not wanted with the proper name.' It may however serve to express contempt.

§§ 18, 19. *The compact was violated in the first instance by the shipment of an insufficient quantity of wine. They had used the money for other purposes, and never even intended to buy it* (at Mende, §§ 10, 20).

18. ὡς ὑπαρχούσης] 'As if

κοντα μνῶν, ὥστ᾽ εἰς τάλαντον ἀργυρίου τὴν τιμὴν εἶναι τοῦ οἴνου καθισταμένην, σὺν τοῖς ἀναλώμασιν, ὅσα ἔδει ἀναλίσκεσθαι εἰς τὴν κατασκευὴν τὴν περὶ τὸν οἶνον· τὰ δὲ τρισχίλια κεράμια ἄγεσθαι ταῦτα εἰς 929 τὸν Πόντον ἐν τῇ εἰκοσόρῳ, ἣν Ὑβλήσιος ἐναυκλήρει.

19 γέγραπται μὲν ταῦτα ἐν τῇ συγγραφῇ, ὦ ἄνδρες δικασταί, ἧς ὑμεῖς ἀκηκόατε· οὗτοι δ᾽ ἀντὶ τῶν τρισχιλίων κεραμίων οὐδὲ πεντακόσια κεράμια εἰς τὸ πλοῖον ἐνέθεντο, ἀλλ᾽ ἀντὶ τοῦ ἠγοράσθαι αὐτοῖς τὸν οἶνον, ὅσον προσῆκε, τοῖς χρήμασιν ἐχρῶντο ὅ τι ἐδόκει τούτοις, τὰ δὲ κεράμια τὰ τρισχίλια οὐδ᾽ ἐμέλλησαν οὐδὲ διενοήθησαν ἐνθέσθαι εἰς τὸ πλοῖον κατὰ τὴν συγγραφήν. ὅτι δ᾽ ἀληθῆ ταῦτα λέγω, λαβὲ τὴν μαρτυρίαν τῶν συμπλεόντων ἐν τῷ αὐτῷ πλοίῳ τούτοις.

they had to offer (i.e. already possessed) security for other thirty minae' (3000 dr.). See Or. 34 § 16. They probably represented the wine as already theirs (purchased, perhaps, but not fully paid for), and lying at the port in Pallene; and this seems the point of ἠγοράσθαι in § 19, 'instead of the wine *having been* bought by them.'

εἰς τάλαντον] The goods were to be twice the value of the loan; 3000 dr. × 2 = 60 minae = 1 talent.

καθισταμένην] Perhaps here we should read τὴν καθισταμένην, 'the price which was agreed for.' Otherwise, we must follow Mr Mayor (p. 244) and others in regarding εἶναι καθισταμένην = καθίστασθαι.—σὺν τοῖς, κ.τ.λ. 'including the expenses which had to be incurred for the vesselling and stowage of the wine.' Kennedy. Comp. Or. 34 § 7, σὺν τῷ ἐπισιτισμῷ. It will be observed that the contract (10—14) contains no clause to this effect.

19. τὰ κεράμια τὰ τρ.] Note the force of the double article: 'all this pretended cargo of the 3000 jars,' &c. So above, § 17, ἡ συγγραφὴ ἡ ναυτική is 'this bond which they pretend to have been bound by (but have violated).' Inf. § 30. ὁ ἀδελφὸς ὁ 'Αρτέμωνος, § 32, τὸ πλοῖον τὸ ναυαγῆσαν, and τὸ οἰνάριον τὸ Κῷον (where incredulity of the existence of a lost cargo is implied), § 52, τοῦ ναυκλήρου τοῦ Φασηλίτου. In these passages irony is perhaps intended to be conveyed. Mr Mayor however (p. 244) says the repetition of the article 'denotes nothing more than a wish to be exact.'

§ 20. *Evidence of the pilot and quartermaster that only* 450 *jars of wine were taken in Hyblesius' ship.*

ΜΑΡΤΥΡΙΑ.

['Ερασικλῆς μαρτυρεῖ κυβερνᾶν τὴν ναῦν ἣν Ὑβλή- 20
σιος ἐναυκλήρει, καὶ εἰδέναι Ἀπολλόδωρον ἀγόμενον ἐν
τῷ πλοίῳ οἴνου Μενδαίου κεράμια τετρακόσια πεντήκοντα, καὶ οὐ πλείω· ἄλλο δὲ μηδὲν ἀγώγιμον ἄγεσθαι
ἐν τῷ πλοίῳ Ἀπολλόδωρον εἰς τὸν Πόντον.

Ἱππίας Ἀθηνίππου Ἁλικαρνασσεὺς μαρτυρεῖ
συμπλεῖν ἐν τῇ Ὑβλησίου νηὶ διοπεύων[k] τὴν ναῦν, καὶ
εἰδέναι Ἀπολλόδωρον τὸν Φασηλίτην ἀγόμενον ἐν τῷ
πλοίῳ ἐκ Μένδης εἰς τὸν Πόντον οἴνου Μενδαίου κεράμια τετρακόσια πεντήκοντα, ἄλλο δὲ μηδὲν φορτίον.

Πρὸς τοῖσδ' ἐξεμαρτύρησεν Ἀρχιάδης[1] Μνησωνί-
δου Ἀχαρνεύς, Σώστρατος Φιλίππου Ἱστιαιόθεν,
Εὐμάριχος Εὐβοίου Ἱστιαιόθεν[m], Φιλτιάδης Κτησίου
Ξυπεταιών, Διονύσιος Δημοκρατίδου Χολλείδης.]

[k] διοπεύων restored by Dindorf, Z and Donaldson (*New Crat.*
§ 433), *Bekk. st.* διοπτεύων Bekker 1824 *cum libris.*
[1] Ἀχράδης Z *cum* F Φ. Ἀρχάδης Bekker.
[m] *om.* Z.

Ἀπολλόδωρον] Sup. § 16, it was Artemo who was to sail with the goods.

διοπεύων] An overlooker or super-cargo. A form of διοπτεύειν, seen also in ὀπιπτεύειν. Aeschylus has βασιλῆς διοποι in Pers. 44 (Hesych. ἐπιμεληταί). And Hesych. has διοπεύειν· ἐπιμελεῖσθαι νεώς.—δίοπος· ἐπίσκοπος, ἄρχων, ναύαρχος, ἐπιστάτης, διόπτης. — διοπτεύειν· κατασκοπεῖν.—[Schol. διοπεύων· ὀπιπτεύων τὰ κατὰ τὴν ναῦν, οἷον δίοπός τις ὤν, ἤγουν κατασκοπῶν. Harpocrat. διοπτεύων (sic)· Δημοσθένης ἐν τῷ κατὰ Λακρίτου. δίοπος λέγεται νεὼς ὁ διέπων καὶ ἐποπτεύων τὰ κατὰ τὴν ναῦν. See Büchsenschütz, *Besitz u. Er-*

werb, p 459 n. S.]

ἐξεμαρτύρησεν] 'Put in a written affidavit on absence at the time,' i.e. when the other depositions were drawn up. On this word there is a note on Aesch. Agam. 1167 (P.) [Or. 46 § 7].—Ἱστιαιόθεν, 'from Histiaea'(Oreus) in Euboea, of which island Nausicrates, the partner of Androcles, was a native, § 10.

Ξυπεταιών] Photius, Ξυπεταίωνες (sic), δῆμος τῆς Κεκροπίδος φυλῆς. Ξυπεταιή, ἀφ' ἧς ὁ δημότης Ξυπεταιών. Hesych. Ξυπετεά· δῆμος τῆς Κ. φ. The proper form is Ξυπετῇ (Steph. Byzant.).—Χολλείδης, Ar. Ach. 406, of the deme Chollidae.

21 Περὶ μὲν οὖν τοῦ πλήθους τοῦ οἴνου, ὅσον ἔδει αὐτοὺς ἐνθέσθαι εἰς τὸ πλοῖον, ταῦτα διεπράξαντο, καὶ ἤρξαντο εὐθὺς ἐντεῦθεν ἀπὸ τοῦ πρώτου γεγραμ- 930 μένου παραβαίνειν καὶ μὴ ποιεῖν τὰ γεγραμμένα. μετὰ δὲ ταῦτ' ἔστιν ἐν τῇ συγγραφῇ ὅτι ὑποτιθέασι ταῦτ' ἐλεύθερα καὶ οὐδενὶ οὐδὲν ὀφείλοντες, καὶ ὅτι οὐδ' 22 ἐπιδανείσονται ἐπὶ τούτοις παρ' οὐδενός. ταῦτα διαρρήδην γέγραπται, ὦ ἄνδρες δικασταί. οὗτοι δὲ τί ἐποίησαν; ἀμελήσαντες τῶν γεγραμμένων ἐν τῇ συγγραφῇ δανείζονται παρά τινος νεανίσκου, ἐξαπατήσαντες ὡς οὐδενὶ οὐδὲν ὀφείλοντες· καὶ ἡμᾶς τε παρεκρούσαντο καὶ ἔλαθον δανεισάμενοι ἐπὶ τοῖς ἡμετέροις, ἐκεῖνόν τε τὸν νεανίσκον τὸν δανείσαντα ἐξηπάτησαν ὡς ἐπ' ἐλευθέροις τοῖς χρήμασι δανειζόμενοι· τοιαῦτα τούτων ἐστὶ τὰ κακουργήματα. ταῦτα δὲ πάντ' ἐστὶ τὰ σοφίσματα Λακρίτου τουτουί. ὅτι δ' ἀληθῆ λέγω καὶ ἐπεδανείσαντο[n] χρήματα παρὰ τὴν συγγραφήν, μαρτυ-

[n] τὰ Z cum Σ.—om. Bekker.

§§ 21, 22. *A further violation of the contract was the raising a new loan on the goods pledged to us, by which transaction both we and the second lender were defrauded.*

ἀπὸ τοῦ πρώτου] 'From the first clause,' as given in § 10, ἐπὶ οἴνου κεραμίοις τρισχιλίοις.

ὑποτιθέασι...ἐλεύθερα] Theophrast. fragm. 97, παρ' οἷς ἀναγραφὴ τῶν κτημάτων ἐστὶ καὶ τῶν συμβολαίων, ἐξ ἐκείνων ἐστὶ μαθεῖν, εἰ ἐλεύθερα καὶ ἀνέπαφα καὶ τὰ αὑτοῦ πωλεῖ δικαίως. S.]

22. ἐπιδανείσονται] Or. 34 § 6.

καὶ ἡμᾶς τε κ.τ.λ.] 'And by this proceeding they not only cheated us and borrowed, without our knowledge or consent, on the security of our property, but they also defrauded that poor youth who lent them the money, by pretending to borrow it on property on which there was no other claim.' ('Leading him to suppose that the property on which they borrowed his money was unencumbered.' Kennedy.)

τοιαῦτα κ.τ.λ.] So τοιαῦται is a predicate inf. § 24. For the use of the article compare Aesch. Theb. 646, τοιαῦτ' ἐκείνων ἐστὶ τἀξευρήματα. (The sentence in Demosthenes is also in iambic verse.) [On Iambic verses in prose cf. Isocr. Paneg. § 170, n. S.]

§ 23. *Affidavit that the second loan was advanced in ignorance of a former loan having been made on the same security.*

ρίαν ἀναγνώσεται ὑμῖν αὐτοῦ τοῦ ἐπιδανείσαντος. λέγε 23
τὴν μαρτυρίαν.

ΜΑΡΤΥΡΙΑ.

["Ἄρατος Ἁλικαρνασσεὺς μαρτυρεῖ δανεῖσαι Ἀπολλοδώρῳ ἕνδεκα μνᾶς ἀργυρίου ἐπὶ τῇ ἐμπορίᾳ ἣν ἦγεν ἐν τῇ Ὑβλησίου νηὶ εἰς τὸν Πόντον καὶ τοῖς ἐκεῖθεν ἀνταγορασθεῖσι, καὶ μὴ εἰδέναι αὐτὸν δεδανεισμένον παρὰ Ἀνδροκλέους ἀργύριον· οὐ γὰρ ἂν δανεῖσαι αὐτὸς Ἀπολλοδώρῳ τὸ ἀργύριον.]

Αἱ μὲν πανουργίαι τοιαῦται τῶν ἀνθρώπων τούτων 24 εἰσίν. γέγραπται δὲ μετὰ ταῦτα ἐν τῇ συγγραφῇ, ὦ ἄνδρες δικασταί, ἐπειδὰν ἀποδῶνται ἐν τῷ Πόντῳ ἃ ἦγον, πάλιν ἀνταγοράζειν χρήματα καὶ ἀντιφορτίζειν° καὶ ἀπάγειν Ἀθήναζε τὰ ἀντιφορτισθέντα, καὶ ἐπειδὰν ἀφίκωνται Ἀθήναζε, ἀποδοῦναι εἴκοσιν ἡμερῶν τὸ ἀργύριον ἡμῖν δόκιμον· ἕως δ' ἂν ἀποδῶσι, κρατεῖν τῶν χρημάτων ἡμᾶς, καὶ ἀνέπαφα ταῦτα παρέχειν

° Σ. ἀντιφορτίζεσθαι Z. Cf. §§ 25, 37.

οὐ γὰρ ἂν δανεῖσαι αὐτὸς] 'For that he would not himself' (i.e. whatever others might have done) 'have lent the money to Apollodorus.' It might be inferred from this that the lending on ἐπιδανεισμὸς was as illegal as the borrowing. He may however only mean, that he would not have lent it unless he had been misinformed about the security.

§§ 24, 5. *Other points in which the bond was broken.* (1) The defendants did not take a counter-cargo from Pontus (§ 11); (2) They did not put us in possession of the ship or goods, for they did not return to the Piraeus at all (§ 28).

ἃ ἦγον] An historical clause, for the actual words of the contract, ἃ ἂν ἀγάγωσι. *All* subjunctives are futures; and the verb in the minor clause is not logically correct in the past tense, unless indeed (as inf. § 26) a transaction is described preceding the event expressed by the subjunctive. But the use under any circumstances is rare, as is the subjunctive itself with πρόσθεν or πρότερον (Thuc. I. 41, Ar. Vesp. 1074).

δόκιμον] (Predicate) 'in current coin.' Kennedy.

ἕως δ' ἂν κ.τ.λ.] 'Pending the payment, *we* are to have possession of the goods, and they on their parts are to give them up to us uninjured (§ 11) till we have got our money back.'

25 τούτους, ἕως ἂν ἀπολάβωμεν. γέγραπται μὲν γὰρ ταῦτα οὑτωσὶ ἀκριβῶς ἐν τῇ συγγραφῇ· οὗτοι δ', ὦ ἄνδρες δικασταί, ἐνταῦθα καὶ ἐπεδείξαντο μάλιστα τὴν ὕβριν καὶ τὴν ἀναίδειαν τὴν ἑαυτῶν, καὶ ὅτι οὐδὲ μικρὸν προσεῖχον τοῖς γράμμασι τοῖς γεγραμμένοις ἐν τῇ συγγραφῇ, ἀλλ' ἡγοῦντο εἶναι τὴν συγγραφὴν ἄλλως ὕθλον καὶ φλυαρίαν. οὔτε γὰρ ἀντηγόρασαν οὐδὲν ἐν τῷ Πόντῳ οὔτε ἀντεφορτίσαντο ὥστε ἄγειν 'Αθήναζε· ἡμεῖς τε οἱ δανείσαντες τὰ χρήματα ἡκόντων αὐτῶν τούτων ἐκ τοῦ Πόντου οὐκ εἴχομεν ὅτου ἐπιλαβοίμεθα οὐδ' ὅτου κρατοῖμεν, ἕως^p κομισαίμεθα τὰ ἡμέτερ'^q αὐτῶν· οὐδ' ὁτιοῦν γὰρ εἰσήγαγον εἰς τὸν λιμένα τὸν 26 ὑμέτερον οὗτοι. ἀλλὰ πεπόνθαμεν καινότατον, ὦ ἄνδρες δικασταί· ἐν γὰρ τῇ πόλει τῇ ἡμετέρᾳ αὐτῶν, οὐδὲν ἀδικοῦντες οὐδὲ δίκην οὐδεμίαν ὠφληκότες τούτοις, σεσυλήμεθα τὰ ἡμέτερ' αὐτῶν ὑπὸ τούτων Φασηλιτῶν ὄντων, ὥσπερ δεδομένων συλῶν Φασηλίταις

p ἕως [ὅτου] Bekk. 1824.   q ἡμέτερα Z.

25. καὶ—μάλιστα] This seems the syntax intended. Mr Mayor, p. 245, thinks ἐνταῦθα καί, 'it was here also that they showed,' is the author's meaning.
ἄλλως ὕθλον] 'Mere trash and nonsense.' There was a proverb γραῶν ὕθλος, 'old wives' fables,' Plat. Theaet. p. 176 B. For ἄλλως Penrose compares Eur. Troad. 476, οὐκ ἀριθμὸν ἄλλως, ἀλλ' ὑπερτάτους Φρυγῶν.
ὅτου—ἕως] In direct narrative, οὐκ ἔχομεν ὅτου κρατῶμεν ἕως ἂν κομισώμεθα. In Latin, non habebamus quod prenderemus donec recepissemus quae essent nostri. The ἂν would have been added to ἕως had the event been still pending; and even with the optative in past narrative it is sometimes added,

as explained at length on Aesch. Pers. 452 (P). Cf. Or. 33 § 8, ὠνὴν ποιοῦμαι (i.e. ἐποιούμην) τῆς νεὼς καὶ τῶν παίδων, ἕως ἀποδοίη τὰς δέκα μνᾶς ἃς δι' ἐμοῦ ἔλαβε.
§§ 26, 27. *Thus we have been robbed of our property in our own city, as if forsooth these Phaselites had the right of reprisal on Athenians! For it is robbery not to pay debts. Here was no dispute about facts, no ambiguity in the terms of the bond. It is simply roguery on their part. When both the contracting parties have made a written agreement, there is an end of it; it only remains for them to act up to the letter of the contract.*
συλῶν] See § 13. Photius (in v. σύλας) cites the sentence

κατ' Ἀθηναίων. ἐπειδὰν γὰρ μὴ ἐθέλωσιν ἀποδοῦναι ἃ ἔλαβον, τί ἄν τις ἄλλο ὄνομ' ἔχοι θέσθαι τοῖς τοιούτοις ἢ ὅτι ἀφαιροῦνται βίᾳ τὰ ἀλλότρια; ἐγὼ μὲν οὐδ' ἀκήκοα πώποτε πρᾶγμα μιαρώτερον ἢ ὃ οὗτοι διαπεπραγμένοι εἰσὶ περὶ ἡμᾶς, καὶ ταῦθ' ὁμολογοῦντες λαβεῖν παρ' ἡμῶν τὰ χρήματα. ὅσα μὲν γὰρ ἀμφισ- 27 βητήσιμά ἐστι τῶν συμβολαίων, κρίσεως δεῖται, ὦ ἄνδρες δικασταί· τὰ δὲ παρ' ἀμφοτέρων ὁμολογηθέντα τῶν συντιθεμένων, καὶ περὶ ὧν συγγραφαὶ κεῖνται ναυτικαί, τέλος ἔχειν ἅπαντες νομίζουσι, καὶ χρῆσθαι προσήκει τοῖς γεγραμμένοις. ὅτι δὲ κατὰ τὴν συγγραφὴν οὐδ' ὁτιοῦν πεποιήκασιν, ἀλλ' εὐθὺς ἀπ' ἀρχῆς ἀρξάμενοι ἐκακοτέχνουν καὶ ἐπεβούλευον μηδὲν ὑγιὲς ποιεῖν, ὑπό τε τῶν μαρτυριῶν καὶ αὐτοὶ ὑφ' ἑαυτῶν[r] ἐλέγχονται οὑτωσὶ καταφανῶς.

Ὃ δὲ πάντων δεινότατον διεπράξατο Λάκριτος 28 οὑτοσί, δεῖ ὑμᾶς ἀκοῦσαι· οὗτος γὰρ ἦν ὁ πάντα ταῦτα διοικῶν. ἐπειδὴ γὰρ ἀφίκοντο δεῦρο, εἰς μὲν τὸ

[r] αὐτῶν Z.

σεσυλήμεθα—ἀλλότρια, omitting some words, τούτων and ὄντων, ὥσπερ before δεδομένων and βίᾳ after ἀναιροῦνται (sic). He refers the passage to the De Corona, by an evident mistake. Cf. Lysias κατὰ Νικομ. Or. 30 § 22, ὁρῶν—Βοιωτοὺς σῦλα ποιουμένους.

οὐδ' ἀκήκοα] i.e. much less have I witnessed.

διαπεπραγμένοι] Observe the medial use of the perfect passive corresponding to the aorist διεπράξαντο. Similarly εἰσπέπρακται in § 44.

27. ὅσα κ.τ.λ.] 'Those contracts which are disputed.' Kennedy. Rather, perhaps, 'such clauses in contracts as are disputable.'

τέλος ἔχειν] 'To be final,' i.e. κύρια or valid.——χρῆσθαι, 'to adopt, carry into effect.'

§§ 28—31. *On returning to Athens, they put the ship into 'Smugglers' Creek,' and there she remained at anchor for nearly a month, while the defendants showed themselves frequently on 'Change. On being asked for payment, they said they were doing all they could to discharge our claims; but finding no goods were forthcoming, I asked Lacritus the reason. He replied, that the ship had been wrecked in the home voyage, and all the goods lost that were to have been conveyed to Athens.*

ὑμέτερον[a] ἐμπόριον οὐ καταπλέουσιν, εἰς φωρῶν δὲ λιμένα ὁρμίζονται, ὅς ἐστιν ἔξω τῶν σημείων τοῦ ὑμετέρου[t] ἐμπορίου. καὶ ἔστιν ὅμοιον εἰς φωρῶν λιμένα ὁρμίσασθαι, ὥσπερ ἄν εἴ τις εἰς Αἴγιναν ἢ εἰς Μέγαρα ὁρμίσαιτο· ἔξεστι γὰρ ἀποπλεῖν ἐκ τοῦ λιμένος τούτου ὅποι ἄν τις βούληται καὶ ὁπηνίκ' ἂν δοκῇ αὐτῷ. 29 καὶ τὸ μὲν πλοῖον ὥρμει ἐνταῦθα πλείους ἢ πέντε καὶ εἴκοσιν ἡμέρας, οὗτοι δὲ περιεπάτουν ἐν τῷ δείγματι τῷ ὑμετέρῳ[u], καὶ ἡμεῖς προσιόντες διελεγόμεθα, καὶ ἐκελεύομεν τούτους ἐπιμελεῖσθαι ὅπως ἂν ὡς τάχιστ' ἀπολάβοιμεν τὰ χρήματα. οὗτοι δ' ὡμολόγουν τε καὶ ἔλεγον ὅτι αὐτὰ ταῦτα περαίνοιεν. καὶ ἡμεῖς τούτοις

[a] ἡμέτερον Z cum Γ A¹.—ὑμέτερον Bekker.
[t] ἡμετέρου Z cum Σ Φ.—ὑμετέρου Bekker.
[u] ἡμετέρῳ Z.

28. ἔξω τῶν σημείων] A flagstaff, perhaps, or some similar signal, was placed to show the limits of the Attic harbours. This was an insignificant creek probably nearly opposite the little island of Psyttaleia, having its nickname from its use to unprincipled traders in evading the custom-duties. It was as much out of the way (says the orator, using hyperbole), as if one should put in at Aegina or Megara (Nisaea). [Bekker's *Anecd.* 315, Φωρῶν λιμένα: ὁ φωρῶν λιμήν ἐστιν ἐν μεθορίῳ τῆς Ἀττικῆς, ἔνθα οἱ λῃσταὶ καὶ κακοῦργοι ὁρμίζονται. Strabo, p. 395, οἱ Κορυδαλεῖς, εἶθ' ὁ φωρῶν λιμὴν καὶ ἡ Ψυττάλεια. Leake (*Athens* II 273) thinks that the words in the text are better suited to the bay of Keratzini than to the more easterly creek of Trapezona, which was perhaps *within* the outworks of the Peiraeus. S.]

ὁπηνίκα] 'At whatever hour he may choose,' i.e. to sneak away in the dark.

29. δείγματι] A place where samples of goods (δείγματα) were shown. See Boeckh, *Publ. Ec.* p. 58. Or. 50 (πρὸς Πολυκλέα), § 24, παραλαβὼν Δεινίαν τὸν κηδεστὴν τὸν ἐμὸν προσέρχεται αὐτῷ ἐν τῷ δείγματι. Ar. Equit. 979, ἐν τῷ δείγματι τῶν δικῶν. Hesych. δεῖγμα τόπος ἐν Ἀθήναις οὕτως καλούμενος. [Harpocrat. τόπος τις ἐν τῷ Ἀθήνησιν ἐμπορίῳ. Leake's *Athens*, I 382. S.]

ἐπιμελεῖσθαι] 'To do all in their power.' The ἄν here, differently from the combination ὅπως ἄν with the subjunctive (sup. § 7) belongs to the optative, and the order of the words might have been ὅπως ὡς τάχιστ' ἄν ἀπολάβοιμεν.——
αὐτά, perhaps αὐτοί, i.e. themselves, without being urged.

p. 933]   ΛΑΚΡΙΤΟΥ ΠΑΡΑΓΡΑΦΗΝ.   73

προσῇμεν, καὶ ἅμ' ἐπεσκοποῦμεν εἴ τι ἐξαιροῦνταί
ποθεν ἐκ τοῦ πλοίου˘ ἢ πεντηκοστεύονται. ἐπειδὴ δ' 30
ἡμέραι τε ἦσαν συχναὶ ἐπιδημοῦσι τούτοις, ἡμεῖς τ'
οὐδ' ὁτιοῦν εὑρίσκομεν οὔτ' ἐξῃρημένον οὔτε πεπεν-
933 τηκοστευμένον ἐπὶ τῷ ὀνόματι τῷ τούτων, ἐνταῦθ'
ἤδη μᾶλλον προσεκείμεθα ἀπαιτοῦντες. καὶ ἐπειδὴ
ἠνωχλοῦμεν αὐτοῖς, ἀποκρίνεται Λάκριτος οὑτοσὶ ὁ
ἀδελφὸς ὁ Ἀρτέμωνος ὅτι οὐκ ἂν οἷοί τ' εἴησαν ἀποδοῦναι, ἀλλ' ἀπόλωλεν ἅπαντα τὰ χρήματα· καὶ ἔφη
Λάκριτος δίκαιόν τι ἔχειν λέγειν περὶ τούτων. καὶ 31
ἡμεῖς, ὦ ἄνδρες δικασταί, ἠγανακτοῦμεν μὲν ͫ ἐπὶ τοῖς
λεγομένοις, πλέον δ' οὐδὲν ἦν ἀγανακτοῦσιν ἡμῖν·
τούτοις γὰρ οὐδ' ὁτιοῦν ἔμελεν. οὐδὲν δ' ἧττον ἠρω-
τῶμεν αὐτοὺς ὅντινα τρόπον ἀπολωλότ' εἴη τὰ χρήματα. Λάκριτος δ' οὑτοσὶ ναυαγῆσαι ἔφη τὸ πλοῖον
παραπλέον ἐκ Παντικαπαίου εἰς Θεοδοσίαν, ναυαγή-
σαντος δὲ τοῦ πλοίου ἀπολωλέναι τὰ χρήματα τοῖς

˘ ἐκ πλοίου Z.   τοῦ addidit Wolf.
ͫ om. Z et Bekk. st. cum libris.   μὲν cum Reiskio Bekk. 1824.

ἐπεσκοποῦμεν] 'We kept our eyes upon them.'
πεντηκοστεύονται] 'Are paying duty on.' Before the goods were landed, they had to pay 2 per cent. (Or. 34 § 7), and thus by the entries made in the books (ἀπογραφαὶ) all imports and exports could be known.
30. προσεκείμεθα] 'We became more urgent in our demand of payment.' Kennedy.
——ἠνωχλοῦμεν, ὀχληροὶ ἐγιγνό-μεθα, 'when we began to be very pressing.'
ὁ ἀδελφὸς ὁ Ἀ.] See sup. § 19.
δίκαιόν τι λέγειν] 'That he could say something to prove it was all right.' This is bitter satire on the Sophist and the Professor of eloquence. Kennedy hardly expresses this, 'and Lacritus said he could assign good ground of excuse.'
31. Παντικαπαίου] Kertsch, in the Crimea. See on Or. 34 § 8.—Θεοδοσία, Strabo, p. 309 (Vol. II p. 425, ed. Meineke), ἔστι δὲ τὸ μεταξὺ τῆς Θεοδοσίας καὶ τοῦ Παντικαπαίου σταδίων περὶ πεντακοσίων καὶ τριάκοντα. [Dem. Lept. § 83 (of Leucon king of Bosporus), προσκατα-σκευάσας ἐμπόριον Θευδοσίαν (sc. Kaffa) ὅ φασιν οἱ πλέοντες οὐδ' ὁτιοῦν χεῖρον εἶναι τοῦ Βοσπόρου (sc. Kertsch) κἀνταῦθ' ἔδωκε τὴν ἀτέλειαν ἡμῖν. S.]

ἀδελφοῖς τοῖς ἑαυτοῦ, ἃ ἔτυχεν ἐν τῷ πλοίῳ ἐνόντα· ἐνεῖναι δὲ τάριχός τε καὶ οἶνον Κῷον καὶ ἄλλ' ἄττα. καὶ ταῦτα ἔφασαν πάντα ἀντιφορτισθέντα μέλλειν 32 αὐτὰ ἄγειν Ἀθήναζε, εἰ μὴ ἀπώλετο ἐν τῷ πλοίῳ. καὶ ἃ μὲν ἔλεγε, ταῦτ' ἦν· ἄξιον δ' ἀκοῦσαι τὴν βδελυρίαν τῶν ἀνθρώπων τούτων καὶ τὴν ψευδολογίαν. πρός τε γὰρ τὸ πλοῖον τὸ ναυαγῆσαν οὐδὲν ἦν αὐτοῖς συμβόλαιον, ἀλλ' ἦν ἕτερος ὁ δεδανεικὼς Ἀθήνηθεν ἐπὶ τῷ ναύλῳ τῷ εἰς τὸν Πόντον καὶ ἐπ' αὐτῷ τῷ πλοίῳ (Ἀντίπατρος ὄνομα ἦν τῷ δεδανεικότι, Κιτιεὺς τὸ γένος)· τό τ' οἰνάριον τὸ Κῷον ὀγδοήκοντα στάμνοι

ἃ ἔτυχεν ἐνόντα] 'Which at that time were on board.'
τάριχος] Strabo, xi p. 493, says of the Rhombites (a river flowing into the *Sea of Azov*) ἐν ᾧ τὰ πλεῖστα ἁλιεύματα τῶν εἰς ταριχείας ἰχθύων. [Cf. Büchsenschütz, *Besitz u. Erwerb*, p. 432. S.]
αὐτὰ] This seems added redundantly, or by a change of syntax from καὶ ταῦτα πάντα ἀντ. ἔχειν, καὶ μέλλειν αὐτὰ ἄγειν. Shilleto (on Thuc. I 91, not. crit.) approves of Schaefer's conjecture ἀπάγειν for αὐτὰ ἄγειν.
§ 32. *Exposure of the pretence about the lost cargo. With the safety of the ship, apart from the cargo, they had no concern by the present bond, for it had been made over as security to another. As for the cargo, part of it was worthless, and part was being conveyed for and at the cost of a farmer at Theodosia.*
τὸ πλοῖον τό] See on § 19. He seems to mean, that if it really was wrecked (which he doubts), the loss could not be pleaded in excuse for non-payment to the plaintiff, because the ship had been mortgaged to Antipater. By ναυαγῆσαν (διεφθάρη, § 33) he must mean such damage as would require the cargo to be taken out for repairing it; for the ship itself was bound by the contract to be the same (τῷ αὐτῷ πλοίῳ, § 11), and it had returned to Athens, § 28. From the contract, § 10, it seems that the security given to Androcles was not the ship, but only the cargo of wine to be taken in at Mende, and the return cargo from the Pontus. Here Antipater is said to have owned the ship as well as to have had the freightage (ναῦλον) made over to him, i.e. the profits of conveying any goods over and above the Mendean wine belonging to Artemo. It seems clear from § 33 that Hyblesius had hired the ship from Antipater, i.e. had borrowed money on it and taken it up for his own trading purposes.—συμβόλαιον, see Or. 34 § 3.
Κιτιεὺς] Of Citium in Cyprus.

ΛΑΚΡΙΤΟΥ ΠΑΡΑΓΡΑΦΗΝ.

ἐξεστηκότος οἴνου, καὶ τὸ τάριχος ἀνθρώπῳ τινὶ γεωργῷ παρεκομίζετο ἐν τῷ πλοίῳ ἐκ Παντικαπαίου εἰς Θεοδοσίαν, τοῖς ἐργάταις τοῖς περὶ τὴν γεωργίαν χρῆσθαι. τί οὖν ταύτας τὰς προφάσεις λέγουσιν; οὐδὲν γὰρ προσήκει. καί μοι λαβὲ τὴν μαρτυρίαν, πρῶτον 33 μὲν τὴν Ἀπολλωνίδου ὅτι Ἀντίπατρος ἦν ὁ δανείσας ἐπὶ τῷ πλοίῳ, τούτοις δ' οὐδ' ὁτιοῦν προσήκει τῆς ναυαγίας, ἔπειτα τὴν Ἐρασικλέους καὶ τὴν Ἱππίου, ὅτι ὀγδοήκοντα μόνον κεράμια παρήγετο ἐν τῷ πλοίῳ.

ΜΑΡΤΥΡΙΑΙ.

[Ἀπολλωνίδης Ἁλικαρνασσεὺς μαρτυρεῖ εἰδέναι δανείσαντα Ἀντίπατρον, Κιτιέα τὸ γένος, χρήματα Ὑβλησίῳ εἰς τὸν Πόντον ἐπὶ τῇ νηὶ ἣν Ὑβλήσιος ἐναυκλήρει, καὶ τῷ ναύλῳ τῷ εἰς τὸν Πόντον· κοινωνεῖν δὲ καὶ αὐτὸν τῆς νεὼς Ὑβλησίῳ, καὶ συμπλεῖν ἑαυτοῦ οἰκέτας ἐν τῇ νηὶ, καὶ ὅτε διεφθάρη ἡ ναῦς, παρεῖναι τοὺς οἰκέτας τοὺς ἑαυτοῦ καὶ ἀπαγγέλλειν ἑαυτῷ καὶ ὅτι ἡ ναῦς κενὴ διεφθάρη παραπλέουσα εἰς Θευδοσίαν ἐκ Παντικαπαίου.

Ἐρασικλῆς μαρτυρεῖ συμπλεῖν Ὑβλησίῳ κυβερ- 34 νῶν τὴν ναῦν εἰς τὸν Πόντον, καὶ ὅτε παρέπλει ἡ ναῦς εἰς Θευδοσίαν ἐκ Παντικαπαίου, εἰδέναι κενὴν τὴν

ἐξεστηκότος] *Vapidi, vappae;* 'that had turned bad.' Hesych. ἐξεστηκὼς οἶνος, ὁ ὀξίνης, i.e. in which the acetous fermentation had taken place.—στάμνοι, the same as κεράμια, as appears from §§ 33, 34.

χρῆσθαι] Either 'to use for his workmen,' or 'for his workmen to use.'

§§ 33, 34. *Evidence of the pilot and others to prove that the defendant had no cargo of his own on board when the ship was wrecked.*

κοινωνεῖν καὶ αὐτὸν] 'That he was himself part-owner.'

παρεῖναι] 'That slaves of his own were present at the time and brought the further report to him that the ship had no cargo when she was wrecked.'

κενή] Not absolutely 'empty' (as it appears from the eighty jars of wine being on board), but 'without any regular cargo stowed in the hold.'

34. The clause αὐτοῦ τοῦ φεύγοντος νυνὶ τὴν δίκην is perhaps an interpolation. There

ναῦν παραπλέουσαν, καὶ Ἀπολλοδώρου αὐτοῦ τοῦ φεύγοντος νυνὶ τὴν δίκην, μὴ εἶναι οἶνον ἐν τῷ πλοίῳ, ἀλλὰ παράγεσθαι τῶν ἐκ τῆς Θευδοσίας τινὶ οἴνου Κῷα κεράμια περὶ ὀγδοήκοντα.

Ἱππίας Ἀθηνίππου Ἁλικαρνασσεὺς μαρτυρεῖ συμπλεῖν Ὑβλησίῳ διοπεύων[x] τὴν ναῦν, καὶ ὅτε παρέπλει ἡ ναῦς εἰς Θευδοσίαν ἐκ Παντικαπαίου, ἐνθέσθαι Ἀπολλόδωρον εἰς τὴν ναῦν ἐρίων ἀγγεῖον ἐν ᾗ δύο καὶ ταρίχους κεράμια ἕνδεκα ἢ δώδεκα καὶ δέρματ' αἴγεια, δύο δέσμας ἢ τρεῖς, ἄλλο δ' οὐδέν.

Πρὸς τοῖσδ' ἐξεμαρτύρησεν Εὐφίλητος Δαμοτίμου Ἀφιδναῖος, Ἱππίας Τιμοξένου Θυμαιτάδης, Σώστρατος Φιλίππου Ἱστιαιόθεν, Ἀρχενομίδης Στράτωνος Θριάσιος, Φιλτιάδης Κτησικλέους Ξυπεταιών.]

35 Ἡ μὲν ἀναίδεια τοιαύτη τῶν ἀνθρώπων τούτων ἐστίν. ὑμεῖς δ', ὦ ἄνδρες δικασταί, ἐνθυμεῖσθε πρὸς ὑμᾶς αὐτοὺς εἴ τινας πώποτ' ἴστε ἢ ἠκούσατε οἶνον

[x] διοπτεύων Bekk. 1824. Cf. § 20.

is no other evidence in the speech, as Kennedy observes, that Apollodorus was joint defendant with Lacritus, nor does it seem likely that he should have been; for, as he alone was liable for Artemo's share (§ 12), Lacritus would hardly have been sued if Apollodorus had not been insolvent. And Kennedy observes "there could have been no great advantage in bringing an action against him, except, perhaps, for the purpose of holding him to bail." He suspects that for αὐτοῦ we should read ἀδελφοῦ.

οἴνου Κῷα κεράμια] For οἴνου Κῴου κερ. Cf. § 10, οἴνου κεραμίοις Μενδαίοις (but in § 20, οἴνου Μενδαίου κεράμια). Ar. Lys. 196, Θάσιον οἴνου σταμνίον. S.]

διοπεύων] § 20.
Ἀπολλόδωρον] Perhaps Ἀπολλοδώρου, 'belonging to Apollodorus.' In § 16 it is said that Artemo was to sail with the goods. See, however, § 20. The middle ἐνθέσθαι may mean that A. 'had it put on board' in his absence.
ἀγγεῖον] 'A hamper,' perhaps. So in Eur. Ion 1412, the ἀντίπηξ or round casket (vidulus) is called ἄγγος.
δέρματα, see Or. 34 § 10.
ἐξεμαρτύρησεν] § 20.
§§ 35—7. *The improbability of the defendant's statement is shown by the custom of exporting wine to, not importing it from, the Pontus. Lacritus' account, that his brother Artemo had lent a friend of his in Pon-*

Ἀθήναζε ἐκ τοῦ Πόντου κατ' ἐμπορίαν εἰσάγοντας, ἄλλως τε καὶ Κῷον. πᾶν γὰρ δήπου τοὐναντίον εἰς τὸν Πόντον ὁ οἶνος εἰσάγεται ἐκ τῶν τόπων τῶν περὶ ἡμᾶς, ἐκ Πεπαρήθου καὶ Κῶ καὶ Θάσιος καὶ Μενδαῖος καὶ ἐξ ἄλλων τινῶν πόλεων παντοδαπός· ἐκ δὲ τοῦ Πόντου ἕτερά ἐστιν ἃ εἰσάγεται δεῦρο. κατεχόμενοι δ' 36 ὑφ' ἡμῶν καὶ ἐλεγχόμενοι εἴ τι περιγένοιτο τῶν χρημάτων ἐν τῷ Πόντῳ, ἀπεκρίνατο Λάκριτος οὑτοσὶ ὅτι ἑκατὸν στατῆρες Κυζικηνοὶ περιγένοιντο καὶ τοῦτο τὸ χρυσίον δεδανεικὼς εἴη ἀδελφὸς αὑτοῦ[y] ἐν τῷ Πόντῳ ναυκλήρῳ τινὶ Φασηλίτῃ, πολίτῃ καὶ ἐπιτηδείῳ ἑαυτοῦ, καὶ οὐ δύναιτο κομίσασθαι, ἀλλὰ σχεδόν τι ἀπολωλὸς εἴη καὶ τοῦτο. ταῦτ' ἐστὶν ἃ ἔλεγε Λάκριτος 37 οὑτοσί. ἡ δὲ συγγραφὴ οὐ ταῦτα λέγει, ὦ ἄνδρες

[y] αὑτοῦ Z.

---

tus 100 staters, contravenes the terms of the bond, that goods should be purchased with the money in Pontus, and brought back to Athens.

κατ' ἐμπορίαν] 'In the way of trade.'

εἰς τὸν Πόντον ὁ οἶνος—Θάσιος] Virg. G. II 91, 'Sunt Thasiae vites.' Fragments of earthenware wine-jars have been found near the harbours of the Northern Euxine, especially the ancient Olbia (at the mouth of the Dnieper), stamped with the names of Rhodes, Cnidus and Thasos (Büchsenschütz, *Besitz u. Erwerb*, pp. 422—4. Cf. Strabo quoted on Or. 34 § 10). In the Leake Collection there are several coins of Peparethus, with the head of Bacchus, and on the reverse a *diota* or *cantharus*, with bunches of grapes. Those of Thasos often have the head of Bacchus or Silenus; those of Mende, on Silenus on the obverse, and on the reverse a vine or a diota. See *Plate of Coins*. Ar. fragm. 301, οἶνον δὲ πίνειν οὐκ ἐάσω Πράμνιον, οὐ Χῖον, οὐχὶ Θάσιον, οὐ Πεπαρήθιον. S.]

ἕτερά ἐστι] Some of these are enumerated in Pers. Sat. V 134, 'saperdas advehe Ponto, Castoreum, stuppas, ebenum, thus, lubrica Coa,' where 'Coa' is interpreted to mean 'silk' or fine linen.

36. κατεχόμενοι] 'Being still detained by us and questioned whether any of the property had been saved in the Pontus.' *Nominativus pendens*, or a careless syntax with the singular Λάκριτος.

στατῆρες Κυζικηνοί] See note on Or. 34 § 23.

οὐ δύναιτο] 'That he was not able to recover it, in fact, that this also might be considered as lost.' Kennedy.

78   XXXV. ΠΡΟΣ ΤΗΝ   [§§ 37—41

δικασταί, ἀλλ' ἀντιφορτισαμένους ἀπάγειν κελεύει
Ἀθήναζε, οὐ δανείζειν τούτους ὅτῳ ἂν βούλωνται ἐν τῷ
Πόντῳ τὰ ἡμέτερα ἄνευ ἡμῶν, ἀλλ' Ἀθήναζε παρέχειν
ἀνέπαφα ἡμῖν, ἕως ἂν ἡμεῖς ἀπολάβωμεν τὰ χρήματα
ὅσ' ἐδανείσαμεν. καί μοι ἀναγίγνωσκε τὴν συγγραφὴν
πάλιν.

ΣΥΓΓΡΑΦΗ.

38   Πότερον, ὦ ἄνδρες δικασταί, δανείζειν κελεύει 937
τούτους ἡ συγγραφὴ τὰ ἡμέτερα, καὶ ταῦτ' ἀνθρώπῳ
ὃν ἡμεῖς οὔτε γιγνώσκομεν οὔθ' ἑοράκαμεν[z] πώποτε,
ἢ ἀντιφορτισαμένους κομίσαι Ἀθήναζε καὶ φανερὰ
39 ποιῆσαι ἡμῖν καὶ ἀνέπαφα παρέχειν; ἡ μὲν γὰρ συγγραφὴ οὐδὲν κυριώτερον ἐᾷ εἶναι τῶν ἐγγεγραμμένων,
οὐδὲ προσφέρειν οὔτε νόμον οὔτε ψήφισμα οὔτ' ἄλλ'
οὐδ' ὁτιοῦν πρὸς τὴν συγγραφήν· τούτοις δ' εὐθὺς
ἐξ ἀρχῆς οὐδὲν ἐμέλησε τῆς συγγραφῆς ταύτης, ἀλλὰ
τοῖς χρήμασιν ἐχρῶντο τοῖς ἡμετέροις ὥσπερ ἰδίοις οὖσιν αὐτῶν· οὕτως εἰσὶν οὗτοι κακοῦργοι σοφισταὶ καὶ
40 ἄδικοι ἄνθρωποι. ἐγὼ δὲ μὰ τὸν Δία τὸν ἄνακτα καὶ

[z] ἑωράκαμεν Z.

§§ 38—40. *If the terms of the loan forbid lending the money in Pontus, that must be regarded as decisive. These Sophists are 'a bad lot.' I don't say it because they have paid for learning eloquence (that is their affair); but if their eloquence is perverted to injustice, they ought to be punished.*

39. ἡ μὲν γὰρ, κ.τ.λ.] '(I ask the question), for whatever the bond says on this point is final.' See § 13.

προσφέρειν] 'To bring to bear against, or as tending to cancel, the bond.'

κακοῦργοι] 'Rogues as So-phists, and dishonest as men.' In Or. 19 § 246 (παραπρ. p. 417) the Sophists are spoken of with contempt: — λογογράφους καὶ σοφιστὰς ἀποκαλῶν τοὺς ἄλλους καὶ ὑβρίζειν πειρώμενος.

40. τὸν Δία τὸν ἄνακτα] See Argum. ad fin. [ἄναξ is a poetical word and is extremely rare in Greek Prose. Perhaps the only other passage where it occurs is Isocr. ix § 72, where Evagoras King of Cyprus is said to have given the name to the younger princes of the royal family, τῶν ἐξ αὐτοῦ γεγονότων οὐδένα κατέλιπεν ἰδιωτικοῖς ὀνόμασι προσ-αγορευόμενον, ἀλλὰ τὸν μὲν

p. 938]   ΛΑΚΡΙΤΟΥ ΠΑΡΑΓΡΑΦΗΝ.   79

τοὺς θεοὺς ἅπαντας, οὐδενὶ[a] πώποτ' ἐφθόνησα οὐδ'
ἐπετίμησα, ὦ ἄνδρες δικασταί, εἴ τις βούλεται σοφι-
στὴς εἶναι καὶ Ἰσοκράτει ἀργύριον ἀναλίσκειν· μαινοί-
μην γὰρ ἄν, εἴ τί μοι τούτων ἐπιμελὲς εἴη. οὐ μέντοι
μὰ Δία οἶμαί[b] γε δεῖν ἀνθρώπους καταφρονοῦντας καὶ
οἰομένους δεινοὺς εἶναι ἐφίεσθαι τῶν ἀλλοτρίων, οὐδ'
ἀφαιρεῖσθαι, τῷ λόγῳ πιστεύοντας· πονηροῦ γὰρ
938 ταῦτ' ἐστι σοφιστοῦ καὶ οἰμωξομένου. Λάκριτος δ' 41
οὑτοσί, ὦ ἄνδρες δικασταί, οὐ τῷ δικαίῳ πιστεύων εἰσελήλυθε ταύτην τὴν δίκην, ἀλλ' ἀκριβῶς εἰδὼς τὰ
πεπραγμέν' ἑαυτοῖς περὶ τὸ δάνεισμα τοῦτο, καὶ ἡγούμενος δεινὸς εἶναι καὶ ῥᾳδίως λόγους ποριεῖσθαι περὶ
ἀδίκων πραγμάτων, οἴεται παράξειν ὑμᾶς ὅποι ἂν
βούληται. ταῦτα γὰρ ἐπαγγέλλεται δεινὸς εἶναι, καὶ
ἀργύριον αἰτεῖ καὶ μαθητὰς συλλέγει, περὶ αὐτῶν τού-

[a] οὐδὲν Z cum Σ.   οὐδενὶ Bekk.
[b] οἴομαι Z. Cf. Veitch, Gk. Vbs. s.v.

βασιλέα καλούμενον, τοὺς δὲ
ἄνακτας τὰς δὲ ἀνάσσας. A
somewhat similar oath is found
in Or. 48 (Olymp.) § 2, μὰ τὸν
Δία τὸν μέγιστον. S.]
τι τούτων] 'Any matters of
that sort,' viz. so little concerning an ἔμπορος.
καταφρονοῦντας] 'Conceited.'
Hesych. καταφρονεῖ· ὑπερηφανεῖ.
But it may be doubted if ἄλλων
has not dropped out.
οἰμωξομένου] 'Who should be
made to smart for it.' Kennedy.
Or, 'who will come to grief,' as
we say. So Ar. Pac. 756 ἑκατὸν
κεφαλαὶ κολάκων οἰμωξομένων.
§§ 41, 42. *Lacritus trusts in
this case to his skill in eloquence, and his cleverness in
making you take his own views
of the matter. His brothers
have been brought up in the
same school, and are therefore
equally dishonest.*
41. εἰδὼς τὰ πεπραγμένα]
'With a full knowledge of (the
dishonesty of) the transactions
they were engaged in.'
ταῦτα γὰρ] 'For this is just
what he professes to be clever
in; for this he asks for money
and collects pupils, engaging to
instruct them on these very
points.' So in Or. 19 § 48 (παραπρεσβ. p. 356), καὶ ἐπαινέσαι
δὲ Φίλιππον ὅτι ἐπαγγέλλεται τὰ
δίκαια ποιήσειν. Here is a distinct charge against the Sophists
of teaching ἀδικία, dishonesty.

μαθητὰς συλλέγει] Apart from
his own brothers Artemo and
Apollodorus, referred to in the
next §, we find one other pupil
of Lacritus in Archias of Thurii,
ὁ κληθεὶς φυγαδοθήρας, 'nick-
named the hunter of exiles,'
from being employed (under the

42 τῶν ἐπαγγελλόμενος παιδεύειν. καὶ πρῶτον μὲν τοὺς ἀδελφοὺς τοὺς αὐτοῦ ἐπαίδευσε τὴν παιδείαν ταύτην, ἣν ὑμεῖς αἰσθάνεσθε πονηρὰν καὶ ἄδικον, ὦ ἄνδρες δικασταί, δανείζεσθαι ἐν τῷ ἐμπορίῳ ναυτικὰ χρήματα καὶ ταῦτ' ἀποστερεῖν καὶ μὴ ἀποδιδόναι. πῶς ἂν γένοιντο πονηρότεροι ἄνθρωποι ἢ τοῦ παιδεύοντος τὰ τοιαῦτα ἢ αὐτῶν τῶν παιδευομένων ; ἐπεὶ οὖνᶜ δεινός ἐστι καὶ πιστεύει τῷ λέγειν καὶ ταῖς χιλίαις δραχμαῖς,
43 ἃς δέδωκε τῷ διδασκάλῳ, κελεύσατε αὐτὸν διδάξαι ὑμᾶς ἢ ὡς τὰ χρήματ' οὐκ ἔλαβον παρ' ἡμῶν, ἢ ὡς λαβόντες ἀποδεδώκασιν, ἢ ὅτι τὰς ναυτικὰς συγγραφὰς οὐ δεῖ κυρίας εἶναι, ἢ ὡς δεῖ ἄλλο τι χρήσασθαι τοῖς χρήμασιν ἢ ἐφ' οἷς ἔλαβον κατὰ τὴν συγγραφήν. τούτων ὅ τι βούλεται πεισάτω ὑμᾶς. καὶ ἔγωγε καὶ αὐτὸς συγχωρῶ σοφώτατον εἶναι τοῦτον, ἐὰν ὑμᾶς πείσῃ τοὺς περὶ τῶν συμβολαίων τῶν ἐμπορικῶν δικάζοντας. ἀλλ' εὖ οἶδ' ὅτι οὐδὲν ἂν τούτων οἷός τ' εἴη οὗτος οὔτε διδάξαι οὔτε πεῖσαι.

ᶜ Σ. ἐπειδὴ Bekk. 1824; ἐπεὶ δ' οὖν Bekk. st.

orders of Antipater, in B.C. 322) to seize the orators who had fled from Athens — amongst others Hyperides and Demosthenes himself. Plutarch, Dem. 28, Ἕρμιππος τὸν Ἀρχίαν ἐν τοῖς Λακρίτου τοῦ ῥήτορος μαθητὴν ἀναγράφει. S.]

42. αἰσθάνεσθε] 'Are aware,' by the present example, perhaps.

διδασκάλῳ] Isocrates, cf. §§ 15, 40.

§ 43. *As he is so clever, perhaps he will undertake to prove to you that black is white and that they did not borrow at all, or that they have paid, or that the bond is waste paper, or that they had a right to use our money as they pleased.*

ἄλλο τι] See on § 17.

τούτων ὅ τι βούλεται κ.τ.λ.] Or. 43 (Macart.) § 41, τούτων ὅ τι βούλεταί τις μαρτυρησάτω αὐτῷ, quoted by Blass, *Att. Ber.* III 505, who ascribes this speech to the same author as Or. 43. S.]

τῶν συμ. τῶν ἐμ.] 'Who sit to try these cases of mercantile contracts.' A mere synonym of δίκαι ἐμπορικαί, and distinct from those questions of international law, or right of appeal from the citizens of one state to the tribunals of another, known as δίκαι ἀπὸ συμβόλων, and συμβολαῖαι δίκαι. The phrase again occurs in § 47.

ΛΑΚΡΙΤΟΥ ΠΑΡΑΓΡΑΦΗΝ.

Χωρὶς δὲ τούτων, φέρε πρὸς τῶν θεῶν, ὦ ἄνδρες 44 δικασταί, εἰ τοὐναντίον συνεβεβήκει[d], μὴ ὁ τούτου ἀδελφὸς ὁ τετελευτηκὼς ἐμοὶ ὤφειλε τὰ χρήματα, ἀλλ' ἐγὼ τῷ τούτου τάλαντον ἢ ὀγδοήκοντα μνᾶς ἢ πλέον ἢ ἔλαττον, ἆρ' ἂν οἴεσθε Λάκριτον τουτονί, ὦ ἄνδρες δικασταί, τοὺς αὐτοὺς λόγους λέγειν οἷσπερ νυνὶ κατακέχρηται, ἢ[e] φάσκειν αὐτὸν οὐκ εἶναι κληρονόμον καὶ ἀφίστασθαι τῶν τοῦ ἀδελφοῦ, καὶ οὐκ ἂν πάνυ πικρῶς εἰσπράττειν με, ὥσπερ καὶ παρὰ τῶν ἄλλων εἰσπέπρακται, εἴ τίς τι ἐκείνῳ τῷ τετελευτηκότι ὤφειλεν ἢ ἐν Φασήλιδι ἢ ἄλλοθί που; καὶ εἴ τις ἡμῶν φεύγων δίκην 45 ὑπὸ τούτου παραγραφὴν ἐτόλμησε παραγράφεσθαι, μὴ εἰσαγώγιμον εἶναι τὴν δίκην, εὖ οἶδ' ὅτι ἠγανάκτει ἂν αὐτὸς καὶ ἐσχετλίαζε πρὸς ὑμᾶς, δεινὰ φάσκων πάσχειν καὶ παρανομεῖσθαι, εἰ μή τις αὐτῷ τὴν δίκην ψηφιεῖται εἰσαγώγιμον εἶναι, ἐμπορικὴν οὖσαν. ἔπειτα, ὦ Λάκριτε, σοὶ μὲν τοῦτο δίκαιον δοκεῖ εἶναι, ἐμοὶ δὲ διὰ τί οὐκ ἔσται; οὐχ ἅπασιν ἡμῖν οἱ αὐτοὶ νόμοι

[d] συμβεβήκει Z cum Σ r A¹, συμβεβήκει καὶ Bekk. (Vid. Or. 34 § 12, n.)
[e] ἢ Z cum Σ. καὶ Bekk.

§§ 44, 45. *Supposing the contrary had happened, that I had owed Lacritus' deceased brother the money which he owed to me; would Lacritus then have relinquished the property, or omitted to sue me? Or again if any one of you had put in a special plea in bar of his claims, would he not have insisted that the case was a mercantile suit, and as such could be tried in this court?*

κατακέχρηται] 'Lavishly uses.' The κατὰ in this verb, which commonly means *abuti*, has the same force as in καταχαρίζεσθαι, καταπροδοῦναι, &c., and means 'to use up,' or, 'use away,' ἀναλίσκειν. But to use in excess is to *abuse*.

εἰσπέπρακται] In the medial sense. See on § 26.

45. αὐτὸς] sc. ὥσπερ νῦν ἡμεῖς ἀγανακτοῦμεν. — παρανομεῖσθαι, that he is being dealt with in a manner not contemplated by the laws.

ἔπειτα, κ.τ.λ.] 'Then, Lacritus, if you consider this just for yourself, why should it not be just for me? Are not the same laws enacted for all? Have not all the same rights in regard to mercantile actions?' Kennedy.

γεγραμμένοι εἰσὶ καὶ τὸ αὐτὸ δίκαιον περὶ τῶν ἐμπο-
46 ρικῶν δικῶν; ἀλλ᾽ οὕτω βδελυρός τίς ἐστι καὶ ὑπερ-
βάλλων ἅπαντας ἀνθρώπους τῷ πονηρὸς εἶναι ὥστ᾽
ἐπιχειρεῖ πείθειν ὑμᾶς ψηφίσασθαι μὴ εἰσαγώγιμον
εἶναι τὴν ἐμπορικὴν δίκην ταυτηνί, δικαζόντων ὑμῶν
νυνὶ τὰς ἐμπορικὰς δίκας. ἀλλὰ τί κελεύεις, ὦ Λάκριτε; μὴ ἱκανὸν εἶναι ἡμᾶς ἀποστερεῖσθαι ἃ ἐδανείσαμεν χρήματα ὑμῖν, ἀλλὰ καὶ εἰς τὸ δεσμωτήριον παρα-
δοθῆναι ὑφ᾽ ὑμῶν προσοφλόντας τὰ ἐπιτίμια, ἐὰν μὴ
47 ἐκτίνωμεν; καὶ πῶς οὐκ ἂν δεινὸν εἴη καὶ σχέτλιον
καὶ αἰσχρὸν ὑμῖν, ὦ ἄνδρες δικασταί, εἰ οἱ δανείσαντες 940
ἐν τῷ ἐμπορίῳ τῷ ὑμετέρῳ χρήματα ναυτικὰ καὶ ἀπο-

46. ψηφίσασθαι] This shows that the granting a παραγραφή was by voting, as in an ordinary verdict.

δικαζόντων ὑμῶν νυνὶ τὰς ἐμπορικὰς δίκας] The courts of Commerce held their sittings during the season of the year in which navigation was suspended. Cf. Or. 33 § 23, αἱ δὲ λήξεις τῶν δικῶν τοῖς ἐμπόροις ἔμμηνοί εἰσιν ἀπὸ τοῦ βοηδρομιῶνος μέχρι τοῦ μουνυχιῶνος (i.e. from about September to April), ἵνα παραχρῆμα τῶν δικαίων τυχόντες ἀνάγωνται. The present passage helps to fix the date of the speech. We know that in B.C. 355, the date of Xenophon's treatise on the Revenue of Athens (III 3), this prompt settlement of commercial cases had not yet been introduced; for he proposes by way of remedy that a prize should be given to the officer of the harbour who gave the most expeditious and equitable decision. But in B.C. 343-2, the date of the speech on Halonnesus, the improved system had already come into force, as the speaker (Hegesippus) referring to the times of Amyntas says, ἐμπορικαὶ δίκαι οὐκ ἦσαν ὥσπερ νῦν ἀκριβεῖς αἱ κατὰ μῆνα. (Dem.) Or. 7 § 12. Cf. Introd. p. 52, and note on Or. 37 § 2. S.]

ἱκανὸν εἶναι] i.e. ἀρκεῖν, ἅλις εἶναι.

προσοφλόντας] 'For having been condemned in costs, and if we fail to pay them.' The ἐπωβελία is meant, which was a penalty of a sixth part of the assessment of the suit (an obolus for every drachma), claimed by the defendant—in this case by Lacritus—if the plaintiff failed to obtain a fifth part of the votes.

§§ 47—9. *If we, exercising the profession of money-lenders in your mart, are to be not only robbed, but fined (with the ἐπωβελία) and imprisoned, for not paying it, it would be a hard case. If our claim cannot be tried here, to what other court can we resort? Certainly not to the Archons, nor the strategi, who have nothing to do with mercantile suits, whereas both I and your brother Artemo are merchants.*

ΛΑΚΡΙΤΟΥ ΠΑΡΑΓΡΑΦΗΝ.

στερούμενοι ὑπὸ τῶν δανεισαμένων καὶ ἀποστερούντων ἀπάγοιντο εἰς τὸ δεσμωτήριον; ταῦτ' ἐστὶν, ὦ Λάκριτε, ἃ τουτουσὶ πείθεις; ἀλλὰ ποῦ χρὴ λαβεῖν δίκην, ὦ ἄνδρες δικασταὶ, περὶ τῶν ἐμπορικῶν συμβολαίων; παρὰ ποίᾳ ἀρχῇ ἢ ἐν τίνι χρόνῳ; παρὰ τοῖς ἕνδεκα; ἀλλὰ τοιχωρύχους καὶ κλέπτας καὶ τοὺς ἄλλους κακούργους τοὺς ἐπὶ θανάτῳ οὗτοι εἰσάγουσιν. ἀλλὰ παρὰ τῷ ἄρχοντι; οὐκοῦν ἐπικλήρων καὶ ὀρφανῶν καὶ τῶν τοκέων τῷ ἄρχοντι προστέτακται ἐπιμελεῖσθαι. ἀλλὰ νὴ Δία παρὰ τῷ βασιλεῖ. ἀλλ' οὐκ ἐσμὲν γυμνασίαρχοι, οὐδὲ ἀσεβείας οὐδένα γραφόμεθα. 48

47. ὑπὸ τῶν δαν., κ.τ.λ.] To be construed with ἀπάγοιντο. 'Should be carried to prison by the fraudulent debtors.' Kennedy. Lit. 'by those who have borrowed and then try to evade payment.'

ἐν τίνι χρόνῳ;] For mercantile suits were held only occasionally, "They were tried before the Thesmothetae during the six winter months, while the ships were laid up in harbour, and the judges were compelled to bring them to a final decision within a month." (Kennedy, argum. against Zen. Or. 32.) Hence they were called ἔμμηνοι δίκαι Or. 33 § 23, quoted on § 46. See the commencement of Or. 33, πρὸς Ἀπατούριον:—τοῖς μὲν ἐμπόροις καὶ τοῖς ναυκλήροις κελεύει ὁ νόμος εἶναι τὰς δίκας πρὸς τοὺς θεσμοθέτας, ἐάν τι ἀδικῶνται ἐν τῷ ἐμπορίῳ ἢ ἐνθένδε πλέοντες ἢ ἑτέρωθεν δεῦρο.—τοῖς ἕνδεκα, 'the criminal court,' the 'eleven' having the custody of as well as the jurisdiction of prisoners on capital charges, οἱ ἐπὶ θανάτῳ (ὑπαγόμενοι). [K. F. Hermann's *Public Antiquities* § 139.]

48. τῷ ἄρχοντι] 'The Archon,' i.e. the ἐπώνυμος. See Or. 37 § 33, ὅσα εἰς ἐπικλήρους, πρὸς τὸν ἄρχοντα. As guardian generally of orphans and heiresses, the chief Archon was the Lord Chancellor of Athens. [Hermann's *Public Ant.* § 138, 6.] It may be questioned if the clause καὶ τῶν τοκέων is not here an interpolation, resulting from a gloss on ὀρφανῶν. Or must we suppose that claims of parents to be maintained by their children (γηροβοσκεῖσθαι) came into the court of the chief archon? [Blass objects to the word τοκεῖς as 'undemosthenic,' *Att. Ber.* III 506. S.]

τῷ βασιλεῖ] The 'King-Archon' represented the religious part of the duties of the king of old, as the Roman Pontifex and Rex Sacrificulus did. The games were a part of the public religion, and so any complaints on that head fell under his cognizance, as well as ἀσέβεια, any kind of disrespect to the gods or the temples. Cf. Androt. p. 601 (Or. 22 § 27), τῆς ἀσεβείας κατὰ ταὐτὰ ἔστιν ἀπάγειν, γράφεσθαι, δικάζεσθαι πρὸς Εὐμολπίδας, φρά-

ἀλλ' ὁ πολέμαρχος εἰσάξει. ἀποστασίου γε καὶ ἀπροστασίου. οὐκοῦν ὑπόλοιπόν ἐστιν οἱ στρατηγοί. ἀλλὰ τοὺς τριηράρχους καθιστᾶσιν[f], ἐμπορικὴν δὲ δίκην 49 οὐδεμίαν εἰσάγουσιν[g]. ἐγὼ δ' εἰμὶ ἔμπορος, καὶ σὺ ἀδελφὸς καὶ κληρονόμος ἑνὸς τῶν ἐμπόρων τοῦ λαβόντος παρ' ἡμῶν τὰ ἐμπορικὰ χρήματα. ποῖ οὖν δεῖ ταύτην εἰσελθεῖν τὴν δίκην; δίδαξον, ὦ Λάκριτε, μόνον δίκαιόν τι λέγων καὶ κατὰ τοὺς νόμους. ἀλλ' οὐκ ἔστιν οὕτω δεινὸς ἄνθρωπος οὐδείς, ὅστις ἂν περὶ τοιούτων πραγμάτων ἔχοι τι δίκαιον εἰπεῖν.

50 Οὐ τοίνυν ταῦτα μόνον, ὦ ἄνδρες δικασταί, δεινὰ ἐγὼ πάσχω ὑπὸ Λακρίτου τουτουί, ἀλλὰ καὶ χωρὶς

[f] οὗτοι εἰσάγοντες εἰς τὸ δικαστήριον, " om. B, in marg. γρ. habent FΦ." Z.
[g] + εἰς τὸ δικαστήριον Σ.

ξειν πρὸς τὸν βασιλέα. [Hermann's *Public Ant.* § 138, 8.]
ὁ πολέμαρχος] In early times, he was the Minister of War and even the chief commander, like Callimachus of Aphidnae at Marathon, Herod. vi 109 (τὸ παλαιὸν γὰρ Ἀθηναῖοι ὁμόψηφον τὸν πολέμαρχον ἐποιεῦντο τοῖσι στρατηγοῖσι). [Hermann's *Public Ant.* § 138, 10.]
ἀποστάσιον and ἀπροστάσιον were respectively applied to the case of a μέτοικος leaving, or acting without the sanction of, the προστάτης or patron under whom he had been enrolled (ὃν ἐπεγράψατο), and the refusing to be enrolled. Hesych. ἀποστασίου δίκη· κατὰ τῶν προστάτην μὴ ἀπογραψαμένων (l. ἐπιγρ.) μετοίκων.
[Harpocr. εἶδος δίκης κατὰ τῶν προστάτην μὴ νεμόντων μετοίκων. There were two speeches of Hyperides κατ' Ἀρισταγόρας ἀπροστασίου, fragments of which are still extant. S.]
οἱ στρατηγοί] Briefly put

for εἰσιέναι παρὰ τοὺς στρατηγούς.
καθιστᾶσιν] 'They appoint,' 'settle disputes about,' viz. by taking cognizance of and hearing claims respecting the ἀντίδοσις, or offer of exchange of property. Or. 42 § 5, τοῦ γὰρ μεταγειτνιῶνος μηνὸς τῇ δευτέρᾳ ἱσταμένου ἐποίουν οἱ στρατηγοὶ τοῖς τριακοσίοις τὰς ἀντιδόσεις. Hence the phrase ἀντιδιδόναι τριηραρχίαν, Mid. p. 539 (Or. 21 § 78).
49. The article before ἐμπορικὰ seems at least unnecessary to the sense. Perhaps however we should read ἐμπορικὰ τὰ χρήματα, 'who got from us money to be used in trade.'
οὕτω δεινὸς] 'So clever.' Again a stroke of satire against the Sophists, whom Plato so often calls δεινοὶ ἄνδρες.
§ 50. *It is fortunate that the bond expressly stated that the money was lent* 'to Pontus and back to Athens.' *For otherwise he might have carried his*

p. 941] ΛΑΚΡΙΤΟΥ ΠΑΡΑΓΡΑΦΗΝ. 85

τοῦ ἀποστερεῖσθαι τὰ χρήματα[h] εἰς τοὺς ἐσχάτους ἂν
κινδύνους ἀφικόμην τὸ τούτου μέρος, εἰ μή μοι ἡ συγ-
941 γραφὴ ἐβοήθει ἡ πρὸς τούτους, καὶ ἐμαρτύρει ὅτι εἰς
τὸν Πόντον ἔδωκα τὰ χρήματα καὶ πάλιν Ἀθήναζε.
ἴστε γὰρ[i], ὦ ἄνδρες δικασταί, τὸν νόμον ὡς χαλεπός
ἐστιν, ἐάν τις Ἀθηναίων ἄλλοσέ ποι σιτηγήσῃ ἢ Ἀθήναζε, ἢ χρήματα δανείσῃ εἰς ἄλλο τι[k] ἐμπόριον ἢ τὸ
Ἀθηναίων, οἷαι ζημίαι περὶ τούτων εἰσίν, ὡς μεγάλαι
καὶ δειναί. μᾶλλον δ' αὐτὸν ἀνάγνωθι αὐτοῖς τὸν 51
νόμον, ἵν' ἀκριβέστερον μάθωσιν.

ΝΟΜΟΣ.

[Ἀργύριον δὲ μὴ ἐξεῖναι ἐκδοῦναι Ἀθηναίων καὶ
τῶν μετοίκων τῶν Ἀθήνησι μετοικούντων μηδενί, μηδὲ
ὧν οὗτοι κύριοί εἰσιν, εἰς ναῦν ἥτις ἂν μὴ μέλλῃ ἄξειν
σῖτον Ἀθήναζε, καὶ τἆλλα τὰ γεγραμμένα περὶ ἑκάσ-

[h] + καὶ Z.   [i] γὰρ δή που Bekk. 1824.
[k] om. Z et Bekk. st. cum Σ.

application for a special plea against me, the law forbidding the lending of money for any other mart than Athens.
τὸ τούτου μέρος] 'As far as he was concerned,' i.e. as far as he could imperil me by making me pay the ἐπωβελία (§ 46) and succeeded in quashing my suit by a παραγραφή. Cf. Soph. Trach. 1215, οὐ καμεῖ τοὐμὸν μέρος, 'you shall not suffer through deficiency on my part.' ['C'est là un artifice oratoire. La loi dont il s'agit ne pouvait pas s'appliquer aux cas de force majeure.' Dareste. S.]
ἐάν τις, κ.τ.λ.] Cf. Or. 34 §37, and Lycurg. adv. Leocr. § 27, οἱ ὑμέτεροι νόμοι τὰς ἐσχάτας τιμωρίας ὁρίζουσιν ἐάν τις Ἀθηναίων ἄλλοσέ ποι σιτηγήσῃ ἢ ὡς ὑμᾶς.

Hermann Privatalt. § 45, 17 = p. 433 Blümner. S.] See Boeckh, P. E. pp. 56 and 85 (Lewis, ed. 2).
ἄλλοσε ἢ Ἀθήναζε] This was the worst form of 'protection,' since it tended to make corn a monopoly at Athens.
51. ὧν οὗτοι κύριοί εἰσι] viz. any slave or agent in their employ.
καὶ τἆλλα τὰ γ.] Equivalent to our form "and so on," "et cetera." Only one or two clauses are quoted. But the law, as remarked on § 10, is spurious. The phrase ἐκδοῦναι, for προέσθαι or δανεῖσαι, is by no means common, though ἔκδοσις seems sometimes so used. (Boeckh, P. E. p. 132.)

του αὐτῶν¹. ἐὰν δέ τις ἐκδῷ παρὰ ταῦτ', εἶναι τὴν φάσιν καὶ τὴν ἀπογραφὴν τοῦ ἀργυρίου πρὸς τοὺς ἐπιμελητάς, καθὰ περὶ τῆς νεὼς καὶ τοῦ σίτου εἴρηται, κατὰ ταῦτα. καὶ δίκη αὐτῷ μὴ ἔστω περὶ τοῦ ἀργυρίου, ὃ ἂν ἐκδῷ ἄλλοσέ ποι ἢ 'Αθήναζε· μηδὲ ἀρχὴ εἰσαγέτω περὶ τούτου^m μηδεμία.]

52 Ὁ μὲν νόμος, ὦ ἄνδρες δικασταί, οὕτω χαλεπός ἐστιν· οὗτοι δ' οἱ μιαρώτατοι ἀνθρώπων ἁπάντων, γεγραμμένου^n διαρρήδην ἐν τῇ συγγραφῇ 'Αθήναζε πάλιν ἥκειν τὰ χρήματα, εἰς Χίον ἐπέτρεψαν καταχθῆναι ἃ ἐδανείσαντο 'Αθήνηθεν παρ' ἡμῶν. δανειζομένου γὰρ ἐν τῷ Πόντῳ τοῦ ναυκλήρου τοῦ Φασηλίτου ἕτερα χρήματα παρά τινος Χίου ἀνθρώπου, οὐ φάσκοντος δὲ τοῦ Χίου δανείσειν, ἐὰν μὴ ὑποθήκην λάβῃ ἅπανθ' ὅσ' ἦν περὶ τὸν ναύκληρον, καὶ ἐπιτρέπωσι ταῦτα οἱ πρότερον δεδανεικότες, ἐπέτρεψαν ταῦτα ὑποθήκην γενέσθαι τῷ Χίῳ τὰ ἡμέτερα καὶ κύριον ἐκεῖνον γενέ- 942

53 σθαι ἁπάντων, καὶ οὕτως ἀπέπλεον ἐκ τοῦ Πόντου

¹ καὶ τἄλλα—αὐτῶν. 'Seiunximus haec verba a reliquis cum nobis viderentur non esse legis ipsius.' Z.
^m τούτων Bekk. 1824.
^n 'corrig. γεγραμμένον διαρρήδην, quum esset diserte scriptum.' Cobet, Miscellanea Critica p. 86; idem dederat Bekker 1824.

τὴν φάσιν] The action for contraband trading. —ἐπιμελητάς, sc. λιμένων, or ἐμπορίου, the overseers or harbour-masters. [They were ten in number. See Meier and Schömann, p. 86.] —ἀπογραφή, see Or. 34 § 7.
§§ 52—4. Clear and explicit as the terms of the law are, they have been violated by taking the ship (from Thieves' harbour) to Chios at the instance of a Chian merchant who had lent them money on our goods at the Pontus. And those who break the law do indirectly injure the citizens generally.
τοῦ ναυκλήρου τοῦ Φ.] See sup. § 19.
περὶ τὸν ναύκληρον] 'With, and in custody of, the skipper.' The word ἅπαντα is emphatic: he would have the whole cargo, and therefore the property of Androcles was included. Such a transaction appears to have been legal, provided the consent of the former lenders was obtained.

p. 942] ΛΑΚΡΙΤΟΥ ΠΑΡΑΓΡΑΦΗΝ. 87

μετὰ τοῦ Φασηλίτου ναυκλήρου καὶ μετὰ τοῦ Χίου τοῦ δεδανεικότος, καὶ ὁρμίζονται ἐν φωρῶν λιμένι, εἰς δὲ τὸ ὑμέτερον⁰ ἐμπόριον οὐχ ὡρμίσαντο. καὶ νυνὶ, ὦ ἄνδρες δικασταὶ, τὰ Ἀθήνηθεν δανεισθέντα χρήματα εἰς τὸν Πόντον καὶ πάλιν ἐκ τοῦ Πόντου Ἀθήναζε εἰς Χίον κατηγμένα ἐστὶν ὑπὸ τούτων. ὅπερ οὖν ἐν ἀρχῇ 54 ὑπεθέμην τοῦ λόγου, ὅτι καὶ ὑμεῖς ἀδικεῖσθε οὐδὲν ἧττον τῶν δόντων ἡμῶν τὰ χρήματα. σκοπεῖτε δ', ὦ ἄνδρες δικασταὶ, πῶς συναδικεῖσθεᴾ, ἐπειδάν τις τῶν νόμων τῶν ὑμετέρων κρείττων ἐγχειρῇ εἶναι καὶ τὰς συγγραφὰς τὰς ναυτικὰς ἀκύρους ποιῇ καὶ καταλύῃ, καὶ τὰ χρήματα τὰ παρ' ἡμῶν εἰς Χίον ᾖ διαπεσταλκώς, πῶς οὐκ ἀδικεῖ ὁ τοιοῦτος ἄνθρωπος καὶ ὑμᾶς;

⁰ ἡμέτερον Z cum ΣΦ.—ὑμέτερον Bekk. Cf. § 28.
ᴾ πῶς οὐκ ἀδικεῖσθε Bekk. 1824.

53. ἐν φωρῶν λιμένι] See § 28.
κατηγμένα] Cf. § 52, καταχθῆναι. Aeschylus has προσηγμένον, 'brought up' (beached) by windlasses or capstans, said of a ship. Suppl. 441.
54. ὅπερ—σκοπεῖτε δ'] 'This then is precisely what I took for granted at the beginning of my address.' Mr Mayor suggests the placing of a comma instead of a period at τούτων, 'goods have been taken by them to Chios, proving the truth of my remark that the city itself loses.' In this case it would surely be better to omit οὖν. There seems to be something wrong in this passage. Either ὅτι should be omitted, or, if it be retained, we should read σκοπεῖτε ἐκ τῶνδε for σκοπεῖτε δ' ὦ κ.τ.λ. 'What I said at first, that you also are wronged, consider from this point of view (that ye may see) how you share in the wrong done; (for) when a man attempts to make himself superior to your laws, surely he does involve you in a common injury.' Even the clause πῶς συναδικεῖσθε might be omitted without detriment to the sense.
[With the whole passage cf. Or. 48 § 55 αὗται (the speaker's wife and daughter) γάρ εἰσιν αἱ ἀδικούμεναι οὐχ ἧττον ἐμοῦ, ἀλλὰ καὶ μᾶλλον. πῶς γὰρ οὐκ ἀδικοῦνται ἢ πῶς οὐ δεινὰ πάσχουσιν, ἐπειδὰν ὁρῶσι...αὗται δὲ...ἔχωσιν ἅπαντα, πῶς οὐκ ἐκεῖναι μᾶλλον ἔτι ἀδικοῦνται ἢ ἐγώ; Blass (Att. Ber. III 505), who quotes this parallel, attributes the present speech to the same author as Or. 48. S.]

διαπεσταλκώς] A happy term for 'dispatching goods to different destinations other than what the law allows.' Mr Penrose fails to see the true force of the διά in composition.

XXXV. ΠΡΟΣ ΤΗΝ ΛΑΚ. ΠΑΡ. [§§ 55, 56

55 Ἐμοὶ μὲν οὖν ἐστιν, ὦ ἄνδρες δικασταί, πρὸς τούτους ὁ λόγος· τούτοις γὰρ ἔδωκα τὰ χρήματα. τούτοις δ' ἔσται πρὸς τὸν ναύκληρον ἐκεῖνον τὸν Φασηλίτην, τὸν πολίτην τὸν αὑτῶν, ᾧ φασὶ δανεῖσαι τὰ χρήματα ἄνευ ἡμῶν παρὰ τὴν συγγραφήν· οὐδὲ γὰρ ἡμεῖς ἴσμεν τίνα ἐστὶ τὰ πεπραγμένα τούτοις πρὸς τὸν ἑαυτῶν πο-
56 λίτην, ἀλλ' αὐτοὶ οὗτοι ἴσασιν. ταῦτα ἡγούμεθα δίκαια εἶναι, καὶ ὑμῶν δεόμεθα, ὦ ἄνδρες δικασταί, βοηθεῖν ἡμῖν τοῖς ἀδικουμένοις, καὶ κολάζειν τοὺς κακοτεχνοῦντας καὶ σοφιζομένους, ὥσπερ οὗτοι σοφίζονται. καὶ ἐὰν ταῦτα ποιῆτε, ὑμῖν τε αὐτοῖς τὰ συμφέροντα ἔσεσθε ἐψηφισμένοι, καὶ περιαιρήσεσθε τῶν πονηρῶν ἀνθρώπων τὰς πανουργίας ἁπάσας, ἃς ἔνιοι πανουργοῦσι περὶ τὰ συμβόλαια τὰ ναυτικά.

§§ 55, 6. *The case now lies between me and the defendants: it is for them to deal with Hyblesius the skipper, who is their own countryman, and must be sued in their courts. We have no knowledge of any transactions between them. It is the duty of the judges to deal severely with fraud in defence of mercantile interests.*

ᾧ φασὶ δανεῖσαι] § 36.

ἔσεσθε ἐψηφισμένοι] The Greeks have no tense corresponding to the Latin future perfect indicative, *fuero*, &c. They use therefore ἔσομαι with a past participle, as Aesch. Suppl. 454, λέξον, τίν' αὐδὴν τήνδε γηρυθεῖσ' ἔσει; Soph. Ant. 1067, νέκυν νεκρῶν ἀμοιβὸν ἀντιδοὺς ἔσει. Cobet gives a great many examples in p. 321 of his *Variae Lectiones*.

περιαιρήσεσθε] 'You will rid yourselves of all the villainous artifices of these unprincipled men.' Kennedy translates 'you will deprive the swindlers of those artifices,' &c. But it is more probable that αἱρήσομαι (like λέξομαι, τιμήσομαι &c.) is here passive = αἱρεθήσομαι. The idiom is here the same as in the more familiar ἀφαιρεθῆναί τι.

OR. XXXVII.

ΠΑΡΑΓΡΑΦΗ ΠΡΟΣ ΠΑΝΤΑΙΝΕΤΟΝ.

This is an important and rather difficult speech. As conveying much and curious information about mining operations and the laws which regulated them, it is unique in the writings of the orators, though Xenophon touches upon the subject, if the treatise περὶ πόρων, 'on the Athenian Revenues,' is rightly attributed to him. Dismissing for the present any discussion on this topic[1],

---

[1] The student will find ample information upon it in Kennedy's long and careful Introduction, p. 219—24 (in Vol. IV of his Translation of Demosthenes), and in Boeckh's *Dissertation on the silver mines of Laurion* in p. 615—678 of the "Public Economy," translated by Lewis, Ed. 2. [See also K. F. Hermann's *Lehrbuch der Griechischen Privataltertümer*, § 14, 17, and Büchsenschütz, *Besitz und Erwerb im Griechischen Alterthume*, pp. 98—103. In the time of Strabo (fl. B.C. 24) the silver mines were nearly exhausted: IX 23, p. 399, τὰ δ' ἀργυρεῖα τὰ ἐν τῇ Ἀττικῇ κατ' ἀρχὰς μὲν ἦν ἀξιόλογα νυνὶ δ' ἐκλείπει· καὶ δὴ καὶ οἱ ἐργαζόμενοι τῆς μεταλλείας ἀσθενῶς ὑπακουούσης τὴν παλαιὰν ἐκβολάδα (unsmelted ores left by the old workers, the Cornish 'attle') καὶ σκωρίαν ('slag') ἀναχωνεύοντες εὕρισκον ἔτι ἐξ αὐτῆς ἀποκαθαιρόμενον ἀργύριον, τῶν ἀρχαίων ἀπείρως καμινευόντων. The right to work this refuse ore (as well as the slag) was from 1869 to 1873 one of the points in dispute between the Greek government and a commercial company, MM. Roux et Serpierei. An interesting account of the origin of the quarrel, with some correspondence thereon, may be found in the *Times* for 9th, 10th, 12th and 16th Oct. 1872, and 10th Aug. 1875; and a lively description of a visit to the works of one of the Greek companies is given in Mahaffy's *Rambles and Studies in Greece*, pp. 117—131, 1876. In April 1886, by the kindness of MM. Serpieri and Pellissier, Mr Sandys visited some of the more ancient portions of the extensive mines of the French company which sends its lead to Newcastle, and its zinc to Swansea and Antwerp. S.]

we shall endeavour to state the nature and grounds of the action as briefly and clearly as the somewhat complex and involved argument allows.

The plea is preferred by one Nicobulus for a παραγραφὴ against certain unreasonable claims made upon him, as he considers them, by Pantaenetus, who is in effect the plaintiff. He had charged Nicobulus with damaging his works, with taking away ore and smelted silver from his slaves, with taking possession of the mine for non-payment of money advanced to him by Nicobulus in conjunction with Evergus, and with other outrages (§ 33). The case is made more intricate by the numerous transfers of the mining property (or "sett," as it is now technically called) to various owners, who still retain a lien upon it. The successive proprietors of the mine were (1) Telemachus, § 5; (2) Pantaenetus, § 22; (3) Mnesicles, who holds the conveyance in his own name, as having lent money on security of it, § 5; (4) Nicobulus and Evergus, who obtained the transfer direct from Mnesicles, as the mortgagee; (5) Pantaenetus again, but *under lease* to the last-mentioned proprietors; (6) the nominees of Pantaenetus, who bought it at his urgent request from Nicobulus, § 16.

To pay for the mine, and perhaps to carry on operations, Pantaenetus had at the outset borrowed money from Mnesicles (§ 4) and other parties. On this account, the mine is transferred to Mnesicles, who is thenceforth the real vendor, πρατήρ. But, on Mnesicles requiring to be paid, Pantaenetus a second time borrows money, viz. from Nicobulus and Evergus, who consent to purchase the mine in their turn from Mnesicles, at the desire of the nominal owner Pantaenetus, on condition of getting their interest, in the form of rent, from the profits of the mine, of which he becomes the lessee under

ΠΡΟΣ ΠΑΝΤΑΙΝΕΤΟΝ. 91

them, § 5. At this juncture, of course, Nicobulus and Evergus are the real owners of the mine; but by a special clause, Pantaenetus has the power of redemption, or resuming actual ownership, within a certain time.

The transaction being concluded, Nicobulus goes abroad for a time, and during his absence Evergus, failing to obtain the promised rent as interest, takes possession on his own account, and apparently with undue rigour, of the mine, the slaves, and even of the ore raised. For this Pantaenetus eventually brings an action against him (probably on some technical ground of illegality[1]), and obtains a verdict, with the heavy damages of two talents. (§ 46.)

Nicobulus, on his return to Athens, is surprised to find Evergus in possession of the mine, he being still unpaid, and additional creditors against the mine, i.e. against Pantaenetus (whether real or fictitious) now coming forward. It is at length arranged that both Evergus and Nicobulus shall be paid their claims in full, and the mine shall pass into other hands. Nicobulus takes the precaution to get a release and discharge from all further demands on the part of Pantaenetus (i.e. as the former lessee), and this release is made the principal ground of the present παραγραφή. Not so Evergus, however, who (as above mentioned) was prosecuted and condemned for the seizure of the property on his own account. It is clear that if he also had obtained an acquittance, Pantaenetus could have had no legal ground for the suit against him. An action is now brought against Nicobulus, who is the defendant in the suit. Pantaenetus says that he aided and abetted Evergus in getting wrong-

---

[1] Evergus ought to have acted, perhaps strictly in agreement with Nicobulus, or have waited for his return, or to have dis- trained only for the value of the mine. See on § 5, and Arg. 50—4. He is said πλημμελεῖν, § 26.

ful possession of the property, and he seeks to obtain damages from him. But Nicobulus resists the claim, relying on the release he had got under the hand of Pantaenetus. Another point of the παραγραφή is, that this is not properly a mining suit, and therefore cannot be tried among other δίκαι μεταλλικαί. (§ 35—6.)

Pantaenetus makes an unfair use of the popular dislike of money-lenders. He urges this point in § 52, μισοῦσιν Ἀθηναῖοι τοὺς δανείζοντας, and declares that Nicobulus is arrogant and personally offensive. But Nicobulus says he is not a professional money-lender who cares only for profit, but "a private gentleman with capital at his disposal," who is willing to oblige his friends by a loan.

The chief difficulty, perhaps, lies in understanding how Pantaenetus contrived to get a verdict against Evergus; for it is clear that it is on the merits of this case, and the success that had attended it, that the further action is filed against Nicobulus.

The late Mr Kennedy's Introduction should be in the hands of the student. As an eminent barrister, who was thoroughly versed in both the English and the Attic law, he has disentangled the case with great skill, though he considers it as still obscure on several points.

The date of the speech is approximately determined by the mention in § 6 of the Archonship of Theophilus, viz. B.C. 347. [The speech probably belongs to the year 345, A. Schaefer, *Dem. u. s. Zeit*, III 2, pp. 206, 332; Blass, *Att. Ber.* III 420. Both of these able critics accept it as a genuine work of Demosthenes. The contrary view is held by Sigg and G. Krueger (Halle), 1876, whose arguments have been refuted in detail by A. Hoeck (Berlin) 1878. S.]

XXXVII.

ΠΑΡΑΓΡΑΦΗ ΠΡΟΣ ΠΑΝΤΑΙΝΕΤΟΝ.

ΥΠΟΘΕΣΙΣ.

Πανταίνετος παρὰ Τηλεμάχου τινὸς ἐργαστήριον μεταλλικὸν ἐν Μαρωνείᾳ (τόπος δὲ οὗτος τῆς Ἀττικῆς) καὶ μετὰ τοῦ ἐργαστηρίου τριάκοντα τὸν ἀριθμὸν οἰκέτας ὠνούμενος, δανείζεται παρὰ μὲν Μνησικλέους τάλαντον, παρὰ δὲ Φιλέου καὶ Πλείστορος πέντε καὶ 5
τετταράκοντα μνᾶς. καὶ ἦν ὠνητὴς ἐγγεγραμμένος ὁ

1. *Argument* ἐργαστήριον μεταλλικὸν] 'Mining works.' We have ἐργαστήριον συκοφαντῶν, 'a gang of informers,' in Or. 39 § 2, and the word properly includes the slaves, though special mention of them follows, as below, τὸ ἐργαστήριον καὶ τὰ ἀνδράποδα. In § 4 it is ἐργαστήριον ἐν τοῖς ἔργοις, where Kennedy renders it 'a pit.' [At the present day, *Ergasteria* is in common use in Attica as an alternative name for the modern mining-village of *Lavrion*. S.]

2. Μαρωνείᾳ] 'The mining district, besides the demi Anaphystus, Besa, Amphitrope, and Thoricus, contained several places which were not demi, as Laureium, Thrasyllum, Maroneia, Aulon' (Leake's *Demi*, p. 274).—The place may perhaps be identified with some ruins five miles N. of Sunium. S.]

Boeckh, in his Dissertation on the Mines of Laurion (*P. Econ.* p. 619, trans. Lewis[2]) notices the identity of this name with the Maronea in Thrace, a colony of the Chians, said to be so called from the eponym hero (or wine-god) Μάρων. He thinks that through Chios the name may have passed from Attica into Thrace. See inf. § 4.

6. ὠνητής] 'The name of Mnesicles was written in the bond as the purchaser (viz. from Telemachus, § 5), and he retained the deeds of sale of the property himself.' In effect, the mine belonged to Pantaenetus, but it was conveyed to Mnesicles as security for the loan. Mnesicles therefore has the right of sale, and in fact does afterwards sell the property to Evergus and

Μνησικλῆς, καὶ τὰς ὠνὰς εἶχεν αὐτός. ὕστερον δὲ ἀπαιτούμενος τὸ ἀργύριον ὁ Πανταίνετος δευτέρους λαμβάνει δανειστὰς, τόν τε παραγραφόμενον νῦν Νικό-
10 βουλον καὶ Εὔεργόν τινα, καὶ τούτοις ὑποθήκην δίδωσι τὸ ἐργαστήριον καὶ τὰ ἀνδράποδα. γραμματεῖον δὲ οὐχ ὑποθήκης, ἀλλὰ πράσεως γράφεται. καὶ γίνεται πρατὴρ καὶ βεβαιωτὴς τοῖς δευτέροις δανεισταῖς ὁ πρότερος δεδανεικὼς ὁ Μνησικλῆς, ὁ τὰς ὠνὰς ἔχων.
15 καὶ μισθοῦσι τῷ Πανταινέτῳ τά τε ἀνδράποδα καὶ τὸ 964 ἐργαστήριον Εὔεργος καὶ ὁ Νικόβουλος, ὡς δεσπόται δῆθεν γεγονότες αὐτοῦ. τοσούτου δὲ μισθοῦσιν ὅσον τὸ δάνειον τόκον ἐποίει· ἐδεδανείκεσαν μὲν γὰρ ἑκατὸν πέντε μνᾶς, ἔδει δὲ κατὰ μνᾶν τόκον εἶναι δραχμήν·
20 ἑκατὸν οὖν καὶ πέντε δραχμὰς λαμβάνειν συνέθεντο· καὶ ἦν τοῦτο τῷ μὲν ἔργῳ τόκος, τῷ δὲ ὀνόματι μίσ-θωσις. τούτων πραχθέντων ὁ μὲν Νικόβουλος ἀπεδή-μησε, παρὰ δὲ τὴν ἀπουσίαν τὴν ἐκείνου Ἀθήνησι

Nicobulus, the latter of whom (as we have seen) is the defendant, and is now maintaining his right to a παραγραφή as against Pantaenetus.

8. ἀπαιτούμενος] Or. 34, arg. n. 16. On being required to repay the loan to Mnesicles, he has recourse to *versura*, or borrowing from another party; who, on Mnesicles being paid, purchase the mine from him, i.e. take over the mine in lieu of the loan, at the desire and with the consent of Pantaenetus.

11. γραμματεῖον κ.τ.λ.] 'And thus the indenture is not a mortgage, but an actual conveyance.' Now therefore Evergus and Nicobulus become the proprietors; and they in turn *lease* to Pantaenetus the property he had originally bought.

17. ὅσον τόκον] They lease it on terms which would just pay the interest of the loan, a drachma per month for every mina lent, or 12 per cent. per annum. Thus, he adds, it was a nominal lease, being in fact merely a way of paying the usual interest.

23. παρὰ] During or pending Nicobulus' absence at Athens Evergus becoming dissatisfied with Pantaenetus for not paying the interest (or rent) regularly, goes to the mine to take possession (cf. Or. 33 § 6, οἱ χρησταὶ κατήπειγον αὐτὸν ἀπαιτοῦντες καὶ ἐνεβάτευον), and even seizes from a servant of Pantaenetus some money that was being conveyed for payment of the royalty to the state.

ΠΡΟΣ ΠΑΝΤΑΙΝΕΤΟΝ.

τάδε γίγνεται. ὁ Εὔεργος ὁ κοινωνὸς τοῦ δανείσματος, αἰτιώμενος τὸν Πανταίνετον ὡς οὐδὲν τῶν συγκειμένων ἐθέλοντα ποιεῖν, ἐλθὼν ἐπὶ τὸ ἐργαστήριον κατεῖχεν αὐτοῦ, καὶ δὴ ἀργύριον φυλάξας ἐκ τῶν μετάλλων Πανταινέτῳ κομιζόμενον, ὅπερ ἔμελλεν εἰς τὸ δημόσιον καταβάλλειν, ἀφείλετο τὸν κομίζοντα οἰκέτην βίᾳ· παρὸ καὶ διπλῆν εἰς τὸ δημόσιον κατέβαλεν, ὡς ἔφη, τὴν καταβολὴν ὁ Πανταίνετος, τῆς προσηκούσης προθεσμίας δι' Εὔεργον ἐκπεσών. ἐπὶ τούτοις καὶ δίκην ἔλαχε τῷ Εὐέργῳ βλάβης, καὶ εἷλεν αὐτόν. ὡς δὲ ἐπανῆκε καὶ ὁ Νικόβουλος ἐκ τῆς ἀποδημίας καὶ δανεισταὶ πολλοί τινες ἀνεφαίνοντο τοῦ Πανταινέτου πρότερον ἀγνοούμενοι, λόγων πολλῶν λεγομένων πέρας συνέβησαν ὥστε Νικόβουλον μὲν καὶ Εὔεργον ἀπολαμβάνοντας ἑκατὸν καὶ πέντε μνᾶς ἀποστῆναι τοῦ ἐργαστηρίου καὶ τῶν ἀνδραπόδων, ταῦτα δὲ τοὺς ἑτέ-

26. κατεῖχεν] In late Greek, this seems to mean 'took possession of,' *obtinuit*, in the sense of εἴχετο.

30. παρὸ, κ.τ.λ.] 'Through which transaction as a further wrong (καὶ) Pantaenetus had to pay the sum due twice over, having exceeded the time allowed for remitting it.'—See Boeckh *Dissert*. &c. p. 665.

[Owing to the intervention of Eubulus, Pantaenetus was thwarted from (ἐκπεσών) paying the 'royalty' by the proper time, viz. the 9th of the 10 πρυτανεῖαι into which the year was divided. Andoc. de Myst. § 73, οἱ μὲν ἀργύριον ὀφείλοντες τῷ δημοσίῳ...τούτοις ἡ μὲν ἔκτισις ἦν ἐπὶ τῆς ἐνάτης πρυτανείας, εἰ δὲ μή, διπλάσιον ὀφείλειν. Cf. Or. 59 § 7, and K. F. Hermann, *Privatalterthümer* § 71, 12 = *Rechtsalterthümer* ed. Thalheim § 16 p. 108. S.]

33. ἔλαχε] sc. Pantaenetus.—εἷλεν, he obtained a verdict. The precise grounds on which he succeeded in this action for damage we are not told, and, as Kennedy says, we cannot determine. (See Introduction.)

36. πέρας] 'At last,' or 'as a final arrangement.'

38. ἑκατὸν καὶ πέντε μνᾶς] viz. the full sum they had jointly lent Pantaenetus.—ἀποστῆναι, 'they were to give up possession.' Cf. Or. 35 § 4.

39. τοὺς ἑτέρους δανείσαντας] The parties (not named) who had furnished Pantaenetus with the money for payment, and who thus obtained the right of sale and the legal conveyance of the mine, § 13. They are called ἕτεροι in contrast with ὁ πρότερος δεδανεικὼς ὁ Μνησικλῆς, supra l. 14.

XXXVII. ΠΑΡΑΓΡΑΦΗ [Argument

40 ρους δανείσαντας ὠνεῖσθαι. πάλιν δὲ οὐκ ἐθελόντων τῶν δανειστῶν ὠνεῖσθαι τὰ κτήματα, εἰ μὴ πρατῆρες αὐτοὶ καὶ βεβαιωταὶ γίγνοιντο Νικόβουλος καὶ Εὔεργος, πείθεται ὁ Νικόβουλος καὶ ὑπ' αὐτοῦ Πανταινέτου, 965 καθά φησιν, ἀξιούμενος, οὐ πρότερον δὲ ἀνεδέξατο,
45 πρὶν τὸν Πανταίνετον ἄφεσιν αὐτῷ παντὸς ἐγκλήματος δοῦναι. ὁ δὲ Πανταίνετος ἔδωκε μὲν τὴν ἄφεσιν καὶ ἐπράθη τὰ κτήματα, οὐδὲν δὲ ἧττον καὶ τούτῳ τὴν αὐτὴν ἥνπερ Εὐέργῳ δίκην εἴληχε, μεταλλικὴν ἐπιγράφων τὴν δίκην, ὡς δὴ τῶν τε τὰ μέταλλα ἐργαζομένων
50 εἷς ὢν καὶ περὶ μέταλλον ἠδικημένος. ἐγκαλεῖ δὲ τῷ Νικοβούλῳ καὶ περὶ τῆς τῶν χρημάτων ἀφαιρέσεως τῶν ὑπὸ τοῦ οἰκέτου κομιζομένων, καὶ περὶ τῆς τοῦ ἐργαστηρίου καὶ τῶν ἀνδραπόδων πράσεως παρὰ τὰς συνθήκας γεγενημένης, καὶ μέντοι καὶ περὶ ἑτέρων
55 τινῶν. ὁ δὲ Νικόβουλος παραγράφεται τὸν ἀγῶνα καθ' ἕνα μὲν ἐκεῖνον νόμον τὸν κελεύοντα, περὶ ὧν ἂν ἄφεσις καὶ ἀπαλλαγὴ γένηται, περὶ τούτων μηκέτι ἐξεῖναι δικάζεσθαι, καθ' ἕτερον δὲ ἐκεῖνον, ὃς διαρρήδην καὶ σαφῶς ὁρίζει περὶ τίνων δεῖ τὰς μεταλλικὰς δίκας

44. ἀνεδέξατο] Nicobulus refused the responsibility of giving a title till Pantaenetus gave him a formal release from all claims. For the title would not have been good if there were any former claims or mortgage upon it. Inf. § 30, οὐδεὶς γὰρ ἤθελε δέχεσθαι τοῦτον πρατῆρα.
47. οὐδὲν ἧττον] i. e. in spite of the release having been given.
48. ἐπιγράφων] Indorsing the action as a 'mining cause'; just as other suits were marked ἐμπορικαί, &c. The defendant pleads this, as one ground for the παραγραφὴ, that it was improperly so indorsed.
53. πράσεως παρὰ τὰς συνθήκας]

There must have been a clause in the bond between Nicobulus the lender and Pantaenetus the borrower, that Nicobulus should not have an absolute title to sell the property. Pantaenetus, it seems, desired to retain the right of redemption.
54. περὶ ἑτέρων τινῶν] See §§ 32, 33.
56. περὶ ὧν ἂν ἄφεσις, κ.τ.λ.] See Or. 36 § 25.
59. περὶ τίνων δεῖ] This anticipates the objection (64) that the plaintiff, Pantaenetus, 'had joined in one plaint various causes of action which could not be tried together before the same tribunal.' Kennedy.

εἰσάγειν, ὧν οὐδὲν πεπονθότα Πανταίνετον ἀτόπως φησὶ μεταλλικὴν δικάζεσθαι δίκην. καὶ μὴν καὶ τρίτον παρέχεται νόμον, ὃς διαιρεῖ περὶ ποίων ἐγκλημάτων ποῖα χρὴ κρίνειν δικαστήρια καὶ ποίας ἀρχὰς εἰσάγειν τὰς δίκας· Πανταίνετον δέ φησι παρὰ τοῦτον ποιεῖν τὸν νόμον, ποικίλα ἐγκλήματα εἰς ταὐτὸν μίξαντα καὶ περὶ πάντων ἐν τῷ μεταλλικῷ δικαστηρίῳ τὴν κατηγορίαν ποιούμενον. τῷ μὲν οὖν περὶ τῆς ἀφέσεως νόμῳ κατ' ἀρχὰς κέχρηται, τοῖς δὲ δύο τοῖς ἑτέροις ἐπὶ τοῦ τέλους, καὶ ἀρχόμενος ἀπὸ τῆς παραγραφῆς καὶ λήγων εἰς ταύτην. ἐν δὲ μέσῳ τὴν εὐθυδικίαν πεποίηκεν, ἧς μέγιστον καὶ ἰσχυρότατόν ἐστιν, ὅτι μηδὲ ἐπιδημῶν ἐτύγχανε τότε Νικόβουλος, ὅτε Πανταίνετος[a] ἔπασχεν ἐκεῖνα, ἐφ' οἷς τότε Εὐέργῳ καὶ νῦν Νικοβούλῳ τὴν δίκην εἴληχεν.

Δεδωκότων, ὦ ἄνδρες δικασταί, τῶν νόμων παραγράψασθαι περὶ ὧν ἄν τις ἀφεὶς καὶ ἀπαλλάξας δικάζηται, γεγενημένων ἀμφοτέρων μοι τούτων[b] πρὸς

[a] om. Z.   [b] τούτων om. Z et Bekk. st.

60. ἀτόπως, κ.τ.λ.] That it is quite out of the way to bring these points into a mining suit. 'That the subject of the dispute did not authorise a mining action.' Kennedy.
68. κέχρηται] viz. as entitling him to bar the action, and plead 'not maintainable.'—ἐπὶ τοῦ τέλους] See §§ 36—38.
70. τὴν εὐθυδικίαν] i.e. τὴν εὐθεῖαν. 'The merits of the case.' Argum. Or. 34. The strongest point in what would constitute an ordinary defence, is the pleading an *alibi* when the alleged outrage took place.
71. ὅτι μηδέ] Observe the solecism, very common in late Greek, for ὅτι οὐδέ. The use of ἐκεῖνα following, as a mere demonstrative antecedent (*ea quae*, &c.), is hardly classical.
p. 966. § 1. *As the laws allow a bar to a suit in all matters in which a discharge and acquittance have been given, I have claimed this right against Pantaenetus. I shall show that he gave me such a discharge; and I shall not allow him to argue, that, if he had really done so, I ought to have put in the παραγραφή, but did not.*
ἀμφοτέρων] Cf. Or. 36 § 25, καὶ γὰρ ἀφῆκε καὶ ἀπήλλαξεν, and

Πανταίνετον τουτονί, παρεγραψάμην, ώς ήκούσατ' άρτίως, μη εισαγώγιμον είναι την δίκην, ουκ οιόμενος δείν αφείσθαι του δικαίου τούτου, ουδ', επειδαν εξελέγξω προς άπασι τοις άλλοις και αφεικότα τούτον εμαυτον και απηλλαγμένον, εγγενέσθαι τούτω μη φάσκειν αληθή με λέγειν, και ποιείσθαι τεκμήριον ώς, είπερ επράχθη τι τοιούτον, παρεγραψάμην αν αυτόν, αλλ' επι ταύτης της σκήψεως εισελθων αμφότερα υμίν επιδείξαι, και ως ουδεν ηδίκηκα τούτον και ως παρα

the note there (cf. § 19 infra). The latter verb implies the release under proper authority (κυρία) from all further trouble or obligation about any matter, as απαλλαγη πόνων, Aesch. Ag. 1, ές το παν σε τωνδ' απαλλάξαι πόνων, Eum. 83. The two words are very often combined, as πάντων αφεθείς των εγκλημάτων και απαλλαγείς, § 16; ων αν αφη και απαλλάξη τις, § 19; ηνίκα αφιέμην υπο τούτου και απηλλαττόμην, § 17. The two acts are very frequently pleaded as the ground of a παραγραφή, e.g. προς Ναυσίμαχον, Or. 38 § 5, ακούετε, ω άνδρες δικασταί, του νόμου σαφως λέγοντος έκαστα, ων μη είναι δίκας· ων έν έστιν, ομοίως τοις άλλοις κύριον, περι ων αν τις αφη και απαλλάξη, μη δικάζεσθαι.
[Or. 38, προς Ναυσίμαχον, contains several striking parallels to the present speech, e.g. 38, § 4, compared with § 18 infr.; also passages in 38, §§ 21 and 22, which are almost identical with §§ 58—60 infr. A. Schaefer, *Dem. u. s. Zeit*, III 2, 210 n. S.]

ουκ οιόμενος] 'Thinking I ought not to forego this right.' There is probably a play on αφείς, 'when he had discharged me from further claims, I was not to be discharged from my own claim against him.'

και απηλλαγμένον] 'And that he had been got rid of.' But it is likely that the two words are an interpolation. The first και is used in reference to προς άπασι τοις άλλοις, but the interpolator was thinking of the formula και αφείς και απαλλάξας. The passive would require a change of subject from τούτον to εμέ. Nor does it seem likely that the passive could here have been used in the medial sense, which is wholly inappropriate.—εγγενέσθαι, εξείναι αυτώ.

τι τοιούτον] viz. το αφείναι με.

αλλ'—επιδείξαι] To supply as the context rather requires, οιόμενος δείν would involve εισελθόντα for εισελθών. Hence we should rather understand δύνασθαι επιδείξαι, or perhaps read επιδείξειν.—επί, 'relying on this plea,' viz. that the action is an illegal one.

ως ουδεν ηδίκηκα] This, as often happens in παραγραφαί, constitutes the ordinary defence in ευθυδικία, or where there is no bar to the action. He enters the court, he says, to plead a παραγραφή, but besides doing this, he will assert his innocence.

ΠΡΟΣ ΠΑΝΤΑΙΝΕΤΟΝ.

τὸν νόμον μοι δικάζεται. εἰ μὲν οὖν ἐπεπόνθει τι τού- 2
των Πανταίνετος ὢν νῦν ἐγκαλεῖ, κατ' ἐκείνους ἂν
τοὺς χρόνους εὐθὺς ἐφαίνετό μοι δικαζόμενος, ἐν οἷς
τὸ συμβόλαιον ἡμῖν πρὸς ἀλλήλους ἐγένετο, οὐσῶν μὲν
ἐμμήνων τούτων τῶν δικῶν, ἐπιδημούντων δ' ἡμῶν
ἀμφοτέρων, ἁπάντων δ' ἀνθρώπων εἰωθότων παρ'
αὐτὰ τἀδικήματα μᾶλλον ἢ χρόνων ἐγγεγενημένων
ἀγανακτεῖν. ἐπειδὴ δὲ οὐδὲν ἠδικημένος, ὡς καὶ ὑμεῖς
οἶδ' ὅτι φήσετε ἐπειδὰν τὰ πεπραγμένα ἀκούσητε, τῷ
κατορθῶσαι τὴν πρὸς Εὔεργον δίκην ἐπηρμένος* συκο-
φαντεῖ, ὑπόλοιπόν ἐστι παρ' ὑμῖν, ὦ ἄνδρες δικασταί,

* ἐπηρμένος Z. ἐπῃρμένος Bekk. et Dind.

§ 2. *If Pantaenetus had really been wronged, he would have brought the action long before this, and when I was at Athens along with Evergus. Men are usually most indignant when the sense of wrong is recent; and the courts meet for cases of this kind every month. The truth is, he was not wronged by me, but put up to this prosecution by having got a verdict against Evergus.*

ἐμμήνων] Kennedy translates, 'as these actions last only for a month.' Or. 33 § 23, αἱ λήξεις τῶν δικῶν τοῖς ἐμπόροις ἔμμηνοί εἰσιν ἀπὸ τοῦ βοηδρομιῶνος μέχρι τοῦ μουνυχιῶνος, i.e. from September till April: Cf. Or. 35 § 46 n. Boeckh (*P. Econ.* ed. 1, pp. 50 and 667, trans. Lewis²) renders it 'monthly suits,' and on p. 667 explains it to mean that "it was necessary that judgment should be given within a month, the object being that the mine-proprietor might not be too long detained from his business." [In his 2nd ed., however, the rendering 'monthly suits' disappears, and the epithet is understood to refer to the 'decision of certain processes within a month from their commencement' p. 72, Lamb]. In Soph. El. 281, ἔμμηνα ἱερά are clearly "monthly offerings."
παρ' αὐτὰ κ.τ.λ.] 'At the very time of the wrongs.' In Or. 32 § 7, for παρὰ τἀδικήματα we should perhaps read παρ' αὐτὰ τἀδικήματα. For the sentiment compare Thuc. III 38, ἀμύνασθαι τῷ παθεῖν ὅτι ἐγγυτάτω κείμενον ἀντίπαλον ὂν μάλιστα τὴν τιμωρίαν ἀναλαμβάνει (where perhaps ὂν is an interpolation: the τιμωρία is μάλιστα ἀντίπαλος when it is recent). So Or. 36 § 53 πλησίον ὄντων τῶν ἀδικημάτων ἐγκαλεῖς.

p. 967. ἐπηρμένος] 'Elated,' put up to it, 'by having carried to a successful issue the suit against Evergus.' Thucydides generally uses ἐπαιρόμενος. Or. 32 § 10, we have τῷ ποτ' ἐπηρμένος οὗτος κατελήλυθε. Eur. Andr. 705, μόχθοισιν ἄλλων καὶ πόνοις ἐπηρμένοι.
παρ' ὑμῖν] 'In your court.'

ἐπιδείξαντα ὡς οὐδ' ὁτιοῦν ἀδικῶ, καὶ μάρτυρας ὧν ἂν λέγω παρασχόμενον, πειράσασθαι σώζειν ἐμαυτόν.

3 δεήσομαι δὲ καὶ μέτρια καὶ δίκαια ὑμῶν ἁπάντων, ἀκοῦσαί τέ μου περὶ ὧν παρεγραψάμην εὐνοϊκῶς καὶ προσέχειν ὅλῳ τῷ πράγματι τὸν νοῦν· πολλῶν γὰρ δικῶν ἐν τῇ πόλει γεγενημένων, οὐδένα πω δίκην οὔτ' ἀναιδεστέραν οὔτε συκοφαντικωτέραν οἶμαι φανήσεσθαι δεδικασμένον ἧς νῦν οὑτοσὶ λαχὼν εἰσελθεῖν τετόλμηκεν. ἐξ ἀρχῆς δ', ὡς ἂν οἷός τε ὦ, διὰ βραχυτάτων ἅπαντα τὰ πραχθέντα διηγήσομαι πρὸς ὑμᾶς.

4 Ἐδανείσαμεν πέντε καὶ ἑκατὸν μνᾶς ἐγὼ καὶ Εὔεργος, ὦ ἄνδρες δικασταί, Πανταινέτῳ τούτῳ ἐπ' ἐργαστηρίῳ τε ἐν τοῖς ἔργοις ἐν Μαρωνείᾳ καὶ τριάκοντα ἀνδραπόδοις. ἦν δὲ τοῦ δανείσματος τετταράκοντα

§ 3. *I only ask for a fair and attentive hearing in showing grounds for a bar to this action: for of all the audacious charges ever tried in an Athenian court this is about the worst.*
δεήσομαι κ.τ.λ.] Or. 38 § 2 δεήσομαι δὲ καὶ δίκαια καὶ μέτρια ὑμῶν ἁπάντων, πρῶτον μὲν εὐνοϊκῶς ἀκοῦσαί μου λέγοντος κ.τ.λ.
πολλῶν γὰρ, κ.τ.λ.] Isaeus, the traditional teacher of Demosthenes, has a similar sentence in Or. 8 § 5, πολλῶν δὲ δικῶν ἐν τῇ πόλει γενομένων, οὐδένες ἀναιδέστερον τούτων οὐδὲ καταφανέστερον ἀντιποιησάμενοι φανήσονται τῶν ἀλλοτρίων. Cf. Dem. in Aph. 1 § 7. S.]
φανήσεσθαι] φανήσεται ὅτι οὐδείς, κ.τ.λ.—δεδικασμένον, in the medial sense, 'has had tried,' 'has brought into court.' The construction of the sentence is rather artificial. More usual would be οἶμαι μηδένα ἂν φανῆναι, but οὐκ οἶμαι οὐδένα is meant.

§§ 4—6. *History of the transaction: I, Nicobulus, with my partner Evergus, lent the defendant 105 minae on the works at Maronea, in order that he might pay off the sum due to Mnesicles and others. Mnesicles, as the mortgagee, accordingly conveys the mine and the slaves to us. The defendant then, in place of paying interest on the loan, agrees to hire the mine of us at a rent amounting to the interest. This agreement being signed, I went off to the Pontus, Evergus staying at home.*
ἐργαστηρίῳ] This word meant any place where works were carried on (see Arg. l. 1); but here the ἔργα, or mining operations, are distinguished from the sheds for dressing or the factory for smelting, &c. Probably we should read ἐργαστηρίῳ τῷ ἐν τοῖς ἔργοις, the τε being both needless and not in accordance with the orator's usual style.
Μαρωνείᾳ] See note on Arg. l. 2.
τετταράκοντα κ.τ.λ.] From § 21 it would seem that Nico-

μὲν καὶ πέντε μναῖ ἐμαί, τάλαντον δ' Εὐέργου. συνέβαινε δὲ τοῦτον ὀφείλειν Μνησικλεῖ μὲν Κολλυτεῖ τάλαντον, Φιλέᾳ δ' Ἐλευσινίῳ καὶ Πλείστορι πέντε καὶ τετταράκοντα μνᾶς. πρατὴρ μὲν δὴ τοῦ ἐργαστηρίου 5 καὶ τῶν ἀνδραπόδων ὁ Μνησικλῆς ἡμῖν γίγνεται· καὶ γὰρ ἐώνητο ἐκεῖνος αὐτὰ τούτῳ παρὰ Τηλεμάχου τοῦ πρότερον κεκτημένου· μισθοῦται δ' οὑτοσὶ[d] παρ' ἡμῶν τοῦ γιγνομένου τόκου τῷ ἀργυρίῳ, πέντε καὶ ἑκατὸν δραχμῶν τοῦ μηνὸς ἑκάστου. καὶ τιθέμεθα συνθήκας, ἐν αἷς ἥ τε μίσθωσις ἦν γεγραμμένη καὶ λύσις τούτῳ παρ' ἡμῶν ἔν τινι ῥητῷ χρόνῳ. πραχθέντων δὲ τού- 6 των ἐλαφηβολιῶνος μηνὸς ἐπὶ Θεοφίλου ἄρχοντος, ἐγὼ μὲν ἐκπλέων εἰς τὸν Πόντον εὐθὺς ᾠχόμην, οὗτος δ'

[d] οὗτος Z.

bulus had lent the smaller sum on the security of the slaves, Evergus the larger sum on that of the mine. Boeckh's account of the transaction (Dissert. p. 655) seems confused: Pantaenetus, he says, had purchased another mine besides that from Mnesicles (§ 22), and "had borrowed on it, viz. 45 minas on the slaves of Nicobulus and a talent on the mine of Evergus." (*From* Nicobulus, &c., he should have said.)

ibid. Note that the Greeks say indifferently πέντε καὶ τετταράκοντα or τετταράκοντα καὶ πέντε, &c.

5. καὶ γὰρ κ.τ.λ.] 'For Mnesicles had also bought the property for Pantaenetus.' For καὶ γάρ see inf. 34. There were two reasons why Mnesicles was the legal vendor; first, he was the mortgagee, and secondly, he was the person in whose name the property had been bought for another. It appears from § 29, that it was by the express desire of the latter that it was sold to Nicobulus and Evergus.

τόκου] 'For the interest accruing on the money.' The word γίγνεσθαι is used in conformity with the proper sense of τόκος, which gives rise to a joke in Ar. Thesm. 845, ἀξία γοῦν εἰ τόκου τεκοῦσα τοιοῦτον τόκον. Cf. Shakspeare's '*breed of barren metal.*' For the genitive see on Or. 34 § 40. The dative also follows the usual construction γίγνεται υἱός τινι ἐκ τινός.

λύσις] 'A power of redemption,' i.e. a right to take back the mine within a certain time on payment of our loan in full.

6. ἐπὶ Θεοφίλου ἄρχοντος] Nicobulus set sail in the spring of B.C. 347, in the ninth month of the Attic year (corresponding to the second half of March and the first half of April). S.]

εἰς τὸν Πόντον] For the purpose of trading, as appears from § 10.

ἐνθάδε ἦν καὶ Εὔεργος. τὰ μὲν δὴ πραχθέντα τούτοις πρὸς αὐτούς, ἕως ἀπεδήμουν ἐγώ, οὐκ ἂν ἔχοιμι εἰπεῖν· οὔτε γὰρ ταὐτὰ λέγουσιν οὔτ' ἀεὶ ταὐτὰ οὗτός γε, ἀλλὰ τοτὲ μὲν[e] ἐκπεσεῖν ὑπ' ἐκείνου βίᾳ παρὰ τὰς συνθήκας ἐκ τῆς μισθώσεως, τοτὲ δ' αὐτὸν αἴτιον ἑαυτῷ[f] πρὸς τὸ δημόσιον γενέσθαι τῆς ἐγγραφῆς, τοτὲ δ' ἄλλ' ὅ τι 7 ἂν βούληται. ἐκεῖνος δ' ἁπλῶς οὔτε τοὺς τόκους ἀπολαμβάνων οὔτε τῶν ἄλλων τῶν ἐν ταῖς συνθήκαις ποιοῦντος οὐδὲν τούτου, ἐλθών, παρ' ἑκόντος τούτου λαβὼν ἔχειν τὰ ἑαυτοῦ· μετὰ δὲ ταῦτ' ἀπελθόντα τοῦτον ἥκειν τοὺς ἀμφισβητήσοντας ἄγοντα, αὐτὸς δ' οὐχ ὑπεξελθεῖν ἐκείνοις, τοῦτον δ' οὐχὶ κωλύειν ἔχειν ὅσαπερ ἐμισθώσατο, εἰ ποιοίη τὰ συγκείμενα. τούτων 8 μὲν δὴ τοιούτους ἀκούω λόγους. ἐκεῖνο δ' οἶδ' ὅτι, εἰ μὲν οὗτος ἀληθῆ λέγει καὶ δεινὰ πέπονθεν, ὥσπερ φη-

[e] μέν φησι Bekk. 1824.   [f] αὐτῷ Z.

τὰ πραχθέντα—πρὸς] See inf. § 19.

ἐκπεσεῖν ὑπ' ἐκείνου] 'That he was ejected from the tenancy (lease) of the works by Evergus.' ἐκπεσεῖν is commonly used as passive of ἐκβαλεῖν. Cf. infr. § 59, ἐκβαλεῖν—ἐκπίπτειν.

πρὸς τὸ δημόσιον] These words are rather obscure. We cannot construe τῆς ἐγγραφῆς πρὸς τὸ δ. 'of being registered as a debtor to the state,' nor is αἴτιον πρός τι a common idiom. Perhaps the words are opposed to the ἰδίᾳ βλάβῃ, 'in a public point of view.' We have, however, γράφειν μίσθωσιν πρός τινα, § 10.

§ 7. *Evergus pleads that, as the defendant did not fulfil his engagement, he went and took possession without protest or opposition from Pantaenetus; but that afterwards (as an expedient for getting the mine out of his hands) Pantaenetus brought other persons who said they had a prior claim on it. These he, Evergus, resisted, while he professed his willingness that Pantaenetus should re-enter his tenancy, provided he acted according to the contract.*

ἁπλῶς] 'His simple and consistent story is that,' &c. This is opposed to οὐ ταὐτὰ λέγουσιν above.

ἥκειν κ.τ.λ.] Cf. Or. 48 § 10, ὑπενοοῦμεν γάρ, ὦ ἄνδρες δικασταί, ἥξειν τινὰς ἀμφισβητήσοντας τῶν τοῦ Κόνωνος καὶ ἑτέρους.

τοῦτον] Accusative of the object; 'Evergus did not prevent Pantaenetus,' &c.

§ 8. *If Pantaenetus was really wronged, as he says, he has got damages as assessed by himself against Evergus. But that is no reason why he should prosecute me who was then absent.*

σὶν, ὑπὸ τοῦ Εὐέργου, ἔχει δίκην ἧς ἐτιμήσατο αὐτός· εἷλε γὰρ αὐτὸν εἰσελθὼν ὡς ὑμᾶς, καὶ οὐ δήπου τῶν αὐτῶν παρά τε τοῦ πεποιηκότος δίκαιός ἐστι δίκην λαβεῖν καὶ παρ' ἐμοῦ τοῦ μηδ' ἐπιδημοῦντος· εἰ δ' ὁ Εὔεργος ἀληθῆ λέγει, σεσυκοφάντηται μὲν, ὡς ἔοικεν, ἐκεῖνος, ἐγὼ δ' οὐδ' οὕτω τῶν αὐτῶν φεύγοιμ' ἂν δίκην εἰκότως. ὡς οὖν ταῦτα πρῶτον ἀληθῆ λέγω, τούτων τοὺς μάρτυρας ὑμῖν παρέξομαι.

ΜΑΡΤΥΡΕΣ.

Ὅτι μὲν τοίνυν καὶ πρατὴρ ἦν ἡμῖν τῶν κτημάτων ὅσπερ ἐξ ἀρχῆς αὐτὸς ἐώνητο, καὶ κατὰ τὰς συνθήκας οὗτος ἐμισθώσατο ἡμέτερον ὂν τὸ ἐργαστήριον καὶ τἀνδράποδα, καὶ οὔτε παρῆν ἐγὼ τοῖς μετὰ ταῦτα πρὸς Εὔεργον τούτῳ πραχθεῖσιν οὔτ' ἐπεδήμουν ὅλως, ἔλαχέ τε δίκην ἐκείνῳ καὶ οὐδὲν πώποθ' ἡμῖν ἐνεκάλει, ἀκούετε τῶν μαρτύρων, ὦ ἄνδρες δικασταί. ἐπειδὴ τοίνυν ἀφικόμην σχεδόν τι πάντ' ἀπολωλεκὼς ὅσα ἔχων ἐξέπλευσα, ἀκούσας καὶ καταλαβὼν τοῦτον μὲν

If Evergus was tried for the offence, (though wrongly, as he says,) I ought not to be tried also for the same.

ἔχει δίκην ἧς κ.τ.λ.] 'He has recovered the sum at which he laid his damages,' Kennedy. The plaintiff is said τιμᾶσθαι, the jury τιμᾶν τινί τινος, and this is the constant use in Demosthenes. But the force of αὐτὸς is, that as Pantaenetus himself fixed the damages, he cannot fairly say they were insufficient.

τοῦ πεποιηκότος] viz. Εὐέργου.

ἐκεῖνος] viz. Εὔεργος.

τῶν αὐτῶν] The law said that a case once decided should not be tried over again (inf. § 18).

§ 9. *Testimony has been given to the facts* (1) *that Mnesicles sold us the mine;* (2) *that Pantaenetus hired it of us;* (3) *that I was absent when he prosecuted Evergus;* (4) *that he then laid no charge against me.*

ἐώνητο] παρὰ Τηλεμάχου, § 5.

§ 10. *On my return, finding Evergus in possession of our joint property, I was annoyed; for either I must take a part in the management with him, or have Evergus my debtor instead of Pantaenetus, and so draw up a new contract with him.*

ἀκούσας καὶ κ.τ.λ.] 'After hearing, and actually finding, that the defendant had given up, and Evergus was in possession of, the property.' The word ἀφισ-

ἀφεστηκότα, τὸν δ' Εὔεργον ἔχοντα καὶ κρατοῦντα ὧν ἐωνήμεθα, θαυμαστῶς ὡς ἐλυπήθην, ὁρῶν τὸ πρᾶγμά μοι περιεστηκὸς εἰς ἄτοπον· ἢ γὰρ κοινωνεῖν ἔδει τῆς ἐργασίας καὶ τῶν ἐπιμελειῶν τῷ Εὐέργῳ, ἢ χρήστην ἀντὶ τούτου τὸν Εὔεργον ἔχειν, καὶ πρὸς ἐκεῖνον πάλιν μίσθωσιν γράφειν καὶ συμβόλαιον ποιεῖσθαι· 11 τούτων δ' οὐδέτερον προῃρούμην. ἀηδῶς δ' ἔχων οἷς λέγω τούτοις, ἰδὼν τὸν Μνησικλέα τὸν πρατῆρα τούτων ἡμῖν γεγενημένον, προσελθὼν ἐμεμφόμην αὐτῷ, λέγων οἷον ἄνθρωπον προὐξένησέ μοι, καὶ τοὺς ἀμφισβητοῦντας καὶ τί ταῦτ' ἐστιν ἠρώτων. ἀκούσας δ' ἐκεῖνος τῶν μὲν ἀμφισβητούντων κατεγέλα, συνελ-

τασθαι is often used (e.g. in Or. 35 § 4) for giving up, or declining to take any property, especially a legacy. Cf. Or. 38 § 7, φασὶ γὰρ οὐκ ἀποδόσθαι τὰ πατρῷα ὧν ἐκομίζοντο χρημάτων, οὐδ' ἀποστῆναι τῶν ὄντων. Or. 21 (Mid.) p. 573 init., ὧν εἷλεν ἀποστὰς, 'having to give up what he had got from another by a verdict.'

ἔχοντα καὶ κρατοῦντα] It would seem from this that Evergus had commenced to carry on the works himself; and this explains what follows.

ἐωνήμεθα] sc. from Mnesicles, § 5.

περιεστηκὸς εἰς ἄτοπον] 'Had come to a pretty pass,' Kennedy.

ἢ χρήστην] If I preferred to be a 'sleeping partner,' I must look to Evergus for paying my share of the loan (45 minae, § 4).

§ 11. *Accordingly, I went to Mnesicles and asked what it all meant, and who these pretended claimants to the mine were. But he only laughed, and said he would take care we should meet them. As for Pantaenetus, he would also see that justice was done by him.*

οἷς λέγω τούτοις] The dative depends on the sense 'being displeased by,' and may therefore be regarded as causal. Cf. Mid. § 108, ἐγὼ γὰρ ἐνηνοχὼς χαλεπῶς ἐφ' οἷς—ὑβρίσθην, ἔτι πολλῷ χαλεπώτερον τούτοις τοῖς μετὰ ταῦτα ἐνήνοχα, where however ἐπὶ may be supplied from the first clause. See Shilleto on Thuc. I 77 § 3.

τὸν πρατῆρα κ.τ.λ.] See § 5. (The τὸν, of course, belongs to γεγενημένον.)

προὐξένησε] 'That he had introduced such a person to me.' Kennedy. To be πρόξενος to a man is to act as his patron and guarantee, and therefore to bring him forward in some relation to others. The accusative depends on the sense, like συκοφαντεῖν τινα, συνευπορεῖν τι, inf. § 49. Euripides has προξενεῖν τι, to introduce a subject for an oracular response, Ion 335, Hel. 146. In Or. 53 (πρὸς Νικοστρ.), § 13, προξενεῖν τινα is used as above.

ΠΡΟΣ ΠΑΝΤΑΙΝΕΤΟΝ.

θεῖν δ' ἔφη τούτους βούλεσθαι πρὸς ἡμᾶς, καὶ συνάξειν αὐτὸς ἡμᾶς, καὶ παραινέσειν τούτῳ πάντα ποιεῖν τὰ δίκαια ἐμοί, καὶ οἴεσθαι πείσειν. ὡς δὲ συνήλθομεν, 12 τὰ μὲν πολλὰ τί δεῖ λέγειν; ἧκον δ' οἱ δεδανεικέναι φάσκοντες τούτῳ ἐπὶ τῷ ἐργαστηρίῳ καὶ τοῖς ἀνδραπόδοις, ἃ ἡμεῖς ἐπριάμεθα παρὰ Μνησικλέους, καὶ οὐδὲν ἦν ἁπλοῦν οὐδ' ὑγιὲς τούτων. πάντα δ' ἐξελεγχόμενοι ψευδῆ λέγοντες, καὶ τοῦ Μνησικλέους βεβαι-
970 οῦντος ἡμῖν, προκαλοῦνται πρόκλησιν ἡμᾶς ὡς οὔ δεξομένους, ἢ κομίσασθαι πάντα τὰ χρήματα παρ' αὐτῶν[g] καὶ ἀπελθεῖν, ἢ διαλῦσαι σφᾶς ὑπὲρ ὧν ἐνεκάλουν, αἰτιώμενοι πολλῷ πλείονος ἄξια ἔχειν ὧν ἐδεδώκειμεν χρημάτων. ἀκούσας δ' ἐγὼ παραχρῆμα, οὐδὲ βουλευ- 13 σάμενος, κομίσασθαι συνεχώρησα, καὶ τὸν Εὔεργον ἔπεισα. ἐπεὶ δ' ἔδει τὰ χρήμαθ'[h] ἡμᾶς ἀπολαμβάνειν καὶ τὸ πρᾶγμ' εἰς τοῦτο προῆκτο, οὐκ ἔφασαν μετὰ

[g] αὐτῶν Z.   [h] χρήματα Z.

τούτους] i.e. οὗτοι οἱ ἀμφισβητοῦντες, οὓς σὺ δέδοικας, βούλονται, ἔφη, συνελθεῖν ὑμῖν (πρὸς ὑμᾶς). Otherwise αὐτοὺς rather than τούτους would have been used.

§ 12. *Well, these claimants came, and affirmed they had lent money to Pantaenetus on the mine. As this was shown to be false, and Mnesicles confirmed us in the possession, they then proposed that we should get back our money from them (on cession of our rights to the mine), or (retaining the mine) pay them their claims on it; for the security was worth more than the money due on it (so that we might wish to retain it).*

διαλῦσαι σφᾶς] 'To settle with one,' is properly to 'untie him from his obligation.' Or. 30 §

8, διαλύειν μὲν ἡμᾶς 'Ονήτωρ οὐδ' ἐπεχείρησεν. — ἐδεδώκειμεν, sc. ἐδανείσαμεν Πανταινέτῳ.

§ 13. *Upon our assenting to receive our money, the claimants refused to pay it unless we sold them the mine; in which they shewed their sense, for they knew we were being vexatiously prosecuted by Pantaenetus.*

παραχρῆμα] 'On the spur of the moment, without even considering the matter.' It is clear that the claiming party, οἱ ἀμφισβητοῦντες, did not expect this result; their offer was not made bona fide, for they did not intend to pay Nicobulus his dues: in fact, their pretended claims seem to have been made only in collusion with Pantaenetus.

XXXVII. ΠΑΡΑΓΡΑΦΗ [§§ 13—16

ταῦτα δώσειν οἱ τότ' ἐκεῖνα ἐπαγγειλάμενοι¹, εἰ μὴ πρατῆρες γιγνοίμεθ' ἡμεῖς τῶν κτημάτων αὐτοῖς, νοῦν ἔχοντες, ὦ ἄνδρες Ἀθηναῖοι, κατ' αὐτό γε τοῦτο· ἑώρων γὰρ ἡμᾶς οἷα ἐσυκοφαντούμεθ' ὑπὸ τούτων ͡ʲ. ὡς οὖν καὶ ταῦτ' ἀληθῆ λέγω, λαβέ μοι καὶ ταύτας τὰς μαρτυρίας.

ΜΑΡΤΥΡΙΑΙ.

14 Ἐπειδὴ τοίνυν τὸ πρᾶγμ' ἐνταῦθ' εἱστήκει, καὶ τὰ μὲν χρήματα οὐ προΐεντο οὓς ἐπήγαγεν οὗτος, ἡμεῖς δ' εἰκότως ἐφαινόμεθα ὧν ἐωνήμεθα κρατεῖν, ἱκέτευεν, ἐδεῖτο, ἠντιβόλει πρατῆρας ἡμᾶς γίγνεσθαι ᵏ. ἀξιοῦντος δὲ τούτου καὶ πολλὰ δεηθέντος ἐμοῦ, καὶ τί οὐ

¹ ἐπαγγελλόμενοι Bekk. 1824. ͡ʲ τούτον Bekk. 1824.
ᵏ γενέσθαι Bekk. 1824.

οἱ τότε κ.τ.λ.] sc. οἱ ἀμφισβητοῦντες, § 7.
κατ' αὐτό γε τοῦτο] 'And on this very point assuredly they showed their wisdom,' viz. in not paying us the money without purchasing from us the absolute property in the mine, since a claim for damages was now being made, which might seriously affect the value of it. Inf. § 30 he says that 'no one would accept Pantaenetus as the vendor.' Of course, the ἡμεῖς preceding is emphatic.
ὑπὸ τούτων] This is rather obscure. The claimants saw that an action was brought against us (Evergus and Nicobulus) by Pantaenetus, and thought that if it went against us we might not have security to offer them. From § 30 it would seem that the purchasers thought they had a full power of sale; and the claiming party accordingly demand that the mine shall be sold to them if they advance the money due. Perhaps we should read ὑπὸ τούτου, for Mnesicles can hardly be included. Kennedy seems to have been nearly right in translating 'for they saw the pettifogging tricks which this man was playing up.' Sup. § 8. Evergus is said σεσυκοφαντῆσθαι.

§§ 14—16. *When the persons introduced by Pantaenetus (§ 11) refused to part with their money, i.e. to pay us, unless we sold the mine, he, the plaintiff, begged us to sell it to them; and at last I assented, wishing to get clear from one who showed by all his conduct that he cared for nothing but his own interests.*
ἐφαινόμεθα κ.τ.λ.] When it was clear that we were rightfully in possession of what we had bought from Mnesicles.
ἐμοῦ] The genitive after δεηθέντος. It seems clear from all this that the οἱ ἀμφισβητοῦντες were mere 'pretenders,' and that Pantaenetus wished to get

p. 971] ΠΡΟΣ ΠΑΝΤΑΙΝΕΤΟΝ. 107

ποιήσαντος; καὶ τοῦθ' ὑπέμεινα. ὁρῶν δ' αὐτὸν, ὦ 15
ἄνδρες Ἀθηναῖοι, κακοήθη, καὶ τὸ μὲν ἐξ ἀρχῆς τοῦ
Μνησικλέους κατηγοροῦντα πρὸς ἡμᾶς, πάλιν δ' ᾧ
φίλος ἦν τὰ μάλιστα, τῷ Εὐέργῳ, τούτῳ προσκεκρου-
κότα, καὶ τὸ μὲν πρῶτον ὡς ἐγὼ κατέπλευσα, ἄσμενον
φάσκοντα ἑορακέναι[1] με, ἐπεὶ δ' ἔδει τὰ δίκαια ποιεῖν,
ἐμοὶ πάλιν δυσκολαίνοντα, καὶ ἅπασι μέχρι τοῦ προ-
λαβεῖν καὶ τυχεῖν ὧν δέοιτο φίλον ὄντα, μετὰ ταῦτα
971 δ' ἐχθρὸν καὶ διάφορον γιγνόμενον, ἠξίουν ἀπαλ- 16
λαττόμενος καὶ πρατὴρ ὑπὲρ τῶν τούτου[m] γιγνόμενος,
πάντων ἀφεθεὶς τῶν ἐγκλημάτων καὶ ἀπαλλαγεὶς,
οὕτω διαλύεσθαι. τούτων δὲ συγχωρηθέντων οὗτος
μὲν ἀφῆκεν ἁπάντων ἐμὲ, ἐγὼ δὲ πρατὴρ, ὥσπερ
ἐδεῖθ' οὗτος, τῶν κτημάτων ἐγιγνόμην, καθάπερ αὐτὸς ἐπριάμην παρὰ Μνησικλέους. κομισάμενος δὲ τὰ
ἐμαυτοῦ, καὶ τοῦτον οὐδ' ὁτιοῦν ἀδικῶν, μὰ τοὺς θεούς,

[1] ἑωρακέναι Z.
[m] τούτου τινῶν Bekk. 1824.

a transference of the mine to them that he might regain possession of it. See on § 31.

15. πάλιν δ', κ.τ.λ.] Examples are given to show that further dealings with Pantaenetus were undesirable, and to account for the giving up the mine in order to get rid of him.

προσκεκρουκότα] Or. 39 § 18, πολλοῖς προσκρούει. In 54 § 3, προσκρούσματα are 'collisions.'

16. πρατήρ] 'If I became a vendor to them in behalf of the plaintiff's property.' Kennedy, 'if I withdrew and assumed the character of vendor in respect of his property.' The property really and bona fide belonged to Nicobulus and Evergus. But, as Mnesicles had originally bought it from Telemachus for Pantaenetus (§ 5), the claimants seem to have preferred to buy it as from the plaintiff, but conveyed to them by Nicobulus.—ἠξίουν—διαλύεσθαι, 'I required that I should come to a settlement with him.' (So Kennedy. Rather, 'I thought it best to come,' &c.)—ἐγκλημάτων, not that Pantaenetus had any real claims against Nicobulus, though he vexatiously prosecuted him. But Nicobulus knew his man, and guarded himself by this instrument against any future claims that Pantaenetus might make in respect of his former occupancy of the mine, even though, as he says just below, he never dreamed that a suit would be filed against him. The legal form, 'a discharge

οὐδ' ἂν εἴ τι γένοιτο[n], ᾠήθην[o] δίκην μοι λαχεῖν ποτὲ τουτονί.

17 Τὰ μὲν δὴ γεγενημένα, καὶ περὶ ὧν οἴσετε τὴν ψῆφον, καὶ δι' ἃ τὴν δίκην συκοφαντούμενος παρεγραψάμην μὴ εἰσαγώγιμον εἶναι, ταῦτ' ἐστιν, ὦ ἄνδρες δικασταί. παρασχόμενος δὲ[p] μάρτυρας, οἳ παρῆσαν ἡνίκα ἀφιέμην ὑπὸ τούτου καὶ ἀπηλλαττόμην, ὡς οὐκ[q] εἰσαγώγιμος ἐκ τῶν νόμων ἐστὶν ἡ δίκη, μετὰ ταῦτ' ἐπιδείξω. καί μοι λέγε ταύτην τὴν μαρτυρίαν.

ΜΑΡΤΥΡΙΑ.

Λέγε δή μοι καὶ τὴν τῶν ἐωνημένων μαρτυρίαν, ἵν' εἰδῆθ' ὅτι τούτου κελεύοντος αὐτὰ ἀπεδόμην οἷς οὗτος ἐκέλευσεν.

ΜΑΡΤΥΡΙΑ.

18 Οὐ τοίνυν μόνον ἡμῖν εἰσιν οὗτοι μάρτυρες ὡς ἀφείμεθα καὶ νῦν συκοφαντούμεθα, ἀλλὰ καὶ Πανταί-

[n] γίγνοιτο Z cum Σ.
[p] +τοὺς Z cum ΣrA¹.
[o] Bekk. ᾠήθην ἂν Z cum Σr.
[q] οὐδ' Bekk. 1824.

from all claims,' was one ground of the παραγραφὴ (§ 1), and it is here mentioned as such.

οὐδ' ἂν εἴ τι γένοιτο] 'I never imagined that, happen what might, he would bring an action against me' (Kennedy). The negative, οὐκ ᾠήθην, is separated from the verb by the strengthening clause or condition. So Eur. Hipp. 654, πῶς ἂν οὖν εἴην κακὸς, ὃς οὐδ' ἀκούσας τοιάδ' ἁγνεύειν δοκῶ; The ἂν, of course, belongs to λαχεῖν, but it is attracted, as usual, to the negative. See Shilleto on Thuc. 1 76 § 4, who remarks, "the desire of the Greeks to show as early as possible that a sentence is intended to be *contingent* in-

duces them not only to construct such sentences as οὐκ ἂν οἶμαι (δοκεῖ) εἶναι, οὐκ ἂν ἔφασαν, but even to place this anticipative ἂν in a wrong clause." The Greeks greatly prefer οὐκ ἂν γένοιτο τοῦτο to οὐ γένοιτ' ἂν τοῦτο, &c.

17. οἷς οὗτος ἐκέλευσεν] viz. in § 14.

§ 18. *The plaintiff himself, by omitting my name in his action against Evergus, is a witness that he has no claim against me. The charge is the same; and if both had been guilty, both would have been prosecuted. But, the case having been tried once, the law forbids it to be tried again.*

p. 972]   ΠΡΟΣ ΠΑΝΤΑΙΝΕΤΟΝ.   109

νετος αὐτός. ὅτε γὰρ λαγχάνων Εὐέργῳ τὴν δίκην εἴασεν ἐμέ, τότ' ἐμαρτύρει οὗτος πρὸς ἐμὲ αὐτῷ μηδὲν ἔγκλημα ὑπόλοιπον εἶναι· οὐ γὰρ ἂν δήπου τῶν αὐτῶν ἀδικημάτων παρόντων ἀμφοῖν[r] ὁμοίως ἐγκαλῶν τὸν μὲν εἴασε, τῷ δ' ἐδικάζετο. ἀλλὰ μὴν ὅτι γ' οὐκ ἐῶσιν οἱ νόμοι περὶ τῶν οὕτω πραχθέντων πάλιν λαγ- 972 χάνειν, οἶμαι[s] μὲν ὑμᾶς καὶ μηδὲν εἰπόντος ἐμοῦ γιγνώσκειν· ὅμως δὲ λέγε αὐτοῖς καὶ τὸν νόμον τουτονί.

ΝΟΜΟΣ.

Ἀκούετε, ὦ ἄνδρες Ἀθηναῖοι, καὶ[t] τοῦ νόμου λέ- 19 γοντος ἄντικρυς, ὧν ἂν ἀφῇ καὶ ἀπαλλάξῃ τις, μηκέτι τὰς δίκας εἶναι. καὶ μὴν ὅτι γ' ἀμφότερ' ἐστὶ πεπρα-

[r] ἀμφοῖν δ' Z cum Σ.
[s] οἴομαι Z. Cf. Veitch, Gk. Verbs, s. v.   [t] om. Z cum Σ.

οὐ γὰρ ἂν κ.τ.λ.] 'For surely, when the same wrongs were before the court, if he had the same charge to bring against both, he would not have passed over the one, and gone to law with the other.'

τῶν οὕτω πραχθέντων] When a legal discharge and acquittance has been given.

ἀλλὰ μὴν—τουτονί] Or. 38 § 4 ὅτι δ' οὐκ ἐῶσιν οἱ νόμοι περὶ τῶν οὕτω πραχθέντων αὖθις δικάζεσθαι, νομίζω μὲν ἅπαντας ὑμᾶς εἰδέναι, κἂν μηδὲν εἴπω περὶ αὐτῶν ἐγώ, βούλομαι δ' ὅμως καὶ τὸν νόμον ὑμῖν αὐτὸν ἀναγνῶναι.

καὶ μηδὲν εἰπόντος] i.e. κἂν ἐγὼ μηδὲν εἴπω.

καὶ τὸν νόμον] Either 'beside my assertion of the fact,' or 'beside the evidence read before.'

§§ 19, 20. *The law then forbids a second trial when the case has once been settled. This prohibition holds good especially in claims settled by consent; for to try these over again is not to* abide by one's own decision, whereas in a verdict on public matters, or actions brought by others, there may be some ground for alleging misdirection. (For the argument compare the whole of § 25 in Or. 36.)

19. ἀκούετε—εἶναι] Or. 38 § 5 ἀκούετε, ὦ ἄ. δ., τοῦ νόμου σαφῶς λέγοντος ἕκαστα, ὧν μὴ εἶναι δίκας, ων ἕν ἐστιν, ὁμοίως τοῖς ἄλλοις κύριον, περὶ ὧν ἄν τις ἀφῇ καὶ ἀπαλλάξῃ, μὴ δικάζεσθαι.

ἄντικρυς] For διαρρήδην, ἁπλῶς, in a plain and straightforward way.

ἀμφότερα] Though a distinction here seems made between ἀφεῖναι and ἀπαλλάξαι, it is probable, as Kennedy remarks, that they are virtually synonyms, and that this formula, which constantly occurs, arose from the surplus verbiage incidental to legal documents. [See, however, note on Or. 36 § 25, referred to *supra* § 1. S.]

γμένα ταῦτα τούτῳ πρὸς ἡμᾶς, ἠκούσατε τῶν μαρτύρων. ἁπάντων μὲν τοίνυν τῶν ἐν τοῖς νόμοις ἀπειρημένων οὐ προσήκει δικάζεσθαι, ἥκιστα[u] δὲ τούτων. ἃ μὲν γὰρ τὸ δημόσιον πέπρακεν[v], ἔχοι τις ἂν εἰπεῖν ὡς
20 ἀδίκως ἦ[w] οὐ προσήκοντα πέπρακεν[v]· καὶ περὶ ὧν ἔγνω τὸ δικαστήριον, ἔστιν εἰπεῖν ὡς ἐξαπατηθὲν τοῦτ' ἐποίησε, καὶ περὶ τῶν ἄλλων τῶν ἐν τῷ νόμῳ καθ' ἑκάστου γένοιτ' ἄν τις εἰκότως λόγος. ἃ δ' αὐτὸς ἐπείσθη καὶ ἀφῆκεν, οὐκ ἔνι δήπουθεν εἰπεῖν οὐδ' αὐτὸν αἰτιάσασθαι ὡς οὐ δικαίως ταῦτ' ἐποίησεν. οἱ μὲν οὖν παρά τι τῶν ἄλλων τούτων δικαζόμενοι τοῖς ὑφ' ἑτέρων δικαίοις ὡρισμένοις οὐκ ἐμμένουσιν, ὁ δ' ὧν ἂν ἀφῇ πάλιν λαγχάνων τοῖς ὑφ' ἑαυτοῦ. διὸ πάντων μάλιστ' ἄξιον τούτοις χαλεπαίνειν.

[u] οὐχ ἥκιστα Bekk. 1824.
[v] Z et Dindf. cum Σ (Cf. Or. 24 § 54 τὸ δημόσιον ἀπέδοτο). πέπραχεν Bekk.   [w] om. Z cum Σ.

τούτῳ πρὸς ἡμᾶς] See Or. 34 § 36, Sup. § 6.
ἁπάντων, κ.τ.λ.] 'In no cases where the laws have forbidden it, ought people to sue, but especially not in these. Of things done by public authority it may be said, that they have been done unjustly or improperly;' Kennedy;—who seems to have followed Bekker's reading πέπραχεν. Of course πέπρακεν is from πιπράσκω, and means that perhaps the state 'has sold what did not really belong to it.'
20. καὶ περὶ τῶν ἄλλων] 'And, with respect to the other cases mentioned in the law, a plausible objection may be raised to every one of them.' Kennedy.
αὐτός] i.e. τις in ἔχοι τις ἂν εἰπεῖν.—οὐκ ἔνι, οὐκ ἔνεστιν ἐν τῷ πράγματι, 'the very nature of the case does not allow him to charge himself with injustice.' For this would be ἑκόντα ἀδικεῖσθαι, which Aristotle (in Eth. Nic. v) shows to be barely possible. Kennedy rather quaintly renders it, 'it does not lie in his mouth surely, to object to his own act, and charge himself with injustice.'—παρά τι, contrary to what is prescribed in other matters than such as are settled by himself. (Or perhaps, 'For any of these other reasons'.) The sentiment here is similarly expressed in Or. 36 § 25.
τοῖς ὑφ' ἑαυτοῦ] sc. ὡρισμένοις οὐκ ἐμμένει, 'He who brings an action again for claims of which he has given a discharge, fails to abide by his own act.'

p. 973] ΠΡΟΣ ΠΑΝΤΑΙΝΕΤΟΝ. 111

Οὐκοῦν ὡς μὲν ἀφῆκέ με πάντων, ὅτε ἐγιγνόμην 21
τῶν ἀνδραπόδων πρατήρ, ἐπέδειξα· ὅτι δ' οὐκ ἐῶσιν
οἱ νόμοι τούτων εἶναι δίκας, ἀκηκόατε ἀρτίως ἀναγι-
γνωσκομένου τοῦ νόμου. ἵνα δ', ὦ ἄνδρες Ἀθηναῖοι,
μή τις οἴηται τοῖς περὶ τῶν πραγμάτων αὐτῶν δικαίοις ἁλισκόμενόν με ἐπὶ τοῦτο ἀποχωρεῖν, καὶ καθ' ἕκαστον ὧν ἐγκαλεῖ βούλομαι δεῖξαι αὐτὸν ψευδόμενον.
λέγε δ' αὐτὸ τὸ ἔγκλημα, ὅ μοι δικάζεται. 22

973   ΕΓΚΛΗΜΑ.

["Εβλαψέ με Νικόβουλος ἐπιβουλεύσας ἐμοὶ καὶ
τῇ οὐσίᾳ τῇ ἐμῇ, ἀφελέσθαι κελεύσας Ἀντιγένην[x] τὸν
ἑαυτοῦ οἰκέτην τὸ ἀργύριον τοῦ ἐμοῦ οἰκέτου, ὃ ἔφερε
καταβολὴν τῇ πόλει τοῦ μετάλλου, ὃ ἐγὼ ἐπριάμην
ἐνενήκοντα μνῶν, καὶ αἴτιος ἐμοὶ γενόμενος ἐγγραφῆναι
τὸ διπλοῦν τῷ δημοσίῳ.]
Ἐπίσχες. ταυτὶ πάντα, ἃ νῦν ἐγκέκληκεν ἐμοὶ, 23

[x] Ἀντιγένη Ζ.

21. ἵνα δὲ κ.τ.λ.] 'That none of you may suppose that I have recourse to this plea because I have the worst of it on the merits of the case.' Kennedy. Cf. Plat. Theaet. p. 179 B, ἐκείνη μοι δοκεῖ, ὦ Σώκρατες, μάλιστα ἁλίσκεσθαι ὁ λόγος, ἁλισκόμενος καὶ ταύτῃ.

22., ὃ ἐγὼ] 'which I the plaintiff had bought for ninety minae.' Kennedy thinks that this sum was due to the state from Telemachus, the original purchaser of the mine (§ 5), but not paid till after the transfer, and perhaps from the profits of working the mine. Boeckh (Dissert., &c. p. 645) remarks on this, "The state granted to private individuals the mines in the Athenian territory on perpetual leases, which might be transferred to a third person by inheritance or sale, and in short by every kind of legal conveyance. The possession was therefore obtained by the payment of a sum of money once for all, as purchase or entrance money." On τὸ διπλοῦν, see Andocides quoted in the note on l. 30 of the ὑπόθεσις. Or. 21 § 43 διπλοῦν τὸ βλάβος ἐκτίνειν, and διπλᾶ τὰ ἁμάρτια Aesch. Ag. 520 (P.). Boeckh, III viii p. 338 = 449 trans. Lamb.

§ 23. *The very same charges he before brought against Evergus, and obtained a verdict. That I was absent when the plaintiff quarrelled with him, I have already proved, and the fact is clear from the charge itself; for he does not say that I did it, only that I ordered a*

πρότερον τὸν Εὔεργον αἰτιασάμενος τὴν δίκην εἷλεν. μεμαρτύρηται μὲν δὴ καὶ ἐν ἀρχῇ μοι τοῦ λόγου πρὸς ὑμᾶς ὡς ἀπεδήμουν, ὅτε τούτοις αἱ πρὸς ἀλλήλους ἐγίγνοντο διαφοραί· οὐ μὴν ἀλλὰ καὶ ἐκ τοῦ ἐγκλήματος τούτου δῆλόν ἐστιν. οὐδαμοῦ γὰρ ὡς ἐγώ τι πεποίηκα τούτων ἔγραψεν, ἀλλ' ὑπογράψας ἐπιβουλεῦσαί με αὐτῷ[y] καὶ τῇ οὐσίᾳ προστάξαι μέ[z] φησι τῷ παιδὶ ταῦτα ποιεῖν, ψευδόμενος· πῶς γὰρ ἐγὼ προσέταξα, ὃς ὅτε ἐξέπλεον τῶν γενησομένων ἐνταῦθ' οὐδ'
24 ὁτιοῦν δήπουθεν ᾔδειν; εἶτα καὶ πόση μωρία, λέγοντα ὡς ἐπεβούλευον ἀτιμῶσαι καὶ τὰ ἔσχατα πρᾶξαι, οἰκέτῃ με ταῦτα προστάξαι γεγραφέναι, ἃ οὐδὲ πολίτης πολίτην δύναιτ' ἂν ποιῆσαι; τί οὖν ἐστι τοῦτο;

[y] αὐτῷ Z.   [z] om. Z cum FΣΦ.

slave to do it. But how could even that be, when I could not possibly have foretold what would happen when I left Athens?
αἱ πρὸς ἀλλήλους] viz. Pantaenetus and Evergus.
ὑπογράψας] 'After premising.' Kennedy. Rather, perhaps, 'having made it a minor, or inferential charge.' Liddell and Scott explain it here 'indorsing it with the title of plot against him and his effects.'
ᾔδειν] The first person of the latter Attic. The older Greeks appear to have declined it ᾔδη, ᾔδησθα, ᾔδειν. See Cobet, Nov. Lect. p. 214. Photius: ᾔδη (ᾔδη)· ἀντὶ τοῦ ᾔδειν. The context seems to show that ᾔδειν is the first person in Ar. Vesp. 635. Cf. Or. 34 § 38, παρῄει n.
§ 24. *He says I laid a plot to disfranchise him. Why, that is more than one citizen can do* to another; much less therefore can a slave. The fact is, as I was myself absent, he was obliged, to make out any case at all, to lay it on my slave.
ἀτιμῶσαι] viz. by making him a debtor to the treasury, § 6. Besides ἀτιμόω, 'to make ἄτιμος,' formed from the adjective, like the Platonic ἀνομοιοῦσθαι, there is ἀτιμάζω, and the anomalous epic form ἀτιμάω, used by Soph. Aj. 1129, as ἀτίειν in the sense of ἀτίζειν is used by Theognis and Aeschylus (Eum. 540).
γεγραφέναι] 'To have written in the indictment that I bade my slave,' &c.
δύναιτ' ἄν] viz. since this could only be done by the state. There is a sort of quibble between the direct and the indirect agency. Kennedy does not well render it, 'which even a citizen would not venture to do to another citizen.'

οὐκ ἔχων, οἶμαι, κατ' οὐδὲν διὰ τὴν ἀποδημίαν εἰς ἐμὲ τούτων ἀνενεγκεῖν τι, συκοφαντεῖν δὲ βουλόμενος, ὡς προσέταξα ἐνέγραψεν· οὐδὲ γὰρ λόγος ἦν, εἰ μὴ τοῦτ' ἐποίησεν. λέγε τἀκόλουθον.

ΕΓΚΛΗΜΑ.

[Καὶ ἐπειδὴ ὤφλον ἐγὼ τῷ δημοσίῳ, καταστήσας 25 Ἀντιγένην[a] τὸν ἑαυτοῦ οἰκέτην εἰς τὸ ἐργαστήριον τὸ ἐμὸν τὸ ἐπὶ Θρασύλλῳ[b] κύριον τῶν ἐμῶν, ἀπαγορεύοντος ἐμοῦ.]

974 Ἐπίσχες. πάλιν ταυτὶ πάντα ὑπ' αὐτοῦ τοῦ πράγματος ἐξελεγχθήσεται ψευδόμενος· γέγραφε γὰρ καταστῆσαι μὲν ἐμέ, ἀπαγορεύειν δὲ αὐτόν[c]. ταῦτα δ' οὐχ οἷόν τε τὸν μὴ παρόντα. οὔτε γὰρ καθίστην ἐγὼ ὅ γε ὢν ἐν τῷ Πόντῳ, οὔτ' ἀπηγόρευεν οὗτος τῷ μὴ παρόντι· πῶς γάρ; πῶς οὖν εἰς ἀνάγκην ἦλθε ταῦθ' 26 οὕτω γράψαι; ὁ Εὔεργος τότ', οἶμαι, πλημμελῶν ὧν δέδωκε[d] δίκην, συνήθως ἔχων ἐμοὶ καὶ γνώριμος ὢν κατέστησε τὸν οἰκέτην οἴκοθεν λαβὼν παρ' ἐμοῦ φυ-

[a] Ἀντιγένη Z.
[c] αὐτόν Z.
[b] Θρασύλλου Bekk. 1824.
[d] ἔδωκε Z cum Σ.

εἰς ἐμὲ] Emphatic.
οὐδὲ λόγος] 'Not the shadow of a case.' Kennedy.
25. ἐπὶ Θρασύλλῳ] 'At Thrasyllus.' See Boeckh, Dissert. p. 619. A site so called from a monument of Thrasyllus, in the district of Maroneia. Harpocration quotes this passage, and adds Ἀττικὸν ἔθος ἀντὶ τοῦ ἐπὶ τῷ Θρασύλλου μνήματι.
[Aeschin. κατὰ Τιμάρχου § 101, ἐργαστήρια δύο ἐν τοῖς ἀργυρείοις, ἐν μὲν ἐν Αὐλῶνι ἕτερον δ' ἐπὶ Θρασύλλῳ. The site is also mentioned in an inscription in the British Museum (Elgin Marbles, cf. Boeckh, Inscr. Gr. 162). S.]
κύριον] 'To take possession of my (the plaintiff's) effects.'
ἐμὲ] The subject; 'That I set him there, and he protested against it.'
τὸν μὴ παρόντα] See on 34, 26, and inf. 28.
26. πλημμελῶν—δίκην] 'When he was committing those trespasses for which he has given satisfaction.' Kennedy. See § 7. This seems an admission that Evergus did exceed his rights in taking possession.
λαβών] 'Took my servant from my house, and placed him

114   XXXVII. ΠΑΡΑΓΡΑΦΗ   [§§ 26—28

λάττειν ὡς αὐτόν. εἰ μὲν οὖν ἔγραψε τἀληθὲς, γέλως ἂν ἦν· τί γάρ, εἰ κατέστησεν Εὔεργος, ἐγώ σε ἀδικῶ; φεύγων δὲ τοῦτο τοιαῦτ᾽ ἠνάγκασται γράφειν, ἵν᾽ ᾖ πρὸς ἐμὲ αὐτῷ τὸ ἔγκλημα. λέγε τὰ ἐφεξῆς.

ΕΓΚΛΗΜΑ.

[Κἄπειτα πείσας τοὺς οἰκέτας τοὺς ἐμοὺς καθίζεσθαι εἰς τὸν κεγχρεῶνα ἐπὶ βλάβῃ τῇ ἐμῇ.]

27   Τουτὶ* παντελῶς ἤδη καὶ ἀναιδές ἐστιν· οὐ γὰρ

* ἐπίσχες. τουτὶ Bekk. 1824.

at his own works to keep guard.' Kennedy.

πρὸς ἐμὲ] That he may so frame the indictment as to render me responsible.

εἰς τὸν κεγχρεῶνα] This probably means 'the granulating mould' (furnace or pit), i.e. the place into which the silver is run when smelted. It appears to have been dropped into water, which gives it a granulated appearance. (So it is often to be seen in the windows of our bullion-shops, and so, in fact, leaden shot is made.) Hence, probably, ἀργυρίου ψακὰς in Ar. Pac. 121. In Eur. Phoen. 1316, ἀσπίδος κεγχρώματα seem to be small round eye-holes in the margin of a shield, so-called from their supposed resemblance to millet-seed. Photius: κεγχρεών, τόπος Ἀθήνησιν (he means 'in Attica'), ἐν ᾧ ἡ ἀργυρῖτις ἐκαθαίρετο κέγχρος (f. ὡς κέγχρος). καὶ ἡ ἀπὸ τῶν ἀργυρείων ἀναφερομένη ἄμμος. Ibid. Κεγχρεών, Δημοσθένης ἐν τῇ πρὸς Πανταίνετον γραφῇ, Κἄπειτα ἔπεισε (sic) τοὺς οἰκέτας τοὺς ἐμοὺς καθέζεσθαι εἰς τὸν κεγχρεῶνα. Harpocr. τὸ καθαριστήριον ὅπου τὴν ἐκ τῶν μετάλλων κέγχρον διέψυχον. Boeckh, however (p. 638), thinks κέγχρος was a kind of dross or efflorescence, consisting chiefly of glazed lead that was got rid of in the refining furnace, thence called κεγχρεών. He identifies it with spuma argenti or lithargyrus and compares the χαλκοῦ ἄνθος (an efflorescence formed on copper when fused after the smelting) described by Dioscorides as κεγχριοειδὲς τῷ ῥυθμῷ. Publ. Econ. p. 640—6, trans. Lewis[2]. "The κεγχρεών at the silver foundries was in fact the foundry where the silver which had been already fused was refined: the impurity detached in this stage was called κέγχρος, and perhaps chiefly consisted of glazed lead; and here the silver was again cooled with water." There seems however little force in his remark (p. 641), "it is not at all probable that silver should have been fused in a granulated form," since this is certainly the practice now. We see something like it in what is known as "frosted silver."

§ 27. *The notion of my persuading (or bribing) the plaintiff's servants is absurd.* Why

μόνον ἐκ τοῦ προκαλεῖσθαι τούτους παραδοῦναι, τοῦτον δὲ μὴ ἐθέλειν, ἀλλὰ καὶ ἐκ πάντων δῆλόν ἐστι ψεῦδος ὄν. τίνος γὰρ ἕνεκ' ἔπειθον[f]; ἵνα νὴ Δί' αὐτοὺς κτήσωμαι. ἀλλ' αἱρέσεώς μοι δοθείσης ἢ ἔχειν ἢ κομίσασθαι τὰ ἐμαυτοῦ, εἱλόμην κομίσασθαι, καὶ ταῦτα μεμαρτύρηται. λέγε δὲ[g] τὴν πρόκλησιν ὅμως.

ΠΡΟΚΛΗΣΙΣ.

Ταύτην τοίνυν οὐχὶ δεξάμενος τὴν πρόκλησιν, 28 ἀλλὰ φυγών, σκέψασθε οἷον εὐθέως μετὰ τοῦτ' ἐγκαλεῖ. λέγε τὸ ἐχόμενον.

ΕΓΚΛΗΜΑ.

[Καὶ κατεργασάμενος τὴν ἀργυρῖτιν, ἣν οἱ ἐμοὶ οἰκέται εἰργάσαντο, καὶ ἔχων τὸ ἀργύριον τὸ[h] ἐκ ταύτης τῆς ἀργυρίτιδος.]

975   Πάλιν[i] ταῦτα πῶς ἔνεστ' ἐμοὶ πεπρᾶχθαι τῷ μὴ

[f] 'edendum est...καὶ ἔπειθον; ut in tali re usitatum est dicere.' Cobet, nov. lect. 606.

[g] δὴ Z cum FΣΦB. δὲ Bekk.

[h] om. Z.   [i] ἐπίσχες. πάλιν Bekk. 1824.

should I? When the offer was made to me either to be paid or to take the slaves, I preferred to be paid (§ 12).

ἐκ τοῦ προκαλεῖσθαι] 'From my having proposed to him to give over to me these slaves of his, and his being unwilling to do so.' Nicobulus would seem to have proposed that Pantaenetus' slaves should be interrogated by torture whether Nicobulus had given them any orders on the subject. See on § 40, where the surrender of a slave by Nicobulus is proposed on the other side.

εἱλόμην κομίσασθαι] See § 13.

28. κατεργασάμενος] 'By reducing (for his own use) the silver-ore which my servants had dug, and keeping the bullion smelted from it.' Hesychius confounds ἀργυρῖτις with ἀργυρίτης when he explains the latter by ἡ ἐκ τῶν ἀναργύρων μετάλλων γῆ. Whether it was sand, or soft earth, or (as Kennedy thinks) stony ore, seems uncertain. The word is used rather often in Xenophon's treatise on Revenues. See Boeckh, Publ. Econ. p. 637, 624, &c. trans. Lewis[2].

πάλιν] 'I ask again, how is it possible that these things should have been done by me, and also (or, any more than) those for which you got a verdict against Evergus?' The

8—2

παρόντι, καὶ περὶ ὧν Εὐέργου κατεδικάσω; λέγε δ᾽
αὐτὸ τὸ ἔγκλημα ἑξῆς[1].

ΕΓΚΛΗΜΑ.

29 [Καὶ ἀποδόμενος τὸ ἐργαστήριον τὸ ἐμὸν καὶ τοὺς
οἰκέτας παρὰ τὰς συνθήκας, ἃς ἔθετο πρὸς ἐμέ[k]].
Ἐπίσχες. τουτὶ πολὺ πάνθ᾽ ὑπερβέβληκε τἆλλα.
πρῶτον μὲν γὰρ παρὰ τὰς συνθήκας φησὶν, ἃς ἔθετο
πρὸς ἐμέ. αὗται δ᾽ εἰσὶ τίνες; ἐμισθώσαμεν τῶν
τόκων τῶν γιγνομένων τούτῳ τὰ ἡμέτερα ἡμεῖς, καὶ
ἄλλο οὐδέν· πρατὴρ μὲν γὰρ ὁ Μνησικλῆς ἡμῖν
30 ἐγεγόνει τούτου παρόντος καὶ κελεύοντος. μετὰ ταῦτα
δὲ τὸν αὐτὸν τρόπον ἡμεῖς ἑτέροις ἀπεδόμεθα, ἐφ᾽
οἷσπερ αὐτοὶ ἐπριάμεθα, οὐ μόνον κελεύοντος ἔτι
τούτου, ἀλλὰ καὶ ἱκετεύοντος· οὐδεὶς γὰρ ἤθελε
δέχεσθαι τοῦτον πρατῆρα. τί οὖν αἱ τῆς μισθώσεως

[1] om. Z et Bekk. st.   [k] με Z cum Σ.

sense seems to be, 'how can I be guilty of acts of which Evergus was found guilty, when he was present while I was absent?' τῷ μὴ παρόντι may be rendered 'if I was not present.' See Or. 34 § 26, and Shilleto, not. crit. on Thucyd. i 118 § 2. So sup. 25, τὸν μὴ παρόντα, τῷ μὴ παρόντι, where the person is definite, but the event or the circumstances are regarded as contingent,—'how could I, when I was not there?' &c. With regard to καὶ, Mr Mayor remarks (p. 246), "it seems to join the two reasons why the speaker was not responsible for the proceedings complained of: 1st, he was absent; 2ndly, Evergus had been already found guilty."

§§ 29, 30. *The nature of the contract entered into between Nicobulus and Evergus on the* one hand, and Pantaenetus on the other:—*Pantaenetus was to have a lease of the mine at a rent equalling the interest of the money lent* (§ 3); *the property being ours by purchase at the express desire of the plaintiff. We sold it again to others, also at the plaintiff's request* (§§ 14, 16), *consequently the "agreement" is not with us, but with the owners of the property.*

29. τῶν τόκων] See § 5.
30. ἐφ᾽ οἷσπερ] 'On the same terms and conditions on which we had bought it.' But these terms are nowhere specified.—καὶ ἱκετεύοντος, see § 14.
οὐδεὶς γάρ] See § 13.
τί οὖν κ.τ.λ.] 'What then has the agreement of lease to do with the question?' Kennedy.—ἐνέγραψας, sc. τῷ ἐγκλήματι.

p. 976]   ΠΡΟΣ ΠΑΝΤΑΙΝΕΤΟΝ.   117

ἐνταῦθα συνθῆκαι; τί τοῦτο, ὦ φαυλότατ' ἀνθρώπων, ἐνέγραψας; ἀλλὰ μὴν ὅτι σοῦ κελεύοντος καὶ ἐφ' οἷσπερ ἐωνήμεθα αὐτοὶ πάλιν ἀπεδόμεθα, λέγε τὴν μαρτυρίαν.

ΜΑΡΤΥΡΙΑ.

Μαρτυρεῖς τοίνυν καὶ σύ· ἃ γὰρ ἡμεῖς πέντε καὶ 31 ἑκατὸν μνῶν ἐωνήμεθα, ταῦθ' ὕστερον τριῶν ταλάντων καὶ δισχιλίων καὶ ἑξακοσίων ἀπέδου σύ· καίτοι τίς ἂν καθάπαξ πρατῆρά σ' ἔχων σοὶ δραχμὴν ἔδωκε μίαν; ἀλλὰ μὴν ὅτι ταῦτ' ἀληθῆ λέγω, κάλει μοι τούτων τοὺς μάρτυρας.

ΜΑΡΤΥΡΕΣ.

Ἔχων μὲν τοίνυν ἣν ἐπείσθη τῶν αὐτοῦ τιμήν, 32 δεηθεὶς δ' ἐμοῦ τότε γενέσθαι πρατῆρα καθ' ὃ συνέβαλον ἀργύριον, αὐτὸς δυοῖν ταλάντοιν προσδικάζεται. καὶ τὰ λοιπὰ τῶν ἐγκλημάτων ἔτ' ἐστὶ δεινότερα. λέγε δή μοι τὸ λοιπὸν τοῦ ἐγκλήματος.

31. πέντε καὶ ἑκατὸν μνῶν] § 4. They had bought the mine for the sum they had lent the defendant. Here the defendant is said to have sold it again for more. The mine had been conveyed at his request to other parties (§ 14), but it is evident that Pantaenetus himself really had an interest in it, and that they were only what is called "cats'-paws," or nominal purchasers. (Boeckh, *P. E.* p. 671, thinks this was a legal, or not unusual, transaction.) The price he got, 206 minae, was as nearly as possible double what Nicobulus and Evergus had bought it for. It was therefore rightly called πολλῷ πλείονος ἄξια in § 12.

καθάπαξ] 'For the sale once for all,' 'for the complete conveyance.' So ἄτιμος ἔσται καθάπαξ, 'once for all,' 'for the single offence,' Mid. p. 524, § 32. Cf. inf. § 50. The sense is, the plaintiff would have no legal title to property which was mortgaged to others. Perhaps we should read in full, and with the accent of emphasis, πρατῆρα σὲ ἔχων.

32. ἣν ἐπείσθη] Which he was persuaded or induced to take, i.e. with no compulsion put upon him.

καθ' ὃ συνέβαλον] 'For the sum which I had lent.' Kennedy. Lit. 'according to the amount (45 minae) that I had advanced.'—δυοῖν ταλάντοιν, i.e. besides the large profits he had made by the sale, § 31. These two talents were for damages alleged, and the same sum in which he had convicted Evergus. §§ 25—8. Cf. § 50.

XXXVII. ΠΑΡΑΓΡΑΦΗ [§§ 33—35

ΕΓΚΛΗΜΑ.

33 Ἐνταυθὶ πόλλ' ἄττα καὶ δεινά μοι ἄλλα ἐγκαλεῖ· καὶ γὰρ αἰκίαν καὶ ὕβριν καὶ βιαίων καὶ πρὸς ἐπικλήρους ἀδικήματα. τούτων δ' εἰσὶν ἑκάστου χωρὶς αἱ δίκαι καὶ οὔτε πρὸς ἀρχὴν τὴν αὐτὴν οὔθ' ὑπὲρ τιμημάτων τῶν αὐτῶν, ἀλλ' ἡ μὲν αἰκία καὶ τὰ τῶν βιαίων πρὸς τοὺς τετταράκοντα, αἱ δὲ τῆς ὕβρεως πρὸς τοὺς θεσμοθέτας, ὅσα δ' εἰς ἐπικλήρους, πρὸς τὸν ἄρχοντα. οἱ δὲ νόμοι καὶ τούτων διδόασι τὰς παραγραφὰς ἀντι-

§ 33. *He also mixes up in his plaint charges that can only be properly tried in other courts.* (See on this subject the important passage in Or. 35, πρὸς Λακρ. § 47.) At this point of the speech a distinct ground for allowing the παραγραφή is discussed, viz. the mixed nature of the complaint.

αἰκίαν καὶ ὕβριν] Cf. Or. 54 § 1, δίκη αἰκίας...ὕβρεως γραφαί. The difference seems to consist in the latter meaning an outrage of any kind against goods or person (Mid. p. 523), the former being assault with battery, or intent to commit personal injury. For αἰκίζειν is properly 'to disfigure' by any kind of mauling or ill-treatment (Aesch. Prom. 467, 178, Soph. Ant. 206). Though ὕβρις also means 'rape,' it may be doubted if Kennedy is right in giving it that meaning here. Generically, it means 'lewdness,' e.g. Aesch. Suppl. 80, 102, but it is applied indefinitely to any brutal outrage. The allusion here is to the charge mentioned inf. § 45.

ὑπέρ] 'For the recovery of the same penalties.'

. *τοὺς τετταράκοντα*] The Forty are not often mentioned. Pho- tius explains it κληρωτή τις Ἀθήνησιν ἀρχὴ τετταράκοντα τὸν ἀριθμόν οἳ τὰς ἰδιωτικὰς δίκας ἐδίκαζον· ἀλλὰ τὰς μὲν ἄχρι δέκα δραχμῶν αὐτοτελεῖς ἦσαν δικάζειν· τὰς δὲ ὑπὲρ ταύτας τοῖς διαιτηταῖς παρεδίδουν. [They are mentioned in Isocr. de Perm. § 237 ἐν δὲ ταῖς τῶν τετταράκοντα (σανίσιν ἀναγκαῖον εἶναι) τούς τ' ἐν τοῖς ἰδίοις πράγμασιν ἀδικοῦντας καὶ τοὺς μὴ δικαίως ἐγκαλοῦντας. Cf. Dem. Timocr. § 112 δικαστὴς κατὰ δήμους (with Wayte's n.) and Meier and Schömann, *Att. Process* pp. 77—82. S.]

τὸν ἄρχοντα] The chief archon; cf. Or. 35 § 47, ἐπικλήρων καὶ ὀρφανῶν τῷ ἄρχοντι προστέτακται ἐπιμελεῖσθαι.

οἱ δὲ νόμοι] 'And the laws allow exceptive pleas to those charges of which the magistrates to whom they were preferred have not cognizance.' Kennedy. The sense is, that a demurrer is allowed for the mere fact of a case being brought before a wrong court. For ἀντιλαγχάνειν see Or. 39 § 38. The εἰσαγωγεὺς was one who lent his name and authority for introducing a suit, and thereby attested that it was brought *bona fide*. It seems also applied to the authorities

λαγχάνειν, περὶ ὧν οὐκ εἰσὶν εἰσαγωγεῖς. λέγε δ' αὐτοῖς τουτονὶ τὸν νόμον.

ΝΟΜΟΣ.

Τοῦτο τοίνυν ἐμοῦ παραγεγραμμένου πρὸς τῇ ἄλλῃ παραγραφῇ, καὶ οὐκ ὄντων εἰσαγωγέων τῶν θεσμοθετῶν ὑπὲρ ὧν λαγχάνει Πανταίνετος, ἐξαλήλιπται καὶ οὐ πρόσεστι τῇ παραγραφῇ. τὸ δ' ὅπως ὑμεῖς σκοπεῖτε· ἐμοὶ μὲν γάρ, ἕως ἂν ἔχω τὸν νόμον αὐτὸν δεικνύναι, οὐδ' ὁτιοῦν διαφέρει· οὐ γὰρ τὸ γιγνώσκειν καὶ συνιέναι τὰ δίκαια ὑμῶν ἐξαλεῖψαι δυνήσεται.

Λαβὲ δὴ καὶ τὸν μεταλλικὸν νόμον· καὶ γὰρ ἐκ τούτου δείξειν οἶμαι[1] οὐκ οὖσαν εἰσαγώγιμον τὴν δίκην, χάριτός τε ὢν μᾶλλον ἄξιος ἢ τοῦ συκοφαντεῖσθαι. λέγε.

ΝΟΜΟΣ.

Οὗτος σαφῶς ὁ νόμος διῄρηκεν ὧν εἶναι δίκας προσήκει μεταλλικάς. οὐκοῦν ὁ μὲν νόμος, ἐάν τις

[1] οἴομαι Z.

or magistrates who give formal leave to bring a suit before them; which in this case had not been done.

§ 34. *The plaintiff has contrived to strike out the plea just mentioned, which I had put in among others. Never mind; the law remains in my favour, and the jury, acting on it, will not fail to do me justice.*

τῇ ἄλλῃ] viz. ὧν ἂν ἀφῇ τις, &c., 19.

τῶν θεσμοθετῶν] The six junior archons, who appear to have generally presided in the chief civil court, the ἡλιαία.

τὸ δ' ὅπως] He seems to intimate that bribery or collusion of some kind had been employed.

ἐξαλεῖψαι] Timocr. p. 712, ταῦτα πάντα Τιμοκράτης ἠφάνισεν ἐξήλειψεν. Tac. Agric. 2, 'scilicet illo igne vocem populi Romani et libertatem senatus et conscientiam generis humani aboleri arbitrabantur.'

καὶ γάρ] 'For even from this'; 'from this also.' Inf. § 58, καὶ γὰρ ἀκούσιοι φόνοι καὶ ὕβρεις, 'for both manslaughter and outrage' &c. The meaning of this formula is too often overlooked; it very rarely, if ever, stands for the simple γάρ. See sup. § 5.—χάριτός τε ὤν, note the

ἐξίλλῃᵐ τινὰ τῆς ἐργασίας ὑπόδικον ποιεῖ· ἐγὼ δ' οὐχ 977
ὅπως αὐτὸς ἐξίλλωⁿ, ἀλλ' ὧν ἄλλος τοῦτον° ἀπεστέρει,
τούτων ἐγκρατῆ κατέστησα καὶ παρέδωκα, καὶ πρατὴρ
36 τούτου δεηθέντος ἐγενόμην. ναί, φησίν· ἀλλὰ κἂν
ἄλλο τι ἀδικῇ τις περὶ τὰ μέταλλα, καὶ τούτων εἰσὶ δίκαι. ὀρθῶς γ', ὦ Πανταίνετε· ἀλλὰ ταῦτα τί ἐστιν;
ἂν τύφῃᵖ τις, ἂν ὅπλα ἐπιφέρῃ, ἂν ἐπικατατέμνῃ τῶν

ᵐ ἐξείλλῃ Z.   ⁿ ἐξείλλω Z cum Σ.   ° om. Z.
ᵖ τυφῇ rA¹. ὑφῆι Σ. ὑφάψῃ FΦ.—τύφῃ Z et Dindorf.

change of subject: 'and that I am deserving of thanks rather than persecution.' Kennedy.
35. ἐξίλλῃ] See Or. 39 § 15. —οὐχ ὅπως, Or. 56 § 43.
ἄλλος] sc. Evergus, § 7.
§ 36. *The defendant has no right to be bringing a mining suit against me, and therefore I plead a bar to his action. The law has defined what charges fall under that head, and to none of these have I made myself liable in any way.*
ἂν τύφῃ τις] From Ar. Vesp. 1079, where Xerxes is described as burning Athens to 'smoke out' the citizens as if they were so many hornets, τῷ καπνῷ τύφων ἅπασαν τὴν πόλιν καὶ πυρπολῶν, it would seem that the misdemeanour here mentioned is either sending smoke into a neighbour's pit to retard or annoy his workmen, or stopping up the ventilation so as to cause bad air. In Mid. p. 568, § 167, we have mention of θυρώματα καὶ ξύλα εἰς τὰ ἔργα τὰ ἀργυρεῖα, which may refer to doors such as might be blocked or fastened up in the mines. Boeckh, who has another reading before him (ἐὰν ὑφάψῃ τις), says "we might either understand the burning of the wood used for supporting the mine, or the setting fire to the ores, for the purpose of undermining the pillars which supported the overlying mass, after they had become infirm." *Publ. Econ.* (p. 672, trans. Lewis²). But ὑφάψῃ seems due to a conjectural correction of the false reading ὑφῆ in Σ. [In a Derbyshire mine in 1833, a quarrel about the right of working a lode of lead ended in several miners being stifled to death with lighted straw. Annual Register 1834, p. 296. S.]
ὅπλα ἐπιφέρειν can only mean the making an armed attack; and it is likely that 'claims' were often made the subject of violent dispute. It cannot refer to the seizure of tools and instruments, as some appear to have thought (See Boeckh, *Dissert.* p. 667). [Among the customs of the Manor of Crich in Derbyshire is the following: 'No miner is to bring an unlawful weapon to the mines, and if it chance that a miner (or any other person whosoever) quarrels upon the mine and fights and draws blood upon the mine, he shall pay the sum of three shillings and fourpence before the sun set.' Bainbridge's *Law of Mines and Minerals*, p. 569. S.]
ἐπικατατέμνειν, like ἐπινέμε-

μέτρων ἐντός. ταῦτ' ἔστι τἄλλα, ὧν οὐδὲν δήπου πέπρακται πρὸς ὑμᾶς ἐμοί, πλὴν εἰ τοὺς κομιζομένους, ἃ προεῖντό σοι, μεθ' ὅπλων ἥκειν νομίζεις. εἰ δὲ ταῦθ' ἡγεῖ^q, πρὸς ἅπαντας τοὺς προϊεμένους τὰ ἑαυτῶν εἰσί σοι δίκαι μεταλλικαί. ἀλλ' οὐ δίκαιον. φέρε γάρ, ὅστις 37 ἂν μέταλλον παρὰ τῆς πόλεως πρίηται, τοὺς κοινοὺς παρελθὼν νόμους, καθ' οὓς καὶ διδόναι καὶ λαμβάνειν πᾶσι προσήκει δίκας, ἐν ταῖς μεταλλικαῖς δικάσεται, ἐὰν^r δανείσηται παρά τού τι; ἄν^s κακῶς ἀκούσῃ; ἂν πληγὰς λάβῃ; ἂν κλοπὴν ἐγκαλῇ; ἂν προεισφο-

q ἡγῇ Z.
r ἂν Z. s παρά του; τί δὲ, ἂν Z. παρά του; ἂν Bekk. st.

σθαι, without much doubt refers to encroaching on the oreground or 'sett' of another, μέτρον. A similar word is ἐπικαταλλαγὴ in Theophrast. Char. 30, αἰσχροκερδείας. Xenophon (de Vectig. § 27) contrasts τὰ κατατετμημένα with ἄτμητα μέταλλα. [Hyperid. Euxenip. col. 44, 17, φήναντος Λυσάνδρου τὸ 'Επικράτους μέταλλον τοῦ Παλληνέως ἐντὸς τῶν μέτρων τετμημένον...οἱ δικασταὶ...ἔγνωσαν ἴδιον εἶναι τὸ μέταλλον, where the boundaries appear to be the limits of the portion unallotted by the state to private individuals. Cf. also Pseudo-Plutarch, vit. Lycurg. ἔκρινε δὲ καὶ Δίφιλον ἐκ τῶν ἀργυρίων μετάλλων τοὺς μεσοκρινεῖς (sc. κίονας, the supporting pillars which also served as boundaries) οἳ ἐβάσταζον τὰ ὑπερκείμενα βάρη ὑφελόντα καὶ ἐξ αὐτῶν πεπλουτηκότα παρὰ τοὺς νόμους καὶ θανάτου ὄντος ἐπιτιμίου ἁλῶναι ἐποίησε. In the local customs of Derbyshire various fines are imposed for working out of limits, unlawful filling up of shafts, &c. Bainbridge's Law of Mines, p. 461. In the ancient mines at Laurium there have been found 'limit columns of the various allotments, with the names of their proprietors, and the prices paid for each; tools of the workmen, chiefly pickaxes; the niches in which they set their lamps, and the lamps themselves' (Murray's Greece, ed. 1884, p. 367). S.]

ἃ προεῖντό σοι] 'Which they had lent you on the risk of getting it back.' See § 14, and also 22.

πρὸς ἅπαντας] For all men wish κομίζεσθαι τὰ ἑαυτῶν.

§ 37. *It is absurd to suppose that, because a dispute has some remote relation to a mine, therefore a mining-suit alone will meet it. No, the ordinary courts will settle it; and 'mining-suits' are reserved for special and comparatively rare contingencies.*

παρελθὼν] 'Shall he pass by, or fail to appeal to, the general laws, and have his plaint settled among (or as one of the) mining suits?'

προεισφοράν] See Or. 39 § 9.

38 ράν μὴ κομίζηται; ἂν ὅλως[t] ἄλλο τι; ἐγὼ μὲν οὐκ οἶμαι, ἀλλὰ τὰς μεταλλικὰς εἶναι δίκας τοῖς κοινωνοῦσι μετάλλου καὶ τοῖς εἰς[u] ἕτερον συντρήσασιν[v] καὶ ὅλως τοῖς ἐργαζομένοις τὰ μέταλλα καὶ τῶν ἐν τῷ νόμῳ τι ποιοῦσι, τῷ δὲ δανείσαντι Πανταινέτῳ, καὶ ταῦτ᾽[w] ἀπειληφότι γλίσχρως καὶ μόλις παρὰ τούτου, οὐκ εἶναι δίκην[x] μεταλλικὴν προσφευκτέον, οὐδ᾽ ἐγγύς.

39 Ὡς μὲν οὖν οὔτ᾽ ἠδίκηκα τοῦτον οὐδὲν οὔτ᾽ εἰσαγώγιμος ἐκ τῶν νόμων ἐστὶν ἡ δίκη, ταῦτ᾽ ἄν τις σκοπῶν ῥᾳδίως γνοίη. οὐδὲν τοίνυν δίκαιον ἔχων οὐδὲ καθ᾽ ἓν λέγειν ὑπὲρ ὧν ἐγκαλεῖ, ἀλλὰ καὶ ψευδῆ 978 γεγραφὼς εἰς τὸ ἔγκλημα καὶ περὶ ὧν ἀφῆκε δικαζόμενος, τοῦ ἐξελθόντος μηνός, ὦ ἄνδρες Ἀθηναῖοι, ἐπειδὴ ἔμελλον εἰσιέναι τὴν δίκην, ἤδη τῶν δικαστηρίων ἐπικεκληρωμένων, προσελθὼν καὶ περιστήσας τοὺς

[t] ἄλλως Z cum Σ.   ὅλως Bekk.
[u] om. Z.   [v] εἰς τὰ τῶν πλησίων Z.
[w] αὖτ᾽ Z cum Σ.
[x] πρὸς δίκην Cobet, nov. lect. 609.

38. συντρήσασιν] Properly, συντετραίνειν is to make a hole into another hole, i.e. to make two holes meet. So in Aesch. Cho. 451, δι᾽ ὤτων δὲ συντέτραινε μῦθον may refer to words entering the double aperture of both ears; and thus the emendation δι᾽ ὤτων δ᾽ ἔσω τέτραινε, however probable, can hardly be regarded as necessary. See also Herod. II. 11, σχεδὸν ἀλλήλοισι συντεραίνοντας τοὺς μυχούς, used of two arms of the Red Sea that converge and join in one.

τῷ δὲ κ.τ.λ.] 'But a man who has lent money to Pantaenetus, and has had the utmost difficulty and trouble to get it back from him, is not to have the further infliction of being made defendant in a mining cause; most decidedly not.' Kennedy.

γλίσχρως] Lit. 'with greediness on his part,' i.e. wish to retain it if possible. The adjective properly means 'sticky,' κολλώδης, Hesych., hence 'importunate,' as in Ar. Ach. 452, νῦν δὴ γενοῦ γλίσχρος, προσαιτῶν, λιπαρῶν τ᾽.

§ 39. *One proof that the plaintiff was conscious of the weakness of his case against me, is a trick which he put upon me respecting the torture of one of my slaves, almost the moment before the trial was about to commence.*

περὶ ὧν ἀφῆκε] viz. which was forbidden by the law, § 19.

ἐπικεκληρωμένων] Like the Roman custom *sortiendi judices*,

ΠΡΟΣ ΠΑΝΤΑΙΝΕΤΟΝ.

μεθ' ἑαυτοῦ, τὸ ἐργαστήριον τῶν συνεστώτων, πρᾶγμα ποιεῖ πάνδεινον· ἀναγιγνώσκει μοι πρόκλησιν 40 μακράν, ἀξιῶν, ὅν φησιν οἰκέτην ταῦτα συνειδέναι, βασανίζεσθαι, κἂν μὲν ᾖ ταῦτ' ἀληθῆ, τὴν δίκην ἀτίμητον ὀφλεῖν αὐτῷ^y, ἐὰν δὲ ψευδῆ, τὸν βασανιστὴν

^y αὐτῷ Z.

and our phrase 'impanelling a jury,' the jury seem, in the age of Demosthenes, to have been selected by lot from the 6000 who were the constituted members of the law-courts. In the time of Aristophanes they drew a letter, A or B, &c., to indicate the court where they were to sit for the day; κληρώσω πάντας, Ar. Eccl. 682, who is speaking of public, not of special or private causes. In Mid. § 13, τὸν ἄρχοντα ἐπικληροῦν ὁ νόμος τοῖς χοροῖς τοὺς αὐλητὰς κελεύει. Whether δικαστηρίων here means precisely the same as δικαστῶν, or whether some courts were open while others were closed, appears uncertain. See Boeckh, *P. E.* pp. 235—6.

περιστήσας] *Cum se stipasset suis.*—τὸ ἐργαστήριον, 'that gang of packed conspirators against justice.' See Argum. init. So Ar. Lysist. 577, καὶ τούς γε συνισταμένους τούτους. Or. 39 § 2. Inf. § 48.

πάνδεινον] For he committed a fraud in altering the terms of a πρόκλησις that had been hastily and rather carelessly drawn up, § 42.

40. μακράν] i.e. the very length of it was confusing, and designed to deceive me.—ἀξιῶν, 'requiring that a certain slave who, he said, was acquainted with the facts, should be put to the question, and that, if the facts which he (i.e. the plaintiff) alleged were true, I should be bound to pay his damages without assessment; if they were false, the questioner, Mnesicles, should estimate the value of the slave.' Kennedy—who says "the account of this transaction is exceedingly obscure." It is plain however that Pantaenetus, who claims a large sum (§ 32) for damages done by or through the order of Nicobulus, here makes an offer to settle the case by torturing a slave belonging to Nicobulus, to find out if such orders were really given. If it should appear they were not, then damages are to be paid (assessed by Mnesicles, who is to conduct the inquiry) for any loss of time or bodily hurt resulting from the torture. This proposal might have been fair enough if a third party, Mnesicles, was allowed to conduct it; but it became unfair when Pantaenetus himself conducted it on purpose to extort evidence in his own favour. [See also Meier and Schömann, *Att. Proc.* p. 188, note 69 ed. Lipsius.]

ἀτίμητος, opposed to τιμητὸς, means 'unassessable,' or where the penalty or amount is fixed by law. In the other case it can be laid at the discretion of the jury. See Mid. p. 543, § 90.— ὀφλεῖν, 'that I should have to pay to him the sum charged in the suit' (two talents).

Μνησικλέα ἐπιγνώμονα εἶναι τῆς τιμῆς τοῦ παιδός. λαβὼν δ' ἐγγυητὰς τούτων παρ' ἐμοῦ, καὶ σημηναμέ-
41 νου τὴν πρόκλησιν ἐμοῦ, οὐχ ὡς δίκαιον ὄν· ποῦ γάρ ἐστι δίκαιον ἐν οἰκέτου σώματι καὶ ψυχῇ ἢ δύο ὠφληκέναι τάλαντα ἢ μηδὲν τὸν συκοφαντοῦντα ζημιοῦσθαι; ἀλλ' ἐγὼ πολλῷ τῷ δικαίῳ περιεῖναι βουλόμενος συνεχώρουν. καὶ μετὰ ταῦτα προσκαλεῖται μέν με τὴν δίκην πάλιν, ἐπειδὴ θᾶττον ἀνείλετο τὰς παρακαταβολάς· οὕτως εὐθὺς ἦν δῆλος οὐδ' οἷς αὐτὸς ὡρί-
42 σατο ἐμμένων δικαίοις. ἐπειδὴ δ' ἥκομεν πρὸς τὸν βασανιστήν, ἀντὶ τοῦ τὴν πρόκλησιν ἀνοίξας δεῖξαι τὰ

ἐπιγνώμονα] Aeschylus has γνώμων ἄκρος, and προβατογνώμων, Ag. 768, 1099. Hesych. ἐπιγνώμων, ἐπόπτης. The term was applied to the inspectors of the sacred olives (Boeckh, *P. E.* p. 305).

ἐγγυητὰς] Sureties that I would abide by the terms of the challenge.

§ 41. *I signed the challenge though I thought it unfair that I should have to pay so much for damages on the testimony of a slave, who might be tortured to death, and made to say anything. But no sooner was this done, than he makes another challenge, again to bring the matter before the jury, though it had in fact been quashed by the former challenge.*

ποῦ γάρ] 'It cannot be right that.' So Eur. Ion 528, ποῦ δέ μοι πατήρ σύ; Heracl. 369, ποῦ ταῦτα καλῶς ἂν εἴη παρά γ' εὖ φρονοῦσιν;

ἢ μηδὲν κ.τ.λ.] It was unfair that his risk should be nothing at all, supposing the result of the torture was in my favour. It would seem from this that in the case of a πρόκλησις, or challenge voluntarily accepted, no fine attended a failure in the case, like the ἐπωβελία in ordinary trials.

πολλῷ τῷ δικαίῳ] i.e. to have on my side a περιουσία, or more than the bare justice necessary for supporting my plea.

ἀνείλετο] It seems that, on cancelling or withdrawing an action, not for a frivolous reason, but by a πρόκλησις or some other way of settling it, the plaintiff was entitled to 'take up' or recover the deposit he had paid into court, the general term for such court fees being πρυτανεῖα. Ar. Nub. 1136. Vesp. 659. Boeckh, p. 345.

§ 42. *The challenge had been drawn up so hastily that I had made no copy of it on my part; and thus he substituted the words 'that I put to the torture' for 'that Mnesicles put to the torture,' &c.*

δεῖξαι] It seems to have been the custom to produce the document before the proceedings commenced, that both parties might consent to the course pursued.

γεγραμμένα καὶ κατὰ ταῦτα πράττειν ὅ τι δόξαι (διὰ γὰρ τὸν θόρυβον τὸν* τότε καὶ τὸ μέλλειν καλεῖσθαι τὴν δίκην τοιοῦτον ἦν· προκαλοῦμαί σε ταυτί· δέχομαι· φέρε δὴ τὸν δακτύλιον· λαβέ· τίς δ' ἐγγυητής; οὑτοσί· οὐδὲν οὔτ' ἀντίγραφον οὔτ' ἄλλο οὐδὲν ἐποιησάμην τοιοῦτον)—ἀντὶ δὲ τοῦ ταῦθ' οὕτως ὥσπερ λέγω πράττειν ἑτέραν ἧκεν ἔχων πρόκλησιν, ἀξιῶν αὐτὸς βασανίζειν τὸν ἄνθρωπον, καὶ ἐπιλαβόμενος εἷλκε, καὶ ἐνέλειπεν οὐδὲν ἀσελγείας. καὶ ἔγωγ' ἐνεθυμή- 43 θην, ὦ ἄνδρες δικασταί, ἡλίκον ἐστὶ πλεονέκτημα τὸ μὴ[a] καταπεπλῆχθαι τὸν βίον. ἐγὼ γὰρ ἐμαυτῷ[b] ταῦτα πάσχειν ἐδόκουν καταφρονούμενος τῷ ἁπλῶς καὶ ὡς πέφυκα ζῆν, καὶ δίκην διδόναι παμμεγέθη ταῦτ' ἀνε-

* om. Z et Bekk. st. cum FΣΦB.   τὸν τότε Bekk. 1824.
* om. Z et Bekk.   καταπεπλάσθαι Emperius laudatus in Bekk. st.
  [b] ἐμαυτὸν Z.

τὸ μέλλειν καλεῖσθαι] sc. ἐπικεκλ. τῶν δικ. § 39. The broken sentences following imply the haste and suddenness of the act, the time pressing, as the plaintiff very well knew. Plautus, Rudens, 171; 'at in vado est: iam facile enabit: eugepae: salva est: evasit ex aqua: iam in litore est.'

τὸν δακτύλιον] The ring for sealing the challenge.

ἑτέραν] Not, perhaps, literally *another*; but the terms agreed on had been so altered that virtually it became another.

ἀσελγείας] He perhaps acted or spoke to Nicobulus, on his protesting, in a rough or blackguardly way.

§ 43. *I now felt that it does not pay in life for a man to be too humble; it was from my own want of spirit and self-assertion that I suffered this wrong.* However, there was no help for it now, so I surrendered the slave to be tortured by the plaintiff himself.

τὸ μὴ καταπεπλῆχθαι] τὸ μὴ καταπλῆγα εἶναι (Arist. Eth. N. ii 7). 'The not being shy.' Kennedy quite alters the sense in translating 'what an immense advantage it is to intimidate people by your style of conduct,' and omitting the μὴ, which indeed is not found in the Mss. The manuscript reading is retained by Bekker, G. H. Schaefer and the Zürich editors. 'Quae sic opinor, vertenda: *quantum sit lucrum sycophantae ita vivere, ut alii metu eius percellantur.*' ut sarcastica sit notatio morum calumniatoris.' G. H. Schaefer. Or. 21 (Mid.) § 194, ὥστε κακῶς λέγων —καταπλήξειν ᾤετο τὸν δῆμον ἅπαντα.—μὴ is a conjecture due to F. A. Wolf, accepted by Reiske and Dindorf.

χόμενος· ὅτι δ' οὖν ἠναγκαζόμην, παρ' ἃ ἡγούμην δίκαια εἶναι, ἀντιπροκαλεῖσθαι, καὶ τὸν οἰκέτην παρεδίδουν. καὶ ὅτι ταῦτ' ἀληθῆ λέγω, λέγε τὴν πρόκλησιν.

ΠΡΟΚΛΗΣΙΣ.

44 Φυγὼν μὲν τοίνυν ταῦτα, φυγὼν δ' ἃ τὸ πρῶτον αὐτὸς προὐκαλέσατο ἔγωγε, ὅ τι ποτ' ἐρεῖ πρὸς ὑμᾶς, θαυμάζω. ἵνα δ' εἰδῆτε ὑφ' οὗ φησὶ καὶ τὰ δεινὰ πεπονθέναι, θεάσασθε. οὗτός ἐστιν ὁ Πανταίνετον ἐκβαλών, οὗτός ἐσθ'° ὁ κρείττων τῶν φίλων τῶν Πανταινέτου καὶ τῶν νόμων. οὐ γὰρ ἔγωγ' ἐπεδήμουν, οὐδ' αὐτὸς ἐγκαλεῖ.

45 Βούλομαι δ' ὑμῖν καὶ δι' ὧν τοὺς πρότερον δικαστὰς ἐξαπατήσας εἷλε τὸν Εὔεργον εἰπεῖν, ἵν' εἰδῆθ' ὅτι καὶ νῦν οὐδὲν οὔτ' ἀναιδείας οὔτε τοῦ ψεύδεσθαι

° ἐστιν Z.

ἀνεχόμενος] ὑπομένων. By patiently enduring all this impudence from him. He wished to be thought μέτριος and ἐπιεικής, but found himself despised as ἄψυχος.

ὅτι δ' οὖν] 'However, as I should have been compelled (lit. as I was being forced by the circumstances) to give a counter-challenge contrary to what I thought was right and fair, I did even offer to give up my slave.' If he had declined to act on this πρόκλησις, duly signed and sealed as it was, he would have had to make another on his part, and one which would have been equally against his own sense of right (οὐχ ὡς δίκαιον, sup. 41). For δ' οὖν, 'be that as it may,' see Aesch. Agam. 34, 217 (P.) Or. 56 § 10, πέρας δ' οὖν—ἐξαιρεῖται τὸν σῖτον, where δ' οὖν means, as usual, 'be that as it may,' leaving the truth of a previous statement undetermined.

44. ἃ τὸ πρῶτον] viz. that Mnesicles, not the plaintiff himself should preside over the torture.—ὅ τι ποτ' ἐρεῖ, I wonder what he will say for himself after being proved to have thus broken his own agreement.

θεάσασθε] 'He exhibits to the jury the slave, Antigenes, a feeble old man, not likely to have committed the outrages complained of.' Kennedy.

ἐκβαλών] See § 25.

§ 45. *To illustrate the man's recklessness in making charges, I will relate how he contrived to convict Evergus at the former trial. He accused him of coming to his house in the country and insulting his daughters who were heiresses, and who, had the story been true at all, would have got redress by appealing to the chief archon.*

παραλείψει. πρὸς δὲ τούτοις καὶ περὶ ὧν ἐμοὶ δικάζεται νυνὶ τὰς αὐτὰς οὔσας ἀπολογίας εὑρήσετε· ὅσπερ ἔλεγχος ἀκριβέστατός ἐστιν ὑπὲρ τοῦ τότ' ἐκεῖνον σεσυκοφαντῆσθαι. οὗτος γὰρ ᾐτιάσατο ἐκεῖνον πρὸς ἅπασι τοῖς ἄλλοις ἐλθόντ' εἰς ἀγρὸν ὡς αὐτὸν ἐπὶ τὰς ἐπικλήρους εἰσελθεῖν καὶ τὴν μητέρα τὴν αὑτοῦ, καὶ τοὺς νόμους ἧκεν ἔχων τοὺς τῶν ἐπικλήρων πρὸς τὸ 980 δικαστήριον. καὶ πρὸς μὲν τὸν ἄρχοντα, ὃν τῶν τοιού- 46 των οἱ νόμοι κελεύουσιν ἐπιμελεῖσθαι καὶ παρ' ᾧ τῷ μὲν ἠδικηκότι κίνδυνος περὶ τοῦ τί χρὴ παθεῖν ἢ ἀποτῖσαι, τῷ δ' ἐπεξιόντι μετ' οὐδεμιᾶς ζημίας ἡ βοήθεια, οὐδέπω καὶ τήμερον ἐξήτασται, οὐδ' εἰσήγγειλεν οὔτ' ἐμὲ οὔτε τὸν Εὔεργον ὡς ἀδικοῦντας, ἐν δὲ τῷ δικαστηρίῳ ταῦτα κατηγόρει καὶ δυοῖν ταλάντοιν εἷλε δίκην. ἦν γὰρ, οἶμαι, κατὰ μὲν τοὺς νόμους προειδότα[d] 47

[d] προϊδόντα Z cum Σ. προειδότα Bekk.

τὰς αὐτὰς ἀπολογίας] viz. the charge of αἰκία and ὕβρις, § 33.
ἐκεῖνον] scil. Evergus.
εἰσελθεῖν] This is illustrated by Mid. p. 540, § 79, εἶτα τῆς ἀδελφῆς ἔτ'· ἔνδον οὔσης τότε καὶ παιδὸς οὔσης κόρης ἐναντίον ἐφθέγγοντο αἰσχρὰ, κ.τ.λ. By the term ἐπίκληρος is meant an unmarried girl who becomes with her fortune the property of her nearest marriageable male relative. To open the door of the γυναικωνῖτις to admit a man, was to take an unwonted liberty; and this seems the point of the charge in the mock-trial Ar. Vesp. 768, ὅτι τὴν θύραν ἀνέῳξεν ἡ σηκὶς λάθρᾳ. Euripides pretends that he would exclude even women-servants, χρῆν δ' ἐς γυναῖκα πρόσπολον μὲν οὐ περᾶν, Hippol. 645.

46. We gain from this passage the important information, that the process before the archon in such cases was by εἰσαγγελία (Or. 34 § 50), and that no penalty attended the failure of the prosecution, like the χίλιαι δράχμαι in the ordinary courts. The meaning is, that if he could have sustained the charge, the plaintiff would certainly have preferred a court where there was no risk. See Boeckh, P. E. p. 357.

ἐξήτασται] This may mean, 'he has had the matter investigated,' in the medial sense. 'Not to this day has he ever appeared before the Archon.' Kennedy. (Mr Mayor, p. 246, regards the passive meaning to be the correct one.)

δυοῖν ταλάντοιν] This shows why he hoped to get the same amount out of Nicobulus, § 32.

§ 47. *Evergus would have easily got off if he had known*

τὴν αἰτίαν, ἐφ' ᾗ κρίνεται, ῥᾴδιον τἀληθῆ καὶ τὰ δίκαια ἐπιδεῖξαντ' ἀποφεύγειν, ἐν δὲ μεταλλικῇ δίκῃ,
περὶ ὧν οὐδ' ἂν ἤλπισεν αὐτοῦ κατηγορηθήσεσθαι, χαλεπὸν παραχρῆμα ἔχειν ἀπολύσασθαι τὴν διαβολήν·
ἡ δ' ὀργὴ παρὰ τῶν ἐξηπατημένων ὑπὸ τούτου δικαστῶν, ἐφ' ᾧ τὴν ψῆφον εἶχον πράγματι, τούτου κατεψη-
48 φίσατο. καίτοι τὸν ἐκείνους ἐξηπατηκότα τοὺς δικαστὰς ἆρ' ὀκνήσειν ὑμᾶς ἐξαπατᾶν οἴεσθε; ἢ πεπιστευ-
κότα εἰσιέναι τοῖς πράγμασιν, ἀλλ' οὐ τοῖς λόγοις καὶ
τοῖς συνεστῶσι μεθ' αὑτοῦ[e] μάρτυσι, τῷ τ' ἀκαθάρτῳ
καὶ μιαρῷ Προκλεῖ, τῷ μεγάλῳ τούτῳ, καὶ Στρατοκλεῖ
τῷ πιθανωτάτῳ πάντων ἀνθρώπων καὶ πονηροτάτῳ,
καὶ τῷ μηδὲν ὑποστελλόμενον μηδ' αἰσχυνόμενον

[e] ἑαυτοῦ Z.

the precise charge he would have to defend himself against. But a 'mining-suit' was trumped up against him; and as other counts (§ 45) were added to rouse the indignation of the jury, he was thus unfairly condemned.

ἔχειν] Here for δύνασθαι. With χαλεπὸν, ἦν is to be repeated from above.

ἡ ὀργὴ] The resentment they felt about the ἐπίκληροι.—ἐφ' ᾧ, κ.τ.λ. 'found him guilty of the charge upon which they sat in judgment.' Kennedy.

§ 48. If then the plaintiff succeeded in deceiving the jury before, will he scruple to deceive you now? Will he not rely for success on the false evidence of his good-for-nothing friends?

τοῖς πράγμασιν] The facts of the case rather than the mere assertions of himself and his witnesses.—συνεστῶσι, 'packed;' see § 39.

τῷ—κλαήσειν] 'In his being ready to cry.' This use of the future (τὸ ποιήσειν facturum esse, &c.) belongs to the later Attic, the Ionic form in -ήσω of κλαίω, or κλάω, common in the earlier dialect (τυπτήσω, χαιρήσω, βαλλήσω, &c.), being retained.—
μηδέν, κ.τ.λ. Cf. Mid. p. 537, § 70, τῷ μηδὲν ὑποστειλαμένῳ πρὸς ὕβριν. The term is perhaps military or nautical; probably the former, in reference to the withdrawal of troops. The origin of the phrase is however rather obscure. Hesych. ὑποστειλάμενος· ὑποκρυψάμενος, φοβηθείς.—ὑποστέλλεσθαι· ἀναδύεσθαι, δολιεύεσθαι, ὑποκρίνεσθαι.—ὑποστέλλεται· φοβεῖται, καὶ τὰ ὅμοια. In De Fals. Leg. p. 415, μετὰ παρρησίας διαλεχθῆναι μηδὲν ὑποστελλόμενον clearly means "without any reserve." Cf. Eur. Orest. 607, ἐπεὶ θρασύνει κοὔχ ὑποστέλλει λόγῳ. Possibly the primary idea was the 'tucking under' or 'cloaking over,' and so hiding

κλαήσειν' καὶ ὀδυρεῖσθαι; καίτοι τοσούτου δεῖς ἐλέου 49
τινὸς ἄξιος εἶναι ὥστε μισηθείης ἂν δικαιότατ' ἀνθρώπων ἐξ ὧν πεπραγμάτευσαι· ὅς γε ὀφείλων μνᾶς
ἑκατὸν καὶ πέντε καὶ οὐχ οἷός τε ὢν διαλῦσαι, τοὺς
ταῦτα συνευπορήσαντας καὶ γενομένους αἰτίους σοι
τοῦ τὰ δίκαια ποιῆσαι τοῖς συμβαλοῦσιν ἐξ ἀρχῆς, χωρὶς ὧν περὶ αὐτὰ τὰ συμβόλαια ἠδικήκεις, καὶ πρὸς
ἀτιμῶσαι⁵ ζητεῖς. καὶ τοὺς μὲν ἄλλους τοὺς δανειζομένους ἴδοι τις ἂν ἐξισταμένους τῶν ὄντων· σοὶ δ' ὁ
συμβεβληκὼς τοῦτο πέπονθε, καὶ δανείσας τάλαντον
δύο ὤφληκε συκοφαντηθείς. ἐγὼ δὲ τετταράκοντα 50

f κλαίησειν Z cum libris. *Cf.* Veitch, *Gk. Verbs.*
g προσατιμῶσαι Z. Or. 39 § 23.

something worn on the person. 'Relying on the whining face and the tears that he can assume so recklessly and so impudently.' Kennedy.

§ 49. *You, however, must not expect to move any by your tears, for you have acted most basely and fraudulently towards those who lent you money in your distress. You have not only cheated them by not paying, but you want to make them debtors to the treasury.*

δεῖς] The second person is rare, though the Greeks often say τοσούτου δέω, &c. See on Or. 40 § 22.

πεπραγμάτευσαι] 'From the shameful actions you have concerned yourself with,' or 'have contrived to bring about.'

ὀφείλων] See § 4.—διαλῦσαι, sc. τοὺς δανείσαντας. See § 12.

τοὺς ταῦτα κ.τ.λ.] 'Those who helped you to raise the ready money and enabled you to satisfy your original creditors.'

ἠδικήκεις] See § 7, τῶν ἐν ταῖς συνθήκαις ποιοῦντος οὐδὲν τούτου.

ἀτιμῶσαι] sc. ὡς ὀφείλοντα. 'To disfranchise him *besides*.' If, with the Zürich editors, we print this as one word προσατιμῶσαι, we must still translate the preposition as a separate word, as in Or. 39 § 23, πρὸς μισεῖν, 22 § 75, τοσοῦτ' ἀπέχει τοῦ τιμῆς τινὸς τυχεῖν ὥστ' ἀπειρόκαλος πρὸς ἔδοξεν, and Aristot. Eth. iv iii 24, πρὸς ὀφλήσει. Inf. § 56, we have δίκην προσοφλεῖν. S.]

καὶ τοὺς κ.τ.λ.] 'And whereas one may generally see those who borrow having to give up their property, now it is the lender to *you* who has to suffer this: he lent you a talent, and for that he has been condemned to pay two by an unjust and vexatious action.'

ὁ συμβεβληκὼς] 'The lender,' 'the maker of the contract.' So Or. 34 § 1, συμβόλαια πολλοῖς συμβάλλοντες, and inf. § 54. He is now speaking of Evergus (τάλαντον Εὐέργου, § 4).—δύο, see § 46.

μνᾶς δανείσας δυοῖν ταλάντοιν ταυτηνὶ φεύγω δίκην. καὶ ἐφ' οἷς δανείσασθαι μὲν οὐδεπώποτ' ἐδυνήθης ἑκατὸν μνῶν πλέον, πέπρακας δὲ καθάπαξ τριῶν ταλάντων καὶ δισχιλίων, εἰς ταῦτα τέτταρα, ὡς ἔοικεν, ἠδίκησαι τάλαντα. ὑπὸ τοῦ ταῦτα; ὑπὸ τοῦ οἰκέτου νὴ Δία[h] τοῦ ἐμοῦ. τίς δ' ἂν οἰκέτῃ παραχωρήσειε πολίτης τῶν αὐτοῦ[i]; ἢ τίς ἂν φήσειεν, ὧν δίκην λαχὼν ᾕρηκεν οὗτος Εὔεργον, τούτων καὶ τὸν ἐμὸν παῖδα ὑπεύθυνον εἶναι προσήκειν; χωρὶς δὲ τούτων αὐτὸς αὑτὸν οὗτος ἀφῆκε τῶν τοιούτων αἰτιῶν ἁπασῶν· οὐ γὰρ νῦν ἔδει λέγειν, οὐδ' εἰς τὴν πρόκλησιν γράφειν ἐν ᾗ βασανίζειν ἐξῄτει, ἀλλὰ λαχόντα ἐκείνῳ τὴν δίκην τὸν κύριον διώκειν ἐμέ. νῦν δ' εἴληχε μὲν ἐμοὶ, κατηγορεῖ δ' ἐκείνου. ταῦτα δ' οὐκ ἐῶσιν οἱ νόμοι· τίς γὰρ πώποτε τῷ δεσπότῃ λαχὼν τοῦ δούλου τὰ πράγματα, ὥσπερ κυρίου, κατηγόρησεν;

51

[h] νὴ τὸν Δία Z.   [i] ἑαυτοῦ Z.

50. δυοῖν ταλάντοιν] viz. for damages, § 32.—καθάπαξ, § 31. The sum mentioned in § 31 is 3 talents and 26 minae. Here he uses a round sum; see Or. 34 §§ 25, 41.

εἰς ταῦτα κ.τ.λ.] 'Upon this property you have sustained damage, as it appears, to the amount of four talents.' Two talents had already been got out of Evergus, and the plaintiff is trying to get two more out of Nicobulus.

παραχωρήσειε] 'Give up.' So in Mid. p. 523, § 28, εἰ δ' ἐγὼ—τῇ πόλει παραχωρῶ τῆς τιμωρίας. This seems little better than a quibble; according to the plaintiff, violence was used by Antigenes in taking the money (§ 22); but perhaps he refers to the occupation of the mine under protest, § 25.

ἢ τίς ἂν κ.τ.λ.] 'Who would say that, when Evergus has already been condemned for them, my slave was also guilty of the same acts?'

§ 51. *Besides, the plaintiff himself has defeated his own purpose by reversing the process he should have adopted; he should have charged the slave with the act direct, and made me indirectly responsible, as his master. But now he has charged me first, and then the slave through me.*

ἐξῄτει] Sup. § 40, ἀξιῶν ὃν φησιν οἰκέτην ταῦτα συνειδέναι, βασανίζεσθαι.

τὸν κύριον] 'His owner.' Very nearly the Latin *dominum*. Ar. Equit. 969, διώξει Σμικύθην καὶ κύριον. [Meier and Schömann p. 573, note 58 ed. Lipsius.]

ὥσπερ κυρίου] As if he had

ΠΡΟΣ ΠΑΝΤΑΙΝΕΤΟΝ.

Ἐπειδὰν τοίνυν τις αὐτὸν ἔρηται "καὶ τί δίκαιον 52 ἕξεις λέγειν πρὸς Νικόβουλον;" μισοῦσι, φησὶν, Ἀθηναῖοι τοὺς δανείζοντας· Νικόβουλος δ᾽ ἐπίφθονός ἐστι, καὶ ταχέως βαδίζει, καὶ μέγα φθέγγεται, καὶ βακτηρίαν φορεῖ· ταῦτα δ᾽ ἐστὶν ἅπαντα, φησὶ, πρὸς ἐμοῦ. καὶ ταῦτ᾽ οὐκ αἰσχύνεται λέγων, οὐδὲ τοὺς ἀκούοντας οἴεται μανθάνειν ὅτι συκοφαντοῦντός ἐστιν[j] λογισμὸς οὗτος, οὐκ ἀδικουμένου. ἐγὼ δ᾽ ἀδικεῖν μὲν 53 οὐδένα τῶν δανειζόντων οἶμαι[k], μισεῖσθαι μέντοι τινὰς ἂν εἰκότως ὑφ᾽ ὑμῶν, οἳ τέχνην τὸ πρᾶγμα πεποιημένοι μήτε συγγνώμης μήτ᾽ ἄλλου μηδενός εἰσιν

[j] + ὁ Z.   [k] οἴομαι Z.

any authority of his own, and was not entirely the tool and property of his master, who is responsible for his actions. 'Who ever commenced an action against the master, and charged the facts against the slave, as if he were his own guardian?' Kennedy.
§§ 52—4. *Unable to substantiate any real charge against me, he will descend to general platitudes against money-lenders; as if that were not in itself a proof that he has nothing better to say.*
·ταχέως βαδίζει κ.τ.λ.] Or. 45 § 77, τῆς μὲν ὄψεως τῇ φύσει καὶ τῷ ταχέως βαδίζειν καὶ λαλεῖν μέγα, οὐ τῶν εὐτυχῶς πεφυκότων ἐμαυτὸν κρίνω· ἐφ᾽ οἷς γὰρ οὐδὲν ὠφελούμενος λυπῶ τινας, ἔλαττον ἔχω πολλαχοῦ. Cf. infr. § 55.— Aristotle, in one of the touches that remind us of the *Characters* of his pupil Theophrastus, ascribes to the μεγαλόψυχος (Eth. IV ix=iii) κίνησις βραδεῖα καὶ φωνὴ βαρεῖα καὶ λέξις στάσιμος. S.]
βακτηρίαν φορεῖ] Theophrast. Char. 21 (Μικροφιλοτιμίας), δει-νὸς κτήσασθαι—βακτηρίας τῶν σκολιῶν ἐκ Λακεδαίμονος. From many passages in Aristophanes (e.g. Vesp. 33, Eccl. 74), as well as from the chorus in the Agamemnon who are said τρίποδας ὁδοὺς στείχειν (80), it is evident that sticks were commonly carried by the more aged at least. [Cf. Lysias 24 § 12, and Eur. H. F. 254; and see Becker's *Charicles*, I 159= p. 87 of English edition, and K. F. Hermann's *Privatalt*. § 24 12=p. 184 ed. Blümner. S.]
53. τέχνην πεποιημένοι] 'Make a trade of it.' Kennedy. From Ar. Eq. 63, where the same phrase occurs, it would seem to mean 'a crafty or cunning trade.'— μήτε συγγνώμης, 'who care neither for humanity nor for anything else but the lust of gain.' Kennedy. The reading seems in some way faulty here; either ἐπιμελεῖς εἰσὶν or φροντίζουσιν would represent the required sense. [The reading of the MSS is supported by the quotation of Priscian II 359, 22 Hertz: 'Attici συγγνώμης οὐκ ἔστιν οὗτος, id est *nemini dat*

ἀλλ' ἢ τοῦ πλείονος. διὰ γὰρ τὸ καὶ δεδανεῖσθαι πολλάκις, μὴ μόνον αὐτὸς τούτῳ δανεῖσαι, οὐδ' ἐγὼ[1] τούτους ἀγνοῶ οὐδὲ φιλῶ, οὐ μέντοι γ' ἀποστερῶ μὰ Δί'
54 οὐδὲ συκοφαντῶ. ὅστις δὲ εἴργασται μὲν ὥσπερ ἐγὼ πλέων καὶ κινδυνεύων, εὐπορήσας δὲ μικρῶν ἐδάνεισε ταῦτα, καὶ χαρίσασθαι βουλόμενος καὶ μὴ λαθεῖν διαρρυὲν αὐτὸν[m] τὸ ἀργύριον, τί τις ἂν τοῦτον εἰς ἐκείνους τιθείη; εἰ μὴ τοῦτο λέγεις, ὡς ὃς ἄν σοι δανείσῃ, τοῦτον δημοσίᾳ μισεῖσθαι προσήκει. λέγε δή μοι τὰς μαρτυρίας, τίς ἐγὼ πρὸς τοὺς συμβάλλοντας ἄνθρωπος καὶ πρὸς τοὺς δεομένους εἰμί.

ΜΑΡΤΥΡΙΑΙ.

55 Τοιοῦτος, ὦ Πανταίνετε, ἐγὼ ὁ ταχὺ βαδίζων καὶ τοιοῦτος σὺ ὁ ἀτρέμας. ἀλλὰ μὴν περὶ τοῦ ἐμοῦ γε βαδίσματος ἢ τῆς διαλέκτου τἀληθῆ πάντ' ἐρῶ πρὸς ὑμᾶς, ὦ ἄνδρες δικασταί, μετὰ παρρησίας. ἐγὼ

[1] +αὐτὸς Z cum ΣτΑ[1].   [m] αὐτὸν Z.

veniam. μισεῖσθαι—πλείονος. Sallustius in Iugurthino: homines multarum imaginum ac nullius stipendii (85, 10).' S.]
The sense of μήτε (as different from οὔτε) would, as usual, be given by the Latin *nihil curent* instead of *curant.*—δεδανεῖσθαι, i. e. δανείσασθαι.
ἀποστερῶ] As Shilleto remarks on Thuc. I 69, and as indeed is well known, this is not 'to deprive,' but 'to keep back from another what is due.' Our monosyllable 'to rob' renders it fairly well.
54. πλέων] See Or. 34 § 30. —εὐπορήσας δὲ, 'and who has lent at interest his small profits in order to accommodate his friends, and that his money may not be imperceptibly frittered away.' Kennedy. (More closely, 'from a wish not only to oblige, but to prevent his money from slipping through his fingers without being aware of it.')—εἰς ἐκείνους, why should he be classed with those others who τέχνην πεποίηνται?
σοὶ δανείσῃ κ.τ.λ.] A very hard hit indeed.
τίς ἐγὼ κ.τ.λ.] Here, as in Or. 39 § 25, τίς=ποῖος.

§§ 55, 6. *The evidence just read has shown that I am not a hard or dishonest man, though it happens that I walk quickly and you walk gently. I am sorry I cause annoyance to others, but I am what nature made me, and no man can alter that.*

p. 983] ΠΡΟΣ ΠΑΝΤΑΙΝΕΤΟΝ. 133

γὰρ οὐχὶ λέληθα ἐμαυτὸν, οὐδ' ἀγνοῶ οὐ τῶν εὖ πεφυκότων κατὰ ταῦτα ὧν ἀνθρώπων, οὐδὲ τῶν λυσιτελούντων
ἑαυτοῖς[n]. εἰ γὰρ ἐν οἷς μηδὲν[o] ὠφελοῦμαι ποιῶν, λυπῶ
τινὰς, πῶς οὐκ ἀτυχῶ κατὰ τοῦτο τὸ μέρος; ἀλλὰ τί 56
χρὴ παθεῖν; ἂν τῷ δεῖνι δανείσω, διὰ ταῦτα δίκην
προσοφλεῖν; μηδαμῶς. κακίαν γὰρ ἐμοὶ καὶ πονηρίαν
οὔθ' οὗτος προσοῦσαν οὐδεμίαν δείξει οὔθ' ὑμῶν τοσούτων ὄντων οὐδὲ εἷς[p] σύνοιδεν. τἆλλα δὲ ταῦθ' ἕκαστος
ἡμῶν, ὅπως ἔτυχε, πέφυκεν, οἶμαι. καὶ φύσει μάχε-
983 σθαι μὲν ἔχοντα οὐκ εὔπορόν ἐστιν (οὐ γὰρ ἂν ἀλλή-
λων διεφέρομεν οὐδέν), γνῶναι δ' ἰδόντα ἕτερον καὶ
ἐπιπλῆξαι ῥᾴδιον. ἀλλὰ τί τούτων ἐμοὶ πρὸς σὲ, Παν- 57
ταίνετε; πολλὰ καὶ δεινὰ πέπονθας; οὐκοῦν εἴληφας
δίκην. οὐ παρ' ἐμοῦ γε; οὐδὲ γὰρ ἠδικήθης οὐδὲν ὑπ'

[n] ἐμαυτῷ Z et Bekk. st. cum libris. ἑαυτοῖς Bekk. (1824) et
Dindf. cum Reiskio.
[o] οὐδὲν Bekk. 1824.   [p] οὐδεὶς Z.

τῶν εὖ πεφυκότων] 'One of those favoured in these respects by nature.' For a parallel to the whole of this passage, see Or. 45 § 77 quoted above, § 52 n. So strong was the Greek appreciation of τὸ καλὸν that they associated moral with merely physical qualities.—ἑαυτοῖς seems a necessary correction for ἐμαυτῷ, which would require τῶν λυσ. to be a genitive of quality in the neuter.

56. τἆλλα ταῦτα] These other qualities which are bodily and not mental.

ἔχοντα] 'Since one has it,' i.e. a particular form and shape assigned to him. [Ar. Vesp. 1457 τὸ γὰρ ἀποστῆναι χαλεπὸν φύσεος, ἢν ἔχοι τις ἀεί. S.]—οὐ γὰρ ἂν κ.τ.λ. '(and that he should have such is a necessity): for,' &c.

γνῶναι δ' ἰδόντα] 'Though it is easy enough to remark and criticise them in another.' Kennedy. Hesych. ἐπιπλήξειν· ἐπελθεῖν, ἐπιτιμῆσαι, ὑβρίσαι. He is supposed to refer to Il. XXIII. 580, καί μ' οὕτινά φημι ἄλλον ἐπιπλήξειν Δαναῶν. As however the explanations are given in the aorist and not in the future, it is probable that the present passage is referred to. The use is rare. In Eur. Or. 922, ἀνεπίπληκτον ἠσκηκὼς βίον, the variant ἀνεπίληπτον is derived from Hesychius.

57. τί τούτων] 'Which of these personal failings of mine affects the question between you and me?'

οὐ παρ' ἐμοῦ γε] 'Not from me, do you say? Of course not; you were not wronged by me, or you would not have given me the release, nor pass-

134 XXXVII. ΠΑΡΑΓΡΑΦΗ [§§ 57—60

ἐμοῦ. οὐ γὰρ ἄν ποτ' ἀφῆκας, οὐδ', ὅτ' Εὐέργῳ προῃροῦ λαγχάνειν, εἴασας ἐμέ, οὐδὲ πρατῆρα ἠξίωσας ὑποστῆναι τόν γε δεινά σε καὶ πολλὰ[q] εἰργασμένον. εἶτα καὶ πῶς ἂν ὁ μὴ παρὼν μηδ' ἐπιδημῶν ἐγὼ τί σε ἠδί-
58 κησα; εἰ τοίνυν ὡς οἷόν τε μέγιστ' ἠδικῆσθαι δοίη τις αὐτῷ καὶ ἐρεῖν ἅπαντα τἀληθῆ περὶ τούτων νυνί, ἐκεῖνό γ' οἶμαι[r] πάντας ἂν ὑμᾶς ὁμολογῆσαι, ὅτι πολλὰ συμβέβηκεν ἠδικῆσθαί τισιν ἤδη μείζω τῶν εἰς χρήματα γιγνομένων ἀδικημάτων· καὶ γὰρ ἀκούσιοι φόνοι καὶ ὕβρεις εἰς ἃ μὴ δεῖ καὶ πολλὰ ἄλλα τοιαῦτα γίγνεται. ἀλλ' ὅμως ἁπάντων τούτων ὅρος καὶ λύσις τοῖς
59 παθοῦσι τέτακται τὸ πεισθέντας ἀφεῖναι. καὶ τοῦθ' οὕτω τὸ δίκαιον ἐν πᾶσιν ἰσχύει ὥστε, ἂν ἑλών τις ἀκουσίου[s] φόνου καὶ σαφῶς ἐπιδείξας μὴ καθαρὸν με-

[q] μέγαλα Bekk. 1824.
[r] οἴομαι Z.   [s] ἐκουσίου Bekk. 1824.

ed by me when you resolved (were making up your mind) to commence an action against Evergus, nor required one who had done you the many grievous wrongs you pretend, to promise to sell you the property.'

ὑποστῆναι] The omission of εἶναι in this idiom is remarkable. So in Aesch. Eum. 195, κἄπειθ' ὑπέστης αἵματος δέκτωρ νέου. Shilleto has given some examples on Thuc. I 32 § 4.

§ 58. *But, if I had really wronged him ever so much, and if all he intends to say against me were true, this at least is certain, that worse wrongs have been condoned by others, and so made no longer actionable.*

καὶ γάρ] See on § 34.

ἀλλ' ὅμως] 'Yet in all these cases the law has appointed one limit and one end of the dispute in the settlement by mutual consent.'

§ 59. *The strongest case of this is seen in the law which acquits even a homicide if the dying man forgives him.*

ἀκουσίου] This, the manuscript reading, is more probable than Reiske's conjecture ἑκουσίου, which is adopted by Bekker, followed by Kennedy; for it is not likely that deliberate and intentional murder would be pardoned.—μὴ καθαρόν, that he is ἐναγής, or has contracted a guilt requiring formal expiation.—αἰδεῖσθαι, 'to show mercy to a suppliant,' is almost a technical term. [The whole of this passage εἰ τοίνυν—τὸν αὐτόν ἐστιν, and § 60 εἶθ' ὑπὲρ—καταλυθήσεται, is repeated almost verbatim—a practice not very uncommon with Demosthenes, in Or. 38 §§ 21 and 22, where the words ἂν ἑλών τις ἀκουσίου φόνου, κ.τ.λ. (though one MS the codex Bavaricus has ἑκουσίου)

τὰ ταῦτ' αἰδέσηται καὶ ἀφῇ, οὐκέτ' ἐκβαλεῖν κύριος τὸν αὐτόν ἐστιν. οὐδέ γ', ἂν ὁ παθὼν αὐτὸς ἀφῇ τοῦ φόνου, πρὶν τελευτῆσαι, τὸν δράσαντα, οὐδενὶ τῶν λοιπῶν συγγενῶν ἔξεστιν ἐπεξιέναι, ἀλλ' οὓς ἐκπίπτειν καὶ φεύγειν, ἂν ἁλίσκωνται, καὶ τεθνάναι προστάττουσιν οἱ νόμοι, τούτους, ἂν ἀφεθῶσιν, ἅπαξ ἁπάντων ἐκλύει τῶν δεινῶν τοῦτο τὸ ῥῆμα. εἶθ' ὑπὲρ μὲν 60 ψυχῆς[t] καὶ τῶν μεγίστων οὕτως ἰσχύει καὶ μένει τὸ ἀφεῖναι, ὑπὲρ δὲ χρημάτων καὶ ἐλαττόνων ἐγκλημάτων ἄκυρον ἔσται; μηδαμῶς. οὐ γὰρ εἰ μὴ τῶν δικαίων ἐγὼ παρ' ὑμῖν τεύξομαι, τοῦτ' ἔστι δεινότατον, ἀλλ' εἰ πρᾶγμα δίκαιον ὡρισμένον ἐκ παντὸς τοῦ χρόνου νῦν καταλυθήσεται[u] ἐφ' ἡμῶν.

[t] τῆς ψυχῆς Z.
[u] καταλύσετε Z cum B.   Sed cf. Or. 38 § 22 νῦν καταλυθήσεται.

support the reading adopted in the text. Cf. Or. 23, Aristocr., § 72, τὸν ἁλόντα ἐπὶ ἀκουσίῳ φόνῳ φεύγειν ἕως ἂν αἰδέσηταί τινα τῶν ἐν γένει τοῦ πεπονθότος, also ib. § 77. S.]

ἐκβαλεῖν] 'To procure his banishment,' contrasted with ἐκπίπτειν καὶ φεύγειν, infr.

οὐδὲ—οὐδενί] See on Or. 34 § 1.

τοῦτο τὸ ῥῆμα] "This expression, 'I forgive.'" Plat. Phileb. p. 20 B, τὸ γὰρ εἰ βούλει ῥηθὲν λύει πάντα φόβον ἑκάστων πέρι, i. e. that single phrase '*if you please*' does away with all fear in every one of these questions.

60. εἰ πρᾶγμα κ.τ.λ.] 'Your abolishing in our time a sound rule of practice established ages ago.' Kennedy. The defendant closes his speech with putting forward prominently, and by pointed examples, the legal efficacy of *acquittance* in barring further proceedings; and it is evident that this is the plea on which he mainly relies in bringing his παραγραφὴ against the claims of Pantaenetus.

ἐφ' ἡμῶν] The last two words are omitted in Or. 38 § 22, and indeed are hardly necessary, as νῦν is quite sufficient as a contrast to ἐκ παντὸς τοῦ χρόνου. Perhaps we should here read ὑφ' ὑμῶν, 'by your present decision.'

OR. XXXIX.

ΠΡΟΣ ΒΟΙΩΤΟΝ ΠΕΡΙ ΤΟΥ ΟΝΟΜΑΤΟΣ.

THIS speech turns on a point involving some curious questions in the rights of citizenship. It is primarily this: whether two sons of the same father, both enrolled as citizens, have a legal right to the same name. The civil disabilities resulting from it are described in detail; and although such difficulties could hardly arise with us, who use a plurality of names, the Athenian custom of describing a person solely by one name[1], with the addition of that of his father and *deme* (borough or parish), made it impossible, in such cases as election by lot to any office, or the appointment to any service, to know,

---

[1] "The peculiar system of the Romans enabled them to associate with the individual's name an intimation of his clan and his family. But the Greeks, without such help, endeavoured to make a single name indicate as much as possible concerning the individual's relationship. Thus a Mantias names his son Mantitheus, preserving one element of his name, and varying the remainder. This method was exceedingly common, as appears from the witness of epitaphs, such as Δημοφῶν Δημο- νίκου, Σωγένης Σωκράτους, Φιλοξενίδης Φιλοκράτους, &c.—Nor can it have been an accident that in Demosthenes' family there should be so many persons named from δῆμος. The name Demosthenes was borne by his father, Demon by an uncle and a cousin, Demophon by an uncle, Demochares and Demomeles by several of his kinsmen. We trace in this the democratic and political bias of the family." Rev. E. L. Hicks in *Nineteenth Cent.* no. 61, pp. 391, 398.

ΠΡΟΣ ΒΟΙΩΤΟΝ ΠΕΡΙ ΤΟΥ ΟΝΟΜ. 137

publicly at least, which of the two was intended. It is distinctly affirmed in §§ 32 and 40, that no Athenian citizen ever called two sons of his own by the same name.

To remove this practical difficulty an action is brought by Mantitheus, the son of Mantias, of the deme Thoricus, and of a daughter of Polyaratus (Or. 40 § 24), against his half-brother, by name Boeotus. This man was the son of another woman, Plango, who, though but the mistress of Mantias, was an Athenian citizen; and the citizenship descended to the progeny of ἀστοὶ on both sides, even without the legal form of marriage[1]. It appears from the speech that Mantias had, either in reality or in pretence, felt some doubts about this Boeotus, and another brother called, after the mother's father, Pamphilus, being his sons by Plango. Boeotus, however,—at what age is uncertain,—had been persuaded by his friends to represent himself as an injured man[2], and to insist on being recognised as the son of Mantias, and as entitled to the rights of citizenship. Mantias was reluctant, but an action was threatened to compel him. Unwilling, for some political reasons, to appear in a public trial, he endeavoured to settle the matter by πρόκλησις, i.e. by proposing that Plango should declare

[1] Adoption, or recognition of parentage by the father, was however necessary. Mr Kennedy assumes that Mantias must subsequently have married Plango; for he says, "had she never been more than a concubine, her sons could not have had heritable rights" (Introd. p. 253). That they did share in the property with Mantitheus, is clear; see § 6, and Or. 40 § 48. But it is not clear that this was not an arrangement effected by sufferance or compromise, rather than a positive legal right. The passage in Or. 40 § 9, οὐδὲ τῆς μητρὸς τῆς ἐμῆς ἀποθανούσης ἠξίωσεν αὐτὴν εἰς τὴν οἰκίαν παρ' ἑαυτὸν εἰσδέξασθαι, seems nearly conclusive against Mantias having subsequently married her.

[2] From § 18 it seems likely that he had enlisted popular sympathy; and this may in some degree explain the probable result of the trial in his favour.

on oath before an arbitrator, whether Boeotus and Pamphilus were her sons by Mantias or not. She had assured him privately that if the oath on the affirmative were tendered to her, she would decline to take it; and it had been further arranged, that a sum of money should be paid to her for so declining it. She, however, had unexpectedly sworn that they *were* her sons by Mantias; and thus Mantias was obliged to enter both sons in the clans (φρατρίαι or 'families'), according to the established rule of the *first* enrolment or registration of citizens' children, which usually took place at an early age. It was then that the name of Boeotus was given to the elder, that of Pamphilus to the younger son. However, before the *second* enrolment into the register of citizens (in the γραμματεῖον ληξιαρχικὸν) had taken place, Mantias died. Boeotus then, dissatisfied with the name (which, though taken from his maternal uncle, he pretended had been given him in contempt[1]), contrived to get himself registered as Mantitheus. The true Mantitheus resents this: he had, in filial obedience, recognised his half-brothers, taken them to live with him after his father's death, and acknowledged them as his co-heirs. But he insists on his sole right to the name of Mantitheus. Both in this and in the next speech, which is intimately connected with it, examples are given in which real inconvenience had resulted from the two having the same name.

It seems that Boeotus had founded his claim on his elder birth (ὡς δὴ πρεσβύτερος ὤν, § 27). Mantitheus does not affirm that he is himself older in years, but pleads that his registration in the phratry took place before that of Boeotus; and he contends that the precedence in being inscribed in the city register should be dated from that time.

[1] § 27. Compare the proverb Βοιωτία ὗς, in Pind. Ol. vi 90.

ΠΕΡΙ ΤΟΥ ΟΝΟΜΑΤΟΣ. 139

The precise age or period at which Boeotus procured his enrolment into his clan or phratry is not stated. It appears, however, that he was old enough to co-operate with (μεθ' ἑαυτοῦ κατασκευάσαι, § 2) a party who undertook the management of the affair. At whatever age an adoption took place, the registration in a phratry was required (Ar. Ach. 146; cf. Ran. 418).

That the plaintiff Mantitheus lost his cause seems probable from Or. 40 §§ 17, 18. It is there stated that Mantitheus brought an action against his brother by the name of Boeotus to recover the dower of his mother. This cause was given against Boeotus by the arbitrator; but he had denied that this was his name, and said that he was Mantitheus, not Boeotus[1]. This could not have been said,—unless in open contempt of court,—if he had been adjudged, in the present trial, to retain the name of Boeotus.

[Had the plaintiff gained his cause we may be quite sure that in his subsequent speech περὶ προικὸς (Or. 40) he would have expressly asserted that it had been legally decided that the name of Mantitheus belonged to himself alone. Further, in the latter part of § 18 of that speech, the suit περὶ προικὸς is described as directed against the defendant under the name of Mantitheus[2]. Hence Dionysius of Halicarnassus rightly calls the first speech πρὸς Βοιωτὸν ὑπὲρ τοῦ ὀνόματος and the second πρὸς Μαντίθεον περὶ προικός[3]. It may be interesting to add that, in

---

[1] οὔτε ἠντιδίκει τότε παρών, οὔτ' ἔφη με καταδιαιτήσασθαι τὴν δίκην αὐτοῦ· οὐ γὰρ εἶναι Βοιωτὸν αὐτῷ ὄνομα, ἀλλὰ Μαντίθεον. (Or. 40 § 18.)

[2] Or. 40 § 18 τὴν αὐτὴν ταύτην δίκην λαχὼν αὐτῷ Μαντιθέῳ...νῦν εἰς ὑμᾶς καταπέφευγα.

[3] Both speeches were carefully discussed by him in the lost portions of his treatise on Demosthenes. All that remains of that discussion may be found in his treatise on Deinarchus §§ 11—13, where he combats on chronological grounds the notion that the speech περὶ τοῦ ὀνόματος was written by the later Attic orator Deinarchus, and assigns it to the archonship

140 ΠΡΟΣ ΒΟΙΩΤΟΝ ΠΕΡΙ ΤΟΥ ΟΝΟΜ.

an inscription referring to a date shortly after B.C. 342, or at least eight years after the present trial, both the elder and the younger Mantitheus are mentioned with Pamphilus as heirs of Mantias[1]. The date of the speech is determined within narrow limits by the reference to the battle of Tamynae (§ 16 n.), which may perhaps be placed in the spring of B.C. 350. The trial probably took place in the autumn of that year[2]. S.]

of either Thessalus (Ol. 107, 2=B.C. 351—0) or Apollodorus (Ol. 107, 3=B.C. 350—49). A. Schaefer, *Dem. und seine Zeit*, III 2, p. 222 ff., and Boeckh's *Staatshaushaltung der Athener* (2nd German ed.) I, p. 680—1 =p. 675 trans. Lamb. See also Blass, *Att. Ber.* III 288, 416, where it is observed that Dionysius was misled by a false reading Πύλας for Ταμύνας in § 16, the former referring to the Athenian naval expedition to Thermopylae in Ol. 106, 4

=B.C. 353—2. Blass assigns the speech to the year 348.
[1] The inscription (as restored by Boeckh, *Urkunden über das Seewesen* X^d 4—12; cf. p. 380 f.) is as follows : Μαντ[ίας Θορίκιος], ταμία[s γενόμενος εἰς τὰ νεώ]ρια Κα- -[ἄρχοντος]· ὑπὲρ το[ύτου ἀπέδω]καν κλη[ρονόμοι] Πάμφιλος [Θορίκιος] ΗΗΗΔΠⱵ, Μαντίθεος Θ[ορίκ](ιος)- -, Μαντίθεος [Θο- ρίκ](ιος)- -. A. Schaefer, *u. s.* pp. 214, 220.
[2] A. Schaefer, *u. s.* p. 223.

XXXIX.

ΠΡΟΣ ΒΟΙΩΤΟΝ ΠΕΡΙ ΤΟΥ ΟΝΟΜΑΤΟΣ.

ΥΠΟΘΕΣΙΣ.

Μαντίας, εἷς τῶν πολιτευσαμένων Ἀθήνησι, γήμας γυναῖκα κατὰ τοὺς νόμους ἐκ ταύτης παῖδα ἐκτήσατο τὸν νυνὶ δικαζόμενον· προσῄει δέ τινι Πλαγγόνι κατ'

Argument. ll. 1—7. 'Mantias, one of those who had formerly held office at Athens, had married a wife according to the legal forms, and had by her a son, the same (Mantitheus) who now brings the action. But he had formed a connexion with one Plango, an Attic citizen, from a passion he had conceived for her. She bore him two sons, who on attaining their full age went to law with Mantias, claiming to be recognised by him as their father. Mantias pleaded against the claim at first, but afterwards adopted the youths, as no other course remained to him in consequence of an offer of his own which he had made to Plango, deceived by a solemn promise of hers.'

1. Μαντίας] A minor politician and public speaker. Cf. § 3, πολιτευομένου, and Aristot. Rhet. II 23, περὶ τῶν τέκνων αἱ γυναῖκες πανταχοῦ διορίζουσι τἀληθές· τοῦτο μὲν γὰρ Ἀθήνησι Μαντίᾳ τῷ ῥήτορι ἀμφισβητοῦντι πρὸς τὸν υἱὸν ἡ μήτηρ ἀπέφηνεν. The evidence of inscriptions proves that he was treasurer of the Athenian dockyards about 360 B.C., and concerned in the registration of vessels in the harbour of Munychia; at a later date (after 342 B.C.) his heirs had to discharge a debt incurred by him in those duties. (Cf. § 25, τίς ἦν χρηματιστὴς ὁ πατήρ.) See note 1 on p. 140, and Arnold Schaefer's *Dem. und seine Zeit,* III 2, p. 214. S.]

2. γυναῖκα] The lawful wife of Mantias was the widow of Cleomedon, son of the famous demagogue Cleon. Or. 40 § 6. S.]

3. προσῄει] Here the *plus-quam perfectum,* 'he had had connexion.' The name Πλαγγόνι is perhaps a ὑποκόρισμα, as the word means 'Dolly.' Hesych. πλαγγών· κηρινόν τι κοροκόσμιον. The fact of this woman being ἀστή, not δούλη or ξένη, made the sons legitimate, if acknowledged by the father, even if the marriage was not κατὰ νόμους.

142   XXXIX. ΠΡΟΣ ΒΟΙΩΤΟΝ   [Argument

ἐρωτικὴν ἐπιθυμίαν, Ἀττικῇ γυναικί. ταύτης δύο υἱεῖς
5 ἀνδρωθέντες ἐδικάζοντο τῷ Μαντίᾳ, ἑαυτῶν εἶναι πατέρα φάσκοντες· ὁ δὲ ἀντέλεγεν. ἔπειτα ἀναλαμβάνει 994
τοὺς παῖδας ἀναγκασθεὶς ἀπὸ ἰδίας προκλήσεως, ἣν
ἀπατηθεὶς ἐποιήσατο. προὐκαλέσατο μὲν γὰρ τὴν
Πλαγγόνα ὀμόσαι περὶ τῶν παίδων, εἰ ὄντως εἰσὶν ἐξ
10 αὐτοῦ, ὑποσχόμενος, εἰ ὀμόσειεν, ἐμμένειν τῷ ὅρκῳ·
προὐκαλέσατο δὲ ἀπατηθεὶς ὡς οὐ δεξομένης τὸν ὅρκον
τῆς γυναικός· ὑπὲρ τούτου γὰρ καὶ μισθὸν αὐτῇ συχνὸν
ἐπηγγείλατο. ὡς δέ φησιν ὁ τὸν λόγον λέγων, καὶ
ὠμωμόκει ἡ Πλαγγὼν αὐτῷ λάθρᾳ προτεινόμενον τὸν
15 ὅρκον μὴ δέξεσθαι. προκαλεσαμένου τοίνυν παραβᾶσα

There was a law (Arg. ad Or. 57, πρὸς Εὐβουλίδ.) to the effect that the names of those who were not born of both father and mother who were citizens, should be struck off the register; τοὺς μὴ γεγονότας ἐξ ἀστοῦ καὶ ἐξ ἀστῆς ἐξαλείφεσθαι. So Or. 48 § 53, Ὀλυμπιόδωρος γὰρ οὑτοσὶ γυναῖκα μὲν ἀστὴν κατὰ τοὺς νόμους τοὺς ὑμετέρους οὐδεπώποτ' ἔγημεν, οὐδ' εἰσὶν αὐτῷ παῖδες οὐδ' ἐγένοντο.

6. ἀναλαμβάνει] Suscipit, 'acknowledges as his own.'

8. ἀπατηθεὶς] The grammarian goes on to explain this. He first explains προκλήσεως, and then προὐκαλέσατο ἀπατηθείς. Mantias had wished not to recognise the sons; and Plango, induced by a promise of money, had given a pledge that, on the oath being tendered to her, she would swear they were *not* by him. But she (induced perhaps by her affection for them, or perhaps by a still larger bribe on their part) had sworn just the contrary, viz. that they *were* her sons by Mantias.

ib. προὐκαλέσατο] This word, 'to make a formal offer,' governs a double accusative, τί τινα. So πολλὰ προκαλουμένου, sc. τὸν ἔρωτα, in Ar. Ach. 984. Or. 30, πρὸς Ὀνήτ. § 1, πολλὰ καὶ δίκαια προκαλεσάμενος ἀμφοτέρους, and προκαλεῖσθαί τινα πρόκλησιν, Or. 56 § 17.

10. ἐμμένειν] 'promising to abide by the oath,' i.e. whichever way she should make the declaration, and even against his own wish or belief.

12. ὑπὲρ τούτου] sc. τοῦ μὴ ὀμόσαι αὐτήν.

14. λάθρᾳ] Construe with καὶ ὠμωμόκει, not with προτεινόμενον. She had even sworn privately, i.e. she had even gone so far as to swear. Such a compact was fraudulent and illegal, and for that reason, perhaps, secretly made.

ib. προτεινόμενον] 'When offered.' Perhaps προτεινομένου, i.e. αὐτοῦ, 'should he offer it.'

15. προκαλεσαμένου] 'When he called upon her to make her declaration on oath.'—συνθήκας, the pledges she had given that she would decline to take the oath.

P. 994] ΠΕΡΙ ΤΟΥ ΟΝΟΜΑΤΟΣ. 143

τὰς συνθήκας δέχεται τὸν ὅρκον. καὶ οὕτω μὲν
ἀναγκάζεται τοὺς παῖδας ἀναλαβεῖν, μετὰ τοῦτο δὲ[a]
τετελεύτηκεν. ὁ τοίνυν ἐκ τῆς νόμῳ γαμηθείσης
γυναικὸς παῖς δικάζεται τῷ ἑτέρῳ τῶν εἰσποιηθέντων
περὶ τοῦ ὀνόματος, λέγων αὐτὸν Βοιωτὸν καλεῖσθαι 20
προσήκειν, ὅπερ ἐξ ἀρχῆς ὠνομάζετο, καὶ μὴ Μαντί-
θεον· τοῦτο γὰρ αὐτῷ[b] παρὰ τοῦ πατρὸς ἐξ ἀρχῆς τεθεῖσθαι τοὔνομα. αὐτόθεν μὲν οὖν δόξειεν ἄν τις φιλο-
πράγμων καὶ φιλόνεικος ὑπὲρ προσηγοριῶν διαφερό-
μενος· ὁ μέντοι λόγος ἱκανὰς ἀποδείξεις παρέχεται τοῦ 25
καὶ δημοσίᾳ καὶ ἰδίᾳ βλαβερὰν εἶναι τὴν ὁμωνυμίαν.

[a] μετὰ δὲ τοῦτο Z.   [b] αὐτῷ Z.

18. τετελεύτηκεν] 'He died.' So the perfect is sometimes used by the grammarians, e.g. πέπομφε, Arg. ad Or. 34 § 31. [The pf. ('dies and is now dead') is influenced by the present construction δέχεται...ἀναγκάζεται, &c. Prof. Kennedy.]
19. εἰσποιηθέντων] 'Who had been admitted by adoption into the roll of the citizens.'
22. τοῦτο γὰρ αὐτῷ] If we read αὐτῷ, τοῦτο must mean Boeotus. If αὑτῷ, then Mantitheus: 'For *this* name had been given to himself, Mantitheus, by his father.'
23. τεθεῖσθαι] Here put passively. The Attic writers of the best age used κεῖσθαι in preference. [The only instances of τεθεῖσθαι as passive quoted by Veitch, *Gk. Verbs*, are Ar. fragm. 304, ἀμφοδον ἐχρῆν αὐτῷ τεθεῖσθαι τοὔνομα, which *may* be middle, and Demades 12, τοὺς ὅρους τῆς Λακωνικῆς τεθειμένους, which is from a spurious speech by a late Rhetorician. For its correct use, as a middle, cf. § 40,

ὅστις ταὐτὸν ὄνομα τέθειται, and for the passive, Isaeus III 32 (ὄνομα) ὑπὸ τοῦ πατρὸς κείμενον. (Isocr. ad Dem. § 36 n.) S.]
ib. αὐτόθεν] *Prima facie*, as we say; lit. from the facts of the case itself. 'From a casual view of the matter, a man might be thought litigious and quarrelsome in disputing about names and titles; but the speech itself supplies good proofs that the having the same name is seriously inconvenient both on public and on private grounds.' The former of these are summed up §§ 7—12, the latter §§ 13—18.
§§ 1—5. *Statement of the reasons why the present action is unavoidable. It is not brought in ignorance that I shall be blamed for going to law about a name; but the consequences of two persons bearing the same name are grave and serious. The defendant on a former occasion got up a plot with some disreputable persons, pretending to have suffered a wrong, and so he contrived, by an in-*

XXXIX. ΠΡΟΣ ΒΟΙΩΤΟΝ [§§ 1—3

Οὐδεμιᾷ φιλοπραγμοσύνῃ μὰ τοὺς θεούς, ὦ ἄνδρες δικασταί, τὴν δίκην ταύτην ἔλαχον Βοιωτῷ, οὐδ' 995 ἠγνόουν ὅτι πολλοῖς ἄτοπον δόξει τὸ δίκην ἐμὲ λαγχάνειν, εἴ τις ἐμοὶ ταὐτὸν ὄνομα οἴεται δεῖν ἔχειν· ἀλλ' ἀναγκαῖον ἦν ἐκ τῶν συμβησομένων, εἰ μὴ τοῦτο 2 διορθώσομαι, ἐν ὑμῖν κριθῆναι. εἰ μὲν οὖν ἑτέρου τινὸς οὗτος ἔφη πατρὸς εἶναι καὶ μὴ τοὐμοῦ, περίεργος ἂν εἰκότως ἐδόκουν εἶναι φροντίζων ὅ τι βούλεται καλεῖν οὗτος[c] ἑαυτόν. νῦν δὲ λαχὼν δίκην τῷ πατρὶ τῷ

[c] αὐτὸς Z.

genious fraud, to induce my father to recognise him and his brother as his own sons by another woman. He had hoped she would not swear to his being hers by him; but she did swear it, and they were accordingly enrolled in the phratry as his. And now, my father being dead, he has gone and entered himself in the city register by an altered name, which is the name that I had previously received.

οὐδεμιᾷ κ.τ.λ.] 'It was not from any fondness for lawsuits, I protest by all the gods, gentlemen of the jury, that I brought this action against Boeotus, nor could I be ignorant that to many it will seem strange conduct in me to bring an action at all, just because another chooses to have the same name as myself; yet it was necessary, from the consequences that are sure to ensue if I do not get this matter set right, to stand a trial before you.' The *proeme* is unusually brief, but it sets forth the case in a very clear and businesslike way.—ἐν τινι (or rather ἐν τισι) κρίνεσθαι is the regular idiom, as δίκην λαγχάνειν is the familiar term for 'bringing an action,' derived from the obtaining leave (originally by drawing lots) to bring on the suit on a certain day. The bringing the action actually into court is technically δίκην εἰσελθεῖν or εἰσιέναι. For κριθῆναι we might rather have expected διαδικάσασθαι: κριθῆναι, however, is virtually middle.

2. περίεργος] 'meddlesome,' 'fussy.' The περί has the sense that it bears in περισσός, περιγενέσθαι, περιεῖναι, περιούσιος, of 'superfluity;' but it is not easy to explain it.

νῦν δέ] 'But as it is, the case stands thus. He brought a suit against my father, and after getting up a gang of informers on his side—Mnesicles, whom I dare say you all know well enough, and Menecles, the wretch who got the poor girl Ninus convicted, and some others of that sort—he went into court, declaring he was Mantias' son by the daughter of Pamphilus, and that he was being shamefully treated, and robbed of his rights as a citizen.' Of the conviction of Ninus, probably by ψευδομαρτυρία, little certain is known; but it was evidently regarded as a public

ἐμῷ καὶ μεθ' ἑαυτοῦ κατασκευάσας ἐργαστήριον συκοφαντῶν, Μνησικλέα τε, ὃν ἴσως γιγνώσκετε πάντες, καὶ Μενεκλέα τὸν τὴν Νίνον[d] ἑλόντα ἐκεῖνον, καὶ τοιούτους τινάς, ἐδικάζεθ' υἱὸς εἶναι φάσκων ἐκ τῆς Παμφίλου θυγατρὸς καὶ δεινὰ πάσχειν καὶ τῆς πατρίδος ἀποστερεῖσθαι. ὁ πατὴρ δὲ (πᾶσα γὰρ εἰρήσεται 3 ἡ ἀλήθεια, ὦ ἄνδρες δικασταὶ) ἅμα μὲν φοβούμενος εἰς δικαστήριον εἰσιέναι, μή τις οἷα ὑπὸ πολιτευομέ-

[d] Νῖνον Z.

scandal. We should expect Νινῶν, or Νινώ, as ἡ Νίνος is a strange form for a woman's name. Allusion is made to this person, who was a priestess, in Παραπρ. § 281, where the schol. says she was put to death, ὡς φίλτρα ποιούσης τοῖς νέοις. See Mr Heslop's note *ibid.* [Dionys. Halic. *Deinarchus* 11, Μενεκλῆς ὁ τὴν ἱέρειαν Νίνον ἑλών. Cf. Josephus adv. Apion. II 37 § 4, ed. Müller 1877, νῦν μὲν γάρ τινα ἱέρειαν ἀπέκτειναν, ἐπεί τις αὐτῆς κατηγόρησεν, ὅτι ξένους ἐμύει θεούς, which is supposed to refer either to Ninus (Foucart, *Des Associations religieuses chez les Grecs*, 1873 p. 132), or to Theoris (Plutarch, Dem. 14). Like Πλαγγών, the name probably means 'Dolly.' Cf. Νάνα, Νάννιον, Ναννώ (in Pape-Benseler's *griech. Eigennamen*). S.]

ἐργαστήριον] See Or. 37, *Argum.*, and *ibid.* § 39, περιστήσας τοὺς μεθ' ἑαυτοῦ, τὸ ἐργαστήριον τῶν συνεστώτων. In the parallel passage of Or. 40 § 9 we have παρασκευασάμενος ἐργαστήριον συκοφαντῶν. For ἐκεῖνον, 'that notorious man,' comp. Or. 35 § 6, Θρασυμήδης ὁ Διοφάντου υἱός, ἐκείνου τοῦ Σφηττίου. In Or. 40 § 32, it is Menecles who is charged with being the real author of the whole plot.—υἱὸς εἶναι, i.e. the son of Mantias, and not of some other man, as Mantias wished him to be thought.

ἐκ τῆς Παμφίλου θυγατρός] Or. 40 § 20, Παμφίλου...ὃς ἦν πατὴρ τῆς Πλαγγόνος.

3. μή τις κ.τ.λ.] 'Lest some one, resenting some annoyance he had received elsewhere (i.e. not in court) from Mantias when in office, should confront him here.' Mantias had evidently been unpopular in his administration (cf. note on ὑπόθεσις, l. 1), and was afraid lest some one should pay off an old score by giving evidence against him if he disclaimed the relationship before the dicasts. From Or. 40 § 37, it seems that Mantias had been an ambassador or πρόξενος to the Mytileneans, or in some way had performed a public service for which they had voted him a reward. To avoid the risk of meeting his political enemies in court, he had made a πρόκλησις, or offer of settling the matter, by the summary process of denying the parentage, before an arbitrator, or perhaps in presence of the Archon, on the testimony of Plango on her oath.

146   XXXIX. ΠΡΟΣ ΒΟΙΩΤΟΝ [§§ 3—6

νου ἑτέρωθί που λελυπημένος ἐνταυθὶ[e] ἀπαντήσειεν αὐτῷ[f], ἅμα δ᾽ ἐξαπατηθεὶς ὑπὸ τῆς τουτουὶ μητρὸς ὀμοσάσης αὐτῆς ἢ μὴν, ἐὰν ὅρκον αὐτῇ[g] διδῷ περὶ τούτων, μὴ ὀμεῖσθαι, τούτων δὲ πραχθέντων οὐδὲν ἔτι ἔσεσθαι αὐτοῖς, καὶ μεσεγγυησαμένης ἀργύριον, ἐπὶ τούτοις δίδωσι τὸν ὅρκον. ἡ δὲ δεξαμένη οὐ μόνον 4 τοῦτον, ἀλλὰ καὶ τὸν ἀδελφὸν τὸν ἕτερον πρὸς τούτῳ κατωμόσατο ἐκ τοῦ πατρὸς εἶναι τοῦ ἐμοῦ. ὡς δὲ τοῦτ᾽ ἐποίησεν, εἰσάγειν εἰς τοὺς φράτερας ἦν ἀνάγκη τούτους καὶ λόγος οὐδεὶς ὑπελείπετο. εἰσήγαγεν, ἐποιή-

[e] ἐνταυθοῖ Z.   [f] αὐτῷ Z.   [g] αὐτῇ Z.

ὀμοσάσης αὐτῆς] 'Who had voluntarily sworn that, if any one should tender her an oath (lit. an object to swear by), she would decline to take it.' The terms διδόναι and δέξασθαι ὅρκον are well known, if only from Aesch. Eum. 429, ἀλλ᾽ ὅρκον οὐ δέξαιτ᾽ ἄν, οὐ δοῦναι θέλει. We might render μὴ ὀμεῖσθαι 'that she would swear they were not,' and this seems the more idiomatic meaning. The author of the Argument, however, says ὡς οὐ δεξομένης τὸν ὅρκον, and τὸν ὅρκον μὴ δέξεσθαι.—οὐδὲν ἔτι, κ.τ.λ. 'That, this being done, all connexion between them should cease.' The transaction here mentioned is more fully described in Or. 40 §§ 10, 11. —μεσεγγυήσασθαι is 'to get a sum of money placed in the hands of a third party' (in sequestro deponere). Mantias had promised that she should receive a certain sum on the condition of fulfilling her promise. [Harpocr. μεσεγγύημα: τὸ ὁμολογηθὲν ἀργύριον παρ᾽ ἀνδρὶ μέσῳ γινομένῳ ἐγγυητῇ τῆς ἀποδόσεως. Hermann, Privatalt. § 68, note 20=Rechtsalt. ed. Thalheim p. 91, quotes Antiph. de Chor. § 50, Lysias adv. Philocr. § 6, Isocr. de Soph. § 5. S.]

4. κατομόσασθαι] Lit. 'to swear by a given object.' Hence the genitive in Ar. Equit. 660, κατὰ χιλίων εὐχὴν ποιήσασθαι, and ἐπαράσασθαι κατ᾽ ἐξωλείας, ὀμνύναι κατὰ παίδων (Or. 54 § 38). Compare καταγοράσαι, 'to buy goods as against a loan of money,' Or. 34 § 7. The primary idea must have been adverse action against some one.

φράτερας] After the adoption, the first enrolment into the families took place; a politico-religious ceremony. Ar. Ach. 145, ὁ δ᾽ υἱὸς, ὃν Ἀθηναῖον ἐπεποιήμεθα, ᾖρα φαγεῖν ἀλλᾶντας ἐξ Ἀπατουρίων, i.e. ἐγγράφεσθαι εἰς τοὺς φράτερας. [Harpocr. Ἀπατούρια: ἑορτή τις παρ᾽ Ἀθηναίοις ἣν ἄγουσι Πυανεψιῶνι ἐφ᾽ ἡμέρας δ᾽ κ.τ.λ. Id. φράτερες: Δημ. περὶ τοῦ ὀνόματος. φρατρία ἐστὶ τὸ τρίτον μέρος τῆς φυλῆς, φράτερες δὲ οἱ τῆς αὐτῆς φρατρίας μετέχοντες. Hermann's Political Antiquities, § 99. S.] Cobet, Var. Lect. p. 350, shows that φράτερες is the true form, not φράτορες.

ΠΕΡΙ ΤΟΥ ΟΝΟΜΑΤΟΣ.

σατο, ἵνα τἀν μέσῳ[h] συντέμω, ἐγγράφει τοῖς Ἀπατουρίοις τουτονὶ μὲν Βοιωτὸν εἰς τοὺς φράτερας, τὸν δ' ἕτερον Πάμφιλον· Μαντίθεος δ' ἐνεγεγράμμην ἐγώ. συμβάσης δὲ τῷ πατρὶ[i] τελευτῆς πρὶν τὰς εἰς τοὺς δημότας ἐγγραφὰς γενέσθαι, ἐλθὼν εἰς τοὺς δημότας οὑτοσὶ ἀντὶ Βοιωτοῦ Μαντίθεον ἐνέγραψεν ἑαυτόν[j]. τοῦτο δ' ὅσα βλάπτει ποιῶν πρῶτον μὲν ἐμέ, εἶτα δὲ[k] καὶ ὑμᾶς, ἐγὼ διδάξω, ἐπειδὰν ὧν λέγω παράσχωμαι μάρτυρας.

ΜΑΡΤΥΡΕΣ.

Ὃν μὲν τοίνυν τρόπον ἡμᾶς ἐνέγραψεν ὁ πατήρ, ἀκηκόατε τῶν μαρτύρων· ὅτι δ' οὐκ οἰομένου τούτου δεῖν ἐμμένειν, δικαίως καὶ ἀναγκαίως ἔλαχον τὴν δίκην,

[h] τἀμμέσῳ Z.   [i] +της Z.
[j] αὑτόν Z.   [k] om. Bekk. 1824.

Βοιωτόν] 'By the name of Boeotus.' If this was the name given at the Apaturia, when the first enrolment took place, the name Mantitheus could not be substituted for it at the second enrolment among the ἀστοί, viz. when, on passing the δοκιμασία, the young men were entered on the γραμματεῖον ληξιαρχικόν. Cf. Or. 30 § 6, ἐπειδὴ τάχιστ' ἀνὴρ εἶναι δοκιμασθείην.

ἐνεγεγράμμην] 'I had before been enrolled (in the phratries) as Mantitheus.' Therefore he had a prior claim to the name.

5. εἰς τοὺς δημότας ἐνέγραψεν] The enrolment of Boeotus in the later register was fraudulent, and succeeded only because his father was dead. See Or. 40 § 34. Such an event argues some carelessness in the keeping of the state registers. [See Hermann's *Political Antiquities*, § 121, and A. Schaefer, *Dem. u. s. Zeit*, III 2, 19—38. S.]—

τοῦτο δέ, κ.τ.λ. i.e. τοῦτο ποιῶν ὅσα βλάπτει ἐμέ, κ.τ.λ.

6. ἐμμένειν] To abide by the name, Boeotus, which his father thought fit to give him. δικαίως, κ.τ.λ. to be construed with ἔλαχον.—ἐγὼ γάρ, κ.τ.λ. 'for, of course, *I* am not such a dolt nor so inconsiderate as to have consented to take a third share of my father's property, (though all of it was coming into my possession,) on the ground that my father had adopted these men, and to rest content with that, and then to go and quarrel with one so near of kin about a name, were it not that our changing our name (i.e. my changing mine) was likely to bring serious discredit and the charge of want of proper spirit, while his having the same name with me was on many accounts impossible.'

10—2

τοῦτ' ἤδη δείξω. ἐγὼ γὰρ οὐχ οὕτω δήπου σκαιός εἰμι ἄνθρωπος οὐδ' ἀλόγιστος ὥστε τῶν μὲν πατρῴων, ἃ πάντα ἐμὰ ἐγίγνετο, ἐπειδήπερ ἐποιήσατο τούτους ὁ πατήρ, συγκεχωρηκέναι τὸ τρίτον νείμασθαι μέρος καὶ στέργειν ἐπὶ τούτῳ, περὶ δ' ὀνόματος ζυγομαχεῖν, εἰ μὴ τὸ μὲν ἡμᾶς μεταθέσθαι μεγάλην ἀτιμίαν ἔφερε καὶ ἀνανδρίαν, τὸ δὲ ταὐτὸν ἔχειν τοῦτον ἡμῖν ὄνομα διὰ πόλλ' ἀδύνατον ἦν.

7 Πρῶτον μὲν γάρ, εἰ δεῖ τὰ κοινὰ τῶν ἰδίων εἰπεῖν

σκαιὸς...ἀλόγιστος] 'Stupid and unreasonable.'
ἐγίγνετο] 'Which were becoming mine,' before my father was driven to adopt them.
τὸ τρίτον μέρος] Or. 40 § 48, κἀγὼ μὲν διὰ τὴν τούτων μητέρα τὰ δύο μέρη τῆς οὐσίας ἀφαιρεθεὶς ὅμως αἰσχύνομαι λέγειν περὶ ἐκείνης τι φλαῦρον.
ζυγομαχεῖν] 'To wrangle,' 'to carry on a family quarrel,' a metaphor either from two rowers on the ζυγόν (cross-bit) of a trireme, or from two animals under the yoke. Hesiod, Opp. 439 οὐκ ἂν τώ γ' ἐρίσαντε κατ' αὔλακα καμμὲν ἄροτρον ἄξειαν, τὸ δὲ ἔργον ἐτώσιον αὖθι λίποιεν. It is from the latter simile that the author of the proeme to the Iliad says ἐξ οὗ δὴ τὰ πρῶτα διαστήτην ἐρίσαντε Ἀτρείδης τε ἄναξ ἀνδρῶν καὶ δῖος Ἀχιλλεύς. Hesych. ζυγομαχεῖν· τὸ τοῖς οἰκείοις διαφέρεσθαι. It is a verb of the later Attic, used by Menander.

§§ 7—12. *An enumeration of the anomalies and confusion that would result in the state from two citizens bearing the same name.* (1) Supposing some public service is imposed; which of the two is to perform it? (2) Or which of the two is to pay the penalty for refusing to perform it? (3) The same may occur if the name is entered on the list of contributors, or in the military list, or for any public function to which the archon or other authorities are nominating fitting persons. It would be possible, but it would also be illegal, to distinguish them by adding the name of the mother. (4) Or suppose a judge or umpire were nominated; who is to know which is summoned? (5) If, on the other hand, the appointment is not a burden, but an honour, there would be no way of knowing which of the two was elected by the lot, unless indeed a mark is put on it; and even then the meaning of the mark would only be known to a very few. (6) If the two should enter into a compact that the lot drawn for the one should be counted for the election of the other; that would violate the law which orders, under penalty of death, that "no citizen shall have more than one lot drawn on his behalf."

7. τὰ κοινά] 'To mention public before private difficulties, in what way shall the state impose the duty, if there is anything to be done,' i.e. any burden or liturgy to be performed?

πρότερον, τίν' ἡμῖν ἡ πόλις ἐπιτάξει τρόπον, ἄν τι δέῃ ποιεῖν; οἴσουσι[1] νὴ Δία οἱ φυλέται τὸν αὐτὸν τρόπον ὅνπερ καὶ τοὺς ἄλλους. οὐκοῦν Μαντίθεον Μαντίου Θορίκιον οἴσουσιν, ἐάν[m] χορηγὸν ἢ γυμνασίαρχον ἢ ἑστιάτορα ἢ ἐάν τι τῶν ἄλλων φέρωσιν. τῷ δῆλον οὖν ἔσται πότερον σὲ φέρουσιν ἢ ἐμέ; σὺ μὲν γὰρ φήσεις 8 ἐμέ, ἐγὼ δὲ σέ. καὶ δὴ καλεῖ μετὰ τοῦθ' ὁ ἄρχων, ἢ

[1] ἢ οἴσουσι—ἄλλους; Z.   [m] ἄν Z.

The state, as the master, gives its orders on the subject as its slave. Ἐπιτάσσειν is the technical word in this sense, whereas προστάσσειν is used of *general* commissions, orders, or appointments; in poetry even τάσσειν, as φωνεῖν ἐτάχθην πρὸς σοφοῦ διδασκάλου, Aesch. Eum. 269. We have οἰκέτῃ προστάξαι in Or. 37 § 24, but the more common word is ἐπιτάξαι. So ἐπιταττόμενος φοιτᾷς, Ar. Vesp. 686.—οἴσουσι, 'the members of the tribe will propose the name (or 'will return us') by the same formula as they adopt for the citizens in general,' i. e. by the name of the person with the addition of his father and his deme or ward (borough).

χορηγόν] 'Choral-Steward.' Prof. Kennedy.

ἑστιάτορα] [Harpocr. ἑστιάτωρ: ὁ τράπεζάν τισι παρατιθείς. Δημ. ἐν τῷ πρὸς Βοιωτόν. εἰστιῶν τὰς φυλὰς οἱ μὲν ἐθελονταί, οἱ δὲ κληρωτοί, ὡς ὁ αὐτὸς ῥήτωρ δηλοῖ ἐν τῷ κατὰ Μειδίου (p. 565, 10?). S.] One of the public duties was to give an annual dinner (probably in the Prytaneum), at the cost of some wealthy citizen, to the members of his tribe. See on this (and the other λειτουργίαι) Wolf's Preface to the Leptines, p. 45, ed. Beatson. Wolf indeed says "to the men of his tribe on days of sacrifice and on feast-days;" but it is obvious that this requires some limitation. Boeckh (*Publ. Ec.* p. 465, trans. Lewis[2]) thinks the *hestiatores* were appointed according to the amount of property in some regular succession which is unknown to us. He thinks there may have been two thousand guests, and the cost nearly 700 drachmas. It may perhaps be doubted if the entertainment was so general, and not in fact limited to the fifty βουλευταί in each tribe.— The gymnasiarchs (Boeckh, p. 462) had to maintain and pay those persons who were training for the celebration of the festivals, as well as to provide the requisite food for the combatants and the requisite decorations for the exhibition.

8. σὺ μὲν γάρ] As we neither of us shall like the duty, we shall try to shift it on to each other's shoulders.

καὶ δή] 'And now suppose,' as in Eur. Med. 386, καὶ δὴ τεθνᾶσι, and often elsewhere.

μετὰ τοῦτο] After the refusal to serve. By the words πρὸς ὅντιν' ἂν ᾖ ἡ δίκη, 'before whatever judge the cause is brought,' we must infer that the liturgies were appointed and enforced by different authorities.

πρὸς ὄντιν'ⁿ ἂν ᾖ ἡ δίκη. οὐχ ὑπακούομεν. οὐ λειτουργοῦμεν. πότερος° ταῖς ἐκ τῶν νόμων ἔσται ζημίαις ἔνοχος; τίνα δ' οἱ στρατηγοὶ τρόπον ἐγγράψουσιν, ἂν εἰς 997 συμμορίαν ἐγγράφωσιν, ἢ ἂν τριήραρχον καθιστῶσιν; 9 ἢ ἂν στρατεία τις ᾖ, τῷ δῆλον ἔσται πότερός ἐσθ' ὁ κατειλεγμένος; τί δέ, ἂν ἄλλη τις ἀρχὴ καθιστῇ εἰς

ⁿ ὅντινα Z.   ° πότερος οὖν Bekk. 1824.

οὐχ ὑπακούομεν, 'we refuse to obey the summons,' and 'do not accept the service,' i. e. we show contempt of court and incur a penalty.

τίνα δ' οἱ στρατηγοὶ κ.τ.λ.] 'In what manner will the war office (the War-Commission of the ten generals) enter us, if they are entering the names for a tax-company?' Prof. Kennedy.

εἰς συμμορίαν] Each of the ten tribes of the Athenians returned a list of an hundred and twenty, who were the richest of their members. Each of these lists was equally divided, and thus there were in all twenty classes called συμμορίαι, each of sixty persons. The twelve hundred thus collected were again divided into two parts, each of six hundred men, and each of these again into two; so that there were four divisions in all, of three hundred each. Now these three hundred, who surpassed the more numerous remainder in wealth, took the lead in contributions; and on urgent occasions of war they paid down the subsidy required, and collected it back from the poorer members at some time less unfavourable; and thus they had them submissive to their dictation on all points. (Wolf, Introd. to Leptines, p. 49, ed. Beatson.) See

Or. 37 § 37, ἂν προεισφορὰν μὴ κομίζηται. These classes were, of course, a shifting list, according to the changes of fortune and the census of the citizens. Whether a certain number only in each tribe could be put in the first or richest class, may be doubted; but the rich tribes would reasonably bear a greater share of the state burden than the poorer ones. The subject is fully explained by Boeckh, *Publ. Ec.*, Bk. IV. chap. xiii.

9. ὁ κατειλεγμένος] 'The person entered on the military list,' 'enlisted.' Here also the technical term was ἐγγράφειν. The constant changes made in this list by the taxiarchs caused a great deal of trouble and annoyance. Ar. Pac. 1179, δρῶσιν οὐκ ἀνασχετά, τοὺς μὲν ἐγγράφοντες ἡμῶν, τοὺς δ' ἄνω τε καὶ κάτω ἐξαλείφοντες δὶς ἢ τρίς.

τί δέ;] Like *Quid!* 'Or again!' ἀρχή] 'The authorities,' 'the magistrate,' like *magistratus*, used of the public officer as well as his office. Aeschin. Ctesiph. § 21, ἀρχὴν ὑπεύθυνον μὴ ἀποδημεῖν. Cic. II Phil. § 52, consulibus reliquisque imperiis et potestatibus. Caesar B. C. III 32, plena lictorum et impe-riorum provincia. Juv. x 100, Gabiorum potestas (cf. the Italian *podesta*). S.]

ΠΕΡΙ ΤΟΥ ΟΝΟΜΑΤΟΣ.

λειτουργίαν, οἷον ἄρχων, βασιλεύς, ἀθλοθέται, τί σημεῖον ἔσται πότερον καθιστᾶσιν; προσπαραγράψουσι νὴ Δία τὸν ἐκ Πλαγγόνος, ἂν σὲ ἐγγράφωσιν, ἂν[p] δ' ἐμὲ, τῆς ἐμῆς μητρὸς τοὔνομα. καὶ τίς ἤκουσε πώποτε, ἢ κατὰ ποῖον νόμον προσπαραγράφοιτ' ἂν τοῦτο τὸ παράγραμμα ἢ ἄλλο τι πλὴν ὁ πατὴρ καὶ ὁ δῆμος; ὧν ὄντων ἀμφοῖν τῶν αὐτῶν πολλὴ ταραχὴ συμβαίνει. φέρε, εἰ δὲ κριτὴς καλοῖτο Μαντίθεος Μαντίου 10 Θορίκιος, τί ἂν ποιοῖμεν; ἢ βαδίζοιμεν ἂν ἄμφω; τῷ γὰρ ἔσται δῆλον πότερον σὲ κέκληκεν ἢ ἐμέ; πρὸς Διός, ἂν δ' ἀρχὴν ἡντινοῦν ἡ πόλις κληροῖ, οἷον βουλῆς ἢ θεσμοθέτου ἢ τῶν ἄλλων, τῷ δῆλος ὁ λαχὼν ἡμῶν ἔσται; πλὴν εἰ[q] σημεῖον, ὥσπερ[r] ἄλλῳ τινὶ, τῷ

[p] ἐὰν Z.   [q] εἰ μὴ Sr.   εἰ Z et Dindf.   [r] 'Fortasse ὡς.' Sauppe.

ἀθλοθέται] Boeckh, *Publ. Ec.* p. 216, "For the games there were the athlothetæ, who had the particular care of the great Panathenæa, though probably with the exception of the sacrifices." ['Prize-managers,' 'Stewards of the Games.' Pollux, ἀθλοθέτας, ἕνα κατὰ φυλὴν ἑκάστην. S.]

κατὰ ποῖον νόμον] 'By what law could this special description be added to the usual form, or indeed *any* other than that of the father and the deme?' This was the invariable description of a citizen, as given below, Μαντίθεος Μαντίου Θορίκιος.— ποῖος, as usual, follows τίς, or καὶ τίς, implying incredulity of some statement.

10. κριτής] This seems rather a general term. The δικασταὶ answer more nearly to the Roman *judices*; and the president was usually one of the Archons, as at Rome the Praetor. The Athenians had not, as Bp. Thirlwall remarks, "that nice distinction which is so familiar to us between the province of the judge and jury." Perhaps an arbitrator is here meant, or an umpire in any dispute, public or private. [A judge in any games, any theatrical or other contest: and *not* a law officer. Prof. Kennedy.] The subject to κέκληκεν may be ὁ ἄρχων, or ὁ κρινόμενος.

κληροῖ] The subjunctive; and the same is also the present indicative and optative of verbs in -όω. 'If the state is appointing to any office by lot.' The middle voice is used of the person who obtains it, κληροῦται, *sortitur*, or εἴληχε.—θεσμοθέτου, one of the six minor archons; 'the office of Thesmothet.' To this genitive, which is more familiar as an English than a Greek use, τῶν ἄλλων is attracted; we should rather expect either ἤ τινα τῶν ἄλλων (ἀρχῶν), or ἢ ἄλλην τινά.

χαλκίῳ προσέσται· καὶ οὐδὲ τοῦθ' ὁποτέρου ἐστὶν οἱ πολλοὶ γνώσονται. οὐκοῦν ὁ μὲν ἑαυτόν, ἐγὼ δ' ἐμαυ- 11 τὸν φήσω τὸν εἰληχότ' εἶναι. λοιπὸν εἰς τὸ δικαστήριον ἡμᾶς εἰσιέναι. οὐκοῦν ἐφ' ἑκάστῳ τούτων δικαστήριον ἡμῖν ἡ πόλις καθιεῖ, καὶ τοῦ μὲν κοινοῦ καὶ ἴσου, τοῦ τὸν λαχόντ' ἄρχειν, ἀποστερησόμεθα, ἀλλήλους δὲ πλυνοῦμεν, καὶ ὁ τῷ λόγῳ κρατήσας ἄρξει. καὶ πότερ' ἂν βελτίους εἴημεν τῶν ὑπαρχουσῶν δυσκολιῶν ἀπαλλαττόμενοι ἢ καινὰς ἔχθρας καὶ βλασφημίας ποι-

τῷ χαλκίῳ] It appears from this that the lot was a piece of bronze or copper. The diminutive is used as in χρυσίον, ἀργύριον, meaning a piece of the metal as distinct from its nature as bullion. Some difficulty has been raised as to the meaning of the σημεῖον here spoken of. Kennedy thinks there is an allusion to marking the ticket as in the impanelling of jurors; but he seems to confound it with the σύμβολον which each dicast received on entering the court where he was to sit (Boeckh, *P. E.* p. 235). The sense here is quite simple, if we suppose ὥσπερ ἄλλῳ τινί to mean any other common article or chattel that could be distinguished by the owner's private mark. If there are two persons called Mantitheus, only a special mark on the lot (which would be informal) could indicate which of the two was drawn. Even that mark, he adds, could only be known privately to the person who made it. [In Iliad VII 175, each of the nine Greek heroes, in drawing lots for single-combat with Hector, scratches a mark on his own lot, with a view to its identification, κλῆρον ἐσημήναντο ἕκαστος, and ib. 187, ἐπιγράψας κυνέῃ βάλε. Here,

the χαλκία are apparently small plates of bronze, identical with πινάκια of § 12. Thus, each person eligible by lot for any κληρωτὴ ἀρχὴ (like that of θεσμοθέτης) would have his full name (e. g. Μαντίθεος Μαντίου Θορίκιος) inscribed on a separate χαλκίον; these χαλκία would be put into an urn or other vessel and then drawn by the superintending officer. S.]

11. λοιπόν] The only course remaining is to go into court to try our rights.—καθιεῖ (Attic form of καθίσει), the state will order a court to sit for us, as on a special occasion.

πλυνοῦμεν] 'We shall abuse each other.' A singular expression, used more than once by Aristophanes, as Ach. 381, κακυκλοβόρει κἄπλυνεν. Plut. 1061, πλυνόν με ποιῶν ἐν τοσούτοις ἀνδράσιν. Hesych. πλύνεται· βλασφημεῖται, λοιδορεῖται. (Phot. λοιδορεῖται, αἰσχρῶς ὑβρίζεται.) Id. πλυνὸν, καταπλυντήριξε, καὶ πλυνθήσομαι· Ἀττικοὶ ἐπὶ τῶν λοιδοριῶν λέγουσι.

ἀπαλλαττόμενοι] 'By trying to get rid of our existing difficulties,' viz. by settling this dispute about the name. δυσκολιῶν, 'dissensions,' C. R. Kennedy; 'resentments,' H. W. Moss.

βλασφημίας] ' Recrimina-

ούμενοι; ἃς πᾶσα ἀνάγκη συμβαίνειν, ὅταν ἀρχῆς ἢ τινος ἄλλου πρὸς ἡμᾶς αὐτοὺς ἀμφισβητῶμεν. τί δὲ, 12 998 ἂν ἄρα (δεῖ γὰρ ἄπανθ᾽ ἡμᾶς ἐξετάσαι) ἅτερος ἡμῶν πείσας τὸν ἕτερον, ἐὰν λάχῃ, παραδοῦναι αὐτῷ τὴν ἀρχήν, οὕτω κληρῶται; τὸ δυοῖν πινακίοιν τὸν ἕνα κληροῦσθαι τί ἄλλο ἐστίν; εἶτ᾽ ἐφ᾽ ᾧ θάνατον ζημίαν ὁ νόμος λέγει, τοῦθ᾽ ἡμῖν ἀδεῶς ἐξέσται πράττειν; πάνυ γε· οὐ γὰρ ἂν αὐτὸ ποιήσαιμεν. οἶδα κἀγώ, τὸ γοῦν κατ᾽ ἐμέ· ἀλλ᾽ οὐδ᾽ αἰτίαν τοιαύτης ζημίας ἐνίους ἔχειν καλόν, ἐξὸν μή.

tions,' 'mutual imputations.' Prof. Kennedy. Perhaps for βλαψιφημίας. Eur. Ion 1189, βλασφημίαν τις οἰκετῶν ἐφθέγξατο.
12. ἂν ἄρα] Si forte. Hence the parenthetic clause is added.
δυοῖν πινακίοιν] Kennedy translates, 'and what is this but one man balloting with two balls?' But this involves a confusion between appointment by drawing lots, which is here meant, and election by *tacita suffragia* or ballot, which was rarely resorted to (see Schömann de Comitiis, p. 125). S.] The πινάκια are slips of wood, which may have been in use when the law in question was drawn up. [Harpocr. πινάκια· τὰ καθιέμενα ἀντὶ κλήρων ὑπὸ τῶν κληρουμένων· ἔοικε δ᾽ εἶναι ταῦτα χαλκᾶ ὡς ὑποσημαίνει Δ. ἐν τῷ περὶ ὀνόματος. The lexicographer is doubtless here referring to τῷ χαλκίῳ in § 10. Cf. Photius, πινάκιον· σύμβολον δικαστικόν, χαλκοῦν ἢ πύξινον. S.] At other times the bean, κύαμος, was adopted. Cf. Hdt. VI 109 ὁ κυάμῳ λαχών, and Thuc. VIII 69 οἱ ἀπὸ τοῦ κυάμου βουλευταί. Hence Δῆμος is called κυαμοτρώξ, Ar. Equit. 41. Hesych. κύαμος· ὅσπριον ἢ ὁ κλῆρος.
ἐξὸν μή] 'When they need not,' 'when they might avoid it,' lit. 'it being in their power *not* to have it.' So Mid. p. 538, καὶ ταῦτ᾽ εἰς οἰκίαν ἐλθὼν ἐπὶ δεῖπνον, οἷ μὴ βαδίζειν ἐξῆν αὐτῷ.
§§ 13—18. *Enumeration of the many private inconveniences that must result from two having the same name. These are classed under eight heads.* (1) *If, from the questionable company this half-brother of mine keeps, he should be induced to bring an action against some one, and should get fined, failing in the attempt, which of us is to be registered as a debtor for non-payment?* (2) *If the debt remains still unpaid, why are his children rather than mine to be held liable?* (3) *In an action for ejectment, why will it be his name that is written in the archon's books rather than mine?* (4) *The same may be said of being a defaulter in the income tax.* (5) *And of any action brought, or any unpleasant report circulated about 'Mantitheus.'* (6) *Or if he should be indicted for refusing to serve in the army, and make some such lame excuse for staying at home*

154   XXXIX. ΠΡΟΣ ΒΟΙΩΤΟΝ   [§§ 13, 14

13   Εἶεν. ἀλλὰ ταῦτα μὲν ἡ πόλις βλάπτεται· ἐγὼ δ᾽
ἰδίᾳ τί; θεάσασθε ἡλίκα*, καὶ σκοπεῖτε ἄν τι δοκῶ λέ-
γειν· πολὺ γὰρ χαλεπώτερα ταῦτα ὧν ἀκηκόατ᾽ ἐστίν.
ὁρᾶτε μὲν γὰρ ἅπαντες αὐτὸν χρώμενον, ἕως μὲν ἔζη,
Μενεκλεῖ καὶ τοῖς περὶ ἐκεῖνον ἀνθρώποις, νῦν δ᾽ ἑτέροις ἐκείνου βελτίοσιν οὐδὲν καὶ τὰ τοιαῦτ᾽ ἐζηλωκότα
καὶ δεινὸν δοκεῖν εἶναι βουλόμενον· καὶ νὴ Δία ἴσως
14 ἔστιν. ἂν οὖν προϊόντος τοῦ χρόνου τῶν αὐτῶν τι ποι-

ᵃ Bekk. om. Z cum pr. Σ.

as he actually did make of late. (7) Or if he be called upon to prove his claims to citizenship, which, from the circumstances of his adoption, is a contingency far from improbable. (8) Lastly, if he should be indicted for perjury, and not appear in court, it might be said that I was the culprit, as no one would see him convicted.
13. ἀλλά] At enim. 'It will be said that in the above matters it is the state which is injured; what harm does it do to me individually?' viz. that I should make it thus a personal matter, and subject myself to the charge of being quarrelsome and litigious (§ 1). C. R. Kennedy does not give quite the same sense: 'Well: I have shown the damage which the state suffers. What is my own private damage?' And Prof. Kennedy observes that ἀλλὰ νὴ Δία is more usual in the former sense.—ἡλίκα, sc. βλάπτομαι, 'in how grave and serious matters.'
χρώμενον] Familiariter utentem.—Μενεκλεῖ, the man mentioned above as having convicted 'poor Ninus.' Perhaps we should read ἑωρᾶτε.—ἕως ἔζη, during the lifetime of Menecles. —ἴσως ἔστιν, 'I dare say he is' clever in his own sense of the word, i.e. πανοῦργος. Plat. Theaet. p. 176 D, τῷ οὖν ἀδικοῦντι καὶ ἀνόσια λέγοντι ἢ πράττοντι μακρῷ ἄριστ᾽ ἔχει τὸ μὴ συγχωρεῖν δεινῷ ὑπὸ πανουργίας εἶναι. The words τὰ τοιαῦτα ἐζηλωκότα, 'aspiring to the same fame as they attained,' seem to show that successful oratory in unjust actions was the object of their ambition. Kennedy perceives this, and renders δεινὸν εἶναι βουλόμενον 'he wishes to be thought an orator.' The word is as commonly applied in irony to the ῥήτορες as to the σοφισταί. The meaning is, that the man may imitate his worthless companions and turn συκοφάντης against honest people, but fail some day to establish the prosecution, and be fined a thousand drachmas for not getting a fifth part of the votes. In private actions, (and also in φάσεις, which were public,) the ἐπωβελία (an obol for every drachma), and in public suits, a fine of 1000 drachms, was imposed on the plaintiff if in either case he failed to get a fifth part of the votes. (Boeckh, P. E. pp. 346, 350, 363.) See Or. 56 § 4.

p. 998]   ΠΕΡΙ ΤΟΥ ΟΝΟΜΑΤΟΣ.   155

εἶν τούτοις ἐπιχειρῇ (ἔστι δὲ ταῦτα γραφαὶ, φάσεις^t, ἐνδείξεις, ἀπαγωγαὶ,) εἶτ' ἐπὶ τούτων τινὶ (πολλὰ γάρ ἐστι τἀνθρώπινα^u, καὶ τοὺς πάνυ δεινοὺς ἑκάστοτε, ὅταν πλεονάζωσιν, ἐπίστασθ' ὑμεῖς κοσμίους ποιεῖν) ὄφλῃ τῷ δημοσίῳ, τί μᾶλλον οὗτος ἐγγεγραμμένος

^{t} Bekk. om. Z cum Σ.
^{u} Bekk. ἐστ' ἀνθρώπινα Z cum Σ.

14. γραφαὶ] Public indictments of any sort.—φάσεις, presentments or prosecutions for importing or exporting or possessing contraband goods. The bringing of this action is called φαίνειν in Ar. Ach. 819, 908. So ἐνδεικνύναι, εἰσαγγέλλειν, are used for prosecuting by other special processes. Boeckh (*Publ. Econ.* p. 368, trans. Lewis²) observes that "a peculiar circumstance occurred in the phasis, as being a public suit. In this form of proceeding it must be inferred from the circumstances of the case that the defendant, if he lost his cause, paid the fine, and also the epobelia, if he did not obtain the fifth part of the votes: the plaintiff indeed had no reason to apprehend the first payment, but if he was unsuccessful in his suit, he was in the same case compelled to pay the epobelia; and if he did not obtain the fifth part of the votes, i. e. in the very case in which he was subject to the epobelia, he was forced to pay to the state the usual fine of 1000 drachmas." [φάσεις, ἐνδείξεις, may be approximately rendered 'fiscal and criminal informations.' Prof. Kennedy.]

ἐνδείξεις] Actions for holding any office when a person was legally disqualified by being ἄτιμος, or a public debtor (Timocr. p. 707). Lex. Rhetor.

Cant. ἔνδειξις φάσεως διαφέρει. ὅτι τὴν μὲν ἔνδειξιν δύναται ἀντιλέγεσθαί, οἷον, ἀνέδειξεν (l. ἐνέδειξεν) 'Αριστογείτονα Δημοσθένης, ὅτι λέγει ὁ φάσκων οὐκ ὀφείλει (qu. ὅτι λέγει, φάσκων οὐκ ὀφείλειν, 'alleging that he has no right to speak in the assembly'), φάσις δέ ἐστιν ὅταν φαίνῃ τῶν δημοσίων ἔχοντά τινα μὴ πριώμενον (πριάμενον).—ἀπαγωγαὶ, 'arrests,' i.e. the carrying men off to the authorities at once as guilty of some offence. See Androt. (Or. 22) p. 601, ἔρρωσαι, καὶ σαυτῷ πιστεύεις· ἄπαγε· ἐν χιλίαις δ' ὁ κίνδυνος. Timocr. Or. 24 § 146, ὅσων ἔνδειξίς ἐστιν ἢ ἀπαγωγή. See Boeckh, *P. E.* p. 389.

[Pollux: ἔνδειξις δὲ ἦν πρὸς τὸν ἄρχοντα ὁμολογουμένου ἀδικήματος μήνυσις οὐ κρίσεως ἀλλὰ τιμωρίας δεομένου...καὶ αὕτη μὲν γίγνεται περὶ τῶν οὐ παρόντων, ἡ δὲ ἀπαγωγὴ ὅταν τις ὃν ἔστιν ἐνδείξασθαι μὴ παρόντα, τοῦτον παρόντα ἐπ' αὐτοφώρῳ λαβὼν ἀπαγάγῃ...μάλιστα δὲ τοὺς ὀφείλοντας τῷ δημοσίῳ ἐνεδείκνυσαν ἢ τοὺς κατιόντας ὅποι μὴ ἔξεστιν, ἢ τοὺς ἀνδροφόνους (VIII 49). S.]

πλεονάζωσιν] 'When they do not keep within due bounds.' He intimates that the dicasts are very knowing in discriminating mere συκοφαντία for private ends, and in discouraging them by imposing the fines for 'not-proved.'

ἐγγεγραμμένος] Entered in

156   XXXIX. ΠΡΟΣ ΒΟΙΩΤΟΝ [§§ 14—16

ἔσται ἐμοῦ ; ὅτι νὴ Δία εἴσονται πάντες* πότερός ποτε
15 ὤφλεν. καλῶς. ἂν δὲ, ὁ τυχὸν γένοιτ᾽ ἂν, χρόνος διέλθῃ καὶ μὴ ἐκτισθῇ τὸ ὄφλημα, τί μᾶλλον οἱ τούτου
παῖδες ἔσονται τῶν ἐμῶν ἐγγεγραμμένοι, ὅταν τοὔνομα καὶ ὁ πατὴρ καὶ ἡ φυλὴ καὶ πάντ᾽ ᾖ ταὐτά ; τί δ᾽,
εἴ τις δίκην ἐξούλης αὐτῷ λαχὼν μηδὲν ἐμοὶ φαίη πρὸς

* Bekk. cum Σ (in margine).   om. Z cum Σ.

the register of debtors to the public treasury, as not having paid the fine. Cf. Or. 53 § 14, ἐγγράφει τῷ δημοσίῳ ἐξακοσίας καὶ δέκα δραχμάς.—ὅτι, κ.τ.λ., 'because, of course (it will be said) all will know which of us brothers was condemned to pay.' It will be a matter of notoriety which was the συκοφάντης, and which had to suffer the consequences.

15. χρόνος] 'If time should elapse (not 'if the time should expire') and the fine be not paid; why should his sons be entered as debtors rather than mine?' There seems a euphemism in χρόνος διέλθῃ. See Boeckh, p. 391.

ὄφλημα] Hesychius χρεώστημα. The word is formed as if from ὀφλέω, a secondary present from the aorist ὀφλεῖν, like εἰδήσω from εἶδον, ἐνισπήσω, χραισμήσω from ἐνισπεῖν, χραισμεῖν, τυχήσω from τυχεῖν (inf. § 25), παρασχήσω from παρασχεῖν. Photius (Lex. in v.) says the Attics wrote ὀφλεῖν, not ὀφλεῖν.

δίκην ἐξούλης] An action to make him give up property which he refuses to cede in contempt of court. Actio rei judicatae, Boeckh, P. E. p. 377. The word ἐξούλη, from ἐξειλεῖν, ἐξείλειν, ἐξίλλειν, properly meant 'the keeping of another out of his rights'; and the action of ἐξούλη was brought against

the person guilty of the act. So Demosthenes served Midias with this process when he refused to pay the fine for κακηγορία, Mid. p. 540. As for the form of the word, the root Fελ (εἴλειν, ἴλλειν, pilus, wool, &c.) passed into οὖλος, used of crisp or closely compacted hair, by the influence of the F. The forms ἰλλός, ἴλλεσθαι (Soph. Antig. 340), ἰλλάδες (our willows perhaps), in Il. xiii 572, ἐξίλλειν, Or. 37 § 35, all point to the original idea of close packing or pressing together. From the form of the root with (dropped) sibilant instead of the F, came silva, Sila, ἴλη, probably ὕλη from the dense growth. Compare Scaptesula for σκαπτὴ ὕλη. In Or. 30, πρὸς Ὀνήτορα ἐξούλης, Onetor is prosecuted for refusing to cede the estates which the law had adjudged to Demosthenes. [Cf. K. F. Hermann, Privatalt. § 71, 13, p. 116 of Rechtsalt. ed. Thalheim; Buttmann's Lex. § 44, 10; and esp. G. Curtius, Gr. Etym. §§ 527 and 660. S.]

μηδὲν ἐμοί κ.τ.λ.] 'Should say that he had no claim against me, but, having got the writ duly signed (or registered by the Archon), should enter the name of Mantitheus, why should he have his name written more than mine?' Kennedy translates 'suppose a man sues him in ejectment, not pretending to have

p. 999] ΠΕΡΙ ΤΟΥ ΟΝΟΜΑΤΟΣ. 157

999 αὐτὸν εἶναι, κυρίαν δὲ ποιησάμενος ἐγγράψαι, τί μᾶλλον ἂν εἴη τοῦτον ἢ ἐμὲ ἐγγεγραφώς; τί δ', εἴ τινας εἰσφορὰς μὴ θείη; τί δ', εἴ τις ἄλλη περὶ τοὔνομα γί- 16
γνοιτο ἢ λῆξις δίκης ἢ δόξα ὅλως ἀηδής; τίς εἴσεται
τῶν πολλῶν πότερός ποτε οὗτός ἐστι, δυοῖν Μαντιθέοιν ταὐτοῦ πατρὸς ὄντοιν; φέρε, εἰ δὲ^w δίκην ἀστρατείας φεύγοι, χορεύοι δὲ ὅταν στρατεύεσθαι δέῃ; καὶ
γὰρ νῦν, ὅτε εἰς Ταμύνας παρῆλθον οἱ ἄλλοι, ἐνθάδε

^w Bekk.   φέρε δὲ, εἰ Z cum Σr.

any claim against me, and afterwards, when he has established his right in the suit, enters the record of the judgment: why will the judgment be entered against Boeotus rather than me?' The meaning of ἐγγράψαι is somewhat uncertain, for we do not know all the circumstances of this peculiar action.
16. λῆξις δίκης κ.τ.λ.] 'Any filing of a suit or, in a general way, any unpleasant report,' 'any scandal.'
δίκην ἀστρατείας] 'An action for non-service,' i. e. for refusing to serve when a person's name is placed on the military κατάλογος. [Aeschin. 1 § 29, τὰς στρατείας μὴ ἐστρατευμένος. Dem. Or. 24 § 103, ἂν ἀστρατείας τις ὄφλῃ......τοῦτον δεδέσθαι. The Roman *detrectatio militiae*, Livy III 69. S.] This was but slightly different from either δειλίας φεύγειν, Ar. Ach. 1129, or λιποστρατίου, λιποταξίου, Mid. p. 548. In these latter cases there was generally actual desertion or running away from the ranks. [In Dem. 24 § 119, we have τοῖς ἀνδροφόνοις, τοῖς ἀστρατεύτοις, τοῖς λείπουσι τὰς τάξεις, and in Aeschin. 3 § 175, ὁ Σόλων ἐν τοῖς αὐτοῖς ἐπιτιμίοις ᾤετο δεῖν ἐνέχεσθαι τὸν ἀστράτευτον καὶ τὸν λελοιπότα τὴν τάξιν καὶ τὸν δειλὸν ὁμοίως. The 14th and 15th Orations of Lysias, in prosecution of the younger Alcibiades, are entitled λιποταξίου and ἀστρατείας respectively. Such prosecutions were instituted by the ten generals, or (perhaps, though the next section scarcely proves it) by the ταξίαρχοι, and were public indictments (γραφαί) and not private suits (δίκαι). The term δίκη must therefore be here used in its generic sense, and not in its more limited meaning. (See introd. to the above speeches of Lysias in Frohberger's *Ausgewählte Reden des Lysias*, and Meier and Schömann, *Attischer Process* p. 364.) S.]
εἰς Ταμύνας] A town in Euboea where the Athenians led by Phocion gained a victory over Callias tyrant of Chalcis, B.C. 350. In Mid. p. 550 and 558 mention is made of the slightly later expedition to Argusae in Euboea, and the cowardice of Midias in the matter, and his complicity with Plutarchus, tyrant of Eretria. [Demosthenes tried to dissuade the Athenians from undertaking the expedition, and was fully justi-

158   XXXIX. ΠΡΟΣ ΒΟΙΩΤΟΝ [§§ 16—18

τοὺς χόας ἄγων ἀπελείφθη καὶ τοῖς Διονυσίοις κατα-
μείνας ἐχόρευεν, ὡς ἅπαντες ἑωρᾶτε οἱ ἐπιδημοῦντες.
17 ἀπελθόντων δ᾽ ἐξ Εὐβοίας τῶν στρατιωτῶν λιποταξίου προσεκλήθη, κἀγὼ ταξιαρχῶν τῆς φυλῆς ἠναγ-

fied in so doing. Aeschines however fought bravely as a hoplite at Tamynae, and was sent to Athens to carry the first news of Phocion's victory. His rival was reproached by his enemies for having been absent from the battle, and at the instigation of Meidias he was threatened with an indictment for deserting his post (Or. 21 §103, ἐγράψατο λιποταξίου). The expedition seems to have taken place late in February, and in March we find Demosthenes choregus at the Dionysia (when he was brutally insulted by Meidias); an engagement which may have enabled him to obtain leave of absence. (A. Schaefer, *Dem. u. s. Zeit* II 74—80, and Grote, *H. G.* chap. 88.) S.]

παρῆλθον] 'Entered'; so ὅτε Ἀλέξανδρος παρῄει ἐς Θήβας, Or. 34, p. 918, and frequently δόμους παρελθεῖν in tragedy. The proper meaning is, 'to go past the door-keeper,' and so to get into a closed building. (See note on 34 § 38.) So παριέναι is 'to admit,' 'to allow to pass in,' Eur. Heracl. 153, Suppl. 468, Plat. Phaed. p. 90 E. [*Proficisci agmine facto, castra movere*, to march, to advance from one place to another, Mitchell's ed. of Reiske's *Indices*. 'The other day when the rest of the troops *appeared before* (went on the campaign to) Tamynae.' Prof. Kennedy. Curtius *H. G.* V 269, 'when they came to Tamynae, they suddenly found themselves surrounded in a gorge by the enemy.' Plut. Dem. 12, Aeschin. III 86 τὸ στρατόπεδον εἴς τινας δυσχωρίας κατακεκλειμένον. S.]

τοὺς χόας] 'He was left at home keeping the feast of the χόες' ('the feast of flagons,' the second day of the Anthesteria). [Harpocr. Δημοσθένης ἐν τῷ περὶ τοῦ ὀνόματος. ἑορτή τις ἦν παρ᾽ Ἀθηναίοις ἀγομένη Ἀνθεστηριών (half of February and March) δωδεκάτῃ. φησὶ δὲ Ἀπολλόδωρος Ἀνθεστήρια μὲν καλεῖσθαι κοινῶς τὴν ὅλην ἑορτὴν Διονύσῳ ἀγομένην, κατὰ μέρος δὲ Πιθοίγια, Χόας, Χύτρους. S.]—ἐχόρευεν, 'he was serving in the chorus at the Dionysia' (in March), which entitled him to exemption from service legally, but it was often adopted by cowards as an excuse. Kennedy neatly renders it, 'dancing as a chorister when he should be campaigning.'

ἑωρᾶτε κ.τ.λ.] Dem. himself was *choregus* at this festival. Cf. εἰς Ταμύνας n. S.]

λιποταξίου] 'for desertion'; here applied to the offence committed by one who, by staying in Athens, failed to take the place assigned him in the ranks of his regiment, Meier and Schömann, p. 365, note 779, ed. Lipsius. See Wayte on Timocr. § 103. S.]

17. ταξιαρχῶν] Mantitheus, as taxiarch, and having the duty of drawing up the military list (Ar. Pac. 1173), was subject to the odium of having his own name and his father's, Μαντίθεος Μαντίου, made the subject of an

P. 999]   ΠΕΡΙ ΤΟΥ ΟΝΟΜΑΤΟΣ.   159

καζόμην κατὰ τοῦ ὀνόματος τοῦ ἐμαυτοῦ πατρόθεν
δέχεσθαι τὴν λῆξιν· καὶ εἰ μισθὸς ἐπορίσθη τοῖς δικαστηρίοις, εἰσῆγον ἄν[x] δῆλον ὅτι. ταῦτα δ' εἰ μὴ σεση-
μασμένων ἤδη συνέβη τῶν ἐχίνων, κἂν μάρτυρας ὑμῖν 18
παρεσχόμην. εἶεν. εἰ δὲ ξενίας προσκληθείη ; πολλοῖς
δὲ προσκρούει, καὶ ὃν ἠναγκάσθη τρόπον ὁ πατὴρ
ποιήσασθαι αὐτόν, οὐ λέληθεν. ὑμεῖς δ', ὅτε μὲν τοῦτον οὐκ ἐποιεῖτο ὁ πατήρ, τὴν μητέρα ἀληθῆ λέγειν
ἡγεῖσθε αὐτοῦ· ἐπειδὰν δ' οὕτω γεγονὼς οὗτος ὀχλη-

[x] ἂν Z et Dindf. cum Σr.   ἄν με Bekk.

action in consequence of his brother's cowardice. But the taxiarchs are themselves accused of being runaways in action, φεύγειν πρῶτοι, Pac. 1177, so that perhaps the action here mentioned as a monstrous case was not wholly without precedent.

εἰ μισθὸς ἐπορίσθη] This shows that legal business was sometimes suspended from the poverty of the treasury. [This financial embarrassment was the result of the attempt to recover Euboea. Dem. (De Pace, § 5) describes it as a πόλεμος ἄδοξος καὶ δαπανηρός.—Each of the dicasts received three obols a day, and each court consisted of at least 500 dicasts, involving an expenditure of 250 drachmae, or about £10 daily. S.]

18. τῶν ἐχίνων] The ἐχῖνοι were cases or vases for holding documents and affidavits, generally in connexion with appeals against arbitrations (Or. 48, p. 1108, τὰ ἀντίγραφα ἐμβαλέσθαι εἰς τὸν ἐχῖνον). These were sealed up before the trial, and when sealed they were not allowed to be opened till the day of the trial. See Or. 54 § 27, and Or. 45 § 17, ἐχρῆν αὐτὸ τὸ γραμματεῖον εἰς τὸν ἐχῖνον ἐμβαλεῖν. In the present case, the event is described as immediately following the departure of the army from Euboea, and immediately preceding the trial; so that the date of the speech is determined within narrow limits.—μάρτυρας, perhaps μαρτυρίας, i.e. written evidence.

ξενίας] If he should be summoned or called on to prove his right to the citizenship. That is not an unlikely event, he adds, since he has many enemies, and the tale of his forced adoption is no secret.

οὕτω γεγονώς] i.e. ἀστός. 'With his birth thus established,' Kennedy. 'You, the judges, then thought he was wronged, and listened to his mother who asserted his legitimacy; but now that you find him so troublesome as a citizen, you will begin to think the father was right in denying the paternity.' The inference left to be drawn is, that the father had good reasons for not wishing to acknowledge such a son.

ρὸς ᾖ, πάλιν ὑμῖν ποτὲ δόξει ἐκεῖνος ἀληθῆ λέγειν. τί δ᾽, εἰ ψευδομαρτυριῶν ἁλώσεσθαι προσδοκῶν ἐφ᾽ οἷς ἐρανίζει τούτοις τοῖς περὶ αὐτόν, ἐρήμην ἐάσειε τελεσθῆναι τὴν δίκην; ἆρά γε μικρὰν ἡγεῖσθε βλάβην, ὦ ἄνδρες Ἀθηναῖοι, ἐν κοινωνίᾳ τὸν ἅπαντα βίον τῆς τούτου δόξης καὶ τῶν ἔργων εἶναι;

19 Ὅτι τοίνυν οὐδ᾽ ἃ διεξελήλυθα ὑμῖν μάτην φοβοῦμαι, θεωρήσατε. οὗτος γὰρ ἤδη καὶ γραφάς τινας, ὦ ἄνδρες Ἀθηναῖοι, πέφευγεν, ἐφ᾽ αἷς οὐδὲν αἴτιος ὢν ἐγὼ συνδιαβάλλομαι, καὶ τῆς ἀρχῆς ἠμφισβήτει⁷ ἣν ὑμεῖς ἐμὲ ἐχειροτονήσατε², καὶ πολλὰ καὶ δυσχερῆ διὰ τὸ ὄνομα συμβέβηκεν ἡμῖν, ὧν, ἵν᾽ εἰδῆτε, ἑκάστων μάρτυρας ὑμῖν παρέξομαι.

ΜΑΡΤΥΡΕΣ.

20 Ὁρᾶτε, ὦ ἄνδρες Ἀθηναῖοι, τὰ συμβαίνοντα, καὶ

⁷ ἠμφεσβήτει Z.   ᶻ ἐπεχειροτονήσατε Bekk. 1824.

ἐφ᾽ οἷς ἐρανίζει] 'On the strength of some of the services he so freely lends to his friends.' For this doctrine of ἔρανος, or receiving from others the same treatment that you give to them, see Mid. (Or. 21 § 184). The meaning is, as his friends tell any lies to serve him, so he does the same for them; but that some day he may be in danger of being convicted for giving false evidence, and so let a judgment go against him by default, not daring to appear. [Harpocration s. v. ἐρανίζοντες paraphrases the sentence thus: ἀντευποιεῖ ἀποδιδοὺς τὴν ἴσην βοήθειαν αὐτοῖς, ἣν κἀκεῖνοί ποτε παρέσχον ψευδομαρτυρήσαντες ὑπὲρ αὐτοῦ. S.] It is not however quite clear whether τελεσθῆναι means καθ᾽ αὑτοῦ or κατά τινος, i.e. from default of evidence that he does not give. The sense probably is, that an action of ψευδομαρτυρία is brought against him, and he dares not rebut it, but allows it to go against himself by not appearing in court.

§ 19. *These fears are not merely imaginary, for he has actually been defendant in some public actions by which I have been compromised, though quite undeservedly on my part.*
καὶ τῆς ἀρχῆς κ.τ.λ.] 'Nay, he even put in a claim against me for holding the office to which you had elected me.' He alludes perhaps to the office of Taxiarch, § 17. Or. 40 § 34. The genitive is used like ἐγκαλεῖν τινος, to lay claim to a thing.

20. συμβαίνοντα] 'What actually does occur,' or 'is every day occurring.'

τὴν ἀηδίαν τὴν ἐκ τοῦ πράγματος. εἰ τοίνυν μὴᵃ ἀηδὲς ἦν ἐκ τούτων μηδ' ὅλως ἀδύνατον ταὐτὸν ἔχειν ὄνομα ἡμῖν συνέβαινεν, οὐ δήπου τοῦτον μὲν δίκαιον τὸ μέρος τῶν ἐμῶν χρημάτων ἔχειν κατὰ τὴν ποίησιν, ἣν ὁ πατὴρ αὐτὸν ἀναγκασθεὶς ἐποιήσατο, ἐμὲ δ' ἀφαιρεθῆναι τοὔνομα, ὃ βουλόμενος καὶ οὐδ' ὑφ' ἑνὸς βιασθεὶς ἔθετο. οὐκ ἔγωγε ἡγοῦμαι. ἵνα τοίνυν εἰδῆτε ὅτι οὐ μόνον εἰς τοὺς φράτερας οὕτως, ὡς μεμαρτύρηται, ὁ πατὴρ τὴν ἐγγραφὴν ἐποιήσατο, ἀλλὰ καὶ τὴν δεκάτην ἐμοὶ ποιῶν τοὔνομα τοῦτο ἔθετο, λαβέ μοι καὶ ταύτην τὴν μαρτυρίαν.

ΜΑΡΤΥΡΙΑ.

Ἀκούετε, ὦᵇ ἄνδρες Ἀθηναῖοι, ὅτι ἐγὼ μέν εἰμιᶜ 21 ἐπὶ τοῦ ὀνόματος τούτου πάντα τὸν χρόνον, τουτονὶ

ᵃ μηδὲν Z.
ᵇ om. Z cum Σ.   ᶜ Σ. ἦν Bekk. 1824.

εἰ τοίνυν] 'Well, now, even if there were no such disagreeable consequences of these disputes, and if it did not prove so absolutely impossible for us to have the same name, yet surely it would not be fair for him to have his share of the property by virtue of the adoption which my father made, because he could not help it, but for me to be deprived of that name which he gave me of his own accord and under constraint from no one.' The antithesis between the reluctant and the voluntary act is rather forced; but antithesis was the soul of ῥητορική.

τὴν δεκάτην ποιῶν] 'In keeping the tenth day after the birth,' when the child was named. He shows that the name Mantitheus was conferred on him even before the enrolment into the phratries. [Or. 40 § 28, Arist.

Aves 922, οὐκ ἄρτι θύω τὴν δεκάτην ταύτης ἐγώ; καὶ τοὔνομ' ὥσπερ παιδίῳ νῦν δὴ 'θέμην. See Becker's Charicles II 6, or p. 219 of English Abridgment, and Hermann, Privatalt. § 32, notes 15 and 16 = p. 283 ed. Blümner. S.]

§ 21. The name Mantitheus therefore is mine only; Boeotus properly belongs to the other. That name was given by his father, who is now deceased, and whose will and pleasure in the matter ought to be respected. Had the father lived, he certainly would have made the second and later entry by the same name, Boeotus. It is unreasonable to compel a father to adopt you, and then, after his decease, to undo the very acts of his which resulted from the adoption.——ἐπί, 'in possession of this name.'

δὲ Βοιωτὸν εἰς τοὺς φράτερας, ἡνίκ᾽ ἠναγκάσθη, ἐνέγραψεν ὁ πατήρ· ἡδέως τοίνυν ἐροίμην ἂν αὐτὸν ἐναντίον ὑμῶν· εἰ μὴ ἐτελεύτησεν ὁ πατήρ, τί ἄν ποτε ἐποίεις πρὸς τοῖς δημόταις; οὐκ ἂν εἴας σε αὐτὸν[d] ἐγγράφειν Βοιωτόν; ἀλλ᾽ ἄτοπον δίκην μὲν λαγχάνειν τούτου, κωλύειν δὲ πάλιν. καὶ μὴν εἴ γ᾽ εἴας αὐτόν, ἐνέγραψεν ἄν σε εἰς τοὺς δημότας, ὅπερ εἰς τοὺς φράτερας. οὐκοῦν δεινόν, ὦ γῆ καὶ θεοί, φάσκειν μὲν ἐκεῖνον αὐτοῦ πατέρα εἶναι, τολμᾶν δ᾽ ἄκυρα ποιεῖν ἃ ἐκεῖνος ἔπραξε ζῶν.

22 Ἐτόλμα τοίνυν πρὸς τῷ διαιτητῇ πρᾶγμα ἀναιδέστατον λέγειν, ὡς ὁ πατὴρ αὐτοῦ δεκάτην ἐποίησεν ὥσπερ ἐμοῦ καὶ τοὔνομα τοῦτ᾽ ἔθετο αὐτῷ[e], καὶ μάρ-

1001

[d] σὺ αὐτὸν Z cum pr. Σ.   σεαυτὸν Bekk.
[e] αὐτῷ Z.

ἡνίκ᾽ ἠναγκάσθη] opposed to πάντα τὸν χρόνον, i.e. 'and that not till he was forced.'

πρὸς τοῖς δημόταις] 'At,' or in presence of, 'the members of the ward in which you were to be enrolled as a citizen.'—οὐκ ἂν εἴας, 'would you have objected to his registering you as Boeotus? But surely it is strange conduct first to bring an action for this, and then afterwards to try to prevent it. And yet, if you had let him, he would have entered you by the same name among the wards-men as he had before into the phratries.'

φάσκειν] 'Is it not a shame for Boeotus to be always saying that Mantias (ἐκεῖνον) was his father, and yet to presume to make null and void what Mantias effected in his lifetime?' viz. the enrolment of Boeotus under that name.

§§ 22—4. *Boeotus told the arbitrator that his father had named him Mantitheus in his infancy, and he tried to prove this by the evidence of some who could have known nothing about it. But first, the father did not think the boy was his son, and so did not give him the name; and secondly, if he had, he would hardly have altered it afterwards to Boeotus, even if he had a quarrel with the mother. Moreover, he used to go to school in a different tribe from myself, which he would not have done if his mother had thought herself wronged, as he pretends she did, by the father not acknowledging Boeotus as his son.*

αὐτοῦ] Construe with δεκάτην. Hesych. δεκάτην θύομεν. τῇ δεκάτῃ ἡμέρᾳ τὰ ὀνόματα τοῖς βρέφεσιν ἐτίθεσαν· ὁ δὲ Ἀριστοτέλης τῇ ἑβδόμῃ φησί. Of course, the inference is, that if he kept the tenth day after the birth, it was because he acknowledged the child.

p. 1001]   ΠΕΡΙ ΤΟΥ ΟΝΟΜΑΤΟΣ.   163

τυράς τινας παρείχετο, οἷς ἐκεῖνος οὐδεπώποτε ὤφθη χρώμενος. ἐγὼ δ' οὐδένα ὑμῶν ἀγνοεῖν οἶμαι[f] ὅτι οὔτ' ἂν ἐποίησε δεκάτην οὐδεὶς παιδίου μὴ νομίζων αὑτοῦ δικαίως εἶναι, οὔτε ποιήσας καὶ στέρξας, ὡς ἂν υἱόν τις στέρξαι, πάλιν ἔξαρνος ἐτόλμησε γενέσθαι. οὐδὲ 23 γὰρ εἴ τι τῇ μητρὶ πρὸς ὀργὴν ἦλθε τῇ τούτων, τούτους ἂν ἐμίσει, νομίζων αὑτοῦ εἶναι· πολὺ γὰρ μᾶλλον εἰώθασιν, ὧν ἂν ἑαυτοῖς διενεχθῶσιν ἀνὴρ καὶ γυνή, διὰ τοὺς παῖδας καταλλάττεσθαι[g] ἢ δι' ἃ ἂν[h] ἀδικηθῶσιν ὑφ' αὑτῶν, τοὺς κοινοὺς παῖδας πρὸς μισεῖν[i]. οὐ τοίνυν ἐκ τούτων ἔστιν ἰδεῖν μόνον ὅτι ψεύσεται, ταῦτ' ἂν λέγῃ, ἀλλὰ πρὶν ἡμέτερος φάσκειν συγγενὴς εἶναι, εἰς Ἱπποθωντίδα ἐφοίτα φυλὴν εἰς παῖδας χορεύσων·

[f] οἴομαι Z.
[g] καταλλάττεσθαι Bekk. st. cum Σ.   διαλλάττεσθαι Bekk. 1824 cum libris ceteris (cf. Or. 40 § 29).
[h] Bekk.   δι' ἂν Z (δι' ἂν Σ).
[i] προσμισεῖν Z.   Cf. Or. 37 § 49.

οἷς ἐκεῖνος κ.τ.λ.] Or. 40 § 28, οὗτός γε εἰς τοῦτο τόλμης ἥκει ὥστε φησὶ τὸν πατέρα μου δεκάτην ὑπὲρ αὑτοῦ ἑστιᾶσαι· καὶ περὶ τούτου μόνον Τιμοκράτους καὶ Προμάχου ἐμβέβληται μαρτυρίας, οἳ οὔτε γένει προσήκουσί μου τῷ πατρὶ οὐδέν, οὔτε φίλοι ἦσαν ἐκείνῳ.

χρώμενος] Familiariter utens.
—μὴ νομίζων, nisi putasset.—
δικαίως, fairly and honestly, without fraud or collusion.

ἔξαρνος] i.e. so that an action became necessary to compel him to recognise the child.

23. πρὸς ὀργὴν ἦλθε] The tragic phrase is ἐλθεῖν δι' ὀργῆς, δι' ἔχθρας, &c. The argument here is in answer to the allegation that Boeotus was repudiated by the father in spite to the mother.

πολὺ γὰρ κ.τ.λ.] 'For it is far more common with man and wife, in any differences that they may have had with each other, to be reconciled for the sake of their children, than through any wrongs they may have suffered from each other, to dislike their common offspring besides.' This passage is repeated almost verbatim, in Or. 40 § 29.—διὰ τοὺς παῖδας must be carefully distinguished from διὰ τῶν παίδων, 'through the agency (or medium) of their children.'—ὧν ἂν, sc. ἐκείνων (or τῶν) ἅ, &c. The genitive depends on the sense of καταλλάττεσθαι, as Soph. Aj. 744, θεοῖσιν ὡς καταλλαχθῇ χόλου.

πρὸς μισεῖν] πρός, i.e. in addition to disliking each other, to hate their common children into the bargain. See note on Or. 37 § 49.

24 καίτοι τίς ἂν ὑμῶν οἴεται τὴν μητέρα πέμψαι τοῦτον εἰς ταύτην τὴν φυλὴν δεινὰ μὲν, ὥς φησιν, ὑπὸ τοῦ πατρὸς πεπονθυῖαν, δεκάτην δ᾽ εἰδυῖαν πεποιηκότα ἐκεῖνον καὶ πάλιν ἔξαρνον ὄντα; ἐγὼ μὲν οὐδέν᾽ ἂν οἶμαι. εἰς γὰρ τὴν Ἀκαμαντίδα ὁμοίως ἐξῆν σοι φοιτᾶν, καὶ ἐφαίνετ᾽ ἂν οὖσ᾽ ἀκόλουθος ἡ φυλὴ τῇ θέσει τοῦ ὀνόματος. ὡς τοίνυν ταῦτ᾽ ἀληθῆ λέγω, τούτων μάρτυρας ὑμῖν τοὺς συμφοιτῶντας καὶ τοὺς εἰδότας παρέξομαι.

ΜΑΡΤΥΡΕΣ. 1002

25 Οὕτω τοίνυν φανερῶς παρὰ τὸν τῆς αὐτοῦ μητρὸς ὅρκον καὶ τὴν τοῦ δόντος ἐκείνῃ τὸν ὅρκον εὐή-

24. τίς ἂν κ.τ.λ.] The ἂν, which belongs to πέμψαι=ἔπεμψεν ἂν, undergoes the same hyperbaton as in οὐκ ἂν οἴομαι γενέσθαι, &c. The argument is, that by sending Boeotus to learn dancing in another tribe than that to which Mantias belonged, viz. her own tribe, she virtually admitted that he was not Mantias' son, and that Mantias had not owned him. Boeckh, *Publ. Ec.* p. 121, observes, "The tribes at Athens were bound to provide for a part of the instruction in music and gymnastic exercises, and they had their own teachers, by whom the youth of the whole tribe were instructed; in the other schools each person paid, but how much we are not informed." This inference seems a little far-fetched. Nothing more is said, than that the mother sent the boy to learn dancing to a school of her own tribe; which was very natural, if the boy was, as Mantitheus intimates, not believed by the mother herself to be Mantias' child. The argument seems worth little, anyhow, as a ground for logical inference of parentage.

ἀκόλουθος] 'Consistent with' (or possibly, 'consequent on') the (pretended) giving of the name Mantitheus by your father. —φοιτᾶν and συμφοιτηταί are the common terms for 'going to school' and 'school-fellows.'

§§ 25, 6. *Not content with his success in getting himself enrolled as a citizen, Boeotus has brought against me sundry claims for money due from his father, i.e. as co-heir. But, if the tale of the mother was true, that Mantias kept her, and maintained two establishments, he could not have left much money, not being a man remarkable for his successes in trading.*

οὕτω φανερῶς κ.τ.λ.] 'Having thus clearly as I have shown found a father through the oath which his mother took, and the simple credulity of him who tendered it to her, and so having been (registered as) born in the tribe Acamantis instead of the tribe Hippothontis, the defend-

p. 1002] ΠΕΡΙ ΤΟΥ ΟΝΟΜΑΤΟΣ. 165

θείαν πατρὸς τετυχηκὼς καὶ[j] ἀνθ' Ἱπποθωντίδος ἐν Ἀκαμαντίδι φυλῇ γεγονὼς οὐκ ἀγαπᾷ Βοιωτὸς οὑτοσί, ἀλλὰ καὶ δίκας ἐμοὶ δύ' ἢ τρεῖς εἴληχεν ἀργυρίου πρὸς αἷς καὶ πρότερόν μ' ἐσυκοφάντει. καίτοι πάντας οἶμαι τοῦθ' ὑμᾶς εἰδέναι, τίς ἦν χρηματιστὴς ὁ πατήρ. ἐγὼ 26 δ' ἐάσω ταῦτα. ἀλλ' εἰ δίκαια ὀμώμοκεν ἡ μήτηρ ἡ τούτων, ἐπ' αὐτοφώρῳ συκοφάντην ἐπιδεικνύει τοῦτον ταῖς δίκαις ταύταις. εἰ γὰρ οὕτω δαπανηρὸς ἦν ὥστε γάμῳ γεγαμηκὼς τὴν ἐμὴν μητέρα ἑτέραν εἶχε γυναῖκα, ἧς ὑμεῖς ἐστέ, καὶ δύ' οἰκίας ᾤκει, πῶς ἂν ἀργύριον τοιοῦτος ὢν κατέλιπεν;

Οὐκ ἀγνοῶ τοίνυν, ὦ ἄνδρες Ἀθηναῖοι, ὅτι Βοι- 27 ωτὸς οὑτοσὶ δίκαιον μὲν οὐδὲν ἕξει λέγειν, ἥξει δ' ἐπὶ

[j] om. Z cum Σr.

ant Boeotus is not content with this, but has also brought against me two or three suits for money, besides those which he formerly trumped up against me.'—τετυχηκώς, an Ionic and Homeric form, as if from τυχέω, a secondary present from the aorist τυχεῖν (see on § 15), retained its place even in the later Attic. But the regular Attic future is τεύξομαι, e.g. Or. 37, fin., εἰ μὴ τῶν δικαίων ἐγὼ παρ' ὑμῖν τεύξομαι. τετευχὼς occurs in Mid. § 150.—γεγονώς, cf. sup. § 18, ἐπειδὰν οὕτω γεγονὼς οὗτος ὀχληρὸς ᾖ.

πρὸς αἷς] i.e. πρὸς ἐκείναις ἅς, where ἅς is a cognate accusative after ἐσυκοφάντει. The actions alluded to are apparently those described in Or. 40 §§ 16, 17, for the mother's dowry, and other claims.

26. τίς χρηματιστής] sc. ποῖος, 'what sort of money-maker,' i.e. ὡς φαῦλος. [For τίς used as ποῖος, Shilleto, on Fals. Leg. § 15, quotes the present passage (translating it, 'what sort of an economist') and Or. 37, Pant. § 69, λέγε δή μοι τὰς μαρτυρίας, τίς ἐγώ...ἄνθρωπος εἰμί, followed by τοιοῦτος...ἐγώ.—For Mantias' character as an indifferent man of business cf. n. on ὑπόθεσις, l. 1. S.]

ἐπ' αὐτοφώρῳ] sc. ὄντα συκοφάντην. 'It thereby proves him to be *ipso facto* (as we say) dishonest in bringing these actions,' viz. since no money could have been due to him from the father, sc. ἐάν τι οὗτοι τῶν πατρῴων ἐπιζητῶσι, Or. 40 § 15.

δύ' οἰκίας] A wife seems only to have insisted on the mistress living apart. Hence Deianira's grievance in Soph. Trach. 376, τίν' εἰσδέδεγμαι πημονὴν ὑπόστεγον λαθραῖον; and ibid. 537, κόρην γὰρ—παρεισδέδεγμαι φόρτον ὥστε ναυτίλος.—τοιοῦτος ὤν, i.e. οὕτω δαπανηρός.

§§ 27, 8. *Having no sound excuse to allege for his conduct, Boeotus will pretend that the name (meaning 'bumpkin') was*

ταῦθ' ἅπερ ἀεὶ λέγει, ὡς ἐπηρέαζεν ὁ πατὴρ αὐτῷ[k] πειθόμενος ὑπ' ἐμοῦ, ἀξιοῖ δ' αὐτὸς ὡς δὴ πρεσβύτερος ὢν τοὔνομ' ἔχειν τὸ τοῦ πρὸς πατρὸς πάππου. πρὸς δὴ ταῦτα ἀκοῦσαι βέλτιον ὑμᾶς βραχέα. ἐγὼ γὰρ οἶδα τοῦτον, ὅτε οὔπω συγγενὴς ἦν ἐμοί, ὁρῶν ὥσπερ ἂν ἄλλον τινὰ οὑτωσί, νεώτερον ὄντα ἐμοῦ καὶ συχνῷ, ὅσα ἐξ ὄψεως, οὐ μὴν ἰσχυρίζομαι τούτῳ· καὶ γὰρ εὐ-
28 ηθες. ἀλλ' εἴ τις ἔροιτο Βοιωτὸν τουτονί, ὅτ' ἐν Ἱπποθωντίδι φυλῇ ἠξίου χορεύειν, οὔπω τοῦ πατρὸς εἶναι φάσκων τοῦ ἐμοῦ υἱός, τί σαυτὸν ἔχειν δικαίως ἂν θείης ὄνομα; εἰ γὰρ Μαντίθεον, οὐκ ἂν διὰ τοῦτό γε 1003 φαίης ὅτι πρεσβύτερος εἶ ἐμοῦ. ὃς γὰρ οὐδὲ τῆς φυλῆς τότε σοι προσήκειν ἡγοῦ τῆς ἐμῆς, πῶς ἂν τοῦ γε

[k] αὐτῷ Z.

given him by his father at my instigation on purpose to insult him. He says he is the elder, and has a claim to his grandfather's name. Why, I myself remember him a mere lad when I was grown up. And if one asked him what his name ought to have been at the time when he claimed the right of being sent to school in my tribe, he cannot say it was Mantitheus, as the senior; for if that had been so, he would not have been sent to the tribe Acamantis at all.

ἐπηρέαζεν] So Hor. Epist. II 1, 244, 'Boeotûm in crasso iurares aere natum.' Pind. Ol. VI 90, Βοιωτίαν ὗν. Cf. Mid. § 14, καὶ παρηκολούθησε παρ' ὅλην τὴν λειτουργίαν ἐπηρεάζων μοι συνεχῶς.

πρὸς πατρὸς κ.τ.λ.] The son usually took the name of the grandfather on the father's side. [Cf. Or. 40 § 6, where Cleon's name is given to his grandson. Arist. Aves 282 Ἱππόνικος Καλλίου κἀξ Ἱππονίκου Καλλίας. Nub. 65, ἐγὼ δὲ τοῦ πάππου 'τιθέμην Φειδωνίδην. (See Becker's Charicles II 7, or p. 219 of English Abridgment.) Similarly the kings of Cyrene were named Battus and Arcesilas alternately for eight generations. S.]

οἶδα τοῦτον...ὁρῶν] 'I remember seeing him, quite casually as one would any other (i.e. not at all as a brother), much younger than myself, to judge by his look.'

τούτῳ] i.e. the argument from mere appearance.

28. τῆς φυλῆς τῆς ἐμῆς] The genitive appears to depend on ἀμφισβητεῖν to be supplied from the next clause, 'you did not think you had any right to put in a claim to my tribe.' The argument is this: Boeotus, by the very fact of his going contentedly to school in a different tribe from mine, proves that he could not then have been called Mantitheus because he was my

πάππου τοῦ ἐμοῦ ἠμφισβήτεις[1]; ἔτι δ', ὦ ἄνδρες Ἀθη- 29
ναῖοι, τὸν μὲν τῶν ἐτῶν ἀριθμὸν οὐδεὶς οἶδεν ὑμῶν·
ἐγὼ μὲν γὰρ ἐμοὶ πλείονα, οὗτος δ' ἑαυτῷ φήσει· τὸν
δὲ τοῦ δικαίου λόγον ἅπαντες ἐπίστασθε. ἔστι δ' οὗτος τίς; ἀφ' οὗ παῖδας ἐποιήσατο τούτους ὁ πατήρ, ἀπὸ
τούτου καὶ νομίζεσθαι. πρότερον τοίνυν ἐμὲ εἰς τοὺς
δημότας ἐνέγραψε Μαντίθεον, πρὶν εἰσαγαγεῖν τοῦτον
εἰς τοὺς φράτερας. ὥστ' οὐ τῷ χρόνῳ μόνον, ἀλλὰ καὶ
τῷ δικαίῳ πρεσβεῖον ἔχοιμ' ἂν ἐγὼ τοὔνομα τοῦτ' εἰκότως. εἶεν. εἰ δέ τίς σ' ἔροιτο[m] "εἰπέ μοι, Βοιωτέ, πόθεν 30
νῦν Ἀκαμαντίδος φυλῆς γέγονας καὶ τῶν δήμων[n] Θορίκιος καὶ υἱὸς Μαντίου, καὶ τὸ μέρος τῶν ὑπ' ἐκείνου
καταλειφθέντων ἔχεις," οὐδὲν ἂν ἄλλ' ἔχοις εἰπεῖν
πλὴν ὅτι κἀμὲ[o] ζῶν ἐποιήσατο Μαντίας. τί τεκμήριον,
εἴ τίς σε ἔροιτο, ἢ μαρτύριόν ἐστί σοι τούτου; εἰς τοὺς
φράτεράς με εἰσήγαγε, φήσειας ἄν. τί οὖν σε ἐνέγρα-

[1] ἠμφεσβήτεις Z.   [m] σ' ἔροιτό τις Z cum Σ.
[n] τὸν δῆμον Bekk. 1824.   [o] Bekk. cum rA¹B. καὶ ἐμὲ Z.

senior; for if he had claimed the name on that ground, he would have claimed my tribe too.

§ 29. *As mere assertion on either side will not prove our respective ages, it will be the fairest way to reckon from the date of the adoption. Now it can be shown that I had been registered in the state-books (after the δοκιμασία), and that by the name Mantitheus, before he had been entered even in the phratries. So that by the mere right of prior entry (τῷ δικαίῳ) I should reasonably claim the name of Mantitheus on the ground of seniority.*

νομίζεσθαι] viz. παῖδας αὑτοῦ. 'We will say nothing about the δεκάτη, but argue only on the dates of our registration.'

πρεσβεῖον] The prerogative of primogeniture. Or. 36 § 35, πρεσβεῖα τὴν συνοικίαν ἔλαβε κατὰ διαθήκην.

§§ 30, 31. *Boeotus claims citizenship and a share of the property by virtue of his registration. But he was registered by the name Boeotus; and it would be ungrateful in him to disown the name now which conferred such privileges on him.*

φυλῆς γέγονας] As sup. § 25, ἐν Ἀκαμαντίδι φυλῇ γεγονώς.—
τῶν δήμων, lit. 'Of the demi, a member of that called Thoricus.' [τῶν δήμων, the reading of Σ, is supported against τὸν δῆμον by Plato, Euthyphro 2 B, τῶν δήμων Πιθεύς. S.]

ψεν ὄνομα, εἴ τις ἔροιτο, Βοιωτὸν ἂν εἴποις· τοῦτο γὰρ εἰσήχθης. οὐκοῦν δεινὸν εἰ τῆς μὲν πόλεως καὶ τῶν ὑπ' ἐκείνου καταλειφθέντων διὰ τοὔνομα τοῦτο μέτεστί σοι, τοῦτο δ' ἀξιοῖς ἀφεὶς ἕτερον μεταθέσθαι σαυτῷ. φέρ', εἴ σε ὁ πατὴρ ἀξιώσειεν ἀναστὰς ἢ μένειν ἐφ' οὗ σε αὐτὸς ἐποιήσατο ὀνόματος ἢ πατέρ' ἄλλον σαυτοῦ φάσκειν εἶναι, ἆρ' οὐκ ἂν μέτρια ἀξιοῦν δοκοίη; ταῦτα τοίνυν ταῦτα ἐγώ σε ἀξιῶ, ἢ πατρὸς ἄλλου σαυτὸν[p] παραγράφειν, ἢ τοὔνομα ἔχειν ὃ ἐκεῖνος ἔδωκέ σοι. νὴ Δί', ἀλλ' ὕβρει καὶ ἐπηρείᾳ τινὶ τοῦτο ἐτέθη σοι. ἀλλὰ 1004 πολλάκις μὲν, ὅτ' οὐκ ἐποιεῖτο ὁ πατὴρ τούτους, ἔλεγον οὗτοι ὡς οὐδὲν χείρους εἰσὶν οἱ τῆς μητρὸς τῆς τούτου συγγενεῖς τῶν τοῦ πατρὸς τοῦ ἐμοῦ. ἔστι δ' ὁ Βοιωτὸς ἀδελφοῦ τῆς τούτου μητρὸς ὄνομα. ἐπειδὴ δ' εἰσάγειν ὁ πατὴρ τούτους ἠναγκάζετο, ἐμοῦ προεισηγμένου

[p] σεαυτόν Z.

§ 31. *If your father were to come to life, he might fairly ask you either to retain the name he gave you, or to give up the claim you made to be his son. My request is similar; keep the name he gave you, or, if you must be Mantitheus, which is my name, don't sign yourself* Μαντίθεος Μαντίου.

ἀφείς] *Omisso hoc nomine.*—μεταθέσθαι, ἄλλο ὄνομα ἐπιθέσθαι.

ἀναστάς] If he were now to rise up, as if conjured by magic art. So Plato, Theaet. p. 171 D, εἰ αὐτίκα ἐντεῦθεν ἀνακύψειε μέχρι τοῦ αὐχένος, sc. Πρωταγόρας. That this is the meaning seems probable from an engraving on an antique gem, representing a head rising up out of the floor, and a person standing by with a magic wand.—ἐφ' οὗ, the cognate accusative is implied, 'to remain in possession of the name by which he adopted you.'

παραγράφειν] 'To sign yourself.' Kennedy. This seems the technical word in this sense; cf. § 9. [Rather, 'to *add* to your name (or signature) that of another father.' S.] The middle voice, of course, has quite a different meaning, 'to put in a special plea.'

§§ 32, 3. *The name Boeotus, we shall be told, was given in insult. Why, this man and his brother used to boast of their good family; and, in fact, Boeotus is the name of his uncle by his mother's side. It was because I had forestalled the name Mantitheus that the other name was given to him, and without the least intention of putting a slight upon him. You compel us to say that you deserved the name you so dislike, by your own insulting and boorish treatment of your father's memory and intentions.*

p. 1004] ΠΕΡΙ ΤΟΥ ΟΝΟΜΑΤΟΣ. 169

Μαντιθέου, οὕτω τοῦτον εἰσάγει Βοιωτόν, τὸν ἀδελφὸν δ' αὐτοῦ Πάμφιλον. ἐπεὶ σὺ δεῖξον ὅστις Ἀθηναίων ταὐτὸν ὄνομα τοῖς αὐτοῦ παισὶν ἔθετο δυοῖν. κἂν δείξῃς, ἐγὼ συγχωρήσω δι' ἐπήρειάν σοι τοῦτο τοὔνομα θέσθαι τὸν πατέρα. καίτοι εἴ γε τοιοῦτος 33 ἦσθα ὥστε ποιήσασθαι μὲν σαυτὸν ἀναγκάσαι, ἐξ ὅτου δ' ἀρέσεις ἐκείνῳ τρόπου μὴ σκοπεῖν, οὐκ ἦσθα οἷον δεῖ τὸν προσήκοντα εἶναι περὶ τοὺς γονέας, οὐκ ὢν δὲ οὐκ ἐπηρεάζου δικαίως ἄν, ἀλλ' ἀπωλώλεις[q]. ἦ δεινόν γ' ἂν εἴη, εἰ κατὰ μὲν τῶν ὑπὸ τοῦ πατρὸς αὐτοῦ νομιζομένων παίδων οἱ περὶ τῶν γονέων ἰσχύσουσι νόμοι, κατὰ δὲ τῶν αὑτοὺς εἰσβιαζομένων ἄκοντας ποιεῖσθαι ἄκυροι γενήσονται.

[q] ἀπολώλεις Z.

ἐπεὶ σὺ δεῖξον] 'Else, *you* must prove.' For this use of ἐπεὶ implying a suppressed clause, e.g. 'if you deny it,' cf. Soph. El. 352, ἐπεὶ δίδαξον, and Ar. Vesp. 72, ἐπεὶ τοπάζετε. S.]
33. καίτοι κ.τ.λ.] 'And yet, if you were so perverse as to compel your father to adopt you, and yet not to consider how you might please him, you did not behave as so near a relative should do towards his parents; and as you did not, you deserved to be not only spoken of with contempt, but even to be put to death. For it would be hard indeed, if the laws about parents are to be in force against those who are recognised by the father himself as his sons, but are to become null and void against those who force their fathers to adopt them against their will.'

ἐκείνῳ] Of a deceased person this is used where αὐτῷ would have been used of one living. See on Or. 40 § 28.

This is a common use, answering to our phrase 'the *late* so and so;' but it is apt to be overlooked. Properly, 'the man there,' ἐκεῖ, viz. in the other world, opposed to οὗτος, 'here before us.'

οἷον κ.τ.λ.] Construe οἷον δεῖ εἶναι περὶ τ. γ., as a man is said to be δίκαιος περὶ πόλιν, &c.

νόμοι] The laws of Draco seem to have been still in force, though perhaps in abeyance. Like the Jews, the patriarchal traditions of the Greeks induced them to hold the dignity and authority of a parent in a very sacred light. See Aesch. Suppl. 708, τὸ γὰρ τεκόντων σέβας, τρίτον τόδ' ἐν θεσμίοις δίκας γέγραπται μεγιστοτίμου. In Ar. Vesp. 377, μὴ πατεῖν τὰ ταῖν θεαῖν ψηφίσματα refers to this, but ψηφίσματα stands for some other word like μυστήρια.

εἰσβιαζομένων] This is used for ἀναγκαζόντων rather with reference to an alien forcing himself upon the state, like the ora-

34 Ἀλλ', ὦ χαλεπώτατε Βοιωτὲ, μάλιστα μὲν ὧν πράττεις πάντων παῦσαι, εἰ δ' ἄρα μὴ βούλει, ἐκεῖνό γε πρὸς Διὸς πείθου· παῦσαι μὲν σαυτῷ παρέχων πράγματα, παῦσαι δ' ἐμὲ συκοφαντῶν, ἀγάπα δ' ὅτι σοι πόλις, οὐσία, πατὴρ γέγονεν. οὐδεὶς ἀπελαύνει σε ἀπὸ τούτων, οὔκουν ἔγωγε. ἀλλ' ἂν μὲν[r], ὥσπερ εἶναι φῇς ἀδελφὸς, καὶ τὰ ἔργα ἀδελφοῦ ποιῇς, δόξεις εἶναι συγγενὴς, ἂν δ' ἐπιβουλεύῃς, δικάζῃ, φθονῇς, βλασφημῇς, δόξεις εἰς ἀλλότρια ἐμπεσὼν ὡς οὐ προσ-

[r] om. Z cum Σ.

tor in Eur. Orest. 904, who is called, probably in reference to the demagogue Cleophon, Ἀργεῖος, οὐκ Ἀργεῖος, ἠναγκασμένος, and ὁ μὲν γὰρ οὐκ ὢν ἀστὸς ἐσβιάζεται, Ar. Av. 32. ['Those who force their parents to adopt them against their will.' Prof. Kennedy.]

§ 34. *Do therefore, most troublesome Churl (as you tell us your name means), do stop and give neither yourself nor me any further trouble. If you want to be thought my brother in reality and not merely in name, act like a brother. Otherwise, people will think you have got possession of property that you had no real claim to.*

ἀλλ', ὦ χαλεπώτατε Βοιωτὲ] Hermogenes περὶ ἰδεῶν, I 11 p. 325 Spengel: οὔτε τραχύτητι οὔτε σεμνότητι οὔτε λαμπρότητι οὔτε ἀκμῇ χρήσαιτο ἄν τις ἀκριβῶς ἐν ἰδιωτικοῖς· σφοδρότητι μέντοι ἔστιν ὅπου, καὶ ταύτῃ μετὰ ἤθους τινὸς, ὡς ἐν τῷ, ἀλλ', ὦ χαλεπώτατε Βοιωτέ, δύναται χρῆσθαι. S.]

οὔκουν ἔγωγε] 'Nor do I,' Kennedy. Here, as frequently, the γε gives its emphasis to the οὖν, and so the formula means οὐκ ἐγὼ γοῦν, 'at all events not I.' So Soph. Oed. Col. 924, οὔκουν ἔγωγε, σῆς ἐπεμβαίνων χθονὸς, οὐδ' εἰ τὰ πάντων εἶχον ἐνδικώτατα, οὔθ' εἷλκον οὔτ' ἂν ἦγον.

ἐπιβουλεύῃς κ.τ.λ.] 'If you go on plotting thus,' &c. So κλάῃ καὶ ὀδύρηται inf.—ὡς οὐ προσήκουσιν, i. e. as not properly your own,—as not belonging to you. There may have been a saying, that money badly acquired was generally badly spent [cf. Cic. Phil. II 65 'male parta male dilabuntur']. At all events, a bad use of property was thought to be a proof that it was not rightly obtained. Cf. Or. 21 (in Mid.) 150 τὸ τῆς φύσεως βάρβαρον ἀληθῶς καὶ θεοῖς ἐχθρὸν ἕλκει καὶ βιάζεται, καὶ φανερὸν ποιεῖ τοῖς παροῦσιν ὥσπερ ἀλλοτρίοις, ὅπερ ἐστὶν, αὐτὸν χρώμενον.

§§ 35, 6. *It was not I who did you wrong, since I followed my father's wish in the matter throughout. That I did so, is proved by the privileges you possess; neither I nor any one else wants to take them from you. You can retain them, nay, you can go to law with me, if you please, by the name Boeotus. In fact, it is your own interest to be called by that name; for you would not like to have it said,*

1005 ἤκουσιν οὕτω χρῆσθαι. ἐπεὶ ἔγωγ' οὐδ' εἰ τὰ μάλιστα 35
ὁ πατὴρ ὄντα σε αὑτοῦ μὴ ἐποιεῖτο ἀδικῶ[s]. οὐ γὰρ
ἔμοιγε προσῆκεν εἰδέναι τίνες εἰσὶν υἱεῖς ἐκείνου, ἀλλ'
ἐκείνῳ δεῖξαι τίνα ἐμοὶ νομιστέον ἔστ' ἀδελφόν. ὃν
μὲν τοίνυν οὐκ ἐποιεῖτό σε χρόνον, οὐδ' ἐγὼ προσῆ-
κονθ' ἡγούμην, ἐπειδὴ δ' ἐποιήσατο, κἀγὼ νομίζω.
τί τούτου σημεῖον; τῶν πατρῴων ἔχεις τὸ μέρος μετὰ
τὴν τοῦ πατρὸς τελευτήν· ἱερῶν, ὁσίων μετέχεις· ἀπά-
γει σε οὐδεὶς ἀπὸ τούτων. τί βούλει; ἂν δὲ φῇ δεινὰ
πάσχειν καὶ κλάῃ[t] καὶ ὀδύρηται καὶ κατηγορῇ ἐμοῦ,
ἃ μὲν ἂν[u] λέγῃ, μὴ πιστεύετε· οὐ γὰρ δίκαιον μὴ περὶ
τούτων[v] ὄντος τοῦ λόγου νυνί[w]· ἐκεῖνο δ' ὑπολαμβάνετε, ὅτι οὐδὲν ἔστ' αὐτῷ ἧττον δίκην λαμβάνειν
Βοιωτῷ κληθέντι. τί οὖν φιλονεικεῖς; μηδαμῶς· μὴ 36
ἔχε οὕτω πρὸς ἡμᾶς ἐθελέχθρως· οὐδὲ γὰρ ἐγὼ πρὸς

[s] οὐκ ἀδικῶ Bekk. 1824.   [t] κλαίῃ Z. Cf. Veitch, Greek Vbs.
[u] ἂν μὲν Z (ἂν μὲν Σ).   [v] τούτου Z cum ΣrA¹.
[w] τοῦ νυνί Z.   νυνὶ Bekk. st. cum rA¹.

by 'way of distinction, that you are the Mantitheus who forced his father to adopt him.
εἰ τὰ μάλιστα] 'If ever so much,' i.e. if it is ever so true that your father declined to acknowledge you though you were his son.
οὐ γὰρ] i.e. I might have wronged you if his recognition of you had depended on me.
ἱερῶν, ὁσίων] Religious privileges as well as those of the state (secular or political). The first depended on the enrolment into the phratriae, the latter on that into the γραμματεῖον ληξιαρχικόν. So Timocr. p. 703, § 9, τῶν ἱερῶν μὲν χρημάτων τοὺς θεοὺς, τῶν ὁσίων δὲ τὴν πόλιν ἀποστερεῖ. Thuc. II 52, ἐς ὀλιγωρίαν ἐτράποντο καὶ ἱερῶν καὶ ὁσίων ὁμοίως.

ἃ μὲν ἂν λέγῃ] 'Whatever he may say, don't believe him.' Our idiom perhaps is, 'don't believe what he says,' though the phrases are not really identical. He means, τοῖς μὲν λεγομένοις μὴ πιστεύετε, ἐκεῖνο δὲ, &c.—μὴ περὶ τούτων ὄντος, 'siquidem hac de re nunc non disputatur.' (See Shilleto, not. crit. on Thuc. I 118 § 2.)— ὑπολαμβάνετε, 'give him this answer; that he can get satisfaction just as well by the name Boeotus.'
36. ἐθελέχθρως] 'Wishful of enmity.' A singular and rare compound. The adjective is quoted from Cratinus (Frag. incert. 103). A word of similar character is φιλαπεχθήμων, in Timocr. p. 701 § 6.

σὲ, ἐπεὶ καὶ νῦν, ἵνα μηδὲ τοῦτο λάθῃ σε, ὑπὲρ σοῦ λέγω[x] μᾶλλον, ἀξιῶν[x] μὴ ταὐτὸν ἔχειν ὄνομα ἡμᾶς, ἢ ἐμαυτοῦ[y]. εἰ γὰρ μηδὲν ἄλλο, ἀνάγκη τὸν ἀκούσαντα ἐρέσθαι πότερος, δύ᾽ ἂν ὦσι Μαντίθεοι Μαντίου. οὐκοῦν, ὃν ἠναγκάσθη ποιήσασθαι, σὲ ἂν[z] λέγῃ, ἐρεῖ. τί οὖν ἐπιθυμεῖς τούτων; ἀνάγνωθι δέ μοι λαβὼν δύο ταυτασὶ μαρτυρίας, ὡς ἐμοὶ Μαντίθεον καὶ τούτῳ Βοιωτὸν ὁ πατὴρ ὄνομ᾽ ἔθετο.

ΜΑΡΤΥΡΙΑΙ.

37 Λοιπὸν ἡγοῦμαι τοῦθ᾽ ὑμῖν ἐπιδεῖξαι, ὦ ἄνδρες Ἀθηναῖοι[a], ὡς οὐ μόνον εὐορκήσετε, ἂν ἃ ἐγὼ λέγω ψηφίσησθε, ἀλλὰ καὶ ὡς οὗτος αὐτὸς αὑτοῦ κατέγνω Βοιωτὸν, ἀλλ᾽ οὐ Μαντίθεον ὄνομα δικαίως ἂν ἔχειν. 1006 λαχόντος γὰρ ἐμοῦ τὴν δίκην ταύτην Βοιωτῷ Μαντίου Θορικίῳ, ἐξ ἀρχῆς τ᾽ ἠντιδίκει[b] καὶ ὑπώμνυτο ὡς ὢν

[x] Bekker. λέγων μ. ἀξιῶ Z. λέγειν μ. ἀξιῶ FΣΦ.
[y] ἢ ἐμαυτοῦ Bekk. 1824 cum marg. Σ.   om. Z cum Σ.
[z] ἐὰν Z.   [a] δικασταί Bekk. 1824.   [b] ἠντεδίκει Z.

τούτων] Such inconveniences and causes of reproach as I have described.

§§ 37, 8. One proof that he considered his name to be really Boeotus and not Mantitheus is, that under the former name he both accepted the action I brought, and moved for a rule for a new trial against the decision of the arbitrators.

[§ 39 is closely connected with § 36, and the two intervening sections must have been inserted after the arbitration, shortly before the trial. Blass Att. Ber. III 417. S.]

ἃ ἐγὼ λέγω] 'What I say,' i.e. rather than what he says. So Plato, Theaet. p. 161 B, σὺ κάλλιον, ὦ Σώκρατες, λέγεις. This explains the important texts S. Matth. 27. 11, S. John 18. 34.

κατέγνω] Lit. 'gave a verdict against himself to the effect that he would rightly have the name Boeotus and not Mantitheus.'

ἠντιδίκει καὶ ὑπώμνυτο] 'He at once accepted service of the suit, and put in an oath that he was unable to attend.' The ὑπωμοσία is here spoken of as one of the many evasions adopted by those who endeavoured to thwart justice. From Ar. Plut. 725, it is clear that it was occasionally put in as an aegrotat, a certificate of illhealth. Compare Mid. p. 541, § 84. Or. 48 § 25.

p. 1006] ΠΕΡΙ ΤΟΥ ΟΝΟΜΑΤΟΣ. 173

Βοιωτὸς καὶ τὸ τελευταῖον ἐπεὶ οὐκέτι ἐνῆν αὐτῷ διακρούσασθαι, ἐρήμην ἐάσας καταδιαιτῆσαι, σκέψασθε πρὸς θεῶν τί ἐποίησεν· ἀντιλαγχάνει μοι τὴν μὴ οὖ- 38 σαν Βοιωτὸν αὐτὸν προσαγορεύσας. καίτοι ἐξ ἀρχῆς τε ἔδει ἐᾶν αὐτὸν τελέσασθαι τὴν δίκην κατὰ Βοιωτοῦ, εἴπερ μηδὲν προσῆκεν αὐτῷ τοῦ ὀνόματος, ὕστερόν τε μὴ αὐτὸν φαίνεσθαι ἐπὶ τῷ ὀνόματι τούτῳ ἀντιλαγχάνοντα τὴν μὴ οὖσαν. ὃς οὖν αὐτὸς αὑτοῦ κατέγνω δικαίως εἶναι Βοιωτός, τί ὑμᾶς ἀξιώσει τοὺς ὀμωμοκότας ψηφίζεσθαι; ὡς δὲ ταῦτ' ἀληθῆ λέγω, λαβέ μοι τὴν ἀντίληξιν καὶ τὸ ἔγκλημα τουτί.

ΑΝΤΙΛΗΞΙΣ. ΕΓΚΛΗΜΑ.

Εἰ μὲν τοίνυν οὗτος ἔχει δεῖξαι νόμον ὃς ποιεῖ κυ- 39 ρίους εἶναι τοὺς παῖδας τοῦ ἑαυτῶν ὀνόματος, ἃ λέγει

ἐάσας κ.τ.λ.] He let the arbitrators give judgment against him by default (compare Mid. ut sup.), and then moved for a new trial under the name of Boeotus. The phrase ἀντιλαγχάνειν τὴν μὴ οὖσαν means to obtain a new trial of the reference (Kennedy, Appen. x, p. 398), i.e. to set aside a verdict on the ground that it is wrong, and therefore that the trial is null and void, non-existent, as it were. Mid. p. 543 § 90, ἀλλὰ τὴν μὴ οὖσαν ἀντιλαχεῖν αὐτῷ ἐξῆν δήπου. [Pollux: ὁπόταν τις παρὰ διαιτηταῖς παραγραψάμενος καὶ ὑπομοσάμενος νόσον ἢ ἀποδημίαν, εἰς τὴν κυρίαν μὴ ἀπαντήσας ἐρήμην ὄφλῃ, ἐξῆν ἐντὸς δέκα ἡμερῶν τὴν μὴ οὖσαν ἀντιλαχεῖν, καὶ ἡ ἐρήμη ἐλύετο, ὡς ἐξ ἀρχῆς ἐλθεῖν ἐπὶ διαιτητήν (viii 60). (Hudtwalcker über die Diaeteten, p. 99 ff.) S.]

38. προσαγορεύσας] See note on Isocr. Paneg. § 25, προσειπεῖν. S.]

ἐξ ἀρχῆς] 'He ought to have let me get the original action to go against Boeotus, if he had no claim to the name at all, and not to come forward himself afterwards to ask for a new rule by this name.' Compare a similar argument in Or. 40 § 18.

The subject of τελέσασθαι seems to be ἐμέ. Kennedy translates, 'he should in the first instance have allowed the suit to proceed to its termination against Boeotus.' But it may be suggested that τετελέσθαι is the true reading. Cf. Or. 38 (πρὸς Ναυσιμ.) 18, δεινὸν ἂν εἴη εἰ——εἰκοστῷ νῦν ἔτει δίκην τελέσαισθ' ὑμεῖς.

τί ἀξιώσει κ.τ.λ.] 'What verdict will he expect you on your oaths to give?' i.e. it is not very likely you will decide that he ought to be called Mantitheus.

§ 39. If he can show a law that gives children a right to name themselves, then you will

νῦν οὗτος, ὀρθῶς ἂν ψηφίζοισθε. εἰ δ' ὁ μὲν νόμος, ὃν πάντες ἐπίστασθε ὁμοίως ἐμοί, τοὺς γονέας ποιεῖ κυρίους οὐ μόνον θέσθαι τοὔνομα ἐξ ἀρχῆς, ἀλλὰ κἂν πάλιν ἐξαλεῖψαι βούλωνται καὶ ἀποκηρῦξαι, ἐπέδειξα δ' ἐγὼ τὸν πατέρα, ὃς κύριος ἦν ἐκ τοῦ νόμου, τούτῳ μὲν Βοιωτὸν, ἐμοὶ δὲ Μαντίθεον θέμενον, πῶς ὑμῖν 40 ἔστιν ἄλλο τι πλὴν ἁγὼ λέγω ψηφίσασθαι; ἀλλὰ μὴν ὧν γ' ἂν μὴ ὦσι νόμοι[c], γνώμῃ τῇ δικαιοτάτῃ δικάσειν ὀμωμόκατε, ὥστ' εἰ μηδεὶς ἦν περὶ τούτων κείμενος νόμος, κἂν οὕτω δικαίως πρὸς ἐμοῦ τὴν ψῆφον ἔθεσθε. τίς γάρ ἐστιν ὑμῶν ὅστις ταὐτὸν ὄνομα τοῖς αὑ- 1007 τοῦ παισὶ τέθειται δυοῖν[d]; τίς δ', ᾧ μήπω παῖδες εἰσὶ,

[c] νόμοι ὦσι Z.   [d] Σ (cf. § 32). δυοῖν οὖσιν Bekk. 1824.

properly vote for him; but if the law gives fathers the fullest power over both the name and the property of sons, and if Mantias did legally call me by one name and him by another, how can you, if you act by the law, refuse my request?

ἐξαλεῖψαι] To erase it from the list of citizens. So Cleon is said in making a certain speaker ἄτιμος, τὸν Γρύττον ἐξαλεῖψαι, Ar. Equit. 877. So also Or. 37 § 34.—ἀποκηρῦξαι, ἀπειπεῖν, to disclaim or disinherit him. The absolute power of the father over the status of the son was the same in both the Attic and the Roman law.

['Révoquer publiquement.' ἀποκήρυξις signifie ici tout simplement la proclamation par la voix du héraut. Les lexicographes donnent encore à ce mot un autre sens, celui de la répudiation du fils par le père. Mais voyez à ce sujet les judicieuses observations de Van den Es, *de iure familiarum apud Athenienses*, p. 125—135.' Da-reste.]

§§ 40, 1. *In default of the express command of the law, you are bound (i.e. by the terms of your oath) to vote as you think most just; so that even on this ground you ought to vote for me. No father ever does or ever will give the same name to two sons, so that what you think is right for your own children you ought to think is right also for me.*

ὧν ἂν μὴ ὦσι νόμοι] The oath of the heliasts in Timocr. (Or. 24) p. 746 commences with ψηφιοῦμαι κατὰ τοὺς νόμους. [Pollux VIII 122, ὁ δ' ὅρκος ἦν τῶν δικαστῶν περὶ μὲν ὧν νόμοι εἰσί, ψηφιεῖσθαι κατὰ τοὺς νόμους, περὶ δὲ ὧν μὴ εἰσί, γνώμῃ τῇ δικαιοτάτῃ. S.]

πρὸς ἐμοῦ] 'On my side,' virtually the same as πρὸ ἐμοῦ. So Soph. Trach. 150, ἤτοι πρὸς ἀνδρὸς ἢ τέκνων φοβουμένη.

τέθειται] In the usual medial sense. Cf. ὑπόθεσις 1. 23 n.— ᾧ μήπω κ.τ.λ. 'cui nondum sint liberi.'

θήσεται^e· οὐδεὶς δήπου. οὐκοῦν ὃ δίκαιον τῇ γνώμῃ 41
τοῖς ὑμετέροις αὐτῶν παισὶν ὑπειλήφατε, τοῦτο καὶ
περὶ ἡμῶν εὐσεβὲς γνῶναι. ὥστε καὶ κατὰ τὴν δικαιο-
τάτην γνώμην καὶ κατὰ τοὺς νόμους καὶ κατὰ τοὺς
ὅρκους καὶ κατὰ τὴν τούτου προσομολογίαν ἐγὼ μὲν
μέτρια ὑμῶν, ὦ ἄνδρες Ἀθηναῖοι, δέομαι καὶ δίκαια
ἀξιῶ, οὗτος δ' οὐ μόνον οὐ μέτρια, ἀλλ' οὐδ' εἰωθότα
γίγνεσθαι.

^e τίs—θήσεται *in margine a correctore additum habet* Σ, *om.* Z.

41. εὐσεβὲς] 'Your duty in accordance with your oath.' For this technical sense, see the note on Eur. Med. 755. Hipp. 656, 1309 (P.).

τὴν τούτου προσομολογίαν] The admission he made, by accepting the action, § 37.

The grounds for a verdict of the dicasts in his favour are briefly summed up again; the law, their sense of right, their oath to decide by that sense, and the defendant's own admission that Boeotus was and is his name.

OR. XL.

ΠΡΟΣ ΒΟΙΩΤΟΝ ΠΕΡΙ ΠΡΟΙΚΟΣ ΜΗΤΡΩΙΑΣ.

THE parties in this suit are the same as in the preceding. The action now brought against the defendant is for a sum of money claimed out of the general property as due exclusively to Mantitheus, viz. a talent as the dower of his mother, to which he had a legal claim (§ 59). The dispute seems to have been an old one; for in §§ 3 and 18 the plaintiff says that after a lapse of eleven years he has come into court, all attempts to settle the matter by arbitration having failed. The claim was evidently first made by Mantitheus soon after his father's death. He had recognised his two half-brothers as co-heirs, and was willing to let them take a third share each, though perhaps he was not legally bound to do this[1]. But he asserted his right to the talent over and above his own third part. Upon this Boeotus makes a counter-claim to

---

[1] In Or. 39 § 6, he says, συγκεχωρηκέναι τὸ τρίτον νείμασ- θαι μέρος, as if it were a voluntary concession on his part. But in § 13 of the present speech he says he acknowledged Boeotus and Pamphilus in obedience to the law, though they were not his brothers. From which we may infer, not, as Kennedy thinks, that Mantias must have married Plango after the death of his first wife, but that the adoption by the father entitled them to a share in the property. Indeed, this is virtually asserted in Or. 39 §§ 6, 20, 30. It appears likely that this would carry with it a legal claim (§ 59) to Plango's property under the title of προῖκα, or dowry.

ΠΡΟΣ ΒΟΙΩΤΟΝ ΠΕΡΙ ΠΡΟΙ. ΜΗ. 177

the same sum, τὴν ἴσην προῖκα[1], due to himself from his mother Plango (§ 14), and, as it seems, to some further property due from his father (§ 15). He thought, no doubt, that his brother would decline to risk an action for a still larger demand than that which he had himself made, and which might go against him; and in default of direct evidence, he trusted probably to vague, indirect, and purposely misleading inferences (παραγωγαὶ, § 21), to establish the allegation that Plango had a fortune. This, however, is denied and disproved by counter-testimony by Mantitheus.

For the time being, the dispute seems to have been settled by the division of the bulk of Mantias' personal property, reserving only the slaves and the family house (οἰκία), the former for the sake of evidence on either side, the latter for payment of the claims, whichever side should prove to have a right to them.

This agreement being made, the cross-suits appear to have at once commenced. Each claimed his mother's dower out of the residuary property. The case was referred to an arbitrator Solon (§ 16), who however died before the decision could be given, in consequence of the delays and evasions of Boeotus. The latter then brings a fresh action against Mantitheus, and Mantitheus renews his old claim against Boeotus, and by that name. There are grounds for believing[2] the man had established his right to the name of Mantitheus: anyhow, when the case went against him as Boeotus, he denied that this was his name and took no notice whatever of the decision (§§ 17, 18). Consequently, the real Mantitheus is compelled to sue him again in the eleventh year, in the court. Boeotus, it would seem, had changed his claim for Plango's

[1] In § 20 it is said that Plango's dower was more than 100 minae. (See the note on § 14.)
[2] See Introd. Or. 39 ad fin.

dower to a demand for some other property, which is not specified[1]; but his motive was the same, to cancel one demand by another, and he probably made that demand which he thought he could best establish on the slaves' evidence.

That Boeotus had played the bully for a long time, and made many vexatious claims on his brother, is clear from the evidence adduced. He had behaved so badly, in fact, that Mantitheus had been compelled to leave his own home. Many instances are given in which the old quarrel about the name had led to most disagreeable results and misunderstandings. In truth, throughout both the speeches the *animus* manifested on both sides is as bad as possible. In § 57 the plaintiff intimates that he had fears of being poisoned if he had continued to live in the same house. And he even takes pains to show that he did not believe the defendants were his father's sons at all. He regards the whole affair of the forced adoption as a scandalous fraud.

In one part of the present speech (§§ 8—12) the orator repeats, with some slight addition to the details, the subject of the preceding action about the name. The argument against the present claim of Boeotus turns (§§ 20—24) on the improbability of his mother's father, who died a debtor to the state, having left any money over and above, that could have come to Mantias after the confiscation of the property. On the other hand, it is shown

---

[1] § 17, οὐ νῦν περὶ ἐκείνων εἴληχέ μοι δίκην οὐδεμίαν, ἀλλὰ περὶ ἄλλων τινῶν. There is some obscurity on this point which is not fully cleared up in the course of the speech. Perhaps the arbitrators' decision in favour of Mantitheus had released him from the payment of Plango's dower; and so it was thought unsafe to make precisely the same demand in a new action. From § 3, ἕνεκα τῆς δίκης ταύτης, it appears likely that some other claims were trumped up for the sake of furnishing the matter of a cross-suit.

ΠΡΟΙΚΟΣ ΜΗΤΡΩΙΑΣ. 179

(§§ 24, 25) that Mantitheus' mother was a lady of property, the daughter of Polyaratus, and sister of the wife of Chabrias. Her first husband was a son of Cleon (§ 25), and it is argued that such a man was not likely to have married a penniless wife. Her brothers too were men of wealth and honour who were not likely to have seen their sister wronged (§ 25).

The precise date of the action is uncertain. That the misconduct of Boeotus had gone on for eleven years after the death of Mantias is expressly stated (§ 3). And from § 34 it is also clear that the enrolment by the name of Mantitheus instead of Boeotus had been made after some at least of his vexatious proceedings (μετὰ ταῦτα Μαντίθεον ἑαυτὸν ἐγγράψας εἰς τοὺς δημότας). In § 35 however he speaks of the action περὶ τοῦ ὀνόματος having been already brought; and there is nothing in the present speech to indicate how soon afterwards the trial about the dowry was commenced.

[The present trial seems to have taken place in the eleventh year after the death of Mantias, who according to the evidence of inscriptions (see note 1 on p. 140) was alive at the end of Ol. 105, 3 = B.C. 357. The earliest possible date for his death is Ol. 105, 4 = B.C. 356, which would give us Ol. 108, 2 = B.C. 347—6 as the probable date of the present trial. This conclusion is supported by other details minutely stated by Arnold Schaefer (*Dem. u. s. Zeit* III 2, 224), and coincides with a passage of Dionysius of Halicarnassus[1], placing the trial περὶ

---

[1] Dionys. (on Deinarchus, § 13 p. 666, 1) πρὸς Μαντίθεον περὶ προικός· 'Πάντων ἐστὶν ἀναιρότατον.' οὗτος ἀκολουθεῖ τῷ προτέρῳ λόγῳ καὶ πολλὰ ἔχει κατὰ λέξιν ταὐτά, ἃ εἴη ἂν τοῦ αὐτοῦ ῥήτορος, ἔξω τῆς Δεινάρχου ἡλικίας. [καὶ γὰρ οὔ] πολλοῖς ἔτεσιν ὕστερον ἠγώνισται τὸν ἀγῶνα ὁ κατήγορος, ἀλλὰ δύο ἢ τρισίν, ὡς ἀκριβέστερον περὶ αὐτῶν ἐν τῇ Δημοσθένους γραφῇ δεδηλώκαμεν. The restoration in brackets is due to Sauppe.—For a minor chronological point, see on § 37.

XL. ΠΡΟΣ ΒΟΙΩΤΟΝ ΠΕΡΙ

προικὸς *two or three* years after the trial περὶ ὀνόματος, which probably belongs to B.C. 350.

Arnold Schaefer (*u. s.* pp. 225—6) holds the present speech inferior to the speech περὶ ὀνόματος both in grasp of subject-matter and in style and expression. The writer was clearly familiar with the earlier speech, and several closely parallel passages occur in the two orations, which are in some cases better expressed in the earlier speech (cf. Or. 39 § 23 with 40 § 29; 39 § 2 with 40 § 9). For these and similar reasons he concludes that the περὶ προικὸς was not written by Demosthenes. Having in the former case availed himself of the help of Demosthenes without success, the plaintiff may have resorted to another advocate in the latter. In frequency of hiatus and in absence of rhythm the speech is unlike the genuine work of Demosthenes; and, for these and other reasons, Blass agrees with Schaefer in regarding it as the work of another writer. *Att. Ber.* III 453. S.]

ΠΡΟΙΚΟΣ ΜΗΤΡΩΙΑΣ.   181

[The following tables may illustrate some of the genealogical details involved in the case:

Clegenetus of Κυδαθήναιον.
|
CLEON Or. 40 § 25 (the demagogue, *ob.* B.C. 422).
|
Cleomedon, § 6 + Daughter*, § 6 ———— Menoxenus, §§ 6, 25.   Polyaratus of Χολαργός
(whose second (§§ 6 and 24)
husband was (*ob.* soon after B.C. 399).
MANTIAS). |
 ———————————————
 | | | |
Cleon   Three   Daughter, § 24   Bathyllus, §§ 6, 25.   Periander, § 6
(§ 6 *ad fin.*).   daughters.   (married to   (trierarch in
Eryximachus   B.C. 357).
whose sister
is wife of the   Polyaratus of Χο-
famous general   λαργός (trierarch
Chabrias).   in Samian war
B.C. 322).

Pamphilus (§ 20) of Κειριάδαι.
|
Boeotus, § 23.   Hedylus, § 23.   Euthydemus, § 23.   PLANGON + Mantitheus of Θορικός.
(*ob.* B.C. 356?)
|
BOEOTUS (or Mantitheus the elder).   Pamphilus,   MANTIAS   Daughter* of Polyaratus
§ 11. | and widow of Cleomedon.
 —————————
 | |
MANTITHEUS   Son (died early, § 7).
(the younger).
|
Daughter, § 13.

(Cf. A. Schaefer, *u. s.* pp. 211—4.)   S.]

XL.

ΠΡΟΣ ΒΟΙΩΤΟΝ ΠΕΡΙ ΠΡΟΙΚΟΣ ΜΗΤΡΩΙΑΣ.

ΥΠΟΘΕΣΙΣ.

Καὶ οὗτος παρὰ τοῦ αὐτοῦ καὶ πρὸς τὸν αὐτὸν ὁ λόγος εἴρηται. καὶ τὰ μὲν ἄλλα πάντα ταὐτά, ἡ Πλαγγὼν, ὁ ὅρκος, ἡ τῶν παίδων ἀναγκαία ποίησις. ἀποθανόντος δὲ τοῦ Μαντίου οἱ παῖδες ὄντες τρεῖς, 5 Μαντίθεος ὁ ἐκ τῆς νόμῳ γαμηθείσης καὶ Βοιωτὸς καὶ Πάμφιλος οἱ ἐκ τῆς Πλαγγόνος, ἐνέμοντο τὴν οὐσίαν. φάσκοντος δὲ τοῦ Μαντιθέου προῖκα ἑαυτῷ μητρῴαν ὀφείλεσθαι, Βοιωτὸς καὶ Πάμφιλος καὶ αὐτοὶ προικὸς ἠμφισβήτουν, ὡς καὶ τῆς Πλαγγόνος εἰσενεγκα-
10 μένης εἰς τὸν οἶκον τοῦ Μαντίου μνᾶς ἑκατόν. συνέδοξεν οὖν αὐτοῖς νείμασθαι πάντα ἐπ' ἴσης πλὴν τῆς οἰκίας, ἵν' ὁποτέρων ἂν ἡ μήτηρ φανῇ προῖκα εἰσενεγκαμένη, τούτοις ἀπὸ τῆς οἰκίας ἀποδοθῇ τὸ ἀργύριον, καὶ πλὴν τῶν ἀνδραπόδων, ὅπως οἱ περὶ τὸν

Argument. 1. 9, ἠμφισβήτουν] 'Put in a counter-claim to a dower, on the plea that Plango also (their mother) had brought into the family-property of Mantias 100 drachmae.' Both the mothers being dead, as well as the father, their respective children claim the dower that each had contributed. The question mainly turns on the fact of either or both having brought a dower. Mantitheus, when the property was being shared, claimed his mother's money over and above his share. It is clear that he regarded Boeotus' demand as a mere device for cancelling his account against the common property.

εἰσενεγκαμένης] A technical word in this sense. So Or. 42 § 27, μενούσης μοι τῆς μητρὸς ἐν τῷ οἴκῳ καὶ ζώσης καὶ προῖκα ἐπενεγκαμένης. See also inf. §§ 19, 59, 60.

14. By οἱ περὶ Βοιωτὸν,

ΠΡΟΣ ΒΟΙΩΤΟΝ ΠΕΡΙ ΠΡΟΙ. ΜΗ.

1008 Βοιωτὸν, ἐὰν ἐπιζητῶσί τι τῶν ἔνδον, ἔχωσιν ἔλεγχον. 15 μετὰ δὲ ταῦτα ἀντενεκάλεσαν ἀλλήλοις, ὁ μὲν Μαντίθεος ὑπὲρ τῆς μητρῴας οὐσίας, ἐκεῖνοι δὲ ὑπὲρ ἄλλων τινῶν. καὶ ὁ διαιτητὴς Μαντιθέου μὲν ἀπεδιαίτησε, Βοιωτοῦ δὲ κατεδιαίτησεν ἐρήμην. λαγχάνει δὴ Μαντίθεος καὶ εἰς τὸ δικαστήριον αὐτῷ τὴν αὐτὴν δίκην, 20 ἀπαιτῶν τὴν προῖκα.

Πάντων ἐστὶν ἀνιαρότατον, ὦ ἄνδρες δικασταί, ὅταν τις ὀνόματι μὲν ἀδελφὸς προσαγορευθῇ τινῶν,

'Bœotus' party,' himself, his brother Pamphilus, and their friends are meant. See Or. 39 § 2. If they should afterwards put in a further claim on any property in the house, with the exception of the slaves, such claims would be refuted by their having been paid and a release given by them. By ἔχωσιν ἔλεγχον he means ἔχωσιν ᾧ ἐλέγχωνται as well as ᾧ ἐλέγχωσιν. Otherwise, *both* parties would hardly have consented to this reservation. The reason why the slaves were reserved appears from § 15, viz. that the question by torture might be put to them, as belonging to both parties alike, if any further claims to property should be made, ἐάν τι ἐπιζητῶσι.

16. μετὰ ταῦτα] After this agreement had been made, that future claims should be paid out of the common property, &c. Bœotus, it seems, thereupon dropped his claim to Plango's dower, and asserted his right to ἄλλα τινα, perhaps thinking that he could make use of the evidence of the slaves in his favour. See § 17.

18. ἀπεδιαίτησε] He gave the decision in favour of Mantitheus, and against Boeotus by default (§ 17). Mantitheus, therefore, fortified by this decision, on Boeotus' refusal to pay, brings the same suit into court, requiring payment of the money, i.e. of the dower.

20. καὶ εἰς τὸ δ.] 'He brings the same suit *also* into court:' apparently because Boeotus disregarded the arbitrators' decision, on the plea that not Boeotus, but Mantitheus was his name (§ 18). [For λαγχάνειν δίκην εἰς δικαστήριον cf. 59 (Neaer.) § 98 λαγχάνουσι δίκην τοῖς Λακεδαιμονίοις εἰς τοὺς Ἀμφικτύονας χιλίων ταλάντων. S.]

§§ 1—5. *Statement of the hardships the plaintiff has had to bear. First, he has been deprived of two-thirds of his rightful property by the forced recognition of his illegitimate half-brothers. Next, he has been ejected by them from his own home; and thirdly, they withhold the payment of his mother's dower, which he now requires as a portion for a marriageable daughter.*

πάντων κ.τ.λ.] 'Nothing is more painful, gentlemen of the

τῷ δ' ἔργῳ ἐχθροὺς ἔχῃ τούτους, καὶ ἀναγκάζηται πολλὰ καὶ δεινὰ παθὼν ὑπ' αὐτῶν εἰσιέναι εἰς δικαστήριον, ὃ νῦν ἐμοὶ συμβέβηκεν. οὐ γὰρ μόνον ἀτύχημά μοι ἐξ ἀρχῆς ἐγένετο, διότι Πλαγγὼν ἡ τούτων μήτηρ ἐξαπατήσασα τὸν πατέρα μου καὶ ἐπιορκήσασα φανερῶς ἠνάγκασεν αὐτὸν ὑπομεῖναι τούτους ποιήσασθαι, καὶ διὰ τοῦτο τὰ δύο μέρη τῶν πατρῴων ἀπεστερήθην· ἀλλὰ πρὸς τούτοις ἐξελήλαμαι μὲν ἐκ τῆς πατρῴας οἰκίας ὑπὸ τούτων, ἐν ᾗ καὶ ἐγενόμην καὶ ἐτράφην καὶ εἰς ἣν οὐχ ὁ πατὴρ αὐτοὺς, ἀλλ' ἐγὼ τελευτήσαντος ἐκείνου παρεδεξάμην, ἀποστεροῦμαι δὲ τὴν προῖκα τῆς ἐμαυτοῦ μητρὸς, περὶ ἧς νυνὶ δικάζομαι, αὐτὸς μὲν τούτοις δίκας ὑπὲρ ὧν ἐνεκάλουν μοι πάντων δεδωκώς, πλὴν εἴ τινα νῦν ἕνεκα τῆς δίκης

jury, than for a man to be addressed in name as 'brother' to certain persons, but in fact to have them his enemies, and to be compelled, from the many cruel wrongs he has suffered from them, to come into your court. This is now my case.' The usual antithesis of λόγος and ἔργον is slightly changed, because ὄνομα refers to the specific title or name of 'brother.' And hence the dative is used, though προσαγορεύεσθαι ὄνομα is a more common syntax. See inf. §§ 18, and 20, ὅτι ποτ' ἄλλο χαίρει προσαγορευόμενος. [On the form προσαγορευθῇ cf. note on Or. 55 § 4. S.]

2. ἐπιορκήσασα φανερῶς] 'By manifest perjury.' Kennedy. See Or. 39 § 4.

ὑπομεῖναι] "Graviter additum est ad significandum quam invitus homo mulieri cesserit." G. H. Schaefer.

ἐξελήλαμαι] His brother had behaved so badly that he could not continue to live in the same house. See § 56 fin.

εἰς ἥν κ.τ.λ.] 'Into which they were admitted, not by my father' (i.e. which might have given some apparent right to their claim to the property), 'but by myself after his death.' Kennedy gives a slightly different turn to the sense, 'and in which I received them after my father's death, though he in his lifetime would never admit them to it.' The point seems to be, that the half-brothers have abused a reluctant concession. Their legal right, at least, is not clear, the marriage of Mantias with Plango being left uncertain.

3. δίκας δεδωκώς] 'Though I had given them satisfaction on all matters (plural) in which they made any claim, except indeed some trifling ones which they have wrongfully made the grounds of a cross-suit (or counter-suit) on account of this

p. 1009] ΠΕΡΙ ΠΡΟΙΚΟΣ ΜΗΤΡΩΙΑΣ. 185

ταύτης ἀντειλήχασί μοι συκοφαντοῦντες, ὡς καὶ ὑμῖν ἔσται καταφανές, παρὰ δὲ τούτων ἐν ἔνδεκα ἔτεσιν οὐ δυνάμενος τυχεῖν τῶν μετρίων, ἀλλὰ νῦν εἰς ὑμᾶς[a] καταπεφευγώς. δέομαι οὖν ἁπάντων ὑμῶν, ὦ ἄνδρες 4 δικασταί, μετ᾿ εὐνοίας τέ μου ἀκοῦσαι οὕτως ὅπως ἂν δύνωμαι λέγοντος, κἂν ὑμῖν δοκῶ δεινὰ πεπονθέναι, συγγνώμην ἔχειν μοι ζητοῦντι κομίσασθαι τἀμαυτοῦ, ἄλλως τε καὶ εἰς θυγατρὸς ἔκδοσιν· συνέβη γάρ μοι[b] δεηθέντος τοῦ πατρὸς ὀκτωκαιδεκέτη γῆμαι, καὶ διὰ τοῦτο εἶναί μοι θυγατέρα ἤδη ἐπίγαμον. ὥστ᾿ ἐμοὶ μὲν 5 δικαίως ἂν ἀδικουμένῳ διὰ πολλὰ βοηθήσαιτε, τούτοις δ᾿ εἰκότως ἂν ὀργίζοισθε· οἵτινες, ὦ γῆ καὶ θεοί, ἐξὸν αὐτοῖς τὰ δίκαια ποιήσασι μὴ εἰσιέναι εἰς δικαστήριον, οὐκ αἰσχύνονται μὲν ἀναμιμνήσκοντες ὑμᾶς εἴ τι ᾖ ὁ

[a] ὑμᾶς Bekk. 1824 (cf. § 18). ὑμᾶς βοηθοὺς Z et Bekk. st. cum Σ.
[b] Bekk. μοι γὰρ Z cum FΦ et pr. Σ.

action,' i.e. that they may seem to be claimants themselves instead of defendants. The disputes had been referred to arbitration before Solon and another, inf. § 16.—ἕνεκα τῆς δίκης, i.e. for the mere purpose of getting up a claim against my demand for the dowry.

οὐ δυνάμενος] Referring to δικάζομαι. 'I have been unable for eleven years to obtain from them fair treatment (or, a fair settlement of my claims), and so at last I have recourse to you.'

τῶν μετρίων] 'My just and reasonable demands.'—ἔνδεκα ἔτεσιν, cf. § 18.

4. ὅπως ἂν δύνωμαι κ.τ.λ.] An apology for want of skill in pleading, as in Or. 34 § 1; the fact being suppressed that the speech was really composed for him by another.

συγγνώμην ἔχειν μοι] To show me all reasonable consideration; to make allowance for my feelings and language under the circumstances which I shall describe.

εἰς ἔκδοσιν] 'For a marriage portion for my daughter,' who is ἐπίγαμος, nubilis, 'marriageable,' § 57. The gloss of Hesychius, ἐπίγαμος· πατρῷος, is difficult to explain. The technical term was ἐπιδοῦναι προῖκα, §§ 6, 56.

[On προίξ, see Hermann's Privatalt. § 30, 14 to 22 = p. 263 ed. Blümner, also § 65, 15 to 17 = p. 66 of Rechtsalt. ed. Thalheim; and Becker's Charicles III p. 293—7 = p. 480 of Engl. abridgment. S.]

5. ἐξὸν—μὴ] 'When they need not have come into court at all.' See Or. 39 § 12.

πατὴρ ἡμῶν μὴ ὀρθῶς διεπράξατο ἢ οὗτοι εἰς ἐκεῖνον ἥμαρτον, ἀναγκάζουσι δ' ἐμὲ δικάζεσθαι αὐτοῖς. ἵνα δ' ἀκριβῶς εἰδῆτε ὡς οὐκ ἐγὼ τούτου αἴτιος εἰμί[c], ἀλλ' οὗτοι, ἐξ ἀρχῆς ὑμῖν, ὡς ἂν ἐν βραχυτάτοις δύνωμαι, διηγήσομαι τὰ πραχθέντα.

6 Ἡ γὰρ μήτηρ ἡ ἐμή, ὦ ἄνδρες δικασταί, θυγάτηρ μὲν ἦν Πολυαράτου Χολαργέως, ἀδελφὴ δὲ Μενεξένου καὶ Βαθύλλου καὶ Περιάνδρου. ἐκδόντος δ' αὐτὴν τοῦ πατρὸς Κλεομέδοντι τῷ Κλέωνος υἱεῖ, καὶ προῖκα τάλαντον ἐπιδόντος, τὸ μὲν πρῶτον τούτῳ συνῴκει· γενομένων δ' αὐτῇ τριῶν μὲν θυγατέρων, υἱοῦ δ' ἑνὸς 1010 Κλέωνος[d], καὶ μετὰ ταῦτα τοῦ ἀνδρὸς αὐτῇ τελευτήσαντος, ἀπολιποῦσα τὸν οἶκον καὶ κομισαμένη τὴν 7 προῖκα, πάλιν ἐκδόντων αὐτὴν τῶν ἀδελφῶν Μενεξένου καὶ Βαθύλλου (ὁ γὰρ Περίανδρος ἔτι παῖς ἦν) καὶ τὸ τάλαντον ἐπιδόντων συνῴκησε τῷ ἐμῷ πατρί.

[c] ὡς ἐγὼ αἴτιος οὐκ εἰμί Z. (ὡς οὐκ ἐγὼ αἴτιος οὐκ εἰμί Σ.) ἐγὼ τούτου Bekk. cum margine Σ.

[d] Bekk. om. Z cum Σ.

μὴ ὀρθῶς διεπράξατο] 'Any act which my father improperly committed.' He somewhat curtly alludes to the paternal peccadilloes mentioned in Or. 39 § 26. Perhaps certain political misdoings are included. *Ibid.* § 3.

§§ 6, 7. *The family history. My mother had been married before to Cleomedon, a son of Cleon, with the dower of a talent. After his death, her brothers gave her to my father Mantias, with the same dower, to which I (my younger brother by her being dead) am now the sole claimant.*

Πολυαράτου] Cf. § 24. In B.C. 409 he held a financial office, as is shown by an inscription concluding with the words Ἑλληνοταμίᾳ Ἀναιτίῳ Σφηττίῳ καὶ παρέδρῳ [Π]ολυαράτῳ Χολαργεῖ. Boeckh, *Publ. Ec.* II vii p. 245 trans. Lamb. S.]

Χολαργέως] Hesych. Χολαργῆς· δῆμος φυλῆς Ἀκαμαντίδος. Arist. Ach. 855, Λυσίστρατός τ' ἐν τἀγορᾷ Χολαργέων ὄνειδος. More is said of these brothers inf. § 25.

τῷ Κλέωνος υἱεῖ] See *Arg.* Or. 39, n. 1. On Cleon, the famous demagogue, see further in § 25.

ἐπιδόντος] Cf. Isaeus de Pyrrhi hered. § 51, μήτε τὸ δέκατον μέρος ἐπιδοὺς ἐκδοῦναι τῇ γνησίᾳ θυγατρὶ τῶν πατρῴων. S.]

κομισαμένη] 'Receiving back.' Kennedy.

καὶ γίγνομαι αὐτοῖς ἐγώ τε καὶ ἄλλος ἀδελφὸς νεώτερος ἐμοῦ, ὃς ἔτι παῖς ὢν ἐτελεύτησεν. ὡς δ' ἀληθῆ λέγω περὶ τούτων ὑμῖν, πρῶτον τοὺς μάρτυρας παρέξομαι.

ΜΑΡΤΥΡΕΣ.

Τὴν μὲν τοίνυν μητέρα τὴν ἐμὴν οὕτως ὁ πατήρ 8 μου γήμας εἶχε γυναῖκα ἐν τῇ οἰκίᾳ τῇ ἑαυτοῦ, ἐμέ τε ἐπαίδευε καὶ ἠγάπα, ὥσπερ καὶ ὑμεῖς ἅπαντες τοὺς ὑμετέρους παῖδας ἀγαπᾶτε. τῇ δὲ τούτων μητρὶ Πλαγγόνι ἐπλησίασεν ὅντινα δή ποτ' οὖν τρόπον· οὐ γὰρ ἐμὸν τοῦτο λέγειν ἐστί. καὶ οὕτως οὐ πάντα γε ἦν 9 ὑπὸ τῆς ἐπιθυμίας κεκρατημένος, ὥστ' οὐδὲ τῆς μητρὸς τῆς ἐμῆς ἀποθανούσης ἠξίωσεν αὐτὴν εἰς τὴν οἰκίαν

§§ 8—10. *Mantias treated his lawful wife with all affection, and me also her son; while Plango the mistress and her brats held quite a secondary place, and were not acknowledged at all; nay, even on the death of his wife, he would have nothing to say to them. It was only when Boeotus being grown up had conspired with some good-for-nothing friends of his to defraud me, and by their advice had brought a suit against my father to compel him, that he reluctantly acknowledged the children of the mistress; and the defendant gained his end by the perjury of the woman in collusion with Menecles.*

ὥσπερ καὶ ὑμεῖς] An appeal to the feelings of the judges, and a compliment to their character. The *argumentum ad misericordiam* is similarly seen in §§ 4, 5.

ὅντινα—τρόπον] This must mean that he does not know and does not care to inquire how the connexion arose [45 § 3].—ἐπλησίασεν, 'he had formed a connexion with' [Isaeus 3 § 10], a common sense of πελάζειν. Aesch. Suppl. 300, οὐκοῦν πελάζει Ζεὺς ἐπ' εὐκραίρῳ βοΐ. Soph. Trach. 17, πρὶν τῆσδε κοίτης ἐμπελασθῆναί ποτε. Eur. Andr. 25, πλαθεῖσ' Ἀχιλλέως παιδί. Hence the Spartan word πλᾶτις, 'a wife,' Ar. Ach. 132.

9. οὕτως οὐ—ὥστ' οὐδὲ κ.τ.λ.] *Adeo non prorsus cupidine victus ut ne mortua quidem matre domo eam ad se receperit.* We may construe either οὐ πάντα, in the sense of μετρίως (C. R. Kennedy, 'he was so far under restraint'), or οὐ κεκρατημένος πάντα, 'not wholly (or in all his impulses) overcome by his passion.' The general sense is, 'and though he was very fond of her, he refused to give either her or her sons any formal recognition.' ['He was not *so* mastered by his passion, as to introduce her to live with him in his house.' Prof. Kennedy.]

παρ' ἑαυτὸν εἰσδέξασθαι, οὐδὲ τούτους, ὡς υἱεῖς εἰσὶν
αὐτοῦ, πεισθῆναι· ἀλλὰ τὸν μὲν ἄλλον χρόνον οὗτοι
διῆγον οὐκ ὄντες τοὐμοῦ πατρός, ὡς καὶ ὑμῶν οἱ
πολλοὶ ἴσασιν, ἐπειδὴ δ' οὑτοσὶ[e] αὐξηθεὶς καὶ μεθ'
αὑτοῦ[f] παρασκευασάμενος ἐργαστήριον συκοφαντῶν,
ὧν ἡγεμὼν ἦν Μνησικλῆς καὶ Μενεκλῆς ἐκεῖνος ὁ τὴν
Νίνον ἑλών, μεθ' ὧν οὗτος ἐδικάζετό μου τῷ πατρὶ
10 φάσκων υἱὸς εἶναι ἐκείνου. συνόδων δὲ γιγνομένων
πολλῶν ὑπὲρ τούτων, καὶ τοῦ πατρὸς οὐκ ἂν φάσκοντος πεισθῆναι ὡς οὗτοι γεγόνασιν ἐξ αὐτοῦ, τελευτῶσα 1011
ἡ Πλαγγών, ὦ ἄνδρες δικασταί, (πάντα γὰρ εἰρήσεται
τἀληθῆ πρὸς ὑμᾶς) μετὰ τοῦ Μενεκλέους ἐνεδρεύσασα
τὸν πατέρα μου καὶ ἐξαπατήσασα ὅρκῳ ὃς μέγιστος
δοκεῖ καὶ δεινότατος παρὰ πᾶσιν ἀνθρώποις εἶναι,

[e] Bekk. οὗτος Z cum ΣΦ.
[f] Bekk. μετὰ αὑτοῦ Z. (μεταυτοῦ Σ.)

τὸν μὲν ἄλλον χρόνον] 'In the *first* instance.'

οὐκ ὄντες] The meaning is, that they were not sons at all till a later period, when they were legally made so by adoption.

ἐπειδὴ δ' κ.τ.λ.] There is no proper apodosis, which was intended to be at τελευτῶσα ἡ Πλαγγών, in § 10. It would be better perhaps to place not a full stop, but a mark of *aposiopesis*, or break in the sense, after ἐκείνου. Shilleto cites this passage, not. crit. on De Fals. Leg. p. 333, where a long and irregular sentence begins with ἐπειδὴ δέ.

παρασκευασάμενος] In Or. 39 § 2, where much the same words occur in a more regularly constructed sentence (cf. Introd. p. 180), he uses μεθ'

ἑαυτοῦ κατασκευάσας, 'having got them to act with himself against his own father.'

10. οὐκ ἂν φάσκοντος] i.e. φάσκοντος ὅτι οὐκ ἄν ποτε πεισθείη. Mantias does not say 'he never will be persuaded to acknowledge them,' but he does not believe they are his sons at all. This is a strong point in the case, if a true assertion. He only adopted them ultimately because he was compelled by the law.

τελευτῶσα] 'At last.' So in Soph. Ant. 260, κἂν ἐγίγνετο πληγὴ τελευτῶσ', Or. 54 § 26.

ἐνεδρεύσασα] The accusative rather depends on ἐξαπατήσασα than on this participle. It is remarkable that a quotation follows from Il. xv 37 ἴστω—Στυγὸς ὕδωρ, ὅστε μέγιστος Ὅρκος δεινότατός τε πέλει μακάρεσσι θεοῖσιν.

p. 1011] ΠΕΡΙ ΠΡΟΙΚΟΣ ΜΗΤΡΩΙΑΣ. 189

ὡμολόγησε τριάκοντα μνᾶς λαβοῦσα τούτους μὲν τοῖς αὑτῆς ἀδελφοῖς εἰσποιήσειν υἱεῖς, αὐτὴ δ', ἂν πρὸς τῷ διαιτητῇ προκαλῆται αὐτὴν ὁ πατήρ μου ὀμόσαι ἢ μὴν τοὺς παῖδας ἐξ αὐτοῦ γεγονέναι, οὐ δέξεσθαι[h] τὴν πρόκλησιν· τούτων γὰρ γενομένων οὔτε τούτους ἀποστερήσεσθαι τῆς πόλεως[i], τῷ τε πατρί μου οὐκέτι δυνήσεσθαι αὐτοὺς πράγματα παρέχειν τῆς μητρὸς αὐτῶν οὐ δεξαμένης τὸν ὅρκον. συγχωρηθέντων δὲ 11

[h] οὐ δέξεσθαι Dindf. et Z cum Σ.   οὐ δέξασθαι rA¹.   μὴ δέξασθαι FΦ.   μὴ δέξεσθαι Bekk.
[i] Bekk. 1824.   πολιτείας Z et Bekk. st. cum Σ et γρ. FΦB.

τριάκοντα μνᾶς λαβοῦσα] 'She promised, on the receipt of 30 minae, that she would get her brothers to adopt the defendants as their sons (lit. 'bring them into the phratries as sons to her brothers'), but that she herself, if my father should challenge her before the arbitrator to swear that the children were in very truth by him, would decline to accept the challenge.' The transaction is related in Or. 39 § 3; but Plango is there said μεσεγγυήσασθαι ἀργύριον. For εἰσποιεῖν, 'to cause a child to be adopted,' see Or. 43 (πρὸς Μακαρτ.) § 15, ἐμοὶ γὰρ οὐκέτι οἷόν τ' ἦν, ὦ ἄνδρες δικασταί, κυρίῳ ἐγγεγράφθαι, εἰσπεποιηκότι τὸν παῖδα εἰς τὸν οἶκον τὸν Εὐβουλίδου· Or. 44 (πρὸς Λεωχ.) § 34, οὐκ ἐπιλογισάμενος—ὅτι οἱ εἰσποιητοὶ οὐκ αὐτοὶ ὑφ' αὑτῶν, ἀλλ' ὑπὸ τῶν εἰσποιουμένων καθίστανται. Hence the word was opposed to the natural relation, and meant θετός, νόθος, ἔξωθεν γεγενημένος, as Hesychius explains it.

οὐ δέξεσθαι] Madvig Gk. Synt. § 205. Virtually this is ὡμολόγησεν ὅτι οὐ δέξοιτο. With the infinitive, μὴ would be the usual idiom.

οὔτε τούτους] As long as the three boys were enrolled in the phratries, their citizenship would be secured to them; while, if enrolled as the sons of Plango's brothers, they could no longer claim to be the sons of Mantias, and he would be rid of all further trouble from them. For πράγματα παρέχειν, i.e. ἐνοχλεῖν, a common expression, it is hardly necessary to cite inf. § 35, κακά μοι παρέχων ἠνάγκασέ με λαχεῖν αὐτῷ δίκην. Mid. § 17, p. 520, κακὰ καὶ πράγματα ἀμύθητά μοι παρέχων διετέλεσεν. Ar. Vesp. 312, τί με δῆτ', ὦ μελέα μῆτερ, ἔτικτες, ἵν' ἐμοὶ πράγματα βόσκειν παρέχῃς; (This is said to be from the Theseus of Euripides. The original probably was, ἵνα σοι πράγματα βόσκειν παρέχω, 'to give you trouble in maintaining me.')

§§ 11, 12. *Plango violated her promise and declared on oath that the defendants were my father's sons; and so he was compelled, though seriously an-*

190   XL. ΠΡΟΣ ΒΟΙΩΤΟΝ   [§§ 11—14

τούτων τί ἂν ὑμῖν μακρολογοίην; ὡς γὰρ πρὸς τὸν διαιτητὴν ἀπήντησε, παραβᾶσα πάντα τὰ ὡμολογημένα ἡ Πλαγγὼν δέχεταί τε τὴν πρόκλησιν καὶ ὄμνυσιν ἐν τῷ Δελφινίῳ ἄλλον ὅρκον ἐναντίον τῷ προτέρῳ, ὡς καὶ ὑμῶν οἱ πολλοὶ ἴσασι· περιβόητος γὰρ ἡ πρᾶξις ἐγένετο. καὶ οὕτως ὁ πατήρ μου διὰ τὴν ἑαυτοῦ πρόκλησιν ἀναγκασθεὶς ἐμμεῖναι τῇ διαίτῃ ἐπὶ μὲν τοῖς γεγενημένοις ἠγανάκτει καὶ βαρέως ἔφερε, καὶ εἰς τὴν οἰκίαν οὐδ' ὡς εἰσδέξασθαι τούτους ἠξίωσεν, εἰς δὲ τοὺς φράτερας ἠναγκάσθη εἰσαγαγεῖν. καὶ τοῦτον 12 μὲν ἐνέγραψε Βοιωτόν, τὸν δ' ἕτερον Πάμφιλον. ἐμὲ δ' εὐθὺς ἔπεισε περὶ ὀκτωκαίδεκ' ἔτη γεγενημένον τὴν Εὐφήμου γῆμαι θυγατέρα, βουλόμενος παῖδας ἐξ ἐμοῦ γενομένους ἐπιδεῖν. ἐγὼ δ', ὦ ἄνδρες δικασταί, νομίζων

noyed at the result, to enrol them as such in the phratries. I then, at my father's request, married at the age of 18.

πρὸς τὸν δ.] The accusative is used from the notion of going to court to meet some one by agreement. So inf. § 17, οὐκ ἀπαντήσαντος πρὸς τὸν διαιτητήν, and §§ 38, 39, where the same formula occurs, as Mr Mayor points out, p. 247.

Δελφινίῳ] This court is not often mentioned; it was said to be attached to a temple of Apollo at Athens, and probably was specially used in cases of solemn attestation respecting birth-right. [Harpocr. s.v. ’Αθήνησιν ἱερὸν Ἀπόλλωνος, ἔνθα ἦν καὶ τὸ ἐν Δελφινίῳ δικαστήριον· Δημ. ἐν τῷ πρὸς Βοιωτόν. S.] To this perhaps Or. 54 (κατὰ Κον.) § 26 refers, πρὸς τὸν λίθον ἄγοντες καὶ ἐξορκίζοντες—ἐξ ἑταίρας εἶναι παιδίον αὐτῷ τοῦτο, though ὁ λίθος is generally understood of the altar in the Acropolis. See Or. 23 (κατ' Ἀριστ.) § 74.

ἡ πρᾶξις] Rather unusual for τὸ πρᾶγμα, but the way of doing it, rather than the thing done, is described.

διὰ τὴν ἑαυτοῦ πρόκλησιν] Not from any will of his own, but from his folly in trusting the oath of such a woman as Plango.

12. ἐπιδεῖν] 'To live to see.' This, with ἐπιδών § 13, is a good example of a remarkable, but not uncommon, sense of the verb. Another is Aesch. Agam. 1538, ἰὼ γᾶ, γᾶ, εἴθε μ' ἐδέξω, πρὶν τόνδ' ἐπιδεῖν ἀργυροτοίχου δροίτας κατέχοντα χαμεύναν. Herod. vi 52, ἐπιδόντα δὲ τὸν Ἀριστόδημον τὰ τέκνα, νούσῳ τελευτᾶν. Mantias, on being compelled to adopt the sons of Plango, induced his legitimate son to marry, in order to perpetuate the descent through him as the rightful heir. We may infer from εὐθὺς and βουλόμενος ἐπιδεῖν

p. 1012] ΠΕΡΙ ΠΡΟΙΚΟΣ ΜΗΤΡΩΙΑΣ. 191

1012 δεῖν καὶ πρότερον καὶ ἐπειδὴ οὗτοι ἐλύπουν αὐτὸν δικαζόμενοι καὶ πράγματα παρέχοντες, ἐμὲ τοὐναντίον εὐφραίνειν ἅπαντα ποιοῦνθ' ὅσ' ἐκείνῳ χαριεῖσθαι μέλλοιμι, ἐπείσθην αὐτῷ. γήμαντος δέ μου τὸν τρό- 13 πον τοῦτον ἐκεῖνος μὲν τὸ θυγάτριόν μοι ἐπιδὼν γενόμενον, οὐ πολλοῖς ἔτεσιν ὕστερον ἀρρωστήσας ἐτελεύτησεν· ἐγὼ δ', ὦ ἄνδρες δικασταί, ζῶντος μὲν τοῦ πατρὸς οὐδὲν ᾤμην δεῖν ἐναντιοῦσθαι αὐτῷ, τελευτήσαντος δ' ἐκείνου εἰσεδεξάμην τε τούτους εἰς τὴν οἰκίαν καὶ τῶν ὄντων ἁπάντων μετέδωκα, οὐχ ὡς ἀδελφοῖς οὖσιν (οὐδὲ γὰρ ὑμῶν τοὺς πολλοὺς λελήθασιν ὃν τρόπον οὗτοι γεγόνασιν), νομίζων δ' ἀναγκαῖον εἶναί μοι, ἐπειδὴ ὁ πατὴρ ἐξηπατήθη, πείθεσθαι τοῖς νόμοις τοῖς ὑμετέροις. καὶ οὕτως ὑπ' ἐμοῦ εἰς τὴν οἰκίαν 14 εἰσδεχθέντες, ὡς ἐνεμόμεθα τὰ πατρῷα, ἀξιοῦντος ἐμοῦ

that Mantias was either advanced in life or consciously infirm, though below Mantitheus says he fell ill and died οὐ πολλοῖς ἔτεσιν ὕστερον.

καὶ πρότερον καὶ ἐπειδὴ κ.τ.λ.] 'As before, so especially now when the defendants were beginning to annoy him.'

ὅσα] Supply ποιῶν.

§§ 13, 14. *Though my father would not receive them under his roof, I did so after his decease, not wishing to oppose the law, which had recognised them as my brothers. It was then that they met my claim to my mother's dower by a counter-claim on the property for the same amount in right of their mother Plango.*

ἐναντιοῦσθαι] He did not care (so he pretends) to oppose his father's expressed dislike to admit the adopted sons to live with him.

οὐχ...οὖσιν] 'Not as being really my brothers,' contrasted with ὃν τρόπον γεγόνασιν ('the manner in which they have *become* so,' or 'in what manner they have been born.' Prof. Kennedy).

λελήθασιν] He might have said οὐ λέληθεν, but the Greeks, as is well known, prefer in these idioms the personal use of the verb, e.g. δίκαιος εἶ ποιεῖν, ἔοικας ποιήσειν, &c. The matter was περιβόητον, 'notorious,' § 11, and so the jury are now supposed to know all about it. [Aristotle's allusion, quoted on p. 141, implies that the facts were noised abroad. S.]

ἐξηπατήθη] He uses a word which has more of bitterness even than ἠναγκάσθη.

14. εἰσδεχθέντες] Here the aorist of a deponent has a passive sense as well as form. See a paper by R. Shilleto in the *Journal of Philology*, XIII p. 151. (A good example, omitted by him, is Eur. Hec. 448,

ἀπολαβεῖν τὴν τῆς μητρὸς προῖκα ἀντενεκάλουν καὶ
οὗτοι, καὶ ἔφασαν ὀφείλεσθαι καὶ τῇ αὐτῶν μητρὶ τὴν
ἴσην προῖκα. συμβουλευσάντων δ' ἡμῖν τῶν παρόντων
τὰ μὲν ἄλλα πάντα ἐνειμάμεθα, τὴν δ' οἰκίαν καὶ τοὺς
παῖδας τοὺς διακόνους τούς^j τοῦ πατρὸς ἐξαιρέτους
15 ἐποιησάμεθα, ἵν' ἐκ μὲν τῆς οἰκίας, ὁποτέροις ἂν ἡμῶν
φαίνηται ὀφειλομένη ἡ προὶξ, οὗτοι αὐτὴν κομίσωνται, ἐκ δὲ τῶν παίδων κοινῶν ὄντων, ἐάν τι οὗτοι
τῶν πατρῴων ἐπιζητῶσι, πυνθάνωνται, καὶ βασανί-
ζοντες αὐτοὺς καὶ ἄλλῳ ὅτῳ ἂν τρόπῳ βούλωνται
ζητοῦντες. ὅτι δὲ καὶ ταῦτ' ἀληθῆ λέγω, ἐκ τούτων
τῶν μαρτυριῶν εἴσεσθε.

^j Bekk. 1824.   om. Z et Bekk. st. cum ΣrA¹.

τῷ δουλόσυνος πρὸς οἶκον κτηθεῖσ'
ἀφίξομαι;)
ἐνεμόμεθα] From Or. 39
§ 6, it would seem that the
property was equally divided between the three brothers, the
house and the slaves being reserved till the claims about the
dower should be adjudicated.
See inf. § 60.
τὴν ἴσην] It does not seem
easy to reconcile this statement
with § 20, where the dower is
fixed at 100 minae (60 minae being a talent). Perhaps the recklessness of Boeotus' statements
is glanced at in the latter passage.
τῶν παρόντων] The friends
who were called in to advise
what should be done. Kennedy
renders it, 'under the advice of
persons who were present.'
τοὺς παῖδας] Either these
words or τοὺς διακόνους read like
an interpolated gloss.
Mr Mayor however remarks
(p. 247) "A reference to the index shows παῖδα διάκονον p.
1155, οἰκέτην διάκονον p. 1359;

and it seems probable from other
passages that διάκονος was a
term applied to a superior class
of servants."
ἐξαιρέτους] 'Specially reserved.' Cf. inf. §§ 56, 60.
15. ἵνα κ.τ.λ.] 'In order
that, to whichever side of us
the dower should appear to be
due, that party might recover
it from (the value of) the house;
and that if the defendants should
put in a further claim to any of
my father's effects, they might
make inquiry respecting it from
the slaves, as common property,
either by torturing them or by
looking into the matter in any
other way they may please.'
The exact sense of ἐπιζητῶσι is
rather obscure. Kennedy translates, 'should these men want
to search for any of our father's
effects.' It might be, that they
supposed some property had
been concealed, and that the
slaves knew where it was; but
it might also mean that (as in
Or. 36 § 14) some small effects

p. 1013] ΠΕΡΙ ΠΡΟΙΚΟΣ ΜΗΤΡΩΙΑΣ.

ΜΑΡΤΥΡΙΑΙ.

Μετὰ ταῦτα τοίνυν οὑτοί τ' ἐμοὶ δίκας ἔλαχον 16 ὑπὲρ ὧν ἐνεκάλουν κἀγὼ τούτοις ὑπὲρ τῆς προικός. καὶ τὸ μὲν πρῶτον παραγραψάμενοι Σόλωνα Ἐρχιέα διαιτητὴν τούτῳ ἐπετρέψαμεν δικάσαι περὶ ὧν ἐνεκαλοῦμεν ἀλλήλοις· ὡς δ' οὐκ ἀπήντων οὗτοι, ἀλλ' ἐφυγοδίκουν καὶ χρόνος διετρίβετο συχνός, τῷ μὲν Σόλωνι συνέβη τελευτῆσαι τὸν βίον, οὗτοι δὲ πάλιν ἐξ ὑπαρχῆς λαγχάνουσί μοι δίκας, καὶ ἐγὼ τούτῳ, προσκαλεσάμενος αὐτὸν καὶ ἐπιγραψάμενος ἐπὶ τὸ

were claimed in addition to the property distributed, and that the slaves would be asked respecting the ownership. And this is the sense in which the term seems to be explained in the Argument, ἐὰν ἐπιζητῶσί τι τῶν ἔνδον.

§§ 16—18. *At first our respective claims were submitted to one Solon for arbitration; but, some delays having intervened, the case was tried afresh, and the suit, which was filed in the name of Boeotus, was given against him. Knowing he was in the wrong, he did not carry the case to a higher court; but he has brought an action for other and fresh claims, denying at the same time that the decision had gone against him, for his name (he said) was not Boeotus. I was thus compelled to file a new bill against him as Mantitheus.*

δίκας ἔλαχον] This seems to refer to the suit mentioned in § 3, πλὴν εἴ τινα νῦν ἕνεκα τῆς δίκης ταύτης ἀντειλήχασί μοι συκοφαντοῦντες.

παραγραψάμενοι] 'Having had his name registered.' See on

Or. 34 § 43. 'Causing him to be inserted in the margin, or at the foot, of the record,' Kennedy; who observes that the arbitrators appear to have been public (κληρωτοί), not private (αἱρετοί); since there was no appeal from the decision of the latter, and the words οὔτε ἐφῆκεν εἰς τὸ δικαστήριον in § 17 imply that there was in this case a power of appeal.

Ἐρχιέα] The name of the deme Ἐρχία occurs, but in a doubtful reading and in a passage of doubtful genuineness, Mid. § 22, Παμμένης Παμμένους Ἐρχιεύς. Photius, Ἐρχιάδαι· Ἐρχία δῆμος τῆς Ἀττικῆς. Hesych. Ἐρχεῖα· δῆμος φυλῆς τῆς Αἰγηῗδος.

ἐφυγοδίκουν] 'Shirked the hearing altogether,' Kennedy. A rare word, if not ἅπαξ εἰρημένον.

πάλιν ἐξ ὑπαρχῆς] Soph. Oed. Tyr. 132, ἀλλ' ἐξ ὑπαρχῆς αὖθις αὔτ' ἐγὼ φανῶ. Hesych. ἐξ ὑπαρχῆς· ἐξ ἀρχῆς.

ἐπὶ τὸ ἔγκλημα] This clause reads like a gloss. 'Having had the name *Boeotus* written upon it,' is the simple sense.

P. S. D. 13

ἔγκλημα Βοιωτόν· τοῦτο γὰρ αὐτῷ ὁ πατὴρ ἔθετο 17 τοὔνομα. περὶ μὲν οὖν ὧν οὗτοί μοι ἐδικάζοντο, παρόντος τούτου καὶ ἀντιδικοῦντος καὶ οὐκ ἔχοντος ἐπιδεῖξαι οὐδὲν ὧν ἐνεκάλουν, ἀπεδιῄτησέ μου ὁ διαιτητής· καὶ οὗτος συνειδὼς αὑτῷ ἀδίκως ἐγκαλοῦντι οὔτε ἐφῆκεν εἰς τὸ δικαστήριον, οὔτε νῦν περὶ ἐκείνων εἴληχέ μοι δίκην οὐδεμίαν, ἀλλὰ περὶ ἄλλων τινῶν, λύσειν τοῖς ἐγκλήμασι τούτοις τὴν δίκην ταύτην οἰόμενος. ἣν δ' ἐγὼ τοῦτον ἐδίωκον τότε περὶ τῆς προικός, ἐπιδημοῦντος τούτου ἐνθάδε καὶ οὐκ ἀπαντήσαντος πρὸς τὸν

ὁ πατὴρ ἔθετο] See Or. 39 § 4. Mantitheus resolved not to acknowledge any other name than Boeotus for his half-brother, although it is more than probable (as before remarked) that he had succeeded in establishing his right to be called Mantitheus. This indeed appears in § 20.

17. παρόντος] See § 31, παρὼν αὐτὸς ὅτε ἀπεδιῄτησέ μου ὁ διαιτητής, and inf. § 55. When he brought the action against me, he appeared before the arbitrator, and accepted the cross-suit which I at the same time brought against him, though his name was entered as Boeotus. But when the suit went against him, then he said he was not Boeotus, but Mantitheus. For ἀποδιαιτᾶν, like ἀπογνῶναί τινα τῆς δίκης, § 39, is to acquit, or give sentence in favour of a person. The full phrase, which occurs in § 55, is ἀποδιαιτᾶν δίκην τινός. The contrary is καταδιαιτᾶν τινος. Cf. Mid. § 85 πείθειν αὐτὸν ἣν κατεδεδιῃτήκει, ταύτην ἀποδεδιῃτημένην ἀποφαίνειν.

ἐφῆκεν] See Or. 34 § 21.— περὶ ἐκείνων, i.e. he has not now made that claim, viz. specially

and exclusively to the dowry of his mother Plango.

τὴν δίκην ταύτην] He thought that my claims to my mother's dower might be set aside by his counter-claim to other property; or at least, that if both claims were allowed, one might cancel the other. See § 3.

τότε] "After the death of Solon each party brought a suit against the other. Boeotus appeared in court as plaintiff, but made no appearance as defendant. This is shown by the antithesis περὶ μὲν οὖν ὧν οὗτοί μοι ἐδικάζοντο—ἣν δ' ἐγὼ τοῦτον ἐδίωκον. It is this second suit, not that before Solon, to which τότε refers." Mr Mayor, p. 248.—ἐπιδημοῦντος, though he was in town and might have appeared if he had liked. This seems to show that in the case of absence abroad, a judgment could not go by default. But there is some obscurity here: the first arbitrator, Solon, died before the decision was given; before the second arbitrator Boeotus did appear (ἀντιδικοῦντος τούτου).—ἐρήμην, so in the same passage of the Midias, τὴν ἔρημον δεδωκότα, sc. δίαιταν.

p. 1014] ΠΕΡΙ ΠΡΟΙΚΟΣ ΜΗΤΡΩΙΑΣ. 195

διαιτητὴν, ἐρήμην κατεδιῄτησεν αὐτοῦ. οὑτοσὶ δ', ὦ 18
ἄνδρες δικασταί, οὔτε ἠντιδίκει τότε παρὼν οὔτ' ἔφη
με καταδιαιτήσασθαι τὴν δίκην αὐτοῦ· οὐ γὰρ εἶναι
Βοιωτὸν αὐτῷ ὄνομα, ἀλλὰ Μαντίθεον, καὶ οὕτως
ὀνόματι ἀμφισβητῶν ἔργῳ τὴν προῖκά με τῆς μητρὸς
ἀποστερεῖ. ἀπορῶν δ' ἐγὼ τί ἄν τις χρήσαιτο τῷ
πράγματι, οὕτω πάλιν τὴν αὐτὴν ταύτην δίκην λαχὼν
αὐτῷ Μαντιθέῳ ἐνδεκάτῳ ἔτει νῦν εἰς ὑμᾶς καταπέ-
1014 φευγα. ὡς δὲ καὶ ταῦτ' ἀληθῆ λέγω, ἀναγνώσεται ὑμῖν
περὶ τούτων μαρτυρίας.

MAPTYPIAI.

"Οτι μὲν τοίνυν, ὦ ἄνδρες δικασταί, ἥ τε μήτηρ 19
μου τάλαντον ἐπενεγκαμένη προῖκα, ἐκδοθεῖσα ὑπὸ
τῶν ἀδελφῶν τῶν αὐτῆς, ὥσπερ οἱ νόμοι κελεύουσι,

18. οὑτοσὶ δὲ κ.τ.λ.] 'Thus the defendant in this (the second) case not only did not appear, though he was in Athens, but he declared I had not got the verdict against *him*, for his name was not Boeotus, but Mantitheus.' See inf. § 34, and Or. 39 § 37. We might have expected οὑτοσὶ δὴ, κ.τ.λ. but the δὲ is really antithetical to περὶ μὲν οὖν ὧν οὗτοι, &c. above.
ὀνόματι ἀμφισβητῶν] 'By disputing (quibbling or cavilling) about a name.' For the antithesis with ἔργῳ, see sup. § 1.
ἀπορῶν κ.τ.λ.] 'As I scarcely knew how such a case was to be dealt with.' Kennedy. Cf. Or. 34 § 46, ἐγὼ δ' οὐκ ἔχω τί χρήσωμαι τοῖς τούτου μάρτυσιν, and 53 § 13.
Μαντιθέῳ] 'As Mantitheus,' i.e. by an altered name. (Or perhaps, 'with Mantitheus *himself*,' in ironical allusion to Boeotus being somebody else. Cf. § 20 *init*. Mr Mayor does not think any irony is meant, but translates (p. 248), "I prosecuted him as being actually Mantitheus,—under the actual name Mantitheus.") If Μαντιθέῳ is not to be regarded as an interpolated gloss, we must conclude that the legal difficulty could only be got over in this way; for the defendant, after his father's death, ἐλθὼν εἰς τοὺς δημότας ἀντὶ Βοιωτοῦ Μαντίθεον ἐνέγραψεν ἑαυτόν, Or. 39 § 5. And the filing of an action against Mantitheus was a virtual acknowledgment that he could now legally claim that name. It is very likely that the trueborn Mantitheus really lost his cause by showing 'contempt of court' in still insisting that Boeotus was the right name. It would doubtless be a hard matter to alter a name once duly inserted in the γραμματεῖον ληξιαρχικόν.
19. ὥσπερ οἱ νόμοι] The brothers were . κύριοι, i. e. had legal disposal, as next of kin,

13—2

συνώκησε τῷ πατρί, καὶ ὃν τρόπον ἐγὼ τούτους εἰσεδεξάμην εἰς τὴν οἰκίαν τοῦ πατρὸς τελευτήσαντος, καὶ ὅτι ἀπέφυγον αὐτοὺς τὰς δίκας ἅς μοι ἐνεκάλουν, ταῦτα μὲν πάντα καὶ μεμαρτύρηται ὑμῖν καὶ ἐπιδέδεικται. Ἴθι δὲ λαβὲ καὶ τὸν περὶ τῆς προικὸς νόμον τουτονί.

ΝΟΜΟΣ.

20   Οὕτω τοίνυν τοῦ νόμου ἔχοντος οἶμαι τουτονὶ Βοιωτὸν ἢ Μαντίθεον, ἢ ὅ τι ποτ' ἄλλο χαίρει προσαγορευόμενος, δικαίαν μὲν ἀπολογίαν καὶ ἀληθινὴν οὐδεμίαν ἕξειν εἰπεῖν, ἐπιχειρήσειν δὲ τῇ τόλμῃ καὶ τῇ θρασύτητι τῇ ἑαυτοῦ πιστεύοντα περιιστάναι τὰς ἑαυτοῦ συμφορὰς εἰς ἐμέ, ἅπερ καὶ ἰδίᾳ ποιεῖν εἴωθε, λέγων ὡς δημευθείσης τῆς τοῦ Παμφίλου οὐσίας, ὃς ἦν πατὴρ τῆς Πλαγγόνος, τὰ περιγενόμενα χρήματα ὁ πατὴρ ὁ ἐμὸς ἔλαβεν ἐκ τοῦ βουλευτηρίου, καὶ οὕτως

of the person and property of their sister. [Lysias 16 § 10, δύο ἀδελφὰς ἐξέδωκα ἐπιδοὺς τριάκοντα μνᾶς ἑκατέρᾳ. S.]

ἀπέφυγον] 'Obtained judgment in the actions which they brought against me.' Kennedy. The double accusative is used as in μετελθεῖν τινα δίκην. See inf. § 42, ἃς ἐγὼ δίκας τοῦτον ἀπέφυγον.

§§ 20, 21. *Having no just plea, he will pretend that his mother Plango was entitled to the residue of her father's confiscated estate, and that my father actually received it, while my mother had no dower at all. But this is mere assertion; for he knows it would not suit his interest to admit that he is acting dishonestly.*

ὅ τι ποτ' ἄλλο] sc. ὄνομα. See on § 1. There is a kind of pettishness in this reluctant admission that there really was some legal ground for disclaiming the name of Boeotus.

ἀληθινήν] 'Genuine,' opposed to πλαστήν, 'fictitious:' while ἀληθῆ is opposed to ψευδῆ.

περιιστάναι] See Or. 37 § 39. The intransitive is more common, as τὸ πρᾶγμα περιέστη εἰς ὑπέρδεινον, &c. See Thuc. I 78, ἐς τύχας φιλεῖ περίστασθαι. Or. 37 § 10, ὁρῶν τὸ πρᾶγμά μοι περιεστηκὸς εἰς ἄτοπον. The meaning seems to be, that he will try to make it appear that my mother's father had been proscribed (by the Thirty, probably); which in fact was the case with *his* mother's father. 'He will try to shift the misfortunes of his own family on my shoulders.' Kennedy.

ἐκ τοῦ βουλευτηρίου] Whether generally or specially, after the

p. 1015] ΠΕΡΙ ΠΡΟΙΚΟΣ ΜΗΤΡΩΙΑΣ. 197

ἀποφαίνειν πειρώμενος τὴν μὲν αὑτοῦ μητέρα ἐπενεγκαμένην προῖκα πλεῖν ἢ ἑκατὸν μνᾶς, τὴν δ' ἐμὴν
ἄπροικον φάσκων συνοικῆσαι. ταῦτα διέξεισιν, ὦ 21
ἄνδρες δικασταί, οὔτε μαρτυρίαν οὐδεμίαν ἐμβεβλημένος ὑπὲρ τούτων οὔτ' ἀγνοῶν ὡς οὐδὲν ὑγιὲς λέγει,
ἀλλ' ἀκριβῶς εἰδὼς ὅτι ὁμολογῶν μὲν ἀδικεῖν ἐν ὑμῖν
1015 οὐδείς πω ἀπέφυγε[k], ψευδόμενος δὲ καὶ παραγωγὰς
λέγων ἤδη τις δίκην οὐκ ἔδωκεν. ἵν' οὖν μὴ ἐξαπατη-
θῆτε ὑπ' αὐτοῦ, βέλτιον εἶναί μοι δοκεῖ βραχέα καὶ
περὶ τούτου πρὸς ὑμᾶς εἰπεῖν. ἐὰν γὰρ λέγῃ ὡς ἡ μὲν 22
ἐμὴ μήτηρ οὐκ ἐπηνέγκατο προῖκα, ἡ δὲ τούτων ἐπη-

[k] Bekk. ἀπέφευγε Σ.

dissolution of the Thirty, the Council had financial duties of this kind, may perhaps be questioned. But it was a rule of Athenian policy that the βουλὴ should have especial jurisdiction in all matters of finance. See Boeckh, *P. Econ.* p. 153—4, trans. Lewis². —τὰ περιγενόμενα, what remained over and above the fine or debt to the treasury, for the payment of which the goods were confiscated. The term is used in Or. 35 § 13, for goods saved from a wreck.

πλεῖν ἢ ἑκατὸν μνᾶς] See on § 14. Of the Attic formula πλεῖν ἢ (not πλέον ἢ) Cobet has collected numerous examples in *Var. Lect.* p. 237.

21. ἐμβεβλημένος] 'Without having filed (or, entered) any affidavit.' In the medial sense, like μαρτυρίαν ἐνεβάλοντο, § 58, lit. 'having caused to be thrown in,' i.e. εἰς τὸν ἐχῖνον. See § 28.—παραγωγάς, arguments to lead away from the real point; 'shuffling excuses.' Kennedy. Hesych. παραγωγαί· ἀπάται, χρή-

σεις. (Perhaps καταχρήσεις.) Or. 23 (κατὰ Ἀριστ.) § 95, ἀπλῆν μὲν, οὐδὲ δικαίαν οὐδ' ἡντινοῦν ἀπολογίαν Ἀριστοκράτης ἕξει λέγειν, παραγωγὰς δὲ τοιαύτας τινὰς ἐρεῖ. ὁμολογῶν κ.τ.λ.] Fals. leg. 215 ἴστε γὰρ δήπου τοῦθ', ὅτι ἀφ' οὗ γεγόνασιν ἄνθρωποι καὶ κρίσεις γίγνονται, οὐδεὶς πώποθ' ὁμολογῶν ἀδικεῖν ἑάλω, ἀλλ' ἀναισχυντοῦσιν, ἀρνοῦνται, ψεύδονται, προφάσεις πλάττονται, πάντα ποιοῦσιν ὑπὲρ τοῦ μὴ δοῦναι δίκην. This passage belongs to a later date than the present speech, but the writers of both may have borrowed from an earlier original, Blass *Att. Ber.* III 453. S.]

περὶ τούτου] Either 'about this matter,' or 'about the family history of the defendant.'

§§ 22, 3. *Pamphilus, in fact, the father of Plango, died indebted to the treasury, and in a sum so large that the sale of his property did not realize it. Besides, had there been any surplus, it must have come to the sons, and not to the daughter.*

198   XL. ΠΡΟΣ ΒΟΙΩΤΟΝ   [§§ 22—25

νέγκατο, ἐνθυμεῖσθ᾽ ὅτι περιφανῶς ψεύδεται. πρῶτον μὲν γὰρ ὁ Πάμφιλος ὁ πατὴρ τῆς τούτου μητρὸς πέντε τάλαντα τῷ δημοσίῳ ὀφείλων ἐτελεύτησε, καὶ τοσούτου ἐδέησε περιγενέσθαι τι τοῖς ἐκείνου παισὶ τῆς οὐσίας ἀπογραφείσης καὶ δημευθείσης ὥστ᾽ οὐδὲ τὸ ὄφλημα πᾶν ὑπὲρ αὐτοῦ ἐκτέτισται¹, ἀλλ᾽ ἔτι καὶ νῦν ὁ Πάμφιλος ὀφείλων τῷ δημοσίῳ ἐγγέγραπται. πῶς οὖν οἷόν τε τὸν ἐμὸν πατέρα χρήματα λαβεῖν ἐκ τῆς Παμφίλου οὐσίας, ἢ οὐδ᾽ αὐτὸ τὸ ὄφλημα ἱκανὴ 23 ἐγένετο τῇ πόλει ἐκτῖσαι; ἔπειτ᾽, ὦ ἄνδρες δικασταί, ἐνθυμεῖσθ᾽ ὅτι εἰ τὰ μάλιστα περιεγένετο τὰ χρήματα ταῦτα, ὥσπερ οὗτοί^m φασιν, οὐκ ἂν ὁ ἐμὸς πατὴρ αὐτὰ ἔλαβεν, ἀλλ᾽ οἱ τοῦ Παμφίλου υἱεῖς Βοιωτὸς καὶ Ἡδύλος καὶ Εὐθύδημος, οἳ οὐκ ἂν δήπου ἐπὶ μὲν τῷ τἀλλότρια λαμβάνειν ὑτιανοῦν ἐποίουν, ὡς καὶ ὑμεῖς

¹ Bekk. ἐκτετῖσθαι e coniectura Z.   (ἐκτετεισθαι Σ.)
^m Bekk. αὐτοὶ Σ cum Z.

And they were not the men to let my father get possession of what belonged to them.

τοσούτου ἐδέησε] Impersonally used: 'so far was it from there being any surplus for his children when the property had been scheduled and publicly sold, that not even the whole of the debt has been discharged on his account.' In Or. 37 § 49, it is personal, τοσούτου δεῖς ἐλέου τινὸς ἄξιος εἶναι ὥστε, κ.τ.λ.—ἀπογραφείσης, after an inventory of it had been made, and a formal return of the goods or property. See Or. 34 § 7. A similar word is ἀπόφασις and ἀποφαίνειν. Or. 42 §§ 1, 9.

ἐγγέγραπται] 'Stands in the register.' Kennedy. Cf. 53 § 14.

23. εἰ τὰ μάλιστα κ.τ.λ.] 'If it were ever so true that this surplus existed.'

ὑτιανοῦν] The common reading before Reiske's edition was ὑτιοῦν, which comes to the same thing. The latter, G. H. Schaefer remarks, is for ὅτι οὖν ἐστίν, the former for ὅτι ἂν οὖν ᾖ. 'They surely were not men who, to get hold of the property of others, would (as you all of you know) have recourse to any artifice, and yet would have tamely allowed my father to have received what belonged to them.' Kennedy translates: 'persons who would go all lengths to get the property of others, as you all know, and of course would never have allowed my father to receive what belonged to them.' The ἂν belongs to both clauses, but the imperfect represents the habitual way of action, the

ΠΕΡΙ ΠΡΟΙΚΟΣ ΜΗΤΡΩΙΑΣ.

ἅπαντες ἴστε, τὰ δ᾽ αὐτῶν τὸν ἐμὸν πατέρα περιεῖδον κομισάμενον. ὅτι μὲν τοίνυν ἥ γε τούτων μήτηρ οὐκ 24 ἐπηνέγκατο προῖκα, ἀλλ᾽ οὗτοι τοῦτο ψεύδονται, ἱκανῶς ὑμᾶς μεμαθηκέναι νομίζω· ὅτι δ᾽ ἡ ἐμὴ μήτηρ ἐπηνέγκατο, ῥᾳδίως ἐγὼ δείξω. πρῶτον μὲν γὰρ Πολυαράτου θυγάτηρ ἦν, ὃς καὶ ὑφ᾽ ὑμῶν ἐτιμᾶτο καὶ πολλὴν οὐσίαν ἐκέκτητο· ἔπειτα μεμαρτύρηται ὑμῖν ὡς καὶ ἡ ἀδελφὴ αὐτῆς τοσαύτην προῖκα ἐπενεγκαμένη Ἐρυξιμάχῳ συνῴκησε, τῷ Χαβρίου κηδεστῇ. πρὸς δὲ τούτοις φαίνεταί μου ἡ μήτηρ τὸ 25 πρῶτον ἐκδοθεῖσα Κλεομέδοντι, οὗ φασι τὸν πατέρα Κλέωνα τῶν ὑμετέρων προγόνων στρατηγοῦντα, Λακεδαιμονίων πολλοὺς ἐν Πύλῳ ζῶντας λαβόντα, μάλιστα πάντων ἐν τῇ πόλει εὐδοκιμῆσαι· ὥστ᾽ οὔτε τὸν ἐκείνου προσῆκεν υἱὸν ἄπροικον αὐτὴν γῆμαι, οὔτε Μενέ-

aorist the single event. A similar syntax occurs inf. § 26.

§§ 24, 5. *That his mother did not bring a dower, but mine did, is easily shown. My mother belonged to a rich family, and married for her first husband the son of the great Cleon. After his death, it was not likely that her wealthy brothers should have withheld her dower; rather, they would have added to it.*

Χαβρίου] The celebrated Athenian general, who married the sister of Eryximachus.

25. φασι...Κλέωνα] The capture of Pylos by Cleon took place more than seventy-five years before this (B.C. 425). Cf. Thuc. IV 28, 29 and Ar. Eq. 55, 702, 740. The preference, even at this late period, for oral instruction rather than for reading written histories, will account for the expression 'they say that Cleon captured the prisoners at Pylos.' Compare λέγεται Ἀλκιβιάδης γενέσθαι, &c. in Mid. § 143. It is not meant, as G. H. Schaefer observes, that a mere vague or uncertain story is referred to. This casual mention of Cleon, and of his reputation for the event, μάλιστα πάντων εὐδοκιμῆσαι, is interesting. Aristophanes, in pure spite, says that ἔλαμψε τῆς τύχης χάριν, 'he became distinguished by favour of fortune,' Vesp. 62. On the importance attached to στρατηγεῖν, see Or. 34 § 50. By τῶν προγόνων it is merely meant that the ancestors of some of the present jury might have served under Cleon.

τὸν ἐκείνου υἱὸν] Not merely 'his son' (Kennedy), but 'the son of that distinguished man, now deceased' (§ 28).—οὐ προσῆκεν, 'it was not consistent with the wealth and position of the family.'

200   XL. ΠΡΟΣ ΒΟΙΩΤΟΝ   [§§ 25—28

ξένον καὶ Βάθυλλον εἰκός ἐστιν, αὐτούς τε οὐσίαν πολλὴν κεκτημένους καὶ Κλεομέδοντος τελευτήσαντος κομισαμένους τὴν προῖκα, ἀποστερῆσαι τὴν ἀδελφὴν τὴν ἑαυτῶν, ἀλλὰ προσθέντας αὐτοὺς ἐκδοῦναι τῷ ἡμετέρῳ πατρί, καθάπερ καὶ αὐτοὶ πρὸς ὑμᾶς καὶ οἱ
26 ἄλλοι μεμαρτυρήκασιν. χωρὶς δὲ τούτων ἐνθυμήθητε διὰ τί ἄν ποτε ὁ πατήρ, εἴπερ ἡ μὲν[n] ἐμὴ μήτηρ μὴ ἦν ἐγγυητὴ μηδ' ἠνέγκατο προῖκα, ἡ δὲ τούτων ἠνέγκατο, τούτους[o] μὲν οὐκ ἔφη αὑτοῦ υἱεῖς εἶναι, ἐμὲ δὲ καὶ ἐποιεῖτο καὶ ἐπαίδευεν; ὅτι νὴ Δί', ὡς οὗτοι φήσουσιν, ἐμοὶ χαριζόμενος καὶ τῇ ἐμῇ μητρὶ τούτους
27 ἠτίμαζεν. ἀλλ' ἐκείνη μὲν ἔτι παῖδα μικρὸν ἐμὲ καταλιποῦσα αὐτὴ τὸν βίον ἐτελεύτησεν, ἡ δὲ τούτων μήτηρ Πλαγγὼν καὶ πρότερον καὶ μετὰ ταῦτα εὐπρε-

[n] Bekk. om. Z cum Σ.   [o] Bekk. τοὺς Z cum Σ.

εἰκός ἐστιν] An argument from the probabilities of the case, which is continued in §§ 26, 7. See on Or. 34 § 14.

αὐτούς] Ipsos; 'they would themselves (i.e. out of their own property) have added to it.' As a mere accusative of the subject, the word would here be superfluous. Reiske proposed, and Schaefer approves, the insertion of ἂν before αὐτούς. Rather we should expect, in this case, ἀλλ' αὐτοὺς ἂν προσθέντας. But this cannot be necessary. (Goodwin's *Moods and Tenses* § 49, 2, note 3.) We know from §§ 6, 7, 19, that a talent was the dower the lady brought both to her first and to her second husband. Hence it does not appear that the brothers really increased the dower, though they may have given her presents beside.

καὶ οἱ ἄλλοι] See § 19.

§§ 26, 27. *The only con-ceivable reason for my father adopting me and disowning my half-brothers was, that my mother was the lawfully affianced and dowered wife, while Plango was without fortune, and but a mistress. For it is not denied that his affection was rather bestowed on their mother; so that he would have preferred, as a matter of choice, to adopt her sons rather than myself, who was but an infant when my mother died.*

ἐγγυητή] 'Affianced,' sc. ἐκδόντων αὐτὴν τῶν ἀδελφῶν, § 7. [The word does not appear to occur elsewhere. Cf. Isaeus III § 70, ἐνεγύα καὶ ἐξεδίδου τὴν γυναῖκα, VI 14, συνοικεῖν ἢ ἐγγυηθεῖσαν κατὰ νόμον ἢ ἐπιδικασθεῖσαν, [Dem.] Or. 46 § 18. Hermann, *Privatalt.* § 30, 7= p. 262 Blümner. S.]

27. εὐπρεπὴς—οὖσα] This clause explains the continuance of the connexion as well as the

ΠΕΡΙ ΠΡΟΙΚΟΣ ΜΗΤΡΩΙΑΣ.

πῆς τὴν ὄψιν οὖσα ἐπλησίαζεν[p] αὐτῷ· ὥστε πολὺ μᾶλλον εἰκὸς ἦν αὐτὸν διὰ τὴν ζῶσαν γυναῖκα, ἧς ἐρῶν ἐτύγχανε, τὸν τῆς τεθνεώσης υἱὸν ἀτιμάζειν, ἢ δι' ἐμὲ καὶ τὴν τετελευτηκυῖαν τοὺς ἐκ τῆς ζώσης καὶ πλησιαζούσης αὐτῷ παῖδας μὴ ποιεῖσθαι. καίτοι οὗτός γ' εἰς τοῦτο τόλμης ἥκει ὥστε φησὶ τὸν πατέρα μου 28 δεκάτην ὑπὲρ αὐτοῦ ἑστιᾶσαι. καὶ περὶ τούτου μόνον Τιμοκράτους καὶ Προμάχου ἐμβέβληται μαρτυρίας, οἳ οὔτε γένει προσήκουσί μου τῷ πατρὶ οὐδὲν οὔτε φίλοι ἦσαν ἐκείνῳ. οὕτω δὲ φανερῶς τὰ ψευδῆ μεμαρτυρή-

[p] Bekk. ἐπλησίασεν Z cum ΣrA¹.

considerable time it had lasted; and it is a necessary part of the argument ἐκ τῶν εἰκότων. The elegance of the Greek and the cleverness of the reasoning here are alike admirable.—ἐπλησίαζεν, see § 8.

ἧς ἐρῶν ἐτύγχανε] 'Whom he was in love with at the time,' —but the imperfect gives the additional sense, 'during all the time.' Properly, τυγχάνω ποιῶν is not 'I happen to be doing,' but 'in doing it I fall in with some particular time,' or coincidence of time. Thus ἔτυχεν ἐξιών means 'he had *just* gone out,' not 'he happened to have gone out,' and in Soph. El. 313 νῦν δ' ἀγροῖσι τυγχάνει is, 'at this present moment he is in the country.' This idiomatic use was pointed out by Donaldson (*New Crat.* § 445), and it is an important remark, though apparently but little attended to.—πλησιαζούσης, i. e. ἔτι συνοικούσης.

§ 28. *Boeotus has the audacity to assert, though he has no credible witnesses to prove it, that his father celebrated the tenth day after his birth, and so acknowledged him as his son. But all of the judges are aware that he did this only from constraint, and because he was threatened with an action.*

δεκάτην ἑστιᾶσαι] In Or. 39 § 22, it is δεκάτην ποιῆσαι. [Cf. Isaeus III § 70, ἐν τῇ δεκάτῃ τῇ ταύτης κληθέντες συνεστιᾶσθαι. S.]

Τιμοκράτους] It has been proposed to identify this Timocrates with the person against whom Demosthenes delivered Or. 24. Arn. Schaefer, *Dem. u. s. Zeit*, III 2, 218. S.]

ἐμβέβληται] See § 21.

ἐκείνῳ] Here also (see § 25) there is a slightly more demonstrative sense than αὐτῷ would bear. It is *illi* rather than *ei*. A person absent, e.g. from death, becomes ἐκεῖνος as pointed to in the distance, as it were, as sup. § 25, inf. § 45, and Or. 39 § 33, ἐξ ὅτου δ' ἀρέσεις ἐκείνῳ (sc. τῷ τετελευτηκότι) μὴ σκοπεῖν. So Or. 36 § 28, Σωκράτης ὁ τραπεζίτης ἐκεῖνος, and 35 § 6, ὁ Διοφάντου υἱός, ἐκείνου τοῦ Σφηττίου. Perhaps we should so render τῶν ἐκείνου, ibid. § 4, 'the property of his deceased brother.'

κάσιν ὥστε ὃν πάντων ὑμῶν εἰδότων οὑτοσὶ δίκην λαχὼν ἄκοντα ἠνάγκασε ποιήσασθαι αὐτόν, τοῦτον οὗτοι, ὥσπερ κλητῆρες, δύο μόνοι ὄντες μαρτυροῦσι 29 δεκάτην ὑπὲρ τούτου ἑστιᾶσαι. οἷς τίς ἂν ὑμῶν πιστεύσειεν; καὶ μὴν οὐδ' ἐκεῖνό γε εἰπεῖν αὐτῷ ἐνδέχεται, ὡς μικρὸν μὲν ὄντα ἐποιεῖτο αὐτὸν ὁ πατήρ, μείζω δὲ γενόμενον τῇ μητρὶ ὀργισθείς τι τῇ τούτων ἠτίμαζε· πολὺ γὰρ δήπου μᾶλλον εἰώθασιν, ὧν ἂν ἐν

Plat. Phaed. p. 89 A, πολλάκις θαυμάσας Σωκράτη οὐ πώποτε μᾶλλον ἠγάσθην ἢ τότε παραγενόμενος. τὸ μὲν οὖν ἔχειν ὅτι λέγοι ἐκεῖνος, ἴσως οὐδὲν ἄτοπον. It is said that the North-western American Indians always speak of 'that dead man,' and think it unlucky to mention his name. So ἐκεῖ is often a euphemism for ἐν Ἀιδου. Young students are very apt to overlook this well-marked distinction. It may be stated as a rule, that neither ἐκεῖνος nor αὐτὸς ever means 'he,' though αὐτὸν regularly means 'him.' In fact, the Greek language has no way of expressing the simple object 'he,' 'she,' 'it' (*is, ea, id*). In the N.T. the usage of ἐκεῖνος seems affected by the Latin idiom. When (as in § 29) ἐκεῖνο means, like *illud*, 'the following fact,' it really points to something not actually present, 'that other thing.' And hence *olim*, the locative of *ole, olle, ille*, means 'at that other time,' i.e. either past or future.

δίκην λαχὼν] See Or. 39 § 2.

ὥσπερ κλητῆρες] 'Like witnesses to a summons, a pair of them only depose,&c.' Kennedy. "Actori reum citanti duo solummodo κλητῆρες (subscriptores) aderant. Hos igitur duos testes ait potius subscriptores quasi esse adversus Mantiam, quam ei testes adfuisse." Reiske. He contrasts the doubtful evidence of two persons only, Timocrates and Promachus, who not being friends or relations had no right to be present at the birth-feast, and who could have known little or nothing about the matter, with the notoriety of the transaction in the forced adoption of Boeotus. Cf. § 59.

29. οἷς τίς ἂν κ.τ.λ.] 'Is there *any* one who, &c.' For this formula, *quibus nemo facile crediderit*, see the note on Aesch. Suppl. 636. (P.)

πολὺ γὰρ μᾶλλον κ.τ.λ.] Boeotus pretends that he is obliged to account for that name having been given him; and he says it was given ὕβρει καὶ ἐπηρείᾳ τινί, Or. 39 § 32, and resulted from some quarrel of his father with Plango, whereas it was really the name of his uncle, Or. 39 § 32. The argument is the same, and very nearly also the words, as in Or. 39 § 23 [where, however, the inelegant reiteration of διὰ in the present passage, διενεχθῶσι...διαλλάττεσθαι...διὰ τοὺς...διὰ τὰς, is partly avoided by the use of καταλλάττεσθαι; and the *hiatus* in γυνὴ καὶ ἀνὴρ obviated by the transposition ἀνὴρ καὶ γυνή. A. Schaefer, per-

p. 1017] ΠΕΡΙ ΠΡΟΙΚΟΣ ΜΗΤΡΩΙΑΣ. 203

αὐτοῖς διενεχθῶσι γυνὴ καὶ ἀνήρ, διαλλάττεσθαι διὰ τοὺς παῖδας ἢ διὰ τὰς πρὸς ἑαυτοὺς ὀργὰς τοὺς κοινοὺς παῖδας πρὸς μισεῖν. ὥστ' ἐὰν μὲν ἐπιχειρῇ ταῦτα λέγειν, μὴ ἐπιτρέπετε αὐτῷ[q] ἀναισχυντεῖν· ἂν δὲ λέγῃ 30 περὶ τῶν δικῶν ἃς ἀπεδιῄτησέ μου ὁ διαιτητής, καὶ φάσκῃ ὑπ' ἐμοῦ ἀπαράσκευος ληφθῆναι, πρῶτον μὲν μέμνησθε ὅτι οὐκ ὀλίγος χρόνος ἐγένετο ἐν ᾧ ἔδει παρασκευάσασθαι αὐτόν, ἀλλ' ἔτη πολλά, ἔπειθ' ὅτι οὗτος ἦν ὁ διώκων τὴν δίκην, ὥστε πολὺ μᾶλλον ἦν εἰκὸς ἐμὲ ὑπὸ τούτου ἀπαράσκευον ληφθῆναι ἢ τοῦτον ὑπ' ἐμοῦ. ἔτι δὲ πάντες ὑμῖν οἱ πρὸς τῷ διαιτητῇ 31 παρόντες μεμαρτυρήκασιν ὡς οὗτος παρὼν αὐτός, ὅτε ἀπεδιῄτησέ μου ὁ διαιτητής, οὔτε ἐφῆκεν εἰς τὸ δικαστήριον ἐνέμεινέ τε τῇ διαίτῃ. καίτοι ἄτοπον δοκεῖ μοι εἶναι, εἰ οἱ μὲν ἄλλοι, ὅταν οἴωνται ἀδικεῖσθαι, καὶ τὰς πάνυ μικρὰς δίκας εἰς ὑμᾶς ἐφιᾶσιν, οὗτος δέ μοι περὶ προικὸς δίκην ταλάντου λαχών, ταύτῃ, ὡς

[q] Bekk. om. Z cum ΣrA[1].

haps hypercritically, regards the sentence before us as inferior in rhythm and elegance to the parallel in the former speech. *Dem. u. s. Zeit*, III 2, 226. S.]

§§ 30, 31. *He will try to account for the suit (his claim to the dowry) being given against him by the arbitrator, by saying that he was not fully prepared with his case. But he had time enough; and he was the plaintiff, not the defendant, who might rather plead 'unpreparedness.' Besides, why did he not appeal, if he thought the verdict was wrong?*

ἂν δὲ λέγῃ] 'Should he go on to talk about the actions,' &c. See §§ 16, 17.

οὐκ ὀλίγος χρόνος] Between the first arbitration, which ended abruptly by the death of the arbitrator Solon, and the second, there had intervened ample time, χρόνος συχνὸς, § 16.

31. παρὼν αὐτός] § 17, παρόντος τούτου καὶ ἀντιδικοῦντος.

ἀδικεῖσθαι] viz. by a wrong decision of a public arbitrator.
—ἐφιᾶσιν, bring the matter by appeal before the Heliaea.

ταύτῃ] sc. τῇ διαίτῃ. 'If he nevertheless abided by, or acquiesced in it, though, according to his own account, it was unjustly given against him.'

§§ 32, 33. *He will tell you, forsooth, that he was not fond of going to law. But it is not so; he showed towards me a temper very different from your forgiving dispositions; he actually took advantage of some*

32 αὐτός φησιν, ἀδίκως καταδιαιτηθεὶς ͬ ἐνέμεινεν. νὴ 1018
Δί', ἀπράγμων γάρ τις ἴσως ἐστὶν ἄνθρωπος καὶ οὐ
φιλόδικος. ἐβουλόμην τἂν, ὦ ἄνδρες δικασταί, τοιοῦτον αὐτὸν εἶναι. νυνὶ δ' ὑμεῖς μὲν οὕτως ἐστὲ κοινοὶ
καὶ φιλάνθρωποι, ὥστ' οὐδὲ τοὺς τῶν τριάκοντα υἱεῖς
φυγαδεῦσαι ἐκ τῆς πόλεως ἠξιώσατε· οὗτος δ' ἐμοὶ
μετὰ Μενεκλέους τοῦ πάντων τούτων ἀρχιτέκτονος
ἐπιβουλεύσας, καὶ ἐξ ἀντιλογίας καὶ λοιδορίας πληγὰς
συναψάμενος, ἐπιτεμὼν τὴν κεφαλὴν αὐτοῦ τραύματος

ͬ Bekk. cum H. Wolf (cf. Or. 21 § 85, 96). ἀποδιαιτηθείσῃ
coniecit Sauppe (ἀποδιαιτηθείσης ΓΑ¹. ἀποδιαιτηθεὶς libri ceteri).

blows that passed between us in a quarrel, and made a cut on his own head in order to make out a case against me before the Areopagus, of wounding with intent to kill! But for the confession of the doctor who was asked, but refused, to lance him, I might have been transported for life.

νὴ Δί', ἀπράγμων ... καὶ οὐ φιλόδικος] 'Oh! to be sure, he is not a man of business and far from litigious!' Prof. Kennedy. Cf. Or. 42 § 12, μέτριον καὶ ἀπράγμονος πολίτου μὴ εὐθὺς ἐπὶ κεφαλὴν εἰς τὸ δικαστήριον βαδίζειν, 36 § 53, 54 § 24. S.]

νυνὶ δέ] 'But as the case is.'

φυγαδεῦσαι] Perhaps this fact is not elsewhere recorded. "The sons, even of such among the Thirty as did not return, were allowed to remain at Athens, and enjoy their rights of citizens unmolested; a moderation rare in Grecian political warfare." Grote, H. G. chap. 66, VI p. 4 (where the present passage only is referred to). It would seem that, after the defeat of the Thirty by Thrasybulus near the Piraeus, B.C. 403, and the peace made by Pausanias, a compromise was made between the oligarchical and democratical parties, since the greater part of the wealthy citizens (the 3000, as they are called) were more or less concerned with and implicated in the tyranny of the Thirty. Cf. § 46, πρὸς τοὺς ἐπὶ τῆς ὀλιγαρχίας πολλοὺς τῶν πολιτῶν ἀκρίτους ἀποκτείναντας διαλλαγέντες. Andocides, de mysteriis, § 90.

συναψάμενος] 'Having concerted a quarrel that should end in blows.' (He 'contrived from words to come to blows.' C. R. Kennedy. 'Managed to get up a fight.' Middle of 'indirect agency.' Prof. Kennedy.) Or perhaps = πλασάμενος, 'having invented a story about blows having been given in consequence of a quarrel.' Wolf inclines to the latter, G. H. Schaefer to the former interpretation; and it is not very easy to decide between them. (Cf. Or. 54 § 19, κατὰ μικρὸν ὑπάγεσθαι ἐκ μὲν λοιδορίας εἰς πληγὰς, ἐκ δὲ πληγῶν εἰς τραύματα.) The plan evidently was, to get up a case against Mantitheus by provok-

εἰς "Αρειον πάγον με προσεκαλέσατο, ὡς φυγαδεύσων ἐκ τῆς πόλεως. καὶ εἰ μὴ Εὐθύδικος ὁ ἰατρός, πρὸς ὃν 33 οὗτοι τὸ πρῶτον ἦλθον δεόμενοι ἐπιτεμεῖν τὴν κεφαλήν, αὐτὸς πρὸς τὴν ἐξ Ἀρείου πάγου βουλὴν εἶπε τὴν ἀλήθειαν πᾶσαν, τοιαύτην δίκην οὗτος ἂν εἰλήφει παρ' ἐμοῦ μηδὲν ἀδικοῦντος, ἣν ὑμεῖς οὐδὲ κατὰ τῶν τὰ μέγιστ' ἀδικούντων ὑμᾶς ἐπιχειρήσαιτ' ἂν ποιήσασθαι. ἵνα δὲ μὴ δοκῶ διαβάλλειν αὐτόν, ἀνάγνωθί μοι τὰς μαρτυρίας.

ΜΑΡΤΥΡΙΑΙ.

Τοῦτον μὲν τοίνυν οὕτω[a] μέγαν καὶ φοβερὸν ἀγῶ- 34

[a] Bekk. 1824. om. Z et Bekk. st. cum Σ.

ing a quarrel, and to procure his banishment, so as to leave the ground clear for the defendant, if not to get possession of a part of his property.

ἐπιτεμών] As ἐντέμνειν, *incidere*, is 'to make a cut *in*,' so ἐπιτέμνειν is 'to make a cut *on*.' The difference, though slight, is real, the latter referring only to a superficial cut. In the present case, the man made an incision on the scalp, pretending to have been wounded by his adversary.

τραύματος] 'Cutting and maiming.' 'Wounding with intent to kill.' For the genitive cf. Ar. Vesp. 1406, προσκαλοῦμαί σ', ὅστις εἶ, πρὸς τοὺς ἀγορανόμους βλάβης τῶν φορτίων, where there is probably an ellipse of δίκην, though all words of this kind, like ἐγκαλεῖν, ἀμφισβητεῖν, &c., have a tendency to take the genitive.

33. οὗτοι] viz. Boeotus and Menecles, the latter of whom is said to have been at the bottom of the whole plot.

μηδὲν ἀδικοῦντος] *Cum essem innocens*, 'without my having wronged him.' Here μὴ is used, not οὐ, by a lax usage, or perhaps the clause is affected by the hypothetical notion, 'he would have got me punished even when I had done no wrong.' Bekker and the Zürich editors read μηδὲν with the MSS instead of the vulg. οὐδέν, which G. H. Schaefer prefers. And in itself οὐδέν is correct, as asserting the present consciousness of innocence as a fact.

διαβάλλειν] 'To be misrepresenting him,' 'to be saying what is untrue of him.' A favourite verb with the Greeks, for which the Romans had no precise equivalent, *calumniari* being hardly used in this sense. So διαβολαί is often used of false impressions or ill-feelings resulting from slander, e.g. Plat. Apol. p. 18. In Phaed. p. 67 E διαβάλλειν has its original sense of putting two persons or things at variance with each other.

§§ 34, 35. *The bringing of so serious a charge against me shows his malignant intentions.*

νά μοι οὐχ ὡς εὐήθης ὤν, ἀλλ' ὡς ἐπίβουλος καὶ κακοῦργος κατεσκεύασεν. μετὰ δὲ ταῦτα ἀντὶ τοῦ ὀνόματος οὗ ἔθετο αὐτῷ ὁ πατὴρ Βοιωτὸν, ὥσπερ καὶ πρὸς ὑμᾶς μεμαρτύρηται, ἐπειδὴ ἐκεῖνος ἐτελεύτησε, Μαντίθεον ἑαυτὸν ἐγγράψας εἰς τοὺς δημότας, καὶ τοῦ αὐτοῦ ἐμοὶ καὶ πατρὸς καὶ δήμου προσαγορευόμενος, οὐ μόνον τὴν δίκην ταύτην, περὶ ἧς νυνὶ δικάζομαι, ἀνάδικον ἐποίησεν, ἀλλὰ καὶ χειροτονησάντων ὑμῶν ἐμὲ ταξίαρχον ἧκεν αὐτὸς ἐπὶ τὸ δικαστήριον δοκι-

On another occasion, when I had been elected to a public office, he claimed it as being the Mantitheus who had obtained the show of hands. This and other vexatious proceedings compelled me to bring my former action against him, and to insist that he should retain his right name, which is Boeotus.

οὐχ ὡς εὐήθης] 'Not as a simpleton,' who might foolishly suppose that a blow received in a quarrel would be visited by a serious penalty. Mr Mayor thinks the word refers to ἀπράγμων in § 32. Kennedy is scarcely correct in translating 'not as a good-natured person.' 'This great and formidable contest he got up against me, not as a man of simple character, but as a plotter and a villain.' Prof. Kennedy.
—κατεσκεύασεν, this is said in reference to ἀπαράσκευον in § 30.

μετὰ ταῦτα] The action just described would seem to have been brought when he was but a boy. See Or. 39 § 5, συμβάσης τῷ πατρὶ τελευτῆς πρὶν τὰς εἰς τοὺς δημότας ἐγγραφὰς γενέσθαι. It appears therefore clear that enrolment even in the phratriae conferred the rights of a citizen, so far as to justify the bringing of a suit.

τοῦ αὐτοῦ πατρὸς καὶ δήμου] See Or. 39 §§ 4 and 9.

. ἀνάδικον] 'To be tried over again.' He alludes to the transaction before the two arbitrators, §§ 16, 17. By saying that his name was Mantitheus in the city-books, he made null and void a verdict given against Boeotus. The adjective is of rare occurrence. Inf. §§ 40 and 42. Or. 24 (κατὰ Τιμοκρ.) § 191, καὶ τὴν μεθ' ὅρκου καὶ λόγου καὶ κρίσεως ψῆφον ἐνηνεγμένην ἀνάδικον καθίστησιν. Hesych. ἀνάδικοι· οὕτως ἐλέγοντο δίκαι εἰς ἀκεραίαν (i. e. de integro, or re integra) ἐγκαθιστάμεναι, ἤτοι διὰ πολιτικὴν αἰτίαν, ἢ τῶν μαρτύρων ἁλόντων ψευδοκατηγόρων. Kennedy (Append. ix p. 394) renders it 'a reversal of a judgment.'

ταξίαρχον] In Or. 39 § 10 this office is not included in the hypothetical cases given of honours conferred by the state and claimed by another under a false name; but it is mentioned ib. § 17. As this particular case had really occurred, it is omitted in the former enumeration. A preliminary examination, probably of a per-

1019 μασθησόμενος, δίκην δὲ ἐξούλης ὠφληκὼς ταύτην οὐκ αὐτὸς ὠφληκέναι φησὶν, ἀλλ' ἐμέ. ὡς δ' ἐν κεφαλαίῳ 35 εἰπεῖν, κακά μοι παρέχων ἠνάγκασέ με λαχεῖν αὐτῷ δίκην περὶ τοῦ ὀνόματος, οὐχ ἵνα χρήματα παρ' αὐτοῦ λάβω, ὦ ἄνδρες δικασταὶ, ἀλλ' ἵν', ἐὰν ὑμῖν δοκῶ δεινὰ πάσχειν καὶ βλάπτεσθαι μεγάλα, οὑτοσὶ καλῆται Βοιωτός, ὥσπερ ὁ πατὴρ αὐτῷ ἔθετο. ὅτι τοίνυν ἀληθῆ καὶ ταῦτα λέγω, λαβέ μοι καὶ τὰς περὶ τούτων μαρτυρίας.

ΜΑΡΤΥΡΙΑΙ.

Πρὸς τούτοις τοίνυν καὶ ὅτι ἐγὼ στρατευόμενος καὶ 36 μετὰ Ἀμεινίου ξενολογήσας[t], ἄλλοθέν τε χρήματα εὐ-

[t] Bekk. στρατολογήσας Z cum pr. Σ.

son's political status, freedom from debts, &c., had to be passed before he was formally installed in such an office, just as he was liable to the εὐθύνη after holding it. [Meier and Schömann, *Att. Process* pp. 200—14. Hermann, *Staatsalt.* § 149. S.]
δίκην ἐξούλης] See Or. 39 § 15.
35. οὐχ ἵνα κ.τ.λ.] Boeotus would say that it was done merely to secure the dower of my mother, he having before evaded payment on the plea of having another name, § 18. This is why the subjunctive is used, and not λάβοιμι, referring only to the past intention.
καλῆται] 'That the defendant may *go on being called* Boeotus.'
§§ 36, 37. *Another unjust action he brought against me when I was on military service and raising money and recruits. He charged me with having extorted a sum of money from the state of Mytilene, and this he did in the interest of the then tyrant, and pretended it was a debt*

due to my father which I had made them pay.
καὶ ὅτι (unless we should read ὅτε, which seems more natural) means 'on the charge that,' and is taken up by περὶ τούτων μοι δικάζεται, below. [εὐπορήσας is not joined with ξενολογήσας but is an explanatory participle. 'Just because, being on military service and having recruited mercenaries with A. (inasmuch as I was well provided with money and had received, &c.), I spent that sum upon those recruits, in order that, &c., he actually brings a suit against me on this score.' Prof. Kennedy.]
μετὰ Ἀμεινίου] He seems to have been a strategus at the time; and perhaps (as the duty of a taxiarch was to raise troops, and draw up the military κατάλογος), Mantitheus then accompanied him as such. [A. Schaefer, *Dem.* III 2, 224, calls him 'an enemy of Athens.' Nothing is known about him. S.]
εὐπορεῖν χρήματα] 'To raise

πορήσας καὶ ἐκ Μυτιλήνης παρὰ τοῦ ὑμετέρου προ-
ξένου Ἀπολλωνίδου καὶ παρὰ τῶν φίλων τῆς πόλεως
λαβὼν τριακοσίους στατῆρας Φωκαεῖς, ἀνήλωσα εἰς
τοὺς στρατιώτας, ἵνα πρᾶξίς τις πραχθείη καὶ ὑμῖν
37 καὶ ἐκείνοις συμφέρουσα, περὶ τούτων μοι δικάζεται ὡς
πατρικὸν κεκομισμένῳ χρέως παρὰ τῆς πόλεως τῆς
Μυτιληναίων, Κάμμῃ τῷ τυραννοῦντι Μυτιλήνης

money' (an expression not strictly correct) must be distinguished from εὐπορεῖν χρημάτων, 'to have ready-money at command.' Cf. Or. 33 § 6, τριάκοντα δὲ μνᾶς ἐδεῖτό μου οὗτος συνευπορῆσαι, and 36 § 57.

παρὰ τῶν φίλων τῆς πόλεως] "Designat partem illam civium Mitylenensium, quae partibus Atheniensium studeret." *Reiske.*

στατῆρας Φωκαεῖς] Boeckh (*Publ. Econ.* p. 23), quoting this passage, says, "the Phocaic stater occurs, both in inscriptions and in writers, as coined money; nor can it be supposed that silver pieces are meant, as the idea of a gold coin is inseparably associated with the name of a Phocaic stater. Its weight is unknown; it passed however as the least valuable gold coin." Thucyd., IV 52, speaks of certain Mitylenean exiles having seized Rhoeteum, and restored it on the receipt of 'two thousand Phocaic staters.' Prof. Churchill Babington (*Catalogue of Leake Greek Coins*, &c. p. 23) describes No. 70 as a "stater of electrum, or pale gold, of Phocaea," and adds "The Phocaean staters are now among the rarest of Greek coins; they are of purer gold and about six grains heavier than the Cyzicene staters." See *Plate of Coins.*

ἵνα πρᾶξις πραχθείη] 'In order that some action might be performed to your and their advantage.' Kennedy.

37. The form χρέως, for the more usual χρέος, is recognised by Hesychius. The use of πατρικὸν (as in πατρικὴ ἔχθρα, βασιλεία Thuc. I 13), and not πατρῷον (as in πατρῷον σκῆπτρον, πατρῷα χρήματα, &c.), is to be noticed.

Κάμμῃ] We hear nothing more of this ruler of Mytilene, nor of the date when he established himself as tyrant. We know however that in B.C. 351 Mytilene was no longer under a democracy, and that in B.C. 347—6 it was restored to the protection and alliance of Athens. These dates point to the beginning of B.C. 347, as probably the latest date for the delivery of the speech. A. Schaefer, *Dem. u. s. Z.* III 2, 224. S.] Mr Mayor remarks (p. 248), "The circumstances referred to are obscure.—I should suppose that Boeotus charges Mantitheus with having recovered money due to his father in Mytilene, in order that he, Boeotus, may claim a share of it, which of course he could not do if it were money supplied by Apollonidas and other friends of Athens for the purpose of levying a force against the tyrant. Such a demand might

ὑπηρετῶν, ὃς καὶ ὑμῖν κοινῇ καὶ ἐμοὶ ἰδίᾳ ἐχθρός ἐστιν. ὅτι δ' ὁ πατὴρ ἡμῶν, ἣν ἐψηφίσαντο αὐτῷ δωρεὰν οἱ Μυτιληναῖοι, εὐθὺς αὐτὸς ἐκομίσατο, καὶ ὡς οὐδὲν ὠφείλετο αὐτῷ χρέως ἐν Μυτιλήνῃ, τῶν ὑμετέρων φίλων παρέξομαι μαρτυρίαν.

ΜΑΡΤΥΡΙΑ.

Ἔχων τοίνυν, ὦ ἄνδρες δικασταί, καὶ ἄλλα πολλὰ 38 καὶ δεινὰ λέγειν, ἃ οὗτος καὶ εἰς ἐμὲ καὶ εἰς ὑμῶν ἐνίους ἡμάρτηκεν, ἀναγκάζομαι διὰ τὸ ὀλίγον εἶναί μοι τὸ ὕδωρ παραλιπεῖν. νομίζω γὰρ καὶ ἐκ τούτων ὑμῖν ἱκανῶς ἐπιδεδεῖχθαι ὡς οὐ τοῦ αὐτοῦ ἀνθρώπου ἐστὶν ἀγῶνα μέν μοι περὶ φυγῆς κατασκευάζειν καὶ δίκας οὐδὲν προσηκούσας δικάζεσθαι, πρὸς δὲ τὸν διαιτητὴν ἀπαντᾶν ἀπαράσκευον. ὥστε περὶ μὲν τούτων ἂν ἐπιχειρῇ λέγειν, οὐκ οἶμαι ὑμᾶς ἀποδέξεσθαι. ἂν δὲ λέγῃ ὡς ἀξιοῦντος αὐτοῦ ἐπιτρέψαι Κόνωνι τῷ 39 Τιμοθέου περὶ ἁπάντων ἐγὼ οὐκ ἐβουλόμην ἐπιτρέπειν, ἐνθυμεῖσθε ὡς ἐξαπατᾶν ὑμᾶς ἐπιχειρήσει. ἐγὼ

be represented as helping Cammes against the Athenians."

ὑπηρετῶν] To rouse the anger of Cammes against both Mantitheus and the Athenians, Boeotus told him that the debt had been extorted from his citizens, under the plea of its being due to the father, in order to aid and abet the popular side in the στάσις against him.

δωρεὰν] This would seem to have been a vote of money for some services performed to the state by Mantias when πολιτευόμενος, Or. 39 § 3.

τῶν ὑμετέρων φίλων] Your political friends, i.e. not of the party of Cammes.

38. *Want of time compels me to pass over other instances of his malice; but I have shown proofs enough that he was not the man to go unprepared into any suit against me.*

ὕδωρ] note on Or. 54 § 36.
ἀγῶνα περὶ φυγῆς] § 32 fin.
—ἀπαράσκευον, § 30 fin.
πρὸς δὲ τὸν κ.τ.λ.] See sup. §11.

§§ 39, 40. *He will tell you, that he made me an offer to settle all the matters under dispute by arbitration. Why, an arbitration had been given, and more than once, in my favour. What motive could I have for disturbing the decision by appealing to another? It is by his insisting on an arbitrator's award that he holds all his present privileges.*

γὰρ περὶ μὲν ὧν αἱ δίκαι οὔπω τέλος εἶχον, ἕτοιμος ἦν ἐπιτρέπειν καὶ Κόνωνι καὶ ἄλλῳ διαιτητῇ ἴσῳ, ὅτῳ οὗτος βούλοιτο· περὶ δὲ ὧν τρὶς πρὸς τὸν διαιτητὴν ἀπαντήσαντος τούτου καὶ ἀντιδικοῦντος ὁ μὲν διαιτητὴς ἀπέγνω μου, οὗτος δὲ τοῖς γνωσθεῖσιν ἐνέμεινεν, ὡς καὶ ὑμῖν μεμαρτύρηται, οὐκ ᾤμην δίκαιον εἶναι
40 ταῦτα πάλιν ἀνάδικα γίγνεσθαι· τί γὰρ ἂν ἦν πέρας ἡμῖν τοῦ διαλυθῆναι, εἰ τὰ κατὰ τοὺς νόμους διαιτηθέντα λύσας ἑτέρῳ διαιτητῇ ἐπέτρεψα περὶ τῶν αὐτῶν ἐγκλημάτων, ἄλλως τε καὶ ἀκριβῶς εἰδὼς ὅτι, εἰ καὶ πρὸς τοὺς ἄλλους μὴ ἐπιεικές ἐστι ταῖς διαίταις ἰσχυρίζεσθαι, πρός γε τοῦτον ἁπάντων δικαιότατον ἦν οὕτω
41 προσφέρεσθαι. φέρε γάρ, εἴ τις αὐτὸν ξενίας γράψαιτο λέγων ὡς διομνύμενος ὁ πατὴρ οὐκ ἔφη τοῦτον υἱὸν

οὔπω τέλος εἶχον] 'Which had received no judicial determination.' Kennedy.
Κόνωνι] The grandson of the well-known general of that name.
ἴσῳ] 'Impartial.' Or. 55 §§ 9, 35.
τρὶς] This does not clearly appear from the account in §§ 16, 17. One of the three cases meant may have been that before Xenippus, § 44.
40. τί γὰρ ἂν ἦν πέρας κ.τ.λ.] 'What definitive settlement could we ever have come to, if I had set aside an award pronounced according to law, and referred the same causes of action to another arbitrator? especially when I knew so well, that, even if it is not equitable to insist on awards against other people, it is perfectly fair to deal in such a way with Boeotus.' Kennedy.
πέρας τοῦ διαλυθῆναι] 'Final settlement,' 'conclusion of our difference,' lit. 'termination consisting of reconciliation.' For this 'genitive of apposition,' in prose mainly confined to the gen. of the infinitive, cf. Hom. Il. III 309, θανάτοιο τέλος, and Thuc. VII 42, πέρας τοῦ ἀπαλλαγῆναι τοῦ κινδύνου. Kühner, Gk. Gr. § 402 d. S.]—ἰσχυρίζεσθαι, i.e. ἐμμένειν.—προσφέρεσθαι, 'to behave towards,' 'to deal with.' Plat. Theaet. p. 151 c, προσφέρου οὖν πρός με ὡς πρὸς μαίας υἱὸν καὶ αὐτὸν μαιευτικόν. Or. 54 (Νικοστρ.) 28, εἴπερ ἐβούλοντο δικαίως προσφέρεσθαι πρὸς ὑμᾶς.
§ 41. Suppose that some one were to bring an action of ξενία (alien birth) against him; what could he plead, but that he had been made a citizen by an arbitrator's decision?
ξενίας] See Or. 39 § 18.
διομνύμενος] There is an allusion to the double oath of both plaintiff and defendant, called διωμοσία. But the meaning here is merely 'on his oath.'

p. 1021] ΠΕΡΙ ΠΡΟΙΚΟΣ ΜΗΤΡΩΙΑΣ. 211

αὐτοῦ εἶναι, ἔσθ' ὅτῳ ἂν ἄλλῳ ἰσχυρίζοιτο πρὸς
ταῦτα ἢ διότι τῆς μητρὸς αὐτῶν ὀμοσάσης καὶ τοῦ
διαιτητοῦ καταγνόντος ἠναγκάσθη ὁ πατὴρ ἡμῶν
ἐμμεῖναι τῇ διαίτῃ; οὐκοῦν δεινὸν εἰ οὗτος, αὐτὸς κατὰ 42
γνῶσιν διαιτητοῦ ὑμέτερος πολίτης γεγενημένος καὶ
1021 πρὸς ἐμὲ τὴν οὐσίαν νειμάμενος καὶ τυχὼν τῶν μετρίων
ἁπάντων, ἃς ἐγὼ δίκας τοῦτον ἀπέφυγον παρόντα καὶ
ἀντιδικοῦντα καὶ τοῖς γνωσθεῖσιν ἐμμένοντα, ταύτας
ἀναδίκους ἀξιῶν γίγνεσθαι δίκαιόν τι δοκοίη λέγειν
ὑμῖν, ὥσπερ, ὅταν μὲν τούτῳ συμφέρῃ, δέον κυρίας
εἶναι[u] τὰς διαίτας, ὅταν δὲ μὴ συμφέρῃ, προσῆκον
τὴν τούτου[v] γνώμην κυριωτέραν γενέσθαι τῶν κατὰ
τοὺς ὑμετέρους νόμους γνωσθέντων. ὃς οὕτως ἐπί- 43
βουλός ἐστιν ὥστε καὶ τὴν δίαιταν ταύτην ἐπιτρέπειν
με προὐκαλεῖτο οὐχ ὅπως ἀπαλλαγῇ πρός με, ἀλλ'
ἵν', ὥσπερ καὶ πρότερον ἕνδεκα ἔτη διήγαγε κακουργῶν,
οὕτω καὶ νῦν τὰ ἀποδιαιτηθέντα μου λύσας ἐξ ἀρχῆς

[u] εἶναι κυρίας Z et Bekker st. cum Σ.   [v] Bekk. τούτων Z cum Σ.

ἢ διότι] for ἢ ὅτι. The Attic Orators (esp. Isocrates) often prefer διότι to ὅτι when a *hiatus* is thereby avoided. Isocr. Paneg. § 48 n. S.]
ὀμοσάσης] See Or. 39 § 4.
42. κατὰ γνῶσιν] 'Through the decision.' It is a peculiarity of the middle Attic to use κατά, 'in accordance with,' quite as a synonym of διά, 'because of.' Thus, the Attics say κατὰ τί ἦλθες; '*Why* have you come?' &c. Any one of the three prepositions κατά, διά, or παρὰ πενίαν may be used to signify 'through poverty,' and κατά more often bears this meaning than is commonly supposed. Mr Wayte on Timocr. § 32 seems not to have noticed this.

ἀξιῶν κ.τ.λ.] Construe ἀξιῶν τὰς δίκας ἀναδίκους γίγνεσθαι, ἃς ἐγὼ τοῦτον ἀπέφευγον, κ.τ.λ. 'in seeking to reverse a judgment against his own claim, which I obtained against him after appearance and argument, and in which he has acquiesced.' Kennedy. See §§ 19, 34.
τὴν τούτου γνώμην] Contemptuously, '*his* judgment, forsooth, of what is right.'
§§ 43, 44. *So crafty is he, that when he made me an offer to go to an arbitrator, it was only done to set aside a former decision and go to law with me again, as he has been doing for years past.*
ἐπιτρέπειν] sc. Κόνωνι, § 39.
λύσας κ.τ.λ.] 'Setting aside

14—2

44 με συκοφαντῇ καὶ τὴν δίκην ταύτην ἐκκρούῃ. τεκμήριον δὲ τούτου μέγιστον· οὔτε γὰρ τὴν πρόκλησιν ἐδέχετο, ἣν ἐγὼ κατὰ τοὺς νόμους προὐκαλούμην αὐτόν, πρότερόν τε Ξενίππῳ, ὃν οὗτος προὐβάλετο διαιτητήν, ἐπιτρέψαντος μου περὶ τῆς τοῦ ὀνόματος δίκης, ἀπηγόρευσεν αὐτῷ μὴ διαιτᾶν. ὅτι δὲ καὶ ταῦτ' ἀληθῆ λέγω, ἐκ τῆς μαρτυρίας καὶ τῆς προκλήσεως εἴσεσθε.

ΜΑΡΤΥΡΙΑ. ΠΡΟΚΛΗΣΙΣ.

45 Ταύτην τοίνυν τὴν πρόκλησιν οὐ δεξάμενος, ἀλλ' ἐνεδρεύων με καὶ τὴν δίκην ὅτι πλεῖστον χρόνον ἐκκρούειν βουλόμενος, κατηγορήσει, ὡς ἐγὼ πυνθάνομαι, οὐ μόνον ἐμοῦ, ἀλλὰ καὶ τοῦ πατρός, λέγων ὡς ἐκεῖνος ἐμοὶ χαριζόμενος πολλὰ τοῦτον ἠδίκησεν. ὑμεῖς δ', ὦ ἄνδρες δικασταί, μάλιστα μὲν, ὥσπερ αὐτοὶ οὐκ ἂν ἀξιώσαιτε κακῶς ἀκούειν ὑπὸ τῶν ὑμετέρων παί-

the judgment of non-suit pronounced for me by the arbitrator.' Kennedy.

44. προὐβάλετο] 'Had proposed,' 'had put forward.'

ἀπηγόρευσεν] 'He gave him notice not to pronounce the award.' Perhaps this means, that he would not hold himself bound by his decision; or, perhaps, he sent him a notice that he did not accept him as arbitrator. [On this form, for which ἀπεῖπεν is commonly used, see note on Or. 55 § 4. S.]

§§ 45, 46. *Not only has he done his best, by these delays and repeated actions, to injure me, but he intends to throw insult on the memory of his own father by saying that he acted unfairly and partially towards me. But it would be strange if citizens who made* an amnesty and have kept it with the Thirty Tyrants, after all their cruelty, should allow the defendant to speak ill of the father with whom he was reconciled in his lifetime, and for whom he got so much more than ever he deserved.

ἐκεῖνος] Like ἐκεῖνον in § 46 fin., used of one deceased; see on § 28.

μάλιστα μὲν κ.τ.λ.] Answered by ἂν δ' ἄρα in § 47, and taken up or repeated by μάλιστα μὲν in the beginning of that paragraph.—βλασφημεῖν, 'to use bad words.' A favourite term with Demosthenes, and used in a very general sense, without regard to the irreligious import which it now bears after the earlier Greek use, e.g. in Eur. Ion 1189.

ΠΕΡΙ ΠΡΟΙΚΟΣ ΜΗΤΡΩΙΑΣ.

δων, ούτω μηδὲ τούτῳ ἐπιτρέπετε περὶ τοῦ πατρὸς βλασφημεῖν· καὶ γὰρ ἂν εἴη δεινὸν εἰ αὐτοὶ μὲν πρὸς τοὺς ἐπὶ τῆς ὀλιγαρχίας πολλοὺς τῶν πολιτῶν ἀκρίτους ἀποκτείναντας διαλλαγέντες ἐμμένετε ταῖς ὁμολογίαις, ὥσπερ χρὴ τοὺς καλοὺς κἀγαθοὺς ἄνδρας, τούτῳ δὲ πρὸς τὸν πατέρα ζῶντα καὶ διαλυθέντι καὶ πολλὰ παρὰ τὸ δίκαιον πλεονεκτήσαντι νῦν μνησικακεῖν ἐπιτρέψετε καὶ κακῶς λέγειν ἐκεῖνον. μηδαμῶς, ὦ ἄνδρες δικασταί, ἀλλὰ μάλιστα μὲν κωλύετ' αὐτὸν ταῦτα ποιεῖν, ἂν δ' ἄρα βιάζηται ὑμᾶς καὶ λοιδορῆται, ἐνθυμεῖσθ' ὅτι αὐτὸς ἑαυτοῦ καταμαρτυρεῖ μὴ ἐξ ἐκείνου γεγενῆσθαι. οἱ μὲν γὰρ φύσει παῖδες ὄντες, κἂν πρὸς ζῶντας τοὺς πατέρας διενεχθῶσιν, ἀλλ' οὖν τελευτήσαντάς γε[w] αὐτοὺς ἐπαινοῦσιν· οἱ δὲ νομιζόμενοι μὲν υἱεῖς, μὴ ὄντες δὲ γένει ἐξ ἐκείνων, ῥᾳδίως

[w] Bekk. om. Z cum ΓΣΦΒ.

46. αὐτοὶ μὲν—τούτῳ δὲ] See sup. § 32. The sentence is antithetical in several points: 'you forgave and still forgive the men who grievously injured the state and your own families; he made up his quarrel with his father, and though he was benefited by him in life, he assails his memory again when dead.' These constructions are an essential feature of Greek rhetoric; but they are quite alien from both our language and our idioms.

μνησικακεῖν] 'To rip open the quarrel and calumniate him.' Kennedy. But ἐκεῖνον might better have been rendered (see § 28) 'that worthy man.' But there is a sort of antithesis with ζῶντα which points rather to the sense 'now that he is no more.'

§ 47. If he persists in his unseemly language against his father, observe that he is merely giving a proof that he is not really his son; for true sons, even if they quarrel in lifetime, speak with respect of their father's memory, while putative sons have no such scruples.

βιάζηται κ.τ.λ.] 'If he should persist in acting in defiance of your wishes and speaking evil of his father.' Kennedy is here not quite correct, 'if he abuse my father in spite of you.' Compare the force of καλῆται in § 35. Properly, βιάζεσθαι is 'to play the bully,' and the construction is τινά τι, as in Aesch. Theb. 1045, αὐδῶ πόλιν σε μὴ βιάζεσθαι τάδε.

ἀλλ' οὖν—γε] At saltem. See Or. 39 § 34.—ῥᾳδίως, ἀδιαφόρως, 'without any concern;' 'they think nothing of quarrelling

μὲν αὐτοῖς διαφέρονται ζῶσιν, οὐδὲν δὲ φροντίζουσι 48 περὶ τεθνεώτων αὐτῶν βλασφημοῦντες. χωρὶς δὲ τούτων ἐνθυμεῖσθε ὡς ἄτοπόν ἐστιν, εἰ οὗτος τὸν πατέρα ὡς ἁμαρτόντα* εἰς αὐτὸν λοιδορήσει, διὰ τὰ ἐκείνου ἁμαρτήματα ὑμέτερος πολίτης γεγενημένος. κἀγὼ μὲν διὰ τὴν τούτων μητέρα τὰ δύο μέρη τῆς οὐσίας ἀφαιρεθεὶς ὅμως ὑμᾶς αἰσχύνομαι λέγειν περὶ ἐκείνης 49 τι φλαῦρον· οὗτος δ', ὃν ἠνάγκασεν αὐτῷ⁷ πατέρα γενέσθαι, τοῦτον οὐκ αἰσχύνεται ψέγων ἐναντίον ὑμῶν, ἀλλ' εἰς τοῦτ' ἀμαθίας ἥκει ὥστε τῶν νόμων ἀπαγορευόντων μηδὲ τοὺς τῶν ἄλλων πατέρας κακῶς λέγειν τεθνεῶτας, οὗτος, οὗ φησιν υἱὸς εἶναι, τοῦτον λοιδορήσει, ᾧ προσῆκε καὶ εἴ τις ἄλλος ἐβλασφήμει 1023 περὶ αὐτοῦ ἀγανακτεῖν.

* Bekk. ἁμαρτάνοντα Z cum ΣrA¹.
⁷ Bekk. ἑαυτοῦ Z cum Σ.

with them while they are alive,' &c.

§§ 48, 49. *Besides, how inconsistent to talk of my father's failings, when those very failings procured him the rights of citizenship! Though I myself have lost two-thirds of my property through his mother Plango, still I say not a word against her; and yet he abuses in your hearing the father who was compelled to adopt him, and by whom therefore he has actually been benefited.*

τὰ ἐκείνου ἁμαρτήματα] There is a play on the double sense of ἁμαρτεῖν, which is often used as a euphemism for the frailties of love. See Eur. Hipp. 464. Suppl. 900.

τὰ δύο μέρη] Boeotus and his brother Pamphilus had got two-thirds, Mantitheus only one-third, Or. 39 § 6.

49. ψέγων] 'Disparaging,'— the exact meaning of the word. It differs from μέμφεσθαι, the former implying the *expression* of dislike or contempt, the latter the *feeling* of dissatisfaction, though it so often has the secondary sense of 'to blame.'

τῶν νόμων κ.τ.λ.] The law of Draco, γονεῖς τιμᾶν, would seem to have been so far extended that an action for κακηγορία could be brought by any one whose father's memory had been unjustly aspersed. [Dem. Or. 20 § 104; Plutarch, Solon, 21; and Lexicon Rhet. Cantab. ἐάν τις κακῶς εἴπῃ τινὰ τῶν κατοιχομένων, κἂν ὑπὸ τῶν ἐκείνου παίδων ἀκούσῃ κακῶς, ὦφλε τῷ δημοσίῳ. S.]

ἀγανακτεῖν] i. e. to show his resentment by proceeding against him. Construe ἐβλασφήμει περὶ αὐτοῦ.

ΠΕΡΙ ΠΡΟΙΚΟΣ ΜΗΤΡΩΙΑΣ.

Οἶμαι δ' αὐτόν, ὦ ἄνδρες δικασταί, ἐπειδὰν τῶν 50 ἄλλων ἀπορῇ, κακῶς τέ με ἐπιχειρήσειν λέγειν καὶ διαβάλλειν πειράσεσθαι, διεξιόνθ' ὡς ἐγὼ μὲν καὶ ἐτράφην καὶ ἐπαιδεύθην καὶ ἔγημα ἐν τῇ τοῦ πατρὸς οἰκίᾳ, αὐτὸς δ' οὐδενὸς τούτων μετέσχεν· ὑμεῖς δ' ἐνθυμεῖσθ' ὅτι ἐμὲ μὲν ἡ μήτηρ παῖδα καταλιποῦσα ἐτελεύτησεν, ὥστε μοι ἱκανὸν ἦν ἀπὸ τοῦ τόκου τῆς προικὸς καὶ τρέφεσθαι καὶ παιδεύεσθαι· ἡ δὲ τούτων 51 μήτηρ Πλαγγών, τρέφουσα μεθ' αὑτῆς τούτους καὶ θεραπαίνας συχνὰς καὶ αὐτὴ πολυτελῶς ζῶσα, καὶ εἰς ταῦτα τὸν πατέρα τὸν ἐμὸν χορηγὸν ἑαυτῇ ὑπὸ τῆς ἐπιθυμίας ἔχουσα καὶ πολλὰ δαπανᾶν ἀναγκάζουσα, οὐκ ἴσα δήπου τῆς ἐκείνου οὐσίας ἐμοὶ ἀνήλωκεν, ὥστε πολὺ μᾶλλον προσήκειν ἐμὲ τούτοις ἐγκαλεῖν ἢ αὐτὸν

§§ 50—2. *In reply to his assertion, that I was brought up in all the comforts and luxuries of home, while he was but a poor outcast, I have to observe that his mother Plango was a most extravagant woman, and that more of my father's property was spent on her and her son than upon my education. So that on that score he is a debtor to me rather than I to him. Great expenses too I incurred in other transactions in the benefit of which he had a share.*

ἀπὸ τοῦ τόκου] Boeckh (*Publ. Ec.* p. 113, Lewis²) estimates this at 720 drachmas according to the customary rate of interest, i. e. twelve per cent.
—ἱκανὸν ἦν, i.e. I had to be content with that comparatively small sum for my education and maintenance.

51. μεθ' αὑτῆς] 'In her own house,' which was separate from that of Mantias.——τούτους, Boeotus and his brother Pamphilus.

χορηγὸν—ἔχουσα] 'Having my father to furnish the means,' Kennedy. Shilleto quotes this with other examples of the use, on De Fals. Leg. p. 408, § 238. Similarly χορηγεῖν and χορηγία were used of supplies in general, by Aristotle and later writers.—[e.g. Ethics I 10 § 15 τοῖς ἐκτὸς ἀγαθοῖς ἱκανῶς κεχορηγημένον and I 8 § 15 οὐ ῥᾴδιον τὰ καλὰ πράττειν ἀχορήγητον ὄντα ('without appliances'); also in the Greek Testament, 2 Cor. ix 10, 1 Pet. iv 11, 2 Pet. i 5 and 11. The word λειτουργία has a similar history. S.]—ὑπὸ, i.e. διὰ τὴν ἐπιθυμίαν.

οὐκ ἴσα ἐμοί] sc. ἀλλὰ πλείω ἐμοῦ.

τούτοις ἐγκαλεῖν] viz. τῆς προικός. I had more reason to demand from them payment of what was due from my mother, than they had to set up a counter claim to Plango's alleged property; since through Plango's influence with my

52 ἐγκλήματ' ἔχειν ὑπὸ τούτων. πρὸς γὰρ τοῖς ἄλλοις εἴκοσι μὲν μνᾶς δανεισάμενος μετὰ τοῦ πατρὸς παρὰ Βλεπαίου τοῦ τραπεζίτου εἰς ὠνήν τινα μετάλλων, ἐπειδὴ ὁ πατὴρ ἐτελεύτησε, τὰ μὲν μέταλλα πρὸς τούτους ἐνειμάμην*, τὸ δάνειον δ' αὐτὸς εἰσεπράχθην, ἑτέρας δὲ χιλίας εἰς τὴν τοῦ πατρὸς ταφὴν παρὰ Λυσιστράτου Θορικίου δανεισάμενος ἰδίᾳ ἐκτέτικα. ὡς δ' ἀληθῆ καὶ ταῦτα λέγω, ἐκ τούτων τῶν μαρτυριῶν εἴσεσθε.

ΜΑΡΤΥΡΙΑΙ.

53 Τοσαῦτα τοίνυν ἐμοῦ ἐλαττουμένου φανερῶς, οὐ-

* Bekk. ἐγένετο Z cum FΣΦB. ('*Cf*. εἴς τινα γίγνεσθαι, Schoemann ad Isaeum 3 § 36. Possis coniicere ἐνέμετο.' Sauppe.)

father they had so much more spent upon them.

52. μετάλλων] See 37 § 5. This was a speculation, of course; he does not say that it did not answer, but only that he had to pay for it, i. e. to the state, probably. Cf. Ar. Equit. 361, where Cleon says: ἀλλὰ σχελίδας ἐδηδοκὼς ὠνήσομαι μέταλλα, and see Boeckh, *Dissert*. p. 650.

πρὸς τούτους ἐνειμάμην] 'I shared the mines with them, while the whole sum borrowed I had to pay myself.' Cf. Or. 39 § 6, and 36 § 10.

εἰς τὴν τοῦ πατρὸς ταφὴν] For examples of the large expenses incurred in this filial duty, see Boeckh, *Publ. Ec.* p. 114.

ἰδίᾳ] 'On my own account,' viz. without their being in any way liable for it. To be construed, perhaps, with both the participle and the verb. Kennedy translates, 'and I have paid them out of my own pocket.'

§§ 53, 54. *With all these advantages on his side, his complaints against my unfairness are not to be listened to. He is just the man to make random assertions without proving them, and to assume that you know what he says is true. Ask him, then, for his proofs, and don't let him shirk the truth by such pretences. Let him follow my example; for I produced witnesses to prove even what really was notorious—the way in which my father was compelled to adopt him.*

ἐλαττοῦσθαί τι] 'To get (or consent to take) less than one's due;' 'to come off second best in a bargain.' Thuc. I 77, καὶ ἐλασσούμενοι γὰρ ἐν ταῖς ξυμβολαίαις πρὸς τοὺς ξυμμάχους δίκαις—φιλοδικεῖν δοκοῦμεν. Hence Aristotle's ἐλαττωτικός, one who is disposed not to press his full claims, but take somewhat less, opposed to ἀκριβοδίκαιος. See Or. 56 § 14.

p. 1024] ΠΕΡΙ ΠΡΟΙΚΟΣ ΜΗΤΡΩΙΑΣ. 217

τοσὶ νῦν σχετλιάζων καὶ δεινοπαθῶν καὶ τὴν προῖκά
με τῆς μητρὸς ἀποστερήσει; ἀλλ᾽ ὑμεῖς, ὦ ἄνδρες
δικασταί, πρὸς Διὸς καὶ θεῶν, μὴ καταπλαγῆτε ὑπὸ
τῆς κραυγῆς τῆς τούτου· πολὺς γάρ, πολὺς καὶ τολ-
μηρός ἐστιν ἄνθρωπος, καὶ οὕτω κακοῦργος ὥστε περὶ
ὧν ἂν μὴ ἔχῃ μάρτυρας[a] παρασχέσθαι, ταῦτα φήσει
ὑμᾶς εἰδέναι, ὦ ἄνδρες δικασταί, ὃ πάντες ποιοῦσιν
οἱ μηδὲν ὑγιὲς λέγοντες. ὑμεῖς οὖν ἐάν τι τοιοῦτον 54
τεχνάζηται, μὴ ἐπιτρέπετε αὐτῷ, ἀλλ᾽ ἐξελέγχετε, καὶ
ὅ τι ἂν μὴ ἕκαστος ὑμῶν εἰδῇ, μηδὲ τὸν πλησίον
νομιζέτω[b] εἰδέναι, ἀλλ᾽ ἀξιούτω τοῦτον ἀποδεικνύναι
σαφῶς ὑπὲρ ὧν ἂν λέγῃ, καὶ μὴ ὑμᾶς φάσκοντα εἰδέναι, περὶ ὧν αὐτὸς οὐδὲν ἕξει εἰπεῖν δίκαιον, ἀποδιδράσκειν τὴν ἀλήθειαν, ἐπεὶ καὶ ἐγώ, ὦ ἄνδρες δικασταί, πάντων ὑμῶν εἰδότων ὃν τρόπον ἀναγκασθεὶς ὁ
πατήρ μου ἐποιήσατο τούτους, οὐδὲν ἧττον δικάζομαι
νῦν αὐτοῖς καὶ μάρτυρας ὑποδίκους παρέσχημαι. καί- 55

[a] Bekk. μαρτυρίας Z cum ΣΑ¹.
[b] Bekk. δοκιμαζέτω Z cum Σ et γρ. ΓΦΒ.

δεινοπαθῶν] The only passage in which the word is found in the Attic orators. S.]
πολὺς] Violent, vehement. Eur. Hipp. 443, Κύπρις γὰρ οὐ φορητός, ἢν πολλὴ ῥυῇ. The repetition of the word may be compared with the formula καλὸς καλός, Theoc. VIII 73, Pind. Pyth. II 73, Plat. Phaedr. p. 228 B, ἰδὼν μὲν ἰδὼν ἤσθη. ib. p. 242 D, δεινόν, ὦ Φαῖδρε, δεινὸν λόγον—ἐκόμισας.
54. μηδὲ—νομιζέτω] 'Let him think that his neighbour does not know it either.'
ἀλλ᾽ ἀξιούτω] 'No! let him require the defendant to prove clearly whatever he may assert, and not to shirk the truth by saying that you know things about which he will not himself be able to bring forward any fair plea.'
ὑποδίκους] 'Responsible for their testimony,' Kennedy. Lit. 'under penalty of being tried for ψευδομαρτυρία, or perjury.' The Ionic passive perfect of παρέχομαι is used in the medial sense. It is formed regularly as if from παρασχέω, a secondary present of παρασχεῖν. See Or. 39 § 15, and 56 § 39.
§§ 55, 56. Boeotus and his brother have this further advantage over me, that they can appeal against an arbitrator's sentence, whereas the decision of the jury against me will be

218   XL. ΠΡΟΣ ΒΟΙΩΤΟΝ   [§§ 55—58

τοι ουκ ίσος γ' ημίν εστίν ο κίνδυνος, αλλ' εμοι μεν,
εάν υμείς νυνι υπό τούτων εξαπατηθήτε, ουκ εξέσται
έτι δικάσασθαι περι της προικός· τούτοις δ', ει φασιν
αδίκως αποδιαιτήσαί μου τον διαιτητήν τας δίκας, και
τότ' εξήν εις υμάς εφείναι^c και νυν εκγενήσεται^d πάλιν,
εάν βούλωνται, παρ' εμού λαβείν εν υμίν το δίκαιον·
56 και εγώ μεν, εάν, ο μη γένοιτο, υμείς με εγκαταλίπητε^e,
ουχ έξω οπόθεν προίκα επιδώ τη θυγατρί, ης τη μεν
φύσει πατήρ ειμι, την δ' ηλικίαν αυτής ει ίδοιτε^f, ουκ
αν θυγατέρα μου, αλλ' αδελφήν είναι αυτήν νομίσαιτε·
ούτοι δέ, εάν υμείς μοι βοηθήσητε, ουδέν εκ των ιδίων
αποτίσουσιν, αλλ' εκ της οικίας τα εμα εμοι αποδώ- 1025
σουσιν, ην εξειλόμεθα μεν κοινή πάντες εις την έκτισιν

^c Bekk. εφιέναι Z cum Σ.
^d Bekk. εγγενήσεται Z cum Σ m. recent. ειτενήσεται m. pr. Σ.
ει γενήσεται FΦB.
^e Bekk. εγκαταλείπητε Z cum ΣrA¹.
^f Bekk. αν ίδητε Z (αν ίδητε άρα ίδοιτε r).

final. And while I have no other hope of portioning my daughter except through your verdict, these men will lose nothing by having to pay, since the house-property they hold has the charge on it of paying the dowry I claim.
αποδιαιτήσαί μου] 'To have given the decision in my favour.' See sup. § 17. There was an appeal (έφεσις) from a public arbitrator; but a case once tried and decided by a jury could not be tried again. As this was across-suit, each claiming something from the other, Boeotus' suit would be still open, even if Mantitheus' had been given against him.
εκγενήσεται] A synonym of έξεσται.
εν υμίν] See 39 § 1.
56. εγκαταλείπειν. Probably it here means, 'if you should leave (have left) me in the hands of the enemy.' So Arist. Eth. Nic. v 4, ει εγκατέλιπε τον παραστάτην (η επαναφορά) επι δειλίαν. Thuc. IV 44, έχοντες τους εαυτών νεκρούς πλην δυοίν, ους εγκατέλιπον ου δυνάμενοι ευρείν. Plat. Symp. p. 179 A, εγκαταλιπείν τα παιδικά η μη βοηθήσαι κινδυνεύοντι. Hesiod ("Εργ. 378) applies it to one who dies with an heir to succeed him, γηραιος δε θάνοις έτερον παίδ' εγκαταλείπων, and so Plato (Symp. p. 208 B). Kennedy is not quite exact in rendering it 'if you abandon me.'
επιδώ] See § 4.
την ηλικίαν αυτής] 'Her size,' *staturam*, G. H. Schaefer. For Mantitheus had married at 18, sup. § 12.
εξειλόμεθα] εξαίρετον εποιησά-

p. 1025] ΠΕΡΙ ΠΡΟΙΚΟΣ ΜΗΤΡΩΙΑΣ. 219

τῆς προικὸς, οἰκοῦντες δ᾽ αὐτὴν οὗτοι μόνοι διατελοῦσιν. οὔτε γὰρ ἁρμόττει μοι θυγατέρα ἐπίγαμον ἔχοντι οἰκεῖν 57 μετὰ τοιούτων, οἳ οὐ μόνον αὐτοὶ ἀσελγῶς ζῶσιν, ἀλλὰ καὶ ὁμοίους αὑτοῖς ἑτέρους πολλοὺς εἰς τὴν οἰκίαν εἰσάγουσιν, οὔτε μὰ τὸν Δί᾽ ἀσφαλὲς εἶναί μοι νομίζω συζῆν τούτοις ἐν τῷ αὐτῷ· ὅπου γὰρ οὕτω φανερῶς μοι ἐπιβουλεύσαντες εἰς Ἄρειον πάγον ἀγῶνα κατεσκεύασαν, τίνος ἂν[g] οὗτοι ἢ φαρμακείας ἢ ἄλλης[h] κακουργίας τοιαύτης ὑμῖν ἀποσχέσθαι[i] δοκοῦσιν; οἵ 58 γε πρὸς τοῖς ἄλλοις (ἀρτίως γὰρ καὶ τοῦτο ἀνεμνήσθην) εἰς τοσαύτην ὑπερβολὴν τόλμης ἥκουσιν ὥστε καὶ Κρίτωνος μαρτυρίαν ἐνεβάλοντο ὡς ἐώνηται τὸ τρίτον παρ᾽ ἐμοῦ μέρος τῆς οἰκίας· ἣν, ὅτι ψευδής ἐστι, ῥᾳδίως εἴσεσθε. πρῶτον μὲν γὰρ οὐχ οὕτω μετρίως ζῇ Κρίτων ὥστε παρ᾽ ἑτέρου οἰκίαν ὠνεῖσθαι, ἀλλ᾽ οὕτω πολυτελῶς καὶ ἀσώτως ὥστε πρὸς τοῖς ἑαυτοῦ καὶ τὰ τῶν ἄλλων ἀναλίσκειν· ἔπειτ᾽ οὐ μαρτυρεῖ τούτῳ νῦν, ἀλλ᾽ ἐμοὶ ἀντιδικεῖ· τίς γὰρ ὑμῶν

[g] Bekk. om. Z cum Σ.
[h] τίνος οὗτοι ἢ φαρμακείας ἂν ᾖ (ἄλλη Σ) κακουργίας τοιαύτης ὑμῖν ἀποσχέσθαι δοκοῦσιν coniecit Sauppe.
[i] τίνος οὗτοι...ἀποσχήσεσθαι coniecit Baiter.

μεθα. Sup. § 15, ἵν᾽ ἐκ τῆς οἰκίας, ὁποτέροις ἂν ἡμῶν φαίνηται ὀφειλομένη ἡ προίξ, οὗτοι αὐτὴν κομίσωνται.
§ 57. The reason why Boeotus is allowed to occupy the house is, that my daughter cannot be allowed to live with such a set. Indeed, I do not consider my own life safe in the hands of such conspirators.
ἐπίγαμον] See § 4.
εἰσάγουσιν] Viz. κωμαστὰς, and such as those described in Or. 54 (κατὰ Κον.) § 7.
ὅπου] See on Or. 34 § 33.
§ 58. Among other falsehoods they have put in an affidavit that a third (i.e. my own) part of the house-property has been sold to Crito. As if such an extravagant fellow was likely to have money for the purchase! Besides, Crito is not so much a witness for the defendant as an opponent of mine, as an interested party.
ἀρτίως γὰρ] This is said as a sort of apology for introducing a new matter, and one in fact alien to the subject.
ἀναλίσκειν] 'Is in the habit of spending.'

οὐκ οἶδεν ὅτι μάρτυρες μέν εἰσιν οὗτοι, οἷς μηδὲν μέτεστι τοῦ πράγματος, περὶ οὗ ἡ δίκη ἐστίν, ἀντίδικοι δ' οἱ κοινωνοῦντες τῶν πραγμάτων, περὶ ὧν ἂν
59 δικάζηταί τις αὐτοῖς; ὃ Κρίτωνι συμβέβηκεν. ἔτι δὲ τοσούτων ὑμῶν ὄντων, ὦ ἄνδρες δικασταὶ, καὶ τῶν ἄλλων Ἀθηναίων πολλῶν, ἄλλος μὲν οὐδεὶς αὐτῷ παραγενέσθαι μεμαρτύρηκε, Τιμοκράτης δὲ μόνος, ὥσπερ ἀπὸ μηχανῆς, μαρτυρεῖ μὲν δεκάτην ἑστιᾶσαι τούτῳ 1026 τὸν ἐμὸν πατέρα, ἡλικιώτης ὢν τοῦ νυνὶ φεύγοντος τὴν δίκην, φησὶ δὲ πάνθ' ἁπλῶς εἰδέναι ἃ δὴ τούτοις

οἷς μηδὲν μέτεστι] Ad quos res parum pertineat, de qua disceptatur. The subjunctivity of the second clause cannot be expressed with the same subtlety in English or in Greek as in Latin. In what way Crito could be truly said κοινωνεῖν τοῦ πράγματος, does not appear. Perhaps Mantitheus regards him as conspiring with Boeotus to get possession of the property: or perhaps some negotiations had passed concerning the sale, which Crito regarded, or pretended to regard, as final and obligatory.

§§ 59—61. *The evidence of Timocrates has been adduced to prove that my father acknowledged Boeotus as his son when an infant ten days old! Why, Timocrates was then only of that age himself; and his evidence is all one-sided. Who then will believe him when he says he knows that Crito bought the house? After all, it is not the house, but the dower, that is contested. I have shown that my mother brought a dower, that it has not been paid, and that the house was charged with the payment of it: it is for him to show the contrary. But don't accept mere talk or vague complaints in place of proofs. As a matter of justice, it is more reasonable that I should have the dower, than that a son of my father's mistress should be allowed to deprive me of it.*

πολλῶν] scil. ὄντων, cum magnus sit numerus, G. H. Schaefer.

ὥσπερ ἀπὸ μηχανῆς] Like a *deus ex machina*, a familiar phrase borrowed from the stage. [We can only approximate to the sense by rendering 'like a friend in need' or 'by a special providence,' or (with Prof. Kennedy) 'like a good angel.' S.]

ἃ δὴ] Quae quidem, ironically. But μαρτυρεῖ should perhaps be ἐμαρτύρει. For this evidence was given when the adoption of Boeotus took place (sup. 28, and 39 § 22); and it should be contrasted with μαρτυρεῖ δὲ νυνὶ just below. It is clear that in both clauses μόνος means 'he is the sole witness.' Kennedy wrongly renders it in the latter, 'Timocrates now declares, that he alone was with Crito when he purchased the house from me.'

ΠΕΡΙ ΠΡΟΙΚΟΣ ΜΗΤΡΩΙΑΣ.

συμφέρει, μαρτυρεῖ δὲ νυνὶ μόνος Κρίτωνι παρεῖναι, ὅτε παρ' ἐμοῦ τὴν οἰκίαν ἐωνεῖτο. ὃ τίς ἂν ὑμῶν πιστεύσειεν; ἄλλως τε καὶ ὅτι[j] οὐ περὶ τῆς οἰκίας, πότερα ἐώνηται αὐτὴν Κρίτων ἢ μή, νυνὶ δικάζομαι, ἀλλὰ περὶ προικὸς, ἣν ἐπενεγκαμένης[k] τῆς μητρὸς οἱ νόμοι κελεύουσιν ἐμὲ κομίζεσθαι. ὥστε καθάπερ ὑμῖν ἐγὼ 60 καὶ ἐκ μαρτυριῶν πολλῶν καὶ ἐκ τεκμηρίων ἐπέδειξα ἐπενεγκαμένην μὲν τὴν μητέρα μου τάλαντον προῖκα, οὐ κομισάμενον δὲ τοῦτ' ἐμὲ ἐκ τῆς πατρῴας οὐσίας, ἐξαίρετον δ' ἡμῖν γενομένην τὴν οἰκίαν εἰς ταῦτα, οὕτω κελεύετε καὶ τοῦτον ἐπιδεικνύναι ὑμῖν ἢ ὡς οὐκ ἀληθῆ λέγω ἢ ὡς οὐ προσήκει μοι κομίσασθαι τὴν προῖκα· περὶ τούτων γὰρ ὑμεῖς νυνὶ τὴν ψῆφον οἴσετε. ἐὰν δὲ 61 μὴ ἔχων περὶ ὧν φεύγει τὴν δίκην μήτε μάρτυρας ἀξιοχρέως παρασχέσθαι μήτ' ἄλλο πιστὸν μηδὲν, ἑτέρους παρεμβάλλῃ λόγους κακουργῶν καὶ βοᾷ καὶ σχετλιάζῃ μηδὲν πρὸς τὸ πρᾶγμα, πρὸς Διὸς καὶ θεῶν μὴ ἐπιτρέπετε αὐτῷ, ἀλλὰ βοηθεῖτέ μοι τὰ δίκαια ἐξ ἁπάντων τῶν εἰρημένων, ἐνθυμούμενοι ὅτι πολὺ δικαιότερόν ἐστι τὴν τῆς ἐμῆς μητρὸς προῖκα τῇ ἐμῇ θυγατρὶ εἰς ἔκδοσιν ὑμᾶς ψηφίσασθαι, ἢ Πλαγγόνα καὶ τού-

[j] Bekk. om. cum rA[1]. [k] Bekk. ἐνεγκαμένης Z cum Σ.

πότερα—ἢ μή] More correctly, perhaps, ἢ οὐ, since it is a direct question of fact. The use of μή is rather irregular: perhaps we may say that πότερα —ἢ μή is equivalent to εἴτε—ἢ μή.
ἐπενεγκαμένης] Cum domum intulerit.
60. ἐξαίρετον] Sup. § 14.
61. παρεμβάλλῃ] 'If he goes on introducing irrelevant topics.' Ar. Vesp. 481, τοῦτο γὰρ παρεμβαλοῦμεν τῶν τριχοινίκων ἐπῶν.
βοηθεῖτέ μοι τὰ δίκαια] This phrase occurs Or. 35 § 5. It is here opposed to παρὰ πάντα τὰ δίκαια in the next sentence; or rather, perhaps, the clause ἐνθυμούμενοι ὅτι, κ.τ.λ. is exegetical of τὰ δίκαια, and the two together stand in contrast.
—ἐξ ἁπάντων, κ.τ.λ., 'which all the reasons I have urged show me to be entitled to.' Kennedy.
Πλαγγόνα] The subject to ἀφελέσθαι. The sentence is neatly rendered by Kennedy, 'than that Plango and her sons,

τοὺς πρὸς τοῖς ἄλλοις καὶ τὴν οἰκίαν τὴν εἰς τὴν προῖκα ἐξαίρετον γενομένην ἀφελέσθαι ἡμᾶς παρὰ πάντα τὰ δίκαια.

adding another injury to those which they have already inflicted, should, contrary to every principle of justice, deprive me of the house, which was specially reserved as a security for the marriage portion.' The wrong already done is that described in § 51.

OR. LVI.

ΚΑΤΑ ΔΙΟΝΥΣΟΔΩΡΟΥ ΒΛΑΒΗΣ.

THE action "against Dionysodorus for damage" relates, like that against Phormio, to a loan on bottomry, and the non-fulfilment of a contract. The case is plain, and involves no serious difficulties, either in the legal points or in the argument; but the speech is one of considerable value as illustrating the nature of the corn-trade at Athens, and the regulations by which it was controlled[1]. Why it is named an action for *damage* is not so clear. The action was, in fact, to enforce the payment, with interest, of a loan, which was repudiated on the plea of injury to the ship. But, as the ship was the security for the money, and it had not been produced for the mortgagees, we may suppose that βλάβη means "loss" in respect of this part of the contract[2]. According to Mr Kennedy[3], any action at the suit of the party injured was a δίκη βλάβης. And as the injury in this case was a wrong done *ex delicto*, and not merely a breach of obligation *ex contractu*, it is entitled κατὰ Διονυσοδώρου and not πρὸς Διονυσόδωρον[4].

[1] See Introd. to Or. 34, p. 1.
[2] [βλάβης is omitted in the MSS A¹ and Σ and by Harpocra-tion s. v. ἀμφοτερόπλουν. S.]
[3] Dem. Append. IX p. 389.
[4] ib. p. 373.

Darius and Pamphilus had lent to Dionysodorus 3000 drachms, to enable him to engage in the corn-trade between Athens and Egypt. The loan was to be repaid, with interest, on the return to Athens (ἀμφοτερόπλους, § 6), and clauses were inserted binding the borrowers to trade only between Athens and Egypt (§§ 6, 42) and to give up the ship on their return, as security for the payment, under penalty of twice the whole amount due (§ 45). They were to have the use of the money for one year, and had no right to extend the time (§§ 3, 45).

Dionysodorus had a partner Parmeniscus, who sailed with the ship to purchase corn in Egypt. They all appear to have been in collusion with Cleomenes (τοῦ ἐν τῇ Αἰγύπτῳ ἄρξαντος, § 7) and had a joint interest in keeping up the price of corn. The agents at Athens used to send advices to those in Egypt, and when corn became cheaper at home through the arrival of cargoes from Sicily or the Pontus, the buyers in Egypt used to send the corn to some other market where it was dearer. It was with this fraudulent intention, which was illegal (§ 3), that the defendants pretended their ship had sprung a leak, and were compelled to put in to Rhodes and unlade the corn, which they also sold there on finding it would fetch a higher price than at Athens (§ 10).

Dionysodorus, who had remained at Athens, was asked by the money-lenders for an explanation of this affair; they did not like to incur the suspicion of being in collusion with Cleomenes (§ 11) and they required the production of the ship. The defendants upon this make an offer to pay the principal and part of the interest, viz. so much of it as was due for the outer voyage and the return voyage as far as Rhodes, on condition of the bond being cancelled, and with it all further obligation (§ 14). This the plaintiffs decline to do, alleging that if the

ΔΙΟΝΥΣΟΔΩΡΟΥ ΒΛΑΒΗΣ.

ship was really wrecked, or in any way seriously disabled, they were bound to submit to the loss; if not, they were entitled to recover the whole sum. And that the ship was not lost is proved by the fact that the defendants afterwards traded with it between Rhodes and Egypt, and that it was even now making voyages (§ 23). If, the plaintiffs argue, the ship had really sprung a leak, the defendants, had they acted honestly, would have brought the ship back to Athens when it had been repaired (§ 40). For all these reasons the conduct of the defendants is denounced as fraudulent and illegal. The offer of partial payment, the plaintiffs say, was made by the defendants with the conviction that it would be refused, διὰ τὰς ὑπούσας αἰτίας (§ 13).

The suit was one of those called ἐμπορικαί, and the plaintiffs press for a verdict in their favour, not only in their own interest, but in that of the whole mercantile community (§ 48). The indignation of the jury is raised by the hint that the defendants are in collusion with Cleomenes. It seems probable that the cause of the scarcity of corn[1] was popularly attributed to this man's cupidity, and the date of the speech may be approximately fixed by the allusion (§ 8) to the high prices in the years 330—326 B.C., and probably to the end of that period, as prices are said to be falling (§ 9).

[In Fynes-Clinton's *Fasti Hellenici*, the speech is approximately assigned to B.C. 329: not before B.C. 331, because the facts occurred Κλεομένους ἐν τῇ Αἰγύπτῳ ἄρξαντος (p. 1285)—who was appointed praefect of Egypt by Alexander, B.C. 331 (Arrian III 5, Dexippus apud Phot. Cod. 82 = p. 200). Cleomenes was charged with the building of Alexandria (Aristot. Oeconom. II

[1] See Introduction to Or. 34, *ad fin.*

33); *vectigalibus Africae Aegyptique praepositus* (Curtius IV 8, 5). He remained in office till he was put to death by Ptolemy, B.C. 323 (Pausan. I 6, 3).

Arnold Schaefer holds that the aorist participle in § 7 (ἦσαν ὑπηρέται... Κλεομένους τοῦ ἐν τῇ Αἰγύπτῳ ἄρξαντος) shows that the ἀρχή of Cleomenes was at an end when the speech was delivered, and he proposes to assign it to the winter of B.C. 322—321, i.e. some few months after the death of Demosthenes; who therefore, he concludes, could not have written the oration. The argument from ἄρξαντος does not appear conclusive, as the aorist need only imply that Cleomenes *was in power at the time* of the transactions described, without showing whether he was still in office or not when the speech was delivered. But, of course, if he were still in office, the most natural tense would have been the present.

Blass, *Att. Ber.* III 522, places the speech in the winter of B.C. 323—322[1], not because the death of Demosthenes falls in October 322, but because that date marks the downfall of the Athenian democracy; a change which would have found some recognition in the speech itself. On the contrary we have a direct reference to the *Demos* in the words οὔτε γὰρ τῷ πλήθει τῷ ὑμετέρῳ συμφέρει τοῦτο (§ 50).

The Zürich editors, while refraining from deciding against the genuineness of the speech, admit that they have doubts on the subject, though they assign no specific reasons[2].

It closes with an appeal to Demosthenes (ἀξιῶ δὲ καὶ τῶν φίλων μοί τινα συνειπεῖν. δεῦρο, Δημόσθενες). A. Schaefer suggests that some early transcriber may have added

[1] So also Schwarze, *De orat. κατὰ Δ.* (Göttingen, 1870) p. 18 f.
[2] Præf. p. xiv '*addimus etiam de Or. 56 nobis videri dubitandum esse.*'

ΔΙΟΝΥΣΟΔΩΡΟΥ ΒΛΑΒΗΣ.

the name to enhance the value of a spurious oration; but it may be remarked that a transcriber with such an object in view is little likely to have added a clause, which might lead an ordinary reader to suppose at first sight that as the speaker appeals to Demosthenes, the speech was *not* written by that orator. If the last clause is genuine, it proves at any rate that the speech was delivered before the death of Demosthenes, and (as Schaefer candidly confesses) it is not *per se* inconsistent with his having himself composed the speech. He is inclined to ascribe it to the same writer as the speeches against Apaturius (33) and Phormio (34). (*Dem. und seine Zeit*, III 2, 311—314.) Blass agrees in regarding the speech as spurious (*Att. Ber.* III 24—55); and there is an elaborate dissertation by P. Uhle, arguing that the writer was the same as that of the speech against Phormio, but different from that of the speech against Apaturius (*Quaestiones de orationum Demostheni falso addictarum scriptoribus* ii 1886). It is accepted as genuine by Weil,. *les Harangues de Dém.* p. xiii, ed. 1881. S.]

Mr Mayor (*Journal of Philology*, VI, p. 251), remarking on the awkward sentence in § 10, says, "This seems to me more unlike Demosthenes than anything in the *Lacritus*. There are many minor points beside which make me doubt the genuineness of this speech."

LVI.

ΚΑΤΑ ΔΙΟΝΥΣΟΔΩΡΟΥ ΒΛΑΒΗΣ.

ΥΠΟΘΕΣΙΣ.

Δαρεῖος καὶ Πάμφιλος Διονυσοδώρῳ δανείζουσι τρισχιλίας δραχμὰς ἐπὶ τῷ πλεῦσαι αὐτὸν εἰς Αἴγυπτον κἀκεῖθεν αὖθις Ἀθήναζε, καὶ λαμβάνουσι μὲν ὑποθήκην τὴν ναῦν, διομολογοῦνται δὲ καὶ τόκους ὅσους
5 ὤφειλον* Ἀθήναζε καταπλεύσαντος Διονυσοδώρου κομίσασθαι. Διονυσόδωρος δὲ ἀναπλέων ἐκ τῆς Αἰγύπτου, τῇ Ῥόδῳ προσσχών, ἐκεῖ τὸν γόμον ἐξέθετο, ὡς μὲν αὐτός φησι, διὰ τὸ ῥαγῆναι τὴν ναῦν καὶ εἶναι

* Bekk. ὤφελον Z.

1. *Argument.* Δαρεῖος] His name is nowhere mentioned in the speech, and it seems to have been preserved by the author of the argument (Libanius) from some source now unknown. [The name is also given by the MSS Σ and B in the following words added at the close of the speech: δαρειω και παμφιλω κατα διονυσοδωρου. He is identified by Boeckh (*Staatshaushaltung*, addenda to 2nd Germ. ed. p. x) with the person mentioned in an inscription referring to the year Ol. 114, 2 = B.C. 323—2: Δαρείῳ [ἐν Σκα]μβωνιδῶ[ν οἰκ]οῦντι Η Η Η...His partner Pamphilus is probably the Egyptian mentioned in Mid. § 163, τὸν μέτοικον ἐξέπεμψε τὸν Αἰγύπτιον Πάμφιλον. Possibly Pamphilus is, like other μέτοικοι, imperfectly acquainted with Greek, and therefore allows Darius to address the court. Boeckh *l.c.* and A. Schaefer, *Dem. u. s. Zeit* III 2, p. 307 n. S.]

2. ἐπὶ τῷ πλεῦσαι] 'With a view to,' or 'on condition of his sailing,' &c.

4. διομολογοῦνται] 'They come to an agreement between themselves and the lender what interest they were to get when Dionysodorus should have sailed back to Athens.' Cf. § 5.

7. ἐξέθετο] The same as ἐξείλετο, Or. 34 (πρὸς Φορμ.) § 8, inf. §§ 10, 20.

ARGUMENT] LVI. ΚΑΤΑ ΔΙΟΝΤΣΟΔΩΡΟΤ. 229

σαθρὰν, ὡς δὲ Δαρεῖος λέγει, διὰ τὸ πυθέσθαι τὸν
σῖτον Ἀθήνησιν εὔωνον ὄντα· τὴν γὰρ ναῦν σῴαν 10
ὑπάρχειν φησὶ καὶ πλεῖν ἔτι καὶ νῦν. οἱ μὲν οὖν
δανείσαντες καὶ[b] κατηγοροῦσι τοῦ Διονυσοδώρου παρα-
βεβηκέναι τὴν συγγραφὴν, διότι τὴν ὑποθήκην, του-
τέστι τὴν ναῦν, οὐ παρέσχεν ἐμφανῆ, καὶ ἀπαιτοῦσιν
αὐτὸν τοὺς ὁμολογηθέντας τόκους τελείους· ὁ δὲ οὐ 15
πάντας ἀποδιδόναι βούλεται, ἀλλὰ πρὸς λόγον τοῦ
πλοῦ τοῦ πλευσθέντος.

Κοινωνός εἰμι τοῦ δανείσματος τούτου, ὦ ἄνδρες
δικασταί. συμβαίνει δ' ἡμῖν τοῖς κατὰ θάλατταν τὴν
1283 ἐργασίαν προῃρημένοις καὶ τὰ ἡμέτερ'[c] αὐτῶν ἐγχειρίζουσιν ἑτέροις ἐκεῖνο μὲν σαφῶς εἰδέναι, ὅτι ὁ δανει-
ζόμενος ἐν παντὶ προέχει ἡμῶν. λαβὼν γὰρ ἀργύριον
φανερὸν καὶ ὁμολογούμενον, ἐν γραμματειδίῳ δυοῖν

[b] Bekk. om. Z.   [c] ἡμέτερα Z.

10. σῴαν ὑπάρχειν] i.e. ἔτι σῴαν εἶναι.
12. καὶ κατηγοροῦσι] They both charge him with having kept back the security illegally (see Or. 34 § 7), and also demand payment of the interest without deduction. The defendants are willing to pay a part, but only in proportion (πρὸς λόγον) to the length of the actual voyage, viz. they wish to deduct that due from Rhodes to Athens.
§ 1. (*Darius speaks.*) '*I am a partner in this loan, and it happens to us, who have made it our profession to trade on sea-securities, and to place our property in the hands of others, to know this full well, that the borrower in every respect has the advantage over us.* (Look at the present case:) *he has got from us money in hard cash and in sterling coin, for which he leaves us, on a promissory note, that cost him a couple of farthings, and a very small scrap of paper, his agreement to do what is right and honest. Whereas we do not (as he does) merely say we will give, but at the time and on the spot do actually give the money to the borrower.*'
κοινωνός] See § 6, from which it appears that the name of Darius was not inserted in the contract.
προῃρημένοις] προαίρεσιν ποιησαμένοις. So § 48, πολλοὶ τῶν κατὰ θάλατταν ἐργάζεσθαι προαιρουμένων, and § 50.—ἐγχειρίζουσιν, i. e. προϊεμένοις.
γραμματειδίῳ] Cf. ἐν γρ. τὰ

χαλκοῖν ἐωνημένῳ καὶ βιβλιδίῳ μικρῷ πάνυ τὴν ὁμολογίαν καταλέλοιπε τοῦ ποιήσειν τὰ δίκαια. ἡμεῖς δ' οὐ φαμὲν δώσειν, ἀλλ' εὐθὺς τῷ δανειζομένῳ δίδομεν 2 τὸ ἀργύριον. τῷ οὖν ποτὲ πιστεύοντες καὶ τί λαβόντες τὸ βέβαιον προϊέμεθα; ὑμῖν, ὦ ἄνδρες δικασταὶ, καὶ τοῖς νόμοις τοῖς ὑμετέροις, οἳ κελεύουσιν, ὅσα ἄν τις ἑκὼν ἕτερος ἑτέρῳ ὁμολογήσῃ, κύρια εἶναι. ἀλλά μοι δοκεῖ οὔτε τῶν νόμων οὔτε συγγραφῆς οὐδεμιᾶς ὄφελος εἶναι οὐδὲν, ἂν ὁ λαμβάνων τὰ χρήματα μὴ πάνυ δίκαιος ᾖ τὸν τρόπον καὶ δυοῖν θάτερον, ἢ ὑμᾶς δεδιὼς 3 ἢ τὸν συμβαλόντα αἰσχυνόμενος. ὧν οὐδέτερον πρόσεστι Διονυσοδώρῳ τούτῳ, ἀλλ' εἰς τοσοῦτον ἥκει τόλμης ὥστε δανεισάμενος παρ' ἡμῶν ἐπὶ τῇ νηὶ τρισχιλίας δραχμὰς ἐφ' ᾧ τε τὴν ναῦν καταπλεῖν

ψευδῆ μαρτυρεῖν, Or. 54 § 37.—
δυοῖν χαλκοῖν, a fourth of an obol.
βιβλιδίῳ] 'sur un tout petit morceau de papier' Dareste, who adds in a note 'c'était bien du papier, c'est-à-dire du papyrus, et nous voyons par là quel en était le prix.'
§ 2. *In doing this, we trust to the law and its administrators, and in particular to the legal principle, that all voluntary compacts are binding. I however have come to the conclusion that the law is of little avail, if a man is dishonest, and defies both it and the lender of the loan.*
τί λαβόντες τὸ βέβαιον] 'What do we get as our security when we part with our money?' Cf. § 15.
προΐεσθαι (or προέσθαι) is the usual term for 'lending on risk,' 'sacrificing on a venture,' the notion being that of flinging away, *projicere*. Cf. Or. 36 § 6. The active is so used in Ar. Nub. 1214.

τὸν συμβαλόντα] The contributor or provider of the loan, thence called συμβολαῖον, from the 'bringing together' of the contracting parties.
§ 3. *But Dionysodorus is not honest: he borrowed under promise of bringing the ship, which was the security, to Athens; and though we ought to have received our money last autumn, he sold the cargo at Rhodes, illegally and contrary to the terms of agreement, and then went back to Egypt and again to Rhodes. But he has never given the security up to us, and he is using our money now for a second year.*
τρισχιλίας] Boeckh (P. Econ. p. 108) observes that we "are not justified in assuming the ship had not a greater value, as at Athens a double pledge was not unfrequently given in cases of bottomry, and therefore its real value might have been as much as a talent" (6000 drachms).

p. 1284] ΔΙΟΝΥΣΟΔΩΡΟΥ ΒΛΑΒΗΣ. 231

Ἀθήναζε, καὶ δέον ἡμᾶς ἐν τῇ πέρυσιν ὥρᾳ κεκομίσθαι τὰ χρήματα, τὴν μὲν ναῦν εἰς Ῥόδον κατεκόμισε καὶ τὸν γόμον ἐκεῖσε ἐξελόμενος ἀπέδοτο παρὰ τὴν συγγραφὴν καὶ τοὺς[d] νόμους τοὺς ὑμετέρους, ἐκ δὲ τῆς Ῥόδου πάλιν ἀπέστειλε τὴν ναῦν εἰς Αἴγυπτον κἀκεῖθεν εἰς Ῥόδον, ἡμῖν δὲ τοῖς Ἀθήνησι δανείσασιν οὐδέπω καὶ νῦν οὔτε τὰ χρήματα ἀποδίδωσιν οὔτε τὸ ἐνέχυρον καθίστησιν εἰς τὸ ἐμφανές, ἀλλὰ δεύτερον ἔτος τουτὶ καρπούμενος τὰ ἡμέτερα, καὶ ἔχων τό τε 4 δάνειον καὶ τὴν ἐργασίαν καὶ τὴν ναῦν τὴν ὑποκειμένην ἡμῖν, οὐδὲν ἧττον εἰσελήλυθε πρὸς ὑμᾶς δηλονότι[e] ὡς ζημιώσων ἡμᾶς τῇ ἐπωβελίᾳ καὶ καταθησόμενος εἰς τὸ οἴκημα πρὸς τῷ ἀποστερεῖν τὰ χρήματα. ὑμῶν οὖν, ὦ ἄνδρες Ἀθηναῖοι, ὁμοίως ἁπάντων δεόμεθα

[d] Bekk. *om.* Z *cum* FΣΦB.

[e] δῆλον ὅτι *Bekker st.* ὅτι in margine manu antiqua additum, Σ. δῆλον Z.

ὥρᾳ] Properly 'the ripening time,' applied to harvest and vintage, and then to the safe time for sailing. In § 30 it is ἡ ὡραία. On the time granted for paying loans on bottomry, see *Publ. Econ.* p. 139.—κεκομίσθαι, middle, 'when we ought to have got back our money in the season of last year.' Kennedy.

ἐκεῖσε] for ἐκεῖ, as in § 25.
τοὺς νόμους] Cf. inf. § 10.
τὸ ἐνέχυρον] i.e. τὴν ὑποθήκην, τὴν ναῦν.

4. τὴν ἐργασίαν] The privilege of trading with it.

τῇ ἐπωβελίᾳ] The fine of one-sixth of the assessment (an obolus for each drachma), if we fail to obtain the fifth part of the votes. (See Boeckh, *Publ. Econ.* p. 356.) In fact, he thinks we shall not only lose our suit (on the ground that the ship was wrecked or disabled), but shall have to pay the fine to him as the defendant, in compensation; and that if we do not pay it, he will get us put into prison till we do. The term καταθέσθαι is used (as in several places by Thucydides) of depositing captives or hostages in a place of security. The use of τὸ οἴκημα for the debtors' prison is remarkable. Hesych. οἴκημα· τὸ δεσμωτήριον. Cf. Or. 32 § 29, εἰ δὲ μὴ κατέστησεν (τοὺς ἐγγυητάς), εἰς τὸ οἴκημα ἂν ᾔει, and 24 §§ 131, 135, 136. For the sense, cf. Or. 35 § 46. Kennedy renders it 'putting us in the lodging.' Boeckh (*Publ. Ec.* p. 366), "carrying it off to his own house." And he adds (p. 370) that this shows (beside Or. 47 § 64) that in private suits the epobelia was received by the successful party and not by the state.

καὶ ἱκετεύομεν βοηθῆσαι ἡμῖν, ἂν' δοκῶμεν ἀδικεῖσθαι. τὴν δ' ἀρχὴν τοῦ συμβολαίου διεξελθεῖν ὑμῖν πρῶτον βούλομαι· οὕτω γὰρ καὶ ὑμεῖς ῥᾷστα παρακολουθήσετε.

5 Διονυσόδωρος γὰρ οὑτοσί, ὦ ἄνδρες Ἀθηναῖοι, καὶ ὁ κοινωνὸς αὐτοῦ Παρμενίσκος προσελθόντες ἡμῖν πέρυσι τοῦ μεταγειτνιῶνος μηνὸς ἔλεγον ὅτι βούλονται δανείσασθαι ἐπὶ τῇ νηί, ἐφ' ᾧ τε πλεῦσαι εἰς Αἴγυπτον καὶ ἐξ Αἰγύπτου εἰς Ῥόδον ἢ εἰς Ἀθήνας. διομολογησάμενοι τοὺς τόκους εἰς ἑκάτερον τῶν ἐμπο-
6 ρίων τούτων. ἀποκριναμένων δ' ἡμῶν, ὦ ἄνδρες δικασταί, ὅτι οὐκ ἂν δανείσαιμεν εἰς ἕτερον ἐμπόριον οὐδὲν ἀλλ' ἢ εἰς Ἀθήνας, οὕτω προσομολογοῦσι πλεύσεσθαι⁸ δεῦρο, καὶ ἐπὶ ταύταις ταῖς ὁμολογίαις

ᶠ ἐὰν Z. ᵍ πλευσεῖσθαι Z.

§§ 5, 6. *The history of the transaction. We were asked by the defendant and his partner last September to lend them money on the security of the ship, and on condition of their sailing to Egypt, and either to Athens or to Rhodes on the return-voyage; and the interest was to be paid at either of these markets. We objected however to their sailing to any other port but that of Athens; and so they borrowed 3000 drachms and signed a bond on these terms. My partner's name indeed was written as the lender, but I had an interest in the loan, though my name did not appear (ἔξωθεν).*

εἰς Ῥόδον ἢ εἰς Ἀθήνας] An alternative of this kind seems to have been commonly allowed in contracts; so Or. 35 § 10, εἰς Μένδην ἢ Σκιώνην. Here their proposal εἰς Ῥόδον was distinctly declined, so that they could not plead ignorance of the lenders' intentions. Boeckh (*Publ. Ec.* p. 56) calls it "an exceedingly oppressive regulation, that no Athenian or alien resident in Attica should lend money upon a vessel which did not return to Athens with a cargo of corn or other commodities," comparing this passage and Lacrit. § 51. He thinks, however, this involves such difficulties, that we must suppose the law is not fully known to us. On the loan called ἑτερόπλους see *ibid.* pp. 57—8.

διομολογησάμενοι] See *Argum.* l. 4.

6. εἰς ἕτερον ἐμπόριον—Ἀθήνας] See Or. 34 § 37.

προσομολογοῦσι] They enter into an additional agreement. See Or. 37 § 49.

p. 1285]   ΔΙΟΝΥΣΟΔΩΡΟΥ ΒΛΑΒΗΣ.   233

δανείζονται παρ' ἡμῶν ἐπὶ τῇ νηὶ τρισχιλίας δραχμὰς ἀμφοτερόπλουν, καὶ συγγραφὴν ἐγράψαντο ὑπὲρ τούτων. ἐν μὲν οὖν ταῖς συνθήκαις δανειστὴς ἐγράφη Πάμφιλος οὑτοσί· ἐγὼ δ' ἔξωθεν μετεῖχον αὐτῷ τοῦ δανείσματος. καὶ πρῶτον ὑμῖν ἀναγνώσεται αὐτὴν τὴν συγγραφήν.

ΣΥΓΓΡΑΦΗ.

Κατὰ ταύτην τὴν συγγραφήν, ὦ ἄνδρες δικασταί, 7 λαβόντες παρ' ἡμῶν τὰ χρήματα Διονυσόδωρός τε οὑτοσὶ καὶ ὁ κοινωνὸς αὐτοῦ Παρμενίσκος ἀπέστελλον τὴν ναῦν εἰς τὴν Αἴγυπτον ἐνθένδε. καὶ ὁ μὲν Παρ-
1285 μενίσκος ἐπέπλει ἐπὶ τῆς νεώς, οὑτοσὶ δὲ αὐτοῦ κατέμενεν. ἦσαν γάρ, ὦ ἄνδρες δικασταί, ἵνα μηδὲ τοῦτ' ἀγνοῆτε, ὑπηρέται καὶ συνεργοὶ πάντες οὗτοι Κλεομένους τοῦ ἐν τῇ Αἰγύπτῳ ἄρξαντος, ὃς ἐξ οὗ τὴν ἀρχὴν παρέλαβεν οὐκ ὀλίγα κακὰ εἰργάσατο τὴν πόλιν τὴν ὑμετέραν, μᾶλλον δὲ · καὶ τοὺς ἄλλους Ἕλληνας, παλιγκαπηλεύων καὶ συνιστὰς τὰς τιμὰς

ἀμφοτερόπλουν] See Or. 34 (πρὸς Φορμ.) § 6. [Harpocration, s. v. Δημ. ἐν τῷ κατὰ Διονυσοδώρου· ὅταν τις ναυτικὸν δανείσῃ δάνειον ἐπὶ τῷ καὶ ἐνθένδε πλεῦσαί ποι κἀκεῖθεν ἐνθάδε, τοῦτο ἀμφοτερόπλουν καλεῖται. S.]
ἐγώ] Darius, who called himself κοινωνὸς τοῦ δανείσματος, § 1.
§ 7. *The narrative continued. The ship accordingly sailed for Egypt with the defendant's partner on board, while he remained at home. The fact is, these men were in collusion with Cleomenes, who had been making a large profit by raising the price of corn.*
Κλεομένους] Boeckh (*Publ. Ec.* p. 84) calls him Alexander's Satrap in Egypt, and he refers to the second book of Aristotle's Oeconomics for other examples of "this notorious corn-dealer's contrivances." Like the Roman governors of provinces, he seems to have looked principally to his own interests. Apparently he had created a monopoly of corn, and so could sell it at his own prices. (See Introduction, p. 225.)
παλιγκαπηλεύων] 'By retailing,' or perhaps 'by petty jobbing.' Hesych. παλιγκάπηλος· ὁ μεταβόλος· ὁ τὸ αὐτὸ ἀεὶ ἀγοράζων καὶ πωλῶν. [Schol. on Ar. Plut. 1156, ὁ ἀπὸ τοῦ ἐμπόρου ἀγοράζων καὶ πωλῶν. (Dem.) 25 § 46, κάπηλος πονηρίας καὶ παλιγκάπηλος καὶ μεταβολεύς. See Büchsenschütz, *Besitz u.*

8 τοῦ σίτου καὶ αὐτὸς καὶ οὗτοι μετ' αὐτοῦ. οἱ μὲν γὰρ αὐτῶν ἀπέστελλον ἐκ τῆς Αἰγύπτου τὰ χρήματα, οἱ δ' ἐπέπλεον ταῖς ἐμπορίαις, οἱ δ' ἐνθάδε μένοντες διετίθεντο τὰ ἀποστελλόμενα· εἶτα πρὸς τὰς καθεστηκυίας τιμὰς ἔπεμπον γράμματα οἱ ἐπιδημοῦντες τοῖς ἀποδημοῦσιν, ἵνα ἐὰν μὲν παρ' ὑμῖν τίμιος ᾖ ὁ σῖτος, δεῦρο αὐτὸν κομίσωσιν, ἐὰν δ' εὐωνότερος γένηται, εἰς ἄλλο τι καταπλεύσωσιν ἐμπόριον. ὅθεν περ οὐχ ἥκιστα, ὦ ἄνδρες δικασταί, συνετιμήθη τὰ περὶ τὸν

Erwerb, p. 455 n. S.]—συνιστὰς 'by settling the prices of corn.' Kennedy translates, 'by buying up corn for resale and keeping it at his own price.' [G. H. Schaefer on p. 219, 20: 'accendens pretia, flagellans annonam.' Prof. Kennedy: 'By regrating and manipulating the price of corn.' In England severe statutes were passed from the time of Edward VI downwards, against all '*regraters*,' '*engrossers*,' and '*forestallers of the market.*' They were repealed in 1772, and the alleged offence of buying up or bargaining for goods on the way to market, to sell them at a higher price, has ceased to be a subject of criminal prosecution. See Adam Smith, *Wealth of Nations*, IV 5, on the corn laws. For part of the Athenian law on the subject, cf. Lysias, Or. 22 κατὰ τῶν σιτοπώλων, esp. § 6, παρεσχόμεθα τὸν νόμον (against engrossing), ὃς ἀπαγορεύει μηδένα τῶν ἐν τῇ πόλει πλείω σῖτον πεντήκοντα φορμῶν συνωνεῖσθαι. S.]

καὶ οὗτοι] Dionysodorus and Parmeniscus. By πάντες οὗτοι above (not ἄμφω), he appears to include other traders.

§ 8. *An exposure of the transactions by which corn had become dearer. Cleomenes' people used to send off cargoes from Egypt, while these men either sailed with them, or staid at home to watch the market and send off advices, so that the corn was always sold in the dearest mart.*

ταῖς ἐμπορίαις] 'With the cargoes.' The dative depends on the ἐπί, meaning that he was guardian and director of them. So Or. 35 § 16, τὸν δ' ἀδελφὸν ἑαυτοῦ 'Αρτέμωνα πλεύσεσθαι ἐπὶ τοῖς χρήμασι, and 32 § 12 ὁ παρ' ἡμῶν ἐπιπλέων.

πρὸς τὰς κ.τ.λ.] 'According to the market (or average) prices.' So Or. 34 § 39, διεμετρήσαμεν ὑμῖν τῆς καθεστηκυίας τιμῆς, inf. § 10.

γράμματα] 'Letters of advice.'

τίμιος] 'Dear,' opp. to ἄξιος, 'cheap.' Ar. Ach. 758, πῶς ὁ σῖτος ὤνιος; M. παρ' ἀμὲ πολυτίματος, ἅπερ τοὶ θεοί.

συνετιμήθη] It appears likely that we should read ἐπετιμήθη, 'the price was raised,' as in Or. 34 § 39. The συν may have crept in from συνιστὰς just above, which some wrongly explained in the same sense. [ἐπετιμήθη was preferred by Wolf, but συνετιμήθη is recognized by Suidas. 'The price

p. 1285] ΔΙΟΝΥΣΟΔΩΡΟΥ ΒΛΑΒΗΣ. 235

σῖτον ἐκ τῶν τοιούτων ἐπιστολῶν καὶ συνεργιῶν. ὅτε 9
μὲν οὖν ἐνθένδε ἀπέστελλον οὗτοι τὴν ναῦν, ἐπιεικῶς
ἔντιμον κατέλιπον τὸν σῖτον· διὸ καὶ ὑπέμειναν ἐν τῇ
συγγραφῇ γράψασθαι εἰς 'Αθήνας πλεῖν, εἰς δ' ἄλλο
μηδὲν ἐμπόριον. μετὰ δὲ ταῦτ', ὦ ἄνδρες δικασταί,
ἐπειδὴ ὁ Σικελικὸς κατάπλους ἐγένετο καὶ αἱ τιμαὶ
τοῦ σίτου ἐπ' ἔλαττον ἐβάδιζον καὶ ἡ ναῦς ἡ τούτων
ἀνῆκτο εἰς Αἴγυπτον, εὐθέως οὗτος ἀποστέλλει τινὰ
εἰς τὴν 'Ρόδον ἀπαγγελοῦντα τῷ Παρμενίσκῳ τῷ
κοινωνῷ τἀνθένδε[h] καθεστηκότα, ἀκριβῶς εἰδὼς ὅτι
ἀναγκαῖον εἴη τῇ νηὶ προσέχειν εἰς 'Ρόδον. πέρας δ' 10
οὖν,—λαβὼν γὰρ ὁ Παρμενίσκος ὁ τουτουὶ κοινωνὸς τὰ

[h] τἀνθάδε Bekk. 1824.

of corn-imports was *manipulated through such letters and complots*,' i.e. the price was managed by a conspiracy. Liddell and Scott unsatisfactorily say 'Pass. *to increase in value, rise in price*;' a meaning which the passive can scarcely bear. Prof. Kennedy.] Mr Mayor (p. 251) suggests that 'to price (or value) together' may indirectly have meant to raise prices which had been kept down by artificial restrictions.

§§ 9, 10. *Corn was dear when they left Athens, so they consented to return to that mart. But supplies from Sicily meanwhile had brought down prices: accordingly advices are sent to intercept the ship on her return voyage at Rhodes, and so, regardless of the penalties in the contract, and the illegality of the act, they dispose of the cargo at Rhodes.*

ὑπέμειναν] 'They made no objection to having it written.'

Σικελικὸς κατάπλους] 'When the Sicilian convoy arrived,' lit. 'When the Sicilian sailing to land took place.' Vessels laden with corn are meant.

ἐπ' ἔλαττον ἐβάδιζον] Or. 32 (Ζηνοθ.) § 25, ὡς δὲ δεῦρο ἥκοντος αὐτοῦ καὶ περὶ ταῦτα πραγματευομένου ἐπανῆκεν ὁ σῖτος ('the price of corn had gone back'), ἄλλην εὐθέως ἔλαβε γνώμην.

ἀνῆκτο] 'Had already set sail for Egypt.'

τἀνθένδε καθεστηκότα] 'The market-prices (current or established prices) here.' Or perhaps, 'that prices here were steady,' as inf. § 10. He uses ἐνθένδε for ἐνταῦθα on account of ἀποστέλλει, according to a very common idiom.

ἀναγκαῖον εἴη] Perhaps to take in water or provisions.

10. πέρας δ' οὖν] 'In fine,' ceterum. See on Or. 37 § 43. Equivalent to ἵνα δὲ μὴ μακρὰ λέγω. The construction of the long sentence following is irregular. He might have said, ἐπειδὴ ἔλαβε ὁ Παρμενίσκος—ἐξαιρεῖται τὸν σῖτον καταφρονήσας κ.τ.λ., and the plural καταφρονήσαντες may have been used because the speaker is

γράμματα τὰ παρὰ τούτου ἀποσταλέντα, καὶ πυθόμενος τὰς τιμὰς τὰς ἐνθάδε τοῦ σίτου καθεστηκυίας, ἐξαιρεῖται τὸν σῖτον ἐν τῇ Ῥόδῳ κἀκεῖ ἀποδίδοται,— 1286 καταφρονήσαντες μὲν τῆς συγγραφῆς, ὦ ἄνδρες δικασταί, καὶ τῶν ἐπιτιμίων ἃ συνεγράψαντο αὐτοὶ οὗτοι καθ' αὑτῶν, ἐάν τι παραβαίνωσι, καταφρονήσαντες δὲ τῶν νόμων τῶν ὑμετέρων, οἳ κελεύουσι τοὺς ναυκλήρους καὶ τοὺς ἐπιβάτας πλεῖν εἰς ὅ τι ἂν συνθῶνται ἐμπόριον, εἰ δὲ μή, ταῖς μεγίσταις ζημίαις εἶναι ἐνόχους. καὶ ἡμεῖς ἐπειδὴ τάχιστα ἐπυθόμεθα τὸ γεγονός, ἐκπεπληγμένοι τῷ πράγματι προσῇμεν τούτῳ τῷ ἀρχιτέκτονι τῆς ὅλης ἐπιβουλῆς, ἀγανακτοῦντες, οἷον εἰκός, καὶ ἐγκαλοῦντες ὅτι διαρρήδην ἡμῶν διορισα-

conscious that he is really describing the acts of two persons in concert. Another, and perhaps a better way of explaining the anomaly is to regard λαβὼν — γὰρ — ἀποδίδοται as parenthetical, and to suppose that πρᾶγμα ποιοῦσι δεινότατον was intended to follow after ἐνόχους, the last word of the paragraph, but was forgotten in the careless composition of a long sentence. G. H. Schaefer would read πέρας δὲ, and καταφρονήσας in both places, while Reiske proposed ἀποδίδονται for ἀποδίδοται.

καθεστηκυίας] This may mean either 'learning the market-prices here' (so Kennedy takes it), or, 'learning that the market here was quiet,' i.e. that prices were about the average. And so Mr Mayor understands it, p. 250. So in Aesch. Pers. 297, λέξον καταστὰς means 'compose yourself and say.' Ar. Equit. 865, ὅταν ἡ λίμνη καταστῇ.

τοὺς ἐπιβάτας] "Must not the word ἐπιβάτης have had some technical sense which does not appear in our lexicons? It seems hardly possible that ordinary passengers should have been liable to the severest punishment if they changed their destination. I understand it of an agent sent in charge of goods." (Mr Mayor, p. 250.) [Similarly in the seventh ed. of Liddell and Scott: 'a merchant on board ship,' 'a supercargo.' See § 24, Or. 34 § 51, and 32 §§ 4, 5. In 50 § 10 it means (as often) 'a marine.' S.]

§ 11. *We, on learning this transaction, had an interview with the defendant, telling him that he had not only violated the compact, but had thrown a suspicion on us of being concerned in a contraband trade, besides having withheld from us the ship, which was our sole security.*

τῷ ἀρχιτέκτονι] So Ar. Pac. 335, πρὸς τάδ' ἡμῖν, εἴ τι χρὴ δρᾶν, φράζε κἀρχιτεκτόνει.

ἀγανακτοῦντες] 'Expressing our indignation.'

p. 1287]   ΔΙΟΝΤΣΟΔΩΡΟΤ ΒΛΑΒΗΣ.   237

μένων ἐν ταῖς συνθήκαις ὅπως ἡ ναῦς μηδαμόσε καταπλεύσεται[1] ἀλλ᾽ ἢ εἰς Ἀθήνας, καὶ[j] ἐπὶ ταύταις ταῖς ὁμολογίαις δανεισάντων τὸ ἀργύριον, ἡμᾶς μὲν ἐν ὑποψίᾳ καταλέλοιπε τοῖς βουλομένοις αἰτιᾶσθαι καὶ λέγειν ὡς ἄρα καὶ ἡμεῖς κεκοινωνήκαμεν τῆς σιτηγίας τῆς εἰς τὴν Ῥόδον, αὐτοὶ δ᾽ οὐδὲν μᾶλλον τὴν ναῦν ἤκουσι κατακομίζοντες εἰς τὸ ὑμέτερον ἐμπόριον εἰς ὃ συνεγράψαντο. ἐπειδὴ δ᾽ οὐδὲν ἐπεραίνομεν ὑπὲρ τῆς 12 συγγραφῆς καὶ τῶν δικαίων διαλεγόμενοι. ἀλλὰ τό γε δάνειον καὶ τοὺς τόκους ἠξιοῦμεν ἀπολαβεῖν τοὺς ἐξ ἀρχῆς ὁμολογηθέντας. οὗτος δ᾽ οὕτως ὑβριστικῶς ἐχρήσατο ἡμῖν ὥστε τοὺς μὲν τόκους τοὺς ἐν τῇ συγγραφῇ γεγραμμένους οὐκ ἔφη δώσειν. "εἰ δὲ βούλεσθ᾽[k]" ἔφη "κομίζεσθαι τὸ πρὸς μέρος τοῦ πλοῦ τοῦ πεπλευσμένου, δώσω ὑμῖν" φησὶ "τοὺς εἰς Ῥόδον τόκους· πλείους δ᾽ οὐκ ἂν δοίην," αὐτὸς ἑαυτῷ[l] νομοθετῶν καὶ οὐχὶ τοῖς ἐκ τῆς συγγραφῆς δικαίοις πειθόμενος. ὡς δ᾽ ἡμεῖς οὐκ ἂν ἔφαμεν συγχωρῆσαι οὐδὲν 13

[1] μηδαμοῦ (Dobree) καταπλευσεῖται Z.
[j] +ὅτι Z. [ὅτι] Bekk. cum Reiskio.   [k] βούλεσθε Z.   [l] αὑτῷ Z.

οὐδὲν μᾶλλον] *Tametsi reditum Athenas ipsi condixissent.* G. H. Schaefer.

§ 12. *When we found it was no use talking about law and justice to such men, we asked them to pay at least the loan and interest agreed upon, though in fact they were also liable to the penalty. The defendant however, refused even this, and offered interest only as far as Rhodes—thus laying down the law for himself.*

ἀλλὰ] *Saltem.*—τοὺς ἐξ ἀρχῆς, viz. the ἀμφοτερόπλους, § 6.

ἐχρήσατο] 'Treated us.' Or. 34 § 46.

κομίζεσθαι] 'To take in payment.'—τὸ πρὸς μέρος, τὸ πρὸς λόγον, 'the moiety in proportion to the voyage actually sailed.'

§ 13. *When we, fearing we should be implicated in the transaction, declined to take the interest offered, he came to us with witnesses to attest that we rejected the proffered payment, knowing perfectly well that we should reject it, and the reasons why.*

οὐκ ἂν ἔφαμεν κ.τ.λ.] The usual *hyperthesis* or attraction of ἂν to the negative = ἔφαμεν ὅτι οὐκ ἂν συγχωρήσαιμεν. See 37 § 16, and 40 § 10.

238   LVI. ΚΑΤΑ   [§§ 13—15

τούτων, λογιζόμενοι ὅτι, ὁπότε τοῦτο πράξομεν, ὁμολογοῦμεν καὶ αὐτοὶ εἰς Ῥόδον σεσιτηγηκέναι, ἔτι μᾶλλον ἐπέτεινεν οὗτος καὶ μάρτυρας πολλοὺς παραλαβὼν προσῄει, φάσκων ἕτοιμος εἶναι ἀποδιδόναι τὸ δάνειον καὶ τοὺς τόκους τοὺς εἰς Ῥόδον, οὐδὲν μᾶλλον, ὦ ἄνδρες δικασταί, ἀποδοῦναι διανοούμενος, ἀλλ' ἡμᾶς ὑπολαμβάνων οὐκ ἂν ἐθελῆσαι ἀπολαβεῖν τὸ ἀργύριον διὰ τὰς ὑπούσας αἰτίας. ἐδήλωσε δ' αὐτὸ τὸ
14 ἔργον. ἐπειδὴ γὰρ, ὦ ἄνδρες Ἀθηναῖοι, τῶν ὑμετέρων πολιτῶν τινες παραγενόμενοι ἀπὸ ταὐτομάτου συνεβούλευον ἡμῖν τὸ μὲν διδόμενον λαμβάνειν, περὶ δὲ τῶν ἀντιλεγομένων κρίνεσθαι, τοὺς δὲ εἰς Ῥόδον τόκους μὴ καθομολογεῖν ἕως^m ἂν κριθῶμεν, ἡμεῖς μὲν

^m ἕως r. τέως Bekker st. cum ΣΦ.

ὁπότε] See Or. 34 § 33.
μᾶλλον ἐπέτεωεν] 'He was still more pressing.' A metaphor, perhaps, from the tuning of a lute, and raising the pitch. Cf. § 24.
μάρτυρας πολλούς] Cf. Or. 34 § 30, σοὶ δ' ἀποδιδόντι τό τε δάνειον καὶ τοὺς τόκους ἀμφοτέρους—πῶς οὐχὶ πολλοὺς ἦν παραληπτέον μάρτυρας;
οὐδὲν μᾶλλον] Used here adverbially, 'not at all the more intending to repay' &c.
ὑπούσας] sc. τῷ ἀπολαβεῖν.
§§ 14—16. That we were right in supposing he never meant to pay, was shown by the result (§ 16). We were advised to take the interest as far as Rhodes, and to file a bill against them to recover the rest. To this we consented, not wishing to seem too hard on the defendant. But when he demanded that the whole claim should be cancelled on payment of part, we declined

that, offering however to cancel it in so far as it was paid. To this he would not consent, and so to this day he has paid us nothing.
ὑμετέρων πολιτῶν] Hence it follows that the speaker and his partner were not citizens, but μέτοικοι. Cf. note on Argument, l. 1. S.]
ἀπὸ ταὐτομάτου] It seems better to construe this with συνεβούλευον, 'volunteered the advice,' than (as Kennedy takes it) with παραγενόμενοι, 'who were accidentally present.' [M. Weil however (Revue Critique, 1876, p. 145) and Mr Mayor, p. 251, agree with Kennedy's rendering. The other rendering would be naturally expressed by αὐτόματοι. S.]
κρίνεσθαι] 'To go to law,' 'to have the matter decided by a jury.'
μὴ καθομολογεῖν] 'Not to accept as full payment.' The κατὰ here seems to have the same

p. 1287] ΔΙΟΝΤΣΟΔΩΡΟΤ ΒΛΑΒΗΣ. 239

ταῦτα συνεχωροῦμεν, οὐκ ἀγνοοῦντες, ὦ ἄνδρες δικασταί, τὸ ἐκ τῆς συγγραφῆς δίκαιον, ἀλλ᾽ ἡγούμενοι δεῖν ἐλαττοῦσθαί τι καὶ συγχωρεῖν, ὥστε μὴ δοκεῖν φιλόδικοι εἶναι, οὗτος δ᾽ ὡς ἑώρα ἡμᾶς ὁμόσε πορευομένους, "ἀναιρεῖσθε" φησὶ "τοίνυν τὴν συγγραφήν." "ἡμεῖς ἀναιρώμεθα; οὐδέν γε μᾶλλον ἢ ὁτιοῦν· ἀλλὰ 15 κατὰ μὲν τἀργύριον, ὃ ἂν ἀποδῷς, ὁμολογήσομεν ἐναντίον τοῦ τραπεζίτου ἄκυρον ποιεῖν τὴν συγγραφήν, τὸ μέντοι σύνολον οὐκ ἂν ἀνελοίμεθα, ἕως ἂν περὶ τῶν ἀντιλεγομένων κριθῶμεν. τί γὰρ ἔχοντες δίκαιον ἢ τί τὸ ἰσχυρὸν ἀντιδικήσομεν, ἐάν τε πρὸς διαιτητὴν ἐάν τε εἰς δικαστήριον δέῃ βαδίζειν, ἀνελόμενοι τὴν συγγραφὴν ἐν ᾗ τὴν ὑπὲρ τῶν δικαίων βοήθειαν

force as in καταγοράζειν, Or. 34 § 7, 'to agree to as against the debt.'

ἐλαττοῦσθαι] 'To take something less than our rights.' See Or. 40 § 53.

ὁμόσε πορευομένους] This may mean, 'Ready to proceed against him,' i.e. inclined to stand on our rights, and not to give up altogether the interest from Rhodes to Athens; and this is the regular meaning of the term, 'to go *at* a person,' as we say, lit. 'in the direction' of ὁμοῦ, i.e. ἐγγύς. Photius, ὁμόσε· ὁμοῦ εἰς τὸν αὐτὸν τόπον· ἢ ἐξ ἐναντίας.—ὁμόσε ταῖς λόγχαις ἰέναι, ἀντὶ τοῦ ἐξ ἐναντίας εἰς τὸ αὐτὸ ἔρχεσθαι. This gloss lends some colour to Kennedy's rendering, 'when the defendant saw that we were closing with his offer.' Mr Mayor also translates (p. 251) 'ready to meet him halfway;' [M. Dareste has; *prêts à le suivre*, and Blass (III 525) notices it as used peculiarly for συγχωροῦντας].

ἀναιρεῖσθε] See Or. 34 § 31.

15. ἡμεῖς κ.τ.λ.] '*We* cancel it! Nothing less likely.' 'The last thing in the world!' Lit. 'not more than we would do anything.'——ἀλλὰ κ.τ.λ. 'No! in proportion to the sum you may have paid, we will agree to cancel the bond in the presence of a banker; but we will not cancel it as a whole, until we have had a verdict given about the amount in dispute. For with what claims of justice, or holding what as our security, shall we join issue, whether we have to go to an arbitrator or to a court, if we cancel the bond in which we have our sole redress in case our rights are refused?' All this is a model for Greek composition, being at once simple and idiomatic. The law said that all voluntary compacts were binding (§ 2): consequently, if the bond had been cancelled, Dionysodorus could have pleaded a demurrer to any further action.

τί ἔχοντες—τὸ ἰσχυρὸν] See § 2.

16 ἔχομεν;" ταῦτα δ' ἡμῶν λεγόντων, ὦ ἄνδρες δικασταί, καὶ ἀξιούντων Διονυσόδωρον τουτονὶ τὴν μὲν συγγραφὴν μὴ κινεῖν μηδ' ἄκυρον ποιεῖν τὴν ὁμολογουμένην καὶ ὑπ' αὐτῶν κυρίαν εἶναι, τῶν δὲ χρημάτων ὅσα μὲν αὐτὸς ὁμολογεῖ, ἀποδοῦναι ἡμῖν, περὶ δὲ τῶν ἀντιλεγομένων ὡς ἑτοίμων ὄντων[n] κριθῆναι, εἴτε βούλοιντο ἐφ' ἑνὶ[o] εἴτε καὶ πλείοσι τῶν ἐκ τοῦ ἐμπορίου, οὐκ ἔφη προσέχειν Διονυσόδωρος τούτων οὐδενί, ἀλλ' ὅτι τὴν συγγραφὴν ὅλως οὐκ ἀνῃρούμεθα ἀπολαμβάνοντες ἃ οὗτος ἐπέταττεν, ἔχει δεύτερον ἔτος τὰ ἡμέ-
17 τερα καὶ χρῆται τοῖς χρήμασι· καὶ ὃ πάντων ἐστὶ δεινότατον, ὦ ἄνδρες δικασταί, ὅτι αὐτὸς μὲν οὗτος

[n] [ὡς] ἑτοίμων ὄντων Bekker st. ὡς ἐν τῷ μέσῳ ὄντων coniecit Weil.
[o] Bekk. ἐφ' ἑνὸς Z cum FΣΦΒ.

§ 16. *On our saying this, and imploring the defendant not to meddle with, much less to cancel, the agreement which he himself admitted to be still binding, but to pay us what he allowed to be due, and declaring that we were ready to accept the arbitration of any one or more of the merchants on 'Change, Dionysodorus declared that he would not listen to any of these terms, but because we were not willing to cancel the bond entirely on receiving the part of our dues which he ordered us to take, he has been keeping what belongs to us and making use of our money now for two years.*

ὡς ἑτοίμων ὄντων] A kind of attraction to ἡμῶν λεγόντων above. = ὡς ἑτοίμων ἡμῶν ὄντων, Reiske. Kennedy follows G. H. Schaefer in translating, "should leave the disputed claim, the amount of which was certain to be decided by one or more commercial men." ("De controversa autem pecunia, ut de qua liquido constaret." Schaefer.) "In the simplest form the sentence would run ἀξιοῦμεν, ὡς ἕτοιμοι ὄντες, κριθῆναι, which, thrown into the (genitive) absolute, becomes ἀξιούντων ὡς ἑτοίμων ὄντων κριθῆναι." (Mr Mayor, p. 251.)
ἐφ' ἑνί] 'Before one arbitrator.' [Fals. leg. § 243 ἐπὶ τοῖς δικασταῖς ἔλεγες, but in this sense the gen. is more common, e.g. 59 § 66 ἐπὶ τοῦ δικαστηρίου. S.]
ἐπέταττεν] i.e. as if he were master and we were but slaves. See Or. 39 § 7.
§ 17. *What is the hardest thing to bear is this, that he is getting bottomry interest for our money, while we can get none out of him; and that too though his transactions are not for Athens, but for Egypt and Rhodes* (i.e. for the trade between those marts).
καὶ ὃ πάντων ἐστὶ δεινότατον... ὅτι] Cf. Or. 55 § 20, ὃ καὶ πάντων ἐστὶ δεινότατον, εἰ κ.τ.λ. Isocr. Paneg. § 128 n. Madvig, *Gr. Synt.* § 197. S.]

παρ' ἑτέρων εἰσπράττει ναυτικοὺς τόκους ἀπὸ τῶν ἡμετέρων χρημάτων, οὐκ Ἀθήνησι δανείσας οὐδ' εἰς Ἀθήνας, ἀλλ' εἰς Ῥόδον καὶ Αἴγυπτον, ἡμῖν δὲ τοῖς δανείσασιν εἰς τὸ ὑμέτερον ἐμπόριον οὐκ οἴεται δεῖν τῶν δικαίων οὐδὲν ποιεῖν. ὅτι δ' ἀληθῆ λέγω, ἀναγνώσεται ὑμῖν τὴν πρόκλησιν ἣν ὑπὲρ τούτων προὐκαλεσάμεθ' αὐτόν.

ΠΡΟΚΛΗΣΙΣ.

Ταῦτα τοίνυν, ὦ ἄνδρες δικασταί, προκαλεσαμένων ἡμῶν Διονυσόδωρον τουτονὶ πολλάκις, καὶ ἐπὶ πολλὰς ἡμέρας ἐκτιθέντων τὴν πρόκλησιν, εὐήθεις ἔφη παντελῶς ἡμᾶς εἶναι, εἰ ὑπολαμβάνομεν αὐτὸν οὕτως ἀλογίστως ἔχειν ὥστ' ἐπὶ διαιτητὴν βαδίζειν, προδήλου ὄντος ὅτι καταγνώσεται αὐτοῦ ἀποτῖσαι τὰ χρήματα, ἐξὸν αὐτῷ ἐπὶ τὸ δικαστήριον ἥκειν φέροντα

18

ναυτικοὺς τόκους] This was larger than other kinds of interest, probably. Thus, in Or. 34 § 23, it is 600 drachms on 2000, while ibid. § 25, the interest according to a land-mortgage is 560 on 3360, or ἔφεκτος, while in Or. 50 (πρὸς Πολυκλ.) § 17, the ναυτικὸς τόκος is ἐπόγδοος.—τὴν πρόκλησιν, see Or. 39, Argum.

οὐκ οἴεται δεῖν] 'He thinks he is not bound.' In this formula, as in οὐ φημί &c., the infinitive is virtually negatived. See § 47. Thuc. I 33 § 3, τὸν δὲ πόλεμον, δι' ὅνπερ χρήσιμοι ἂν εἴημεν εἴ τις ὑμῶν μὴ οἴεται ἔσεσθαι, 'if any of you think the war will not take place,' &c.

§ 18. He, however, ridiculed the idea of going to an arbitrator, who was sure to give sentence against him. He might just as well go into court at once with the money in his hand, and pay it if he was forced, or keep it if he could.

ἐκτιθέντων] i.e. προτιθέντων. As we insert advertisements in newspapers, so notices were posted on the eponym heroes (statues in the agora) of each tribe, that no man might plead ignorance. The present participle expresses the duration, and so represents the imperfect tense. [ἐκθεῖναι (τοὺς νόμους) πρόσθεν τῶν ἐπωνύμων occurs in Or. 20 (Lept.) § 94, and similarly in 24 §§ 18, 23, Aeschin. 3 § 39 and Andoc. 1 § 84; also (of the public announcement of the name of one who had broken his promise to the people) in Isaeus Or. 5 § 38. There is no proof that documents connected with private suits were published in the same place. S.]

εὐήθεις] Isocr. Paneg. § 169 n. S.]

ἐπὶ διαιτητὴν βαδίζειν] cf. § 15 and see note on 53 § 15. S.]

τἀργύριον, εἶτ'ᵖ ἐὰν μὲν δύνηται ὑμᾶς παρακρούσασθαι, ἀπιέναι τἀλλότρια ἔχοντα, εἰ δὲ μή, τηνικαῦτα καταθεῖναι τὰ χρήματα, ὡς ἄνθρωπος οὐ τῷ δικαίῳ πιστεύων, ἀλλὰ διάπειραν ὑμῶν λαμβάνειν βουλόμενος.

19 Τὰ μὲν τοίνυν πεπραγμένα Διονυσοδώρῳ ἀκη- 1289 κόατε, ὦ ἄνδρες δικασταί· οἴομαι δ' ὑμᾶς θαυμάζειν ἀκούοντας πάλαι τὴν τόλμαν αὐτοῦᵍ, καὶ τῷ ποτὲ πιστεύων εἰσελήλυθε δευρί. πῶς γὰρ οὐ τολμηρὸν, εἴ τις ἄνθρωπος δανεισάμενος χρήματα ἐκ τοῦ ἐμπορίου 20 τοῦ Ἀθηναίων, καὶ συγγραφὴν διαρρήδην γραψάμενος ἐφ' ᾧ τε καταπλεῖν τὴν ναῦν εἰς τὸ ὑμέτερον ἐμπόριον, εἰ δὲ μή, ἀποτίνειν διπλάσια τὰ χρήματα, μήτε τὴν ναῦν κατακεκόμικεν εἰς τὸν Πειραιᾶ μήτε τὰ χρήματ' ἀποδίδωσι τοῖς δανείσασι, τόν τε σῖτον ἐξελόμενος ἐν Ῥόδῳ ἀπέδοτο, καὶ ταῦτα διαπεπραγμένος οὐδὲν ἧττον

ᵖ εἶτα Z.   ᵍ Bekk. cum F (τόλμᾰν αὑτοῦ) et Σ (in margine prima manu adscriptum). om. Z.

παρακρούσασθαι] i.e. to induce them to give a verdict in his favour.
§§ 19, 20. *The matter of surprise is, that he should dare to come into court without 'a leg to stand upon.' Here is a man who has borrowed money in the Athenian mart, under a promise to sail back to it or pay a heavy fine, and yet refuses either to pay or to produce the security! He has sold the corn in Rhodes, thereby breaking the law, and yet has the face to appear before a jury.*
20. γραψάμενος] 'Having had a bond drawn up and engrossed on the express condition that the ship shall put into your port, or in default shall pay the amount of the loan twice over.' For the use of the article by which διπλάσια becomes a predicate, compare Aesch. Ag. 520, διπλᾶ δ' ἔτισαν Πριαμίδαι θἀμάρτια.
ἀπέδοτο] Notice the variety of indicatives depending on εἰ, and expressing fact, κατακεκόμικεν, ἀποδίδωσι, ἀπέδοτο, τολμᾷ.
διαπεπραγμένος] This is frequently found in the middle sense (35 § 26; cf. κεκομίσθαι, § 3). Demosthenes, as elsewhere remarked, is fond of using the form of the perfect passive in the middle sense. Thus γέγραμμαι is 'I have impeached,' Timocr. § 17. This closely resembles the transitive verbal adjective (commonly called the past participle) of deponent verbs, *meditatus*, *comitatus*, &c,

p. 1289] ΔΙΟΝΥΣΟΔΩΡΟΥ ΒΛΑΒΗΣ. 243

τολμᾷ βλέπειν εἰς τὰ ὑμέτερα πρόσωπα; ἃ δὴ λέγει 21
πρὸς ταῦτ' ἀκούσατε. φησὶ γὰρ τὴν ναῦν πλέουσαν ἐξ
Αἰγύπτου ῥαγῆναι, καὶ διὰ ταῦτ' ἀναγκασθῆναι καὶ
προσσχεῖν^r εἰς τὴν Ῥόδον κἀκεῖ^s ἐξελέσθαι τὸν σῖτον·
καὶ τούτου τεκμήριον λέγει, ὡς ἄρ' ἐκ τῆς Ῥόδου
μισθώσαιτο πλοῖα καὶ δεῦρ' ἀποστείλειε τῶν χρημάτων ἔνια. ἓν μὲν τοῦτ' ἐστιν αὐτῷ μέρος τῆς ἀπολογίας,
δεύτερον δ' ἐκεῖνο· φησὶ γὰρ ἑτέρους τινὰς δανειστὰς 22
συγκεχωρηκέναι αὐτῷ^t τοὺς τόκους τοὺς εἰς Ῥόδον·
δεινὸν οὖν, εἰ ἡμεῖς μὴ συγχωρήσομεν ταὐτὰ ἐκείνοις.
τρίτον πρὸς τούτοις τὴν συγγραφὴν κελεύειν φησὶν
αὐτὸν^u σωθείσης τῆς νεὼς ἀποδοῦναι τὰ χρήματα, τὴν
δὲ ναῦν οὐ σεσῶσθαι εἰς τὸν Πειραιᾶ. πρὸς ἕκαστον
δὴ τούτων, ὦ ἄνδρες δικασταί, ἀκούσατε ἃ λέγομεν
δίκαια.

^r A¹. προσχεῖν Bekk. Dind. (προσέχειν FΦB).   ^s καὶ ἐκεῖ Z.
^t αὐτῷ Z.   ^u αὐτὸν Z.

not a few of which are also used in a passive sense, as διαπεπραγμένος in tragedy means 'done for.' Mr Mayor says, "it is curious that Demosthenes and Plato seem never to employ the active διαπράσσειν."
τολμᾷ—πρόσωπα;] Or. 34 § 19, εἰς τὰ ὑμέτερα πρόσωπα ἐμβλέποντα. This is one of the parallels quoted by Blass, Att. Ber. III 525, indicating that the present speech was by the same author as that against Phormio. S.]
§§ 21, 22. Now hear his excuse. He pretends that the ship sprang a leak in the voyage from Egypt, and so he was forced to put in at Rhodes and sell the cargo there. And he points to the fact in confirmation, that he had to hire other craft, and send off some of the goods to Athens. Another plea is, that other leaders agreed to take the interest to Rhodes, thereby showing that they believed his story. Thirdly, the contract says, 'if the ship gets safe;' but she did not get safe.

καὶ προσσχεῖν καὶ—κ.τ.λ.] 'That both the putting in to Rhodes and the unlading of the corn (viz. to get at the leak) were matters of necessity with him.' It might have been urged that at least one of these two expedients was unnecessary. Thus in § 42 it is denied that there was any need of going to Rhodes at all.

22. συγκεχωρηκέναι] This may be called a brief expression for συγχωρεῖν δέξασθαι. The simple accusative generally implies the ceding of something to another. So συγκεχωρέναι λα-

23 Πρῶτον μὲν τὸ ῥαγῆναι τὴν ναῦν ὅταν λέγῃ, οἶμαι πᾶσιν ὑμῖν φανερὸν εἶναι ὅτι ψεύδεται. εἰ γὰρ τοῦτο συνέβη παθεῖν τῇ νηί, οὔτ' ἂν εἰς τὴν Ῥόδον ἐσώθη 1290 οὔτ' ἂν ὕστερον πλώϊμος[uu] ἦν. νῦν δὲ φαίνεται εἰς τὴν Ῥόδον σωθεῖσα καὶ πάλιν ἐκεῖθεν ἀποσταλεῖσα εἰς Αἴγυπτον καὶ ἔτι καὶ νῦν πλέουσα πανταχόσε, πλὴν οὐκ εἰς Ἀθήνας. καίτοι πῶς οὐκ ἄτοπον, ὅταν μὲν εἰς τὸ Ἀθηναίων ἐμπόριον δεήσῃ κατάγειν τὴν ναῦν, ῥαγῆναι φάσκειν, ὅταν δ' εἰς τὴν Ῥόδον τὸν σῖτον ἐξελέσθαι, τηνικαῦτα δὲ πλώϊμον[uu] οὖσαν φαίνεσθαι τὴν αὐτὴν ναῦν;

24 Διὰ τί οὖν, φησίν, ἐμισθωσάμην ἕτερα πλοῖα καὶ μετεξειλόμην τὸν γόμον καὶ δεῦρο ἀπέστειλα; ὅτι, ὦ ἄνδρες Ἀθηναῖοι, οὐ τῶν ἁπάντων ἀγωγίμων οὔθ' οὗτος ἦν κύριος οὔθ' ὁ κοινωνὸς αὐτοῦ, ἀλλ' οἱ ἐπιβάται τὰ ἑαυτῶν χρήματ' ἀπέστελλον, οἶμαι, δεῦρο ἐν ἑτέροις πλοίοις ἐξ ἀνάγκης, ἐπειδὴ προκατέλυσαν οὗτοι τὸν πλοῦν· ὧν μέντοι αὐτοὶ ἦσαν κύριοι, οὐ ταῦτ' ἀπέστελλον πάντα δεῦρο, ἀλλ' ἐκλεγόμενοι τίνων αἱ

[uu] πλόϊμος...πλόϊμον Bekker st. cum A¹Σφr.

βεῖν, § 26. The next sentence is quoted in Bekker's Anecdota, p. 144, 16, δεινὸν οὖν εἰ μὴ ἡμεῖς συγχωρήσομεν.

§§ 23—5. First as to the alleged leak. That must be false, because the ship got safe to Rhodes, and is even now sea-worthy. No! the leak only let in water when the ship was wanted at Athens! Secondly, as to the hiring of other craft. Why, he asks, did I do that if the ship could have made the rest of the voyage? Because, gentlemen of the jury, neither he nor his partner was the owner of all the goods: there were passenger-merchants on board who were obliged to forward their goods when these men chose to stop short at Rhodes. As for their own goods, they sent on such only as would fetch a higher price. Otherwise, why was not the corn sent on also? Because corn had got cheaper at Athens. So that this hiring of other craft proves to have been done only in their own interest.

24. ἐκλεγόμενοι] 'Selecting those of which the prices had been raised.' Lit. 'of what goods,' &c. τίνων in this respect differing from ὧν. G. H. Schaefer suggests εἴ τινων.

[The sense implied by τίνων

τιμαὶ ἐπετέταντο. ἐπεὶ τί δήποτε μισθούμενοι ἕτερα 25
πλοῖα, ὥς φατε, οὐχ ἅπαντα τὸν γόμον τῆς νεὼς μετεν-
έθεσθε, ἀλλὰ τὸν σῖτον αὐτοῦ ἐν τῇ ʽΡόδῳ κατελί-
πετε ᵛ; ὅτι, ὦ ἄνδρες δικασταί, τοῦτον μὲν συνέφερεν
αὐτοῖς ἐκεῖσε πωλεῖν· τὰς γὰρ τιμὰς ἐνθάδε ἀνεικέναι
ἤκουον· τὰ δ' ἄλλ' ʷ ἀγώγιμα ὡς ὑμᾶς ἀπέστελλον, ἀφ'
ὧν κερδανεῖν ἤλπιζον. ὥστε τὴν μίσθωσιν τῶν πλοίων
ὅταν λέγῃς, οὐ τοῦ ῥαγῆναι τὴν ναῦν τεκμήριον λέγεις,
ἀλλὰ τοῦ συμφέροντος ὑμῖν.

Περὶ μὲν οὖν τούτων ἱκανά μοι τὰ εἰρημένα· περὶ 26
δὲ τῶν δανειστῶν, οὕς φασι συγκεχωρηκέναι λαβεῖν
παρ' αὐτῶν τοὺς εἰς ʽΡόδον τόκους, ἔστι μὲν οὐδὲν
πρὸς ἡμᾶς τοῦτο. εἰ γάρ τις ὑμῖν ἀφῆκέ τι τῶν αὐτοῦ,
οὐδὲν ἀδικεῖται ὁ πεισθείς ˣ· ἀλλ' ἡμεῖς οὔτ' ἀφείκαμέν
σοι οὐδὲν οὔτε συγκεχωρήκαμεν τῷ πλῷ τῷ εἰς ʽΡόδον,
οὐδ' ἐστὶν ἡμῖν οὐδὲν κυριώτερον τῆς συγγραφῆς.
αὕτη δὲ τί λέγει καὶ ποῖ προστάττει τὸν πλοῦν ποιεῖ- 27
σθαι; Ἀθήνηθεν εἰς Αἴγυπτον καὶ ἐξ Αἰγύπτου εἰς
Ἀθήνας· εἰ δὲ μή, ἀποτίνειν κελεύει διπλάσια τὰ

ᵛ Bekk. κατελείπετε Z cum Σ.   ʷ ἄλλα Z.
ˣ + ἢ ὁ πείσας Z.   (οὔθ' ὁ δοὺς οὔθ' ὁ πείσας γρ. ΦΒΒ.)
[ἢ ὁ πείσας] Bekk.

is 'Making a selection with careful note what the goods were, the prices of which had been enhanced.' Prof. Kennedy. (Cf. his *Studia Sophoclea*, 1 pp. 69—71.) S.]
25. ἀνεικέναι] Intransitively. 'Had given way, relaxed, slackened.' Both this and the preceding word (see § 13) are borrowed from the tuning of a lute.
§ 26. *Thirdly, it is nothing to us if other lenders consented to take less than their due. We did not consent, nor agree to the voyage to Rhodes at all.*

We abide by the words in the bond, which we still hold to be binding on them.
τῷ πλῷ] The dative is much more common with the person, as συγχωρῶ σοι.
§ 27. *The bond specifies a penalty, and if you have incurred it, then you are bound to pay it. It is a self-imposed obligation, and therefore you cannot evade it. You must prove to the judges either that we can claim no rights by the bond, or that you are not bound to act according to it.*

χρήματα. ταῦτ' εἰ μὲν πεποίηκας, οὐδὲν ἀδικεῖς, εἰ δὲ μὴ πεποίηκας μηδὲ κατακεκόμικας τὴν ναῦν ᾿Αθήναζε, προσήκει σε ζημιοῦσθαι τῷ ἐπιτιμίῳ τῷ ἐκ τῆς συγγραφῆς· τοῦτο γὰρ τὸ δίκαιον οὐκ ἄλλος οὐδείς, ἀλλ' αὐτὸς σὺ σαυτῷ ὥρισας. δεῖξον οὖν τοῖς δικασταῖς δυοῖν θάτερον, ἢ τὴν συγγραφὴν, ὡς οὐκ ἔστιν ἡμῖν κυρία, ἢ ὡς οὐ δίκαιος εἶ πάντα κατὰ ταύτην πράττειν.
28 εἰ δέ τινες ἀφείκασί τί σοι καὶ συγκεχωρήκασι τοὺς εἰς ῾Ρόδον τόκους ὅτῳ δήποτε τρόπῳ πεισθέντες, διὰ ταῦτα οὐδὲν ἀδικεῖς ἡμᾶς, οὓς παρασυγγεγράφηκας εἰς ῾Ρόδον καταγαγὼν τὴν ναῦν; οὐκ οἴομαί γε· οὐ γὰρ τὰ ὑφ' ἑτέρων συγκεχωρημένα δικάζουσιν οὗτοι νῦν, ἀλλὰ τὰ ὑπ' αὐτοῦ σοῦ πρὸς ἡμᾶς συγγεγραμμένα. ἐπεὶ ὅτι γε καὶ τὸ περὶ τὴν ἄφεσιν τῶν τόκων, εἰ ἄρα γέγονεν ὡς οὗτοι λέγουσι, μετὰ τοῦ συμφέροντος τοῦ
29 τῶν δανειστῶν γέγονε, πᾶσιν ὑμῖν φανερόν ἐστιν. οἱ γὰρ ἐκ τῆς Αἰγύπτου δανείσαντες τούτοις ἑτερόπλουν

τῷ ἐπιτιμίῳ τῷ ἐκ τῆς συγγραφῆς] 34 § 26; inf. § 44, cf. §§ 12, 34, τοῖς ἐκ τῆς συγγραφῆς δικαίοις.

ὥρισας] Soph. Antig. 452, οἱ τούσδ' ἐν ἀνθρώποισιν ὥρισαν νόμους. See Or. 37 § 20.—οὐ δίκαιος εἶ, οὐ δίκαιόν ἐστί σε κ.τ.λ.

§ 28. *It does not follow that, because some have taken less than their dues, you do not wrong us by withholding ours. The question before the jury is not what they gave up, but what you engaged to pay. In fact, it is easy to see that the lenders in question really consulted their own interest. They could make more by taking the principal with part of the interest at Rhodes, and lending it for another voyage to Egypt.*

The transitive sense of παρα-συγγραφεῖν is irregular. It merely means 'to violate a bond.' But like many verbs of this sort, it takes an accusative of the person affected by the action. Compare συκοφαντεῖν, προξενεῖν τινά τινι (Or. 37 § 11, 53 § 13). It is intransitive, § 34. Similarly, in Or. 54 (κατὰ Κον.) § 2, a man is said παρανενομῆσθαι, and in Παραπρ. § 198, one is said παροινεῖσθαι, and we have πλεονεκτεῖσθαι, ἀριστοκρατεῖσθαι, δημοκρατεῖσθαι, &c.

29. οἱ γὰρ κ.τ.λ.] This serves as the subject to ἀφίκοντο, though it involves a change of subject in οὗτοι. But the writer intended some other construction in what follows than οὐδὲν διέφερεν αὐτοῖς, e.g. ἤθελον or κρεῖττον ἐνόμιζον.

p. 1292] ΔΙΟΝΥΣΟΔΩΡΟΥ ΒΛΑΒΗΣ. 247

τἀργύριον εἰς Ἀθήνας, ὡς ἀφίκοντο εἰς τὴν Ῥόδον καὶ
τὴν ναῦν ἐκεῖσε οὗτοι κατεκόμισαν, οὐδὲν, οἶμαι, διέφερεν αὐτοῖς ἀφεμένοις[y] τῶν τόκων καὶ κομισαμένοις
τὸ δάνειον ἐν τῇ Ῥόδῳ πάλιν ἐνεργὸν ποιεῖν εἰς τὴν
1292 Αἴγυπτον, ἀλλ᾽ ἐλυσιτέλει πολλῷ μᾶλλον τοῦτο ἢ
δεῦρ᾽ ἐπαναπλεῖν. ἐκεῖσε μέν γε ἀκέραιος[z] ὁ πλοῦς, 30

[y] Bekk. ἀφειμένοις Z cum FΦ; ἀφιμένοις Σ.
[z] γὰρ ἀκέραιος Z cum FΦΣ. γε ἀκαριαῖος Bekk. 'ἀκέραιος quidem
neque tutus (ἀκίνδυνος), neque identidem redintegratus, neque nun-
quam interruptus usquam alibi valere videtur; ἀκαριαῖος autem nil
nisi aut momentaneus aut minutissimus significat. Fortasse igitur scribendum: ἐκεῖσε μὲν γὰρ ἀεὶ ὡραῖος ὁ πλοῦς (Hesiodi Op. 628,
663 ὡραῖος πλόος). Huic opponitur infra παραχειμάζειν καὶ περιμένειν τὴν ὡραίαν. Cf. Pindari Isthm. II 42=62 ἐπέρα ποτὶ μὲν
Φᾶσιν θεραίαις (ponto Euxino aestate tantum aperto), ἐν δὲ χειμῶνι
πλέων Νείλου πρὸς ἀκτάς (navigatione e Sicilia ad Aegyptum ne
hieme quidem interclusa).—Hiberno scilicet tempore propter maris
Aegei procellas inter Athenas Rhodumque multo minus tuta est
navigatio, quam inter Rhodum et Aegyptum, ubi ventus fere semper
ab occasu solis spirat, in alterutram partem navigantibus satis com-
modus; aestatis autem tempore quadraginta dies e regione inter
Boream Zephyrumque iacente (sc. e Rhodo ad Aegyptum) perflant
Etesiae (J. Smith, Voyage and Shipwreck of St Paul, pp. 72, 76).
Etiam χειμῶνος prope Cnidum (i.e. iuxta Rhodum) invenimus τὰς
ἀπ᾽ Αἰγύπτου ὁλκάδας (Thuc. VIII 35).' J. E. Sandys.

τῶν τόκων] sc. τῶν ἐς Ἀθήνας, 'giving up the interest due from Rhodes to Athens.'

ἐπαναπλεῖν] 'To make the return voyage.' Or, 'to com-mence a new voyage to Athens' (Kennedy). "Rursus evehi in altum, huc ut appellerent" (G. H. Schaefer).—ἐκεῖσε μέν γε κ.τ.λ. 'For to Egypt the voyage might be made again and again, and they might have traded twice or thrice with the same money; whereas if they had come to Athens, they would have had to winter there, and wait for the sailing-season. So

that in fact those lenders have made additional profit, and have not remitted any of their gains to benefit them. But, for our parts, so far is it from being a question about the interest, that we cannot get back even our principal.'

ἀκέραιος] Properly 'pure' (Eur. Hel. 48, ἀκέραιον λέχος), or 'unimpaired,' ἀκ. δύναμις, Thuc. III 3. But it seems here to take a later sense, analogous to ἐξ ἀκεραίου, de integro, 'anew,' which is quoted from Polybius XXIV 4 § 10 ἵνα δὲ μὴ πάλιν ἐξ ἀκεραίου περὶ πάντων ἀντιλέγοιεν,

καὶ δὶς ἢ τρὶς ὑπῆρχεν αὐτοῖς ἐργάσασθαι τῷ αὐτῷ ἀργυρίῳ· ἐνταῦθα δ' ἐπιδημήσαντας παραχειμάζειν ἔδει καὶ περιμένειν τὴν ὡραίαν. ὥστ' ἐκεῖνοι μὲν οἱ δανεισταὶ προσκεκερδήκασι καὶ οὐκ ἀφείκασι τούτοις οὐδέν· ἡμῖν δ' οὐκ ὅπως περὶ τοῦ τόκου ὁ λόγος ἐστὶν, ἀλλ' οὐδὲ τἀρχαῖα ἀπολαβεῖν δυνάμεθα.

31 Μὴ οὖν ἀποδέχεσθε τούτου φενακίζοντος ὑμᾶς καὶ τὰ πρὸς τοὺς ἄλλους δανειστὰς πεπραγμένα παραβάλλοντος, ἀλλ' ἐπὶ τὴν συγγραφὴν ἀνάγετ' αὐτὸν[a] καὶ τὰ ἐκ τῆς συγγραφῆς δίκαια. ἔστι γὰρ ἐμοί τε λοιπὸν διδάξαι ὑμᾶς τοῦτο καὶ οὗτος ἰσχυρίζεται τῷ αὐτῷ τούτῳ, φάσκων τὴν συγγραφὴν κελεύειν σωθείσης τῆς νεὼς ἀποδιδόναι τὸ δάνειον. καὶ ἡμεῖς ταῦτα οὕτω

[a] Bekk. αὐτὴν Z cum Σ.

ἔγγραπτον ὑπὲρ τῶν ὁμολογουμένων [ἐποιοῦντο], ἐφ' ὃ πάντες ἐπέβαλον τὰς ἰδίας σφραγῖδας. The only other meaning it could here take is 'safe,' 'unharmed,' (*incolumis, tuta navigatio*, G. H. Schaefer). Perhaps however, we should keep ἀκαριαῖος, 'short,' which is the *vulgata lectio*, retained by Bekker. Hesych. ἀκαριαῖον· τὸ βραχύ. τὸ ὀλίγον.— ἀκαριαία ῥιπή (ῥοπὴ Salmasius)· ὀλίγη, μικρά. [Bekker's *Anecdota* p. 203, 25 (λέξεις ῥητορικαί), ἀκαριαῖον: τὸ βραχύ. 363, 28 μικρόν, βραχύ, ῥοπή.] The rarity of the word would partly account for the corruption. The voyage from Egypt to Rhodes, if not really short, is relatively so to a voyage from Egypt to Athens. [But in direct distance it is as 370 miles is to 590; and it took at least four days, Diodorus III 34. S.]

τὴν ὡραίαν] See § 3. The adjective is used like τροπαία, with the ellipse of αὔρα, in Aeschylus, Cho. 775. Apoll. Rh. 3, 1390 μίμνει ἐς ὡραίην.

§ 31. *Don't listen therefore when he tries to cajole you by comparing our conduct with the treatment that others receive, but bring him to book, and his obligation by the contract. I say, obligation; for we both allow that the matter turns on the clause, 'if the ship gets in safe.'*

ἀποδέχεσθε] As frequently ἀνέχεσθαι, this verb takes a genitive, originally perhaps taken absolutely, 'when he says this, don't take it from him,' or 'don't bear it.' Cf. παραπρεσβ. (Or. 19) p. 345 fin., οὔτε τῶν τὰ τρόπαια καὶ τὰς ναυμαχίας λεγόντων ἀνέχεσθαι. [For ἀποδέχεσθαι with the genitive, see Or. 27 Aphob. A § 59; 48 Olymp. § 51; Lysias 14 § 24; Deinarchus 1 § 113 μὴ ἀποδέχεσθε αὐτῶν. S.]

τὰ πρὸς τοὺς ἄλλους δ. πεπραγμένα] What other borrowers do (or perhaps, what he himself does) to other lenders. G. H. Schaefer explains παραβάλλοντος as παράδειγμα ποιουμένου.

p. 1293] ΔΙΟΝΥΣΟΔΩΡΟΥ ΒΛΑΒΗΣ. 249

φαμὲν δεῖν ἔχειν. ἡδέως δ' ἂν πυθοίμην αὐτοῦ σοῦ, 32
πότερον ὡς ὑπὲρ διεφθαρμένης τῆς νεὼς διαλέγει[b] ἢ ὡς
ὑπὲρ σεσωσμένης. εἰ μὲν γὰρ διέφθαρται ἡ ναῦς καὶ
ἀπόλωλε, τί περὶ τῶν τόκων διαφέρει[c] καὶ ἀξιοῖς ἡμᾶς
κομίζεσθαι τοὺς εἰς Ῥόδον τόκους; οὔτε γὰρ τοὺς
τόκους οὔτε τἀρχαῖα προσήκει ἡμᾶς ἀπολαβεῖν. εἰ δ'
ἔστιν ἡ ναῦς σῶα[d] καὶ μὴ διέφθαρται, διὰ τί ἡμῖν οὐκ
ἀποδίδως[e] τὰ χρήματα ἃ συνεγράψω; πόθεν οὖν ἀκρι- 33
βέστατ' ἂν μάθοιτε, ὦ ἄνδρες Ἀθηναῖοι, ὅτι σέσωσται
ἡ ναῦς; μάλιστα μὲν ἐξ αὐτοῦ τοῦ εἶναι τὴν ναῦν ἐν
πλῷ, οὐχ ἧττον δὲ καὶ ἐξ ὧν αὐτοὶ οὗτοι λέγουσιν.
ἀξιοῦσι γὰρ ἡμᾶς τά τε ἀρχαῖα ἀπολαβεῖν καὶ μέρος
τι τῶν τόκων, ὡς σεσωσμένης μὲν τῆς νεώς, οὐ πε-
πλευκυίας δὲ πάντα τὸν πλοῦν. σκοπεῖτε δέ, ὦ ἄνδρες 34
Ἀθηναῖοι, πότερον ἡμεῖς τοῖς ἐκ τῆς συγγραφῆς δικαίοις
χρώμεθα ἢ οὗτοι, οἳ οὔτε εἰς τὸ συγκείμενον ἐμπόριον
πεπλεύκασιν, ἀλλ' εἰς Ῥόδον καὶ Αἴγυπτον, σωθείσης
τε τῆς νεὼς καὶ οὐ διεφθαρμένης ἄφεσιν οἴονται δεῖν

[b] διαλέγῃ Z. [c] διαφέρῃ Z.
[d] σῶς Cobet. Cf. § 37 inf.
[e] Bekk. 1824. οὐ δίδως Z et Bekk. st. cum ΦΣΦ.

§§ 32, 3. *Either the ship was lost, or it got in safe. In the former case, you are exempted from all payment, and have no need to ask us to accept a part. In the latter case, why do you not pay what you promised? That the ship was not lost is proved by its being actually at sea, as well as by the defendants' own admissions; for they want us to accept a part on the ground that it was not lost, but only made part of the voyage.*

διέφθαρται] Combined with ἀπόλωλε, this suggests the sense 'lost' rather than 'damaged' or 'spoiled' by springing a leak; though either gives a good sense.

διαφέρει] 'Do you dispute?' See inf. § 46.

. § 34. *They, of course, say that we are violating the compact by pressing for payment though the ship has been lost. But surely it is they who do so much more plainly, by not sailing into the port agreed upon, by claiming a reduction of the interest though they sailed to Rhodes only, and by making much money through this contraband importation of corn to that mart.*

εὑρίσκεσθαι τῶν τόκων παρασυγγεγραφηκότες, καὶ αὐτοὶ μὲν πολλὰ χρήματ᾽ εἰργασμένοι παρὰ τὴν σιτηγίαν τὴν εἰς Ῥόδον, τὰ δ᾽ ἡμέτερα χρήματ᾽ ἔχοντες καὶ καρπούμενοι δεύτερον ἔτος τουτί. καινότατον δ᾽ ἐστὶ πάντων τὸ γιγνόμενον· τὸ μὲν γὰρ δάνειον τὸ ἀρχαῖον ἀποδιδόασιν ἡμῖν ὡς σεσωσμένης τῆς νεώς, τοὺς τόκους δ᾽ ἀποστερῆσαι οἴονται δεῖν ὡς διεφθαρμένης. καίτοι ἡ συγγραφὴ οὐχ ἕτερα μὲν λέγει περὶ τῶν τόκων, ἕτερα δὲ περὶ τοῦ ἀρχαίου δανείσματος, ἀλλὰ τὰ δίκαια ταῦτα περὶ ἀμφοῖν ἐστι καὶ ἡ πρᾶξις ἡ αὐτή. ἀνάγνωθι δέ μοι πάλιν τὴν συγγραφήν.

ΣΥΓΓΡΑΦΗ[f].

Ἀκούετε, ὦ ἄνδρες Ἀθηναῖοι· Ἀθήνηθεν, φησὶν, εἰς Αἴγυπτον καὶ ἐξ Αἰγύπτου Ἀθήναζε. λέγε τὰ λοιπά.

ΣΥΓΓΡΑΦΗ[g].

Ἄνδρες Ἀθηναῖοι[h], πάνυ ἁπλοῦν ἐστι διαγνῶναι

[f] +[Ἀθήνηθεν εἰς Αἴγυπτον καὶ ἐξ Αἰγύπτου Ἀθήναζε.] Z. delevit Dobree.
[g] +[σωθείσης δὲ τῆς νεὼς εἰς Πειραιᾶ.] Z. delevit Dobree.
[h] ΓΣΦ. δικασταί Bekk. 1824.

ἐργάζεσθαι χρήματα] 'To make money,' is a close coincidence with our idiom, and is a phrase not uncommon.——παρά, 'along of,' i.e. through the carrying of corn to Rhodes.

§ 35. *The very nature of the offer itself is unprecedented: they are willing to repay the loan because the ship arrived safe, but will not pay the interest because she did not* (i.e. reach Athens). *But the bond makes no such distinction between the principal and the interest.*

τὸ δάνειον] Perhaps τοῦ δανείου, which will be the genitive after both. τὸ ἀρχαῖον and τοὺς τόκους. So below it is probable that τοῦ ἀρχαίου τοῦ δανείσματος is the true reading, and that in § 37 δάνειον should be omitted after ἀρχαῖον. G. H. Schaefer would omit τὸ ἀρχαῖον —ἀρχαίου—ἀρχαῖον. Mr Mayor (p. 252) has no difficulty in rendering the vulgate 'the original debt.' Possibly δάνειον in § 37 crept in from a gloss.

§§ 37, 38. *The case then is very simple: the ship was not*

ὑμῖν ὑπὲρ ταυτησὶ¹ τῆς δίκης, καὶ οὐδὲν δεῖ λόγων πολλῶν. ʲἡ ναῦς ὅτι μὲν σέσωσται καὶ ἔστι σῶαʲ, καὶ παρ' αὐτῶν τούτων ὁμολογεῖται· οὐ γὰρ ἂν ἀπεδίδοσαν τό τε ἀρχαῖον δάνειον καὶ τῶν τόκων μέρος τι. οὐ κατακεκόμισται δ'ᵏ εἰς τὸν Πειραιᾶ. διὰ τοῦτο ἡμεῖς μὲν οἱ δανείσαντες ἀδικεῖσθαί φαμεν, καὶ ὑπὲρ τούτου δικαζόμεθα, ὅτι οὐ κατέπλευσεν εἰς τὸ συγκείμενον ἐμπόριον. Διονυσόδωρος δ' οὔ φησιν ἀδικεῖν δι' αὐτὸ 38 τοῦτο· οὐ γὰρ δεῖν αὐτὸν ἀποδοῦναι πάντας τοὺς τόκους, ἐπειδὴ ἡ ναῦς οὐ κατέπλευσεν εἰς τὸν Πειραιᾶ. ἡ δὲ συγγραφὴ τί λέγει; οὐ μὰ Δί' οὐ ταῦθ' ἃ σὺ λέγεις, ὦ Διονυσόδωρε· ἀλλ' ἐὰν μὴ ἀποδιδῷς τὸ δάνειον καὶ τοὺς τόκους ἢ μὴ παράσχῃς τὰ ὑποκείμενα ἐμφανῆ καὶ ἀνέπαφα ἢ ἄλλο τι παρὰ τὴν συγγραφὴν ποιῇς, ἀποτίνειν κελεύει σε διπλάσια τὰ χρήματα. καί μοι λέγε αὐτὸ τοῦτο τῆς συγγραφῆς.

ΣΥΓΓΡΑΦΗ.

['Εὰν δὲ μὴ παράσχωσι τὰ ὑποκείμενα ἐμφανῆ καὶ

¹ ταύτης Z cum ΣΦ.
ʲ⁻ʲ 'legendum ἡ ναῦς (ὅτι μὲν) σῶς ἐστίν, ut paullo ante p. 1292. utilia de hac re notavit Dindorfius ad (Dem.) paginam (Reiskianam) 61, 14 in editione minore' (p. xviii). Cobet, Misc. Crit. p. 514.
ᵏ δὲ Z.

lost, for they offer to pay in part; it did not sail back to the Peiraeus, and that is precisely our grievance, and the ground of this action. The defendant on his part says that is his reason for not paying the whole. But the bond says differently, and imposes a penalty for default.

λόγων πολλῶν] Perhaps ποικίλων, as opposed to ἁπλοῦν. The same antithesis occurs in Eur. Phoen. 469, ἁπλοῦς ὁ μῦθος τῆς ἀληθείας ἔφυ, κοὐ ποικίλων δεῖ

τἀνδίχ' ἑρμηνευμάτων. [Dem. 9 § 37, οὐδὲν ποικίλον οὐδὲ σοφόν, 29 § 1, εἰ μὲν ἐδεῖτο λόγου τινὸς ἢ ποικίλας contrasted with ἁπλῶς δεῖ διδάξαι καὶ διηγήσασθαι. S.]
38. ἀνέπαφα] This word is technically used of goods not seized or intercepted by pirates. See Or. 35 (πρὸς Λακρ.) §§ 11, 24. In Aesch. Suppl. 309,Ἔπαφος ἀληθῶς ῥυσίων ἐπώνυμος (if the verse is genuine), the meaning is that the name was given from ῥυσίων ἐφάπτεσθαι, 'to lay hands on booty.'

ἀνέπαφα, ἢ ποιήσωσί τι παρὰ τὴν συγγραφήν, ἀποδιδότωσαν διπλάσια τὰ χρήματα.]

39 Ἔστιν οὖν ὅποι παρέσχηκας ἐμφανῆ τὴν ναῦν, ἀφ' οὗ τὰ χρήματα ἔλαβες παρ' ἡμῶν, ὁμολογῶν σῶαν[kk] εἶναι αὐτός; ἢ καταπέπλευκας ἐξ ἐκείνου τοῦ χρόνου εἰς τὸ Ἀθηναίων ἐμπόριον, τῆς συγγραφῆς διαρρήδην λεγούσης εἰς τὸν Πειραιᾶ κατάγειν τὴν ναῦν καὶ ἐμ-
40 φανῆ παρέχειν τοῖς δανείσασιν; καὶ γὰρ τοῦτο, ὦ ἄνδρες Ἀθηναῖοι. θεάσασθε τὴν ὑπερβολήν, ἐρράγη ἡ ναῦς, ὥς φησιν οὗτος, καὶ διὰ τοῦτο εἰς Ῥόδον κατήγαγεν αὐτήν. οὐκοῦν τὸ μετὰ τοῦτο ἐπεσκευάσθη καὶ πλώϊμος ἐγένετο. διὰ τί οὖν, ὦ βέλτιστε, εἰς μὲν τὴν Αἴγυπτον καὶ τἄλλα ἐμπόρια ἀπέστελλες αὐτήν, Ἀθήναζε δ' οὐκ ἀπέστειλας οὐδέπω καὶ νυνὶ πρὸς ἡμᾶς τοὺς δανείσαντας, οἷς ἡ συγγραφὴ κελεύει σε ἐμφανῆ καὶ ἀνέπαφον τὴν ναῦν παρέχειν, καὶ ταῦτ' ἀξιούντων
41 ἡμῶν καὶ προκαλεσαμένων σε πολλάκις; ἀλλ' οὕτως 1295

[kk] σῶν Cobet.

§§ 39, 40. *We have never seen the ship that was mortgaged to us from the day we lent you the money, though you say she is 'all right;' she put in at Rhodes and was overhauled, and so was made tight. Then why did she not come to Athens? It was not for want of many urgent requests on our part.*

παρέσχηκας] This seems one of the Ionic forms, like τετύχηκα, formed as from (σχέω) σχήσω, (τυχέω) τυχήσω. See Or. 40 § 54. The epic perfect of ἔχω is ὄχωκα, if the Homeric language is in all cases genuine.

40. καὶ γὰρ τοῦτο] So τεκμήριον δέ is often used absolutely, i.e. without any verb. Mr Mayor refers to Holmes' note on De Coron. p. 268, § 122, where the same formula occurs, and p. 43, l. 15, p. 442, l. 7, p. 568, l. 12, are compared, with ἐπεὶ κἀκεῖνο in p. 1097, l. 5, ἐνθυμητέον being mentally supplied.

ἐπισκευάζειν] the technical term for repairing a ship. (Lit. 'to put fittings to it'), inf. § 43. See Thuc. I 29, ζεύξαντές τε τὰς παλαιὰς ὥστε πλωΐμους εἶναι καὶ τὰς ἄλλας ἐπισκευάσαντες,' i.e. 'after putting new cross-bits to the old triremes, and repairing the rest.' The former word is wrongly rendered by Arnold 'undergirding,' and the latter not less wrongly in Liddell and Scott 'equipping,' 'fitting out.'

§§ 41, 42. *Though in fact*

ἀνδρεῖος εἶ, μᾶλλον δ' ἀναίσχυντος, ὥστε ἐκ τῆς συγγραφῆς ὀφείλων ἡμῖν διπλάσια τὰ χρήματα οὐκ οἴει δεῖν οὐδὲ τοὺς τόκους τοὺς γιγνομένους ἀποδοῦναι, ἀλλὰ τοὺς εἰς Ῥόδον προστάττεις ἀπολαβεῖν, ὥσπερ τὸ σὸν πρόσταγμα τῆς συγγραφῆς δέον κυριώτερον γενέσθαι, καὶ τολμᾷς λέγειν ὡς οὐκ ἐσώθη ἡ ναῦς εἰς τὸν Πειραιᾶ· ἐφ' ᾧ δικαίως ἂν ἀποθάνοις ὑπὸ τῶν δικαστῶν. διὰ 42 τίνα γὰρ ἄλλον, ὦ ἄνδρες δικασταὶ, οὐ σέσωσται ἡ ναῦς εἰς τὸν Πειραιᾶ; πότερον δι' ἡμᾶς τοὺς διαρρήδην δανείσαντας εἰς Αἴγυπτον καὶ εἰς Ἀθήνας, ἢ διὰ τοῦτον καὶ τὸν κοινωνὸν αὐτοῦ, οἳ ἐπὶ ταύταις ταῖς ὁμολογίαις δανεισάμενοι, ἐφ' ᾧ τε καταπλεῖν Ἀθήναζε, εἰς Ῥόδον κατήγαγον τὴν ναῦν; ὅτι δ' ἑκόντες καὶ οὐκ ἐξ ἀνάγκης ταῦτ' ἔπραξαν, ἐκ πολλῶν δῆλον. εἰ γὰρ 43 ὡς ἀληθῶς ἀκούσιον τὸ συμβὰν ἐγένετο καὶ ἡ ναῦς ἐρράγη, τὸ μετὰ τοῦτ', ἐπειδὴ ἐπεσκεύασαν τὴν ναῦν, οὐκ ἂν εἰς ἕτερα δήπου ἐμπόρια ἐμίσθουν[1] αὐτήν, ἀλλ'

[1] Bekk. 1824. ἐμίσθωσαν Z et Bekk. st. cum FΣΦB.

you owe us the whole sum twice over, by incurring the penalty, you have the face to refuse payment even of the interest, and you tell us to be content with that to Rhodes, as if your order, forsooth, was to have greater weight than the bond. Again, you have the face to say, 'she did not get safe in to the Peiraeus.' Well, through whose fault? Was it ours, who required that it should go back or was it theirs, who wilfully and from no necessity at all took it to Rhodes?

πρόσταγμα] 'Dictation.' Like ἐπέταττεν in § 16, an invidious word contrasted with συγγραφή. Similarly, in Isocr. Paneg. § 176 the Peace of Antalcidas is declared to be no equitable compact (συνθῆκαι), and is denounced as dictated (προστάγματα) by the king of Persia. S.]

ἀποθάνοις] The legal penalty for not producing the security was death. See Or. 34 § 50.

42. ἑκόντες καὶ οὐκ ἐξ ἀνάγκης] So Aesch. Eum. 520, ἑκὼν ἀνάγκας ἄτερ δίκαιος ὤν.

§ 43. If the ship really sprung a leak by mere accident, as soon as she had been repaired, he should have taken her to Athens, to make amends for the delay and the inconvenience. But so far from doing that, he did a greater wrong still, and then, as if in mockery of you, he comes into court, thinking that at the worst, he can only be condemned to repay the loan, and that he shall evade the penalty.

254   LVI. ΚΑΤΑ   [§§ 43—45

ὡς ὑμᾶς ἀπέστελλον, ἐπανορθούμενοι τὸ ἀκούσιον σύμπτωμα. νῦν δ' οὐχ ὅπως ἐπανωρθώσαντο^m, ἀλλὰ πρὸς τοῖς ἐξ ἀρχῆς ἀδικήμασι πολλῷ μείζω προσεξημαρτήκασι, καὶ ὥσπερ ἐπὶ καταγέλωτι ἀντιδικοῦντες εἰσεληλύθασιν, ὡς ἐπ' αὐτοῖς ἐσόμενον, ἐὰν καταψηφίσησθε αὐτῶν, τἀρχαῖα μόνον ἀποδοῦναι καὶ τοὺς τόκους. 44 ὑμεῖς οὖν, ὦ ἄνδρες Ἀθηναῖοι, μὴ ἐπιτρέπετε τούτοις^n οὕτως ἔχουσι, μηδ' ἐπὶ δυοῖν ἀγκύραιν ὁρμεῖν αὐτοὺς

^m ἐπηνωρθώσαντο Z. (Cf. Veitch, Gk. Vbs.)
^n τοῖς Bekk. 1824 cum A¹r.

ὡς ὑμᾶς] i.e. Ἀθήναζε.
ἐπανορθούμενοι] 'Doing all they could to repair the unavoidable mischief.' The indicative of the aorist of this verb generally takes the double augment, ἐπηνωρθώσαντο, like ἠφίει, ἠμπίσχεν, &c.
σύμπτωμα] Here synonymous with συμφορά (τὸ συμβὰν above). The word is used by Thuc. IV 36 and is not unfrequent in Aristotle, but this is the only passage in which it is found in Demosthenes. This point is adduced by A. Schaefer (who quotes Phrynichus, p. 248) as bearing on the doubts sometimes entertained on the genuineness of the speech (Dem. u. s. Zeit III 2, p. 311). Cf. Rutherford's New Phrynichus, p. 318. S.]
οὐχ ὅπως] Compare § 30, Or. 34 § 14, and 54 § 22, οὐχ ὅπως ἀπέτρεψεν, —ἀλλ' αὐτὸς ἡγεμὼν γεγένηται. Mid. § 11, οὐ γὰρ ὅπως τὸ σῶμα ὑβρίζεσθαί τινος ἐν ταύταις ταῖς ἡμέραις —ᾤεσθε χρῆναι, ἀλλὰ καὶ κ.τ.λ. i.e. non modo (non), sed, &c.
§ 44. Do not then let these men rest secure in the confidence that they can keep other men's property, if they can get a verdict in their favour, or if

not, that at least they will not be fined. Fine them, we say; for it is not reasonable that you should be more lenient to them than they were to themselves when they consented to the penalty.
ἐπὶ δυοῖν ἀγκύραιν] When a ship came to the shore, she had her stern to the land, where it was fastened by the πρυμνήσιον, and her head to the sea. An anchor, or, in case of rough weather, two anchors from the bows, held her in that position. To ride on one anchor was considered rather insecure. Hence, Helena says in Eur. Hel. 277, ἄγκυρα δ' ἥ μου τὰς τύχας ὤχει μόνη, and Hecuba in the play of that name (80), ὃς μόνος οἴκων ἄγκυρ' ἔτ' ἐμῶν κ.τ.λ. Hence too we see the precise point in Pind. Ol. VI 100, ἀγαθαὶ δὲ πέλοντ' ἐν χειμερίᾳ νυκτὶ θοᾶς ἐκ ναὸς ἀπεσκίμφθαι δύ' ἄγκυραι, which is incorrectly explained in Dr Donaldson's note. [De Cor. p. 240, § 281, οὐκ ἐπὶ τῆς αὐτῆς (sc. ἀγκύρας) ὁρμεῖ τοῖς πολλοῖς. Apostolius, centuria VII 61 in the Paroemiographi Graeci II 412 ἐπὶ δυοῖν ὁρμεῖ: δηλόντι ἀγκύραιν· λέγεται ἐπὶ τῶν ἀστεμφῶς ἐχόντων. Aristides, Panath.

p. 1296] ΔΙΟΝΤΣΟΔΩΡΟΤ ΒΛΑΒΗΣ. 255

1296 ἐᾶτε, ὡς, ἐὰν° μὲν κατορθῶσι, τἀλλότρια ἔξοντας, ἐὰν δὲ μὴ δύνωνται ἐξαπατῆσαι ὑμᾶς, αὐτὰ τὰ ὀφειλόμενα ἀποδώσοντας· ἀλλὰ τοῖς ἐπιτιμίοις ζημιοῦτε τοῖς ἐκ τῆς συγγραφῆς· καὶ γὰρ ἂν δεινὸν εἴη αὐτοὺς μὲν τούτους διπλασίαν καθ' αὑτῶν[p] τὴν ζημίαν γράψασθαι, ἐάν τι παραβαίνωσι τῶν ἐν τῇ συγγραφῇ, ὑμᾶς δ' ἠπιωτέρως ἔχειν πρὸς αὐτούς, καὶ ταῦτ' οὐχ ἧττον ἡμῶν συνηδικημένους.

Τὰ μὲν οὖν περὶ τοῦ πράγματος δίκαια βραχέα 45 ἐστὶ καὶ εὐμνημόνευτα. ἐδανείσαμεν Διονυσοδώρῳ τούτῳ καὶ τῷ κοινωνῷ αὐτοῦ τρισχιλίας δραχμὰς Ἀθήνηθεν εἰς Αἴγυπτον καὶ ἐξ Αἰγύπτου Ἀθήναζε· οὐκ ἀπειλήφαμεν τὰ χρήματα οὐδὲ τοὺς τόκους, ἀλλ' ἔχουσι τὰ ἡμέτερα καὶ χρῶνται δεύτερον ἔτος· οὐ κατακεκομίκασι τὴν ναῦν εἰς τὸ ὑμέτερον ἐμπόριον οὐδέπω καὶ νῦν, οὐδ' ἡμῖν παρεσχήκασιν ἐμφανῆ· ἡ δὲ συγγραφὴ κελεύει, ἐὰν μὴ παρέχωσιν ἐμφανῆ τὴν

° Α¹Σr. ἂν Z.   p Σ. ἑαυτῶν Z.

110, καὶ πάντες ἐπὶ δυοῖν ὁρμεῖν ἔδοξαν οἱ Ἕλληνες, where the Scholiast observes εἴρηται ἐκ μεταφορᾶς τῶν πλεόντων, ὅταν ἢ δυσὶν ἀγκύραις ὁρμίζωνται ἢ ὅταν ἐλλιμενίσωσι μὲν, προσχρῶνται δὲ καὶ ἀγκύρᾳ διὰ πλείστην ἀσφάλειαν. Propert. II 22, 41 'nam melius duo defendunt retinacula navim.' S.]

ἐξαπατῆσαι] A petitio principii, like παρακρούσασθαι in § 18.

αὐτὰ τὰ ὀφειλόμενα] 'Merely the debt owed,' without the ἐπιτίμιον.

οὐχ ἧττον ἡμῶν] Because the taking corn to Rhodes against the laws was a public offence.

§ 45. Recapitulation. Principal points;—the loan was made on clear conditions; it has not been repaid; the ship has never been produced; there is a fine specified for this neglect, and the right of enforcing it rests with one or both partners.

εὐμνημόνευτα] 'Easily recalled to memory:' an ambiguous term, meaning either, 'readily recounted by the speaker,' or 'readily remembered by the hearer.' It is almost certainly the latter, and this is supported by Aristot. Rhet. III 13, where it is said that the ἐπίλογος, one of the objects of which is recapitulation (ἀναμνῆσαι τὰ προειρημένα, ib. 19), is unnecessary in a forensic speech ἐὰν μικρὸς ὁ λόγος ᾖ τὸ πρᾶγμα εὐμνημόνευτον. S.]

ναῦν, ἀποτίνειν αὐτοὺς διπλάσια τὰ χρήματα, τὴν δὲ
46 πρᾶξιν εἶναι καὶ ἐξ ἑνὸς καὶ ἐξ ἀμφοῖν. ταῦτ' ἔχοντες
τὰ δίκαια εἰσεληλύθαμεν πρὸς ὑμᾶς, ἀξιοῦντες τὰ
ἡμέτερα αὐτῶν ἀπολαβεῖν δι' ὑμῶν, ἐπειδὴ παρ' αὐτῶν τούτων οὐ δυνάμεθα. ὁ μὲν παρ' ἡμῶν λόγος
οὗτός ἐστιν. οὗτοι δὲ δανείσασθαι μὲν ὁμολογοῦσι
καὶ μὴ ἀποδεδωκέναι, διαφέρονται δ' ὡς οὐ δεῖ τελεῖν
αὐτοὺς τοὺς τόκους τοὺς ἐν τῇ συγγραφῇ, ἀλλὰ τοὺς
εἰς Ῥόδον, οὓς οὔτε συνεγράψαντο οὔτ' ἔπεισαν ἡμᾶς.
47 εἰ μὲν οὖν, ὦ ἄνδρες Ἀθηναῖοι, ἐν τῷ Ῥοδίων δικαστηρίῳ ἐκρινόμεθα, ἴσως ἂν οὗτοι ἐπλεονέκτουν ἡμῶν,
σεσιτηγηκότες πρὸς αὐτοὺς καὶ καταπεπλευκότες τῇ 1297
νηὶ εἰς τὸ ἐκείνων ἐμπόριον· νῦν δ' εἰς Ἀθηναίους εἰσ-
εληλυθότες καὶ συγγραψάμενοι εἰς τὸ ὑμέτερον ἐμπόριον οὐκ ἀξιοῦμεν ἐλαττωθῆναι ὑπὸ τῶν καὶ ἡμᾶς καὶ
ὑμᾶς ἠδικηκότων.
48 Χωρὶς δὲ τούτων, ὦ ἄνδρες Ἀθηναῖοι, μὴ ἀγνοεῖτε
ὅτι νυνὶ μίαν δίκην δικάζοντες νομοθετεῖτε ὑπὲρ ὅλου
τοῦ ἐμπορίου, καὶ παρεστᾶσι πολλοὶ τῶν κατὰ θά-

---

46. διαφέρονται, ἀμφισβητοῦσι] See § 32.

§ 47. *If this trial were held in a court at Rhodes, perhaps they would have an undue advantage over us, as having frequented that mart, and being known there as corn-factors. But now, as we drew up the compact expressly for your mart, we expect not to be losers by men who have wronged us privately and you publicly.*

συγγραψάμενοι] viz. σιτηγεῖν or καταπλεῦσαι.

οὐκ ἀξιοῦμεν] 'We hardly expect that you will give the advantage to persons who have wronged you as well as ourselves.' Kennedy. Lit. 'we expect not to be worsted (come off worse) by,' &c. See on § 17.

§ 49. *But besides the above arguments in our favour, the present case is anxiously watched by many other merchants; and if their interests are protected, and you show no tolerance for fraud, these men will lend money more freely, and this again will tend to increase your mart.*

παρεστᾶσι] So also in Or. 54 § 41 we have a pointed allusion to the bystanders in court, ὑμῶν ἕνεκα, ὦ ἄνδρες δικασταί, καὶ τῶν περιεστηκότων.

p. 1297] ΔΙΟΝΥΣΟΔΩΡΟΥ ΒΛΑΒΗΣ. 257

λατταν ἐργάζεσθαι προαιρουμένων ὑμᾶς θεωροῦντες πῶς τὸ πρᾶγμα τουτὶ κρίνετε. εἰ μὲν γὰρ ὑμεῖς τὰς συγγραφὰς καὶ τὰς ὁμολογίας τὰς πρὸς ἀλλήλους γιγνομένας ἰσχυρὰς οἰήσεσθε[q] δεῖν εἶναι καὶ τοῖς παραβαίνουσιν αὐτὰς μηδεμίαν συγγνώμην ἕξετε, ἑτοιμότερον προήσονται τὰ ἑαυτῶν οἱ ἐπὶ τοῦ δανείζειν ὄντες, ἐκ δὲ τούτων αὐξηθήσεται ὑμῖν τὸ ἐμπόριον. εἰ 49 μέντοι ἐξέσται τοῖς ναυκλήροις, συγγραφὴν γραψαμένοις ἐφ' ᾧ τε πλεῖν εἰς Ἀθήνας, ἔπειτα κατάγειν τὴν ναῦν εἰς ἕτερα ἐμπόρια φάσκοντας ῥαγῆναι καὶ τοιαύτας προφάσεις ποριζομένους οἵαισπερ καὶ Διονυσόδωρος οὑτοσὶ χρῆται, καὶ τοὺς τόκους μερίζειν πρὸς τὸν πλοῦν ὃν ἂν φήσωσι πεπλευκέναι, καὶ μὴ πρὸς τὴν συγγραφήν, οὐδὲν κωλύσει ἅπαντα τὰ συμβόλαια διαλύεσθαι. τίς γὰρ ἐθελήσει τὰ ἑαυτοῦ προέσθαι, 50 ὅταν ὁρᾷ τὰς μὲν[r] συγγραφὰς ἀκύρους, ἰσχύοντας δὲ τοὺς τοιούτους λόγους, καὶ τὰς αἰτίας τῶν ἠδικηκότων ἔμπροσθεν οὔσας τοῦ δικαίου; μηδαμῶς, ὦ ἄνδρες δικασταί· οὔτε γὰρ τῷ πλήθει τῷ ὑμετέρῳ συμφέρει τοῦτο οὔτε τοῖς ἐργάζεσθαι προῃρημένοις, οἵπερ χρησι-

[q] Bekk. 1824. οἴεσθε Z et Bekk. st. cum FΣΦB.
[r] Bekk. om. μὲν Z cum FΣΦB.

προαιρουμένων] See § 1, and inf. 50.
πῶς κρίνετε] Perhaps κρινεῖτε, which is a marginal reading in the Paris edition and was preferred by Reiske.
ἐπὶ τοῦ δανείζειν] In the profession or practice of moneylending. —αὐξηθήσεται τὸ ἐμπόριον, cf. 34 § 52.
§§ 49, 50. *If on the other hand, ship-owners may violate their bond and take their ship to any port under pretence of its being disabled, and then apportion the interest due to the voyage sailed, there will be an end of all obligation by contract. No man will lend his money if he sees that such lame excuses have weight in court. This is not to your interest, nor to that of traders, who are most important members of the state, and therefore should be protected.*
καὶ μὴ πρὸς τὴν συγγραφήν] Supply ἀποδοῦναι.
50. αἰτίας] The pleas or reasons.

LVI. ΚΑΤΑ ΔΙΟΝΥΣΟΔΩΡΟΥ. [§ 50

μώτατοί εἰσι καὶ κοινῇ πᾶσιν ὑμῖν καὶ ἰδίᾳ τῷ ἐν-
τυγχάνοντι. διόπερ δεῖ ὑμᾶς αὐτῶν ἐπιμέλειαν ποι- 1298
εῖσθαι.

Ἐγὼ μὲν οὖν, ὅσαπερ οἷός τ' ἦν, εἴρηκα· ἀξιῶ δὲ
καὶ τῶν φίλων μοί τινα συνειπεῖν. δεῦρο, Δημόσθενες.

τῷ ἐντυγχάνοντι] 'To all who have dealings with them.' See 34 § 51.

δεῦρο, κ.τ.λ.] See Or. 34, ad fin., καλῶ δὲ καὶ ἄλλον τινὰ τῶν φίλων, ἐὰν κελεύητε. [Or. 58 (Theocrin.) ad fin. βοήθησον ἡμῖν ὁ δεῖνα, εἴ τι ἔχεις, καὶ σύ-νειπε. ἀνάβηθι. Blass, *Att. Ber.* III 524, suggests that the present speech originally ended with δεῦρο ὁ δεῖνα, and that, on the speech finding its way into the Demosthenic collection, ὁ δεῖνα got altered into Δημό-σθενης. A. Schaefer, on the other hand, supposes that it was the mention of Demosthenes that led to its being included among his works (III 2, 314). See Introd. *ad fin.* S.]

INDEX.

The first figure refers to the number of the Speech, the second to the Section.

A.

ἀγγεῖον ἐρίων, 35. 34
ἄγκυρα, ἐπὶ δυοῖν ἀγκύραιν ὁρμεῖν, 56. 44
ἀγὼν τιμητὸς, ἀτίμητος, 37. 40
ἀηδῶς ἔχειν τινί, 37. 11
Ἀθήνησι, Ionic dative, 34. 42
ἀθλοθέται, 39. 9
αἰδεῖσθαι ἱκέτην, 37. 59
αἰκία, 37. 33
αἰκία καὶ ὕβρις, 37. 33
ἀκέραιος, ἀκαριαῖος, 56. 30
ἀκόλουθος, 39. 24
ἀκούσιος φόνος, 37. 59
ἀληθής, ἀληθινὸς, 40. 20
ἁμαρτάνειν = ἐρᾶν, 40. 48
ἀμφοτερόπλους, 34. 6; 56. 6
ἂν follows οὐ, οὐδὲ, 37. 16; 56. 13
ἀνάδικος, 40. 34, 39, 42
ἀναιρεῖν, ἀναιρεῖσθαι συγγραφήν, 34. 31; 56. 14, 15
ἄναξ (in prose), 35. 40
ἀναστῆναι, ἀνακύψαι ἐκ νεκρῶν, 39. 31
ἀνέπαφος, 35. 11, 24; 56. 37, 40
ἀνιέναι, remitti, 56. 25
ἀντιλαγχάνειν τὴν μὴ οὖσαν, 39. 38
— — παραγραφήν, 37. 33
ἀξιοῦν, 56. 46
ἀπαγωγὴ, 39. 14
ἀπαλλάξαι τινά τινος, 37. 1
ἀπαλλαττόμενοι, 39. 11
ἀπογνῶναι δίκης, 34. 45

ἀπογράφειν, ἀποφαίνειν οὐσίαν, 40. 22
ἀπογραφὴ, 34. 7
ἀποδέχεσθαι, ἀνέχεσθαι with gen., 56. 31
ἀποδιαιτᾶν, 40. 17, 55
ἀποδιδράσκειν τὴν ἀλήθειαν, 40. 54
ἀποκηρῦξαι, 39. 39
ἀποστάσιον, ἀπροστάσιον, 35. 48
ἀποστερεῖν, 37. 53
ἀποφυγεῖν τινα δίκην, 40. 19
Arcturus, rising of, 35. 10
ἀργυρῖτις, 37. 28
article repeated with irony, 35. 19
article in predicate, 35. 17, 22
ἀρχή, 39. 9
ἄρχων βασιλεὺς, πολέμαρχος, 35. 48
ἀστοί, definition of resident, 34. 37
ἀστοὶ, sons of, 39 Arg.
— εἰσβιαζόμενοι, 39. 33
ἀστρατεία, 39. 16
ἀτέλεια σίτου, 34. 36
ἀτιμόω, ἀτιμάζω, 37. 24
attraction of the case of a relative, 34 Arg. 1
ἀφεῖναι καὶ ἀπαλλάξαι, 37. 1, 16, 19
ἀφῆκε, ἀφείκαμεν, 56. 26
ἀφίστασθαι τῶν ὄντων, 35. 4; 37. 10

B.

βαδίζειν, 56. 15, 18
βακτηρίαν φορείν, 37. 52
βιάζεσθαί τινα τι, 40. 47
βλασφημεῖν, 40. 45
Blass, quoted, 34. 16; p. 59 &c.
βοηθεῖν τὰ δίκαια, 35. 5; 40. 61
Βόσπορος, 34. 2; 35. 10
Bottomry, loans on, 34 *Arg.*, and 56 *Arg.*
βουλή, manager of finance, 40. 02
Corn-laws, 35. 50; 56. 7

Γ.

Genitive of value or equivalence, 34. 40
— by attraction, 34 *Arg.* 1.
— limitation of time, 35. 11
γλίσχρως, 37. 38
γραμματείδιον, 56. 1
γραφαί, 39. 14
— ἀσεβείας, 35. 48
γράφειν, ἐγγράφειν, πρός τινα, 37. 6
γυμνασίαρχοι, 35, 48; 39. 7
γυναικωνῖτις, seclusion of, 37. 45

Δ.

Dareste, quoted, pp. 12, 62, 174
δὲ in apodosis, 56. 23
δεῖγμα, τό, 35. 29
δεινοπαθῶν, 40. 53
δεκάτην ἑστιᾶσαι, 40. 28
— ποιεῖν, 39. 20
Δελφίνιον, 40. 11
δευτερολογία, 34. 20, 21
δέω, δεῖς, personal, 37. 49
δημότας, ἐγγράφεσθαι εἰς, 39. 5
διαβάλλειν, διαβολαί, 40. 33
διαιτηταί, αἱρετοί, κληρωτοί, 40. 16
διαλῦσαί τινα, 37. 12
διαμετρεῖν, -εῖσθαι, σῖτον, 34. 39
διαμετρεῖσθαι ἄλφιτον, 34. 37
διαπεπραγμένος sensu medio, 35. 26; 56. 20
διαποστέλλειν, 35. 54
διατίθεσθαι φορτία, 34. 9
διδόναι, δέχεσθαι ὅρκον, 39. 3
δίκαι ἐμπορικαί, 35. 46

δικασταί, non-payment of, 39. 17
δίκην εἰσιέναι, 39. 1
— λαγχάνειν, *ibid.*
διομολογεῖσθαι, 56 *Arg.*
διοπεύειν, 35. 20, 34
διότι = ὅτι, 40. 41
διπλοῦν τὸ βλάβος, 37. 22; 56. 20
διωμοσία, διόμνυσθαι, 40. 41
δοκιμασία, 40. 34
δ' οὖν, ceterum, 37. 43

E.

ἔγγειοι τόκοι, 34. 22
ἐγγράφεσθαι εἰς κατάλογον, 39. 9
— — τὸ δημόσιον, 39. 15
— — δημότας, 39. 5
— — συμμορίαν, 39. 8
— — φράτερας, 39. 4
ἐγγυητὸς, 40. 26
ἐγκαλεῖν τινός, 39. 19
— τινί, 40. 51
ἐγκαταλείπειν, 40. 56
ἐθελέχθρως, 39. 36
εἰ οὐ in bimembered sentences, 34. 48
εἰκὸς ἦν, δίκαιον ἦν &c. without ἄν, 34. 15
εἰκόσορος, 35. 10
εἰκότα, τά, 34. 14, 23; 40. 27
εἰλεῖν, ἰλλεῖν, 39. 15
εἰσαγγελία, 34. 50; 37. 46
εἰσαγωγεύς, 37. 33
εἰσποιεῖν υἱόν, 40. 10.
ἐκβολή, 35. 11
ἐκδοῦναι ἀργύριον, 35. 51
— θυγατέρα, 40. 4
ἐκεῖνος, of persons deceased, 40. 28
ἐκκρούειν, 40. 44, 45
ἐκμαρτυρεῖν, 35. 34
ἐκπίπτειν, 37 *Arg.* 1. 30; 37. 59
ἐλαττοῦσθαί τι, 40. 53; 56. 14
ἐλλιμενισταί, 34. 34
ἐμβεβλημένος μαρτυρίαν, 40. 21, cf. §§ 28, 58
Emendations proposed, 34. 6, 12; 35. 17, 18, 29, 49; 37. 2 (32 § 7); 37. 4; 40. 14; 56. 8, 30, 35, 37

INDEX. 261

ἔμμηνος δίκη, 37. 2
ἐμπορικαὶ δίκαι, 35. 46
ἐμφανῆ παρέχειν, 56. 38, 39, 40, 45
ἐνδείξεις, ἐνδεικνύναι, 39. 14
ἐνεδρεύων, 40. 45
ἐντυγχάνειν, ἔντευξις, 34. 51; 56. 50
ἐξαλείφειν ἀστὸν, 39. 39
ἐξεστηκὼς οἶνος, 35. 32
— τοῦ νοῦ, 34 *Arg.* 1. 28
ἐξετάζειν, to make inventory, 34. 8
ἐξὸν μὴ, 39. 12; 40. 4
ἐξούλης δίκη, 39. 15; 40. 34
ἐπαγγέλλεσθαι, 35. 41
ἐπεὶ with imperative, 39. 32
ἐπετέταντο, 56. 24
ἐπὶ, *coram*, 56. 16
ἐπὶ τοῦ δανείζειν, 56. 48
ἐπιβάτης, 56. 10, 24
ἐπίγαμος, 40. 4, 57
ἐπιγνώμων, 37. 40
ἐπιδανεισμὸς, 34. 6
ἐπιδεῖν, 40. 12
ἐπίδοσις, 34. 38
ἐπιδοῦναι, 40. 7
ἐπικατατέμνειν, 37. 36
ἐπίκληροι, 37. 45
ἐπικληροῦν, 37. 39
ἐπιπλεῖν, 56. 8
ἐπιπλήσσειν, 37. 56
ἐπισκευάζειν ναῦν, 56. 40
ἐπισκήπτειν, -εσθαι, 34. 46
ἐπιτάσσειν δούλοις, προστάσσειν, 39. 7
ἐπιτέμνειν, ἐντέμνειν, 40. 33
ἐπιτιμᾶν σῖτον, 34. 39
ἐπωβελία, 35. 46; 39. 13; 56. 4
ἐρανίζειν, 39. 18
ἐργάζεσθαι χρήματα, 56. 34
ἐργαστήριον, 37 *Arg.*; 37. 4; (a gang) 37. 39; 39. 2
ἔρημον καταδιαιτᾶν, δοῦναι, 40. 17
ἑστιάτωρ, 39. 7
ἔσχηκα, ὄχωκα, 56. 39
ἑτερόπλους, 34. 8, 22, 30; 56. 29
εὐθεῖα, εὐθυδικία, 34 *Arg.*; 37 *Arg.* 1. 70
εὐμνημόνευτος, 56. 45

εὐπορεῖν, εὐπορίαι, 34. 51; 40. 36
ἔφεκτος τόκος, 34. 23
ἔφεσις, 34. 21; 40. 55
ἐφόδιον = σκῆψις, 34. 34
ἐφ' ᾧ τε, 56. 3, 5, 20, 42, 49
ἐχῖνος, 39. 18
ἕως, ἕως ἄν, with opt. 35. 25
Famine-prices, 34. 37, 39
Future perfect indic., 35. 56

Z.

ζεῦξαι ναῦν = ἐπισκευάζειν, 56. 40
Ζεὺς ἄναξ, 35. 40
ζυγομαχεῖν, 39. 6

H.

ἤδη, ἤδειν, 34. 12; 37. 23
ᾔειν, ᾖα, 34. 12
ἡλικία, stature, 43. 56
ἡμίεκτον, 34. 37

Θ.

Θάσιος οἶνος, 35. 35
Θεοδοσία, 35. 31
θέσθαι συγγραφὴν παρά τινι, 34. 6
θεσμοθέτης, 39. 10
θηρία, a term of reproach, 34. 52
-θοιτο, -θεῖτο in compounds of τίθεσθαι, 34. 11

I.

ἰδιώτης, 34. 1
ἱερὰ καὶ ὅσια, 39. 35
Ἰσοκράτης, pupils of, 35. 16
ἰσοτελής, 34. 18

K.

καθάπαξ, 37. 31
καθεστηκὸς, 'settled,' 56. 9
καθομολογεῖν, 56. 14
καὶ γὰρ, 37. 34
καὶ τίς, a formula of incredulity, 39. 9
κακίζειν, 34. 62
κατὰ = διὰ, 40. 42
καταγοράζειν, 34. 7; 56. 14
καταλλάσσειν τινὸς, 39. 23
κατάλογος, κατειλεγμένος, 39. 8

καταπεπλῆχθαι τὸν βίον, 37. 43
καταχρῆσθαι, 35. 44
κατομνύναι τινὸς, 39. 4
κεγχρεών, 37. 26
κλαήσω, 37. 48
Κλέων, 40. 25
κλῆροι, 39. 12
κληροῦν, κληροῦσθαι, 39. 10
— δυοῖν πινακίοιν, 39. 12
— κυάμοις, ibid.
κλητῆρες, 40. 28
κρίνεσθαι ἔν τισι, 39. 1
— ἐπί τινος, 56. 16
κρίτης, 39. 10
κύαμοι, in drawing lots, 39. 12
Κυζικηνικὸς στατήρ, 34. 23; 35. 26
Κῷος οἶνος, 35. 31, 34, 35

Λ.

λαγχάνειν δίκην, 39. 1
Λακρίτου μαθηταί, 35. 41
Laurium, pp. 89, 93, 121
λῆξις δίκης, 39. 16
Liddell & Scott, 56. 40
λιποστρατίου, λιποταξίου, 39. 16
λύσις, 37. 5.

Μ.

μακρὰ στοὰ, 34. 37
Μαρωνεία, 37. 4
Mayor, Joseph B., quoted, 34. 6, 31, 38, 47, 49; 35. 17, 18, 19, 25, 54; 37. 28, 46; 40. 11, 14, 17, 18, 34, 37; 56. 10, 14, 16, 20, 35, 40; p. 227
Μένδη, 35. 10, 20, 35
μέρει, 34. 1. [Lysias] 2 § 33 ἐν μέρει, vicissim.
μερίζειν, 56. 49
μεσεγγυήσασθαι, 39. 3
μεταλλικαὶ δίκαι, 37. 36
μετάλλων ὠνή, 40. 52
μετεξειλόμην, 56. 24
μὴ ὅτι, οὐχ ὅτι, 34. 14
μηχανή, ὥσπερ ἀπὸ μηχανῆς, 40. 59
middle sense of perf. pass., 40. 21, 28; 56. 3, 20
Mines of Derbyshire, 37. 36

Mines of Laurium, pp. 89, 93, 121
μνησικακεῖν, 40. 46
μόνος μόνῳ, 34. 32

Ν.

ναύκληρος, 34 Arg. l. 4
ναυτικοὶ τόκοι, 56. 17
νέμεσθαι πρός τινα, 40. 52
νόμοι περὶ γονέων, 39. 33; 40. 49

Ξ.

ξενίας προσκληθῆναι, 39. 18
— γράφεσθαί τινα, 40. 36
ξενολογεῖν, 40. 36
Ξυπεταιών, 35. 20

Ο.

οἰκεῖν Ἀθήνησιν, 34. 37
οἴκημα, carcer, 56. 4
οἰμωξόμενος, 35. 40
ὁμόσε πορεύεσθαι, 56. 14
ὁπότε, 34. 33
ὅρκον διδόναι, δέξασθαι, 39. 3
ὁρμεῖν ἐπὶ δυοῖν ἀγκύραιν, 56. 44
ὁτιοῦν, ὁτιανοῦν, 40. 23
οὐκ superfluous after οὐδὲ, 34. 1
— after εἰ in bimembered sentence, 34. 78
οὔκουν ἔγωγε = ἐγὼ γοῦν οὐκ, 39. 34
οὐ μὴν ἀλλὰ, elliptical, 34. 4
οὐχ ὅτι, μὴ ὅτι, 34. 14
— ὅπως, 56. 43
ὄφλημα, ὀφλεῖν, ὄφλειν, 39. 15

Π.

Παιρισάδης Rex, 34. 8, 36
παλιγκαπηλεύειν, 56. 7
παντελῶς, 56. 18
Παντικαπαῖον, 35. 10, 31; 34. 2
παραγράφειν, 39. 31
παραγράφεσθαι δίκην, 34. 43
— τινα διαιτητήν, 40. 16
παραγραφή, 34 Arg.
— διδ'ναι, 34. 17
παρακαταβολαί, 37. 41
παρακρούσασθαι, 56. 18
παρανομεῖσθαι, 35. 45
παρασυγγραφεῖν τινα, 56. 28

INDEX.

παραχειμάζειν, 34. 8; 56. 30
παραχωρεῖν τινί τινος, 37. 50
παρελθεῖν, παριέναι, intrare, 34. 38; 39. 16.
παρεμβάλλειν λόγους, 40. 61
Parents, laws about, 39. 33
παρέσχηκα, -ημαι, 56. 39; 40. 54
παρέχειν, -εσθαι, 34. 20
πατρικὸς, πατρῷος, 40. 37
πένθος, 34. 10
πεντηκοστεύεσθαι, 35. 30
Πεπάρηθος, 35. 35
πέπομφε, 34 *Arg.* 30
πεπραγμένα τινὶ πρός τινα, 34. 36
περιαιρεθῆναί τι, 35. 56
περίεργος, 39. 2
περιστῆναι εἴς τι, 37. 10
περιστῆσαι τινά τινι, 37. 39
—— τι εἴς τινα, 40. 20
πινάκια, 39. 12
πλεῖν, οἱ πλέοντες, 34. 30; 37. 54
πλεῖν (πλέον) ἢ, 40. 20
πλέον τρισὶ, &c. 34. 25
πλησιάζειν γυναικὶ, 40. 8, 27
πλύνειν = λοιδορεῖν, 39. 11
πλώϊμος, 56. 23, 40
ποῖος after τίς, 39. 9
πολὺς, 'vehement,' 40. 53
πομπεῖον, τὰ πομπεῖα, 34. 39
πρεσβεῖον, 39. 29
προαιρεῖσθαι, 56. 1
προεισφορὰ, 37. 37; 39. 8
προΐεσθαι χρήματα, 56. 2, 50
προῖκα ἐπενέγκασθαι, 40 *Arg.*
—— ἐπιδοῦναι, 40. 4, 6, 56
προκαλεῖσθαί τινά τι, 39 *Arg.*
προξενεῖν τινα, 37. 11
πρὸς = προσέτι, 37. 49; 39. 23
πρός τινα, κατά τινος, 56 *Arg.*
πρός τινος, 39. 41
πρὸς ὀργὴν ἐλθεῖν τινι, 39. 23
προσεδρεύειν, 34. 26
προσκαλεῖσθαί τινά τινος, 40. 32
προσπαραγράφειν, 39. 9
προσφέρεσθαι πρός τινα, 40. 40
πρυτανεῖα ἀνελέσθαι, 37. 41

P.

Relative, attraction of, 34 *Arg.*
ῥῶπος, 34. 9

Σ.

σημεῖα λιμένος, 35. 28
Shilleto, quoted, 34. 6
Σικελικὸς κατάπλους, 56. 9
Sophists, held in contempt, 35. 39
στατῆρες Κυζικηνοί, 34. 23; 35. 36
—— Φωκαεῖς, 40. 36
στοὰ μακρὰ, 34. 37
στρατηγοί, respect for sons of, 34. 50; 40. 25
subjunctives, always future, 35. 24
συγγραφαί, spurious documents in Dem., 35. 10
σῦλαι, 35. 13, 26
συμβαλεῖν συμβόλαια, 34. 1; 37. 49
συμβόλαιον, 34. 3; 56. 2
—— ἐμπορικὸν, 35. 43
σύμβολον, 39. 12
συμμορίαι, 39. 8
συμπλεῖν, 34. 26
σύμπτωμα, 56. 43
συνεστῶτες, οἱ, 37. 39, 48
συνευπορεῖν τι, 37. 49
συνιστάναι τιμὰς σίτου, 56. 7
συντετραίνειν, 37. 38
συντιμᾶν σῖτον, 56. 8
συσσημαίνεσθαι, 35. 15
σώματα, 34. 10
σωτηρία, salvage, 35. 13

T.

Ταμύναι, 39. 16
ταξιαρχεῖν, 39. 17; 40. 34
τάριχος, 35. 31
τέθεικα, 34 *Arg.*
τεθεῖσθαι, κεῖσθαι, 34. 16; 39 *Arg.* l. 23
τεκταίνεσθαι, 34. 48
τεσσαράκοντα, οἱ, 37. 33
τετελεύτηκεν, moritur, mortuus est, 39 *Arg.* l. 18
τετυχηκὼς, τετευχὼς, 39. 25
τεχνάζεσθαι, 40. 54
τέχνην ποιεῖσθαι, 37. 52
τιμᾶν, τιμᾶσθαί τινί τινος, 37. 3
τιμὴ καθεστηκυῖα, 56. 10

τιμητός, ἀτίμητος ἀγών, 37. 40
τίμιος, ἄξιος, carus, vilis, 56. 8
τίς (ποῖος), 39. 26
τοιχωρυχεῖν, 35. 9
τόκος γιγνόμενος, 37. 5
— ἔγγειος, 37. 5
— ἔφεκτος, 34. 23
τριάκοντα, οἱ, 40. 32
τριήραρχον καθιστάναι, 39. 8
τυγχάνω ποιῶν &c., 40. 27
τύφειν, 37. 35

Υ.

ὕβρις, 37. 33
ὕθλος, 35. 25
ὑπαρχή, ἐξ ὑπαρχῆς, 40. 16
ὑπογράψαι, 37. 23
ὑπόδικοι μάρτυρες, 40. 54
ὑποθήκη ἑτέρα, 34. 6; 35. 21
—— penalty for withholding, 34. 7
ὑποστέλλεσθαι, 37. 48
ὑποστῆναι, 37. 57
ὑπωμοσία, 39. 37
Wayte, W., quoted, 34. 21, 50
Weil, H., quoted, 56. 14

Φ.

φάσις, φαίνειν, 39. 14
φενακίζειν, 56. 31
φέρειν τινά, 'to propose,' 39. 7

Φοίνικες, 34. 6
φοιτᾶν, φοιτηταί, 39. 24
φράτερας, ἐγγράφεσθαι εἰς, 39. 4
φυλαί, public schools of the, 39. 24
Φωκαεῖς στατῆρες, 40. 36
Φωρῶν λιμήν, 35. 28

Χ.

χαλκίον, 39. 8
χαλκοῦν, 56. 1
χίλιαι δραχμαί, 39. 13
χόες, feast of the, 39. 16
χορεύειν Διονύσια, 39. 16
χορηγός, 40. 31
χρηματιστής, 39. 25
χρῆσθαι, familiariter uti, 35. 6
— τινί τι, οὐδὲν, &c., 35. 17

Ψ.

ψέγειν, μέμφεσθαι, 40. 49
ψευδομαρτυριῶν, 39, 18

Ω.

ᾠδεῖον, 34. 37
ὠνεῖσθαι μέταλλα, 37. 5; 40. 52
ὥρα, ὡραία, 56. 3, 30
ὡς ἄν, with opt. suppressed, 34. 32

UNIVERSITY PRESS, CAMBRIDGE.
July, 1890.

PUBLICATIONS OF

The Cambridge University Press.

THE HOLY SCRIPTURES, &c.

The Cambridge Paragraph Bible of the Authorized English Version, with the Text revised by a Collation of its Early and other Principal Editions, the Use of the Italic Type made uniform, the Marginal References remodelled, and a Critical Introduction, by F. H. A. SCRIVENER, M.A., LL.D. Crown 4to., cloth gilt, 21s.

THE STUDENT'S EDITION of the above, on *good writing paper*, with one column of print and wide margin to each page for MS. notes. Two Vols. Crown 4to., cloth, gilt, 31s. 6d.

The Lectionary Bible, with Apocrypha, divided into Sections adapted to the Calendar and Tables of Lessons of 1871. Cr. 8vo. 3s. 6d.

The Old Testament in Greek according to the Septuagint. Edited by the Rev. Professor H. B. SWETE, D.D. Vol. I. Genesis—IV Kings. Crown 8vo. 7s. 6d. Vol. II. By the same Editor. [*In the Press*.

The Book of Psalms in Greek according to the Septuagint. Being a portion of Vol. II. of above. Crown 8vo. 2s. 6d.

The Book of Ecclesiastes. Large Paper Edition. By the Very Rev. E. H. PLUMPTRE, Dean of Wells. Demy 8vo. 7s. 6d.

Breviarium ad usum insignis Ecclesiae Sarum. Juxta Editionem maximam pro CLAUDIO CHEVALLON et FRANCISCO REGNAULT A.D. MDXXXI. in Alma Parisiorum Academia impressam : labore ac studio FRANCISCI PROCTER, A.M., et CHRISTOPHORI WORDSWORTH, A.M.

FASCICULUS I. In quo continentur KALENDARIUM, et ORDO TEMPORALIS sive PROPRIUM DE TEMPORE TOTIUS ANNI, una cum ordinali suo quod usitato vocabulo dicitur PICA SIVE DIRECTORIUM SACERDOTUM. Demy 8vo. 18s.

FASCICULUS II. In quo continentur PSALTERIUM, cum ordinario Officii totius hebdomadae juxta Horas Canonicas, et proprio Completorii, LITANIA, COMMUNE SANCTORUM, ORDINARIUM MISSAE CUM CANONE ET XIII MISSIS, &c. &c. Demy 8vo. 12s.

FASCICULUS III. In quo continetur PROPRIUM SANCTORUM quod et Sanctorale dicitur, una cum Accentuario. Demy 8vo. 15s.

FASCICULI I. II. III. complete £2. 2s.

Breviarium Romanum a FRANCISCO CARDINALI QUIGNONIO editum et recognitum iuxta editionem Venetiis A.D. 1535 impressam curante JOHANNE WICKHAM LEGG. Demy 8vo. 12s.

The Pointed Prayer Book, being the Book of Common Prayer with the Psalter or Psalms of David, pointed as they are to be sung or said in Churches. Royal 24mo, cloth, 1s. 6d.

The same in square 32mo. cloth, 6d.

The Cambridge Psalter, for the use of Choirs and Organists. Specially adapted for Congregations in which the "Cambridge Pointed Prayer Book" is used. Demy 8vo. cloth, 3s. 6d. Cloth limp cut flush, 2s. 6d.

The Paragraph Psalter, arranged for the use of Choirs by the Right Rev. B. F. WESTCOTT, D.D., Lord Bp. of Durham. Fcp. 4to. 5s.

The same in royal 32mo. Cloth, 1s. Leather, 1s. 6d.

London: Cambridge Warehouse, Ave Maria Lane.

The Authorised Edition of the English Bible (1611), its Subsequent Reprints and Modern Representatives. By F. H. A. SCRIVENER, M.A., D.C.L., LL.D. Crown 8vo. 7s. 6d.

The New Testament in the Original Greek, according to the Text followed in the Authorised Version, together with the Variations adopted in the Revised Version. Edited by F. H. A. SCRIVENER, M.A., D.C.L., LL.D. Small Crown 8vo. 6s.

The Parallel New Testament Greek and English. The New Testament, being the Authorised Version set forth in 1611 Arranged in Parallel Columns with the Revised Version of 1881, and with the original Greek, as edited by F. H. A. SCRIVENER, M.A., D.C.L., LL.D. Crown 8vo. 12s. 6d. (*The Revised Version is the joint Property of the Universities of Cambridge and Oxford.*)

Greek and English Testament, in parallel columns on the same page. Edited by J. SCHOLEFIELD, M.A. *New Edition, with the marginal references as arranged and revised by* DR SCRIVENER. 7s. 6d.

Greek and English Testament. THE STUDENT'S EDITION of the above on *large writing paper.* 4to. 12s.

Greek Testament, ex editione Stephani tertia, 1550. Sm. 8vo. 3s. 6d.

The Four Gospels in Anglo-Saxon and Northumbrian Versions. By Rev. Prof. SKEAT, Litt.D. One Volume. Demy Quarto. 30s. Each Gospel separately. 10s.

The Missing Fragment of the Latin Translation of the Fourth Book of Ezra, discovered and edited with Introduction, Notes, and facsimile of the MS., by Prof. BENSLY, M.A. Demy 4to. 10s.

The Harklean Version of the Epistle to the Hebrews, Chap. XI. 28—XIII. 25. Now edited for the first time with Introduction and Notes on this version of the Epistle. By ROBERT L. BENSLY. Demy 8vo. 5s.

Codex S. Ceaddae Latinus. Evangelia SSS. Matthaei, Marci, Lucae ad cap. III. 9 complectens, circa septimum vel octavum saeculum scriptvs, in Ecclesia Cathedrali Lichfieldiensi servatus. Cum codice versionis Vulgatae Amiatino contulit, prolegomena conscripsit, F. H. A. SCRIVENER, A.M., LL.D. Imp. 4to. £1. 1s.

The Origin of the Leicester Codex of the New Testament. By J. R. HARRIS, M.A. With 3 plates. Demy 4to. 10s. 6d.

Notitia Codicis Quattuor Evangeliorum Græci membranacei viris doctis hucusque incogniti quem in museo suo asservat Eduardus Reuss Argentoratensis. 2s.

THEOLOGY—(ANCIENT).

Theodore of Mopsuestia's Commentary on the Minor Epistles of S. Paul. The Latin Version with the Greek Fragments, edited from the MSS. with Notes and an Introduction, by H. B. SWETE, D.D. Vol. I., containing the Introduction, and the Commentary upon Galatians—Colossians. Demy Octavo. 12s.

Volume II., containing the Commentary on 1 Thessalonians—Philemon, Appendices and Indices. 12s.

London: Cambridge Warehouse, Ave Maria Lane.

The Greek Liturgies. Chiefly from original Authorities. By C. A. SWAINSON, D.D., late Master of Christ's College. Cr. 4to. 15*s*.

Sayings of the Jewish Fathers, comprising Pirqe Aboth and Pereq R. Meir in Hebrew and English, with Critical Notes. By C. TAYLOR, D.D., Master of St John's College. 10*s*.

Sancti Irenæi Episcopi Lugdunensis libros quinque adversus Hæreses, edidit W. WIGAN HARVEY, S.T.B. Collegii Regalis olim Socius. 2 Vols. Demy Octavo. 18*s*.

The Palestinian Mishna. By W. H. LOWE, M.A. Royal 8vo. 21*s*.

M. Minucii Felicis Octavius. The text newly revised from the original MS. with an English Commentary, Analysis, Introduction, and Copious Indices. By H. A. HOLDEN, LL.D. Cr. 8vo. 7*s*. 6*d*.

Theophili Episcopi Antiochensis Libri Tres ad Autolycum. Edidit Prolegomenis Versione Notulis Indicibus instruxit GULIELMUS GILSON HUMPHRY, S.T.B. Post Octavo. 5*s*.

Theophylacti in Evangelium S. Matthæi Commentarius. Edited by W. G. HUMPHRY, B.D. Demy Octavo. 7*s*. 6*d*.

Tertullianus de Corona Militis, de Spectaculis, de Idololatria with Analysis and English Notes, by G. CURREY. D.D. Crown 8vo. 5*s*.

Fragments of Philo and Josephus. Newly edited by J. RENDEL HARRIS, M.A. With two Facsimiles. Demy 4to. 12*s*. 6*d*.

The Teaching of the Apostles. Newly edited, with Facsimile Text and Commentary, by J. R. HARRIS, M.A. Demy 4to. 21*s*.

The Rest of the Words of Baruch: A Christian Apocalypse of the year 136 A.D. The Text revised with an Introduction by J. RENDEL HARRIS, M.A. Royal 8vo. 5*s*.

The Acts of the Martyrdom of Perpetua and Felicitas; the original Greek Text now first edited from a MS. in the Library of the Convent of the Holy Sepulchre at Jerusalem, by J. RENDEL HARRIS and SETH K. GIFFORD. Royal 8vo. 5*s*.

THEOLOGY—(ENGLISH).

Works of Isaac Barrow, compared with the original MSS. A new Edition, by A. NAPIER, M.A. 9 Vols. Demy 8vo. £3. 3*s*.

Treatise of the Pope's Supremacy, and a Discourse concerning the Unity of the Church, by I. BARROW. Demy 8vo. 7*s*. 6*d*.

Pearson's Exposition of the Creed, edited by TEMPLE CHEVALLIER, B.D. 3rd Edition revised by R. SINKER, D.D. Demy 8vo. 12*s*.

An Analysis of the Exposition of the Creed, written by the Right Rev. Father in God, JOHN PEARSON, D.D. Compiled by W. H. MILL, D.D. Demy Octavo. 5*s*.

Wheatly on the Common Prayer, edited by G. E. CORRIE, D.D. late Master of Jesus College. Demy Octavo. 7*s*. 6*d*.

The Homilies, with Various Readings, and the Quotations from the Fathers given at length in the Original Languages. Edited by G. E. CORRIE, D.D. late Master of Jesus College. Demy 8vo. 7*s*. 6*d*.

Two Forms of Prayer of the time of Queen Elizabeth. Now First Reprinted. Demy Octavo. 6*d*.

Select Discourses, by JOHN SMITH, late Fellow of Queens' College, Cambridge. Edited by H. G. WILLIAMS, B.D. late Professor of Arabic. Royal Octavo. 7*s*. 6*d*.

London: Cambridge Warehouse, Ave Maria Lane.

De Obligatione Conscientiæ Prælectiones decem Oxonii in Schola Theologica habitæ a ROBERTO SANDERSON, SS. Theologiæ ibidem Professor Regio. With English Notes, including an abridged Translation, by W. WHEWELL, D.D. Demy 8vo. 7s. 6d.

Cæsar Morgan's Investigation of the Trinity of Plato, and of Philo Judæus. 2nd Ed., revised by H. A. HOLDEN, LL.D. Cr. 8vo. 4s.

Archbishop Usher's Answer to a Jesuit, with other Tracts on Popery. Edited by J. SCHOLEFIELD, M.A. Demy 8vo. 7s. 6d.

Wilson's Illustration of the Method of explaining the New Testament, by the early opinions of Jews and Christians concerning Christ Edited by T. TURTON, D.D. Demy 8vo. 5s.

Lectures on Divinity delivered in the University of Cambridge. By JOHN HEY, D.D. Third Edition, by T. TURTON, D.D. late Lord Bishop of Ely. 2 vols. Demy Octavo. 15s.

S. Austin and his place in the History of Christian Thought. Being the Hulsean Lectures for 1885. By W. CUNNINGHAM, D.D. Demy 8vo. Buckram, 12s. 6d.

Christ the Life of Men. Being the Hulsean Lectures for 1888. By Rev. H. M. STEPHENSON, M.A. Crown 8vo. 2s. 6d.

The Gospel History of our Lord Jesus Christ in the Language of the Revised Version, arranged in a Connected Narrative, especially for the use of Teachers and Preachers. By Rev. C. C. JAMES, M.A. Crown 8vo. 3s. 6d.

GREEK AND LATIN CLASSICS, &c.

(See also pp. 15—17.)

Sophocles: the Plays and Fragments. With Critical Notes, Commentary, and Translation in English Prose, by R. C. JEBB, Litt. D., LL.D., Regius Professor of Greek in the University of Cambridge.

Part I. Oedipus Tyrannus. Demy 8vo. *Second Edit.* 12s. 6d.
Part II. Oedipus Coloneus. Demy 8vo. *Second Edit.* 12s. 6d.
Part III. Antigone. Demy 8vo. 12s. 6d. *Second Edit.* [*In the Press.*
Part IV. Philoctetes. [*In the Press.*

Select Private Orations of Demosthenes with Introductions and English Notes, by F. A. PALEY, M.A., & J. E. SANDYS, Litt.D.

Part I. Contra Phormionem, Lacritum, Pantaenetum, Boeotum de Nomine, de Dote, Dionysodorum. Cr. 8vo. *New Edition.* 6s.

Part II. Pro Phormione, Contra Stephanum I. II.; Nicostratum, Cononem, Calliclem. Crown 8vo. *New Edition.* 7s. 6d.

Demosthenes, Speech of, against the Law of Leptines. With Introduction and Critical and Explanatory Notes, by J. E. SANDYS, Litt.D. Demy 8vo. 9s.

Demosthenes against Androtion and against Timocrates, with Introductions and English Commentary by WILLIAM WAYTE, M.A. Crown 8vo. 7s. 6d.

The Bacchae of Euripides, with Introduction, Critical Notes, and Archæological Illustrations, by J. E. SANDYS, Litt.D. New Edition, with additional Illustrations. Crown 8vo. 12s. 6d.

London: Cambridge Warehouse, Ave Maria Lane.

An Introduction to Greek Epigraphy. Part I. The Archaic Inscriptions and the Greek Alphabet. By E. S. ROBERTS, M.A., Fellow and Tutor of Gonville and Caius College. Demy 8vo. 18s.

Aeschyli Fabulae.—ΙΚΕΤΙΔΕΣ ΧΟΗΦΟΡΟΙ in libro Mediceo mendose scriptae ex vv. dd. coniecturis emendatius editae cum Scholiis Graecis et brevi adnotatione critica, curante F. A. PALEY, M.A., LL.D. Demy 8vo. 7s. 6d.

The Agamemnon of Aeschylus. With a translation in English Rhythm, and Notes Critical and Explanatory. **New Edition, Revised.** By the late B. H. KENNEDY, D.D. Crown 8vo. 6s.

The Theætetus of Plato, with a Translation and Notes by the same Editor. Crown 8vo. 7s. 6d.

P. Vergili Maronis Opera, cum Prolegomenis et Commentario Critico pro Syndicis Preli Academici edidit BENJAMIN HALL KENNEDY, S.T.P. Extra fcp. 8vo. 3s. 6d.

Essays on the Art of Pheidias. By C. WALDSTEIN, Litt.D., Phil.D. Royal 8vo. With Illustrations. Buckram, 30s.

M. Tulli Ciceronis ad M. Brutum Orator. A Revised Text. Edited with Introductory Essays and Critical and Explanatory Notes, by J. E. SANDYS, Litt.D. Demy 8vo. 16s.

M. Tulli Ciceronis pro C. Rabirio [Perduellionis Reo] Oratio ad Quirites. With Notes, Introduction and Appendices. By W. E. HEITLAND, M.A. Demy 8vo. 7s. 6d.

M. T. Ciceronis de Natura Deorum Libri Tres, with Introduction and Commentary by JOSEPH B. MAYOR, M.A. Demy 8vo. Vol. I. 10s. 6d. Vol. II. 12s. 6d. Vol. III. 10s.

M. T. Ciceronis de Officiis Libri Tres with Marginal Analysis, an English Commentary, and Indices. New Edition, revised, by H. A. HOLDEN, LL.D., Crown 8vo. 9s.

M. T. Ciceronis de Officiis Libri Tertius, with Introduction, Analysis and Commentary by H. A. HOLDEN, LL.D. Cr. 8vo. 2s.

M. T. Ciceronis de Finibus Bonorum libri Quinque. The Text revised and explained by J. S. REID, Litt.D. [*In the Press.*]
Vol. III., containing the Translation. Demy 8vo. 8s.

Plato's Phædo, literally translated, by the late E. M. COPE, Fellow of Trinity College, Cambridge. Demy Octavo. 5s.

Aristotle. The Rhetoric. With a Commentary by the late E. M. COPE, Fellow of Trinity College, Cambridge, revised and edited by J. E. SANDYS, Litt.D. 3 Vols. Demy 8vo. 21s.

Aristotle.—ΠΕΡΙ ΨΥΧΗΣ. Aristotle's Psychology, in Greek and English, with Introduction and Notes, by EDWIN WALLACE, M.A., late Fellow of Worcester College, Oxford. Demy 8vo. 18s.

ΠΕΡΙ ΔΙΚΑΙΟΣΥΝΗΣ. The Fifth Book of the Nicomachean Ethics of Aristotle. Edited by H. JACKSON, Litt.D. Demy 8vo. 6s.

London: Cambridge Warehouse, Ave Maria Lane.

Pindar. Olympian and Pythian Odes. With Notes Explanatory and Critical, Introductions and Introductory Essays. Edited by C. A. M. FENNELL, Litt.D. Crown 8vo. 9s.

— **The Isthmian and Nemean Odes** by the same Editor. 9s.

The Types of Greek Coins. By PERCY GARDNER, Litt.D., F.S.A. With 16 plates. Impl. 4to. Cloth £1. 11s. 6d. Roxburgh (Morocco back) £2. 2s.

SANSKRIT, ARABIC AND SYRIAC.

Lectures on the Comparative Grammar of the Semitic Languages from the Papers of the late WILLIAM WRIGHT, LL.D., Professor of Arabic in the University of Cambridge. Demy 8vo. 14s.

The Divyâvadâna, a Collection of Early Buddhist Legends, now first edited from the Nepalese Sanskrit MSS. in Cambridge and Paris. By E. B. COWELL, M.A. and R. A. NEIL, M.A. Demy 8vo. 18s.

Nalopakhyánam, or, The Tale of Nala; containing the Sanskrit Text in Roman Characters, with Vocabulary. By the late Rev. T. JARRETT, M.A. Demy 8vo. 10s.

Notes on the Tale of Nala, for the use of Classical Students, by J. PEILE, Litt.D., Master of Christ's College. Demy 8vo. 12s.

The History of Alexander the Great, being the Syriac version of the Pseudo-Callisthenes. Edited from Five Manuscripts, with an English Translation and Notes, by E. A. BUDGE, M.A. Demy 8vo. 25s.

The Poems of Beha ed din Zoheir of Egypt. With a Metrical Translation, Notes and Introduction, by the late E. H. PALMER, M.A. 2 vols. Crown Quarto.
    Vol. I. The ARABIC TEXT. Paper covers. 10s. 6d.
    Vol. II. ENGLISH TRANSLATION. Paper covers. 10s. 6d.

The Chronicle of Joshua the Stylite edited in Syriac, with an English translation and notes, by W. WRIGHT, LL.D. Demy 8vo. 10s. 6d.

Kalīlah and Dimnah, or, the Fables of Bidpai; with an English Translation of the later Syriac version, with Notes, by the late I. G. N. KEITH-FALCONER, M.A. Demy 8vo. 7s. 6d.

MATHEMATICS, PHYSICAL SCIENCE, &c.

Mathematical and Physical Papers. By Sir G. G. STOKES, Sc.D., LL.D. Reprinted from the Original Journals and Transactions, with additional Notes by the Author. Vol. I. Demy 8vo. 15s. Vol. II. 15s.
    [Vol. III. *In the Press.*

Mathematical and Physical Papers. By Sir W. THOMSON, LL.D., F.R.S. Collected from different Scientific Periodicals from May, 1841, to the present time. Vol. I. Demy 8vo. 18s. Vol. II. 15s. Vol. III. 18s.

The Collected Mathematical Papers of ARTHUR CAYLEY, Sc.D., F.R.S. Demy 4to. 10 vols.
    Vol. I. 25s. Vol. II. 25s.   [Vol. III. *Nearly ready.*

A History of the Study of Mathematics at Cambridge. By W. W. ROUSE BALL, M.A. Crown 8vo. 6s.

London: Cambridge Warehouse, Ave Maria Lane.

A History of the Theory of Elasticity and of the Strength of Materials, from Galilei to the present time. Vol. I. GALILEI TO SAINT-VENANT, 1639–1850. By the late I. TODHUNTER, Sc.D., edited and completed by Prof. KARL PEARSON, M.A. Demy 8vo. 25s.
Vol. II. By the same Editor. [*In the Press.*

The Elastical Researches of Barre de Saint-Venant (extract from Vol. II. of TODHUNTER's History of the Theory of Elasticity), edited by Professor KARL PEARSON, M.A. Demy 8vo. 9s.

Theory of Differential Equations. Part I. Exact Equations and Pfaff's Problem. By A. R. FORSYTH, Sc.D., F.R.S., Fellow of Trinity College, Cambridge. Demy 8vo. 12s.

A Treatise on the General Principles of Chemistry, by M. M. PATTISON MUIR, M.A. Second Edition. Demy 8vo. 15s.

Elementary Chemistry. By M. M. PATTISON MUIR, M.A., and CHARLES SLATER, M.A., M.B. Crown 8vo. 4s. 6d.

Practical Chemistry. A Course of Laboratory Work. By M. M. PATTISON MUIR, M.A., and D. J. CARNEGIE, M.A. Cr. 8vo. 3s.

A Treatise on Geometrical Optics. By R. S. HEATH, M.A. Demy 8vo. 12s. 6d.

An Elementary Treatise on Geometrical Optics. By R. S. HEATH, M.A. Crown 8vo. 5s.

A Treatise on Dynamics. By S. L. LONEY, M.A. Cr. 8vo. 7s. 6d.

A Treatise on Analytical Statics. By E. J. ROUTH, Sc.D., F.R.S. [*In the Press.*

Lectures on the Physiology of Plants, by S. H. VINES, Sc.D., Professor of Botany in the University of Oxford. Demy 8vo. 21s.

A Short History of Greek Mathematics. By J. GOW, Litt. D., Fellow of Trinity College. Demy 8vo. 10s. 6d.

Notes on Qualitative Analysis. Concise and Explanatory. By H. J. H. FENTON, M.A., F.C.S. New Edit. Crown 4to. 6s.

Diophantos of Alexandria; a Study in the History of Greek Algebra. By T. L. HEATH, M.A. Demy 8vo. 7s. 6d.

A Catalogue of the Portsmouth Collection of Books and Papers written by or belonging to SIR ISAAC NEWTON. Demy 8vo. 5s.

A Treatise on Natural Philosophy. By Prof. Sir W. THOMSON, LL.D., and P. G. TAIT, M.A. Part I. Demy 8vo. 16s. Part II. 18s.

Elements of Natural Philosophy. By Professors Sir W. THOMSON, and P. G. TAIT. *Second Edition.* Demy 8vo. 9s.

An Elementary Treatise on Quaternions. By P. G. TAIT, M.A. *Second Edition.* Demy 8vo. 14s.

A Treatise on the Theory of Determinants and their Applications in Analysis and Geometry. By R. F. SCOTT, M.A. Demy 8vo. 12s.

Counterpoint. A practical course of study. By the late Prof. Sir G. A. MACFARREN, Mus. D. 5th Edition, revised. Cr. 4to. 7s. 6d.

The Analytical Theory of Heat. By JOSEPH FOURIER. Translated with Notes, by A. FREEMAN, M.A. Demy 8vo. 12s.

London: Cambridge Warehouse, Ave Maria Lane.

The Scientific Papers of the late Prof. J. Clerk Maxwell. Edited by W. D. NIVEN, M.A. 2 vols. Royal 4to. £3. 3s. (net.)
The Electrical Researches of the Honourable Henry Cavendish, F.R.S. Written between 1771 and 1781. Edited by J. CLERK MAXWELL, F.R.S. Demy 8vo. 18s.
Practical Work at the Cavendish Laboratory. Heat. Edited by W. N. SHAW, M.A. Demy 8vo. 3s.
Hydrodynamics, a Treatise on the Mathematical Theory of Fluid Motion, by HORACE LAMB, M.A. Demy 8vo. 12s.
The Mathematical Works of Isaac Barrow, D.D. Edited by W. WHEWELL, D.D. Demy Octavo. 7s. 6d.
Illustrations of Comparative Anatomy, Vertebrate and Invertebrate. Second Edition. Demy 8vo. 2s. 6d.
A Catalogue of Australian Fossils. By R. ETHERIDGE, Jun., F.G.S. Demy 8vo. 10s. 6d.
The Fossils and Palæontological Affinities of the Neocomian Deposits of Upware and Brickhill, being the Sedgwick Prize Essay for 1879. By W. KEEPING, M.A. Demy 8vo. 10s. 6d.
The Bala Volcanic Series of Caernarvonshire and Associated Rocks, being the Sedgwick Prize Essay for 1888, by A. HARKER, M.A., F.R.S. Demy 8vo. 7s. 6d.
A Catalogue of Books and Papers on Protozoa, Coelenterates, Worms, etc. published during the years 1861-1883, by D'ARCY W. THOMPSON, M.A. Demy 8vo. 12s. 6d.
A Revised Account of the Experiments made with the Bashforth Chronograph, to find the resistance of the air to the motion of projectiles. By FRANCIS BASHFORTH, B.D. Demy 8vo. 12s.
An attempt to test the Theories of Capillary Action, by F. BASHFORTH, B.D., and J. C. ADAMS, M.A. Demy 4to. £1. 1s.
A Catalogue of the Collection of Cambrian and Silurian Fossils contained in the Geological Museum of the University of Cambridge, by J. W. SALTER, F.G.S. Royal Quarto. 7s. 6d.
Catalogue of Osteological Specimens contained in the Anatomical Museum of the University of Cambridge. Demy 8vo. 2s. 6d.
Astronomical Observations made at the Observatory of Cambridge from 1846 to 1860, by the late Rev. J. CHALLIS, M.A.
Astronomical Observations from 1861 to 1865. Vol. XXI. Royal 4to., 15s. From 1866 to 1869. Vol. XXII. 15s.

LAW.

Elements of the Law of Torts. A Text-book for Students. By MELVILLE M. BIGELOW, Ph.D. Crown 8vo. 10s. 6d.
A Selection of Cases on the English Law of Contract. By GERARD BROWN FINCH, M.A. Royal 8vo. 28s.
Bracton's Note Book. A Collection of Cases decided in the King's Courts during the Reign of Henry the Third, annotated by a Lawyer of that time, seemingly by Henry of Bratton. Edited by F. W. MAITLAND. 3 vols. Demy 8vo. £3. 3s. (net.)
Tables shewing the Differences between English and Indian Law. By Sir ROLAND KNYVET WILSON, Bart., M.A., LL.M. Demy 4to. 1s.

London: Cambridge Warehouse, Ave Maria Lane.

The Influence of the Roman Law on the Law of England.
Being the Yorke Prize Essay for the year 1884. By T. E. SCRUTTON, M.A. Demy 8vo. 10s. 6d.

Land in Fetters. Being the Yorke Prize Essay for 1885. By T. E. SCRUTTON, M.A. Demy 8vo. 7s. 6d.

Commons and Common Fields, or the History and Policy of the Laws of Commons and Enclosures in England. Being the Yorke Prize Essay for 1886. By T. E. SCRUTTON, M.A. Demy 8vo. 10s. 6d.

History of the Law of Tithes in England. Being the Yorke Prize Essay for 1887. By W. EASTERBY, B.A., LL.B. Demy 8vo. 7s. 6d.

History of Land Tenure in Ireland. Being the Yorke Prize Essay for 1888. By W. E. MONTGOMERY, M.A., LL.M. Demy 8vo. 10s. 6d.

History of Equity as administered in the Court of Chancery. Being the Yorke Prize Essay for 1889. By D. M^cKENZIE KERLY, M.A., St John's College. [*Nearly ready.*

An Introduction to the Study of Justinian's Digest. By HENRY JOHN ROBY. Demy 8vo. 9s.

Justinian's Digest. Lib. VII., Tit. I. De Usufructu, with a Legal and Philological Commentary by H. J. ROBY. Demy 8vo. 9s.
The Two Parts complete in One Volume. Demy 8vo. 18s.

A Selection of the State Trials. By J. W. WILLIS-BUND, M.A., LL.B. Crown 8vo. Vols. I. and II. In 3 parts. 30s.

The Institutes of Justinian, translated with Notes by J. T. ABDY, LL.D., and BRYAN WALKER, M.A., LL.D. Cr. 8vo. 16s.

Practical Jurisprudence. A comment on AUSTIN. By E. C. CLARK, LL.D., Regius Professor of Civil Law. Crown 8vo. 9s.

An Analysis of Criminal Liability. By the same. Cr. 8vo. 7s. 6d.

The Fragments of the Perpetual Edict of Salvius Julianus, Arranged, and Annotated by the late BRYAN WALKER, LL.D. Cr. 8vo. 6s.

The Commentaries of Gaius and Rules of Ulpian. Translated and Annotated, by J. T. ABDY, LL.D., and BRYAN WALKER, M.A., LL.D. New Edition by Bryan Walker. Crown 8vo. 16s.

Grotius de Jure Belli et Pacis, with the Notes of Barbeyrac and others; an abridged Translation of the Text, by W. WHEWELL, D.D. Demy 8vo. 12s. The translation separate, 6s.

Selected Titles from the Digest, by BRYAN WALKER, M.A., LL.D.
Part I. Mandati vel Contra. Digest XVII. 1. Cr. 8vo. 5s.

Part II. De Adquirendo rerum dominio, and De Adquirenda vel amittenda Possessione, Digest XLI. 1 and 2. Crown 8vo. 6s.

Part III. De Condictionibus, Digest XII. 1 and 4—7 and Digest XIII. 1—3. Crown 8vo. 6s.

HISTORICAL WORKS.

The Life and Letters of the Reverend Adam Sedgwick, LL.D., F.R.S. (Dedicated, by special permission, to Her Majesty the Queen.) By JOHN WILLIS CLARK, M.A., F.S.A., and THOMAS M^cKENNY HUGHES, M.A. 2 vols. Demy 8vo. 36s.

The Growth of English Industry and Commerce during the Early and Middle Ages. By W. CUNNINGHAM, D.D. Demy 8vo. 16s.

London: Cambridge Warehouse, Ave Maria Lane.

The Architectural History of the University of Cambridge and of the Colleges of Cambridge and Eton, by the late Professor WILLIS, M.A., F.R.S. Edited with large Additions and a Continuation to the present time by J. W. CLARK, M.A. 4 Vols. Super Royal 8vo. £6. 6s.

Also a limited Edition of the same, consisting of 120 numbered Copies only, large paper Quarto; the woodcuts and steel engravings mounted on India paper; of which 100 copies are now offered for sale, at Twenty-five Guineas **net** each set.

The University of Cambridge from the Earliest Times to the Royal Injunctions of 1535. By J. B. MULLINGER, M.A. Demy 8vo. 12s.

—— Part II. From the Royal Injunctions of 1535 to the Accession of Charles the First. Demy 8vo. 18s.

History of the College of St John the Evangelist, by THOMAS BAKER, B.D., Ejected Fellow. Edited by JOHN E. B. MAYOR, M.A., Fellow of St John's. Two Vols. Demy 8vo. 24s.

Scholae Academicae: some Account of the Studies at the English Universities in the Eighteenth Century. By CHRISTOPHER WORDSWORTH, M.A. Demy 8vo. 10s. 6d.

Life and Times of Stein, or Germany and Prussia in the Napoleonic Age, by J. R. SEELEY, M.A. Portraits and Maps. 3 vols. Demy 8vo. 30s.

The Constitution of Canada. By J. E. C. MUNRO, LL.M. Demy 8vo. 10s.

Studies in the Literary Relations of England with Germany in the Sixteenth Century. By C. H. HERFORD, M.A. Crown 8vo. 9s.

Chronological Tables of Greek History. By CARL PETER. Translated from the German by G. CHAWNER, M.A. Demy 4to. 10s.

Travels in Arabia Deserta in 1876 and 1877. By CHARLES M. DOUGHTY. With Illustrations. Demy 8vo. 2 vols. £3. 3s.

History of Nepāl, edited with an introductory sketch of the Country and People by Dr D. WRIGHT. Super-royal 8vo. 10s. 6d.

A Journey of Literary and Archæological Research in Nepal and Northern India, 1884—5. By C. BENDALL, M.A. Demy 8vo. 10s.

Cambridge Historical Essays.

Political Parties in Athens during the Peloponnesian War, by L. WHIBLEY, M.A. (Prince Consort Dissertation, 1888.) Second Edition. Crown 8vo. 2s. 6d.

Pope Gregory the Great and his relations with Gaul, by F. W. KELLETT, M.A. (Prince Consort Dissertation, 1888.) Crown 8vo. 2s. 6d.

The Constitutional Experiments of the Commonwealth, being the Thirlwall Prize Essay for 1889, by E. JENKS, B.A., LL.B. Cr. 8vo. 2s. 6d.

On Election by Lot at Athens, by J. W. HEADLAM, B.A. (Prince Consort Dissertation, 1890.) Crown 8vo. [*In the Press.*

MISCELLANEOUS.

The Literary remains of Albrecht Dürer, by W. M. CONWAY. With Transcripts from the British Museum Manuscripts, and Notes upon them by LINA ECKENSTEIN. Royal 8vo. 21s.

The Collected Papers of Henry Bradshaw, including his Memoranda and Communications read before the Cambridge Antiquarian Society. *With* 13 *facsimiles.* Edited by F. J. H. JENKINSON, M.A. Demy 8vo. 16s.

London: Cambridge Warehouse, Ave Maria Lane.

Memorials of the Life of George Elwes Corrie, D.D. formerly Master of Jesus College. By M. HOLROYD. Demy 8vo. 12s.

The Latin Heptateuch. Published piecemeal by the French printer WILLIAM MOREL (1560) and the French Benedictines E. MARTÈNE (1733) and J. B. PITRA (1852—88). Critically reviewed by JOHN E. B. MAYOR, M.A. Demy 8vo. 10s. 6d.

Kinship and Marriage in early Arabia, by W. ROBERTSON SMITH, M.A., LL.D. Crown 8vo. 7s. 6d.

Chapters on English Metre. By Rev. JOSEPH B. MAYOR, M.A. Demy 8vo. 7s. 6d.

A Catalogue of Ancient Marbles in Great Britain, by Prof. ADOLF MICHAELIS. Translated by C. A. M. FENNELL, Litt.D. Royal 8vo. Roxburgh (Morocco back). £2. 2s.

From Shakespeare to Pope. An Inquiry into the causes and phenomena of the Rise of Classical Poetry in England. By E. GOSSE, M.A. Crown 8vo. 6s.

The Literature of the French Renaissance. An Introductory Essay. By A. A. TILLEY, M.A. Crown 8vo. 6s.

A Latin-English Dictionary. Printed from the (Incomplete) MS. of the late T. H. KEY, M.A., F.R.S. Demy 4to. £1. 11s. 6d.

Ecclesiae Londino-Batavae archivum. TOMVS PRIMVS. ABRAHAMI ORTELII et virorum eruditorum ad eundem et ad JACOBVM COLIVM ORTELIANVM Epistulae,(1524—1628). TOMVS SECVNDVS. EPISTVLAE ET TRACTATVS cum Reformationis tum Ecclesiae Londino-Batavae Historiam Illustrantes 1544—1622. Ex autographis mandante Ecclesia Londino-Batava edidit JOANNES HENRICVS HESSELS. Demy 4to. Each vol., separately, £3. 10s. Taken together £5. 5s. *Net.*

An Eighth Century Latin-Anglo-Saxon Glossary preserved in the Library of Corpus Christi College, Cambridge, edited by J. H. HESSELS. Demy 8vo. 10s.

Contributions to the Textual Criticism of the Divina Commedia. Including the complete collation throughout the *Inferno* of all the MSS. at Oxford and Cambridge. By the Rev. E. MOORE, D.D. Demy 8vo. 21s.

The Despatches of Earl Gower, English Ambassador at the court of Versailles, June 1790 to August 1792, and the Despatches of Mr Lindsay and Mr Monro. By O. BROWNING, M.A. Demy 8vo. 15s.

Rhodes in Ancient Times. By CECIL TORR, M.A. With six plates. 10s. 6d.

Rhodes in Modern Times. By the same Author. With three plates. Demy 8vo. 8s.

The Woodcutters of the Netherlands during the last quarter of the Fifteenth Century. By W. M. CONWAY. Demy 8vo. 10s. 6d.

Lectures on the Growth and Training of the Mental Faculty, delivered in the University of Cambridge. By FRANCIS WARNER, M.D., F.R.C.P. Crown 8vo. 4s. 6d.

Lectures on Teaching, delivered in the University of Cambridge. By J. G. FITCH, M.A., LL.D. Cr. 8vo. 5s.

Lectures on Language and Linguistic Method in the School. By S. S. LAURIE, M.A., LL.D. Crown 8vo. 4s.

Occasional Addresses on Educational Subjects. By S. S. LAURIE, M.A., F.R.S.E. Crown 8vo. 5s.

London: Cambridge Warehouse, Ave Maria Lane.

A Manual of Cursive Shorthand, by H. L. CALLENDAR, M.A. Extra Fcap. 8vo. 2s.

A System of Phonetic Spelling, adapted to English by H. L. CALLENDAR, M.A. Extra Fcap. 8vo. 6d.

A Primer of Cursive Shorthand. By H. L. CALLENDAR, M.A. 6d.

Reading Practice in Cursive Shorthand. Easy extracts for Beginners. St Mark, Pt. I. Vicar of Wakefield, Chaps. I.—IV. Alice in Wonderland, Chap. VII. Price 3d. each.

Essays from the Spectator in Cursive Shorthand, by H. L. CALLENDAR, M.A. 6d.

Gray and his Friends. Letters and Relics in great part hitherto unpublished. Edited by the Rev. D. C. TOVEY, M.A. Crown 8vo. 6s.

A Grammar of the Irish Language. By Prof. WINDISCH. Translated by Dr NORMAN MOORE. Crown 8vo. 7s. 6d.

A Catalogue of the Collection of Birds formed by the late Hugh EDWIN STRICKLAND, now in the possession of the University of Cambridge. By O. SALVIN, M.A., F.R.S. £1. 1s.

Admissions to Gonville and Caius College in the University of Cambridge March 1558—9 to Jan. 1678—9. Edited by J. VENN, Sc.D., and S. C. VENN. Demy 8vo. 10s.

A Catalogue of the Hebrew Manuscripts preserved in the University Library, Cambridge. By the late Dr SCHILLER-SZINESSY. 9s.

Catalogue of the Buddhist Sanskrit Manuscripts in the University Library, Cambridge. Edited by C. BENDALL, M.A. 12s.

A Catalogue of the Manuscripts preserved in the Library of the University of Cambridge. Demy 8vo. 5 Vols. 10s. each.

Index to the Catalogue. Demy 8vo. 10s.

A Catalogue of Adversaria and printed books containing MS. notes, in the Library of the University of Cambridge. 3s. 6d.

The Illuminated Manuscripts in the Library of the Fitzwilliam Museum, Cambridge, by W. G. SEARLE, M.A. 7s. 6d.

A Chronological List of the Graces, etc. in the University Registry which concern the University Library. 2s. 6d.

Catalogus Bibliothecæ Burckhardtianæ. Demy Quarto. 5s.

Graduati Cantabrigienses: sive catalogus exhibens nomina eorum quos gradu quocunque ornavit Academia Cantabrigiensis (1800—1884). Cura H. R. LUARD, S. T. P. Demy 8vo. 12s. 6d.

Statutes for the University of Cambridge and for the Colleges therein, made, published and approved (1878—1882) under the Universities of Oxford and Cambridge Act, 1877. Demy 8vo. 16s.

Statutes of the University of Cambridge. 3s. 6d.

Ordinances of the University of Cambridge. 7s. 6d.

Trusts, Statutes and Directions affecting (1) The Professorships of the University. (2) The Scholarships and Prizes. (3) Other Gifts and Endowments. Demy 8vo. 5s.

A Compendium of University Regulations. Demy 8vo. 6d.

London: Cambridge Warehouse, Ave Maria Lane.

The Cambridge Bible for Schools and Colleges.

GENERAL EDITOR: J. J. S. PEROWNE, D.D., DEAN OF PETERBOROUGH.

"It is difficult to commend too highly this excellent series."—*Guardian*.

Now Ready. Cloth, Extra Fcap. 8vo. With Maps.

Book of Joshua. By Rev. G. F. MACLEAR, D.D. 2s. 6d.
Book of Judges. By Rev. J. J. LIAS, M.A. 3s. 6d.
First Book of Samuel. By Rev. Prof. KIRKPATRICK, B.D. 3s. 6d.
Second Book of Samuel. By Rev. Prof. KIRKPATRICK, B.D. 3s. 6d.
First Book of Kings. By Rev. Prof. LUMBY, D.D. 3s. 6d.
Second Book of Kings. By Rev. Prof. LUMBY, D.D. 3s. 6d.
Book of Job. By Rev. A. B. DAVIDSON, D.D. 5s.
Book of Ecclesiastes. By Very Rev. E. H. PLUMPTRE, D.D. 5s.
Book of Jeremiah. By Rev. A. W. STREANE, M.A. 4s. 6d.
Book of Hosea. By Rev. T. K. CHEYNE, M.A., D.D. 3s.
Books of Obadiah and Jonah. By Arch. PEROWNE. 2s. 6d.
Book of Micah. By Rev. T. K. CHEYNE, M.A., D.D. 1s. 6d.
Books of Haggai, Zechariah & Malachi. By Arch. PEROWNE. 3s. 6d.
Book of Malachi. By Archdeacon PEROWNE. 1s.
Gospel according to St Matthew. By Rev. A. CARR, M.A. 2s. 6d.
Gospel according to St Mark. By Rev. G. F. MACLEAR, D.D. 2s. 6d.
Gospel according to St Luke. By Archdeacon FARRAR. 4s. 6d.
Gospel according to St John. By Rev. A. PLUMMER, D.D. 4s. 6d.
Acts of the Apostles. By Prof. LUMBY, D.D. 4s. 6d.
Epistle to the Romans. Rev. H. C. G. MOULE, M.A. 3s. 6d.
First Corinthians. By Rev. J. J. LIAS, M.A. 2s.
Second Corinthians. By Rev. J. J. LIAS, M.A. 2s.
Epistle to the Ephesians. Rev. H. C. G. MOULE, M.A. 2s. 6d.
Epistle to the Hebrews. By Archdeacon FARRAR, D.D. 3s. 6d.
Epistle to the Philippians. By Rev. H. C. G. MOULE, M.A. 2s. 6d.
General Epistle of St James. By Very Rev. E. H. PLUMPTRE. 1s. 6d.
Epistles of St Peter and St Jude. By the same Editor. 2s. 6d.
Epistles of St John. By Rev. A. PLUMMER, M.A., D.D. 3s. 6d.

Preparing.

Book of Genesis. By Very Rev. the Dean of Peterborough.
Books of Exodus, Numbers and Deuteronomy. By Rev. C. D. GINSBURG, LL.D.

London: Cambridge Warehouse, Ave Maria Lane.

Books of Ezra and Nehemiah. By Rev. Prof. RYLE, M.A.
Book of Psalms. By Rev. Prof. KIRKPATRICK, B.D.
Book of Isaiah. By Prof. W. ROBERTSON SMITH, M.A.
Book of Ezekiel. By Rev. A. B. DAVIDSON, D.D.
Epistle to the Galatians. By Rev. E. H. PEROWNE, D.D.
Epistles to Colossians & Philemon. By Rev. H. C. G. MOULE, M.A.
Epistles to Timothy and Titus. By Rev. A. E. HUMPHREYS, M.A.
Book of Revelation. By Rev. W. H. SIMCOX, M.A.

The Smaller Cambridge Bible for Schools.

The Smaller Cambridge Bible for Schools *will form an entirely new series of commentaries on some selected books of the Bible. It is expected that they will be prepared for the most part by the Editors of the larger series (the Cambridge Bible for Schools and Colleges). The volumes will be issued at a low price, and will be suitable to the requirements of preparatory and elementary schools.*

Now ready. Price 1s. each.

First and Second Books of Samuel. By Rev. Prof. KIRKPATRICK, B.D.
Gospel according to St Matthew. By Rev. A. CARR, M.A.
Gospel according to St Mark. By Rev. G. F. MACLEAR, D.D.
Gospel according to St Luke. By Archdeacon FARRAR, D.D.
Acts of the Apostles. By Prof. LUMBY, D.D. [*In the Press.*

THE CAMBRIDGE GREEK TESTAMENT
FOR SCHOOLS AND COLLEGES

with a Revised Text, based on the most recent critical authorities, and English Notes, prepared under the direction of the General Editor.

J. J. S. PEROWNE, D.D., DEAN OF PETERBOROUGH.

Gospel according to St Matthew. By Rev. A. CARR, M.A. 4s. 6d.
Gospel according to St Mark. By Rev. G. F. MACLEAR, D.D. 4s. 6d.
Gospel according to St Luke. By Archdeacon FARRAR. 6s.
Gospel according to St John. By Rev. A. PLUMMER, D.D. 6s.
Acts of the Apostles. By Prof. LUMBY, D.D. 4 Maps. 6s.
First Epistle to the Corinthians. By Rev. J. J. LIAS, M.A. 3s.
Second Epistle to the Corinthians. By Rev. J. J. LIAS, M.A.
[*Preparing.*
Epistle to the Hebrews. By Archdeacon FARRAR, D.D. 3s. 6d.
Epistle of St James. By Very Rev. E. H. PLUMPTRE, D.D.
[*Preparing.*
Epistles of St John. By Rev. A. PLUMMER, M.A., D.D. 4s.

London: Cambridge Warehouse, Ave Maria Lane.

THE PITT PRESS SERIES.

⁎ *Copies of the Pitt Press Series may generally be obtained in two volumes, Text and Notes separately.*

I. GREEK.

Aristophanes. Aves—Plutus—Ranae. By W. C. GREEN, M.A., late Assistant Master at Rugby School. *Price 3s. 6d.* each.

Euripides. Heracleidæ. With Introduction and Explanatory Notes by E. A. BECK, M.A., Fellow of Trinity Hall. *Price 3s. 6d.*

Euripides. Hercules Furens. With Introduction, Notes and Analysis. By A. GRAY, M.A., and J. T. HUTCHINSON, M.A. 2s.

Euripides. Hippolytus. By W. S. HADLEY, M.A. 2s.

Euripides. Iphigeneia in Aulis. By C. E. S. HEADLAM, B.A. 2s. 6d.

Herodotus. Book V. Edited with Notes and Introduction by E. S. SHUCKBURGH, M.A. 3s.

Herodotus. Book VI. By the same Editor. *Price 4s.*

Herodotus. Book VIII., Chaps. 1—90. By the same Editor. 3s. 6d.

Herodotus. Book IX., Chaps. 1—89. By the same Editor. 3s. 6d.

Homer. Odyssey, Book IX. Book X. With Introduction, Notes and Appendices by G. M. EDWARDS, M.A. *Price 2s. 6d.* each.

Homer. Odyssey, Book XXI. By the same Editor. 2s.

Luciani Somnium Charon Piscator et De Luctu. By W. E. HEITLAND, M.A., Fellow of St John's College, Cambridge. 3s. 6d.

Platonis Apologia Socratis. With Introduction, Notes and Appendices by J. ADAM, M.A. Revised Edition. *Price 3s. 6d.*

—— **Crito.** With Introduction, Notes and Appendix. By the same Editor. *Price 2s. 6d.*

—— **Euthyphro.** By the same Editor. 2s. 6d.

Plutarch's Lives of the Gracchi.—Sulla—Timoleon. With Introduction, Notes and Lexicon by H. A. HOLDEN, M.A., LL.D. 6s. each.

Plutarch's Life of Nicias. By the same Editor. *Price 5s.*

Sophocles.—Oedipus Tyrannus. School Edition, with Introduction and Commentary by R. C. JEBB, Litt.D., LL.D. 4s. 6d.

Xenophon—Agesilaus. By H. HAILSTONE, M.A. 2s. 6d.

London: Cambridge Warehouse, Ave Maria Lane.

Xenophon—Anabasis. With Introduction, Map and English Notes, by A. PRETOR, M.A. Two vols. *Price* 7*s*. 6*d*.
—— —— Books I. III. IV. and V. By the same Editor. *Price* 2*s*. each. Books II. VI. and VII. *Price* 2*s*. 6*d*. each.
Xenophon—Cyropaedeia. Books I. II. With Introduction and Notes by Rev. H. A. HOLDEN, M.A., LL.D. 2 vols. *Price* 6*s*.
—— —— Books III. IV. and V. By the same Editor. 5*s*.
—— —— Books VI. VII. and VIII. By the same Editor.
[Nearly ready.

II. LATIN.

Beda's Ecclesiastical History, Books III., IV. Edited by J. E. B. MAYOR, M.A., and J. R. LUMBY, D.D. Revised Edit. 7*s*. 6*d*.
Caesar. De Bello Gallico Comment. I. With Maps and Notes by A. G. PESKETT, M.A. *Price* 1*s*. 6*d*. Com. II. III. *Price* 2*s*.
—— Comment. I. II. III. *Price* 3*s*. Com. IV. V., and Com. VII. *Price* 2*s*. each. Com. VI. and Com. VIII. *Price* 1*s*. 6*d*. each.
—— De Bello Civili. Comment. I. By the same Editor.
[In the Press.
M. T. Ciceronis de Amicitia.—de Senectute.—pro Sulla Oratio. Edited by J. S. REID, Litt.D., Fellow of Gonville and Caius College. 3*s*. 6*d*. each.
M. T. Ciceronis Oratio pro Archia Poeta. By the same. 2*s*.
M. T. Ciceronis pro Balbo Oratio. By the same. 1*s*. 6*d*.
M. T. Ciceronis in Gaium Verrem Actio Prima. With Notes by H. COWIE, M.A., Fellow of St John's Coll. *Price* 1*s*. 6*d*.
M. T. Ciceronis in Q. Caecilium Divinatio et in C. Verrem Actio. By W. E. HEITLAND, M.A., and H. COWIE, M.A. 3*s*.
M. T. Ciceronis Oratio pro Tito Annio Milone, with English Notes, &c., by JOHN SMYTH PURTON, B.D. *Price* 2*s*. 6*d*.
M. T. Ciceronis Oratio pro L. Murena, with English Introduction and Notes. By W. E. HEITLAND, M.A. *Price* 3*s*.
M. T. Ciceronis pro Cn. Plancio Oratio, by H. A. HOLDEN, LL.D. Second Edition. *Price* 4*s*. 6*d*.
M. Tulli Ciceronis Oratio Philippica Secunda. With Introduction and Notes by A. G. PESKETT, M.A. *Price* 3*s*. 6*d*.
M. T. Ciceronis Somnium Scipionis. With Introduction and Notes. Edited by W. D. PEARMAN, M.A. *Price* 2*s*.
Horace. Epistles, Book I. With Notes and Introduction by E. S. SHUCKBURGH, M.A., late Fellow of Emmanuel College. 2*s*. 6*d*.
Livy. Book IV. With Notes and Introduction by H. M. STEPHENSON, M.A. *Price* 2*s*. 6*d*.
—— Book V. With Notes, Introduction and Map by L. WHIBLEY, M.A. *Price* 2*s*. 6*d*.
—— Book XXI. Book XXII. With Notes, Introduction and Maps. By M. S. DIMSDALE, M.A. *Price* 2*s*. 6*d*. each.

London: Cambridge Warehouse, Ave Maria Lane.

M. Annaei Lucani Pharsaliae Liber Primus. Edited by W. E. HEITLAND, M.A., and C. E. HASKINS, M.A. *1s. 6d.*

Lucretius, Book V. With Notes and Introduction by J. D. DUFF, M.A., Fellow of Trinity College. *Price 2s.*

P. Ovidii Nasonis Fastorum Liber VI. With Notes by A. SIDGWICK, M.A., Tutor of Corpus Christi College, Oxford. *1s. 6d.*

Quintus Curtius. A Portion of the History (Alexander in India). By W. E. HEITLAND, M.A. and T. E. RAVEN, B.A. *3s. 6d.*

P. Vergili Maronis Aeneidos Libri I.—XII. Edited with Notes by A. SIDGWICK, M.A. *Price 1s. 6d. each.*

P. Vergili Maronis Bucolica. With Introduction and Notes by the same Editor. *Price 1s. 6d.*

P. Vergili Maronis Georgicon Libri I. II. By the same Editor. *Price 2s.* **Libri III. IV.** By the same Editor. *Price 2s.*

Vergil. The Complete Works. By the same Editor. Two Vols. Vol. I. containing the Introduction and Text. *3s. 6d.* Vol. II. The Notes. *4s. 6d.*

III. FRENCH.

Bataille de Dames. By SCRIBE and LEGOUVÉ. Edited by Rev. H. A. BULL, M.A. *Price 2s.*

Dix Années d'Exil. Livre II. Chapitres 1—8. Par MADAME LA BARONNE DE STAËL-HOLSTEIN. By the late G. MASSON, B.A. and G. W. PROTHERO, M.A. New Edition, enlarged. *Price 2s.*

Histoire du Siècle de Louis XIV. par Voltaire. Chaps. I.—XIII. Edited by GUSTAVE MASSON, B.A. and G. W. PROTHERO, M.A. *2s. 6d.* Chaps. XIV.—XXIV. *2s. 6d.* Chap. XXV. to end. *2s. 6d.*

Fredégonde et Brunehaut. A Tragedy in Five Acts, by N. LEMERCIER. By GUSTAVE MASSON, B.A. *Price 2s.*

Jeanne D'Arc. By A. DE LAMARTINE. Edited by Rev. A. C. CLAPIN, M.A. New Edition. *Price 2s.*

La Canne de Jonc. By A. DE VIGNY. Edited with Notes by Rev. H. A. BULL, M.A., late Master at Wellington College. *Price 2s.*

La Jeune Sibérienne. Le Lépreux de la Cité D'Aoste. Tales by COUNT XAVIER DE MAISTRE. By GUSTAVE MASSON, B.A. *Price 1s. 6d.*

La Picciola. By X. B. SAINTINE. The Text, with Introduction, Notes and Map. By Rev. A. C. CLAPIN, M.A. *Price 2s.*

La Guerre. By MM. ERCKMANN-CHATRIAN. With Map, Introduction and Commentary by the same Editor. *Price 3s.*

La Métromanie. A Comedy, by PIRON. By G. MASSON, B.A. *2s.*

Lascaris ou Les Grecs du XVE Siècle, Nouvelle Historique, par A. F. VILLEMAIN. By the same. *Price 2s.*

London: Cambridge Warehouse, Ave Maria Lane.

La Suite du Menteur. A Comedy by P. CORNEILLE. With Notes Philological and Historical, by the same. *Price 2s.*

Lazare Hoche—Par EMILE DE BONNECHOSE. With Four Maps. Introduction and Commentary, by C. COLBECK, M.A. *2s.*

Le Bourgeois Gentilhomme, Comédie-Ballet en Cinq Actes. Par J.-B. Poquelin de Molière (1670). By Rev. A. C. CLAPIN, M.A. *1s. 6d.*

Le Directoire. (Considérations sur la Révolution Française. Troisième et quatrième parties.) Revised and enlarged. With Notes by G. MASSON, B.A. and G. W. PROTHERO, M.A. *Price 2s.*

Les Plaideurs. RACINE. With Introduction and Notes by E. G. W. BRAUNHOLTZ, M.A., Ph.D. *Price 2s.*

Les Précieuses Ridicules. MOLIÈRE. With Introduction and Notes by E. G. W. BRAUNHOLTZ, M.A., Ph.D. *Price 2s.*

L'École des Femmes. MOLIÈRE. With Introduction and Notes by GEORGE SAINTSBURY, M.A. *Price 2s. 6d.*

Le Philosophe sans le savoir. Sedaine. Edited with Notes by Rev. H. A. BULL, M.A., late Master at Wellington College. *2s.*

Lettres sur l'histoire de France (XIII—XXIV). Par AUGUSTIN THIERRY. By G. MASSON, B.A. and G. W. PROTHERO. *Price 2s. 6d.*

Le Verre D'Eau. A Comedy, by SCRIBE. Edited by C. COLBECK, M.A. *Price 2s.*

Le Vieux Célibataire. A Comedy, by COLLIN D'HARLEVILLE. With Notes, by G. MASSON, B.A. *Price 2s.*

M. Daru, par M. C. A. SAINTE-BEUVE (Causeries du Lundi, Vol. IX.). By G. MASSON, B.A. Univ. Gallic. *Price 2s.*

Recits des Temps Merovingiens I—III. THIERRY. Edited by the late G. MASSON, B.A. and A. R. ROPES, M.A. Map. *Price 3s.*

IV. GERMAN.

A Book of Ballads on German History. Arranged and Annotated by WILHELM WAGNER, PH. D. *Price 2s.*

A Book of German Dactylic Poetry. Arranged and Annotated by WILHELM WAGNER, Ph.D. *Price 3s.*

Benedix. Doctor Wespe. Lustspiel in fünf Aufzügen. Edited with Notes by KARL HERMANN BREUL, M.A., Ph.D. *Price 3s.*

Culturgeschichtliche Novellen, von W. H. RIEHL. Edited by H. J. WOLSTENHOLME, B.A. (Lond.). *Price 3s. 6d.*

London: Cambridge Warehouse, Ave Maria Lane.

Das Jahr 1813 (THE YEAR 1813), by F. KOHLRAUSCH. With English Notes by WILHEM WAGNER, Ph.D. *Price 2s.*

Der erste Kreuzzug (1095—1099) nach FRIEDRICH VON RAUMER. THE FIRST CRUSADE. By W. WAGNER, Ph.D. *Price 2s.*

Der Oberhof. A Tale of Westphalian Life, by KARL IMMERMANN. By WILHELM WAGNER, Ph.D. *Price 3s.*

Der Staat Friedrichs des Grossen. By G. FREYTAG. With Notes. By WILHELM WAGNER, PH.D. *Price 2s.*

Die Karavane, von WILHELM HAUFF. Edited with Notes by A. SCHLOTTMANN, PH.D. *Price 3s. 6d.*

Goethe's Hermann and Dorothea. By W. WAGNER, Ph.D. Revised edition by J. W. CARTMELL. *Price 3s. 6d.*

Goethe's Knabenjahre. (1749—1759.) **Goethe's Boyhood.** Arranged and Annotated by W. WAGNER, Ph.D. *Price 2s.*

Hauff, Das Bild des Kaisers. By KARL HERMANN BREUL, M.A., Ph.D. *Price 3s.*

Hauff, Das Wirthshaus im Spessart. By A. SCHLOTTMANN, Ph.D., late Assistant Master at Uppingham School. *Price 3s. 6d.*

Mendelssohn's Letters. Selections from. Edited by JAMES SIME, M.A. *Price 3s.*

Schiller. Wilhelm Tell. With Introduction and Notes by KARL HERMANN BREUL, M.A., Ph.D., University Lecturer in German. *2s. 6d.*

Selected Fables. Lessing and Gellert. Edited with Notes by KARL HERMANN BREUL, M.A., Ph.D. *Price 3s.*

Uhland. Ernst, Herzog von Schwaben. With Introduction and Notes. Edited by H. J. WOLSTENHOLME, B.A. (Lond.). *Price 3s. 6d.*

Zopf und Schwert. Lustspiel in fünf Aufzügen von KARL GUTZKOW. By H. J. WOLSTENHOLME, B.A. (Lond.). *Price 3s. 6d.*

V. ENGLISH.

An Elementary Commercial Geography. A Sketch of the Commodities and Countries of the World. By H. R. MILL, Sc.D., F.R.S.E. *1s.*

An Atlas of Commercial Geography. (Companion to the above.) By J. G. BARTHOLOMEW, F.R.G.S. With an Introduction by Dr H. R. MILL. *3s.*

Ancient Philosophy from Thales to Cicero, A Sketch of, by JOSEPH B. MAYOR, M.A. *Price 3s. 6d.*

London: Cambridge Warehouse, Ave Maria Lane.

Bacon's History of the Reign of King Henry VII. With Notes by the Rev. Professor LUMBY, D.D. *Price 3s.*

British India, a Short History of. By Rev. E. S. CARLOS, M.A. 1s.

Cowley's Essays. By Prof. LUMBY, D.D. *Price* 4s.

General Aims of the Teacher, and Form Management. Two Lectures by F. W. FARRAR, D.D. and R. B. POOLE, B.D. 1s. 6d.

John Amos Comenius, Bishop of the Moravians. His Life and Educational Works, by S. S. LAURIE, A.M., F.R.S.E. 3s. 6d.

Locke on Education. With Introduction and Notes by the Rev. R. H. QUICK, M.A. *Price* 3s. 6d.

Milton's Tractate on Education. A facsimile reprint from the Edition of 1673. Edited by O. BROWNING, M.A. *Price* 2s.

More's History of King Richard III. Edited with Notes, Glossary, Index of Names. By J. RAWSON LUMBY, D.D. 3s. 6d.

On Stimulus. A Lecture delivered for the Teachers' Training Syndicate at Cambridge, May 1882, by A. SIDGWICK, M.A. New Ed. 1s.

Outlines of the Philosophy of Aristotle. Compiled by EDWIN WALLACE, M.A., LL.D. Third Edition, Enlarged. 4s. 6d.

Sir Thomas More's Utopia. By Prof. LUMBY, D.D. 3s. 6d.

Theory and Practice of Teaching. By E. THRING, M.A. 4s. 6d.

The Teaching of Modern Languages in Theory and Practice. By C. COLBECK, M.A. *Price* 2s.

The Two Noble Kinsmen, edited with Introduction and Notes by the Rev. Professor SKEAT, Litt.D. *Price* 3s. 6d.

Three Lectures on the Practice of Education. I. On Marking by H. W. EVE, M.A. II. On Stimulus, by A. SIDGWICK, M.A. III. On the Teaching of Latin Verse Composition, by E. A. ABBOTT, D.D. 2s.

VI. MATHEMATICS.

Euclid's Elements of Geometry. Books I. and II. By H. M. TAYLOR, M.A. 1s. 6d.

——— ——— Books III. and IV. By the same Editor. [*In the Press.*

London: C. J. CLAY AND SONS,
CAMBRIDGE WAREHOUSE, AVE MARIA LANE.
Glasgow: 263, ARGYLE STREET.
Cambridge: DEIGHTON, BELL AND CO. **Leipzig:** F. A. BROCKHAUS.

www.ingramcontent.com/pod-product-compliance
Lightning Source LLC
Chambersburg PA
CBHW021958220426
43663CB00007B/871